D0946912

THE OXFORD HANDBOOK OF

HISTORICAL INSTITUTIONALISM

THE OXFORD HANDBOOK OF

HISTORICAL INSTITUTIONALISM

Edited by

ORFEO FIORETOS

TULIA G. FALLETI

and

ADAM SHEINGATE

OXFORD
UNIVERSITY PRESS

Great Clarendon Street, Oxford, OX2 6DP,
United Kingdom

Oxford University Press is a department of the University of Oxford.
It furthers the University's objective of excellence in research, scholarship,
and education by publishing worldwide. Oxford is a registered trade mark of
Oxford University Press in the UK and in certain other countries

First Edition published in 2016
Impression: 1

Published in the United States of America by Oxford University Press
198 Madison Avenue, New York, NY 10016, United States of America

British Library Cataloguing in Publication Data
Data available

Library of Congress Control Number: 2016933999

ISBN 978–0–19–966281–4

Printed in Great Britain by
Clays Ltd, St Ives plc

Acknowledgements

ORGANIZING a large project brings many debts, and rewards. The scholars, teachers, and friends who shaped this project before and during its lifespan are too many to acknowledge separately, though a glance at chapter bibliographies is a good place to start. Several individuals and organizations provided indispensible support in bringing the project to fruition. Dominic Byatt, our editor at Oxford University Press, was an early and enthusiastic supporter without whom this project would not have come about. A November 2013 conference in Philadelphia, mid-way through the project, shaped the core of the volume. We thank Temple University and the University of Pennsylvania for generous assistance. At Temple, we are especially grateful for the support of Teresa Soufas and Kevin Glass in the Dean's Office of the College of Liberal Arts, the Faculty Senate, Ram Mudambi and the Center for International Business and Education Research, Peter Logan and the Center for Humanities at Temple, Richard Immerman and the Center for the Study of Law and Diplomacy, Richard Deeg and the William Alan Jones Fund of the Department of Political Science. At the University of Pennsylvania, we especially thank Edward Mansfield and the Christopher H. Browne Center for International Studies, the Office of the Vice-Provost for Research, and the Dean's Office at the School of Arts and Sciences for their financial support. We also owe a special thanks to Danielle Scherer for being an indispensible project assistant, and to Prakirti Nangia for organizational assistance with the Philadelphia conference. To Sarah Parker and Olivia Wells of OUP, and to Elizabeth Stone, our copy-editor, we extend particular thanks for lending us keen eyes and kind help along the way. Finally, we thank the contributors who with great energy, humor, and patience shared drafts of papers, participated in conference panels in Washington, D.C., Amsterdam, and San Francisco, and with whom we had the privilege of sharing the rewards of academic exchange.

The Editors

Contents

PART III COMPARATIVE POLITICS

PART IV AMERICAN POLITICS

PART VI INTERNATIONAL RELATIONS

List of Figures

List of Tables

Notes on Contributors

Karen J. Alter is Professor of Political Science and Law, Northwestern University, Evanston, IL, and Permanent Visiting Professor, iCourts Center of Excellence, Faculty of Law, University of Copenhagen, Denmark.

Rodrigo Barrenechea is a Ph.D. Candidate, Department of Political Science, Northwestern University.

Sheri Berman is Professor of Political Science, Barnard College, New York, NY, USA.

Mark Blyth is Professor of International Political Economy, Brown University, Providence, RI, USA.

Tim Büthe is Associate Professor of Political Science and Public Policy, and Senior Fellow for the Rethinking Regulation Project at the Kenan Institute for Ethics, Duke University, Durham, NC, USA.

Melani Cammett is Professor of Government, Harvard University, Cambridge, MA, USA.

Giovanni Capoccia is Professor of Comparative Politics, Department of Politics and International Relations, University of Oxford, Oxford, UK.

Teri L. Caraway is Professor of Political Science, University of Minnesota, Twin Cities, Minneapolis, MN, USA.

James Conran is a Ph.D. Candidate, Department of Political Science, Massachusetts Institute of Technology, Cambridge, MA, USA.

Pepper D. Culpepper is Professor of Political Science, European University Institute, San Domenico di Fiesole, Italy.

Richard Deeg is Professor of Political Science, Temple University, Philadelphia, PA, USA.

Tulia G. Falleti is Class of 1965 Term Associate Professor of Political Science University of Pennsylvania, Philadelphia, PA, USA.

Henry Farrell is Associate Professor of Political Science and International Affairs, George Washington University, Washington, D.C., USA.

Martha Finnemore is University Professor of Political Science and International Affairs, George Washington University, Washington, D.C., USA.

Orfeo Fioretos is Associate Professor of Political Science, Temple University, Philadelphia, PA, USA.

Paul Frymer is Professor of Politics, Princeton University, Princeton, NJ, USA.

Daniel J. Galvin is Associate Professor of Political Science and Faculty Fellow at the Institute for Policy Research, Northwestern University, Evanston, IL, USA.

Edward L. Gibson is Associate Dean of Faculty and Professor of Political Science, Northwestern University, Evanston, IL, USA.

Judith Goldstein is Professor of Political Science and Janet M. Peck Professor in International Communication, Stanford University, Palo Alto, CA, USA.

Marie Gottschalk is Professor of Political Science, University of Pennsylvania, Philadelphia, PA, USA.

Anna Grzymala-Busse is Ronald and Eileen Weiser Professor of European and Eurasian Studies, Department of Political Science, University of Michigan, Ann Arbor, MI, USA.

Robert Gulotty is Assistant Professor of Political Science, Department of Political Science, University of Chicago, Chicago, IL, USA.

Peter A. Hall is Krupp Foundation Professor of European Studies in the Department of Government and Minda de Gunzburg Center for European Studies, and Co-Director of the CIFAR Program on Successful Societies, Harvard University, Cambridge, MA, USA.

Oddný Helgadóttir is a Ph.D. Candidate, Department of Political Science, Brown University, Providence, RI, USA.

Eric Helleiner is Faculty of Arts Chair in International Political Economy, University of Waterloo, Waterloo, ON, Canada.

G. John Ikenberry is Albert G. Milbank Professor of Politics and International Affairs, Department of Politics and the Woodrow Wilson School of Public and International Affair, Princeton University, Princeton, NJ, USA.

Alan M. Jacobs is Associate Professor of Political Science, University of British Columbia, Vancouver, BC, Canada.

R. Daniel Kelemen is Professor of Political Science, State University of New Jersey—Rutgers, New Brunswick, NJ, USA.

Desmond King is the Andrew W. Mellon Professor of American Government and Professorial Fellow, Nuffield College, Oxford University, Oxford, UK.

Atul Kohli is David K. E. Bruce Professor of International Affairs and Professor of Politics and International Affairs, Department of Politics and Woodrow Wilson School, Princeton University, Princeton, NJ, USA.

Stephen D. Krasner is Graham A. Stuart Professor of International Studies, Department of Political Science, and Senior Fellow, Freeman Spogli Institute and Hoover Institution, Stanford University, Stanford, CA, USA.

William Kring is a Ph.D. Candidate, Department of Political Science, Brown University, Providence, RI, USA.

Steven Levitsky is Professor of Government, Harvard University, Cambridge, MA, USA.

Julia Lynch is Associate Professor of Political Science, University of Pennsylvania, Philadelphia, PA, USA.

James Mahoney is Gordon Fulcher Professor in Decision-Making, Professor of Sociology, Department of Sociology, and Professor of Political Science, Department of Political Science, Northwestern University, Evanston, IL, USA.

Khairunnisa Mohamedali, Ph.D. Northwestern 2014, is the Resident Ethnographer at Idea Couture, Toronto, Canada.

Abraham L. Newman is Associate Professor, Edmund A. Walsh School of Foreign Service, Georgetown University, Washington, D.C., USA.

Christoph Nguyen is a Post Doctoral Fellow in the Department of Political Science at Southern Denmark University, Odense.

Paul Pierson is Professor and John Gross Endowed Chair, Department of Political Science, University of California-Berkeley, CA, USA.

Elliot Posner is Associate Professor of Political Science, Case Western Reserve University, Cleveland, OH, USA.

Martin Rhodes is Associate Dean and Professor of Comparative Political Economy, Josef Korbel School of International Studies, University of Denver, Denver, CO, USA.

Rachel Beatty Riedl is Assistant Professor of Political Science, Northwestern University, Evanston, IL, USA.

Aytuğ Şaşmaz is a Ph.D. Candidate, Department of Government, Harvard University, Cambridge, MA, USA.

Adam Sheingate is Associate Professor of Political Science, The Johns Hopkins University, Baltimore, MD, USA.

Hillel David Soifer is Assistant Professor of Political Science, Temple University, Philadelphia, PA, USA.

Etel Solingen is Thomas T. and Elizabeth C. Tierney Chair in Peace and Conflict Studies, Political Science, School of Social Sciences, University of California, Irvine, CA, USA.

Sarah Staszak is Assistant Professor of Political Science, The City College of New York, New York, NY, USA.

Sven Steinmo is Research Professor, Robert Schuman Centre for Advanced Studies, European University Institute, San Domenico di Fiesole, Italy.

Larkin Terrie received his Ph.D. in Political Science from Northwestern University, Evanston, IL, USA.

Mark Thatcher is Professor of Comparative and International Politics, London School of Economics and Political Science, London, UK.

Kathleen Thelen is Ford Professor of Political Science, Massachusetts Institute of Technology, Cambridge, MA, USA.

Kellee S. Tsai is Chair Professor and Division Head of Social Science, Hong Kong University of Science and Technology, Kowloon, Hong Kong; and Professor of Political Science, Johns Hopkins University, Baltimore, MD, USA.

Wilfred Wan is JSPS-UNU (Japan Society for the Promotion of Science-United Nations University) Postdoctoral Fellow, UNU Centre for Policy Research and Hitotsubashi University, Tokyo, Japan.

Lucan A. Way is Associate Professor, Department of Political Science, University of Toronto, Toronto, ON, Canada.

Cornelia Woll is Professor of Political Science, Sciences Po, Paris, France.

PART I

INTRODUCTION

CHAPTER 1

HISTORICAL INSTITUTIONALISM IN POLITICAL SCIENCE

ORFEO FIORETOS, TULIA G. FALLETI, AND ADAM SHEINGATE*

POLITICAL Science in the early twenty-first century is characterized by several robust traditions of institutional analysis. To a much greater extent than a generation ago when scholars debated *whether* institutions mattered in shaping politics, the discipline is now defined by multiple approaches to determining *how* and *when* institutions shape political developments. Since the 1990s, historical, rational choice, and sociological varieties of institutional analysis have experienced significant growth in their empirical scope and analytical sophistication. While the three versions of the "new institutionalisms" in Political Science have areas of overlap, they offer different solutions to central challenges that have confronted students of politics over the ages, including how to better understand and explain the complexity of the political world. Former American Political Science Association President Elinor Ostrom remarked in her Nobel Prize lecture that "When the world we are trying to explain ... is not well described by a simple model, we must continue to improve our frameworks and theories so as to be able to understand complexity and not simply reject it" (Ostrom 2010, 436).

Historical institutionalism is a research tradition that examines how temporal processes and events influence the origin and transformation of institutions that govern political and economic relations. Since it emerged in dialogue with other institutionalisms, scholars in the tradition have been consistently committed to Ostrom's goal of improving our understanding and explanations of complex political phenomena. This commitment is evident in historical institutionalism's empirical profile, analytical toolbox, and methodological choices. Empirically, historical institutionalists have focused on enhancing political scientists' understanding of the origins, evolution, and consequences of humanly created institutions across time and place. While early studies emphasized "big questions" (Pierson and Skocpol 2002, 696–698)—such as the origins of the state, the consequences of revolutions and wars, persistent social inequalities, and economic crises—the tradition's empirical purview has grown considerably in the past 25 years as scholars have studied virtually all types of institutions, big and small, at the local, national, and international levels.

This volume takes stock of the growth in the scope of historical institutionalism across multiple subfields of Political Science. In comparative politics, historical institutionalism has been particularly influential and shapes research agendas in a widening array of substantive areas, from research on the modern state, capitalism, law, and economic development to the study of political regimes, political parties, organized societal actors, and public policy. It is central to the study of American political development, focusing on the elusive character of the American state and the legacy of struggles over race and citizenship that animate much of US politics. In the area of European politics, historical institutionalism now informs the study of political parties, the power of organized interest groups, the attributes of welfare states, and the process of European integration. Finally, in international relations (IR) historical institutionalism has influenced contributions on state sovereignty and foreign economic policy, as well as research in international security, international political economy, international law, and global governance.

Analytically, historical institutionalism is distinguished by a conceptual toolbox that draws attention to the role of temporal phenomena in influencing the origin and change in institutions that govern political and economic relations. Scholars emphasize how temporally defined phenomena such as the timing and sequence of events generate formal and informal institutions and how their emergence and change impact public policies and distributions of political authority. Such emphases have helped scholars revisit conventional understandings of both the origin of major institutions as well as articulate why institutions often persist after their original impetus is no longer present. Focusing on temporal phenomena, like critical (historical) junctures and path-dependent trajectories, has helped scholars reveal the far-reaching consequences that institutions may have for the nature of political power and for the strategies, preferences, and identities of actors over time. Attention to temporal phenomena has also helped scholars bridge accounts of political history as a series of punctuated changes followed by high levels of institutional stability with theories of incremental change to explain the sources of complex, overlapping structures of political authority.

The empirical and analytical growth of historical institutionalism has been facilitated by a pluralistic methodological profile. By resisting sharp trade-offs between nuanced empirical accounts and general theories that hold across time and space, historical institutionalists have refined qualitative and comparative research methods to study how processes that unfold over long periods impact distributions of power and policy outcomes. An ambition to study "forests as well as trees" (Pierson and Skocpol 2002, 711) has encouraged historical institutionalists to widen their use of Political Science methodologies over time to include statistical, formal, and interpretive methods as means of striking a balance between explaining general phenomena and understanding specific patterns of political development.

As the world again struggles to understand the origins and effects of economic crises, social revolutions, redistributions of global power, and persistent social inequalities, historical institutionalism is poised to make new contributions. The chapters that follow explore how historical institutionalism has revisited conventional wisdoms, resolved long-standing empirical puzzles, and opened new areas of inquiry in Political Science. They discuss the tradition's contributions to the study of politics, areas where it complements other approaches of institutional analysis, and the extent to which historical institutionalism itself has responded to criticisms directed its way. This introduction sets the stage for those chapters by first detailing the crystallization of historical institutionalism and some of its core features before identifying empirical, methodological, and analytical frontiers in this growing tradition of political analysis.

The Emergence and Crystallization of Historical Institutionalism

Historical institutionalism has deep roots in Political Science. Attention to temporal phenomena, including the role of timing and sequence, is evident in classic works in comparative political economy that examined how the emergence of capitalism and the development of democracy shaped the diverse trajectories of nation-states (e.g., Polanyi 1944; Gerschenkron 1962; Moore 1966). Beginning in the 1980s, as efforts to reinvigorate the state as an object of study dovetailed with a renewed interest in institutions, scholars developed a conceptually more precise understanding of the causal impact of history and institutions on political life. Efforts to "bring the state back in" combined an ontological claim about the state as an object of inquiry in Political Science with a theoretical claim about historical processes and events that shaped the administrative capacities and organizational routines of national bureaucracies (Evans, Rueschemeyer, and Skocpol 1985; see also Nettl 1968; Nordlinger 1982). By the early 1990s, historical institutionalism emerged as a distinct tradition of institutional analysis that addressed an expanding array of topics in Political Science.

The crystallization of historical institutionalism was part of a new turn in the study of institutions in Political Science and the social sciences more generally. Rejecting elements of behavioralism, pluralism, and Marxism that treated formal arrangements of political authority as arenas of group competition or as epiphenomenal of economic relations, the new institutional turn brought attention to how institutions ordered political life through a variety of mechanisms that constituted actors and constrained their behavior (March and Olsen 1984). But as work proceeded to develop more precise analytical tools to study these mechanisms, important differences emerged in how scholars conceived of institutions as well as the role of actors within them (Hall and Taylor 1996; Immergut 1998; Thelen 1999). Whereas some scholars focused on the material interests that created or sustained institutions through the formation of coalitions, other scholars examined the cognitive dimension of institutions, for instance how a set of rules or policies reflected particular ideas or beliefs. At the same time, scholars emphasized different levels of analysis with some focused on macro-structures and institutional assemblages like the welfare state or national economic systems in shaping political outcomes, while other scholars privileged micro-level factors such as how institutions solved collective action problems among rational actors.

Figure 1.1 graphically represents the three new institutionalisms by aligning them along two central dimensions of social science analysis: the macro–micro continuum, and the material–cognitive continuum. Whereas the horizontal axis ranges from an emphasis on structure to a focus on actors, the vertical axis ranges from an emphasis on interests or material resources in politics to a focus on ideas or the role of human cognition.

The figure situates historical institutionalism as it developed in the 1990s in relation to the rational choice and sociological institutional approaches of the time. Scholars working in the tradition of rational choice institutionalism (upper right quadrant) adopted an interest-based, actor-centered approach that conceived of self-interested individuals as selecting institutions based on a set of exogenously given preferences. Institutions were understood to generate stability, or structure-induced equilibrium, by limiting the range of alternatives actors confront (Shepsle 1981). Scholars attentive to the contextual effects of time and place expressed skepticism with how rational choice institutionalism understood the origins and consequences of actor preferences. Rather than fixed and given exogenously, historical institutional scholars argued that temporal processes may generate and reinforce actor preferences, power relations, and patterns of resource

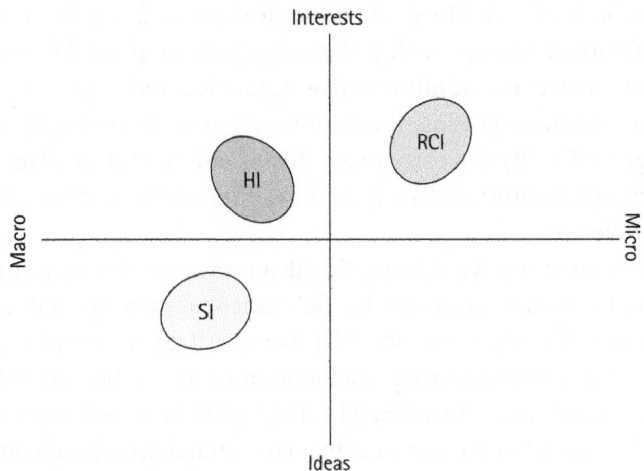

FIGURE 1.1 The Three New Institutionalisms (*c.*1995).

Note: HI=Historical Institutionalism; RCI=Rational Choice Institutionalism; SI=Sociological Institutionalism.

allocation. From this perspective, rationalist models of utility maximizing individuals were ill-equipped to explain the broad array of institutional arrangements governing polities, including those that had unintended and unanticipated consequences. Seeking to explain variations in institutional designs, scholars trained their eyes on the effects of institutions over time, including their consequences on the formation of preferences and the composition of coalitions that formed the basis of political authority.

The 1992 publication of *Structuring Politics: Historical Institutionalism in Comparative Perspective* was an important turning point in the new institutionalisms debate (Steinmo, Thelen, and Longstreth 1992).[1] More than simply coining the term historical institutionalism, the contributors to the volume set to work developing an analytical toolbox for the study of history and politics. This toolbox connected history and politics in theoretical terms, rather than in the empirical and methodological terms which had been the dominant approach among political scientists until then (Steinmo, Thelen, and Longstreth 1992; Pierson 2000). Understood as the rules, norms, and practices that organize and constitute social relations, institutions were examined for their role in creating constraints and opportunities for political action, in distributing political power, and in shaping political preferences over time. The latter was of particular interest as scholars examined the relationship between institutions and political agency.

Kathleen Thelen and Sven Steinmo underscored in the introduction to *Structuring Politics* that "one, perhaps *the*, core difference between rational choice institutionalism and historical institutionalism lies in the question of preference formation" (1992, 9, emphasis in the original). Arguing that institutions shaped individual goals, they noted that institutions often altered preferences and with that the structure of coalitions in ways that could have transformative effects on policy. They explored the role of organizations in shaping such coalitions beyond "aggregate[ing] the endeavor of many individuals" and for their potential role in "ultimately alter[ing]" the preferences of political groups (Hall 1986, 233). In Steinmo's words, "[n]either interests nor value have substantive meaning if abstracted from the institutional context in which humans define them" (Steinmo 1989, 502). Historical institutionalism, then, placed emphasis on the endogenous (institutional) origins of preferences by offering a more structural rendering of the world than rational choice, one in which institutions and organizations, not individual-level traits were the primary building blocks in accounting for political preferences and outcomes.

In exploring the institutional foundations of preferences, historical institutionalists sought a balance between macro- and micro-level theories. While crediting historical institutionalism for its critiques of the "atomistic and anything-goes orientations" of rational choice approaches, Ira Katznelson (1997, 85) expressed concern that the tradition could be sacrificing the theoretical arsenal and parsimony of structural approaches in the sociological tradition. Too contextual an analysis, he suggested, could lead scholars to overlook the impact of large and slow-moving structural processes in favor of idiosyncratic causes. Katznelson (1997, 104) overcame his skepticism, however, and concluded that by adopting a relational perspective that saw "particular clusters of preferences, interests, and identities ... not just as causes; but as causes as well as products," historical institutionalism was "crossing the divide between structure and agency without ... eliminate[ing] the heuristic distinction between the two."

Some of the early historical institutionalist work highlighted the role of ideas in shaping the preferences and goals of political actors and organizations. Several authors in *Structuring Politics*, for example Peter Hall, Desmond King, and Margaret Weir, explored the conditions under which specific political and economic ideas influenced the policy and institutional choices of different countries. Viewing institutions as carriers of ideas that guide action by shaping how individuals and organizations see the world and define their preferences, the emphasis on ideas provided a link between institutional structures and cognitive factors. This link helped scholars resolve a range of puzzles in Political Science research, including why social democratic parties experienced divergent trajectories in interwar Europe (Berman 1998), why liberalism took different paths for much of the twentieth century in the United States and Europe (Blyth 2002), why economic openness persisted despite demands for closure (Goldstein 1994), and why states extended significant governing authority to international organizations (Ikenberry 1992).

The focus on ideas stood in contrast to the materialist and micro-level emphases in rational choice institutionalism and bore a resemblance to sociological approaches exploring relations among political actors and processes of institutional formation and reproduction through cognitive factors such as norms, roles, and repertoires. Like historical institutionalism, the sociological variant (lower left quadrant in Figure 1.1) shared a commitment to detailing the structural role of institutions in shaping political relations. However, the latter placed greater emphasis on cognitive processes such as isomorphism (or mimicry) in which individuals internalize routines or practices perceived as legitimate (DiMaggio and Powell 1983). For early scholars of historical institutionalism, this approach had some limitations. The emphasis on norms and routines was seen to leave too little room for strategic or calculated behavior, and thus risked treating actors like cultural "dopes" who simply enacted organizational routines. The emphasis on cognitive processes in sociological institutionalism was also thought to leave too little room to study power and political contestation. Because an institution was defined by what actors accepted as legitimate and appropriate behavior, historical institutionalists warned that sociological variants paid insufficient attention to the politics and contestation over the structure of institutions themselves (Hall and Taylor 1996, 954).

Through the 1990s, historical institutionalism developed in relation to the rationalist and sociological alternatives. Hall and Taylor (1996) note in their review of the new institutionalisms that the historical variant accepted an eclectic mix of the "calculus" approach embraced by rational choice scholars and the "cultural" approach of sociologists. But they quickly added: "eclecticism has its costs," particularly in terms of "specifying the precise causal chain through which ... institutions [affect] the behaviour they are meant to explain" (Hall and Taylor 1996, 950). This prompted scholars within historical institutionalism to distance themselves from core elements of each alternative and to stake out a position that moved away from the methodological individualism of rational choice and that at the same time was more materialist than sociological institutional variants. Whereas rational choice scholars understood institutions as equilibrium outcomes that emerge from actors' goal-oriented behavior within a specified set of rules, historical institutionalists emphasized how configurations of institutions created in the past structure politics in the present and in ways that often run counter to the interests or preferences of individuals. At the same time, influential scholars within historical institutionalism downplayed (or in some cases rejected outright) the cognitive dimension of institutions. They argued that institutions reflect distributions of material resources and that once established, institutions may continue to structure political affairs and distribute governing authority long after initial conditions do not hold (Skocpol 1995, 105; Thelen 1999). The outcome of scholars' engagement with other traditions during the crystallization of historical institutionalism was that much of the early work placed an emphasis on structural and materialist features.

In articulating the limitations of alternative approaches, historical institutionalism crystallized around a set of claims about the ontological status of institutions and the influence of temporal processes. Scholars argued that institutions were not merely effects of the distribution of preferences or the structure of political constellations at a given moment in time, but that over time institutions also became potential causes behind preferences and patterns of political contestation (Pierson 1993; Katznelson 2003). Scholars further emphasized that causally relevant conditions may interact in varied ways across time and space to produce distinct outcomes that are not anticipated by traditions employing different ontologies (Hall 2003). Historical institutionalists therefore encouraged researchers to pay greater attention to contextual conditions and to study whether, when, and how the same causal mechanisms yield different outcomes across time and space (Falleti and Lynch 2009). These ontological claims, or "fundamental assumptions about the causal structures of the social or political world" (Hall 2003, 374), meant that historical institutionalists resisted a focus on proximate causes because it risked truncating causal narratives at the expense of revealing the original causes of political outcomes. Instead, they favored research designs that covered relatively long time periods and that would ensure that proper attention was given to the interaction and contextual effects that produced distinct patterns of politics across time and space (e.g., Mahoney and Rueschemeyer 2003).

The ontological claims of early historical institutionalists made them methodologically committed to in-depth study of events and cases. They favored methods of agreement and difference among a small number of cases to identify the causal role of institutions. Instead of using historical narratives to illustrate theoretically deduced propositions, historical institutionalists used narratives to identify the mechanisms that shaped political contestation over time. Cognizant that an appreciation for complexity often implies a sacrifice in generalizability (Ragin 1987, 54), and not content with establishing correlation between historical and political phenomena, the methodological enterprise became one of uncovering, through careful study of the empirical record, the mechanisms that linked cause and effect. Historiographical modes of inquiry, counterfactual analysis, and process-tracing informed these efforts and have remained hallmarks of the tradition (e.g., Carpenter 2001; Farhang 2010; Ahmed 2012).

The ontological claims and methodological profile of historical institutionalism are apparent in the conceptual toolbox scholars have relied on as they explore the world of institutions. This toolbox has grown over time, and includes temporal concepts such as critical junctures and path-dependence that have long informed contributions of historical institutionalism, as well as newer concepts like intercurrence and modes of gradual institutional change that have helped scholars refine understandings of the complexity of politics.

Critical Juncture and Path Dependence

In *Shaping the Political Arena*, Collier and Collier (1991) made an early contribution to the historical institutionalist tradition by highlighting the causal effects of critical junctures. Drawing from previous comparative political studies (Lipset and Rokkan 1967; Rokkan 1970), Collier and Collier defined critical juncture "as a period of significant change, which typically occurs in distinct ways in different countries (or in other units of analysis) and which is hypothesized to produce distinct legacies" (1991, 29). While they did not see institutions as having a generative role in shaping the origins of a critical juncture, Collier and Collier argued that variation in the unfolding of critical junctures across contexts held the key to explaining divergent political legacies and outcomes across countries. They stressed the importance of specifying the *duration* of the critical juncture as well as the effecting historical legacies (1991, 31–34), and highlighted that the *timing* of the critical juncture, in relation to other developments, was consequential to subsequent politics. How long critical junctures last (attention to time) as well as when they occur in relation to other events (attention to order and sequence of events) are part of their historical institutional account of political regime outcomes in Latin America. Unlike other types of historical causes, Collier and Collier maintained that critical junctures generate legacies that can reproduce themselves without the enduring presence or recurrence of the originating causes. In the language that would quickly take root, critical junctures marked the beginning of path-dependent processes.

Scholars debate the extent to which critical junctures themselves can be explained by reference to institutions or to other antecedent causes (Pierson and Skocpol 2002; Slater and Simmons 2010), and the degree of agency that stems from these critical moments (Capoccia, this volume). Considering the agency effects of critical junctures, Capoccia and Kelemen (2007, 348) argue that critical junctures are best understood as periods of time that are significantly shorter than the path-dependent processes resulting from them. If critical juncture periods are conceived of as very long periods, the substantial influence of agency that is expected in these periods will be constrained by re-emerging institutional constraints. Capoccia and Kelemen therefore suggest that greater attention be paid to the role of agency and to the *permissive* conditions behind the opening of a specific juncture for this furnishes fuller understandings of how and when political actors upend mechanisms of reproduction, create new institutions, or modify existing ones.

Soifer (2012) adds analytical precision with a distinction between the permissive and the *productive* conditions of critical junctures. Permissive conditions are necessary conditions that loosen institutional or structural constraints on agency or contingency and thus provide the temporal bounds of critical junctures (Soifer 2012, 1574). Productive conditions, on the other hand, act within the context of the permissive conditions to bring about change. They are aspects of the critical juncture that shape initial outcomes and that are subsequently reproduced when the critical juncture comes to a close. In Soifer's account, the emergence of import substitution industrialization (ISI) in Latin American countries in the mid-twentieth century is explained with reference to permissive conditions (collapse of world trade during the Great Depression and World War II), productive conditions (economic nationalist ideas), and a mechanism of reproduction (new political coalition among bureaucrats, domestic elites, and organized labor).

Critical junctures feature extensively within historical institutional scholarship because they may be initial markers of path-dependent processes. After the openness of the critical juncture moment, which enables relatively free agency, a process or sequence of events ensues in which institutions exert their causal force. In the ISI example, once the economic nationalist ideas of Latin American economists shaped policies as a consequence of the permissive conditions generated by the Great Depression and World War II, the corporatist institutions that the emergent populist coalitions of the 1940s and 1950s had created kept the ISI model in place (Soifer 2012), even in the face of major subsequent economic crises (O'Donnell 1973).

Perhaps no concept is more closely associated with historical institutionalism than path dependence. The concept originates in economics (David 1985; Arthur 1994) and has been incorporated extensively into historical institutionalism ever since scholars sought answers to why institutions persist, even after they are no longer efficient. While scholars share a basic understanding of the concept as describing a situation in which reversing a trend (or path) becomes more difficult over time, they have emphasized different causal mechanisms behind such patterns. In one approach, path dependence is understood as self-reinforcing processes "involving positive feedback" (Pierson 2004, 20). From this perspective, it is when extant structures are the source of increasing returns and generate positive (or self-reinforcing) feedback effects to political actors embedded within them that departures or deviations from an existing path become less likely over time (Pierson 2004, 21). Attention to the timing and sequence of developments becomes crucial in such cases since the causal impact of early events is significantly stronger than subsequent events. In Falleti's (2010) study of decentralization reforms in Latin America, for example, the ordering of different types of decentralization policies (administrative, fiscal, and political) in a sequence of reform is highly consequential for political outcomes because early events carry more causal weight in shaping end results.

A second approach to path dependence highlights the role of historical contingency. While in the first approach political actors may purposefully sequence reforms in order to secure desired outcomes, other accounts note that early events that trigger path-dependent processes may even be accidental. Understood as a stochastic process in which the origin of a path dependent process cannot be explained by reference to available theories, attention to contingency provides a foundation for exploring how apparently random, accidental, and small events can have major consequences over time (Mahoney 2000; Mahoney and Schensul 2006, 461). In his study of political regimes in Central America, Mahoney (2001) argues that immediate political contingencies, namely a liberal-conservative elite split during the liberal reform period of the late nineteenth century, explain the choices made by presidents with regards to commercialization of agriculture and the role of the state in the economy and society. Where the split existed (Guatemala, El Salvador, and Nicaragua), the military expanded and presidents pursued radical policy packages with high levels of state coercion, extensive communal land expropriation, and established large-sized agricultural estates. By contrast, where the elite split did not emerge (Costa Rica and Honduras), presidents pursued reformist policies that entailed less state coercion, partial communal land expropriation, and smaller estates.

Mahoney (2000) suggests that path dependence may result from sequences that are characterized by a tightly coupled reaction and counter-reaction dynamic that originates in a contingent breakpoint. What makes reactive sequences path-dependent is not the fact that the direction of the early steps is followed (in fact it is not). Instead, reactive sequences are path-dependent because they begin from contingent events and are followed by closely linked reaction and counter-reaction events that can transform and even reverse the direction of the early steps (Mahoney 2000, 526). The social movements and the contentious politics literatures offer good examples of these type of sequences, such as when political pressure from social movements (a reaction) causes a direct response by the government or state (counter-reaction), which in turn leads to further reactive and counteractive dynamics (e.g., McAdam 1982; Riofrancos 2014).

The extensive attention given to critical junctures and path-dependent processes has led to characterizations of historical institutionalism as a tradition that has favored explanations of change that rest on notions of history as a process characterized by punctutated equilibria, followed by long periods of institutional stability (e.g., Peters, Pierre, and King 2005; see also Baumgartner and Jones 1993). Such characterizations may accurately capture the emphases of specific studies, but overlook that scholars in the tradition have long placed an emphasis on accounting for slow processes of gradual change and overlapping structures of authority rather than on rapid changes and stable orders.

Intercurrence and Modes of Institutional Change

At least since *Structuring Politics* underscored the importance of examining the politics of institutional dynamism (Steinmo et al. 1992, 16–18), and Karen Orren and Stephen Skowronek (1994) encouraged scholars to move beyond the "iconography of order," change has been a central focus in the historical institutionalism tradition. Skeptical of accounts of American politics that contrasted periods of relative stability in electoral coalitions with punctuated moments of change, or critical elections, Orren and Skowronek (1994) introduced the term *intercurrence* to capture the ongoing character of institutional creation, reproduction, and change. Questioning representations of political systems as fully formed entities that emerged at one moment in time, they noted that polities typically are comprised of numerous institutions and policies created at different times, each operating according to its own temporal logic. From this perspective, the non-simultaneity of institutional creation generates "mosaics" of institutions and layered structures of authority that cannot be fitted under descriptions of stable or neatly integrated political orders. Intercurrence describes a condition whereby the "accumulation ... of competing controls within institutions of government" are such that "the normal condition of the polity will be that of multiple, incongruous authorities operating simultaneously" (Orren and Skowronek 2004, 108). As a result, institutions or policies are sometimes ill-fitted to one another or govern according to contradictory imperatives.

The notion of intercurrence, even if not labeled as such, informs studies of American political development that explore how conflicts between multiple institutions and governing arrangements influence the dynamics of American politics. According to Lieberman (2002, 701), for example, American politics is characterized by a "variety of ordered institutional and ideological patterns each with its own origins, history, logic, and pace." Change occurs as the friction between institutions and ideas generates incentives and opportunities for individual political action. As an example, Lieberman points to the rise of affirmative action. Race-based remedies emerged in US employment law despite the 1964 Civil Rights Act, which espoused a race-neutral or color-blind view of discrimination and purposely gave the responsible federal agency very limited enforcement powers. The gap between color-blind ideals and weak institutions invited presidents, bureaucrats, the courts, and various interest groups to fill the breach, resulting in a new set of administrative rules, legal doctrine, and employment practices that gave rise to affirmative action policies.

Attention to the dynamic features of complex institutions is also characteristic of the rapidly growing literature on gradual institutional change. Pointing to the layered quality of institutions and the varying levels of discretion they give individuals to interpret and enforce rules, this literature brings attention to differentiated patterns of institutional growth and the causal mechanisms that produce variations in patterns of incremental change (Sheingate 2014). In distinguishing such patterns from studies of punctuated equilibria and stable orders, Mahoney and Thelen (2010b, 15–22) build on their own (Thelen 2004; Streeck and Thelen 2005) and related historical institutionalist scholarship (Hacker 2005; Schickler 2001) to give particular prominence to four modes of gradual institutional change: *displacement* or the removal of existing rules and the introduction of new ones; *layering* or the introduction of new rules on top of or alongside existing ones; *drift* or the changed impact of existing rules due to shifts in the environment; and *conversion* or the changed enactment of existing rules due to their strategic redeployment. A team of researchers in comparative and American politics finds these patterns of change to be common and identify when incremental modes of change reinforce national and local polities and when they lead to transformative outcomes (Mahoney and Thelen 2010a). Similar dynamics are found in IR, where studies document the role of incremental change in gradually remaking international political and economic institutions (Fioretos 2011a; Farrell and Newman 2014).

By differentiating between modes of gradual change, scholars bring attention to how "everyday" political contests—from small amendments or defection from existing practice, or the reinterpretation and opposition to existing understandings—shape the structure and effects of institutions over time. From this perspective, slow-moving processes of gradual change rather than singular historical break points may be the source of radical change (Pierson 2003). Studies of events that have been characterized as sudden ruptures, such as the global financial crisis of 2008, suggest that these may best be understood as the cumulative outcome of processes of incremental change over several decades. For example, a steady process of market liberalization, supported by an expanding consensus on the advantages of minimal market intervention, created a growing financial market place without a corresponding increase in effective regulatory authority at the domestic or international levels before the crisis (Helleiner 2011). Responses in the aftermath to the crisis, in particular why these failed to meet demand for radical reform, have also been understood in terms of incremental change and attributed to *pre*-crisis institutions that constrained *post*-crisis reforms (e.g., Carpenter 2009; Moshella and Tsingou 2013).

The literatures on gradual institutional change and intercurrence have expanded the analytical toolbox of historical institutionalism and in the process provided new means for understanding and explaining the complexity of the political world. Rather than encouraging scholars to focus on a single institution (or order) abstracted from the broader context in which it operates, these literatures push scholars to identify the points of connection between institutions created or changed at different times and for different purposes. As analytical tools, they thus help historical institutionalists draw attention to temporal and contextual factors that shape agency, including how and when actors exploit the tensions and contradictions between overlapping institutions or institutional layers to promote new or defend existing forms of power and authority.

Developments and Frontiers in Historical Institutionalism

Its growing empirical scope, methodological pluralism, and expanding analytical toolbox has helped to historical institutionalism consolidate its position as one of the three major traditions of institutional analysis in contemporary Political Science. Although scholars in the tradition are united around the importance of studying temporal effects, differences nevertheless exist in the perspectives of its practitioners. There is continued debate among scholars about the degree of dynamism within institutions, the role of actors in institutional accounts, and the relative weight of interests and ideas in the formation of preferences and the explanation of outcomes. Such debate is a mark of a dynamic research agenda and demonstrates that the development of historical institutionalism continues. As scholars debate these issues, opportunities exist to adopt new analytical techniques and methods, to integrate historical institutionalism more closely with related social science disciplines, and to further expand its empirical scope.

Conceptual Debates and Frontiers

Scholars of historical institutionalism have pushed beyond the structural-materialist core of the tradition to yield new insights into the origin, evolution, and transformation of institutions. They have grappled with questions about the relative importance of interests or ideas in institutional accounts (Lieberman 2002). They have stretched the boundaries of historical institutionalism beyond its early contributions by developing more actor-centered approaches (Sheingate 2003; Berk, Galvan, and Hattam 2013; Büthe 2015), as well as how ideas and beliefs structure the way actors interpret the world around them (King and Smith 2005). And they have expanded the boundaries in more structural and materialist directions: Hacker and Pierson's (2010) account of "winner-take-all" politics in the United States, for example, examines how the privileged few effectively captured American institutions in ways that bend public policy toward the material interests of the super-rich. Figure 1.2 illustrates the tradition's growth heuristically, with the shaded areas representing new frontiers within historical institutionalism that extend beyond its original focus.

Figure 1.2 suggests several points of connection between historical institutionalism and other approaches. Historical institutionalists initially criticized rationalist approaches for treating preferences as exogenous to institutions and more sociologically oriented approaches for relying too extensively on macro-structural conditions in accounting for preferences. Instead, they emphasized that careful attention needed to be paid to the interplay between structure and action. This point has become widely

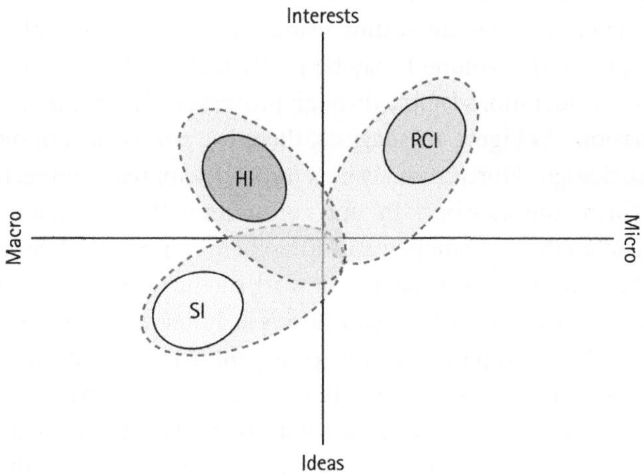

FIGURE 1.2 Frontiers of Institutional Analysis.

Note: HI=Historical Institutionalism; RCI=Rational Choice Institutionalism; SI=Sociological Institutionalism.

accepted among scholars in other traditions and opened room to create new links with other traditions of institutional analysis. In *Preferences and Situations*, for example, Ira Katznelson and Barry Weingast (2005, 1–2) note that a "productive erosion of boundaries has developed" between the historical and rational choice institutionalism, which fosters more common understandings of "how a given institutional milieu both constrains and shapes the repertoire of available preferences." Avner Greif and David Laitin (2004) consider the same intersection in exploring how features of institutions can be self-reinforcing in the short term, but become subject to a gradual and endogenous transformation over the long run. Key to their argument is the concept of a quasi-parameter, which is a set of cognitive beliefs about the world that guide individual behavior. Institutions are stable where such beliefs are robust; that is, they dictate behavior in a wide range of circumstances and in self-enforcing ways. If these beliefs erode, as when situations arise where beliefs cease to provide a course of action, individuals will "experiment or risk deviating from past behavior," resulting in a process of gradual change (Greif and Laitin 2004, 639).

There is an affinity between Greif and Laitin's concept of quasi-parameters and historical-institutionalist modes of gradual change that examine how incremental innovations in rules or their application transform institutions or their effects. Greif and Laitin, however, provide less of an account of institutional *change* than of institutional *breakdown* as the capacity of beliefs to direct behavior weakens over time (Thelen 2004, 30). As a consequence they are unable to distinguish empirically between elements of institutions that are durable from those vulnerable to change (Mahoney and Thelen 2010b, 6). Historical institutionalist work on gradual models of change offer tools to solve that problem and demonstrate the value of embracing the study of long temporal processes when improving explanations and understandings of complex patterns of institutional change.

Historical institutionalism is also well-positioned to engage more directly with sociological approaches to institutions. The sometimes fraught relationship between scholars focused on the material and cognitive dimensions of institutions (see Blyth, Helgadóttir, and Kring, Chapter 8, this volume) may be partly mended by considering how ideas render material considerations legible through processes of communication, coordination, and persuasion. As Figure 1.2 suggests, there is a sizable area of overlap between historical and sociological institutionalism, a multi-disciplinary connection that began with efforts to "bring the state back in" and continues with the ongoing work in comparative historical analysis (Mahoney and Rueschemeyer 2003; Mahoney and Thelen 2015). Within this area one may locate recent work on the evolution of American political parties that explores how party organizations acquired new routines and resources through investments in computer technology and information databases (Galvin 2012; Chapter 18, this volume). Work on the politics of social policy explores how ideas and institutions interact as a neoliberal embrace of the market combined with a paternalistic view of the poor produced a highly punitive set of social programs in the United States (Soss, Fording, and Schram 2011).

The promise of exploring areas of overlap between historical and sociological variants of institutionalism extends beyond national borders. Farrell and Finnemore (Chapter 34, this volume) argue that greater consideration of ideas and norms is particularly important for historical institutionalism within IR because the international system is not as densely institutionalized as domestic polities and effective means to enforce policies are often lacking. Devoting greater attention to how ideas and norms are embedded within international institutions may enhance understandings of the origin of state preferences and why cooperation takes different forms in the modern international system. Work demonstrating how the communication of ideas furthers actors' strategic goals by constraining alternatives, focusing attention, and persuading others may help historical institutionalists gain better understandings of the conditions under which international policy priorities and institutions change (e.g., Blyth 2013; Schmidt 2008; Jabko 2012). Areas of overlap, then, are invitations to continue the exploration of when ideational and material understandings of institutions must be considered side by side in order to gain greater understanding of the complex realities that define politics nationally and internationally.

Methodological Developments

Contemporary historical institutionalism maintains a strong commitment to refining its use of research methods in Politcial Science. This commitment has been spurred on by two research challenges. The first concerns how to determine which of several theories is accurate when they predict similar outcomes. For the new institutionalisms, this equifinality challenge is a question of identifying the extent to which the mechanisms at the center of alternative explanations were present (or absent) in ways that can be said to have caused a specific outcome under some conditions, but not other ones (Hall 2003). As a tradition of middle-range theory that is heavily mechanisms-oriented, resolving this challenge has encouraged historical institutionalists across sub-fields to deepen and refine their use of qualitative methods to leverage historical archives. Galvin (2010) and Carpenter (2001), for example, embrace historiographical methods to offer fine-grained analyses of why the American presidency and bureaucracy followed distinct paths, Ziblatt (2009) and Ahmed (2012) do it to detail the origins of federalism and electoral systems, respectively, and Helleiner (2014) to revisit arguments about the origins of the modern international economic system.

A second challenge that has led historical institutionalists to refine their use of qualitative methods concerns how to identify which of multiple potential historical events gave rise to an outcome. Mahoney, Kimball, and Koivu (2009) ask how one determines which of two or more potential critical junctures is the source of the outcome of interest. Here it is not so much a question of which type of cause is in play, but where in a sequence of events the cause is located. Since when an event takes place may be material for whether other events take place at all, historical institutionalists have sought to refine how they study sequences to better adjudicate which events are proximate in causing political outcomes. Mahoney, Kimball, and Koivu's (2009) "method of sequence elaboration," for example, assists researchers in identifying which of many potential necessary and sufficient causes are the ones that caused events by situating these within different temporal contexts. What Caraway (2004, 455) terms "sequential episodic analysis" and Capoccia and Ziblatt (2010) call a "structured episode" method similarly encourage researchers to carefully analyze distinct episodes in a chain of events in order to ascertain whether purported causes were consistently present and whether they had the anticipated effect. The episodes oriented approach is consistent and complementary with the classic emphasis in historical institutionalism on evolutionary paths, while also making it possible to identify whether any and which of many events mattered in shaping particular trajectories.

While historical institutional research has retained a particular affinity for qualitative methods associated with historiography and process-tracing, researchers have come to embrace a wider array of methods with time. Some of its practitioners have been central to the growth in multi-methods research in Political Science, with studies combining large data-sets and careful process-tracing to improve the precision of case selection and causal inference (Lieberman 2002; Farhang 2010). This has allowed studies to account for a range of empirical patterns, including why the evolution of legislatures has been characterized by "disjointed pluralism" over time (Schickler 2001), and why the structure and strategies of organized interest groups take different forms when facing similar challenges (Martin and Swank 2012). Similarly, a growing body of work employing behavioral methods of survey research and qualitative ethnographic studies have successfully traced policy feedback effects and other institutional legacies to give nuance to diverse patterns of political participation, citizenship, and social relations (Campbell 2003; Mettler and Soss 2004; MacLean 2010).

Incorporating new theoretical insights and refining methods in historical institutionalism could spark additional innovations and new intellectual bridges. For instance, there is an affinity between actor-centered approaches to historical institutionalism and agent-based ones using computer simulations of actors operating under various conditions and constraints in order to probe how actors' decisions produce, reproduce, and transform institutional arrangements over time (Lustick 2011; Lewis and Steinmo 2012). Similarly, network analysis offers a way to incorporate insights from evolutionary theory by examining how relationships among actors are generative of social structures (Farrell and Shalizi 2012). Discourse analysis offers the opportunity to explore a different intersection by providing access to interpretive methodologies that may assist historical institutionalists to better understand how the ideational framing of normative judgments impact support for institutions (Schmidt 2008; Riofrancos 2014). Finally, as Steinmo (Chapter 6, this volume) explores, careful incorporation of experimental methods can help scholars examine previously taken-for-granted assumptions about how institutions structure behavior and how, in turn, individual behavior supports or undermines institutional stability.

Empirical Extensions

From methodological and conceptual refinements, and from greater exchange with other traditions of analysis, come opportunities to extend the empirical scope of historical institutionalism. The vast majority of historical institutionalist work focuses on formal institutions, understood as written and enforceable rules, such as those associated with political constitutions and regulatory frameworks. It is apparent, however, that informal institutions—unwritten understandings and practices—also can have strong consequences for political behavior and preferences (Helmke and Levitsky 2006; Tsai 2006). Political scientists have acknowledged that such institutions matter, but have yet to give such structures their due attention. The importance of considering the role of such institutions is particularly great in the study of developing countries where formal institutions often are relatively weak and informal ones appear more important in structuring social relations (Tsai, Chapter 16, this volume). But also in contexts where formal institutions are plenty is more attention to informal ones warranted. Historical institutionalist theories of incremental change are well-suited for such an undertaking since they include consideration of the informal institutions that are used to negotiate reforms to formal institutions.

Historical institutionalism additionally holds potential for the study of other dimensions of politics that also lack immediate visibility, including institutions that are the source of the structural power that political coalitions wield to secure their preferred policies. Understood generally as the ability to shape the cognitive realities of individuals, structural power often resides in institutions that produce policy biases and that give political groups mobilizational advantages in seeing their preferred policies enacted. Pierson (Chapter 7, this volume) argues that historical institutionalism's emphasis on studying slow-moving processes and constellations of overlapping institutions provide the means to reveal where biases come from and how they are reproduced over time. Recent scholarship in IR points in a similar direction and encourages scholars to look beyond the role of powerful states in shaping the policy prescriptions of international organizations to more carefully study how international bureaucrats mobilize biases with enduring effects for the strategies used by governments (e.g., Barnett and Finnemore 2004). As researchers take on the challenge of explaining why inequalities endure domestically and internationally, despite the availability of new resources and norms of more even distribution, historical institutionalists are well-placed to expand understandings of when and why structural power persists and how it begets other inequalities over time.

Future research may also correct the imbalance that has existed between the study of patterns that lead to the reproduction of institutions and those that may undermine designs. Although initially conceived as a mode of gradual institutional change (Streeck and Thelen 2005), the concept of institutional exhaustion has received much less attention in the literature than layering, conversion, displacement, or drift. Recently, this has begun to change as scholars pay closer attention to how institutions gradually unravel. Jacobs and Weaver (2015) bring attention to how the increasing costs of a policy can undermine crucial sources of institutional support among powerful actors while, at the same time, lead to the perception among mass publics that a failed policy is in need of reform. Busemeyer and Trampusch (2013) explore similar patterns in the context of changing systems and priorities in systems of human capital formation. Attention to exhaustion and other kinds of self-undermining dynamics is also relevant for scholars interested in authoritarian transitions as regimes that initially appear to be quite durable weaken over time as members of a revolutionary cadre die off and key mechanisms of institutional reproduction gradually erode (Levitsky and Way 2013).

Historical institutionalism may also continue to broaden empirical research agendas by serving as a bridge between subfields. Such a bridge has long been in existence between the comparative and American politics subfields and been a source of greater understandings of political developments across countries. More recently it has served as bridge between these subfields and IR (Katznelson and Shefter 2002; Fioretos 2011a). For example, studies have used the tradition to explain the origins of states' preferences over forms of international cooperation, then analyze the effects of the timing and sequence of reforms in determining international bargaining outcomes, and how international institutions impact domestic policy priorities (Farrell and Newman 2010; Fioretos 2011b; Posner 2010). As globalization fosters an increase in the institutions that structure relations among states and these reach more deeply into how domestic polities are managed, historical institutionalism holds much promise for explaining the origins and effects of the complex institutional realities that link international and domestic politics in the twenty-first century.

Finally, the scope of the tradition may be extended by widening the empirical reach of what is conventionally understood as "temporality." The tradition has devoted particular attention to the causal effects of the timing and sequence of reform, and has yet to explore at greater length the potential causal impact on politics of variations in the duration, tempo, and the acceleration of institutional change (Grzymala-Busse 2010). Yet the duration of events may impact time-horizons and discount rates; the speed of change may affect the nature of learning and deliberation; and the extent to which change is accelerating or not may be important for the type of causal mechanisms that are active over time (e.g., tipping points, cascades). To fully identify the potential impact of these temporal factors, future studies may focus on identifying whether and how repeated policy failures or successes impact later reforms, what role institutions play in the tenacity with which historic veto actors and losers from past reform impact patterns of institutional durability and change, and the reasons for why the adoption of new local or global norms vary across time and space. While the baselines used to evaluate the impact of temporal phenomena may vary across areas of research, a richer understanding of such phenomena holds great promise for future studies seeking to formulate nuanced understandings of why complexity remains an enduring feature of modern polities.

Conclusion

Within a generation, historical institutionalism has become a large and diverse analytical and empirical research tradition in Political Science that has tackled core puzzles in the discipline, reinvigorated the study of institutions and history, and developed new areas of research. It is firmly established in areas of research within Comparative, American, European, and International Politics. It is both empirically rich and analytically sophisticated, eschewing convenient trade-offs between these two sides of the social science coin. The chapters that follow very amply demonstrate the growth and vibrancy of historical institutionalism since it crystallized a generation ago. Indeed, and somewhat ironically, the strongest testament to its growth is the reality that not even a comprehensive volume such as this one can fully cover all relevant analytical and empirical developments in the tradition.

The remainder of the volume is divided into five parts, each collecting a set of contributions on distinct aspects of historical institutionalism. Part II details conceptual and methodological foundations of historical institutionalism. Contributors revisit what is meant by "structured politics" (Peter A. Hall, Chapter 2), explore insights into patterns of institutional change (James Conran and Kathleen Thelen, Chapter 3), the role of critical junctures (Giovanni Capoccia, Chapter 5), the exercise of political power (Paul Pierson, Chapter 7), and the relationship between ideas and interests (Mark Blyth, Oddný Helgadóttir, and William Kring, Chapter 8). They further discuss methodological developments in historical institutionalism (James Mahoney, Khairunnisa Mohamedali, and Christoph Nguyen, Chapter 4), including how scholars in this tradition wrestle with causality and make productive use of experimental designs (Sven Steinmo, Chapter 6).

The next four sections are devoted to major subfields within Political Science. Part III explores historical institutionalism's contributions to research in comparative politics, and includes chapters on a wide range of political constructs with empirical illustrations from all corners of the world. It was within comparative politics that historical institutionalism first emerged as a distinct approach to study the effects of institutions on politics. The volume highlights topics that since then have been at the core of the comparative historical institutional agenda, such as the study of the modern developmental state (Atul Kohli, Chapter 9), democratization (Rodrigo Barrenechea, Edward L. Gibson, and Larkin Terrie, Chapter 11), political parties (Rachel Beatty Riedl, Chapter 13), and organized labor (Teri Caraway, Chapter 15). This section also includes chapters on topics that have more recently entered the comparative research agenda, such as the study of competitive authoritarianism (Steven Levitsky and Lucan Way, Chapter 12), the origins of state capacity (Hillel David Soifer, Chapter 10), non-state provision of social welfare (Melanie Cammett and Aytuğ Şamşaz, Chapter 14), and informal institutions (Kellee Tsai, Chapter 16).

In Part IV, contributors explore historical institutionalism in American politics, which has been a major incubator for this approach in Political Science. Often associated with the study of American political development, historical institutionalism has both informed and been informed by the study of the United States. The chapters in this volume continue this tradition by examining the distinctive character of the American state (Desmond King, Chapter 17), the organization of political parties (Daniel Galvin, Chapter 18), the central role of courts (Sarah Staszak, Chapter 19), and the evolution of social policies (Alan Jacobs, Chapter 20). Alongside the focus on American political institutions and policies, the contributions also illustrate how historical institutional approaches address core questions of the American polity, past and present, such as the central place of racial politics, and the yawning gap in income inequality, and the rise of mass incarceration (Paul Frymer, Marie Gottschalk, Chapters 21 and 22, respectively). Together, the chapters illustrate the ongoing vibrancy of research on historical institutionalism and American political development.

Many of the early contributions to historical institutionalism focused on developments in Europe. As European polities have become more internationalized, especially through a lengthy process of European integration, scholars have integrated comparative and international politics to a very significant degree. Chapters in Part V explore areas of research that are tethered relatively closely to national political developments as well as areas that include a very significant dimension of international cooperation. They explore the evolution of European states (Daniel Kelemen, Chapter 23), democracy (Sheri Berman, Chapter 24), institutions of social insurance (Julia Lynch and Martin Rhodes, Chapter 25) and religion (Anna Grzymala-Busse, Chapter 28), business (Pepper Culpepper, Chapter 27), finance (Richard Deeg and Elliot Posner, Chapter 26), market regulation (Mark Thatcher and Cornelia Woll, Chapter 30), as well as supranationalism in the European Union context (Tim Büthe, Chapter 29).

Finally, Part VI explores the contributions and promise of historical institutionalism for research in International Relations across a set of topics, including state sovereignty (Stephen D. Krasner, Chapter 31), global orders (G. John Ikenberry, Chapter 32), and international organizations (Henry Farrell and Martha Finnemore, Chapter 34). Chapters in this section also explore institutional developments in international security cooperation (Etel Solingen and Wilfred Wan, Chapter 33), international law (Karen J. Alter, Chapter 35), trade (Judith Goldstein and Robert Gulotty, Chapter 36), finance (Eric Helleiner, Chapter 37), and other areas of global regulation (Abraham L. Newman, Chapter 38). Together, they detail the contributions that historical institutionalism makes to perennial and new questions in International Relations, while also outlining agendas for future work on international political developments.

Across multiple subfields of Political Science, historical institutionalists have answered enduring empirical questions to the discipline as well as solved new complex puzzles by refining an analytical toolbox and methodological strategies to systematically and rigorously research politics and institutions in time. Since it crystallized as a tradition of political analysis in the early 1990s, its empirical scope has grown greatly to include new areas of research at the local, national, and international levels of politics.

If the past holds lessons for the future, it is that future scholarship will continue to gain from refining analytical concepts, probing new methods, and expanding the empirical horizons of historical institutionalism.

Notes

* For many and engaging conversations about this project, we thank the contributors and Dominic Byatt of Oxford University Press; and for focused feedback on earlier versions of this introduction, we thank Martha Finnemore, Anna Grzymala-Busse, Peter Hall, Cathie Jo Martin, Gabriel Negretto, Hillel David Soifer, Kathleen Thelen, especially Alan Jacobs, as well as participants in the October 2013 Philadelphia conference on Historical Institutionalism in Political Science, the 2013 presentation at CIDE (Mexico), the 2014 Council for European Studies Conference, and the 2014 American Political Science Association Annual Meeting. This introduction is the product of a collaborative partnership that began in 2011. Authors are listed in the same order as the volume masthead and share equal responsibility for the contents of this introduction.

1. Steinmo dates the actual coining of "historical institutionalism" to 1989: "The term came out of a small workshop held in Boulder, Colorado in January 1989" (Steinmo 2008, 136, n. 1). Overviews of the tradition's emergence are found in Thelen 1999; Pierson and Skocpol 2002; Sanders 2006.

References

Ahmed, Amel. 2012. *Democracy and the Politics of Electoral System Choice: Engineering Electoral Dominance*. New York: Cambridge University Press.

Arthur, W. Brian. 1994. *Increasing Returns and Path Dependence in the Economy*. Ann Arbor: University of Michigan Press.

Barnett, Michael and Martha Finnemore. 2004. *Rules for the World: International Organizations in Global Politics*. Ithaca, NY: Cornell University Press.

Baumgartner, Frank B. and Bryan D. Jones. 1993. *Agendas and Instability in American Politics*. Chicago: Chicago University Press.

Berk, Gerald, Dennis C. Galvan, and Victoria Hattam, eds. 2013. *Political Creativity: Reconfiguring Institutional Order and Change*. Philadelphia: University of Pennsylvania Press.

Berman, Sheri. 1998. *The Social Democratic Moment: Ideas and Politics in the Making of Interwar Europe*. New York: Cambridge University Press.

Blyth, Mark. 2002. *Great Transformations: Economic Ideas and Institutional Change in the Twentieth Century*. New York: Cambridge University Press.

Blyth, Mark. 2013. *Austerity: The History of a Dangerous Idea*. New York: Oxford University Press.

Busemeyer, Marius and Christine Trampusch. 2013. "Liberalization by Exhaustion: Transformative Change in the German Welfare State and Vocational Training System." *Zeitschrift für Sozialreform* 59 (3): 291–312.

Buthe, Tim. 2015. Agent-Centric Historical Institutionalism as a Theory of Institutional Change: The Politics of Regulating Competition and Mergers in the European Union, 1955–2010. Manuscript. Duke University.

Campbell, Andrea Louise. 2003. *How Policies Make Citizens: Senior Political Activism and the American Welfare State*. Princeton, NJ: Princeton University Press.

Capoccia, Giovanni and R. Daniel Keleman. 2007. "The Study of Critical Junctures: Theory, Narrative, and Counterfactuals in Historical Institutionalism." *World Politics* 59 (3): 341–369.

Capoccia, Giovanni and Daniel Ziblatt. 2010. "The Historical Turn in Democratization Studies: A New Research Agenda for Europe and Beyond." *Comparative Political Studies* 43 (8/9): 931–968.

Caraway, Teri L. 2004. "Inclusion and Democratization: Class, Gender, Race, and the Extension of Suffrage." *Comparative Politics* 36 (4): 443–460.

Carpenter, D. P. 2001. *The Forging of Bureaucratic Autonomy: Reputations, Networks, and Policy Innovation in Executive Agencies, 1862–1928*. Princeton, NJ: Princeton University Press.

Carpenter, Daniel. 2009. "Institutional Strangulation: Bureaucratic Politics and Financial Reform in the Obama Administration." *Perspectives on Politics* 8 (03): 825–846.

Collier, Ruth Berins and David Collier. 1991. *Shaping the Political Arena: Critical Junctures, the Labor Movement, and Regime Dynamics in Latin America*. Princeton, NJ: Princeton University Press.

David, Paul. 1985. "Clio and the Economics of QWERTY." *American Economic Review* 75: 332–337.

DiMaggio, Paul and Walter Powell. 1983. "The Iron Cage Revisited: Institutional Isomorphism and Collective Rationality in Organizational Fields." *American Sociological Review* 48 (2): 147–160.

Evans, Peter B., Dietrich Rueschemeyer, and Theda Skocpol, eds. 1985. *Bringing the State Back In*. New York: Cambridge University Press.

Falleti, Tulia G. 2010. *Decentralization and Subnational Politics in Latin America*. New York: Cambridge University Press.

Falleti, Tulia G. and Julia Lynch. 2009. "Context and Causation in Political Analysis." *Comparative Political Studies* 49 (9): 1143–1166.

Farhang, Sean. 2010. *The Litigation State: Public Regulation and Private Lawsuits in the U.S.* Princeton, NJ: Princeton University Press.

Farrell, Henry and Abraham L. Newman, eds. 2010. "Special Issue on Market Regulation." *Review of International Political Economy* 17 (4).

Farrell, Henry and Abraham L. Newman. 2014. "Domestic Institutions beyond the Nation State: Charting the New Interdependence Approach." *World Politics* 66 (2): 331–363.

Farrell, Henry and Cosma Shalizi. 2012. Evolutionary Theory and the Dynamics of Institutional Change. Unpublished paper.

Fioretos, Orfeo. 2011a. "Historical Institutionalism in International Relations." *International Organization* 65 (2): 367–399.

Fioretos, Orfeo. 2011b. *Creative Reconstructions: Multilateralism and European Varieties of Capitalism*. Ithaca, NY: Cornell University Press

Galvin, Daniel J. 2010. *Presidential Party Building: Dwight D. Eisenhower to George W. Bush*. Princeton, NJ: Princeton University Press.

Galvin, Daniel. 2012. "The Transformation of Political Institutions: Investments in Institutional Resources and Gradual Change in the National Party Committees." *Studies in American Political Development* 26 (1): 50–70.

Gerschenkron, Alexander. 1962. *Economic Backwardness in Historical Perspective.* New York: Praeger.

Goldstein, Judith. 1994. *Ideas, Interests, and American Trade Policy*. Ithaca, NY: Cornell University Press.

Greif, Avner and David Laitin. 2004. "An Endogenous Theory of Institutional Change." *American Political Science Review* 98 (4): 633–652.

Grzymala-Busse, Anna. 2010. "Time Will Tell? Temporality and the Analysis of Causal Mechanisms and Processes." *Comparative Political Studies* 44 (9), 1267–1297.

Hacker, Jacob S. 2005. "Policy Drift: The Hidden Politics of US Welfare State Retrenchment." In *Beyond Continuity: Institutional Change in Advanced Political Economies*, ed. Wolfgang Streeck and Kathleen Thelen. New York: Oxford University Press, 40–82.

Hacker, Jacob S. and Paul Pierson. 2010. *Winner-Take-All Politics: How Washington Made the Rich Richer, and Turned Its Back on the Middle Class.* New York: Simon and Schuster.

Hall, Peter A. 1986. *Governing the Economy: The Politics of State Intervention in Britain and France*. London: Oxford University Press.

Hall, Peter A. 2003. "Aligning Ontology and Methodology in Comparative Research." In *Comparative Historical Analysis in the Social Sciences*, ed. James Mahoney and Dietrich Rueschemeyer. New York: Cambridge University Press, 373–404.

Hall, Peter A. and Rosemary C. R. Taylor. 1996. "Political Science and the Three New Institutionalisms." *Political Studies* 46: 936–957.

Helleiner, Eric. 2011. "Understanding the 2007–2008 Global Financial Crisis: Lessons From Scholars of International Politcial Economy." *Annual Review of Politcial Science* 14, 67–87.

Helleiner, Eric. 2014. *Forgotten Foundations of Bretton Woods: International Development and the Making of the Postwar Order*. Ithaca, NY: Cornell University Press.

Helmke, Gretchen and Steven Levitsky. 2006. "Informal Institutions in Comparative Research." *Perspectives on Politics* 2 (4), 725–740.

Ikenberry, G. John. 1992. "A World Economy Restored: Expert Consensus and the Anglo-American Postwar Settlement." *International Organization* 46 (1), 289–321.

Immergut, Ellen M. 1998. "The Theoretical Core of the New Institutionalism." *Politics & Society* 26: 5–34.

Jabko, Nicholas. 2012. *Playing the Market: A Political Strategy for Uniting Europe, 1985–2005*. Ithaca, NY: Cornell University Press.

Jacobs, Alan and Kent Weaver. 2015. "When Policies Undo Themselves: Self-Undermining Feedback as a Source of Policy Change." *Governance*. Available at <http://onlinelibrary.wiley.com.proxy1.library.jhu.edu/doi/10.1111/gove.12101/full> (accessed August 18, 2015).

Katznelson, Ira. 1997. "Structure and Configuration in Comparative Politics." In *Comparative Politics: Rationality, Culture, and Structure*, ed. Mark Irving Lichbach and Alan S. Zuckerman. New York: Cambridge University Press, 81–112.

Katznelson, Ira. 2003. "Periodization and Preferences: Reflections on Purposive Action in Comparative Historical Social Science." In *Comparative Historical Analysis in the Social Sciences*, ed. James Mahoney and Dietrich Rueschemeyer. New York: Cambridge University Press, 270–301.

Katznelson, Ira and Martin Shefter, eds. 2002. *Shaped by War and Trade: International Influences on American Political Development*. Princeton, NJ: Princeton University Press.

Katznelson, Ira and Barry Weingast, eds. 2005. "Intersections between Historical and Rational Choice Institutionalism." In *Preferences and Situations: Points of Intersection between*

Historical and Rational Choice Institutionalism, ed. Ira Katznelson and Barry Weingast. New York: Russell Sage Foundation, 1–24.

King, Desmond S. and Rogers M. Smith. 2005. "Racial Orders in American Political Development." *American Political Science Review* 99 (1): 75–92.

Levitsky, Steven and Lucan Way. 2013. "The Durability of Revolutionary Regimes." *Journal of Democracy* 24 (3): 5–17.

Lewis, Orion A., and Sven Steinmo. 2012. "Nested Analysis as a Mixed-method Strategy for Comparative Research." *American Political Science Review* 99 (3): 435–452.

Lieberman, Robert C. 2002. "Ideas, Institutions, and Political Order: Explaining Political Change." *American Political Science Review* 96 (4): 697–712.

Lipset, Seymour and Stein Rokkan. 1967. "Cleavage Structure, Party Systems, and Voter Alignments: An Introduction." In *Party Systems and Voter Alignments: Cross-National Perspectives*, ed. Lipset and Rokkan. New York: Free Press, 1–64.

Lustick, Ian S. 2011. "Taking Evolution Seriously: Historical Institutionalism and Evolutionary Theory." *Polity* 43: 179–209.

McAdam, Doug. 1982. *Political Process and Development of Black Insurgency, 1930–1970*. Chicago and London: University of Chicago Press.

MacLean, Lauren M. 2010. *Informal Institutions and Citizenship in Rural Africa: Risk and Reciprocity in Ghana and Côte D'Ivoire*. New York: Cambridge University Press.

Mahoney, James. 2000. "Path Dependence in Historical Sociology." *Theory and Society* 29 (4): 507–548.

Mahoney, James. 2001. *The Legacies of Liberalism: Path Dependence and Political Regimes in Central America*. Baltimore, MD: Johns Hopkins University Press.

Mahoney, James and Dietrich Rueschemeyer, eds. 2003. *Comparative Historical Analysis in the Social Sciences*. New York: Cambridge University Press.

Mahoney, James and Daniel Schensul. 2006. "Historical Context and Path Dependence." In *The Oxford Handbook of Contextual Political Analysis*, ed. Robert E. Goodin and Charles Tilly. New York and London: Oxford University Press, 454–471.

Mahoney, James and Thelen, Kathleen, eds. 2010a. *Explaining Institutional Change: Ambiguity, Agency, and Power*. New York: Cambridge University Press.

Mahoney, James and Thelen, Kathleen. 2010b. "A Theory of Gradual Institutional Change." In *Explaining Institutional Change: Ambiguity, Agency, and Power*, ed. James Mahoney and Kathleen Thelen. New York: Cambridge University Press, 1–37.

Mahoney, James, and Kathleen Thelen, eds. 2015. *Advances in Comparative Historical Analysis*. New York: Cambridge University Press.

Mahoney, James, Erin Kimball, and Kendra L. Koivu 2009. "The Logic of Historical Explanation in the Social Sciences." *Comparative Politcial Studies* 42 (1): 114–146.

March, James G. and Johan P. Olsen. 1984. "The New Institutionalism: Organizational Factors in Political Life." *American Political Science Review* 78 (3): 734–749.

Martin, Cathie Jo and Duane Swank. 2012. *The Political Construction of Business Interests: Coordination, Growth and Equality*. Cambridge: Cambridge University Press.

Mettler, Suzanne and Joe Soss. 2004. "The Consequences of Public Policy for Democratic Citizenship: Bridging Policy Studies and Mass Politics." *Perspectives on Politics* 2: 55–73.

Moore, Barrington. 1966. *Social Origins of Dictatorship and Democracy: Lord and Peasant in the Making of the Modern World*. Boston: Beacon Press.

Moshella, Manuela and Eleni Tsingou, eds. 2013. *Great Expectations, Slow Transformations: Incremental Change in Post-Crisis Financial Regulation*. Colchester: ECPR Press.

Nettl, J. P. 1968. "The State as a Conceptual Variable." *World Politics* 20: 559–592.

Nordlinger, Eric A. 1982. *On the Autonomy of the Democratic State*. Cambridge, MA: Harvard University Press.

O'Donnell, Guillermo. 1973. *Modernization and Bureaucratic-Authoritarianism: Studies in South American Politics*. Berkeley: University of California Press.

Orren, Karen and Stephen Skowronek. 1994. "Beyond the Iconography of Order: Notes for A New Institutionalism." In *The Dynamics of American Politics: Approaches and Interpretations*, ed. Lawrence Dodd and Calvin Jillison. Boulder, CO: Westview Press, 311–330.

Orren, Karen and Stephen Skowronek. 2004. *The Search for American Political Development*. New York: Cambridge University Press.

Ostrom, Elinor. 2010. "Beyond Markets and States: Polycentric Governance of Complex Economic Systems." In *The Nobel Prizes 2009*, ed. Karl Grandin. Stockholm: Nobel Foundation, 408–444.

Peters, B. Guy, Jon Pierre, and Desmond S. King. 2005. "The Politics of Path Dependence: Political Conflict in Historical Institutionalism." *Journal of Politics* 67 (4): 1275–1300.

Pierson, Paul. 1993. "When Effect Becomes Cause: Policy Feedback Effect and Political Change." *World Politics* 45 (4), 595–628.

Pierson, Paul. 2000. "Not Just What, but *When*: Timing and Sequence in Political Processes." *Studies in American Political Development* 14, 72–92.

Pierson, Paul. 2003. "Big, Slow-Moving, and . . . Invisible: Macrosocial Process in the Study of Comparative Politics." In *Comparative Historical Analysis in the Social Sciences*, ed. James Mahoney and Dietrich Rueschemeyer. New York: Cambridge University Press, 177–207.

Pierson, Paul. 2004. *Politics in Time: History, Institutions, and Social Analysis*. Princeton, NJ: Princeton University Press.

Pierson, Paul and Theda Skocpol. 2002. "Historical Institutionalism in Contemporary Political Science." In *Political Science: State of the Discipline*, ed. Ira Katznelson and Helen V. Milner. New York and Washington D.C.: W.W. Norton and American Political Science Association, 693–721.

Polanyi, Karl. 1944. *The Great Transformation: The Origins of Our Time*. Boston: Beacon Press.

Posner, Elliot. 2010. "Sequence as Explanation: The International Politics of Accounting Standards." *Review of International Political Economy* 17 (4): 639–664.

Ragin, Charles. 1987. *The Comparative Method*. Oakland, CA: University of California Press.

Riofrancos, Thea. 2014. "Contesting Extraction: State-Making, Democracy and Large Scale Mining in Ecuador." Ph.D. Dissertation, Department of Political Science, University of Pennsylvania, Philadelphia, PA.

Rokkan, Stein. 1970. *Citizens, Elections, and Parties*. New York: David McKay.

Sanders, Elizabeth. 2006. "Historical Institutionalism." In *The Oxford Handbook of Political Institutions*, ed. R. A. W. Rhodes, Sarah A. Binder, and Bert A. Rockman. London: Oxford University Press, 39–55.

Schickler, Eric. 2001. *Disjointed Pluralism: Institutional Innovation and the Development of the U.S. Congress*. Princeton, NJ: Princeton University Press.

Schmidt, Vivian. 2008. "Discursive Institutionalism: The Explanatory Power of Ideas and Discourse." *Annual Review of Political Science* 11: 303–326.

Sheingate, Adam D. 2003. "Political Entrepreneurship, Institutional Change, and American Political Development." *Studies in American Political Development* 17 (2): 185–203.

Sheingate, Adam D. 2014. "Institutional Dynamics and American Political Development." *Annual Review of Political Science* 17 (1): 461–477.

Shepsle, Kenneth. 1981. "Institutional Equilibrium and Equilibrium Institutions." In *Political Science: The Science of Politics*, ed. Herbet F. Weisberg. Washington, D.C.: American Political Science Association and Agathon Press, 51–81.

Schickler, Eric. 2001. *Disjointed Pluralism: Institutional Innovation and the Development of the U.S. Congress*. Princeton, NJ: Princeton University Press,

Skocpol, Theda. 1995. "Why I am an Historical Institutionalist." *Polity* 28 (1), 103–106.

Skocpol, Theda and Paul Pierson. 2001. "Historical Institutionalism in Contemporary Political Science." In *Political Science: State of the Discipline*, ed. Ira Katznelson and Helen V. Milner. New York: Norton, 693–721.

Slater, Dan and Erica Simmons. 2010. "Informative Regress: Critical Antecedents in Comparative Politics." *Comparative Political Studies* 43 (7): 886–917.

Soifer, Hillel David. 2012. "The Causal Logic of Critical Junctures." *Comparative Political Studies* 45 (12), 1572–1597.

Soss, Joe, Richard C. Fording, and Sanford Schram. 2011. *Disciplining the Poor: Neoliberal Paternalism and the Persistent Power of Race*. Chicago: Chicago University Press.

Steinmo, Sven. 1989. "Political Institutions and Tax Policy in the United States, Sweden, and Britain." *World Politics* 41 (4): 500–535.

Steinmo, Sven. 2008. "Historical Institutionalism." In *Approaches and Methodologies in the Social Sciences: A Pluralist Perspective*, ed. Donatella Della Porta and Michael Keating. New York: Cambridge University Press, 118–138.

Steinmo, Sven, Kathleen Thelen, and Frank Longstreth, eds. 1992. *Structuring Politics: Historical Institutionalism in Comparative Analysis*. Cambridge: Cambridge University Press.

Streeck, Wolfgang and Kathleen Thelen, eds. 2005. *Beyond Continuity: Institutional Change in Advanced Political Economies*. New York: Oxford University Press.

Thelen, Kathleen. 1999. "Historical Institutionalism in Comparative Politics." *Annual Review of Political Science* 2: 369–404.

Thelen, Kathleen. 2004. *How Institutions Evolve: The Political Economy of Skills in Germany, Britain, the United States, and Japan*. New York: Cambridge University Press.

Tsai, Kellee. 2006. "Adaptive Informal Institutions and Endogenous Institutional Change in China." *World Politics* 59 (1): 116–141.

Ziblatt, Daniel. 2009. "Shaping Democratic Practice and the Causes of Electoral Fraud: The Case of Nineteenth-Century Germany." *American Political Science Review* 103, 1–21.

PART II

FOUNDATIONS

CHAPTER 2

POLITICS AS A PROCESS STRUCTURED IN SPACE AND TIME

PETER A. HALL*

WHAT do we see when we look at the political world across space and time? In large measure, that depends on what we are looking for and the lens through which we look. This is as true of Political Science today as it was of seventeenth-century scientists looking for phlogiston through rudimentary microscopes. Our methods and assumptions about what we should see, notably about causal structures in the world, condition what we find. In this chapter, I consider the value of seeing politics as a process that is structured across space and time, a perspective closely associated with historical institutionalism.

Analysts working within this school of thought have long been interested in the issue of how politics might be structured across space and time. Their initial formulations were inspired by a reaction against behavioral models that saw politics as interest group conflict, sometimes conditioned by political culture, but largely unmediated by institutional structures (Steinmo, Thelen, and Longstreth 1992). Historical institutionalists brought the state back in as an institutional field capable of structuring, as well as responding to, group conflict; and, under the influence of research on neo-corporatism, they went on to argue that the institutional structures organizing capital and labor condition such conflict, giving rise to national or regionally specific patterns of action and policy (Evans, Rueschemeyer, and Skocpol 1985; Goldthorpe 1984; Hall 1986; Immergut 1998; Thelen 1999). These analyses provided influential explanations for many types of phenomena in comparative politics and international relations, and subsequent work has expanded the optic to include a range of ways in which other institutions and ideas might structure politics.

In minimalist terms, to say that politics is a structured process is simply to suggest that the behavior of political actors and the outcomes of political conflict are conditioned, not only by variables whose values change fluidly across time and space, but also by factors that are relatively stable for discrete periods and often divergent across cases. Thus, it highlights certain kinds of context effects (Falleti and Lynch 2009; Goertz 1994). To take such an approach means embracing models of the polity that acknowledge the impact on political action of the social, economic, and political structures in which actors are embedded at a particular time or place and considering how events not only affect the immediate outcome of interest but also restructure the institutional or ideological setting in ways that condition outcomes in later periods of time. One of the principal contributions of historical institutionalism has been to draw our attention to the structural dimensions of political analysis.

In this chapter I outline the limitations of alternative views of politics and consider what it means to see politics as a process structured across space and time with an emphasis both on macro-structures and on the micro-foundations of such an approach. I then take up one of the principal dilemmas generated by such a perspective, which has been thrown into sharp relief by a second wave of work in historical institutionalism, namely, the problem of explaining how institutions that are to some extent plastic can nonetheless contribute to the structuring of the political world. The chapter closes with some overarching conclusions about the importance of looking for patterns in politics.

The Alternative View

Many features of Political Science today militate against seeing politics as a structured process. In the study of comparative politics, for instance, an alternative posture is encouraged by the popularity of panel-based estimation techniques with cross-national and time-series components. Such techniques are appealing because they allow for statistical estimations in cross-national settings where the relevant number of country cases is small. However, these estimation techniques encourage assumptions about the structure of causal relations that militate against seeing politics as a process that is structured by context effects specific to particular places or by various kinds of syncopation in time. That is because those techniques imply unit homogeneity, namely, that, *ceteris paribus*, a change of the same magnitude in the independent variable will produce the same change in the dependent variable in all cases, and that the most relevant *ceteris* are indeed *paribus*, namely all the factors impinging on both the outcome and the explanatory variables have been fully specified in the estimation.

Although a limited number of period and interaction effects can be included in such estimations, in practice, they rarely are. It is difficult, for instance, to include the impact of institutions that are stable over long periods of time or interaction effects operating in some periods but not others. Thus, as they are typically used, these techniques imply a political world in which outcomes are driven by a relatively small set of causal factors operating largely independently of one another and with consistent causal force across space and time. Their popularity promotes images of the polity as a homogenous plane, without historical texture, in which ancillary institutional or ideological developments are relatively unimportant and the fundamental determinants of political action are broadly universal in form.

For example, studies that ask whether levels of social spending are driven by the partisan complexion of government often construe political parties as actors with a consistent identity over time. Some assume that all political parties on the left or right of the political spectrum can be treated as equivalent units regardless of the country or context in which they operate. Social democracy is often seen as a homogenous force operating in the same way across space and time (Brady et al. 2003). Similar assumptions are made about important economic factors, such as levels of economic openness. The usual presumption is that a given increase in exposure to trade has the same effect on redistribution in 1966, say, as it does in 2006 and equivalent impact regardless of the country in which it is occurring.[1]

In some instances, these are defensible assumptions, but they militate against investigation into the context effects that structure the impact of a variable in particular places or times; and they neglect the possibility that the most important impact of a key economic or political event may derive, not from its immediate effects on the outcome of interest, but from the ways in which it restructures the institutional or ideological setting, thereby affecting outcomes in later periods of time. The seminal work of Pierson (2004) draws our attention to this point.

To take a simple illustration, suppose we are interested in the impact of a shift from Conservative to Labour governance on British social or economic policy. We might assess that by calculating the average effects of a shift in governance based on the values taken by indicators for these policies under Labour and Conservative governments throughout the postwar period. For some purposes, that may be useful. But, as the person who is drowning in a river that averages three feet deep soon realizes, such observations hide as much as they reveal. Will that technique generate adequate explanations for what a Labour government does when it takes office in 1945 as compared with one taking office in 1997? In principle, this approach assumes they will do roughly the same thing. In fact, the policies of those two Labour governments were radically different because of variation in key features of historical context, including the ideological frameworks and institutional practices current at each juncture. How well do we understand the impact of Labour governance without taking such factors into account?

In this regard, it is instructive to compare how contemporary analyses treat the impact of changes in the international economy on levels of public spending with Cameron's (1978) analysis of such issues. Many recent studies look for annual changes in spending in response to annual changes in international capital flows or exposure to trade—often to conform to the requirements of panel-based estimations (Garrett 1995; Alderson and Nielsen 2002). We can question whether the lag-structure in such specifications models even the immediate effects of economic integration in plausible terms (Iversen and Cusack 2000). However, these models also neglect the possibility that the most important consequences of economic openness may flow from its structural effects on the economic or institutional environment that show up only over the long term. For instance, Cameron argues that the principal effect on public spending of increasing international economic integration at the turn of the twentieth century operated via the ways in which it altered the structure of the political economy. He argues that integration fostered forms of industrial concentration, which encouraged the development of more powerful trade unions and employers associations, thereby encouraging a neo-corporatist politics favorable to the expansion of public spending in subsequent decades (see also Katzenstein 1985).

Cameron's analysis may not be correct in all respects, but it reveals types of causal paths missed by studies that do not consider how economic or political developments shift the basic structures within which political contestation takes place (Pierson 2004). In the contemporary literature, politics is often presented as a process driven by small sets of variables of timeless importance operating relatively independently of each other and with the same effect regardless of historical context. There is some value in looking for such "portable truths" that apply, in principle, across all times and places (Campbell 1975; Przeworski and Teune 1970). But there is also a case for approaching politics as a field structured across space and time.

Seeing Politics as a Structured Process

What does it mean to view politics as a process structured across space and time? Seeing politics as a structured process entails operating from models of the polity that acknowledge the most important social, economic, and political structures in which actors are embedded, the interaction effects generated by these structures, and the corresponding variation across space and time to which such effects give rise. These models do not give up the aspiration to generality central to social science, but emphasize the importance of securing *effective* generalizations, namely, ones that incorporate relevant interaction effects into assessments of the impact of the explanatory variables and specify with care the scope conditions relevant to the analysis, defined partly in terms of the presence of such structural factors.

The broader literature in comparative politics already provides evidence that politics is structured *across space*, by types of welfare states and varieties of capitalism (Esping-Andersen 1990; Hall and Soskice 2001; Amable 2003). The power resources approach to redistribution, for instance, sees class relations as structural features of a polity that evolve to structure politics differently across countries (O'Connor and Olsen 1998). There is also widespread recognition that politics is structured *across time*. It is now widely accepted, for instance, that the politics of social policy has been different in the post-industrial era than it was in the industrial era (Iversen and Wren 1998; Pierson 2001). It is but a short step from such observations to the acknowledgment that, when social democratic parties move into government, the results may be different in 1997 than they were in 1945. There is a case for inquiring more deeply into how such structures shift over time. As Pierson (2004) has noted, we miss much of what explains political outcomes if we do not take into account these "big, slow-moving processes."

When considering how politics might be structured, at issue are, not only the macro-structures of politics, but the adequacy of the micro-foundations we employ. One of the most prevalent approaches in Political Science adopts what might be described as a Schumpeterian set of micro-foundations. From this perspective, political actors are seen as atomistic and calculating individuals, endowed with certain resources, but connected to others mainly by strategic interaction driven by efforts to coordinate so as to secure more resources. Models built on such assumptions can be highly revealing, especially about the ways in which institutions condition coordination (Shepsle 2006).

However, as economists now recognize, the assumptions of such a model fly in the face of a century of empirical findings in psychology, anthropology, and sociology (Elster 2007). Although riven by debates, those disciplines are united on at least one point. They all see human beings, not as atomistic individuals connected only by strategic interaction, but as relational actors deeply connected to one another by social networks, organizational structures, common practices, and shared meaning systems, which influence them in multi-faceted ways (Hall and Lamont 2013).

To accept the import of this point, we do not have to adopt the view of Foucault (1970) that the actors themselves are constituted by such structures or Althusser's (1971) contention that actors are subjects of ideology because it is ideology that allows them to be acting subjects (Clemens and Cook 1999). It would be a step forward to observe that the ideas common to a community of discourse are likely to influence how an actor interprets the proposals she receives, much as the particular set of political parties she is offered influences her strategic calculations about which one to support. To see political actors as relational actors implies *ipso facto*, that their actions cannot be explained without reference to multiple dimensions of the relations in which they are embedded. Although scholars have developed sophisticated formulations about such structures, ranging from Marxian concepts of class (Giddens 1973; Parkin 1974) to Bourdieu's (1977) theories of practice, virtually all such formulations refer to three constitutive elements of the connections between actors. These are institutional practices, shared cognitive frameworks, and network relations.

Institutional practices can be defined as regularized routines with a rule-like quality in the sense that the actors expect the practices to be observed (Hall and Thelen 2009, 9). Institutions connect actors because they reflect and depend on mutual expectations. They may be formal, if codified by the relevant authorities, or informal, which is to say observed by mutual agreement. They may, but need not, be backed by sanctions. So defined, this category encompasses a wide variety of institutions, ranging from those associated with marriage to those regulating wage bargaining. The core point is that actors do not wander aimlessly in the world. They negotiate their way through the transactions of each day by means of institutional practices. Therefore, we cannot explain their actions without reference to these practices.

Shared cognitive frameworks are sets of ideas with implications for action. They may be normative, thereby carrying prescriptive power, or cognitive, in the sense that they describe how various features of the world work. Goldstein and Keohane (1993) distinguish between *worldviews* composed of the conceptual building blocks of possibility, *principled beliefs*, specifying what is right and wrong, and *causal beliefs* describing how effects follow from causes. These frameworks are reflected in symbolic representations and shared narratives as well as other forms of discourse. They condition collective as well as individual action in realms as diverse as those of environmental movements and international monetary policymaking (Bouchard 2003; Poletta 2006; McNamara 1999).

Network relations are composed of the ties people have to others by virtue of regular contact or communication with them. These relations may be informal or organized by sets of rules. Thus, I include organizations under this rubric as well as networks in which interaction is more informal. Multiple dimensions of network relations condition their impact, including the number and character of their members, the frequency of contact between them, the depth and content of mutual knowledge such contacts convey, and the density or location of their nodes of interaction (Scott 1988; Wellman and Berkowitz 2006). Networks condition capacities for collective as well as individual action in many spheres ranging from the management of childcare to the coordination of international regulation (Eberlein and Newman 2008; Padgett and Powell 2012)

Although these three elements of social relations are conceptually separate, it should be apparent that their social force often derives from how they operate in tandem. Network relations are often consequential because of the cognitive frameworks they promote (Emirbayer and Goodwin 1994). What organizations induce people to do is dependent on the institutional practices they endorse (Meyer and Rowan 1977). By specifying the understandings that make mutual expectations possible, cognitive frameworks provide crucial underpinning for institutional practices (Chwe 2003). All three of these elements *structure* the interactions people have with each other, creating order out of behavior that might otherwise be shapeless or chaotic.

Just *how* these elements structure action is, of course, an issue at the heart of all perspectives on politics as a structured process. My objective is not to resolve that problem but to argue it deserves a central place in the problematics of Political Science. Politics should be approached with sensitivity to the multi-faceted ways in which individuals are connected to one another. All too often, analysts fasten on one feature of the structures in which actors are embedded without regard for the ways in which other such features may be mediating its effects. Where the objective is to illustrate how one facet of such structures conditions action, this approach may be helpful. But, when the goal is to explain an important outcome, such as levels of inequality across nations or the policies that address it, where multiple structural effects are likely to be operating in tandem, to emphasize one without considering others may be misleading.

The value of seeing politics as thickly, rather than thinly, structured can be seen in the leverage it offers over issues of preference formation, a crucial topic in Political Science (Katznelson and Weingast 2007). Influenced by Schumpeterian models, political scientists often think of actors' preferences in binary terms. That is to say, actors are said to have a set of *fundamental preferences* generally seen as universal, such as preferences for more income or power, plus a set of *strategic preferences* over the choices they have to make in any given situation.[2] Strategic preferences are usually said to be conditioned by the ways in which the institutional setting supports cooperation in contexts of strategic interaction. This formulation has generated revealing analyses about some of the ways in which institutions condition action. However, there is an increasingly obvious terrain between fundamental and strategic preferences, in which a good deal of preference formation takes place that is not well explained by such models. We understand reasonably well why an actor interested in increasing his income, who believes that a particular party program will do so, might vote for one party rather than another given a particular set of electoral rules. But current formulations do not tell us much about why that actor gives priority to increasing his income or why s/he believes one party is more likely to do so; yet those judgments are also crucial to the decision to choose one party over another.

Thus, we can advance our understanding of preference formation by incorporating more of the structural dimensions of politics into the analysis. Instead of assuming actors with narrow material interests that arise unambiguously from the world, we might posit actors with multiple goals, reflected in multivariate preference functions, who attach weights to each of those goals in the context of a decision situation. The process whereby those weights are attached can then be modeled as a function of salient features of the institutional, ideological or social context in which the actor is situated (Hall 2009). The preferences of workers over unemployment benefit schemes, for instance, may vary with the skill structures of national production regimes, and the positions taken by parties toward social security reform may be affected by their knowledge of foreign experience with such schemes (Iversen and Soskice 2001; Weyland 2008; Linos 2013). Cognitive frameworks popular in specific times and places can explain why an actor thinks one party program is more likely than another to advance his interests (Jacobs 2010; Berman 2001; McNamara 1999). We still have much to learn about how these dimensions of social relations impinge on such judgments. To do so, however, we have to begin from models of politics as a process structured in more ways than simple coordination models allow.

These observations are especially important to cross-national inquiry because nation-states generate distinctive institutional and ideological fields that persist over long periods of time. The institutional practices, cognitive frameworks, and network relations characteristic of a country constitute something like its *social ecology*. This term implies that distinctive outcomes are often generated by *interaction* among various elements of social relations and the durability of some elements may depend on the presence of others. Absent an appropriate set of cognitive frameworks, for instance, it may be difficult to sustain certain types of institutions (Streeck 2009).

In short, in order to understand cross-national or regional variation in macro-outcomes, such as levels of inequality, redistribution, state intervention, social cohesion, or democratic stability, there is a strong case for moving beyond explanations that turn on two or three dispositive variables toward analyses focused on the social ecologies of countries and how they are built. These analyses need not be abstruse or ornate. Their defining feature would be an effort to describe how politics is structured in each locality, attentive to how institutional practices, cognitive frameworks, and network relations interact. There are already some models for how that type of inquiry can enhance our understanding of comparative politics (Katznelson and Zollberg 1986; Pontusson 1988) and international relations (Fioretos 2011; Krotz and Schild 2013).

Politics Structured in Time

Of course, politics is structured not only in space but in time (Pierson 2004). By this, I mean that some outcomes may be more likely in some kinds of temporal contexts than in others and similar causal factors may have more impact in some periods than in others. There are at least two senses in which politics might be said to be structured in time.

The first emphasizes the distinctiveness of specific historical periods that follows from variation across them in the social ecology of political relations. At specific moments in time, politics may be structured by distinctive complexes of institutions, social networks, or cognitive templates. The causal factors driving social policy, for instance, may differ from one era to another. This proposition calls into question images of politics as a seamless terrain in which variables operate with consistent force regardless of historical context and draws our attention to period effects.

However, there is a second sense in which politics may be structured over time, which puts less emphasis on the historical specificity of a given period and more on the general distinctions that can be drawn between different types of historical periods. Here the issue is whether history should be seen as a constant flux or as a syncopated process divided into different eras marked, for instance, by their relative openness to institutional or ideological change. Such distinctions are important because the kinds of causal factors driving politics might vary across each type of period.

Historical institutionalists have developed a number of formulations to describe how politics is structured over time. The two most influential are built on concepts of critical junctures and path dependence. Following Krasner's (1984) argument that politics reflects a "punctuated equilibrium," many scholars adopted the view that history can be divided into moments of critical juncture, when developments largely exogenous to institutions render those institutions more pliable, and intervening periods of stability, when the institutions established at critical junctures structure political outcomes (Collier and Collier 1991; Capoccia and Keleman 2007). To understand processes of institutional change running over longer periods, scholars devised conceptions of path dependence, based on the contention that positive feedback effects arising from the entrenched entitlements, coordination effects, or network externalities generated by institutions alter the attractiveness of the options facing political actors profoundly enough to foreclose some paths of political development, while making movement along others more likely (Mahoney 2000; Pierson 2004).

Over the past decade, however, deeper exploration of how institutions change has yielded a "second wave" of work in historical instituitionalism—exemplified in the collective volumes of Streeck and Thelen (2005) and Mahoney and Thelen (2009). This second wave has been immensely fruitful. It provides more dynamic analyses of institutions attentive to historical context, generates a host of new propositions about how institutions evolve, and illuminates many of the intricate relationships between institutions and social coalitions. However, this new focus on institutional change has brought historical institutionalists face to face with a paradox: the more attention they devote to the factors that shape institutions, the more they call into question the power of institutions to shape politics (Riker 1980). We might call this the paradox of plasticity.

Three of the formulations advanced with great elegance by Streeck and Thelen (2005) bring this paradox into sharp relief. First, they suggest that institutions should be seen as active objects of political contestation and instruments in the hands of political actors, thereby calling into question the proposition that institutions structure politics in more fundamental ways than an instrument normally would (Streeck and Thelen 2005, 15). Some years ago, Geertz (1964) chastised political scientists for treating ideology in similar terms as a "mask or a weapon" rather than as a constitutive component of action

Second, Streeck and Thelen (2005, 22) observe that there are a multiplicity of institutions in every field, frequently layered on top of another (see also Fligstein and McAdam 2012). Thus, what actors can do is not tightly constrained by the range of available institutions. Instead, actors choose which institutions to use and mold them to their purposes. If institutions are so plentiful and plastic, however, it becomes difficult to understand why they should be seen as factors structuring behavior rather than simply as instruments in the hands of actors whose behavior is driven by something else.

In much the same way, the perspicacious acid of Streeck and Thelen's (2005, 8, 18) analysis dissolves the conceptual frameworks used by earlier institutionalists to understand how politics is structured over time. They take issue with the notion that major institutional changes occur mainly at critical junctures, separated by periods of normal politics, in favor of the view that highly consequential institutional changes often result from incremental steps taken on a continuous basis (see also Palier 2005). This perspective is almost certainly correct, but it gives up the leverage that the critical junctures approach once had over the issue of how to explain when institutions structure conflict and when they are structured by it, leaving us without a clear sense of how politics is structured, if at all, over time.

As a result, historical institutionalists need to rethink the basis for their long-standing claim that politics is a structured endeavor. They confront a paradox of plasticity. The problem becomes one of explaining how institutions that are to some extent plastic can nonetheless contribute to the structuring of the political world.

Institutions and Social Coalitions

As I see it, the key to resolving this problem lies in taking seriously another of the central insights in this second wave of historical institutionalism, namely, its insistence on seeing institutions as the product of social coalitions. The core propositions are that institutions are created by social coalitions composed of actors powerful in the relevant arena and persist only as long as they retain an ample supporting coalition, even if the composition of that coalition changes over time. This contention appears in Swenson's (2001) studies of industrial relations and social policymaking and Thelen's (2004) path-breaking work on systems for skill formation. A coalitional perspective on institutions may seem uncontroversial. As a statement about the conditions underpinning institutional persistence and change, however, it stands in contrast to prominent alternatives attributing the durability of institutions to taken-for-granted logics of appropriateness or to the equilibrium qualities of institutions that promote coordination (cf. March and Olsen 1989; Calvert 1995; Thelen 2004, chapter 1)

This coalitional perspective directs our attention to the problem of how new social coalitions are formed. Although an old problem in political studies, this is one about which we have relatively few general theories. But careful consideration of it reveals dimensions of politics that address the paradox of plasticity.

At a basic level, the formation of new coalitions must involve a process in which multiple actors reinterpret their interests in ways that allow them to join together behind a common project and then assemble the power resources necessary to ensure that the views of the coalition are addressed (Offe and Wiesenthal 1986). How do actors reach a new set of views about their interests? To this question, some accounts cite shifts in material circumstances, on the assumption that actors are motivated by perceptions of economic interest that emerge from changes in the material world. Where this is correct, understanding the formation of new coalitions is easy.

However, as even Karl Marx acknowledged, perceptions of interest rarely arise unambiguously from the world. They emerge from processes of interpretation. Thus, such barebones accounts typically understate the difficulties confronting those who want to form a new coalition sufficiently powerful to implement major institutional changes. In most cases, discontent with existing institutions has to reach certain levels. Actors have to be convinced they should abandon procedures with which they are familiar to enter uncertain territory. They have to develop new interpretations of their circumstances, agree that specific types of reforms are likely to address their problems, find ways of proceeding collectively, and assemble the relevant power resources. Sometimes, they have to be persuaded to enter costly contests for power.

In other words, even within a delimited arena of policymaking, the process whereby a new coalition forms behind important institutional changes is far from mechanical. A wide range of factors have to line up and many of these, including the availability of certain ways of thinking about policy, the presence of particular economic conditions or an increase in the salience of certain issues, will be features of a particular conjuncture rather than durable features of the political setting. To borrow a term from Ragin (1989), the process whereby new coalitions pushing for major institutional changes are formed entails "multiple conjunctural causation"—an image that conforms well to empirical accounts of the processes of coalition formation that produced institutional change in multiple realms, ranging from the reform of health care to the reversal of economic policies (Skocpol 1979; Starr 1984; Immergut 1992; Hall 1993).

Several implications follow from this view of major institutional change as the product of coalition formation in contexts of multiple conjunctural causation. The first is that institutional changes analogous to the episodes of "reform" described by Thelen (2004) are likely to take place in concentrated bursts at particular conjunctures. Small-scale institutional change marked by "defection from below" or "reform from above" may well be continuous in most domains, but major institutional changes are likely to require exceptional circumstances, because change of this magnitude depends on coalitions that are especially difficult to build. They cannot be constructed at all points in time.

The second implication is that conjunctures of major institutional change are likely to be characterized by a particular kind of politics, intrinsically more open than usual and driven by a number of factors not always prominent in the determination of political outcomes. Several scholars have made such observations. Swidler (1986) notes, for instance, that ideology often becomes more important in unsettled moments, when standard "strategies for action" have been discredited. Sewell (2005) sees a role in such contexts for "transformative events" that act as catalysts for large-scale change in worldviews and institutions. Some scholars of American politics have described the politics of "critical realignment" as divergent from those of normal politics (Burnham 1971; cf. Mayhew 2002).

Note that there are some differences between this perspective and older views that associate institutional change with "critical junctures" in which the institutions across multiple spheres change in tandem, as they sometimes do following major wars, revolution, or when nation-states are formed. The conjunctures I describe are rarely so "critical" and often limited to a single policy domain. This is not a "big bang" theory suggesting that many political institutions often change together (cf. Orren and Skowronek 2004). It posits conjunctures less sweeping in scope but still transformative in specific domains of politics.

There are some appealing features to this view. There is a robust role for agency in the process, since institutional reform is seen as the product of actors who join together for that purpose, and this approach accommodates the possibility that some actors may be prime movers in coalition formation, while others play supporting roles (Korpi 2006). Moreover, this perspective reveals how the political imagination of a particular era can leave its mark on history, as the institutions that emerge from the worldviews and context for decision-making at a particular conjuncture go on to structure practices in subsequent periods.

This perspective also directs our attention to the ways in which the incremental institutional changes that take place during periods of stability can condition the timing of critical junctures and the course of events during them. As Thelen (2004) has observed, growing discontent with an institution may lead to "defection" from its practices, giving rise to changes in its operation that precipitate a conjuncture of coalition-building on behalf of more concerted reforms. The character of reform at such junctures may also be conditioned by the kinds of incremental institutional change that precede them. Morrison (2011) argues, for instance, that key features of the 1832 British Reform Act were made possible by gradual changes in the institutional arrangements regulating relations between Parliament and the Crown.

In short, while moving away from the radical disjunctions posited by theories of critical junctures, this perspective still sees history as a syncopated process, divided into conjunctures when concerted efforts are made to put important new institutional frameworks into place and periods in which those frameworks provide a relatively stable structure for politics or policymaking.[3] The timing and pace at which such conjunctures appear will vary across institutional fields, but there is a role for conjuncture in the creation of structures. Moreover, by stressing the coalitional underpinnings of institutions, we lay the groundwork for more nuanced analyses of how the politics of stability conditions what happens during junctures of concerted reform.

Explaining Stability

How, then, are periods of relative institutional stability to be explained? This question takes us back to the paradox of plasticity. If institutions are creatures of coalitions rather than the residues of economic or ideological circumstances, the answer must turn on why the coalition on which an institution depends might remain relatively stable over some period of time. Why might coalitional politics be more orderly in some periods than at others?

That issue, in turn, invites us to consider how institutions and coalitions might be mutually reinforcing. The core point is that, although created by social or political coalitions, many institutions have features that help to consolidate the very coalitions that keep them in place. Indeed, this may be one of the most important ways in which institutions structure politics. Of course, some institutions are more stable than others, and the mechanisms consolidating support can vary across institutional fields; but the literature points to five mechanisms whereby institutions sustain the coalitions on which their own existence depends.

The first is based on the benefits a new set of institutions provides. A social program that confers benefits on a particular class of recipients is the paradigmatic case, although analogous processes pertain to many kinds of taxing, spending, and regulatory regimes. As Pierson (2004) notes, actors may come to see those benefits as entitlements. Thus, the benefits that accrue from an institution and the shifts in worldview about social justice that often accompany them can underpin institutions (Hall 2016). Reinforcing this mechanism is a general feature of human behavior. As Kahneman and Tverseky (1979) report, people are typically more concerned about losing something they already have than about gaining something they do not yet have, even if the latter is of greater value. That helps explain why actors offered another policy promising even larger benefits may not switch their allegiances as often as a simple interest-based calculus might suggest (Fioretos 2011). Mechanisms based on entitlement are likely to operate most powerfully in contexts where institutions deliver a substantial set of visible and well-defined benefits.

A second follows from the levels of uncertainty usually present about what outcomes will flow from institutional reform. Uncertainty in "instrumental beliefs" about what effects will follow from a change of policy may lead actors to hesitate before shifting their support away from existing arrangements whose impact is well known (Goldstein and Keohane 1993). As Shepsle (1989) notes, where the issue is whether to endorse new procedures for making decisions, this "wedge of uncertainty" is likely to be even greater. Even if actors can see an immediate gain from changing those procedures, they can rarely anticipate fully how other matters will be treated under them and thus whether procedural change will benefit them in the long term. Mechanisms based on uncertainty are likely to be especially important to sustaining institutions in technically complex policy areas or where the decision rules that confer power over the allocation of resources are at stake (Blyth 2007).

A third set of mechanisms turns on how institutions distribute power. As Moe (2005) observes, many institutions do not simply resolve collective action problems—they also distribute power in ways that privilege the social coalition that put them in place (Knight 1992). Institutional arrangements dictating who has jurisdiction over a topic, the composition of agendas, or the decision-rules used to resolve issues can all bias decision-making in directions that privilege the coalition that created those institutions (Marshall and Weingast 1988). Although legislators elected via one set of rules sometimes alter them, they do so rarely and not usually to their own disadvantage. Existing institutions often also limit the power resources available to actors likely to challenge them. Political institutions responsive to the affluent, for instance, may reduce the power of trade unions or alter rules in such a way as to discourage political participation by those on low incomes (Gilens 2012). Mechanisms that distribute power underpin many of the institutions distributing economic resources in society.

As Pierson (2004) has noted, a fourth set of mechanisms flow from the network or coordination effects generated by institutions. Institutions such as policy regimes often induce actors to make investments in new kinds of assets or behaviors in order to secure the benefits offered by the institution. To take advantage of a regulatory regime, for instance, firms may invest in particular endeavors. Citizens may invest in certain sets of skills to take advantage of available production regimes or adjust their saving for retirement in light of existing tax policies. Where it is costly to change such investments, these actors are likely to provide continuing support for the institutional arrangements that induced them. Mechanisms based on these kinds of coordination effects operate with special force in the political economy, where actors often make substantial investments or resources based on existing regulatory regimes and institutional structures.

A fifth mechanism turns on the potential for institutional complementarities (Hall and Soskice 2001). The level of benefits actors derive from a set of institutions governing some endeavors can depend on the presence of institutions governing other sets of endeavors. In such cases, actors will join a coalition dedicated to changing one set of institutions only if they can anticipate that a successful coalition can also be formed to make corresponding changes in another institutional arena. Even when that first coalition is feasible, the other may be difficult to construct, either because it entails mobilizing actors without a stake in the first arena or because conditions in other arenas continue to make existing institutions attractive there. Thus, institutional complementarities often act as impediments to institutional reform. This mechanism can be found both in the polity and in the economy. Swenson (2001) argues that institutional arrangements in industrial relations affected the willingness of Swedish and American employers to support reforms to social policy. Goyer (2006) finds that efforts to reform corporate governance in France and Germany turned on variations in the character of labor relations in each country, while Büthe and Mattli (2011) argue that a government's posture toward the institutions governing international standards depends on its domestic institutions for standard-setting.

In sum, there are a variety of ways in which institutions can consolidate the coalitions on which their existence depends. Together, these mechanisms help to explain why, despite a certain amount of continuous institutional adjustment, it still makes sense to see the political world as one characterized by periods of considerable institutional stability punctuated by conjunctures of more intense contestation and institutional change.

Implications for the Study of Politics

The primary objective of this chapter is to encourage scholars to cultivate a greater sensitivity to the overarching models of politics that lie behind their analyses. Instead of thinking about political explanation as a matter of identifying a short list of variables that might impinge on an outcome, we should also be thinking about how these variables interact with one other within specific contexts to form distinctive patterns of politics across space and time. Rather than treating key features of the institutions, cognitive frameworks, and network relations that structure politics as background factors whose effects wash out across cases, we should take seriously the possibility that they may be conditioning the relevant outcomes.

This perspective does not militate against the use of statistical methods for testing propositions about politics. However, it suggests estimations should be used more creatively with an eye to interaction and period effects. In many instances, it may be useful to move beyond fixed effects estimations toward multilevel hierarchical models and to take care when specifying the time-lags associated with causal factors. The effects of the latter may show up only over long periods of time, while others may acquire causal force only after they reach certain thresholds (Abbott 1988; Huber and Stephens 2001; Pierson 2004).

By the same token, we should be cautious about the conclusions that can be drawn from experimental methods. In some instances, such methods allow the analyst to isolate the impact of a key causal factor. But the effects revealed by an experiment occur within a specific situational context that may not generalize to all times and places.

Cross-cultural experimentation can sometimes capture contextual effects. However, many kinds of experiments direct our attention away from the macro-level factors structuring politics toward models that ascribe political outcomes to behavioral traits which, when taken as universal determinants of action, tend to read the effects of structural context out of politics (Deaton 2010; Woolcock 2013).

To understand the syncopation of politics, we also need to think more systematically about the pace at which conjunctures of reform occur and what precipitates them. By moving beyond models focused on critical junctures of very large-scale change, we can consider temporal syncopation of more subtle types. We also know what to look for if we see institutions as the products of social or political coalitions. We should be developing further theories about why coalitions form or break apart and considering why the incremental adjustments that sustain such coalitions occur in some cases but not others. In part, this can be an inquiry about how actors acquire and sustain "strategic capacities."[4]

Similarly, it may be possible to discern differences between the types of politics found during periods of relative institutional stability and unsettled conjunctures, based on how the politics of coalition formation varies across each kind of period. That entails developing a longitudinal perspective on issues that are often considered in purely cross-sectional terms (Lieberman 2001; Pierson 2004; Capoccia and Keleman 2007). For this purpose, it can be revealing to look at contemporary politics through the lens of political development. Following Thelen (2004) and Capoccia and Ziblatt (2010), we might see some outcomes as products of the institutional or ideological structures put in place by a succession of episodes, which appear, not as blips on the radar screen of history, but as moments when the political imagination of particular times and places is etched into longer-term processes of political development.

In short, to see politics as a process structured across space and time brings history back into Political Science, as an active process unfolding over time rather than simply as the terrain on which to find another set of cases (Pierson 2004; Katznelson 2003; Haydu 1998). This perspective does not mean political scientists have to become historians. The search is still for fruitful generalizations, notably about the factors conditioning the formation of coalitions and institutional or ideological development. However, the result can be deeper and more realistic models of politics.

Notes

* An earlier version of this chapter was presented to the 2010 Annual Meeting of the American Political Science Association. It is influenced by the work of Paul Pierson, Kathleen Thelen, Bruce Morrison, Daniel Ziblatt, Frieda Fuchs, Thomas Ertman, and William Sewell, to whom I am grateful for intellectual companionship over many years. For helpful comments, I thank Marius Busemeyer, Charlotte Cavaillé, Orfeo Fioretos, Hans-Jürgen Puhle, and Wolfgang Streeck. The CIFAR Successful Societies Program and a

World Politics Fellowship at Princeton University provided support while this chapter was written.

1. Whether such effects are consistent over time can be assessed using conventional statistical techniques, but often they are not. Fixed effects specifications can control for the impact of country-specific factors on the outcome, but do not automatically evaluate the impact of country-specific factors on the impact of other causal variables.
2. In principle, actors can be endowed with other kinds of fundamental preferences, including ones that are not material, but, in practice, relatively few political scientists assume such preferences.
3. Note that a conjuncture is defined here by the effort to assemble a new coalition behind major institutional reforms as compared to views that define a conjuncture as "a period of significant change" (Collier and Collier 1991, 29).
4. David Soskice has long emphasized the importance of "strategic capacity" in such contexts.

References

Abbott, Andrew. 1988. "Transcending Linear Reality." *Sociological Theory* 6 (2): 169–186.

Alderson, Arthur, Arthur S., and Francois Nielsen. 2002. "Globalization and the Great U-Turn: Income Inequality Trends in 16 OECD Countries." *American Journal of Sociology* 107: 1244–1299.

Althusser, Louis. 1971. *Essays on Ideology*. London: Verso.

Amable, Bruno. 2003. *The Diversity of Modern Capitalism*. Oxford: Oxford University Press.

Berman, Sheri. 2001. "Ideas, Norms and Culture in Political Analysis." *Comparative Politics* 33 (2): 231–250.

Blyth, Mark. 2007. "Beyond the Usual Suspects: Ideas, Uncertainty and Building Institutional Orders." *International Studies Quarterly* 51 (4): 761–777.

Bouchard, Gerard. 2003. *Raison et Contradiction: Le Mythe au Secours de la Pensée*. Quebec: Editions Nota Bene/Cefan.

Bourdieu, Pierre. 1977. *Outline of a Theory of Practice*. Cambridge: Cambridge University Press.

Brady, David, Evelyne Huber, Stephanie Mollwer, François Nielsen, and John D. Stephens. 2003. "Distribution and Redistribution in Postindustrial Democracies." *World Politics* 55 (2): 193–228.

Burnham, Walter Dean. 1971. *Critical Elections and the Mainsprings of American Politics*. New York: Norton.

Büthe, Tim and Walter Mattli. 2011. *The New Global Rulers: The Privatization of Regulation in the World Economy*. Princeton, NJ: Princeton University Press.

Calvert, Randall. 1995. "Rational Actors, Equilibrium and Institutions." In *Explaining Social Institutions*, ed. Jack Knight and Iai Sened. Ann Arbor: University of Michigan Press, 57–94.

Cameron, David. 1978. "The Expansion of the Public Economy: A Comparative Analysis." *American Political Science Review* 72 (December): 1243–1261.

Campbell, Donald C. 1975. "Degrees of Freedom and the Case Study." *Comparative Political Studies* 8 (2): 178–193.

Capoccia, Giovanni and Daniel R. Keleman. 2007. "The Study of Critical Junctures: Theory, Narrrative and Counterfactuals in Historical Institutionalism." *World Politics* 59 (3): 341–369.

Capoccia, Giovanni and Daniel Ziblatt. 2010. "The Historical Turn in Democratization Studies: A New Research Program and Evidence from Europe." *Comparative Political Studies* 43 (8–9): 931–968.

Chwe, Michael Suk-Young. 2003. *Rational Ritual: Culture, Coordination and Common Knowledge*. Princeton, NJ: Princeton University Press.

Clemens, Elizabeth S. and James M. Cook. 1999. "Politics and Institutionalism: Explaining Durability and Change." *Annual Review of Sociology* 25: 441–466.

Collier, David and Ruth Berins Collier. 1991. *Shaping the Political Arena: Critical Junctures, the Labor Movement and Regime Dynamics in Latin America*. Princeton, NJ: Princeton University Press.

Deaton, Angus. 2010. "Instruments, Randomization and Learning about Development." *Journal of Economic Literature* 48: 424–455.

Eberlein, Burkard and Abraham L. Newman. 2008. "Escaping the International Governance Dilemma: Incorporated Transgovernmental Networks in the European Union." *Governance* 21 (1): 25–52.

Elster, Jon. 2007. *Explaining Social Behavior: More Nuts and Bolts for the Social Sciences*. New York: Cambridge University Press.

Emirbayer, Mustafa and Jeff Goodwin. 1994. "Network Analysis, Culture and the Problem of Agency." *American Journal of Sociology* 99 (6): 1411–1454.

Esping-Andersen, Gosta. 1990. *Three Worlds of Welfare Capitalism*. Princeton, NJ: Princeton University Press.

Evans, Peter, Dietrich Rueschemeyer, and Theda Skocpol, eds. 1985. *Bringing the State Back In*. New York: Cambridge University Press.

Falleti, Tulia G. and Julia F. Lynch. 2009. "Context and Causal Mechanisms in Political Analysis." *Comparative Political Studies* 42 (9): 1143–1166.

Fioretos, Orfeo. 2011. *Creative Reconstructions: Multilateralism and European Varieties of Capitalism after 1950*. Ithaca, NY: Cornell University Press.

Fligstein, Neil and Doug McAdam. 2012. *A Theory of Fields*. New York: Oxford University Press.

Foucault, Michel. 1970. *The Order of Things*. New York: Pantheon.

Garrett, Geoffrey. 1995. "Capital Mobility, Trade and the Domestic Politics of Economic Policy." *International Organization* 49 (4): 657–687.

Geertz, Clifford. 1964. *The Interpretation of Cultures*. New York: Basic Books.

Giddens, Anthony. 1973. *The Class Structure of the Advanced Societies*. London: Hutchinson.

Gilens, Martin. 2012. *Affluence and Influence: Economic Inequality and Political Power in America*. Princeton, NJ: Princeton University Press.

Goertz, Gary. 1994. *Contexts of International Politics*. New York: Cambridge University Press.

Goldstein, Judith and Robert O. Keohane, 1993. "Ideas and Foreign Policy: An Analytical Framework." In *Ideas and Foreign Policy*, ed. Judith Goldstein and Robert O. Keohane. Ithaca, NY: Cornell University Press, 3–30.

Goldthorpe, John, ed. 1984. *Order and Conflict in Contemporary Capitalism: Studies in the Political Economy of Western European Nations*. Oxford: Clarendon Press.

Goyer, Michel. 2006. "The Transformation of Corporate Governance in France." In *Changing France: The Politics That Markets Make*, ed. Pepper Culpepper, Peter A. Hall, and Bruno Palier. London: Palgrave Macmillan, 80–104.

Hall, Peter A. 1986. *Governing the Economy: The Politics of State Intervention in Britain and France*. New York: Oxford University Press.

Hall, Peter A. 1993. "Policy Paradigms, Social Learning and the State: The Case of Economic Policy-Making in Britain." *Comparative Politics* 25 (April): 275–296.

Hall, Peter A. 2009. "Historical Institutionalism in Rationalist and Sociological Perspective." In *Explaining Institutional Change*, ed. James Mahoney and Kathleen Thelen. New York: Cambridge University Press, 204–223.

Hall, Peter A. 2016. "The Political Sources of Social Solidarity." In *Social Solidarity in Diverse Societies*, ed. Keith Banting and Will Kymlicka. Oxford: Oxford University Press (forthcoming).

Hall, Peter A. and Michèle Lamont. 2013. "Why Social Relations Matter to Politics and Successful Societies." *Annual Review of Political Science* 16: 49–71.

Hall, Peter A. and David Soskice, eds. 2001. *Varieties of Capitalism: The Institutional Foundations of Comparative Advantage*. Oxford: Oxford University Press.

Hall, Peter A. and Kathleen Thelen. 2009. "Institutional Change in Varieties of Capitalism." *Socio-Economic Review* 7: 7–34

Haydu, Jeffrey. 1998. "Making Use of the Past: Time Periods as Cases to Compare and as Sequences of Problem-Solving." *American Journal of Sociology* 104: 339–371.

Huber, Evelyne and John D. Stephens. 2001. *Development and Crisis of the Welfare State: Parties and Policies in Global Markets*. Chicago: University of Chicago Press.

Immergut, Ellen. 1992. *Health Politics: Interests and Institutions in Western Europe*. New York: Cambridge University Press.

Immergut, Ellen. 1998. "The Theoretical Core of the New Institutionalism." *Politics and Society* 26 (1): 5–34.

Iversen, Torben and Thomas Cusack. 2000. "The Causes of Welfare State Expansion: Deindustrialization or Globalization." *World Politics* 52: 313–349.

Iversen, Torben and David Soskice. 2001. "An Asset Theory of Social Policy Preferences." *American Political Science Review* 95 (4): 875–893.

Iversen, Torben and Anne Wren. 1998. "Equality, Employment and Budgetary Restraint." *World Politics* 50 (July): 507–546.

Jacobs, Alan. 2010. "How Do Ideas Matter? Mental Models and Attention in German Pension Politics." *Comparative Political Studies* 42 (2): 252–279.

Kahneman, Daniel and Amos Tversky. 1979. "Prospect Theory: An Analysis of Decision under Risk." *Econometrica* 47: 263–291.

Katzenstein, Peter. 1985. *Small States in World Markets: Industrial Policy in Europe*. Ithaca, NY: Cornell University Press.

Katznelson, Ira. 2003. "Periodization and Preferences: Reflections on Purposive Action in Comparative Historical Social Science." In *Comparative Historical Analysis in the Social Sciences*, ed. James Mahoney and Dietrich Ruschemeyer. New York: Cambridge University Press, 270–301.

Katznelson, Ira and Barry R. Weingast, eds. 2007. *Preferences and Situations: Points of Intersection between Historical and Rational Choice Institutionalism*. New York: Russell Sage Foundation.

Katznelson, Ira and Aristide Zollberg, eds. 1986. *Working Class Formation*. Princeton, NJ: Princeton University Press.

Knight, Jack S. 1992. *Institutions and Social Conflict*. New York: Cambridge University Press.

Korpi, Walter. 2006. "Power Resources and Employer-Centered Approaches in Explanations of Welfare States and Varieties of Capitalism: Protagonists, Consenters and Antagonists." *World Politics* 58 (January): 167–206.

Krasner, Stephen D. 1984. "Approaches to the State: Alternative Conceptions and Historical Dynamics." *Comparative Politics* 16 (2): 243–266.

Krotz, Ulrich and Joachim Schild. 2013. *Shaping Europe: France, Germany and Embedded Bilateralism from the Elysée Treaty to Twenty-First Century Politics*. Oxford: Oxford University Press.

Lieberman, Evan. 2001. "Causal Inference in Historical Institutional Analysis: A Specification of Period Strategies." *Comparative Political Studies* 34 (9): 1011–1035.

Linos, Katerina. 2013. *The Democratic Foundations of Policy Diffusion*. New York: Oxford University Press.

McNamara, Kathleen. 1999. *The Currency of Ideas: Monetary Politics in the European Union*. Ithaca, NY: Cornell University Press.

Mahoney, James. 2000. "Path Dependence in Historical Sociology." *Theory and Society* 29: 507–548.

Mahoney, James and Kathleen Thelen. 2009. *Explaining Institutional Change*. New York: Cambridge University Press.

March, James G. and Johan P. Olsen. 1989. *Rediscovering Institutions: The Organizational Basis of Politics*. New York: Free Press.

Marshall, William J. and Barry R. Weingast. 1988. "The Industrial Organization of Congress, or Why Legislatures, Like Firms, Are Not Organized as Markets." *Journal of Political Economy* 96 (1): 132–163.

Mayhew, David. 2002. *Critical Realignments: A Critique of an American Genre*. New Haven, CT: Yale University Press.

Meyer, John W. and Brian Rowan. 1977. "Institutionalized Organizations: Formal Structure as Myth and Ceremony." *American Journal of Sociology* 83 (2): 340–363

Moe, Terry. 2005. "Power and Political Institutions." *Perspectives on Politics* 3 (2): 215–234.

Morrison, Bruce W. 2011. "Channeling the 'Restless Spirit of Innovation': Elites, Masses, and the Institutional Contribution to Partial Democracy in Britain." *World Politics* 63 (4): 678–710.

O'Connor, Julia S. and Gregg M. Olsen, eds. 1998. *Power Resource Theory and the Welfare State: A Critical Approach*. Toronto: University of Toronto Press.

Offe, Claus and Helmut Wiesenthal. 1986. "Two Logics of Collective Action: Theoretical Notes on Social Class and Political Form." In *Disorganized Capitalism*, ed. Claus Offe. Cambridge, MA: The MIT Press.

Orren, Karen and Stephen Skowronek. 2004. *The Search for American Political Development*. New York: Cambridge University Press.

Padgett, John F. and Walter W. Powell. 2012. *The Emergence of Organizations and Markets*. Princeton, NJ: Princeton University Press.

Palier, Bruno. 2005. "Ambiguous Agreement, Cumulative Change: French Social Policy in the 1990s." In *Beyond Continuity: Institutional Change in Advanced Political Economies*, ed. Wolfgang Streeck and Kathleen Thelen. Oxford: Oxford University Press, 127–144.

Parkin, Frank. 1974. *The Social Analysis of Class Structure*. London: Tavistock Publications.

Pierson, Paul, ed. 2001. *The New Politics of the Welfare State*. New York: Oxford University Press.

Pierson, Paul. 2004. *Politics in Time*. Princeton, NJ: Princeton University Press.

Poletta, Francesca. 2006. *It Was Like a Fever: Storytelling in Protest and Politics*. Chicago: University of Chicago Press.

Pontusson, Jonas. 1988. *Swedish Social Democracy and British Labour: Essays on the Nature and Conditions of Social Democratic Hegemony*. Ithaca, NY: Cornell Western Societies Program.

Przeworski, Adam and Henry Teune. 1970. *The Logic of Comparative Social Inquiry* New York: Wiley.

Ragin, Charles. 1989. *The Comparative Method: Moving Beyond Quantitative and Qualitative Strategies*. Berkeley: University of California Press.

Riker, William. 1980. "Implications from the Disequilibrium of Majority Rule for the Study of Institutions." *American Political Science Review* 74 (2): 432–446.

Scott, John. 1988. "Social Network Analysis." *Sociology* 22 (1): 109–127.

Sewell, William H. 2005. *Logics of History: Social Theory and Social Transformation*. Chicago: University of Chicago Press.

Shepsle, Kenneth. 1989. "Studying Institutions: Some Lessons from the Rational Choice Approach." *Journal of Theoretical Politics* 1: 131–147.

Shepsle, Kenneth. 2006. "Rational Choice Institutionalism." In *Oxford Handbook of Political Institutions*, ed. Sarah Binder, R. A. W. Rhodes, and Bert A. Rockman. Oxford: Oxford University Press, 23–38.

Skocpol, Theda. 1979. *States and Social Revolutions*. New York: Cambridge University Press.

Starr, Paul. 1984. *The Social Transformation of American Medicine: The Rise of a Sovereign Profession and a Vast Industry*. New York: Basic Books.

Steinmo, Sven, Kathleen Thelen, and Frank Longstreth, eds. 1992. *Structuring Politics*. New York: Cambridge University Press.

Streeck, Wolfgang. 2009. *Re-Forming Capitalism: Institutional Change in the German Political Economy*. Oxford: Oxford University Press.

Streeck Wolfgang and Kathleen Thelen. 2005. "Introduction: Institutional Change in Advanced Political Economies." In *Beyond Continuity: Institutional Change in Advanced Political Economies*, ed. Wolfgang Streeck and Kathleen Thelen. Oxford: Oxford University Press, 1–39.

Swenson, Peter. 2001. *Capitalists against Markets*. New York: Oxford University Press.

Swidler, Ann. 1986. "Culture in Action: Symbols and Strategies." *American Sociological Review* 51: 273–286.

Thelen, Kathleen. 1999. "Historical Institutionalism in Comparative Politics." *Annual Review of Political Science* 2: 369–404.

Thelen, Kathleen. 2004. *How Institutions Evolve*. New York: Cambridge University Press.

Wellman, Barry and S. D. Berkowitz, eds. 2006. *Social Structures: A Network Approach*. New York: Cambridge University Press.

Weyland, Kurt. 2008. "Toward a New Theory of Institutional Change." *World Politics* 60 (2): 281–314.

Woolcock, Michael. 2013. "Using Case Studies to Explore the External Validity of Complex Development Interventions." *Evaluation* 19 (3): 229–249.

CHAPTER 3

INSTITUTIONAL CHANGE

JAMES CONRAN AND KATHLEEN THELEN*

THE analysis of change does not come easily to institutionalists, for its opposite—stability—is more or less built into the very definition of the term institution. Accordingly, the foundational works in the institutionalist tradition frequently assume institutional stability and exploit the cross-sectional (often cross-national) diversity of institutional arrangements to demonstrate the explanatory power of institutions regarding a vast range of outcomes. This chapter tracks the emergence of a relatively new body of literature to show how institutionalists have begun, in the past decade or two, to grapple more directly with the question of how and why institutions themselves change. The emphasis will be primarily on historical institutionalists, but other varieties of institutionalism are drawn upon in the hope that the resulting contrasts can help illustrate what is distinctive about an historical-institutionalist approach to these problems, while also highlighting commonalities and complementarities across these traditions. This approach is especially appropriate since not the least of historical institutionalism's strengths is the "pivotal position" in dialogue and synthesis across these approaches facilitated by its relatively "eclectic" style (Hall and Taylor 1996, 940, 957; see also Hall 2010).

Institutional Analysis as Comparative Statics

The traditional comfort zone of institutional analysis is "comparative statics," in which institutions are invoked as the independent (or sometimes intervening) variable to explain some outcome. Peter Gourevitch, author of one important early work in this vein, once remarked that happiness for a comparativist is a crisis that strikes different countries simultaneously: in such moments we see how common international "shocks" (in his case economic crises) are mediated in crucial ways by domestic institutions. The default orientation for institutionalists is thus to think of institutions as exercising causal force by refracting common problems in different ways. Institutions, then, stand between macro-structural forces—such as class, industrialization, globalization, geography, mass opinion, or the international system—emphasized by a range of more "structural-functionalist" theories, and the relevant outcomes of interest (e.g., class-based political mobilization, welfare state programs, trade and market liberalization, economic growth, or war and peace).

Institutionalists have typically argued that such outcomes were at best underdetermined by such "structural" forces, and that institutions provided the missing meso-level piece of the explanatory puzzle. In establishing the causal force of institutions, therefore, it was helpful to assume or demonstrate the *non-plasticity* of institutions, lest they be dismissed as merely epiphenomena, themselves determined by macro-structural factors. Indeed, with this in mind, a good institutionalist research design might well deliberately restrict the timeframe of the study to a period during which such non-plasticity could be accepted. This holds not just for historical institutionalists but for all varieties of institutionalism—not least because all were to some degree a reaction against pluralism and behavioralism on the one hand and the various forms of structural-functionalism on the other—in both disputes half the battle was demonstrating the "autonomy" of institutions (notably the state). A few examples can illustrate.

Rational Choice Institutionalism

In his seminal article "Institutional Equilibrium and Equilibrium Institutions," Kenneth Shepsle describes institutions as "[s]tanding between the individual qua bundle of tastes and the alternatives comprising available social choices." Their function is to determine "the set of choosing agents, the manner in which their preferences may be revealed, the alternatives over which preferences may be expressed, the order in which such expressions occur, and generally the way in which business is conducted" (Shepsle 1986, 51–52).

In so doing, institutions produce "structure-induced equilibrium" (Shepsle 1979), where unstructured (pre-institutionalist) social choice models predicted only an empirically implausible chaos of endless "cycling" (Arrow 1951).[1] Other core works in the rational choice (RC) tradition showed how institutions allow actors to achieve joint gains through cooperation (e.g., Keohane 1984; Weingast and Marshall 1988). Krehbiel (1998) showed how voting rules promoted "gridlock" in the US Congress while Tsebelis (2002) offered a general theory of how the "configuration of veto players"—that is, institutional rules plus key actors' preferences—constrain outcomes. In both modeling approach and empirical application, these works were characterized mostly by comparative statics, with change emerging only exogenously (e.g., via an election that changes the "pivotal players").

Sociological Perspectives

From a perspective in organizational sociology, DiMaggio and Powell (1983) declared that institutions—particularly state authorities and professional networks—were displacing markets as the Weberian "iron cage," powerfully shaping individual behavior and organizational forms in a homogenizing manner. Notably, their mechanisms of "isomorphic institutional change" (coercive, mimetic, and normative), actually describe *convergence* of individual *organizations* on the forms and practices pressed upon them by higher-level institutions ("organizational fields"). At the *institutional* level the relevant variation was cross-sectional, focused on differences between different (more or less "structurated") such organizational fields and how this led to more or less isomorphism within the field.

March and Olsen (1984, 738) offered a more political-sociological institutionalism, but one still centered on institutional effects. Far from being simply an arena for contending social forces (as in pluralist accounts) or mere tools of societal groups (as Marxists among others implied), institutions such as legislatures, courts, and bureaucracies were "also collections of standard operating procedures and structures that define and defend interests," thus "political actors in their own right." In the sociological tradition institutions are often seen as shaping behavior not, as in RC institutionalism, by structuring the "pay-offs" faced by rational actors but rather by providing "rationalized scripts"; thus Dobbin (1994) argued that nineteenth-century American, British, and French railway policies were decisively shaped by the different templates offered by their respective political constitutions. Again the focus is on institutions as stable independent variables shaping more malleable outcomes.

Historical Institutionalism

Finally, the foundational works in historical institutionalism (HI)—Gourevitch (1986), Katzenstein (1985), and many others—likewise tracked the ways in which different institutional configurations shaped interests, strategies and behaviors in ways that produced distinctive (often cross-national) outcomes. Again, the emphasis was on diversity of outcomes across cases characterized by different—but stable over time—institutional arrangements—that is, comparative statics. Arguably, HI was always better placed to turn its attention to institutional origin and change. All institutionalists by definition attribute important causal effects to institutions, but anti-functionalism—the belief that institutions themselves cannot be explained solely by their (contemporary) effects—is virtually a definitional trait of HI. HI therefore always allowed space for inquiry into the historical origins of institutions, a question of somewhat antiquarian interest in RC institutionalism, where institutions were often seen as coordination mechanisms serving contemporary efficiency purposes. Indeed the "historical" character of "comparative statics" in HI rested in the assumption that institutions come in a meaningful sense "from the past." This may have rendered them fixed and exogenous in a sometimes problematic way (see below), but it at least left the question of institutional origins one worth asking with an open mind.

Nevertheless, the main tendency of HI was also to focus on the effects of institutions assumed to be themselves stable. This tendency is understandable: if institutions did not possess causal power over other outcomes, then there would be little interest in explaining their origins or development. And if institutions did not exhibit some persistence over time, then it would be harder to identify these causal effects. Yet institutionalists have naturally turned to the question of how institutions have themselves been shaped.

Punctuated Equilibrium as the Default Theory of Change

Against this backdrop of assumed institutional stability, it comes as no surprise that when institutions became the dependent variable, the default approach—again, across all varieties of institutionalism—was to characterize particular institutional arrangements as emanating from some exogenous shock. In practice this implied a model of "punctuated equilibrium," characterized by long spells of institutional stability "punctuated" by exogenous and often wholesale institutional change (Krasner 1988).

Rationalist varieties of institutionalism did this almost by definition. One of the defining features of RC institutionalism is its view of institutions as coordinating mechanisms sustaining distinct behavioral equilibria (Levi 1997, 27; Scharpf 1997, 10; Shepsle 1989, 145). Indeed once RC scholars turned from the effects of institutions to their causes, institutions that had previously been seen to *induce* behavioral equilibria, were now conceptualized as *being themselves equilibria*. Embracing this view meant that institutional change involved the breakdown of one equilibrium and a shift to a new one. From such a perspective, however, change necessarily emerges from outside the institutional equilibrium in question. While well disposed to explain outcomes by reference to rational actors operating within stable institutional settings, therefore, RC institutionalism seemed ill-suited to explain *transitions* from one equilibrium to another. As some prominent RC scholars put it, such transitions "seem to defy rational forms of analysis" (Bates et al. 1998, 604–605).

Thus, for example, Weingast (1997) offers a model of "the foundations of democracy and the rule of law," in which two "self-enforcing" equilibria are possible, depending on the expectations of rulers and subjects about others' behavior—one leading to tyranny, the other to limited government. When it comes to his illustrative example of the Glorious Revolution, Weingast declares neutrality as to why the key event precipitating the English *transition* from a tyrannical to a liberal equilibrium—the seemingly "off-equilibrium" decision of James II to expropriate some of his Tory allies—came about, delegating the matter to the historians (1997, 252–253). In fact, precisely these limitations have been the source of complementarities with HI; RC institutionalists have little choice but to agree with Pierson (2000, 264) that, at least when it comes to choices among multiple equilibria, "we have to go back and look."

The new institutionalism in sociology conceives of institutions as informal conventions or collective cognitive scripts, emphasizing how these norms or scripts are reproduced through socialization and enacted in a manner so routine and "taken for granted" that they are in some sense beyond conscious scrutiny. Because institutions embody shared cultural understandings ("interpretive frames") of the way the world works (Meyer and Rowen 1977; Scott 1995), political actors extract causal designations from the world around them and these cause and effect understandings inform their approaches to new problems (DiMaggio and Powell 1991; Dobbin 1994). Specific organizations come and go, but emergent institutional forms will tend to be "isomorphic" with (i.e., resembling and similar in logic to) existing ones because even when policymakers set out to redesign institutions, they are limited in what they can conceive of by these internalized cultural constraints. As DiMaggio and Powell (1991, 10–11) put it, "[i]nstitutionalized arrangements are reproduced because individuals often cannot even conceive of appropriate alternatives (or because they regard as unrealistic the alternatives they can imagine)."

The characteristic mode of change here is that of *diffusion*, which is either purely formal—a matter of "myth and ceremony" largely "decoupled" from actual practices (Meyer and Rowan 1977)—or produces at most *convergence* on a dominant model. This rather limited mode of change, as Scott (2005, 471) puts it, "excludes crucial phases in the institutionalization process which has, necessarily, a beginning and an end as well as a middle." In other words, while diffusion rarely involves perfect replication, it is a mode of change that neglects more radical forms of institutional innovation as well as the demise of once-dominant institutional forms.

When it comes to more substantive change, the implicit model in sociological institutionalist work again involves the breakdown of one set of understandings or conventions in favor of new ones due to some disruption of the organizational field, or through the entry of new actors operating on a different logic who are able to disrupt usual routines and impose their preferred alternative. As DiMaggio and Powell (1991, 111) put it, "[w]hen organizational change does happen it is likely to be episodic and dramatic, responding to institutional change at the macrolevel."

Finally, historical institutionalists have also traditionally explained change in punctuated equilibrium terms. The core idea behind many HI accounts was that key political and economic institutions emerged in the context of some historical choice point—once in place, they are stable and structure the subsequent logic of political development. One sees this in the language of "critical junctures"—decisive moments that occur in the (sometimes distant) past from which alternative possible paths "branch" in divergent and irreversible directions (e.g., Collier and Collier 1991). While such "path dependent" historical trajectories can, as Mahoney (2000) points out, take the form of more or less deterministic causal chains (in the manner of Moore [1966]), processes of institutional *consolidation* (theorized in terms of "increasing returns" by Pierson [2000]) have probably featured more commonly. Thus institutional development takes the form of long stretches of institutional stability or even "stasis," periodically interrupted by episodes of relatively rapid innovation. These moments of innovation are, further, usually associated with some kind of exogenous shock—revolution, defeat in war, regime change, and so forth—that opens the door for institutional transformation. This was again a model of sharply discontinuous change, and one that drew a rather bold line between the logic of institutional reproduction and that of institutional change.

While work in this vein has offered important insights into the origins of a range of institutions, at least two (related) caveats can be raised. First, as Pierson (2004, 72) emphasizes, post-juncture "path dependence" (or institutional equilibrium) needs to be demonstrated rather than assumed. Only effective "mechanisms of reproduction" make the initial choice point a uniquely "critical" one; accordingly the relevant conceptual tools ("sunk costs," "increasing returns," etc.) must be "applied, not just invoked" (Thelen 1999, 391). Simply assuming institutions to be "sticky" by definition begs much of the question, as well as resting on an understanding of the nature of institutions that is called into question by recent developments in institutional theory described below.

Second, while truly and demonstrably "critical" junctures no doubt occur,[2] accounts based upon them tend to be distinctly *non-institutionalist*. Institutions appear to emerge from a largely non- or pre-institutional landscape—precisely the image of political life the various "new institutionalisms" sought to combat. Notably, the concept has often been linked to questions about the relative weight of "agency" and "structure" in different historical phases (e.g., Katznelson 2003). Indeed, there are affinities between the ontology of critical junctures and the Leninist concept of a "revolutionary situation" during which radical historical change becomes temporarily possible. With this, Lenin rejected not only gradualism (Bernstein's "evolutionary socialism"), but also the structural-determinism of classical Marxism. Just as the Bolsheviks thought to suspend the "laws of motion" discovered by Marx in the reading room of the British Library (not for nothing did Gramsci call October "the revolution against Karl Marx's *Capital*"), so too do historical institutionalists attenuate their institutionalism when they propose critical juncture-based accounts of institutional origin.

But, as Ostrom (1990, 140) pointed out, all social action occurs against a backdrop of structuring rules of some kind, rendering a strong distinction between the "origin" of an institution (as though from an institutional *tabula rasa*) and institutional *change* hard to sustain. This point retains much of its force even if, unlike Ostrom, one considers only formal institutions. The new theories of change described in the next section are thus more truly *institutionalist* theories of institutional change, identifying causes of institutional change that are themselves at least partly institutional.

In sum, previous "punctuated" formulations offer theories of institutional *birth* as distinct from institutional *change*. This is an exciting, sometimes epoch-shaping mode of institutional change. But it is only *one type* of such change, and surely not the most frequent or even necessarily the most consequential.

Institutional Change

In the last decade or two, initial steps have been taken toward the development of a conceptual framework for institutional change in all its forms. While arising specifically out of engagement with the problem of change, this research agenda has also contributed to a deeper conceptualization of institutions themselves. HI's constitutive concern with the contextually structured and historically unfolding nature of all political life (Hall, Chapter 2, this volume) naturally draws attention to what Pierson (2004) calls "gaps" that exist from the start or emerge over time between the intended "design" of an institution and its on-the-ground implementation and effects. These "gaps" have several sources, all of which are relevant for the study of institutional change:

1. *Limits of institutional design*: cognitive and informational limitations mean that institutional designers or rule-makers never fully foresee or control the uses to which their creations are put.
2. Even if political actors were "unboundedly rational," gaps would emerge between their ideals and reality because institution building is almost always a matter of political *compromise*. Institutions and rules are often left deeply ambiguous by the coalitions of (often conflicting) interests that preside over their founding. As Schickler's (2001) work shows, institutions also often reflect conflicting goals that over time come to be balanced in quite different ways.
3. Because institutions instantiate *power*, they are contested. Losers in one round do not necessarily disappear but rather survive and find ways not just to circumvent and subvert rules, but to occupy and redeploy institutions not of their own making.
4. *Time*: the institutions we are interested in have often been around for quite a while—longer than the time horizons and even political lives of most individual actors. What a rule "says" is only ever established in a specific temporal context and with reference to the particular circumstances to which the rule is to be applied. Changes in that context can therefore open up tremendous space for reinterpretations that are very far from the intent of the designers who are often long gone or much weakened—though conflicts over these issues can commence as soon as a rule is decided—and this provides an important mechanism by which a rule is over time "clarified" but also, in practice, modified.

Whatever the source of these gaps (cognitive limits, political compromise or contestation, the passage of time and accompanying changes in actors and/or context), they are where historical institutionalists instinctively look to understand how institutions change over time. They are the site of political contestation over what institutions are and what they do. They are the wellspring, therefore, of institutional change.

Other institutionalist traditions have not been entirely blind to these issues, but do tend to understate their implications or even to rule out these "gaps" by definition.

Rational Choice

The institutions-as-equilibria version of RC seems to leave little room for these gaps between the design of the institution and the behavior under it. Instead, the very notion of institution collapses into the behaviors it induces, making it hard to think about institutions as sites of conflict, and thus endogenous change.

However, Shepsle (2010), a founding father of this approach, notes that it does allow for four kinds of change. One is a change in the "primal environment" in which an institution exists—an exogenous shock. The other three sources of rule change are partly endogenous however: first, rule-makers can explicitly include amendment rules (e.g., Article V of the US Constitution); second (and again formally licensed by the existing rules) come "suspensions" of rules, such as provisions for emergency powers in constitutions or "escape clauses" in treaties. Finally, and more pertinent to the kinds of new historical institutionalist approaches outlined below, rules may simply be *broken*. Shepsle, however, suggests rule-breaking may actually render institutions *more* robust to formal revision—an equilibrium that can bend is less likely to break (16–17). This is a view that historical institutionalists, as we will see, at least qualify.

Shepsle concludes his essay with a stark recognition of a core difficulty (first raised by Riker [1980]) for the "equilibrium institutions" approach, namely that the "primal environment"—that is, the world—may not facilitate equilibrium: "we have two diametrically opposed circumstances—the potential disequilibrium in the primal environment on the one hand, and the structure-induced equilibrium of a well-functioning institution on the other. What we observe in many empirical settings, however, seems to be something in between, neither the chaos of the former nor the stability of the latter . . . The puzzle is how to account for this in-between state of affairs" (Shepsle 2010, 17).

Two of the scholars in this tradition who have thought most about issues of change are Avner Greif and David Laitin, who acknowledge the difficulties equilibrium-based models have accommodating endogenous sources of change: "a self-enforcing institution is one in which each player's behavior is a best response. The inescapable conclusion is that changes in self-enforcing institutions must have an exogenous origin" (Greif and Laitin 2004, 633). Their innovation comes in the form of institutional feedback effects that either expand or reduce the set of situations in which an institution is self-enforcing, in other words the scale of exogenous, parameter-shifting shocks it could sustain. Thus they essentially redefine some of the exogenous parameters of the institutions they study as endogenous variables ("quasi-parameters").

In the short run, quasi-parameters operate "as if" they were exogenously set parameters. In fact, however, they are directly albeit gradually altered by behavior endogenous to the institution, in ways that can render the institution itself either self-reinforcing or self-undermining over the long-run. Because of actors' limited knowledge, scarce attention and coordination problems (similar to the first "gap" above), they are either unaware of or do not immediately respond to gradually changing quasi-parameters, thus sustaining the equilibrium in the short run (Greif and Laitin 2004, 636–639).

While Greif and Laitin provide a conceptual language for rational choice scholars to describe *endogenous* institutional change, however, this does not necessarily imply such change will manifest itself *incrementally*. In fact Greif and Laitin see such long-term developments as *underlying* the pattern of "punctuated equilibrium" portrayed by previous scholars: institutions remain self-enforcing for long periods, even as they slowly undermine themselves, becoming gradually more fragile to exogenous shocks *or* (in the case of more endogenous change) the actions of reformers and risk-takers. Thus "change is in actuality evolutionary but apparently abrupt, typically associated with a 'crisis' revealing that the previous behavior is no longer an equilibrium" (639). The resulting model of change resembles the "tipping point" or threshold effects identified by Pierson (2004, 82)—events with "slow" causes and "quick" outcomes.

For one RC institutionalism classic, however, institutional change was "overwhelmingly incremental" and, furthermore, always heavily conditioned by the existing institutional landscape (through its influence on preferences and relative prices), and in that sense endogenous (North 1990, 89–94). A key reason for this is that North (like Ostrom) includes *informal* rules and norms among the relevant institutions—these tend to be less open to abrupt, deliberate, or wholesale change than formal institutions. Thus even the biggest of formal institutional bangs, such as revolutions, lead to far less change than might appear on the formal institutional surface (North 1990, 6; see also Roland 2004)—a conclusion already reached by Tocqueville in his 1856 study of the French Revolution.[3]

In more formal institutional settings, the widely used "principal-agent" RC framework might seem to suggest gaps between rules and implementation. Here, actors' cognitive and informational limitations as well as the existence of "multiple principals" with divergent interests are the source of agency "slack" (e.g., Copelovitch 2010). RC institutionalism's roots in "new institutional economics," however, encourage a highly voluntarist view of institutions as Pareto-efficient solutions to various kinds of collective action problems. "The essence of institutions," for Weingast (2002, 670), "is to enforce mutually beneficial exchange and cooperation." It is hard to see why such institutions would ever be overthrown or undermined by organized action from within. It is unsurprising, then, that in practice the "central thrust" of principal-agent analysis "has involved developing maps from particular types of informational problems to the best possible institutional solutions" (Huber and Shipan 2002, 26).

The functionalist flavor of such an approach forecloses possibilities for change that might have been opened up by its original problematic. Moe, one of the RC scholars most cognizant of the power-distributive nature of institutions, begins to reopen this space by recognizing that the principal-agent approach is "constructed . . . as though bureaucrats are atomized and powerless except for the private information that works in their favor, and as though their principals are imposed on them exogenously and come with their own independent objective functions." As a result, the ability of "bureaucrats" (e.g., teachers via their public sector unions in his empirical analysis) to shape the very institutional rules that (supposedly) define their scope for action—making their principals "agents of the agents"—is missed (Moe 2006, 5–6).[4] Besides being a classic HI-style example of policy feedback (Pierson 1994), the larger point is that neither rules *nor who gets to be a rulemaker* are determined once and for all, but are rather continually contested. Moe does not draw out fully the broader implications of this more "politicized" account of institutional design and development, but they are at the heart of HI approaches to institutional change.

Sociological Institutionalism

In sociological institutionalism, meanwhile, cognitive limitations have been central—perhaps, indeed, *à outrance*, leaving it open to the classic critique of sociology's "over-socialized" ontology (Wrong 1961) populated by "cultural dopes" (Garfinkel 1984). Where institutions are conceived of as scripts that individuals enact through their behavior, there is little possible gap between the institution and the behavior it shapes—the behavior instantiates the institution.

Nevertheless, scholars in the sociological tradition have also begun to address this theoretical deficit. The "new institutionalism's" characteristic mode of change—diffusion—has continued to receive much attention and not exclusively from sociologists. This tradition's central concern with cognitive processes (and limitations) has indeed itself enjoyed much "diffusion" in recent years, particularly in the neo-behavioralist research programs that have thrived in economics and Political Science, often deploying experimental methods (see Steinmo, Chapter 6, this volume). The growing popularity of these ideas has however also manifested itself in an increasingly sophisticated (and again cross-disciplinary) literature on *institutional* (or sometimes quasi-institutional policy) diffusion (Dobbin, Simmons, and Garrett 2007; Linos 2013; Weyland 2008).

Much recent work on change in sociological institutionalism also attempts to make room for change by taking a heavily "agentic" turn, emphasizing the importance of "institutional entrepreneurs" (e.g., Lawrence, Suddaby, and Leca 2009). Some of this work (often bridging to recent HI approaches outlined below) point to the possibility that the existing institutional landscape can act as a resource rather than a constraint, for example by providing raw material for "institutional bricolage," defined by Campbell (2010, 98) as "the rearrangement or recombination of institutional principles and practices in new and creative ways."

Fligstein and McAdam have also sought more theoretical room for change within the sociological tradition, describing DiMaggio and Powell's "new institutionalism" as "really a theory of how conformity occurs in already existing fields" (2012, 28). Their remedy is to emphasize the potentially destabilizing interconnections between different institutional "fields." Such fields are subject to exogenous (but regular, given their mutually embedded nature) shocks that can be exploited by internal "challengers," laying the basis for "[c]onstant low-level contention and incremental change" (Fligstein and McAdam 2012, 12, 19). The affinities between such recast images of institutional life and recent developments in HI should become clear below.

Historical Institutionalism

HI approaches to institutional change have taken different tacks but all share the core understanding of institutions as (a) the legacy of concrete historical processes and (b) the object of ongoing contestation. The first point means that institutions have some life of their own; while actors often assess institutions in light of their (anticipated) effects, especially as these concern their perceived self-interest, all the well-rehearsed reasons for institutional "stickiness" do indeed often apply, so that at any given point in time institutions will be in some sense suboptimal.[5] The second point implies that even to the degree institutions *are* "optimal," they are typically only so for some coalition of interests at some particular time. Together they imply a strong rejection of functionalist accounts.

Both these core positions again recall Pierson's point: for historical institutionalists, one really does have to "go back and look" if one wants to explain the character of contemporary institutions—rather than through backward induction from apparent functions the institution may serve today. This is what makes historical institutionalism *historical*. A classic HI approach has been to "expose" the reality behind functionalist or other teleological stories, in the spirit of antecedents such as Moore (1966), who challenged the "Whig history" of a smooth evolution of English liberal democracy with a much more conflictual account. Thus Streeck and Yamamura (2001) and Thelen (2004) have highlighted the conflict-ridden origins of the institutions identified by Hall and Soskice (2001) as crucial to securing "coordination" equilibria, while Ahmed (2013) "goes back and looks" at the (again conflictual) process of electoral system choice during late nineteenth- and early twentieth-century European democratization, rejecting more functionalist "joint gains" views. Unlike rationalist accounts whose analytical starting point (even, as Moe [2005] points out, when they analyze highly conflictual events) is the *coordinating* functions of institutions, historical institutionalists think about institutions first and foremost as *distributional* instruments, fraught with implications for the allocation and exercise of political power.

From this shared core, HI scholars have developed different approaches in theorizing institutional change.

Institutional Interactions ("Intercurrence") as a Source of Institutional Change

Classic precursors of HI emphasized the causal significance of sequencing and timing in political life, highlighting deeply consequential patterns of interaction between different but contemporaneous political and economic processes in shaping macro-institutional arrangements such as political regime-type (Moore 1966), the institutional underpinnings of industrialization (Gerschenkron 1962), party systems (Lipset and Rokkan 1967) or bureaucratic autonomy (Shefter 1977). More recently, Orren and Skowronek (among others) build on this tradition. Their emphasis on "historical process" over "equilibrium order" in their conceptualization of institutions yields a distinctive approach to institutional change.

Since they emerge from a succession of particular historical conflicts and constellations, institutions—both singly and as constellations—juxtapose different logics of political order, each with their own temporal underpinnings (Orren and Skowronek 1994, 320). For this reason, the various pieces do not necessarily fit into a coherent, self-reinforcing, let alone functional, whole; change thus comes from the interactions of different institutional orders within a society, as instability in one institutional layer disrupts order in others (Orren and Skowronek 1994, 321). Such immanently emerging institutional tensions (what they call "intercurrence") drive institutional evolution in a process largely beyond the control of specific historical agents.

Institutional Reproduction and Institutional Change as Two Sides of the Same Coin

Although the path dependence literature was mostly about institutional stability, it also—somewhat ironically—inspired insights into the sources of institutional change. Understanding the different mechanisms that account for the *persistence* of particular institutional arrangements implicitly reveals points of potential vulnerability, suggesting which kinds of external events and processes are likely to produce institutional *change*. In other words, if different institutions rest on different mechanisms of reproduction (including power-political foundations), then the processes likely to disrupt them will also be different, though predictable.

This insight is the key to understanding why common international trends frequently have such different domestic consequences, disrupting previously stable patterns in some countries while washing over others seemingly without effect (Locke and Thelen 1995). For example, Esping-Andersen's (1990) three welfare regimes—liberal, social-democratic, and conservative-corporatist—rest on different political coalitions and rely on different mechanisms of reproduction. This means that each is differently affected by particular common trends. For instance, changes in gender relations and family structures are likely to *reinforce* elements of the universalistic and liberal welfare states (which both, though in different ways, support and rely upon female labor-force participation), while these same changes are likely to create new *frictions and contradictions* for conservative welfare states, which are premised on the single-breadwinner model of the family. Similarly, the "institutional complementarities" Hall and Soskice see as underpinning the different "varieties of capitalism" also imply the potential for liberalization in one institutional domain (e.g., traditionally "patient" capital markets) to "unravel" coordination in others (e.g., collaborative industrial relations) (Hall and Soskice 2001: 63–64).

These examples resonate with Orren and Skowronek's notion of intercurrence: institutions change because they are inextricably bound up with the operations of other institutions and forces themselves developing according to their own logic. The path dependence literature oriented primarily toward explaining institutional stability can therefore be harnessed to add predictive precision to Orren and Skowronek's insights about different, often conflictual processes interacting over time. Not all such "collisions" are consequential, only those that disrupt the specific mechanisms of reproduction on which particular institutions rest. In contrast to punctuated equilibrium models that separate the question of stability from the question of change, these perspectives on change reveal institutional stability and institutional change as two sides of the same coin: the explanation of political change rests upon an analysis of the foundations of political stability (Thelen 1994).

Strategies of Change under Institutional Constraints: Layering and Drift

The two sets of arguments discussed in the previous section were mostly about the interaction of large-scale processes, often beyond the control of individual or even collective actors, and their impact on existing institutional arrangements—often in the form of unintended, knock-on consequences. Other historical institutionalists have charted how institutional change can be the product of conscious *strategies*, working within and around the constraints that produce path dependence, thereby exploring the relationship between agency and structure in processes of institutional change. Eric Schickler's arguments about *layering* are illustrative. Layering occurs when new rules are attached to existing ones in ways that affect how the old rules structure behavior (Schickler 2001). In this way, even if it is not possible to replace institutions outright, change occurs through seemingly marginal amendments, revisions, or additions to existing institutions or rules that have downstream implications for how the original institutions operate.

Sometimes these changes are intended—or at least advertised—as a way of saving or shoring up the existing system. The classic example concerns reform of social security systems which seemed, as Pierson (1994) argued, politically unassailable. But, Hacker (2004) showed, reformers were able to *add* a "layer" of individual retirement accounts alongside the regular public system. The mechanism of change is not that people "defect" to the individual system in the sense of opting out of the public system altogether; rather as the individual component grows relative to the existing public system, a social insurance program becomes increasingly defined by individualized risk (and less redistributive). This in turn might be expected to undermine support for the public component over the longer run, laying the foundation for possible outright displacement of a once impregnable institution.

Another important example of change emerging through the deliberate strategies of agents operating in highly institutionalized (hence constrained) environments is Hacker's (2005) concept of *drift*, which describes a situation in which formal rules are stable but the environment shifts in ways that alter their operation. Hacker's primary examples are social programs in the US, which have often been resistant to rollbacks but have not adapted to cover new risks that have emerged. A de facto shrinkage in welfare coverage therefore occurs even in the absence of formal retrenchment, because institutions and rules have not been updated. Note that the failure to adapt policy-institutions to their changing environment is not an oversight or the result of generic institutional "inertia," but rather a matter of deliberate, contested, and not-so-benign neglect. Such strategies will be especially viable in political environments with multiple veto players (Mahoney and Thelen 2010), and it is therefore no surprise that Hacker's concept has been formalized by scholars of American politics who model how rational legislators might take account of *ex ante* unpredictable environmental drift when delegating authority to bureaucratic agencies (Callander and Krehbiel 2014).

In grappling with this question of change within institutional constraints, the challenge has been to inject agency into institutional accounts, but in a way that generates *portable* propositions to identify broader patterns. One route has been to ask how prevailing structures influence the kinds of strategies most likely to succeed in specific institutional contexts. Thus Mahoney and Thelen (2010) and Hacker, Pierson, and Thelen (2015) have developed propositions concerning the specific characteristics of the existing institution and of the broader political environment under which one mode of change is more likely to emerge than others.

Endogenous Change: Conversion

The previous discussions of intercurrence, mechanisms of reproduction, and drift and layering have dealt with the occurrence of change in institutionally rich, path-dependent environments. These processes were also partially *endogenous* forms of institutional change, that is, arising out of particular features of the institutions concerned. Change was also partly *exogenous* in these cases however, with environmental change, the addition of "parallel" institutional elements or change in connected but distinct institutional domains playing crucial roles. Other work, however, addresses more strictly *endogenous* institutional change. Again, the point of departure is the distributional rather than the efficiency function of institutions. Whereas in equilibrium accounts, institutions are held together by voluntarism and shared self-interest, in HI institutions are typically political settlements involving the exercise of power and the dominance of some groups over others.

This power-distributional element, however, implies an immanent potential for change (Mahoney 2000, 523)—many of the actors whose "cooperative" behavior constitutes RC's institutional equilibria, are reluctant compliers at best, forced into obeisance by the prospect of punishment or the infeasibility—for the time being—of more favorable institutional arrangements (Moe 2005). HI has never forgotten that institutional outcomes have losers. And these losers often do not go away (Thelen 1999, 385); they live to fight another day, and they typically carry out this fight from *within* the institutions whose imposition they unsuccessfully resisted, as *participants* in the (apparent) equilibrium. From within, they seek to renegotiate and reinterpret the rules and expectations associated with an institution, sometimes succeeding in gradually but radically transforming its form and effects.

Conversion occurs when rules on the books remain the same but are interpreted and enacted in new ways. Identified cases include the German system of vocational training, which, from its pro-artisanal roots in the late nineteenth century, was made to serve the ends first of the industrial sector and then specifically of organized labor, even as the core of the system showed much continuity in the face of world-historic exogenous shocks (Thelen 2004). In a far-removed area, Ding (1994) questions the popular state-civil society dichotomy used to analyze transitions from Communism by highlighting the conversion of state-controlled "pseudo-social" organizations into "instruments . . . against the party-state." These organizations "were set up by the communist regime for its own use but were gradually co-opted by critical forces for counter purposes, all the while keeping up the protective façade that these were still party-state institutions" (Ding 1994, 299).[6]

In general, this mode of change problematizes *enforcement* and above all recognizes that *interpretation* is often highly political and thus conflictual. Rules, even when formally codified, are never simply applied, but always interpreted, enforced, and enacted—and by actors with divergent and conflicting interests. This is why courts can be such influential (and unpredictable) actors, and why lawyers find such gainful employment (Streeck and Thelen 2005, 14–15); it is also, however, why the rulings of courts are themselves rarely more than the end of the beginning of any social conflict, as Rosenberg (2008) argues in the cases of abortion and civil rights in the US. The broader point is perhaps most obvious with macro-institutions such as constitutions, which encompass such a range of political "transactions" that they can only ever be radically incomplete "contracts." Here affinities with RC institutionalism are again apparent. For example, Moe and Howell (1999) explain the growth of presidential power by reference to the wide scope for "presidential unilateralism" provided by the ambiguities and silences of the US Constitution. But explaining the degree to which such powers have actually been exercised (and for what ends) would require an historical approach more attentive to the constraints (and opportunities) implied by a denser institutional environment (e.g., Skowronek 1993) than that usually deployed in RC analysis.

All this was an insight central to the "old" institutionalism in sociology (e.g., Selznick 1949). There, internalized but conceivably alterable (or violable) *norms* were central (DiMaggio and Powell 1991, 15). In the newer version, institutions involve *cognitive* templates that individuals enact, presumably without considering non-compliance (Streeck and Thelen 2005, 11). By contrast, in HI's power-centered view of institutions, the need to impose and enforce rules carries its own dynamic of change.

Conclusion

Recent historical institutionalist work on institutional change moves beyond previous "punctuated equilibria" formulations that conceived of institutional change as predominantly arising from exogenous shocks that cause old patterns to break down, creating space into which some new pattern or equilibrium emerges. In so doing, such work also moves beyond the question of whether agency trumps structure or the other way around and instead seeks mid-range explanations that situate agents within a context that shapes the plausible strategies available to them—but which they may also be able to change. Institutions constrain action but do not eliminate agency—indeed they enable it. In political life, unstructured agency is as unthinkable as are structures with no agents. Recognizing this in the study of institutional change allows analytical weight to be assigned to strategy, conflict, and agency *all* the time and not just in the very rare moments when structures break down entirely.

Notes

* We thank Peter Hall, Julia Lynch, and other participants in this project, especially Tulia Falleti and Orfeo Fioretos, for valuable comments on a previous version of this chapter. The chapter draws in part on Thelen's previous work with Wolfgang Streeck (Streeck and Thelen 2005) and with James Mahoney (Mahoney and Thelen 2010).

1. Shepsle's terminology describes institutions as "structures," but as above they intermediate between "macro-structures"—the "raw" or "pre-institutional" structure of preferences—and outcomes.
2. Capoccia and Keleman (2007) offer useful conceptual and methodological guidance for identifying them. Critical junctures have also been theorized with increasing sophistication (e.g., Hall, Chapter 2, this volume), partly in response to these critiques.
3. But Greif and Kingston (2011, 24–25) critique such use of informal rules to explain non-conformity with formal rules as "a leap of faith that invokes a mysterious and scientifically untestable explanation for the observed behavior."
4. Precisely this point is the central theme in Carpenter's (2001) landmark study.
5. This rejection of what March and Olsen (1984, 737; see also Fioretos 2011, 376–380) called "the efficiency of history"—the view that institutions are optimal equilibria for society or at least the most powerful social groups—is arguably a core condition for any real institutionalism. Without it, it is hard to make a case for institutional effects being exogenous.
6. For a sustained comparison of the different political dynamics associated with drift and conversion, see Hacker, Pierson, and Thelen (2015).

References

Ahmed, Amel. 2013. *Democracy and the Politics of Electoral System Choice: Engineering Electoral Dominance.* New York: Cambridge University Press.

Arrow, Kenneth. 1963 [1951]. *Social Choice and Individual Values.* New York: Wiley.

Bates, Robert H., Rui JP De Figueiredo, and Barry R. Weingast. 1998. "The Politics of Interpretation: Rationality, Culture, and Transition." *Politics and Society* 26: 221–256.

Callander, Steven and Keith Krehbiel. 2014. *Gridlock and Delegation in a Changing World.* SSRN Scholarly Paper. Rochester, NY: Social Science Research Network. Available at <http://papers.ssrn.com/abstract=2083840> (accessed March 26, 2014).

Campbell, John L. 2010. "Institutional Reproduction and Change." In *Oxford Handbook of Comparative Institutional Analysis*, ed. Glenn Morgan and John Campbell. New York: Oxford University Press, 87–115.

Capoccia, Giovanni and R. Daniel Kelemen. 2007. "The Study of Critical Junctures: Theory, Narrative, and Counterfactuals in Historical Institutionalism." *World Politics* 59 (03): 341–369.

Carpenter, Daniel P. 2001. *The Forging of Bureaucratic Autonomy: Reputations, Networks, and Policy Innovation in Executive Agencies, 1862–1928*. Princeton, NJ: Princeton University Press.

Collier, Ruth Berins and David Collier. 1991. *Shaping the Political Arena*. Princeton, NJ: Princeton University Press.

Copelovitch, Mark S. 2010. "Master or Servant? Common Agency and the Political Economy of IMF Lending." *International Studies Quarterly* 54 (1): 49–77.

DiMaggio, Paul J. and Walter W. Powell. 1983. "The Iron Cage Revisited: Institutional Isomorphism and Collective Rationality in Organizational Fields." *American Sociological Review* 48(2): 147–160.

DiMaggio, Paul J. and Walter W. Powell, eds. 1991. *The New Institutionalism in Organizational Analysis*. Chicago: University of Chicago Press.

Ding, Xueliang L. 1994. "Institutional Amphibiousness and the Transition from Communism: The Case of China." *British Journal of Political Science* 24 (3): 293–318.

Dobbin, Frank. 1994. *Forging Industrial Policy: The United States, Britain, and France in the Railway Age*. Cambridge and New York: Cambridge University Press.

Dobbin, Frank, Beth Simmons, and Geoffrey Garrett. 2007. "The Global Diffusion of Public Policies: Social Construction, Coercion, Competition, or Learning?" *Annual Review of Sociology* 33: 449–472.

Esping-Andersen, Gosta. 1990. *The Three Worlds of Welfare Capitalism*. Cambridge: Polity.

Fioretos, Orfeo. 2011. "Historical Institutionalism in International Relations." *International Organization* 65 (02): 367–399.

Fligstein, Neil and Doug McAdam. 2012. *A Theory of Fields*. New York: Oxford University Press.

Garfinkel, Harold. 1984. *Studies in Ethnomethodology*. Cambridge: Polity Press.

Gerschenkron, Alexander. 1962. *Economic Backwardness in Historical Perspective*. Cambridge, MA: Belknap Press of Harvard University.

Gourevitch, Peter Alexis. 1986. *Politics in Hard Times: Comparative Responses to International Economic Crises*. 1st edition. Ithaca, NY: Cornell University Press.

Greif, Avner and Christopher Kingston. 2011. "Institutions: Rules or Equilibria?" In *Political Economy of Institutions, Democracy and Voting*, ed. Norman Schofield and Gonzalo Caballero. Berlin: Springer, 13–43.

Greif, Avner and David D. Laitin. 2004. "A Theory of Endogenous Institutional Change." *American Political Science Review* 98 (04): 633–652.

Hacker, Jacob S. 2004. "Privatizing Risk without Privatizing the Welfare State: The Hidden Politics of Social Policy Retrenchment in the United States." *American Political Science Review* 98 (02): 243–260.

Hacker, Jacob S. 2005. "Policy Drift: The Hidden Politics of US Welfare State Retrenchment." In *Beyond Continuity: Institutional Change in Advanced Political Economies*, ed. Wolfgang Streeck and Kathleen Thelen. New York: Oxford University Press, 40–82.

Hacker, Jacob S., Paul Pierson, and Kathleen Thelen. 2015. "Drift and Conversion: Hidden Faces of Institutional Change." In *Advances in Comparative Historical Analysis*, ed. James Mahoney and Kathleen Thelen. New York: Cambridge University Press, 180–209.

Hall, Peter A. 2010. "Historical Institutionalism in Rationalist and Sociological Perspective." In *Explaining Institutional Change: Ambiguity, Agency, and Power*, ed. James Mahoney and Kathleen Thelen. New York: Cambridge University Press, 204–223.

Hall, Peter A. and David Soskice. 2001. *Varieties of Capitalism: The Institutional Foundations of Comparative Advantage*. New York: Oxford University Press.

Hall, Peter A. and Rosemary C. R. Taylor. 1996. "Political Science and the Three New Institutionalisms." *Political Studies* 44 (5): 936–957.

Huber, John D. and Charles R. Shipan. 2002. *Deliberate Discretion? The Institutional Foundations of Bureaucratic Autonomy*. New York: Cambridge University Press.

Katzenstein, Peter J. 1985. *Small States in World Markets: Industrial Policy in Europe*. Ithaca, NY: Cornell University Press.

Katznelson, Ira. 2003. "Periodization and Preferences: Reflections on Purposive Action in Comparative Historical Social Science." In *Comparative Historical Analysis in the Social Sciences*, ed. James Mahoney and Dietrich Rueschemeyer. New York: Cambridge University Press, 270–301.

Keohane, Robert O. 1984. *After Hegemony: Cooperation and Discord in the World Political Economy*. Princeton, NJ: Princeton University Press.

Krasner, Stephen D. 1988. "Sovereignty: An Institutional Perspective." *Comparative Political Studies* 21 (1): 66–94.

Krehbiel, Keith. 1998. *Pivotal Politics: A Theory of US Lawmaking*. Chicago: University of Chicago Press.

Lawrence, Thomas B., Roy Suddaby, and Bernard Leca. 2009. *Institutional Work: Actors and Agency in Institutional Studies of Organizations*. New York: Cambridge University Press.

Levi, Margaret. 1997. "A Model, a Method, and a Map: Rational Choice in Comparative and Historical Analysis." In *Comparative Politics: Rationality, Culture, and Structure*, ed. Mark Irving Lichbach and Alan S. Zuckerman. Cambridge: Cambridge University Press, 19–41.

Linos, Katerina. 2013. *The Democratic Foundations of Policy Diffusion: How Health, Family, and Employment Laws Spread Across Countries*. New York: Oxford University Press.

Lipset, Seymour M. and Stein Rokkan. 1967. "Cleavage Structures, Party Systems, and Voter Alignments: An Introduction." In *Party Systems and Voter Alignments: Cross-National Perspectives*, ed. Seymour M. Lipset and Stein Rokkan. New York: The Free Press, 1–64.

Locke, Richard M. and Kathleen Thelen. 1995. "Apples and Oranges Revisited: Contextualized Comparisons and the Study of Comparative Labor Politics." *Politics and Society* 23: 337–368.

Mahoney, James. 2000. "Path Dependence in Historical Sociology." *Theory and Society* 29 (4): 507–548.

Mahoney, James and Kathleen Thelen. 2010. "A Theory of Gradual Institutional Change." In *Explaining Institutional Change: Ambiguity, Agency, and Power*, ed. James Mahoney and Kathleen Thelen. New York: Cambridge University Press, 1–37.

March, James G. and Johan P. Olsen. 1984. "The New Institutionalism: Organizational Factors in Political Life." *American Political Science Review* 78 (3): 734–749.

Meyer, John W. and Brian Rowan. 1977. "Institutionalized Organizations: Formal Structure as Myth and Ceremony." *American Journal of Sociology* 83 (2): 340.

Moe, Terry M. 2005. "Power and Political Institutions." *Perspectives on Politics* 3 (02): 215–233.

Moe, Terry M. 2006. "Political Control and the Power of the Agent." *Journal of Law, Economics, and Organization* 22 (1): 1–29.

Moe, Terry M. and William G. Howell. 1999. "The Presidential Power of Unilateral Action." *Journal of Law, Economics, and Organization* 15 (1): 132–179.

Moore, Barrington. 1966. *Social Origins of Democracy and Dictatorship*. Boston, MA: Beacon.

North, D. 1990. *Institutional Change and Economic Performance*, Cambridge: Cambridge University Press.

Orren, Karen and Stephen Skowronek. 1994. "Beyond the Iconography of Order: Notes for a New Institutionalism." In *The Dynamics of American Politics: Approaches and Interpretations*, ed. Lawrence C. Dodd and Calvin Jillison. Boulder, CO: Westview Press, 311–330.

Ostrom, Elinor. 1990. *Governing the Commons: The Evolution of Institutions for Collective Action*. Cambridge: Cambridge University Press.

Pierson, Paul. 1994. *Dismantling the Welfare State? Reagan, Thatcher and the Politics of Retrenchment*. New York: Cambridge University Press.

Pierson, Paul. 2000. "Increasing Returns, Path Dependence, and the Study of Politics." *American Political Science Review* 94 (2): 251–267.

Pierson, Paul. 2004. *Politics in Time: History, Institutions, and Social Analysis*. First edition. Princeton, NJ: Princeton University Press.

Riker, William H. 1980. "Implications from the Disequilibrium of Majority Rule for the Study of Institutions." *The American Political Science Review* 74 (2): 432.

Roland, Gérard. 2004. "Understanding Institutional Change: Fast-Moving and Slow-Moving Institutions." *Studies in Comparative International Development* 38 (4): 109–131.

Rosenberg, Gerald N. 2008. *The Hollow Hope: Can Courts Bring about Social Change?* Chicago: University of Chicago Press.

Scharpf, Fritz Wilhelm. 1997. *Games Real Actors Play: Actor-Centered Institutionalism in Policy Research*. Boulder, CO: Westview Press.

Schickler, Eric. 2001. *Disjointed Pluralism: Institutional Innovation and the Development of the U.S. Congress*. Princeton, NJ: Princeton University Press.

Scott, W. Richard. 1995. *Organizations and Institutions*. Thousand Oaks, CA: Sage.

Scott, W. Richard. 2005. "Institutional Theory: Contributing to a Theoretical Research Program." In *Great Minds in Management: The Process of Theory Development*, ed. Ken G. Smith and Michael A. Hitt. New York: Oxford University Press, 460–484.

Selznick, Philip. 1949. *TVA and the Grass Roots: A Study of Politics and Organization*. Berkeley: University of California Press.

Shefter, Martin. 1977. "Party and Patronage: Germany, England, and Italy." *Politics & Society* 7 (4): 403–451.

Shepsle, Kenneth A. 1979. "Institutional Arrangements and Equilibrium in Multidimensional Voting Models." *American Journal of Political Science* 23 (1): 27–59.

Shepsle, Kenneth A. 1986. "Institutional Equilibrium and Equilibrium Institutions." *Political Science: The Science of Politics* 51: 51.

Shepsle, Kenneth A. 1989. "Studying Institutions Some Lessons from the Rational Choice Approach." *Journal of Theoretical Politics* 1 (2): 131–147.

Shepsle, Kenneth A. 2010. "The Rules of the Game: What Rules? Which Game." In *Prepared for the Conference on the Legacy and Work of Douglass C. North, St. Louis*. Available at <http://scholar.harvard.edu.libproxy.mit.edu/kshepsle/files/north_paper_2010.pdf> (accessed March 26, 2014).

Skowronek, Stephen. 1993. *The Politics Presidents Make: Leadership from John Adams to Bill Clinton*. Cambridge, MA: Harvard University Press.

Streeck, Wolfgang and Kathleen Thelen. 2005. "Introduction: Institutional Change in Advanced Political Economies." In *Beyond Continuity: Institutional Change in Advanced*

Political Economies, ed. Wolfgang Streeck and Kathleen Thelen. New York: Oxford University Press, 1–39.

Streeck, Wolfgang and Kōzō Yamamura. 2001. *The Origins of Nonliberal Capitalism: Germany and Japan in Comparison*. Ithaca, NY: Cornell University Press.

Thelen, Kathleen. 1994. "Beyond Corporatism: Toward a New Framework for the Study of Labor in Advanced Capitalism." *Comparative Politics* 27 (1): 107–124.

Thelen, Kathleen. 1999. "Historical Institutionalism in Comparative Politics." *Annual Review of Political Science* 2(1): 369–404.

Thelen, Kathleen. 2004. *How Institutions Evolve: The Political Economy of Skills in Germany, Britain, the United States, and Japan*. New York: Cambridge University Press.

Tsebelis, George. 2002. *Veto Players: How Political Institutions Work*. Princeton, NJ: Princeton University Press.

Weingast, Barry R. 1997. "The Political Foundations of Democracy and the Rule of Law." *American Political Science Review* 91 (2): 245–263.

Weingast, Barry R. 2002. "Rational-Choice Institutionalism." In *Political Science: The State of the Discipline*, ed. Ira Katznelson and Helen V. Milner. New York: W.W. Norton and Company, 660–692.

Weingast, Barry R. and William J. Marshall. 1988. "The Industrial Organization of Congress; Or, Why Legislatures, like Firms, Are Not Organized as Markets." *Journal of Political Economy* 96 (1): 132–163.

Weyland, Kurt. 2008. "Toward a New Theory of Institutional Change." *World Politics* 60 (2): 281–314.

Wrong, Dennis H. 1961. "The Oversocialized Conception of Man in Modern Sociology." *American Sociological Review* 26 (2): 183–193.

CHAPTER 4

CAUSALITY AND TIME IN HISTORICAL INSTITUTIONALISM

JAMES MAHONEY, KHAIRUNNISA MOHAMEDALI, AND CHRISTOPH NGUYEN*

HISTORICAL institutionalism (HI) is inherently concerned with both causality and time. The concern with causality grows out of the field's quest to explain substantively important outcomes in historical cases. HI researchers ask *case-oriented* and *historical* causal questions in which the focus is often on occurrences in particular times and places. For example, Anthony Chen's (2009) book asks, "What caused affirmative action in employment in the United States?"; Julian Go's (2011) work is directed at the question: "Why did the United States and Britain pursue similar modes of empire building?"; and Tulia Falleti (2010) investigates the following issue: "What explains variation in the power of subnational governments following decentralization reforms in Argentina, Colombia, Brazil, and Mexico?" HI studies such as these pose historical puzzles and then work to unravel them by identifying the causes of the outcomes under study.

The concern with time grows from the fact that HI researchers employ a mode of explanation in which *sequence and temporal structure matter*. Thus, Chen (2009) argues that US affirmative action in employment was rooted in a reactive sequence of events triggered by partisan conflict over fair employment and conservative initiatives during a critical juncture in the 1940s; Go (2011) uncovers a remarkably similar causal sequence with characteristic stages driving empire building in the United States and Britain; and Falleti's (2010) explanation emphasizes differences in the relative timing of decentralization reforms across her Latin American cases. The concern with time has put HI scholarship at the forefront of a broader effort to bring temporality into study of politics (e.g., Pierson 2004; Thelen 2004).

In this chapter, we examine HI's dual concern with causality and time through an analysis of three concepts that are central to this field: critical junctures, gradual change, and path dependence (including both self-reinforcing and reactive sequences). The analysis of these concepts illustrates alternative ways in which temporality and causality come together in HI research. Our goal in discussing these concepts is to make more explicit and more formal the logic underlying studies that use these "causal-temporal" concepts. To do so, a central component of our analysis will involve the use of graphs that depict time, events, and causality. We explore how graphs can make clearer the logic underlying the study of critical junctures, gradual change, and path dependence. In addition, we raise the possibility that graphs offer a convenient and efficient way to summarize the often complex arguments of leading substantive works in the HI tradition.

Depicting Causes and Time with Graphs

We begin by introducing our graphical approach to causation and temporality. This approach captures visually the ways in which HI scholars often treat causes as filters that exist at different points in time and that may combine together to direct cases toward some outcomes and not toward others.

Causes as Filters

In the effort to explain specific outcomes in particular cases, HI researchers often understand causes as conditions that are *necessary* for specific outcomes (i.e., the outcome counterfactually would not have occurred without the cause) and/or as conditions that combine together with other conditions to create *packages* of causes that are *sufficient* for specific outcomes (i.e., combinations of interacting causes that generate outcomes). This logic-based approach to causality grows naturally from the concern of HI researchers with identifying the causes of historical outcomes in specific cases (Goertz and Mahoney 2012).

A common way to illustrate a necessary condition is with a set diagram in which the outcome is a *subset* of the necessary condition (e.g., Ragin 2000). For example, Figure 4.1a depicts severe ethnic divisions as a necessary condition for genocide: countries with genocides are a subset of countries with severe ethnic divisions. To depict this relationship in causal terms, one can separate the two sets and introduce a causal arrow, as in Figure 4.1b. The assumption in this figure is that country cases travel horizontally across space, such that they must first acquire membership in the set "severe ethnic divisions" to subsequently obtain membership in the set "genocide." With this structure, it is quite natural to think of the causal set (i.e., severe ethnic divisions) as a *filter* through which a case must pass in order to obtain membership in the outcome set. This idea of a filter can be illustrated by transforming the causal set and the outcome set into simple vertical lines, as in Figure 4.1c. We will use this filter approach to diagramming causal relations in this chapter.

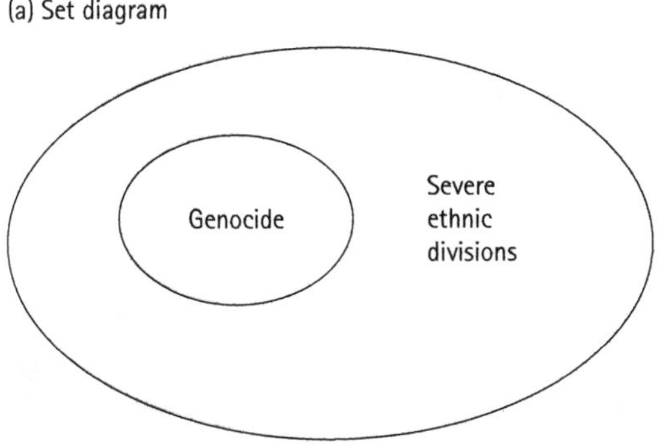

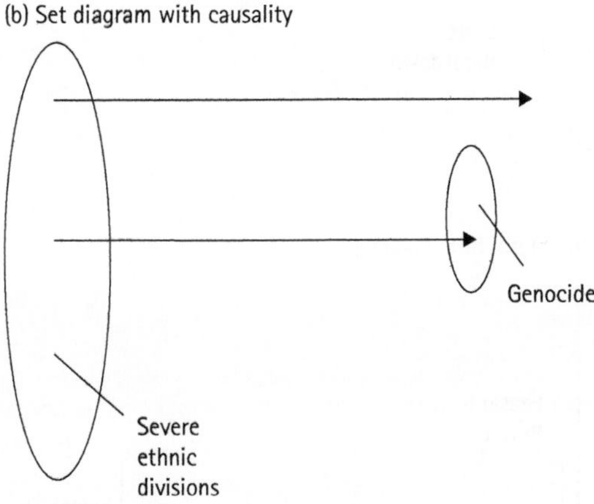

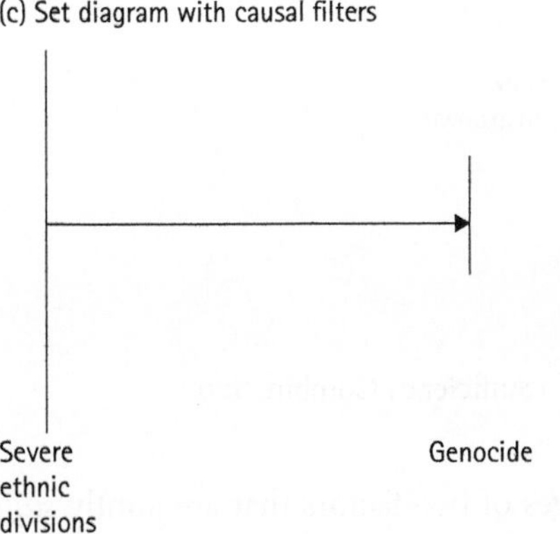

FIGURE 4.1 Depictions of a Necessary Condition

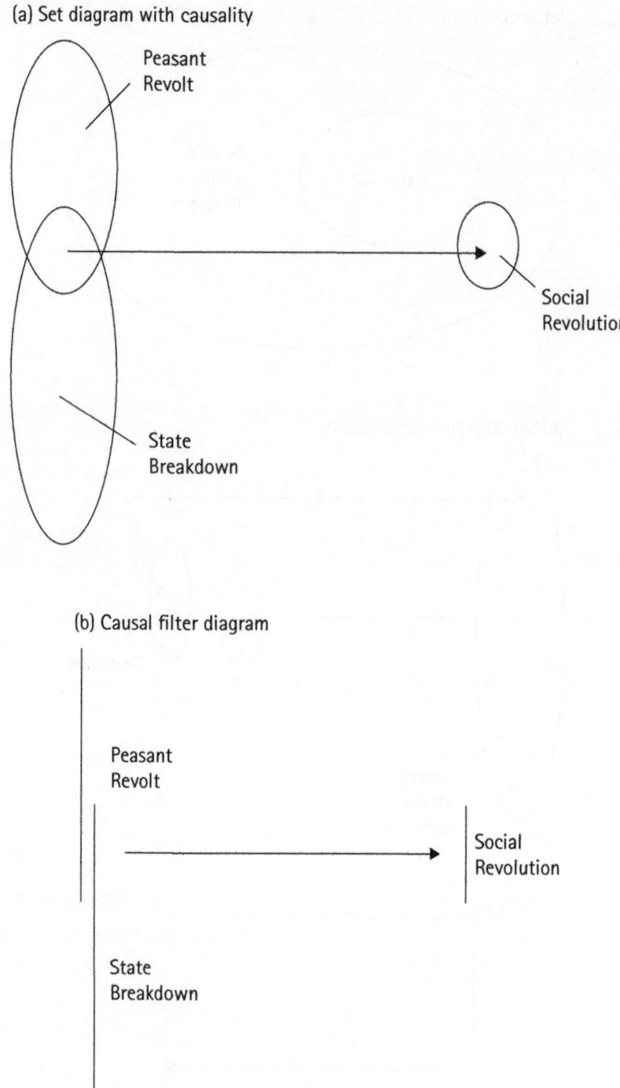

FIGURE 4.2 Depictions of a Sufficiency Combination

Simple causal packages of two factors that are jointly *sufficient* for an outcome can also be depicted with set diagrams.[1] In Figure 4.2a, the combination of "conditions for peasant revolt" and "conditions for state breakdown" is sufficient for social revolution (Skocpol 1979). That is, cases that obtain membership in *both* peasant revolt *and* state breakdown will experience a social revolution. This diagram shows how the causal combination is a subset in relationship to the outcome. Again, one can depict this relationship using the filter metaphor, as in Figure 4.2b. Passing through a sufficient condition filter (in this case, a causal combination) ensures that a case will arrive at a particular outcome.

Situating Causes in Time

HI scholars generally eschew cross-sectional explanations. Instead, their explanations identify causal conditions that are located at multiple points in time. They suggest that adequate explanation requires taking seriously the unfolding of causal processes over time. As a result, HI work is almost inherently process-oriented and mechanism-oriented. In addition, HI scholars are sensitive to other temporal concepts, such as duration (e.g., how long a given event lasts) and causal ordering (e.g., whether *A* occurs before or after *B*). For example, in the context of historical Southeast Asia, Slater (2005) shows that if contentious politics erupted before an authoritarian regime had been inaugurated, a durable authoritarian regime was the result. If, however, contentious politics occurred after the authoritarian regime was in place, then durable authoritarianism could not be sustained.

One can capture visually these ideas by adding a temporal component to the filter diagrams introduced above. Figure 4.3a presents two causal conditions—*X* and *Z*—that are jointly sufficient for the outcome *Y*. The duration of the conditions is depicted by their horizontal lengths, as indicated by the horizontal line extending forward in time. Thus, condition *X* is a necessary condition for outcome *Y* (i.e., a case must pass through *X* to arrive at *Y*); it begins at time 10 and endures until time 40, when the outcome either takes place or does not. Condition *Z* is not necessary for *Y*, but it can combine with *X* to ensure that *Y* will occur. In the figure, condition *Z* starts at time 30 and ends at time 40. A case that passes through *X* and also subsequently passes through *Z* will experience *Y* at time 38. For instance, consider Martin and Swank's (2012) argument that the presence of centralized (as opposed to federal) governments (*Z*) and the introduction of proportional representation/multiparty systems (*X*) lead to the establishment of encompassing and macro-corporatist employer associations (*Y*). Cases first must acquire centralized governments and then subsequently proportional representation/multiparty systems to experience the outcome of interest.

Figure 4.3b considers the possibility that condition *Z* occurs before condition *X*. In this instance, *X* has the same relationship to *Y* as in Figure 4.3a—that is, *X* is a necessary condition that endures until *Y* occurs (or not). However, in the example, *X* is now temporally proximate to *Y*. This version also includes filters for the absence of conditions: ~ *X* (i.e., not *X*) is represented by a dashed line. In the illustration, the occurrence of condition *Z* takes place before *X* and no longer helps to produce outcome *Y* even with the subsequent presence of *X*. In fact, in this example, the occurrence of *Z* *before* *X* ensures that *Y* will *not* occur. The comparison of Figures 4.3a and 4.3b is intended to illustrate how the same causal package can have an opposite effect depending on the order in which conditions within that causal package occur. The combination of *XZ* yields *Y*, whereas the combination of *ZX* yields ~*Y*. To return to Slater's analysis of durable authoritarian

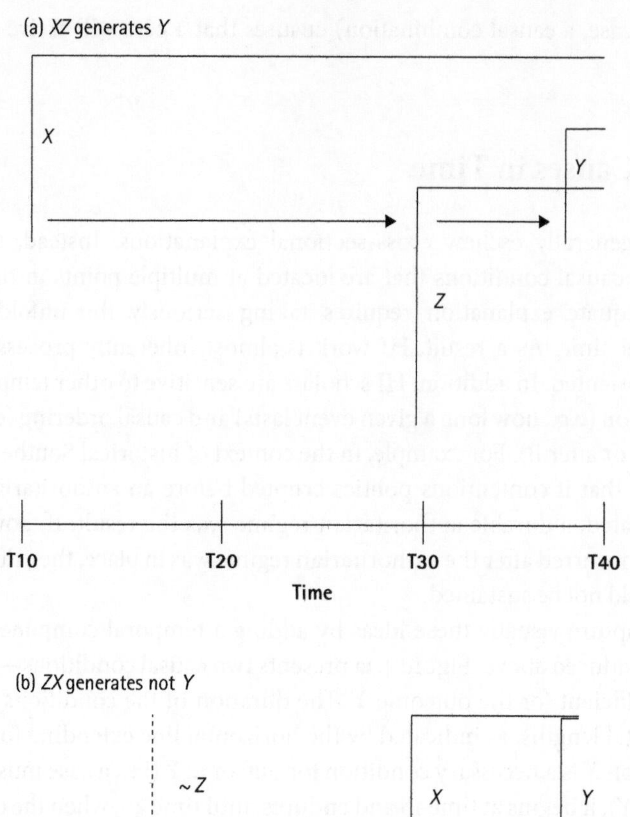

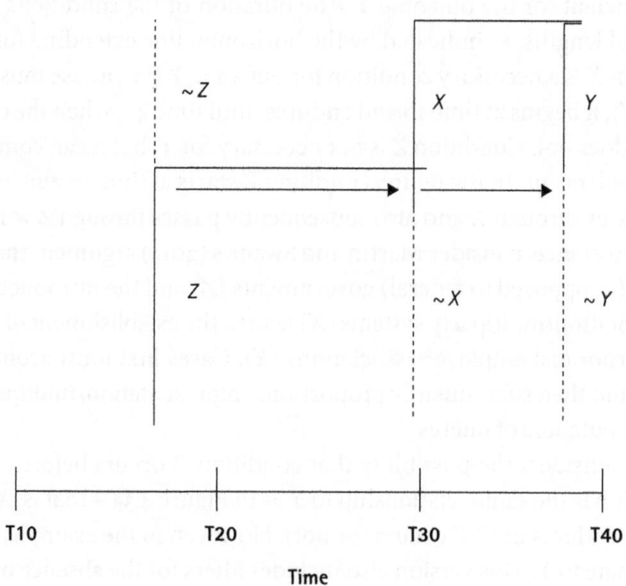

FIGURE 4.3 Causal Filters with Temporal Component

regimes: contentious politics followed by the inauguration of an authoritarian regime (*XZ*) results in a durable authoritarianism (*Y*). However, when the inauguration of an authoritarian regime precedes contentious politics (*ZX*), the outcome is not durable authoritarianism (~*Y*).

THE CAUSAL LOGIC OF PUNCTUATED VERSUS INCREMENTAL CHANGE

In this section, we explore how causal filters and diagrams can shed new light on the logic of two kinds of change central to the HI field: critical junctures and gradual change. Critical junctures are relatively brief episodes during which: (a) the range of possible outcomes that might take place in the future briefly but dramatically expands; and (b) events occur that quickly close off future possibilities and set into motion processes that track specific future outcomes. By contrast, gradual changes occur incrementally over relatively long periods of time, such that a series of events slowly moves a case toward a specific outcome.

Critical Junctures

One way of defining a critical juncture calls central attention to its temporal components. A critical juncture is a relatively short period in time during which an event or set of events occurs that has a large and enduring subsequent impact. Crucial here is that the duration of a critical juncture is *brief* compared to the duration of the causal processes and/or final outcome that it triggers (Capoccia and Keleman 2007). One possibility is presented in Figure 4.4a. In this example, passing through the critical juncture *X* is necessary for the outcome *Y*, which endures for a long period of time. For instance, Solingen and Wan (Chapter 33, this volume) demonstrate how brief interludes of nuclear non-compliance had long-lasting effects for the state of international non-proliferation agreements.

Another possibility is offered in Figure 4.4b. Here passing through the critical juncture *X* is necessary for a series of subsequent causal steps that track and culminate in a relatively brief final outcome. In this latter case, the duration of the legacy is mostly composed of the causal processes connecting the critical juncture to the outcome of interest. In both Figures 4.4a and 4.4b, the occurrence of *X* is "critical" because the case has to pass through this filter if it is to experience *Y*. In fact, in both examples, passing through the critical juncture filter comes close to ensuring that *Y* will occur.

Another (compatible) way to conceptualize critical junctures calls attention to agency, contingency, and the range of possible future outcomes. Here critical junctures are periods in time marked by "openings" when the range of possible future outcomes available to actors is large. Critical periods conclude with "closings" in which the range of possible future outcomes has been limited. A critical juncture is thus an episode in time characterized by a brief loosening in "the constraints of structure ... allow[ing] for agency or contingency to shape divergence from the past, or divergence across cases" (Soifer 2012). The aftermath of a critical juncture is marked by deep and perhaps increasing constraints on agency and the range of outcomes that can occur. The events of critical junctures close off future possibilities.

(a) Enduring post-critical juncture outcome

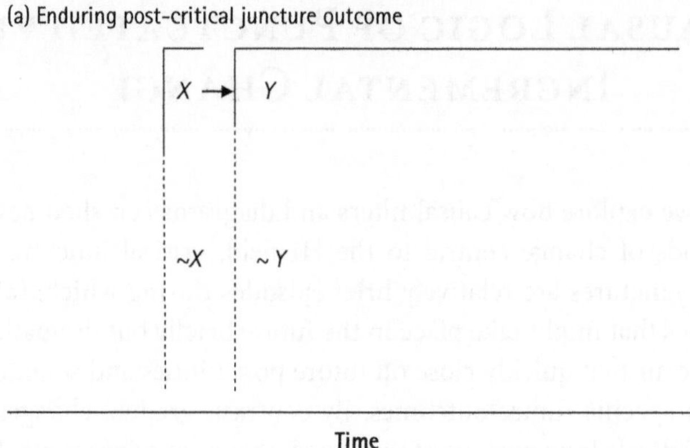

(b) Extended post-critical juncture causal process

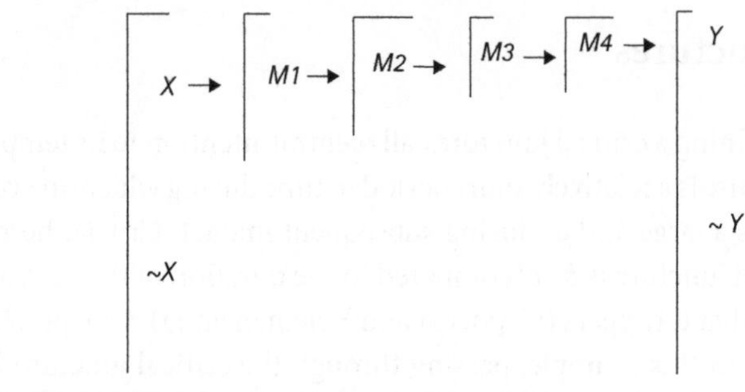

FIGURE 4.4 Temporality of Critical Junctures

Figure 4.5 provides one way of thinking about this opening-closing understanding of critical junctures. The figure illustrates how the critical juncture *X* is a necessary condition for a series of possible outcomes—*A*, *B*, and *C*. Without *X*, these outcomes are not possible, and *X* does not initially close off any possible outcome (including *D*). The figure also illustrates how, at end of the critical juncture, some of these outcomes are closed off (e.g., *C* and *D*), and how one specific outcome (*A*) is now being tracked through causal processes set into motion by the critical juncture. While this diagram cannot capture all aspects of agency and contingency associated with critical junctures, it does capture the idea that critical junctures open up and then close off possible outcomes. It also captures the temporal component of critical junctures by illustrating how the critical juncture is a brief episode in comparison to its legacy.

Thinking in terms of diagrams also allow us to understand better the methodological issues that arise in assessing the relative causal contribution of critical junctures versus antecedent conditions. The problem here is that HI scholars often lack a good way of discussing the extent to which a critical juncture is a clean break from the past versus entangled in a jumble of significant antecedent factors (see Slater and Simmons 2010).

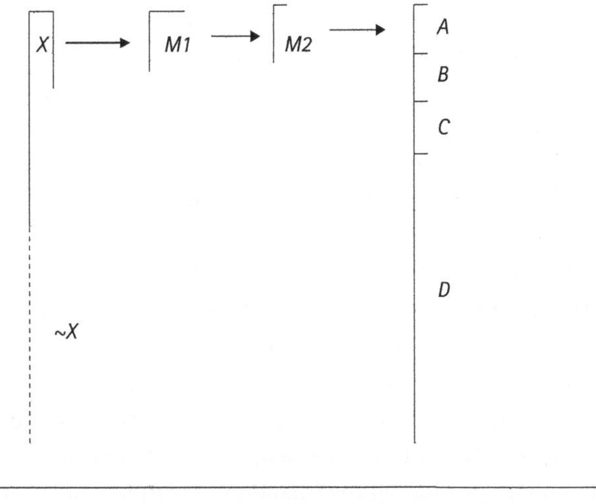

FIGURE 4.5 Opening and Closing of Possible Outcomes during Critical Junctures

Our view is that the best candidates for critical junctures are usually "important" necessary conditions, defined as necessary conditions that come close to also being sufficient for an outcome (see Ragin 2008; Goertz 2006; Mahoney 2008.

With a filter diagram, an important necessary condition has only a slightly larger vertical length than the outcome it helps explain. Thus, passing through the critical juncture filter is not only essential for the outcome, but also comes relatively close to ensuring the outcome, including the intervening causal processes that link the critical juncture to the outcome. By contrast, while various antecedent conditions may have been necessary for the final outcome, they are not critical junctures because they are not important in the sense of coming close to also being sufficient for the final outcome under study. They are, rather, large filters that allow for a wide range of possible outcomes. For example, in 1827, the British Prime Minister's stroke and his successor's sudden death a few months later were antecedent conditions that were necessary but not sufficient for British democratization (Ertman 2010). The disarray caused by these sudden changes in leadership opened the space for reform acts to be instituted, but did not narrow the possible trajectories British institutional reforms could take.

Although antecedent conditions cannot be more important causal filters than a critical juncture itself, they can nevertheless play a supporting role in a critical juncture explanation. One possibility is that antecedent conditions help explain some aspect of the main outcome that the critical juncture does not, even though the antecedent conditions are overall less important causes. These conditions might be labeled "critical antecedents" (see Slater and Simmons 2010), and we can think of them as filters prior to a critical juncture that play an independent role in directing a case toward an outcome, though secondary next to the critical juncture. For instance, in Gingrich's (2011) analysis of variations in market structures, the existing health, education, and care systems are critical antecedents: they help explain variation in the outcomes of market reform in welfare states but play a secondary role to the sudden rise in the political prominence of welfare services, which offered a critical juncture for incumbent parties to institute their preferred market reforms.

Another possibility is that antecedent conditions help explain the critical juncture, but they do not add independent weight toward the outcome of interest themselves. These antecedent conditions are "causes of the critical juncture," but they are not critical antecedents because they do not have a distinctive or direct role in generating the outcome of interest. In Ertman's (2010) analysis of British democratization, the Prime Minister's stroke and his successor's death within the space of a few months in 1827 caused a critical juncture in British democratization. The unexpected upheavals in political leadership triggered an opening from 1828 to 1835, during which numerous reform acts, including the Great Reform Act of 1832, could be passed. However, this antecedent condition did not directly contribute to producing the final outcome of lasting reforms in parliamentary representation and reduced discrimination against religious minorities.

Gradual Change

Theories and arguments about gradual change in the HI literature assume various forms. Some formulations take issue with the sharp separation between stability and change that appears in literature emphasizing exogenous shocks, crises, and punctuations (Thelen 2004; Streeck and Thelen 2005). Proponents of gradual change point out that change and stability are really "two sides of the same coin" in that stability assumes and requires change. A case may experience a given outcome across time, but this continuity occurs only because various changes have taken place. One cannot understand the continuity without also appreciating the change (Mahoney and Thelen 2010).

It is useful to think about this argument in terms of evolving necessary/sufficient condition filters. For illustration, let us assume that we seek to explain the persistence of *Y*, and some factor *A* is essential for the production of *Y* over time. This factor *A* is a necessary condition that repeatedly helps produce *Y*; it is a *constant cause*, in the language of Stinchcombe (1968), and it must be present if *Y* is to be maintained. However, *A* is not sufficient for *Y*, and it must combine with other *time-variant causes* to generate *Y*. Depending on the historical context, these other required causes will be different: at time 1, *A* must combine with *B* and *C* to produce *Y* (i.e., $ABC \rightarrow Y$); at time 2, *A* combines with *C* and *D* (i.e., $ACD \rightarrow Y$); at time 3, *A* combines with *D* and *E* (i.e., $ADE \rightarrow Y$); and so on. Thus, while *Y* is stable over time, the specific causal package that produces this stability changes over time.

Galvin (2010) uses a mechanism of gradual change with constant and time-variant causes to explain why the Republican Party, unlike the Democratic Party, evolved into a vertically integrated, technologically sophisticated national political machine with impressive capacities to activate local grassroots networks. The president's perceptions of his party's competitive standing—a time-variant cause—and the party's competitive standing—a constant cause during the period under analysis—combine together as a package to explain the outcome.

It is also possible to think of the outcome *Y* itself as needing to change over time in order to persist. For example, let us imagine that *Y* is an institution or an organization—such as a university, government, or constitution—and we are impressed by its endurance. However, the entity that endures has changed gradually over time, and this gradual change is crucial to its endurance. That is, the entity would not have endured if it had not changed over time. In some cases, a core set of attributes may persist, and other features around this core evolve to preserve stability. For example, if the stable trait is *A*, we could imagine the defining features of the institution as evolving as follows: *ABCD—ACDE—ADEF—AEFG*. From start to finish, the only common feature is *A*. We could also imagine stability in which no common core is preserved; that is, the features of the institution gradually change over time such that it possesses none of its original features: *ABCD—BCDE—CDEF—DEFG—EFGH*. Because the changes are slow and piecemeal, however, we perceive the entity as experiencing persistence and stability. This stability depends on the gradual changes that occurred over time; instability would have ensued without these slowly accumulating changes.

These two patterns of gradual change can be brought together in graphical form (see Figure 4.6). In Figure 4.6, a series of different combinations of factors reproduce outcome *Y*. At time 1, *A* and *B* are individually necessary and jointly sufficient for *Y*. At time 2, however, *A* is no longer necessary for *Y*. In fact, the continued maintenance of *A* would ensure the absence of *Y*. Instead, at time 2, the combination of *B* and *C* are individually necessary and jointly sufficient for *Y*. At time 3, the combination of *C* and *D* are

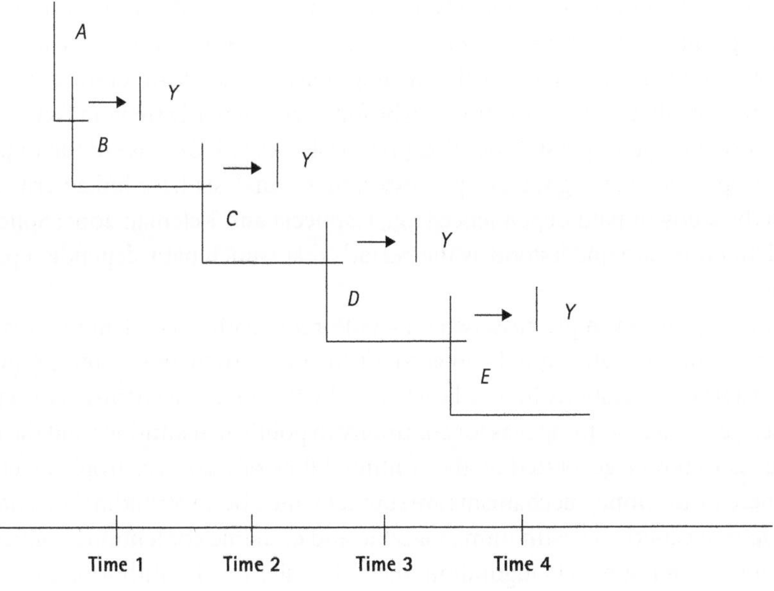

FIGURE 4.6 Process of Gradual Change

individually necessary and jointly sufficient for *Y*, and so on. Thus, the causes required for the reproduction of *Y* vary across time. In addition, this figure suggests that *Y* itself changes gradually over time. One can see this by the shifting vertical space occupied by *Y*. In other words, what it means to be *Y* is not constant in this depiction; it evolves gradually over time. As an example, consider Thelen's (2004) study of skill formation, which highlights how initial arrangements change and adapt over time. While initial conditions remain important, her work emphasizes that repeated, small adjustments can also fundamentally alter the institutional landscape.

Path Dependence

In this section, we consider how ideas of necessary and sufficient conditions, causal filters, and sequential graphs can help HI scholars better conceptualize the phenomenon of path dependence. In doing so, we examine two different kinds of sequences that can exhibit path dependence: (a) self-reinforcing sequences marked by increasing returns dynamics; and (b) reactive sequences that exhibit backlash dynamics.

Self-Reinforcing Sequences

One core definition of path dependence views the phenomenon in terms of positive feedback or increasing returns (Arthur 1994; David 1985; Pierson 2004). With path dependence, each step in a particular direction makes it more likely that a unit will continue to follow that same direction. Over time, it becomes harder and harder to reverse course. Typically, with this conception of path dependence, the early steps are crucial in leading a unit down a particular path. Ensuing steps then serve to reinforce the already high probability that a given direction will be followed. The early steps, in fact, may completely close off certain possibilities that previously existed. Because of the importance of early steps in increasing returns processes, many analysts have linked critical junctures to the study of path dependence (e.g., Capoccia and Keleman 2007; Soifer 2012). Critical junctures are understood as the periods that launch path-dependent processes of change.

Slater (2005), for example, uses two self-reinforcing path dependent processes—one institutional and one attitudinal—to account for the entrenchment and perpetuation of authoritarian institutions in Southeast Asia. Institutional mechanisms of reproduction operate through a strong bias for continuity in political institutions and the increasing returns to power generated by the continual flow of resources from society to the state. These institutional mechanisms are supplemented by an attitudinal mechanism of reproduction: experience with unmanageable and endemic contentious politics before the authoritarian regime's inauguration makes it easier for the authoritarian regime to

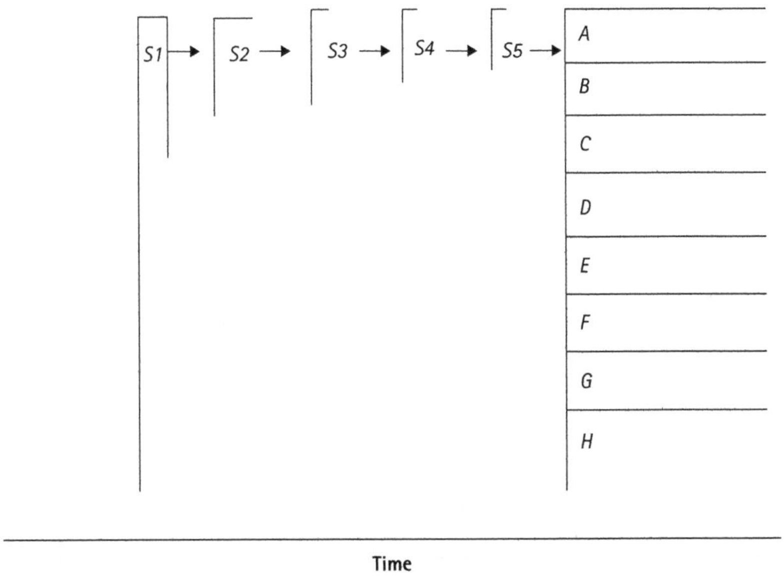

FIGURE 4.7 Path Dependence as Increasing Returns

cultivate and maintain anti-democratic attitudes over the long-run. With time, reversing authoritarian rule becomes more and more difficult.

Figure 4.7 offers one way of diagramming the logic of path dependence as increasing returns. In this figure, one begins with conditions that allow for a wide spectrum of different outcomes (*A*, *B*, ... *H*). An initial critical juncture step then dramatically contracts the range of possibilities, eliminating most outcomes. Subsequent steps increasingly start to track the specific outcome *A*. Each step feeds into the next, reinforcing the direction established during the previous step. Although at no point is outcome *A* ensured, it becomes more and more likely over time.

Three observations are worth making in conjunction with this discussion of Figure 4.7. First, the focus of much of the literature on path dependence concerns the mechanisms through which increasing returns dynamics operate. That is, scholars work to specify the causal logic through which each step toward a particular outcome makes it increasingly likely that the outcome will occur. To do so, they often draw on utilitarian theory and assumptions about pay-offs and relative benefits over time (Arthur 1994; David 1985; Pierson 2004). However, as the Slater example above suggests, this logic can also be codified with other theoretical orientations, including increasing returns to power or legitimacy (Mahoney 2000). Second, it is worth noting that the increasing returns dynamics that follow a critical juncture could be viewed as processes of gradual change. After a critical juncture, intermediate steps unfold slowly over time with each one of them making only a small contribution in moving a case to a specific outcome. Thus, while a path-dependent process begins with a sudden change, it can then become a slow-moving process of incremental shifts.

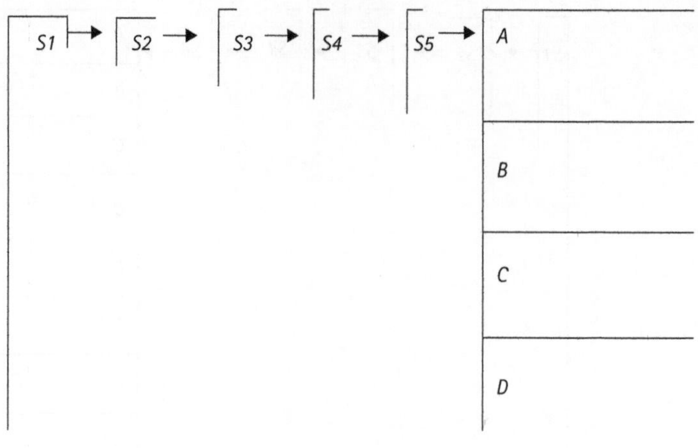

FIGURE 4.8 Path Dependence as Deterministic Increasing Returns

Finally, it is worth noting that one can model path dependence as increasing returns using a deterministic causal structure. For example, in Figure 4.8, the initial step (*S1*) selects a particular pathway that is sufficient for *A*. *S1* completely closes out all other possibilities. The intermediate steps keep the unit on track toward the destined outcome of *A*. Each intermediate step is sufficient for each subsequent step, and each step brings us closer and closer to achieving sufficiency *and* necessity for *A*.

Reactive Sequences

Many HI scholars apply the concept of path dependence to sequences that do not exhibit increasing returns and positive feedback. Their intuition is that the core feature of path dependence is not self-reinforcement per se. Rather, the core feature of path dependence is the existence of a chain of tightly coupled and causally connected events that make up the trajectory linking a critical juncture period to a final outcome of interest. Path dependence thus can also be characterized by *reactive sequences*.

Reactive sequences are chains of tightly coupled events in which each event is a cause of each subsequent event. These sequences are "reactive" both because they move *quickly* from one event to the next and because they are marked by *backlash processes* in which *reversals can take place.* Each step in a reactive sequence therefore is not associated with positive feedback and movement in a particular direction. A given step may in fact bring a case back to a previous choice point, and at a later point in time a case may go down a road that was once bypassed. These reversals and backlashes can be necessary

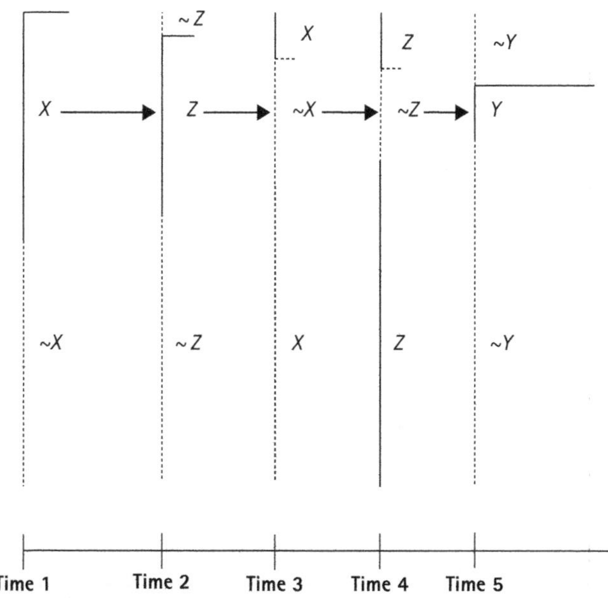

FIGURE 4.9 Path-Dependent Reactive Sequence

ingredients in directing a case toward a specific final outcome of interest. Posner's (2010) explanation for the rise of international accounting standards is an example of the role that sequence and reactivity can play. Posner shows that despite the United States' first-mover advantage and a strong financial industry, the back-and-forth of emulation and bargaining between US and EU regulators ultimately led to the creation of a multi-national, and more importantly privately run, standard-setting body.

Figure 4.9 offers a simple depiction of the causal logic of a path-dependent reactive sequence with backlash dynamics. In the figure, the initial step at time 1 is the selection of *X* rather than ~*X*. In many understandings of path dependence, this selection must be marked by a high level of contingency, such that small events or chance dynamics drive the selection of *X* rather than ~*X*. As the causal filter structure makes clear, the initial selection of *X* is highly consequential: it is *necessary* for the outcome *Y* at time 5. The backlash component of the diagram is captured by the event at time 3, when the case experiences ~*X* rather than *X*. As the diagram illustrates, passing through ~*X* at time 3 is also necessary for *Y*. To arrive at *Y*, in other words, the case must experience backlash in the sense that it reverses its original selection and adopts another choice. Clearly, the sequencing of events matters greatly in this example: selecting ~*X* at time 1, or *X* at time 3, would have produced ~*Y*. The path-dependent aspect of the example is illustrated in the way in which the case increasingly tracks outcome *Y* over time: each necessary condition filter (*X*, *Z*, ~ *X*, ~ *Z*) comes closer and closer to being sufficient for *Y*.

Finally, Figure 4.10 presents an example of a reactive sequence in which the causal logic runs through sufficiency rather than necessity. This example parallels Figure 4.9 except that each causal filter is sufficient for each subsequent filter. Thus, selecting (or

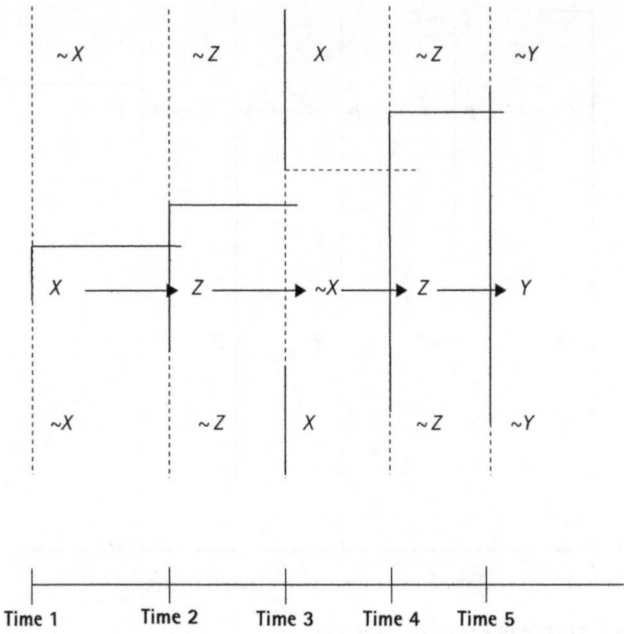

FIGURE 4.10 Path Dependence with Sufficiency

passing through) *X* at time 1 is sufficient for *Y* because it ensures that units will select (or pass through) ~*X* at time 3, which is also sufficient for *Y*. As the figure shows, each step comes closer and closer to being necessary in addition to being sufficient for the final outcome.

Conclusion

In this chapter, we have sought to clarify the logic of several important temporal-causal concepts in the field of historical institutionalism. To do so, we have used graphs in which both time and causality are depicted visually. We have suggested that HI scholars implicitly treat causes as filters through which cases may pass. In some instances, a case must pass through a given filter in order to experience the outcome of interest. In other instances, if a case passes through a given filter or combination of filters, it is assured of experiencing the outcome of interest. In still other cases, passing through a filter makes it more likely that a case will experience an outcome but not does guarantee this result. For many outcomes, the essential requirement is that a case pass through a specific combination of multiple filters. The diagrams that we have constructed allow one to represent all of these causal possibilities.

The diagrams also capture various dimensions of temporality. They illustrate how different causes are located at different points in time and are marked by different durations. By capturing temporality with horizontal lines, the diagrams show how critical junctures are brief episodes that launch enduring outcomes and that narrow the range of possible outcomes a case may experience. The diagrams can also depict patterns of gradual change and path-dependent processes marked by increasing returns or the logic of reactive sequences, all of which can be hard to define and specify without the aid of visual diagrams.

Perhaps above all else, this chapter has shown how, in the field of historical institutionalism, causality and temporality are inherently linked to one another. To make sense of the patterns of change studied in this field, one must ask questions about the nature of both the causal processes and the temporal processes that constitute the pattern of change. This chapter has provided new tools for describing and understanding these processes.

Notes

* We would like to thank Tulia Falleti and Elisabeth Wood for helpful comments on previous drafts of this chapter.

1. Causal packages with several causes defy easy graphical representation.

References

Arthur, W. Brian. 1994. *Increasing Returns and Path Dependence in the Economy*. Ann Arbor, MI: University of Michigan Press.

Capoccia, Giovanni and Daniel Keleman. 2007. "The Study of Critical Junctures: Theory, Narrative, and Counterfactuals in Historical Institutionalism." *World Politics* 59 (3): 341–369.

Chen, Anthony S. 2009. *The Fifth Freedom: Jobs, Politics, and Civil Rights in the United States, 1941–1972*. Princeton, NJ: Princeton University Press.

David, Paul A. 1985. "Clio and the Economics of QWERTY." *American Economic Review* 75 (2): 332–337.

Ertman, Thomas. 2010. "The Great Reform Act of 1832 and British Democratization." *Comparative Political Studies* 43 (8–9): 1000–1022.

Falleti, Tulia G. 2010. *Decentralization and Subnational Politics in Latin America*. New York and Cambridge: Cambridge University Press.

Galvin, Daniel J. 2010. *Presidential Party Building: Dwight D. Eisenhower and George W. Bush*. Princeton, NJ: Princeton University Press.

Gingrich, Jane. 2011. *Making Markets in the Welfare State: The Politics of Varying Market Reforms*. Cambridge: Cambridge University Press.

Go, Julian. 2011. *Patterns of Empire: The British and American Empires, 1688 to the Present*. Cambridge: Cambridge University Press.

Goertz, Gary. 2006. "Assessing the Trivialness, Relevance, and Relative Importance of Necessary or Sufficient Conditions in Social Science." *Studies in Comparative International Development* 41: 88–109.

Goertz, Gary and James Mahoney. 2012. *A Tale of Two Cultures: Qualitative and Quantitative Research in the Social Sciences*. Princeton, NJ: Princeton University Press.

Mahoney, James. 2000. "Path Dependence in Historical Sociology." *Theory and Society* 29 (4): 507–548.

Mahoney, James. 2008. "Toward a Unified Theory of Causality." *Comparative Political Studies* 41: 412–436.

Mahoney, James and Kathleen Thelen. 2010. "A Theory of Gradual Institutional Change." In *Explaining Institutional Change: Ambiguity, Agency, and Power*, ed. James Mahoney and Kathleen Thelen. Cambridge: Cambridge University Press, 1–37.

Martin, Cathie Jo and Duane Swank. 2012. *The Political Construction of Business Interests: Coordination, Growth, and Equality*. New York: Cambridge University Press.

Pierson, Paul. 2004. *Politics in Time: History, Institutions, and Social Analysis*. Princeton, NJ: Princeton University Press.

Posner, Elliot. 2010. "Sequence as Explanation: The International Politics of Accounting Standards." *Review of International Political Economy* 17 (4): 639–664.

Ragin, Charles C. 2000. *Fuzzy-Set Social Science*. Chicago: University of Chicago Press.

Ragin, Charles C. 2008. *Redesigning Social Inquiry: Fuzzy Sets and Beyond*. Chicago: University of Chicago Press.

Skocpol, Theda. 1979. *States and Social Revolutions: A Comparative Analysis of France, Russia, and China*. Cambridge: Cambridge University Press.

Slater, Dan. 2005. *Ordering Power: Contentious Politics and Authoritarian Leviathans in Southeast Asia*. Cambridge: Cambridge University Press.

Slater, Dan and Erica Simmons. 2010. "Informative Regress: Critical Antecedents in Comparative Politics." *Comparative Political Studies* 43 (7): 886–917.

Soifer, Hillel David. 2012. "The Causal Logic of Critical Junctures." *Comparative Political Studies* 45 (12): 1572–1597.

Stinchcombe, Arthur L. 1968. *Constructing Social Theories*. New York: Harcourt.

Streeck, Wolfgang and Kathleen Thelen. 2005. "Introduction: Institutional Change in Advanced Political Economies." In *Beyond Continuity: Institutional Change in Advanced Political Economies*, ed. Wolfgang Streeck and Kathleen Thelen. Oxford: Oxford University Press.

Thelen, Kathleen. 2004. *How Institutions Evolve: The Political Economy of Skills in Germany, Britain, the United States, and Japan*. Cambridge: Cambridge University Press.

CHAPTER 5

CRITICAL JUNCTURES

GIOVANNI CAPOCCIA*

THE concept of critical juncture (and synonyms such as "crisis," "turning point," "unsettled times") has a long pedigree in historical institutionalism. Although, as discussed in this chapter, different definitions of the concept have been used in the literature, the minimum common denominator among all of them is the focus on what can be called "distal historical causation": events and developments in the distant past, generally concentrated in a relatively short period, that have a crucial impact on outcomes later in time. More broadly, this approach has been used in a wide range of disciplines, from medicine to sociology, to account for outcomes as diverse as individual life histories, the development of groups and organizations, and the evolution of entire societies (e.g., Swidler 1986, 280). In Political Science, the concept has been most systematically developed and applied in the area of historical institutionalism (and, more generally, in comparative historical analysis). Indeed, the concept of critical juncture, and the underpinning logic of distal historical causation, is often applied in the analysis of the historical development of *institutions*, broadly defined as including organizations, formal rules, public policies, as well as larger configurations of connected institutional arrangements such as political regimes and political economies.

The first use of the concept in comparative historical analysis is to be found in the classic work of Seymour Martin Lipset and Stein Rokkan tracing the roots of the origins of Western European party systems to three "crucial junctures" in the history of each nation (Lipset and Rokkan 1967, 37–38). Lipset and Rokkan argued that the variety of party systems in Western European democracies that existed the 1960s was the outcome of a set of ordered consequences of "decisions and developments" which occurred in crucial junctures, located much earlier in history. The concept of critical juncture became a crucial part of the toolbox of scholars interested in the study of institutional development with the seminal study by Ruth Berins Collier and David Collier on modes of labor incorporation in Latin America (1991). Berins Collier and Collier argue that polities, when faced with the challenge of incorporating mass labor, opted in some cases for a state-led and in other cases for a party-led labor incorporation. These different options had important long-term legacies in terms of regime outcome (Berins Collier and Collier 1991). Comparative studies that apply a similar logic and that have followed in the footsteps of Berins Collier and Collier include, among others, the work of James Mahoney (2002) and Evan Lieberman (2003) discussed later in this section.

With respect to Lipset and Rokkan's seminal volume, a crucial theoretical innovation of these works is that they explicitly cast their studies as examples of a *more general* approach to the analysis of institutional development, in which critical junctures give rise to *path-dependent* processes. Indeed, these authors typically link their work to research on path dependence in institutional economics, imported into Political Science from the work of Douglass North, Brian Arthur and Paul David (Berins Collier and Collier 1991, 27; Mahoney 2002, 7; Lieberman 2003, 23; see also, more generally, Pierson 2004). The explicit connection of the critical juncture approach to the theory of path dependence provided powerful theoretical tools for the analysis of distal historical causation. The emphasis placed in path dependence theory on mechanisms of institutional reproduction, dynamics of increasing returns, and network effects lent powerful theoretical support to the thesis that decisions and developments located in the distant past can have a long-lasting effect on institutional arrangements.[1] At the same time, the insight drawn from path dependence in economics and sociology that "small and contingent events," although generally of insignificant influence during periods of institutional reproduction, can instead play a crucial role at the beginning of an institutional path (e.g., Mahoney 2000, 536; Pierson 2004, 44; see also Soifer 2012), induced scholars in Political Science to theorize explicitly that during critical junctures different possibilities of development are possible, and that prior structural conditions do not necessarily determine the type and direction of subsequent institutional developments (Goldstone 1998; Mahoney 2000). By underscoring the existence and plausibility of different options that were consequential for subsequent institutional development, these scholars implicitly switched from an *ex post* analytical perspective, evident in the early work of Lipset and Rokkan, to an *ex ante* perspective, which, albeit only implicitly in some work, considered not only the institutional path taken, but also the paths not taken, although plausible at the time.

Although these contributions are at times couched in structuralist language not dissimilar from earlier work (see, e.g., the explicit references to Lipset and Rokkan [1967] as well as to Barrington Moore [1966] in Berins Collier and Collier [1991]), a consequence of the theoretical move from *ex post* to *ex ante* is to focus on political agency and choice as an important factor in selecting among the options available at the time of the critical juncture. According to Berins Collier and Collier, the importance of agency and choice varies: some critical junctures can entail "considerable discretion," while in others "the presumed choice appears deeply embedded in antecedent conditions" (Berins Collier and Collier 1991, 27). In his comparative study of the political development of Central America, Mahoney (2002) defines more explicitly critical junctures as "choice point[s] when a particular option is adopted among two or more alternatives" given by antecedent historical conditions. Mahoney emphasizes the importance of agency and meaningful choice: "in many cases, critical junctures are moments of relative structural indeterminism when willful actors shape outcomes in a more voluntaristic fashion than normal circumstances permit . . . these choices demonstrate the power of agency by revealing how long-term development patterns can hinge on distant actor decisions of the past" (Mahoney 2002, 8; see also Katznelson 2003, 282–283). Lieberman, in his comparative analysis of the development of fiscal systems in Brazil and South Africa, clearly underscores not only that plausible alternatives to the constitutional choices made in the two cases were available to decision-makers, but also that had these alternatives been selected, Brazil and South Africa would have been very different forms of "tax states" (Lieberman 2003, 78–105).

Taking stock of these debates, Giovanni Capoccia and Daniel Kelemen (2007) offer a systematic theorization of critical junctures in historical institutionalism, underscoring that analogies to economic processes in which a series of small events leads to a state of "lock-in" are often inadequate for capturing processes of institutional creation in politics. Even in moments of social and political fluidity, the decisions of some actors are often more influential than those of others in steering institutional development: rather than a focus on cumulative small events, a focus on decision-making by powerful actors is likely to be more useful in the analysis of critical junctures.[2] They anchor the discussion of critical junctures in the analysis of institutions more broadly by arguing that scholars should endeavor to specify precisely the *unit of analysis* with respect to which the "juncture" is argued to be "critical." One common approach in the literature has been to identify relatively brief periods of momentous political, social, or economic upheaval and to assert, in a general sense, that these constitute critical junctures (e.g., Ebbinghaus 2005, 16; Dion 2010, 34). Even during periods of massive social and political upheaval, however, certain institutions may well remain unaffected (Thelen 2004; Streeck and Thelen 2005, 8–9). Conversely, even during periods of stability for a domestic or international regime as a whole, critical junctures may be faced by particular institutions; institutions are certainly inter-connected but critical junctures may occur as relatively discrete phenomena that do not have an immediate impact on the broader political environment. This discussion provides the foundation for a definition of critical junctures that turns on the relaxation of structural (i.e., economic, cultural, ideological, organizational) conditions of political action. Critical junctures are defined as "*relatively* short periods of time during which there is a *substantially* heightened probability that *agents' choices* will affect the outcome of interest" (Capoccia and Kelemen 2007, 348). The reference to "relatively short periods of time" captures the fact that the duration of the juncture must be brief relative to the duration of the path-dependent process that follows (Capoccia and Kelemen 2007, 350–351). The absolute duration of a critical juncture has an impact on the ability of actors to behave freely and to affect future institutional arrangements: the longer the juncture, the higher the probability that political decisions will be constrained by a re-emerging structural constraint. The reference to "*substantially* heightened probability" captures the increased causal importance of agency during the critical juncture when compared to the historical phases before and afterwards. This definition captures both the notion that, for a brief period, agents face a *broader than normal* range of feasible options and that their choices among these options are *likely to have a significant impact* on the path-dependent development of an institution.

The expanded causal role of agency leads to more solid foundations for the analysis of *contingency*, a key element of critical juncture analysis as postulated by path dependence theory in economics (e.g., David 2000), sociology (e.g., Mahoney 2000) and Political Science (e.g., Pierson 2000). Drawing from Isaiah Berlin's work, Capoccia and Kelemen define contingency in the analysis of critical junctures as "the study of what happened in the context of *what could have happened*" (Berlin 1974, 176; italics added).[3] Hence, in this approach, contingency has two important characteristics. First, it is linked to the analysis of agency and choices during critical junctures and points to the intrinsic plausibility of the twofold counterfactual argument that actors could have taken different decisions, and had they done so, this would have had important consequences for the institutional outcome of interest.[4] Second, this conception of contingency underscores the fact that the range of plausible alternative options during critical junctures—in Berlin's words, "what could have happened"—is not infinite: the range of options is defined by prior conditions even though, within the limits of those conditions, actors have real choices. This conceptualization of contingency in the context of critical juncture analysis presents two important advantages. On the one hand, it detaches the concept from notions of randomness (Bennett and Elman 2006). On the other hand, it offers precise methodological guidance, bringing into focus the key tasks of the analyst. In the analysis of critical junctures, the scholar should reconstruct the context of the critical juncture and, through the study of historical sources, establish who were key decision-makers, what choices were *historically* available and not simply *hypothetically* possible, how close actors came to selecting an alternative option, and what likely consequences the choice of an alternative option would have had for the institutional outcome of interest (Capoccia and Kelemen 2007, 355).

This generation of empirical and theoretical studies on critical junctures set the stage for the current use of the concept in historical institutionalism, broadly defining the study of critical junctures as the analysis of the politics of institutional change during a relatively brief phase which is characterized by the availability of different courses of action capable of affecting future institutional development in the longer term.[5] As reviewed below, scholars using this popular approach to the study of institutional development have emphasized different elements. Some scholars have focused on the importance of the "structural" antecedent conditions to the critical juncture—broad impersonal factors such as socio-economic conditions, diffuse cultural orientations, the organization of public powers—in driving the institutional outcome of the juncture; others have instead focused more explicitly on the role of political agency during the critical juncture, emphasizing either political interaction and decision-making by key actors or the strategies designed to embed and legitimize new institutions through ideational change. In the next section, I briefly review and discuss exemplary works in all three traditions.

Approaches to Critical Juncture Analysis

The Role of Antecedent Conditions

Some approaches to the analysis of critical junctures, while not denying the role of agency and choice, emphasize the importance of antecedent structural conditions—impersonal factors such as the socio-economic conditions, class and social alliances, diffuse cultural orientations, and the like—in generating the institutional outcome of interest. Building on classic works in the field with a similar emphasis (e.g., Lipset and Rokkan 1967), recent theoretical contributions have explicitly picked up this theoretical thread, arguing that a critical juncture framework is most appropriate for analyzing situations in which a "common exogenous shock" affects a set of cases (typically countries), causing them to "diverge" as a consequence of the combination of their pre-existing structural configurations and the common shock. For example, Daron Acemoglu and James Robinson, in their analysis of why some societies develop "inclusive" institutions (which favor growth) while others develop "extractive" institutions (which favor predatory elites and stifle growth) define a critical juncture as a "major event or confluence of factors [which disrupts] the existing balance of political and economic power in a nation" (Acemoglu and Robinson 2012, 106), magnifies small, pre-existing institutional differences, and causes nations to "drift apart" along different paths of development.

These works emphasize that post-critical juncture "divergence" is driven by antecedent conditions rather than by decisions and events that take place during the critical juncture.[6] Dan Slater and Erica Simmons, for example, argue that the impact of "critical antecedents"—variation between cases before a common critical juncture—"combines with agency" during critical junctures to produce the outcome of interest (Slater and Simmons 2010, 889).[7] Tulia Falleti and Julia Lynch contrast views of critical junctures that emphasize contingency and, in their account, "delink" critical junctures from contexts, with "classical examples of critical juncture analysis" which instead "embed critical junctures in a richly detailed context" (Falleti and Lynch 2009, 1155, citing among others the works by Lipset and Rokkan and Berins Collier and Collier mentioned above). Soifer, in a recent thoughtful contribution, emphasizes the importance of "permissive" and "productive" prior conditions in generating institutional change during a critical juncture. He underscores the potential causal role of agency and contingency but stresses that he is "agnostic" on the relative importance of such factors versus structural conditions during a critical juncture in generating the outcome of interest (Soifer 2012, 1593). These contributions are powerful reminders for those who employ the critical juncture framework in cross-country analyses to not assume too easily that the background conditions of their cases are similar. Cases may differ in significant ways prior to a critical juncture, and these different initial conditions may have important consequences for the political dynamics that produce the institutional outcome of the critical juncture (e.g., Slater 2011).[8]

The Politics of Institutional Formation

In agency-based accounts of critical junctures, scholars generally take great care to embed the range of choices available to decision-makers within the historical social and political context and to reconstruct carefully the historical plausibility and political viability of the different options (e.g., Katznelson 2003, 277, 282; Capoccia and Kelemen 2007, 355–357). An approach that emphasizes contingent choices, in the sense explained above, and the causal role of agency is not only perfectly compatible with, but indeed *requires* a careful reconstruction of the background conditions and the more immediate context of key decisions during the critical juncture. While not denying the importance of agency and choice, the structural approaches discussed above tend, to use Stathis Kalyvas' phrase, to "black-box" agency, emphasizing the importance of prior conditions rather than the political interactions and decisions leading to the selection of a path of institutional development. The reason typically given for this focus is that the analysis of strategic interaction and political choices during critical junctures is impervious to generalization and the goal of advancing theory on political and institutional development, a goal which in this view is more easily achieved by focusing on the antecedent structural conditions of a critical juncture (Slater and Simmons 2010).

This approach, however, carries the risk of being uninformative in those cases in which the connection between macro-structural antecedent conditions and the strategic interactions and political choices that lead to the adoption of an institutional arrangement is not direct (e.g., Greif 2006). There are three possible sources of this causal ambiguity that have been identified in the literature: first, macro-structural conditions broadly favorable to the adoption of certain institutions may fail to produce institutional innovation if the groups supportive of such innovation are not mobilized by political actors; second, even though "favorable" macro-structural conditions may be present and institutional innovation is possible and, indeed, attempted, it may be narrowly missed; third, even though actor preferences may be linked to antecedent structural conditions, the institutional outcome that emerges from strategic interaction during the critical juncture may *not* correspond with the individual preferences of any of the actors. In all these cases, analyzing the *politics of institutional formation* becomes crucial to understanding institutional development. In the remainder of this section I illustrate these three points with brief examples.

An illustration of the first pattern is Thomas Ertman's recent analysis of the 1832 Reform Act in Great Britain, which he explains as the outcome of a critical juncture in which a "fundamental, unforeseen transformation of a political regime occur[ed] over a relatively short period of time as a result of decisions of a small number of actors" (Ertman 2010, 1001). In his careful reconstruction of the tumultuous political interactions of the years 1827–1835, Ertman underscores the importance of political choices and in particular "the central significance of personal choices made by Peel and Wellington" (Ertman 2010, 1009); at the same time, he embeds this detailed analysis of political agency in the structural cleavages that characterized British politics in that period, in particular the emancipation of religious minorities and the fight against "Old Corruption." Ertman makes clear that these cleavages had been prominent in British politics for several decades, that "demand for parliamentary reform were present at both the popular and elite level since the mid-18th century," and that "the intensity of such demands fluctuated substantially, rising during periods of economic distress and/or budget crisis, but falling during times of national emergency or prosperity" (Ertman 2010, 1008). Hence, Ertman goes on to argue, the reforms of 1827–1835, and in particular the 1832 Reform Act, were not the result of a "long and continuous build-up pressure," as others have maintained (e.g., Morrison 2011) but rather of a series of decisions and political interactions, made in the relevant political context of the time. In sum, Ertman's analysis shows that structural conditions that supported demand for parliamentary reform were *present* in earlier periods but did *not* lead to reform; he underscores that even though background conditions are necessary to understand the parameters of choice during critical junctures, the initiatives of influential actors were crucial in mobilizing and creating coalitions to foster institutional change.

Moving to the second of the three types of difficulties created by the structural-antecedents approach, the analytical focus on agency and contingency in the theory of critical junctures raises the possibility that the political struggle over the choice of different institutional options during a critical juncture may result in *re-equilibration* rather than change—what Capoccia and Kelemen call a "near-miss" critical juncture (Capoccia and Kelemen 2007, 350–351). As Capoccia and Kelemen argue, a logical consequence of stressing the importance of contingency (in the "Berlin-ian" sense discussed above) as a defining element of critical junctures is that, as counterintuitive as it may seem, change is not a necessary element of a critical juncture. If change was proposed, considered, and narrowly rejected, thereby reinstating the previous path of institutional development, there is no reason that such a period should not be considered a critical juncture. Some critical junctures may well result in re-equilibration of an institution. This approach provides scholars with potentially important "negative cases"—that is, cases in which institutional change was possible but did not happen[9]—that increase the leverage of the analysis. One recent example of the application of "near-miss" critical junctures, in which change is possible and plausible but is not achieved, is Curt Nicholls and Adam Myers's work revisiting Stephen Skowronek's (1993) theory of "reconstructive presidency" in the United States (Nicholls and Myers 2010). Nicholls and Myers argue that not all presidents who are "unaffiliated with a vulnerable regime" have seized the opportunity to transform the political order—that is, shift the main axis of partisan cleavage and assemble a new majority coalition. Presidents may fail to do so, in which case reconstruction may still happen but only in a much more protracted way (Nicholls and Myers 2010). By bringing the concept of "near-miss" critical junctures to bear on the theory of reconstructive presidency, Nicholls and Myers propose a fresh analytical perspective and attain new empirical results, thus achieving theoretical and empirical progress on a terrain that seemed well trodden (Nicholls and Myers 2010, 831).

Finally, focusing on political interaction and decision-making during critical junctures may uncover situations in which the institutional outcome does not reflect the preferences of any specific actor, nor even falls within the "winset" of the institutional preferences of any one set of actors (Tsebelis 2002). For example, Kalyvas' analysis of the interactions between conservative elites and the Catholic Church that led to the formation of confessional parties in Western Europe shows how the choices and strategies of key actors were decisive for the outcome of party formation and non-formation, and argues that antecedent conditions had at best an indirect impact on whether a confessional party was formed or not. (For example, he shows that in the case of France, despite the presence of the "right" structural conditions, a confessional party did not emerge.) Kalyvas leverages a large amount of historical evidence to show that both the Catholic Church and conservative politicians, on the basis of a rational assessment of costs and benefits, *opposed* the formation of confessional parties. Confessional party formation was the unintended outcome of the strategic moves made by both actors in response to the liberal anticlericalism of the late nineteenth century (Kalyvas 1996, 262). Where formed, such parties went on to play a crucial role in Western European mass politics during the twentieth century.

In these and other analyses, the politics of institutional change—the strategies and choices adopted by key actors—are firmly embedded in their historical context. At the same time, these analyses demonstrate that the institutional outcomes of critical junctures are not structurally pre-determined and at the same time are not idiosyncratic or random. In particular, the analysis of critical junctures in the context of a structured comparison—either cross-sectional as in the work of Kalyvas or longitudinal as in the work of Nicholls and Myers—can offer important leverage for building and testing theories on the origins of specific institutions, and can generate theoretical insights that can guide the analysis of critical junctures in the development of similar institutional arrangements in other comparable contexts.

Ideational Change and the Legitimation of New Institutions

Another important approach to critical junctures underscores the role of *ideational change* in producing institutional outcomes Also in this approach the role of the politics of institutional formation takes on an important causal role, but the peculiarity vis-à-vis the approaches reviewed above consists in the emphasis on the strategies of public legitimation of institutional change. For example, in their work on the comparative study of macroeconomic crises, Hogan and Doyle characterize critical junctures as encompassing an initial economic dislocation and subsequent ideational change. New policy ideas to tackle the economic problem are promoted by individual and collective actors such as international agencies, academics, bureaucrats, and elected politicians; once a sufficient consensus has consolidated around these new ideas, radical policy change happens (Hogan 2006; Hogan and Doyle 2007).[10] Probably the best example in this tradition of analysis of critical junctures, however, is the work of Mark Blyth. He analyzes the critical junctures of the Great Depression and the economic downturn of the 1970s in Western democracies with the aim of explaining why new political economy institutions emerge after economic crises. Blyth argues that economic crises are not simply a reflection of the "objective" fact of economic dislocation (e.g., deflation or negative growth), but are also socially constructed by powerful actors to be crises and, more importantly, to be *crises of a certain type*. The same actors then promote new institutions to "solve" the so-defined crisis (Blyth 2002). Hence, in his view, the *politics of ideas* is what matters during a critical juncture (Blyth 2007) and what ultimately determines the institutional outcome: a group of actors—in his account collective actors such as the state, decisive in the 1930s, or business, decisive in the 1970s[11]—acts politically to impose on other groups a particular definition of the crisis, and therefore what institutions it takes to "solve" the crisis. When such ideational battle is won, collective action to build new institutions is undertaken (Blyth 2002).

Although this approach to critical junctures has been particularly popular in the analysis of economic crises and macroeconomic policy, the central contention is that the *ideational terrain* is where the main political battles are fought during a critical juncture. In this view, political actors seek to create and diffuse legitimacy for new institutional arrangements, a political strategy that in principle is applicable to other types of institutions too, which do not necessarily or primarily involve distributional conflict (Hogan and Doyle 2007, 884). An example is Ron Krebs's recent work (Krebs 2010). Drawing on a long-standing theme of the literature of the domestic effects of war, Krebs argues that wars are critical junctures for executive power institutions (Kier and Krebs 2010, 15). Focusing on what he calls "limited wars" (i.e., small-scale wars), he argues that the effect of war on executive powers depends only in part on the objective characteristics of the war itself such as duration, cost, level of resource extraction by the state, and extent of societal sacrifice. Rather, whether or not executive powers will increase turns largely on how the purpose and the outcome of a war is framed by national leaders in the public debate. In particular, Krebs argues that limited wars can be framed as transformational or restorative. Transformational wars aim, in essence, to "civilize." Since the high standards and expectations of the promoters of such wars typically exceed the outcomes of war, they are often followed by pressures for institutional reform. Restorative wars are instead generally not followed by institutional reform, since the gap between ideals and institutions is less salient. Crucially, what makes a limited war transformative or restorative is how national leaders frame it in the public arena, thus providing legitimacy either for radical institutional reform of executive powers, or for the consolidation of existing institutions (Krebs 2010).

Similar to the work that emphasizes strategic interaction and political choice, "ideational" approaches to critical junctures emphasize the agency of influential actors, which seek to take advantage of a fluid and uncertain situation to build new institutions. The distinctive feature of ideational approaches is their conceptualization of the interests and the preferences of important actors: interests are not objectively given by an actor's position vis-à-vis the class structure, the market, or other objective structural or institutional conditions but, to a large extent, are *culturally constructed.* This process of construction is the key characteristic of the politics of institutional formation during critical junctures. Powerful collective actors seek to promote, diffuse, and entrench certain ideas in the public sphere, ideas which both define the crisis and provide an institutional recipe to "solve" it, and in so doing they must seek to bring around social groups with different "objective" interests (Blyth 2002, esp. 152–166 and 209–219). These authors insist that since interests are constructed and recast during critical junctures, they are *not* determined by antecedent conditions—and neither is the institutional outcome of the critical juncture. Referring to the economic crisis of the 1970s, during which business successfully promoted anti-inflationary and monetarist policies and transformed the opposing interests of other groups, Blyth argues: "other agents' interests had to be reinterpreted so that they became homologous with business', a homology that was neither obvious *nor structurally determined*" (Blyth 2007, 86, italics added; see also Blyth 2003).

Alternatives to Critical Junctures in the Analysis of Institutional Development: Weak Institutions and Processes of Endogenous Change

To summarize the argument thus far, historical institutionalists have defined critical junctures as moments of openness for radical institutional change, in which a relatively broad range of options are available and can plausibly be adopted. The range, of course, is not infinite: antecedent conditions typically define and limit the possible options. In critical junctures, however, actors operate with a significant margin of maneuver and have increased possibilities for influencing institutional formation: in some cases they can influence the outcome directly, while in other cases their interactions may lead to unexpected results that none of the actors originally intended. Since the institutional outcome of critical junctures is not determined by macro-structural antecedents, the *politics of institutional formation*—strategies and choices of political leaders, decision-making processes, coalition-building, acts of political contestation, waves of public debate—typically take on a central role. Scholars of critical junctures have endeavored, in particular through comparative analysis, to analyze systematically the interactions, strategies, types of coalitions, and ideational debates that give rise to specific institutional arrangements, and have reached insightful conclusions on the origins of important institutions.

In line with this theoretical approach, the study of critical junctures consists essentially in the theory-driven and historically grounded analysis of the politics of institutional formation in moments of political openness during which different options are available to actors and are in principle politically viable. The political history of every country, however, is replete with events, decisions of political leaders, political alliances, the rise of new normative frames for public debate, and other occurrences which, in the language of the French historians of the *Annales* School would be labeled as rather insignificant *histoire événementielle*. What justifies the high cost of detailed, intensive, and time-consuming historical analysis of such events during critical junctures—costs which are compounded in comparative analysis—is the leverage provided for distal causation: the theoretical claim that understanding the politics of a critical juncture is crucial for explaining the origins of an institutional arrangement, which then stays in place for a long time afterwards.

As mentioned in the introductory section of this chapter, typically the reference to institutional path dependence is key to understanding the distal causation that motivates the conceptualization and study of critical junctures: indeed, critical junctures are often an essential part of analyses of path-dependent institutions (Capoccia and Kelemen 2007). As an important tradition of analysis in historical institutionalism has argued, many institutional arrangements are path dependent, namely give rise to endogenous mechanisms of reproduction and positive feedback that sustain them and keep them in place, limiting or bounding change. This view has been applied to the analysis of institutional development in sociology (e.g., Goldstone 1998; Mahoney 2000; see also Abbott 1988, 173) and Political Science (e.g., Pierson 2000). Path-dependent institutional outcomes, therefore, have a composite causal structure: they are the effect both of the mechanisms of institutional reproduction that sustain the trajectory of their development, and of the events of the critical juncture responsible for selecting, in the first place, the path taken.

However powerful the idea of path dependence is in historical institutionalism, recent scholarship in the field has shown important limitations of the approach and has argued that in many cases it does not offer a realistic theoretical image of institutional development. Given the close connection between critical junctures and path dependence, this research also questions indirectly the importance of critical junctures in theories of institutional development. In the last part of this chapter, I review briefly two strands of this scholarship: analyses of "weak institutions" and theories of gradual, endogenous institutional change. Space limitations do not make it possible to do justice to their nuances and complexities; the purpose of this section is to illustrate how and why the concept of critical juncture as discussed above plays a very limited, if any, role in these approaches.

Critical juncture analysis affords limited traction in the analysis of the development of "weak institutions" (Levitsky and Murillo 2005, 2009). Steven Levitsky and Victoria Murillo argue that most theories (notably historical institutional theories) of institutional development were developed in relation to the politics of advanced industrialized democracies, in which the assumption that formal rules either reflect or generate shared expectations about how others will behave is typically correct. They note that this assumption often does *not* hold in most of the developing world, where formal rules are often neither stable nor consistently enforced. Institutional strength, which consists of the level of enforcement and the patterns of stability of formal rules, should be conceptualized as a variable and not as a constant. In their view, this makes historical institutionalist theories largely inapplicable to the developing world, where the "politics of institutional weakness" is often the typical pattern (Levitsky and Murillo 2005).

Relevant for the present discussion is that institutional weakness inhibits path dependence, at least in the sense of institutional self-reinforcement, for which "institutional strength" (defined as a high level of enforcement and a pattern of sufficient stability over time) is a necessary condition: "When institutional arrangements persist (and are enforced) over time … actors develop expectations of stability and consequently invest in skills, technologies and organizations that are appropriate to those institutions … As these investments accumulate, existing arrangements grow increasingly attractive relative to their alternatives, thereby raising the cost of institutional replacement … Where formal institutions are repeatedly overturned or rendered ineffective, actors may develop expectations of instability … Consequently, they will be less likely to invest in those institutions or develop skills and technologies appropriate to them, thereby keeping the cost of overturning the rules low" (Levitsky and Murillo 2009, 123). Under conditions of institutional weakness, institutional change is most likely to take the form of "breakdown and replacement" (Levitsky and Murillo 2009, 128). As a consequence, critical juncture analysis, which examines political struggles over institutional design in brief moments of relative openness and uncertainty, offers little leverage in this context—because the institutional arrangements resulting from such struggle would not be long-standing (or would remain unenforced), and another struggle would be likely to ensue shortly afterwards to bring about new formal rules and overturn the existing ones.[12]

Theories of endogenous institutional change (Hacker 2004; Thelen 2004; Streeck and Thelen 2005; Mahoney and Thelen 2010; Hacker, Pierson, and Thelen 2015) take their lead from what they define as the difficulty that path dependence theories have in explaining institutional change. Theories of institutional path dependence have a stability bias, relegating change to exogenous shocks. In the effort to incorporate change in a theoretical account of institutional development, scholars have therefore identified several patterns of endogenous institutional change that take place gradually but over the long run transform radically an institution, either through piecemeal reform (layering) or reinterpretation (conversion). Scholars in this tradition have shown that such forms of gradual institutional change are very common, and have provided broad empirical support for their theoretical propositions.

This influential approach to institutional change is founded theoretically on the conceptualization of institutions as *arenas of conflict*, rather than as equilibria, as is the case in path dependence theory (albeit implicitly in many accounts). Institutions are constantly reshaped and reinterpreted by groups vying for power, trying to bend the institution to their priorities and preferences. To be sure, theorists of endogenous institutional change do underscore that institutional development does sometimes follow the pattern of punctuated equilibrium, with moments of openness and rapid change (i.e., critical junctures) followed by phases of stability (e.g., Streeck and Thelen 2005, 9). However, when institutions develop according to the patterns of long-term, gradual, endogenous and transformative change such as conversion and layering, critical junctures have no place in the analysis: if institutions are constantly vulnerable to piecemeal modification and reinterpretation by the actors involved, and their shape, nature, and impact change continuously in accordance with shifts in power and influence among the actors involved (Mahoney and Thelen 2010), then there is little reason to study in detail the politics of their initial creation. The analytical attention shifts rather to the long-term process of gradual but transformative institutional change and the patterns and processes of such change. Indeed, and *pour cause*, the concept of critical juncture (and synonyms) does not play an important analytical role in the literature on gradual institutional change.

Conclusion

In historical institutionalism, critical junctures are conceptualized as moments of structural indeterminacy and fluidity during which several options for radical institutional innovation are available, one (including possibly institutional re-equilibration) is selected as a consequence of political interactions and decision-making, and this initial selection carries a long-lasting institutional legacy. In this process, actors have real choices and the institutional outcome, albeit constrained by antecedent conditions and the range of politically feasible options, is not pre-determined by such conditions. Critical junctures underscore the point made by Greif (2006, 33) that "institutional analysis is about situations in which more than one behavior is physically and technologically possible."

The study of critical junctures consists of theory-driven analysis of the *politics of institutional formation* in moments of political openness and fluidity: the various types of political processes through which institutional choices are made: strategic interaction, coalition-building, norm-generating strategies aimed at influencing the perception of the legitimacy of institutional innovations by rule-takers, and choices made by powerful political leaders. These processes unfold in a well-defined context in which several options for institutional change are politically viable. Based on these theoretical premises, scholars have endeavored, often successfully, to offer *systematic* analyses of institutional origins, generally through either cross-sectional or longitudinal comparisons of critical junctures. These analyses have generated key theoretical insights on the origins of important institutions and can guide research on other, comparable cases.

The justification for such detailed historical and comparative study of political processes during critical junctures is to be found in the circumstances that critical junctures have long-term legacies, typically conceptualized, in historical institutionalism, in terms of path dependence. The logic of path dependence highlights the long-term consequences of the selection of one institutional option over the other historically available options during relatively rare moments of political openness. Even though theories of gradual institutional change and of variation in institutional strength have posed a challenge to path dependence approaches to institutional development—and indirectly to critical juncture analysis—the concept continues to be used both in theoretical contributions (e.g., Soifer 2012) and empirical analyses (e.g., Nunn 2009). At the same time, the challenges posed by other traditions of analysis to the usefulness of critical junctures as a theoretical concept in the toolbox of historical institutionalism should not be underestimated. The ubiquitousness of gradual, endogenous, and transformative institutional change, which has been amply documented and is rooted in a theory and a definition of institutions as arenas of conflict, suggests that in many cases the analytical traction offered by critical junctures may be limited. Similarly, weak institutional enforcement and high instability, typical of much of the developing world, render institutions either less consequential or, by underscoring the changing ways in which formal rules may be used in practice, renders the reasons for the in-depth study of their origins less compelling than in the context of more developed polities. To be sure, these approaches are not mutually exclusive: they may be applicable in different circumstances. However, more robust theorization is needed on the *conditions* under which each of them applies—in particular on the conditions which encourage the path-dependence logic of adaptive expectations and specific investments, thus raising the cost of institutional reversal, and the conditions which, instead, produce incremental but transformative institutional change by virtue of continuous strategic action over time on the part of actors vying for power.[13] Theoretical advancement on this front would also clarify the scope of applicability, limitations, and potential of the concept of critical junctures in historical institutionalism.

Notes

* I thank Tulia Falleti and Dan Kelemen for comments on a previous version of this chapter.

1. The theoretical literature on path dependence is very extensive and its discussion goes beyond the scope of this essay. In institutional economics and economic history, key contributions are by North (1990, 1994); Arthur (1989, 1994); David (1985, 1994, 2000, 2007). In economic geography, apart from Arthur's work cited above, an important contribution is by Krugman (1991). In sociology, important theoretical contributions are by Goldstone (1998) and Mahoney (2000). For the use of the concept of path dependence in the field of international relations, see Fioretos (2011). A formalization of the concept is in Page (2006). In Political Science, a seminal contribution is by Pierson (2000).
2. Even Paul David's (2000) classic example of the "direction of traffic," in which a series of individual decisions of car drivers cumulate to bring the system into what he calls a "trapping region" (i.e. a universal rule of keeping right or left), once analyzed historically, reveals the importance of authoritative political decisions rather than the accumulation of individual determinations (Capoccia and Kelemen 2007, 354).
3. Mahoney, in an important piece, also emphasizes the importance of contingency in critical junctures, conceiving it as a factor whose explanation "appears to fall outside of existing scientific theory" (Mahoney 2000, 514; see also Bennett and Elman 2006). More generally on the importance of contingency in the study of politics, see Shapiro and Bedi (2006).

4. On rules for assessing the plausibility of counterfactual arguments in Political Science, see e.g., Fearon (1991); Tetlock and Belkin (1996); Lebow (2000, 2010); Levy and Goertz (2007).
5. As discussed below, these options include re-equilibration, that is, near-miss change (Capoccia and Kelemen 2007).
6. Acemoglu and Robinson argue, however, that although "existing economic and political institutions ... delineate what is politically feasible" during critical junctures, the outcome of critical junctures is "not predetermined but contingent" (Acemoglu and Robinson 2012, 110).
7. Even though not all the "critical antecedents" that Slater and Simmons discuss in their examples refer to impersonal macro-conditions, clarifying the importance of such structural factors in shaping the outcomes of critical junctures seems to be a recurring concern in their elaboration (see Slater and Simmons 2010, 887, 892–895, and 905).
8. More problematic seems to be the reference to "divergence" as a defining element of critical junctures emphasized by these scholars: despite the popularity of this view (e.g., Slater and Simmons 2010, 888; Soifer 2012, 1593; Acemoglu and Robinson 2012, 106), it bears reminding here that "divergence" between cases is *a potential consequence* of critical junctures. In order to have analytical traction, the concept of critical juncture—like any other concept—needs to be defined independently from its empirical consequences. On this see Capoccia (2015).
9. Soifer (2012) considers such situations as "crises without change" (i.e. not critical junctures), and encourages comparisons with critical junctures, thus addressing the same theoretical problem in the context of a partially different framework. Near misses are also an important feature of "episode analysis," an approach to the analysis of sequences of asynchronous punctuated institutional change in different institutional arenas of the polity developed in Capoccia and Ziblatt (2010).
10. One problematic aspect in Hogan's work is that his analysis of critical junctures is explicitly disassociated from the long-lasting legacies of the events and decisions taken during the critical juncture (e.g., Hogan 2006, 664). To be sure, classifying macroeconomic dislocations as more or less severe along certain indicators (and reserving the notion of critical juncture to the most severe ones) may serve classificatory purposes. However, if the concept is applied to the analysis of long-term institutional and policy development, this approach raises the question of why one should study in detail events and decisions whose effects are not long lasting and may well be reversed immediately afterwards. I return to this point in the next section.
11. Blyth does not attribute agency to abstract entities. For example, his account of how American and Swedish business promoted neoliberal ideas to both define and point to a "solution" to the 1970s economic crisis is extremely precise in detailing the internal dynamics within the business world, showing how important donors, organizations, foundations, conservative media and other actors acted in a concerted fashion to promote pro-business ideas. His historical analysis shows empirically that in the critical juncture of the 1970s, business "acted as a class" (Blyth 2002).
12. In this line of theorization, however, critical juncture analysis could play a role in explaining patterns of institutional *instability*: a period of initial institutional failure, which, as Levitsky and Murillo (2009, 123) put it, may be the product of "historically contingent circumstances (including sheer bad luck)" may induce actors to develop expectations for future instability and lack of enforcement, and lock a polity into a path of institutional weakness. This theoretical thread, although promising, has not yet been fully articulated by scholars of weak institutions.
13. I discuss some of the relevant issues in Capoccia (2012).

References

Abbott, Andrew. 1988. "Transcending General Linear Reality." *Sociological Theory* 6 (2), 169–186.

Acemoglu, Daron and Robinson, James A. 2012. *Why Nations Fail: The Origins of Power, Prosperity and Poverty*. New York: Crown Business.

Arthur, W. Brian. 1989. "Competing Technologies, Increasing Returns, and Lock-in by Historical Events." *The Economic Journal* 99 (March), 116–131.

Arthur, W. Brian. 1994. *Increasing Returns and Path Dependence in the Economy*. Ann Arbor, MI: University of Michigan Press.

Bennett, Andrew and Colin Elman. 2006. "Complex Causal Relations and Case Study Methods: The Example of Path Dependence." *Political Analysis* 14 (3): 250–267.

Berins Collier, Ruth and David Collier. 1991. *Shaping the Political Arena: Critical Junctures, the Labor Movement, and Regime Dynamics in Latin America*. Princeton, NJ: Princeton University Press.

Berlin, Isaiah. 1974. "Historical Inevitability." In *The Philosophy of History*, ed. Patrick Gardiner. London: Oxford University Press, 161–186.

Blyth, Mark. 2002. *Great Transformations: Economic Ideas and Institutional Change in the Twentieth Century*. Cambridge: Cambridge University Press.

Blyth, Mark. 2003. "Structures Do Not Come With an Instruction Sheet: Interests, Ideas and Progress in Political Science." *Perspectives on Politics* 1 (4): 695–706.

Blyth, Mark. 2007. "When Liberalisms Change: Comparing the Politics of Inflations and Deflations. Neoliberalism: National and Regional Experiments with Global Ideas." In *Neoliberalism: National and Regional Experiments with Global Ideas*, ed. Ravi K. Roy, Arthur T. Denzau, and Thomas D. Willet. London: Routledge, 71–96.

Capoccia, Giovanni. 2012. "Historical Institutionalism and the Politics of Institutional Change." Manuscript, University of Oxford.

Capoccia, Giovanni. 2015. "Critical Junctures and Institutional Change." In *Advances in Comparative Historical Analysis*, ed. James Mahoney and Kathleen Thelen. Cambridge: Cambridge University Press, 147–179.

Capoccia, Giovanni and Daniel R. Kelemen. 2007. "The Study of Critical Junctures: Theory, Narrative and Counterfactuals in Institutional Analysis." *World Politics* 59 (3): 341–369.

Capoccia, Giovanni and Daniel Ziblatt. 2010. "The Historical Turn in Democratization Studies: A Research Agenda for Europe and Beyond." *Comparative Political Studies* 43 (8/9): 931–968.

David, Paul. 1985. "Clio and the Economics of QWERTY." *American Economic Review* 75 (May): 332–337.

David, Paul. 1994. "Why Are Institutions the 'Carriers of History'? Path Dependence and the Evolution of Conventions, Organizations and Institutions." *Structural Change and Economic Dynamics* 5 (2), 205–220.

David, Paul. 2000. "Path Dependence, Its Critics and the Quest for 'Historical Economics.'" Manuscript, Oxford and Stanford.

David, Paul. 2007. "Path Dependence: A Foundational Concept for Historical Social Science." *Cliometrica* 1 (2), 91–114.

Dion, Michelle L. 2010. *Workers and Welfare: Comparative Institutional Change in Twentieth-Century Mexico*. Pittsburgh, PA: University of Pittsburgh Press.

Ebbinghaus, Bernhard. 2005. "When Less Is More: Selection Problems in Large-N and Small-N Cross-national Comparison." *International Sociology* 20 (2): 133–152.

Ertman, Thomas. 2010. "The Great Reform Act of 1832 and British Democratization." *Comparative Political Studies* 43 (8/9): 1000–1022.

Falleti, Tulia G. and Julia F. Lynch. 2009. "Context and Causal Mechanisms in Political Analysis." *Comparative Political Studies* 42 (9): 1143–1166.

Fearon, James. 1991. "Counterfactuals and Hypothesis Testing in Political Science." *World Politics* 43 (2): 169–195.

Fioretos, Orfeo. 2011. "Historical Institutionalism in International Relations." *International Organization* 65 (2): 367–399.

Goldstone, Jack A. 1998. "Initial Conditions, General Laws, Path Dependence, and Explanation in Historical Sociology." *American Journal of Sociology* 104 (3): 829–845.

Greif, Avner. 2006. *Institutions and the Path to the Modern Economy: Lessons from Medieval Trade*. New York: Cambridge University Press.

Hacker, Jacob. 2004. "Privatizing Risk without Privatizing the Welfare State: The Hidden Politics of Social Policy Retrenchment in the United States." *American Political Science Review* 98 (2): 243–260.

Hacker, Jacob, Paul Pierson, and Kathleen Thelen. 2015. "Drift and Conversion: Hidden Faces of Institutional Change." In *Advances in Comparative Historical Analysis*, ed. J. Mahoney and K.Thelen. Cambridge: Cambridge University Press, 180–209.

Hogan, John W. 2006. "Remoulding the Critical Juncture Approach." *Canadian Journal of Political Science* 39 (3): 657–679.

Hogan, John W. and David Doyle. 2007. "The Importance of Ideas: An *A Priori* Critical Junctures Framework." *Canadian Journal of Political Science* 40 (4): 883–910.

Kalyvas, Stathis N. 1996. *The Rise of Christian Democracy in Europe*. Ithaca, NY: Cornell University Press.

Katznelson, Ira. 2003. "Periodization and Preferences: Reflections on Purposive Action in Comparative Historical Social Science." In *Comparative Historical Analysis in the Social Sciences*, ed. J. Mahoney and D. Rueschemeyer. Cambridge: Cambridge University Press, 270–303.

Kier, Elizabeth and Ron Krebs. 2010. "Introduction: War and Democracy in Comparative Perspective." In *War's Wake: International Conflict and the Fate of Liberal Democracy*, ed. Elizabeth Kier and Ron Krebs. New York: Cambridge University Press, 1–21.

Krebs, Ron. 2010. "International Conflict and the Constitutional Balance: Executive Authority after War." In *War's Wake: International Conflict and the Fate of Liberal Democracy*, ed. Elizabeth Kier and Ron Krebs. New York: Cambridge University Press, 187–210.

Krugman, Paul. 1991. "Increasing Returns and Economic Geography." *Journal of Political Economy* 99 (3).

Lebow, Richard Ned. 2000. "What's So Different about a Counterfactual?" *World Politics* 52 (4): 550–585.

Lebow, Richard Ned. 2010. *Forbidden Fruit: Counterfactuals and International Relations*. Princeton, NJ: Princeton University Press.

Levitsky, Steven and Victoria Murillo, eds. 2005. *Argentine Democracy*. University Park, PA: Pennsylvania State Press.

Levitsky, Steven and Victoria Murillo. 2009. "Variations in Institutional Strength." *Annual Review of Political Science* 12: 115–133.

Levy, Jack and Gary Goertz. 2007. *Explaining War and Peace: Case Studies and Necessary Condition Counterfactuals*. New York: Routledge.

Lieberman, Evan S. 2003. *Race and Regionalism in the Politics of Taxation in Brazil and South Africa*. Cambridge: Cambridge University Press.

Lipset, Seymour M. and Stein Rokkan. 1967. "Cleavage Structures, Party Systems, and Voter Alignments." In *Party Systems and Voter Alignments: Cross-National Perspectives*, ed. Seymour M. Lipset and Stein Rokkan. New York: Free Press, 1–64.

Mahoney, James. 2000. "Path Dependence in Historical Sociology." *Theory and Society* 29 (4): 507–548.

Mahoney, James. 2002. *Legacies of Liberalism*. Baltimore, MD: Johns Hopkins University Press.

Mahoney, James and Kathleen Thelen. 2010. *Explaining Institutional Change: Ambiguity, Agency, and Power*. New York: Cambridge University Press.

Moore, Barrington, Jr. 1966. *The Social Origins of Democracy and Dictatorship*. Boston, MA: Beacon Press.

Morrison, Bruce. 2011. "Channeling the Restless Spirit of Innovation." *World Politics* 63 (4): 678–710.

Nicholls, Curt and Adam S. Myers. 2010. "Exploiting the Opportunity for Reconstructive Leadership: Presidential Responses to Enervated Political Regimes." *American Politics Research* 38 (5): 806–841.

North, Douglass C. 1990. *Institutions, Institutional Change and Economic Performance*. Cambridge: Cambridge University Press.

North, Douglass C. 1994. "Economic Performance through Time." *American Economic Review* 84 (3): 359–368.

Nunn, Amy. 2009. *The Politics and History of AIDS Treatment in Brazil*. New York: Springer.

Page, Scott. 2006. "Path Dependence." *Quarterly Journal of Political Science* 1: 87–115.

Pierson, Paul. 2000. "Increasing Returns, Path Dependence, and the Study of Politics." *The American Political Science Review* 94 (2): 251–268.

Pierson, Paul. 2004. *Politics in Time: History, Institutions, and Social Analysis*. Princeton, NJ: Princeton University Press.

Shapiro, Ian and Sonu Bedi. 2006. *Political Contingency: Studying the Unexpected, the Accidental, and the Unforeseen*. New York: New York University Press.

Skowronek, Stephen. 1993. *The Politics Presidents Make: Leadership from John Adams to George Bush*. Cambridge, MA: Belknap Press of Harvard University Press.

Slater, Dan. 2011. *Ordering Power*. New York: Cambridge University Press.

Slater, Dan and Erica Simmons. 2010. "Informative Regress. Critical Antecedents in Comparative Politics." *Comparative Political Studies* 43 (7): 886–917.

Soifer, Hillel David. 2012. "The Causal Logic of Critical Junctures." *Comparative Political Studies* 45 (12): 1572–1597.

Streeck, Wolfgang and Kathleen Thelen. 2005. "Introduction. Institutional Change in Advanced Political Economies." In *Beyond Continuity: Institutional Change in Advanced Political Economies*, ed. Wolfgang Streeck and Kathleen Thelen. Oxford: Oxford University Press, 1–39.

Swidler, Ann. 1986. "Culture in Action." *American Sociological Review* 51: 273–286.

Tetlock, Philip and Aaron Belkin, eds. 1996. *Counterfactual Thought Experiments in World Politics*, Princeton, NJ: Princeton University Press.

Thelen, Kathleen. 2004. *How Institutions Evolve: The Political Economy of Skills in Germany, Britain, the United States, and Japan*. Cambridge: Cambridge University Press.

Tsebelis, George. 2002. *Veto Players: How Political Institutions Work*. New York and Princeton, NJ: Russell Sage and Princeton University Press.

CHAPTER 6

HISTORICAL INSTITUTIONALISM AND EXPERIMENTAL METHODS

SVEN STEINMO*

Historical institutionalism (HI) grew out of an interest in explaining variation. When we began asking ourselves why policies and politics differed so much across nations and over time, political institutions forced themselves into the center of the analysis. Institutions, we argued, *structured* politics. By now, this basic insight has become commonplace. Even if this was once an innovative contribution, today few would argue against the proposition that institutions are important because they structure strategic incentives and constraints.

But we also know that institutions do not *determine* outcomes (nor do they determine the path of history). This is not only because humans create and can change institutions, but also because human beings come to the institutions they inhabit with prior expectations and cognitive biases that affect how they will work within these institutions and adapt them to their local circumstance. We know, for example, that you cannot simply plant a set of institutions on a population (whether mid-twentieth-century Japan or early twenty-first-century Afghanistan) and expect to easily predict how these institutions will be interpreted, used, and/or manipulated.

I believe that to understand the actual policy choices made in different countries, we must examine the *interaction* between history, political institutions, public policies, and citizens' preferences. I have been cognizant of the fact that both what the state actually does, and how it does it, must affect citizens' attitudes and perceptions of what their state *ought to do*. The truth, however, is that political scientists have never really been able to test this argument.

In this chapter I argue that one way of testing HI theories is to integrate some of the methods and techniques of experimental social science into our analysis. Certainly, much of what historical institutionalists are interested in is not available to field or laboratory experiments—precisely because they are in the past. But for those who would use history to explain outcomes and variation in the modern world, experimental methods and reasoning may be an appropriate addition to our toolboxes.

In my view, at the core of *historical* institutionalism is the insight that history matters not just because it provides different contexts in which rational actors made choices, but because history affects actors' beliefs, values, and preferences. History matters for our understanding of politics because history provides experience and experience can change the beliefs and preferences of citizens and their elites. But, if we are honest with ourselves, we typically do not have the tools to test these propositions.

Willing to Pay? Combining HI and Experiments in the Study of the Welfare State

Let me try to clarify what I mean through a simple example that motivates my current research:

All modern welfare states face a set of very difficult challenges as they adapt to the demographic, economic, and fiscal pressures of the early twenty-first century. These include: (a) fiscal pressures of an aging "core" population; (b) political challenges of maintaining public support for adequate social welfare and education in the context of growing ethnic diversity; (c) growing public frustration with and even distrust of bureaucratic state institutions and political authority; (d) intense pressures to reduce (or at least not increase) taxes for politically powerful constituencies; and (e) the continuing pressures to move from manufacturing-based economies toward service-based economies. These competing pressures deeply constrain the political choices available to policymakers in all advanced democratic nations. It is simply not true, however, that these forces push all democratic states in the same direction. Quite the contrary: the empirical evidence suggests that modern democracies are maintaining quite different policy trajectories—even in the face of broadly similar political, economic, and fiscal pressures.[1]

We know that citizens in different countries respond differently to the question, "Are you willing to pay higher taxes in order to provide better health or education services to those who need them?" (Svallfors 2011; Taylor-Gooby 1995). But the fact is that we do not truly know why citizens in different societies respond differently to this question. It is reasonable to *assume* that they answer differently because they have different expectations of how their tax money will be spent. It is also possible that they have different perceptions of the fairness of the tax system, beliefs about how consistently it is enforced, and/or there are different social norms with respect to tax compliance. These all seem like reasonable assumptions. Yet we do not know which of these explanations is correct because while we can make correlations between attitudes and policy outcomes and/or we can rely on anecdotal evidence in support of our claims, no one has actually been able to test the ways citizens in different countries *think about* policy choices, and how different institutions shape these choices.

The current state of traditional welfare state research (within which we find taxation policy) focuses on (a) public policy comparisons of regime types (e.g., how taxes and public spending are structured in different countries) and their evolutionary histories, and (b) citizens' attitudes toward taxation. But we do not know how to link these related issues, as surveys cannot give us a fine enough measure to understand perceptions of taxes or the real trade-off citizens are willing to make. At the same time, while we have made assumptions that try to draw linkages between the structure of a given nation's systems and citizens' willingness to pay for them in different national contexts, we have not been able to test these assumptions. In short, we do not really know *why* citizens' willingness to pay taxes varies in different countries. We have even less purchase on the questions of what types of taxes citizens might be willing to pay in different countries, and/or on what kinds of trade-offs they are willing to make to help fund social security.

These are very basic questions which, in my view at least, have hugely important implications for all advanced democracies as we enter an era of increased competition, ever tighter budgetary constraint and, finally, aging demographics.

In order to test these relationships I am now conducting a series of experiments in different countries in which we examine the different trade-offs individuals in different societies make under different conditions. We focus on two sets of redistributive policy issues: taxation and public pensions. Space does not permit a full elaboration of the precise questions asked in each experiment, but the chief purpose is to build a series of scenarios that will allow us to test how different institutional contexts frame or shape citizens' decisions and thereby better understand how they perceive and process different policy choices and trade-offs.

To be sure, developing nuanced tests of these basic propositions in different national contexts takes time and a rather subtle understanding of the national context itself. In short, to effectively test these ideas we need to understand the workings of the national political institutions, tax and welfare systems as well as their history and political cultures.

Pension systems provide an excellent example. All welfare states today feature some mix of various pension systems (often called "pillars") in which a basic public pension can be combined with various occupational pension systems and various tax-subsidized private savings schemes. We also know that there is very widespread support for social spending on pensions and the aged in all advanced countries. At the same time, it is quite clear that the enormous costs of these pension systems demands fiscal restraint. I submit that in order to better understand what I will call "the room for maneuver" available in different polities, we need to better understand the citizen's beliefs and expectations about how collective action problems are best managed, and the extent to which norms of equity and responsibility are assumed and reinforced. In short, some policy choices may be available in Sweden that are not available, politically, in Italy, for example, *because of the ways citizens think about these public policies and the political institutions which produce them.*

In my current project, historical institutionalist country specialists are working intensively with the experimentalists, both so that we can refine the experiments in ways that make them more realistic within different national contexts, and equally importantly so that we can build experiments that test the specific hypotheses generated by the country specialists. The strength of the comparative institutional scholar is that he or she has a much deeper understanding of not only the formal institutions in a given country but also the informal norms and expectations that are likely present in that country. The strength of the experimental scientist is that he or she is better positioned to design specific experiments that will enable us to test for differences in norms, expectations, perceptions of fairness, attitudes toward redistribution, and willingness to pay. The foundational idea of this project is that by combining these strengths we will be able to build better models to test the arguments and assumptions made by historical institutionist country specialists, and thereby build better and more verifiable theories for explaining cross-national variation. It is my experience that different institutional and policy structures have different implications—or at least salience—in different national contexts. We want to know if this is true and how they are perceived.[2] Economists and psychologists have attempted to conduct experiments in diverse cultural and institutional settings, but absent the substantive historical and institutional knowledge which the historical institutionalists bring to bear, such experiments remain too abstract. Indeed, many economists remain surprised that there is variation in behavior that cannot be explained by purely institutional incentives and constraints.

Experiments and Institutions—New Methods, New Answers

Significant advances have been made using experimental methods in the social sciences that have helped researchers better understand the cognitive processes that individuals use when making choices. Early work using these experimental technologies was developed by psychologists, but economists were quick to realize that these techniques could be used to test many of their assumptions about human decision-making (Smith 2008). The bulk of research has not supported the simple notions of man as a rational self-interested decision-maker (Gintis et al. 2006; Kahneman, Slovic, and Tversky 1982) and has instead led to a far more nuanced and complex understanding of how and why individuals come to their decisions. The evidence points quite clearly to the claim that most humans are motivated by several forces including self-interest, the desire for social acclaim, and respect for hierarchy, for example. The empirical evidence also demonstrates that there are different distributions of these basic patterns both within populations and between different populations.

Early experimental research by economists tried to explore the base preferences of individuals across time and space. At first they thought they had discovered "multiple equilibria," but soon they also realized that these "equilibria" were dynamic. These works have led to growing interest in the ways in which different cultural national "contexts" affect the decision processes of individuals (see, for example, Cummings et al. 2004, Elster 1999; Bowles et al. 2003; Frey and Meier 2004; Gintis et al. 2006; Alm 2010). The most interesting work in this area is currently being done by those who have accepted the overwhelming empirical evidence showing that human rationality is not only bounded (Simon) but also framed by a complex set of other considerations and/or limitations. Vernon Smith, one of the founders of this field (and Nobel Laureate for his work here) has argued that rationality is "ecologically bounded." In other words, even what is "rational" is framed cognitively by the ecology in which we make decisions. James Alm, one of the leaders in the field, puts the matter rather bluntly: "These are all issues for which the standard neoclassical paradigm gives clear-cut theoretical answers. However, these 'answers' are often misleading or wrong. Testing behavioral public economics notions in the laboratory presents the possibility of demonstrating behavioral responses that are more accurate and realistic, that show the relevance of social context and social process in decisions, and that have the 'external validity' necessary for policy formulation" (Alm 2010, 648).

It is precisely "context" which Political Science (and especially historical institutionalism) can bring to the table. Historical institutionalism *is* the study of the "ecology" of political decisions. Economists and psychologists have become skilled in design and have developed these experimental methods to a greater extent than we have done in Political Science. Political scientists, however, have paid much closer attention to examining and understanding the specific institutional structures, decision-making processes and historical contexts that frame these choices. In my view, both our understanding of how institutions frame and/or structure individual choices, and our understanding of the real institutional choices available in different polities will be greatly enhanced if we can bring these different kinds of expertise together.

Thus, what I hope to accomplish with this line of research is to fuse the basic insights and methods of comparative historical and institutional analysis with the insights and methods of experimental research design. I am precisely interested in how political institutions and public policy regimes, as well as citizens' experiences, *shape the ways they think about political choices*.

Comparative historical analysis has furnished us great insights into the relationship between political institutions and public policies in different countries. Furthermore, work in comparative historical tax policy and fiscal sociology has provided significant insight into how and why different political systems have developed different tax systems (Prasad 2006; Peters 1991; Peters 1979; Steinmo 1993, 2002). However, a number of important questions remain regarding the relationship between citizens' attitudes toward taxation and the state which comparative historical analysis simply cannot answer. To take a specific example: we know that Swedes have a higher rate of tax compliance than the Italians. We can speculate as to why this is, but comparative historical analysis cannot disentangle the multiple plausible explanations or variables. For example, it is plausible that different compliance rates are related to any or all of the following factors:

- Italians may have less fear of being caught for tax evasion than Swedes.
- Italians may believe that no one else pays their taxes and therefore they do not develop the social norm saying that they ought to pay.
- Italians, even more than Swedes, may believe that they do not receive adequate benefits for the taxes they pay and therefore are more hostile to paying their taxes.
- Italians may believe that their politicians are corrupt, or more corrupt than the Swedish believe theirs to be, and therefore are not willing to pay their taxes.
- Italians may have more negative experiences from their interactions with the state than Swedes do.
- Italians may believe that the rich get away without paying their taxes (even more than Swedes) and therefore feel that the tax burden is unfair and are hence unwilling to pay their taxes.

Indeed, it may be some combination of all of these variables that explains Italy's low tax compliance rate. It is my hope that by controlling for specific variables and testing them in various controlled settings we can learn which of these variables is the most salient and under which conditions. Up to this point, no one that I am aware of has attempted to systematically test and compare the underlying understandings of political choices in countries as diverse as Italy, Sweden, or the United States. As above, we may *think* we know what is going on in citizens' minds when they consider political choices or their willingness to pay taxes, or the choice about which kind of pension reforms they are willing to accept, but we do not know much about their real perceptions. Similarly, we can construct narratives that attempt to explain why some Americans today seem willing to bankrupt their country out of a visceral disgust for "politicians" and/or the current president. But I think we should be careful before we assume that we know what is going on in their minds (Frank 2004).

Are Italians more "selfish" or more like individualistic utility maximizers than Swedes, for example? I do not think so. But it does seem that many Italians have come to believe a narrative about their country and its leaders. Consequentially, reformers and leaders are trapped into sub-optimal choices. In a country in which an estimated 30 per cent of gross domestic product (GDP) is hidden in the black, it is difficult to raise the revenue to balance the budget. In a country where public servants believe their bosses are *ladri*, (thieves) how should they behave? When the Prime Minister Mario Monti claimed in 2011 that "Italians do not pay their taxes," many Italians asked themselves, "why should I?" It is not that Italians do not follow rules, or abide by norms, nor is it that they do not care for each other. It is instead that social rules and norms are not necessarily coincident with country's laws.

I, like many reading this volume I suspect, am quite uncomfortable with national stereotypes and simplistic "culturalist" arguments. I am very much an institutionalist.

I strongly believe that institutions can and do shape behavior and that most of the time people can and do respond to incentives and constraints. But at the same time, I am no longer satisfied with institutional explanations that give short shrift to people's beliefs and biases and/or pretend as if material interests and institutional constrains/incentives can tell us enough. It is impossible to live in Italy for five years, as I have now done, and not believe that citizens' perceptions of their society, and their behavior toward the collective, are a part of Italy's governance problem. In short, it is *not* just "The Institutions, Stupid!" (Watts and Steinmo 1995).

I think we can and should go further toward empirically testing the relationship between institutional rules, historical/cultural context, and policy choices. Doing so will allow us to move beyond the tired debates pitting these interests vs. ideational explanations against one another and toward a better and more nuanced understanding of the ways in which institutional rules structure policy choices, and the ways in which cognitive frames shape how institutions are perceived, manipulated, and interpreted. Finally, moving in this direction and looking at the interactive relationship between ideas, interests, and institutions will enable us to develop a better understanding of institutional change generally and why welfare states appear to maintain their distinctiveness despite pressures for convergence.

The few cross-country studies done by behavioral economists to date have shown that differences in tax compliance are related to differences in both social and institutional factors. Experimental studies have shown that the willingness to contribute in public good scenarios increases when individuals believe that they will receive a "fair" return. (What is "fair," of course, can vary across cultural contexts as well as according to the rules through with the redistribution is made.) Interestingly, analyses of the effects of horizontal equity have produced mixed results in different national contexts. We know that part of the explanation for this variance has to do with variation in sanctions (the risk of being caught), perceptions of others' behavior, social norms, and tax rates (Torgler 2002). There is also evidence to suggest that high trust societies are more likely to be high tax-compliant societies. "More experiments should be done to get better insights," Torgler concludes. "It would be interesting to expand the cross-country studies to analyze equity considerations" (Torgler 2002). Indeed, as Feld and Frey point out, "most studies treat 'tax morale' as a black box without discussing or even considering how it might arise or how it might be maintained. It is usually perceived as being part of the meta-preferences of taxpayers and used as the residuum in the analysis capturing unknown influences to tax evasion. The more interesting question then is which factors shape the emergence and maintenance of tax morale" (Feld and Frey 2002, 88–89).

James Alm, perhaps the world's leading scholar using experimental economics to explore tax policy issues, summarizes the major findings in the tax compliance literature as follows: (a) Perceptions of audit rates affect compliance; (b) tax rates affect compliance (e.g., perceptions of fiscal inequity); (c) simplicity versus complexity affects compliance, and finally; (d) process (versus outcomes) affects compliance—in other words, the decision-making institutions used to build or design the tax system in the first place seem to also affect citizens' willingness to comply. "Compliance is driven by far more than the purely financial considerations of detection and punishment, but in ways that are not yet fully understood" (Alm 2010, 647). Equally importantly for our purposes here, Alm's survey of this literature indicates that citizens' perception of the benefits side of the state may also affect compliance rates:

> [e]ven though individual behavior in uncertain environments has been extensively studied in the laboratory, the broader behavioral implications of government-provided social insurance have been almost completely neglected. Linking the public good aspects of social insurance programs with their uncertainty effects seems an especially promising area of research .... In short, I believe that the future prospects for the application of experimental methods to behavioral public economics are exciting and unlimited. The challenge here is to design precise experiments that parallel the essential elements of the naturally occurring world that are of interest, so that the experiments can demonstrate the external validity necessary to inform policy. (Alm 2010, 649)

Political scientists have generated substantial evidence indicating that there is wide variation in the willingness to pay taxes (and also the proclivity to avoid taxes) across countries (Edlund 1999; Svallfors 1997; Taylor-Gooby 1995). These differences are correlated with levels of social trust (PIPA 2006; Rothstein 2005) as well as with perceptions of the benefit side of the budget (Coughlin 1980; Svallfors 1997; Taylor-Gooby 1995). Stefan Svallfors and Jonas Edlund for example, have argued variously that Swedes' willingness to pay high taxes is a result of the fact that they believe that they get more out of the taxes they pay than, for example, Americans or Italians (Scholz and Lubell 1998; Edlund 1999; Svallfors 1997; Taylor-Gooby 1985). It is also reasonable to expect, as some scholars have argued, that citizens are willing to pay taxes if they believe that public spending is allocated fairly and efficiently (Rothstein 1998). But the truth is we do not know if this is correct or not.

The key problem for Political Science is that institutions are endogenous to the political system (Steinmo 2010). Using experiments, we may be able to isolate specific institutional variables and thereby unravel the endogeneity problem. In order to test these assumptions we need to conduct experiments that can control for the multiple intersecting variables that contribute to citizens' willingness to pay taxes. In so doing we will learn much more than the general perceptions or attitudes toward government and taxation. We can also learn what kinds of tax systems citizens have the greatest hostility to, and why. Moreover, by conducting these experiments as trade-offs, especially intergenerational and inter-temporal trade-offs, we can learn which kinds of trade-offs (taxes and benefits) are more or less acceptable or preferable, in different national welfare state context, and why.

History, Institutions, and Cognitive Frames

Understanding how institutions shape and frame people's preferences and consequently their choices should be at the heart of explaining variation. Moreover, developing a better understanding of how and to what extent specific institutions shape and modify people's decisions may allow us to reform and adapt institutions in a more effective and measured way. While it is widely acknowledged that "ideas" are important, the relation between institutions and people's understanding or "cognitive mind" is far less well known (Conte and Castelfranchi 2006; D'Andrade 1993; Jacobsen 1995). Institutions are rules allowing people to solve collective problems (North 1990; Thelen 2003). In order to grasp how these informal rules can change and evolve, the cognitive properties and patterns behind individuals' (inter)-actions must be taken into account (Bowles, Choic, and Hopfensitzd 2003; Hall 1997; Lieberman 2002).

The mind is not a blank slate on which cultural, normative, and social information is simply recorded: different individuals have different beliefs, values and preferences and these internal representations affect the way in which information is stored and organized (Checkel 1999; Young 1998). This social information is not simply copied and passively stored in people's minds: when information is transmitted from an individual to another, several—even though slight—modifications take place and these differences allow institutions to change and evolve.

Curiously, however, few scholars to date—from either "side" of the institutionalist camp—has specifically been able to test empirically the relationship between institutional rules, historical/cultural context, and policy choices. Doing so will allow us to move toward a better and more nuanced understanding of the ways in which institutional rules structure policy choices, and the ways in which cognitive frames shape how institutions are perceived, manipulated and interpreted. Finally, moving in this direction and looking at the interactive relationship between ideas, interests, and institutions will enable us to develop a better understanding of institutional change generally and why welfare states appear to maintain their distinctiveness despite pressures for convergence.

Why Experimental Methods?

There can be no gainsaying that experiment methods are rapidly gaining ground in Political Science (Green and Gerber 2002). Nevertheless, many political scientists will find the proposition that we can bridge Historical and Behavioral traditions strange ... or perhaps even objectionable. But if we consider that each of these approaches is centrally interested in causation, the *why* questions, perhaps this proposition is not so strange after all. Morton and Williams (2010), in their recent survey of the field, credit the New Institutionalism itself for the recent growth of experiments and experimental reasoning in Political Science: "Political science research has also begun to focus more the effects of institutions on political behavior. The 'new institutionalism' contends that institutions matter and influence norms, beliefs, actions of individuals." They suggest that, "*[i]n some cases*, experimental research is a better way to evaluate these institutional differences" (Morton and Williams 2010, 15, my emphasis).

In my view there is an affinity between experimental Political Science and Historical Institutionalist scholarship precisely because they share what Morton and Williams call "experimental reasoning." The very point of comparative historical analysis is to examine the alternative routes taken, the counterfactuals, and the junctures in which policies and institutions change. What made HI distinctive from traditional institutional analysis was the use of comparative historical analysis—not description. What makes experimental Political Science different from traditional behavioralist approaches is in fact the same thing: Both are interested in the "why?" questions. Each offers a distinctive approach to developing and testing *causal* theories.

John Gerring and Rose McDermott recently argued that qualitative research is at its best when it conceptualizes case studies "according to an experimental template." Furthermore, they suggest, "We wish to enlist the experimental ideal as a way of identifying the strengths and weaknesses of all research into causal analysis ... In particular, we have suggested a reconceptualization of research design in terms of the extent to which projects deviate from the classic experiment" (Gerring and McDermott 2007, 698). But why should we stop here? It strikes me that the ideal "multi-method" approach would combine institutional analysis and experiments precisely so that we can test the propositions generated in our historical work.

Suzanne Mettler's recent book, *The Submerged State*, is an excellent example of just such an approach. Her deep historical analysis offers rich examples of how Americans' perceptions of governmental activism have been clouded by the subterranean ways in which the government often pursued its policy goals *and* how these perceptions become traps which ensnare policymakers who would reform and change these structures. She convincingly argues that this government by "smoke and mirrors," has perceptual and even cognitive consequences (Mettler 2011, 24) and then tests these propositions using some of the techniques suggested here. "Survey research and experiments" she concludes, "enable us to examine questions such as which types of policy designs make the workings of government evident to citizens; how citizens can be informed about policies such that they can form opinions about them; and what kinds of information permit them to establish view in keeping with their values and interests" (Mettler 2011, 30).

Theda Skocpol concluded her oft-cited essay "Why I am an Historical Institutionalist" saying, "I believe that causal analysis and hypothesis testing about variations are the way to proceed methodologically. It is not enough just to explore how people talk or think. We must also find patterns in what they do" (Skocpol 1995, 105). Certainly, Skocpol was referring to historical patterns of behavior, but I submit that experiments can be another way that we examine how people actually behave in different conditions.

To be sure, the "conditions" of an experiment (especially in a laboratory experiment) are different from the real world. To start off with, the "subjects" know that they are participating in an experiment and this may itself alter their behavior. Additionally, the subject pools for most experiments (with perhaps the exception of so called "Population Based Survey Experiments") may represent biased samples from the whole population (Mutz 2011). This is why good experimental work needs to be driven by both good theory and sound empirical observation. Experiments are a data generating process where the researcher manipulates different environments and situations (the so-called "experimental treatment") in order to test the treatments' influence on the outcome. These methods allow the researcher to test relationships, whereas other more conventional research methods have shown significant problems isolating and identifying causality. Where for example survey research provides us with an insight into covariance, it does not provide us with causality. In experiments we can intervene in the actual data generating process, thereby enabling ourselves to identify and hold causal links constant. This is not possible with regular, already generated observational data (Green and Gerber 2002). But absent the foundational questions and insights drawn from "observational data" experimental research can fall into the trap of demonstrating the obvious. At first, it was interesting to see how experiments demonstrated the inadequacy of thin rational choice models, but by now even economists are interested in situating their experiments in the real world. As these techniques and methods advance they move closer to the social scientist that has long studied real institutions and the people who populate them.

Nobel Laureate and APSA's President Elinor Ostrom frequently argued in favor of adding experimental to the social scientist's toolbox.

> When conducting field research, one of the frustrating aspects is that so many variables are involved that one is never certain that one has isolated the specific variable—or limited set of variables—that causes an outcome. A good way to understand which components of a common-pool resource situation affect behavior and outcomes, and how, is to study a simplified version in an experimental laboratory. In the laboratory, the researcher carefully establishes the specific components of the theoretical situation to be studied and controls other variables so they do not confound the analysis... To test theory adequately, we need to use methods that together combine external and internal validity.... We always learn more from multiple research modes than we learn by relying on one method alone. Further, experimental research enables us to test the impact of specific variables in repeated controlled settings—something that is not available to scholars studying only field settings .... One gains external validity in doing field research, but internal validity in the laboratory. When political scientists use both methods related to one set of theoretical questions, advances in our understanding are multiplied. (Ostrom 2007, 1)

In a recent paper by Falk and Heckman (2009), titled, "Lab Experiments Are a Major Source of Knowledge in the Social Sciences," they argue similarly that:

> Causal knowledge requires controlled variation. In recent years, social scientists have hotly debated which form of controlled variation is most informative. This discussion is fruitful and will continue. In this context it is important to acknowledge that empirical methods and data sources are complements, not substitutes. Field data, survey data, and experiments, both lab and field, as well as standard econometric methods can all improve the state of knowledge in the social sciences. There is no hierarchy among these methods and the issue of generalizability of results is universal to all of them. (cited in Roth 2010, 22)

Like Ostrom, my interest is not in replacing classical methods in Political Science with experimental work. Quite the contrary, I believe that we can and should augment our work with these techniques because these methods can help us gain purchase on several kinds of questions that more traditional methods (e.g., the ones I have used in my career) cannot. It should be noted that historical institutionalism has always been sensitive to causal inference. Comparative case study methods have been a preferred tool for these scholars precisely because they are one way of controlled variation. However, HI has traditionally operated at a macro- or meso-level of aggregation.[3] But, if we are considering what steps we might want to take next and/or how we can build onto our foundations, adding behavioral and even micro-level analysis may be one way to go.

History, Institutions, and Cognitive Frames

Many institutionalist scholars have already taken steps toward integrating social, cognitive, and institutional analysis and thus offer less reductionist perspectives that view institutions as "complexes" of rules rather than unified, seamless, and consistent constraints. Instead of focusing exclusively on either structure or agency, scholars increasingly recognize how interactions between the two drive change.

Thelen cites John Ferejohn's work as an example, arguing that "culturally shared understandings and meanings" are crucial to selecting among the many possible strategic equilibria (Ferejohn 1991, 285).

> In social action, human agents make strategic or allocative choices while simultaneously enacting (ontologically) prior understandings about the nature of the strategic situation in which they find themselves, the characteristics or identities of the players (including themselves), and the common understandings or expectations as to how the game will be played. Thus, when it comes to explaining action, rational accounts, no less than interpretive ones, must appeal to principles external to the individual agents. (Ferejohn 1991, 285, cited in Thelen 1999, 376).

As Blyth, Lieberman, Lewis and Steinmo, Mahoney, Streeck, and Thelen and many others have pointed out in multiple publications in recent years, institutionalists have revised their conception of institutions from one that viewed institutions as independent, self-reinforcing, and essentially stable constraints on behavior to one that views institutions as sets of rules embedded within the broader institutional milieu of a polity. In order to better explain change, institutionalists have also embraced their complexity (Blyth 2002; Lewis and Steinmo 2012; Lieberman 2002; Mahoney and Thelen 2009; Streeck 2009)

These scholars are giving increasing attention to the "interaction" between institutional structures and agents. For example, Henry Farrell (2009) focuses on the interaction of agent strategies with institutional rules by looking at the conditions under which agents take actions promoting institutional change. In general, rational-choice scholars have developed a more nuanced, bottom-up view of agent preferences and the complexities of decision-making, in part because they are more attuned to the ways that agents interact with and respond to institutional stimuli (Katznelson and Weingast 2005; McDermott, Fowler, and Smirnov 2008).[4]

An earlier generation of comparativist scholars examined differences in preferences and implicitly argued that policies varied in different democratic countries because the citizens in those countries wanted different outcomes (Almond and Verba 1989). These scholars essentially argued against the broader historical and/or Marxist traditions, believing that in democracies at least, governments respond to the preferences and opinions of their citizens. The institutionalist scholars, along with more power based rational-choice scholars took issue with this, perhaps naïve, set of assumptions. As "new" institutionalists we argued that politics and policy outcomes were rarely the product of expressed public preferences. Moreover, we cleverly pointed out, citizens' preferences are rarely clear. Indeed, what citizens want, even in a democracy, cannot be so easily separated from the policies that their governments pursue (Rothstein 1998, 1085).

Farrell and Finnemore, as well as Blyth (Chapters 8 and 34, this volume) speak to the biases in our own historical institutionalist tradition, pointing out that the "ideational" side of the HI tradition has not been well represented in the mainstream. Perhaps this is because historical institutionalists did not have the tools or methods to test the basic propositions that an ideational account suggests. It is indeed ironic that scholars from both the behavioralist and rationalist traditions have begun to use these methods and to test what I, frankly, consider to be historical institutionalism's basic insights—that in order to understand how institutions work and change, we need to better understand what people who constitute these institutions believe and how they behave.

In short, to test the proposition that ideas and institutions are inter-related, we need to look into the black box. Before we can really understand how institutions really work, how they change, and why that change can be so difficult we need to understand more about the human mind (or more accurately, human mind*s*). Instead of seeing actors as rational decision-makers constrained and incentivized by institutional structures, we should explore the iterative relationship between human preferences and the institutions in which they are raised. Combining diverse research traditions and methodologies will allow us to better examine the dynamic relationships between ideas, interests, and institutions and thus help us better understand variation in policies and preferences across cultures and over time.

Notes

* For comments on an earlier draft of this chapter, the author thanks Giulia Andrighetto and Adam Sheingate.

1. For example, despite intense "tax competition" in Europe, tax burdens have not fallen in recent years: Indeed, the average tax burden in the Organisation for Economic

Co-Operation and Development (OECD) grew from 33.5% in 1990 to 38.5% in 2007. Even in the heavily taxed EU-15 countries tax burdens have remained quite stable, growing from 38.2% in 1990 to 38.7% in 2007. Similarly, there is great pressure on health spending in the OECD, and while we have seen the introduction of some privatization in several countries there is no evidence to suggest that the various systems are "converging" on a common policy.

2. An important distinction is "between-subject" and "within-subject"-designs. Between subject design applies one treatment to all subjects and compares them. Within-subject design applies many different treatments to each subject. We conduct both between *and* within subject design in order to attempt to single out both individual differences and manipulate the data by holding more variables constant.
3. I thank Adam Sheingate for this observation.
4. It seems to me that the interaction between individuals' perceptions, preferences and institutions that are at the core of concepts such as "positive and negative feedback" (Pierson 2000), "friction" (Lieberman 2002), as well as "layering and conversion" (Thelen 2004).

References

Alm, James. 2010. "Testing Behavioral Economics Theories in the Laboratory." *National Tax Journal* 63 (4): 535–658.

Almond, Gabriel A. and Sidney Verba. 1989. *The Civic Culture: Political Attitudes and Democracy in Five Nations*. Sage.

Blyth, Mark. 2002. *Great Transformations: Economic Ideas and Institutional Change in the Twentieth Century*. New York: Cambridge University Press.

Bowles, Samuel, Jung-Kyoo Choi, and Astrid Hopfensitz. 2003. "The Co-Evolution of Individual Behaviors and Social Institutions." *Journal of Theoretical Biology* (223): 135–147.

Checkel, Jeffrey. 1999. "Norms, Institutions, and National Identity in Contemporary Europe." *International Studies Quarterly* 43: 83–114.

Conte, Rosaria and Cristiano Castelfranchi. 2006. "The Mental Path of Norms." *Ratio Juris* 19 (4): 501–517.

Coughlin, Richard. 1980. *Ideology, Public Opinion, Welfare Policy: Attitudes Towards Taxing and Spending in Industrial Societies*. Berkeley: Institute of International Studies.

Cummings, R. G., J. Martinez-Vaszquez, M. McKee, and B. Torgler. 2004. "Effects of Culture on Tax Compliance: A Cross Check of Experimental and Survey Evidence." In CREMA Working Paper Series. Basel.

D'Andrade, Roy. 1993. "Cultural Cognition." In *Foundations of Cognitive Science*, ed. Michael Posner. Cambridge, MA: MIT Press, 795–830.

Edlund, Jonas. 1999. "Trust in Government and Welfare Regimes: Attitudes to Redistribution and Financial Cheating in the USA and Norway." *European Journal of Political Research* 35: 341–370.

Elster, Jon. 1999. *Strong Feelings: Emotion, Addiction, and Human Behavior*. Cambridge, MA: MIT Press.

Falk, Armin and James Heckman. 2009. "Lab Experiments Are a Major Source of Knowledge in the Social Sciences." *Science* 326 (5952): 535–538.

Farrell, Henry. 2009. *The Political Economy of Trust: Institutions, Interests and Inter-Firm Cooperation in Italy and Germany*. Cambridge and New York: Cambridge University Press.

Ferejohn, John. 1991. "Rationality and Interpretation: Parliamentary Elections in Early Stuart England." In *The Economic Approach to Politics*, ed. Kristen Monroe. New York: Harper Collins, 279–305.

Feld, B. and L. Frey. 2002. "Trust Breeds Trust: How Taxpayers Are Treated." *Economics of Governance* 3 (2): 87–99.

Frank, Thomas. 2004. *What's the Matter With Kansas? How Conservatives Won the Heart of America*. New York: Henry Holt and Co.

Frey, Bruno S. and Stephan Meier. 2004. "Social Comparisons and Pro-Social Behavior: Testing 'Conditional Cooperation' in a Field Experiment." *American Economic Review* 94: 1717–1722.

Gerring, John and Rose McDermott. 2007. "An Experimental Template for Case Study Research." *American Journal of Political Science* 51 (3): 688–701.

Gintis, Herbert, Samuel Bowles, Robert Boyd, and Ernst Fehr, eds. 2006. *Moral Sentiments and Material Interests: The Foundations of Cooperation in Economic Life (Economic Learning and Social Behavior)*. Cambridge, MA: MIT Press.

Green, Donald and Alan Gerber. 2002. "Reclaiming the Experimental Tradition in Political Science." In *Political Science: The State of the Discipline*, ed. Helen Milner and Ira Katznelson. New York: Norton, 832–835.

Hall, Peter. 1997. "The Role of Interests, Institutions and Ideas in Comparative Political Economy of the Industrialized Nations." In *Comparative Politics: Rationality, Culture and Structure*, ed. Mark Lichbach and Alan Zucherman. New York: Cambridge University Press, 174–207.

Jacobsen, J. K. 1995. "Much Ado About Ideas: The Cognitive Turn in Economic Policy." *World Politics* 47 (January): 283–310.

Kahneman, Daniel, Paul Slovic, and Amos Tversky, eds. 1982. *Judgement Under Uncertainty: Heuristics and Biases*. New York: Cambridge University Press.

Katznelson, Ira and Barry Weingast. 2005. "Intersections between Historical and Rational Choice Institutionalism." In *Preferences and Situations*, ed. Ira Katznelson and Barry Weingast. New York: Cambridge University Press, 1–24.

Katznelson, Ira and Barry R. Weingast. 2005. *Preferences and Situations: Points of Intersection between Historical and Rational Choice Institutionalism*. New York: Russell Sage Foundation.

Lewis, Orion and Sven Steinmo. 2012. "How Institutions Evolve: Evolutionary Theory and Institutional Change." *Polity* 44 (3): 314–339.

Lieberman, Robert. 2002. "Ideas, Institutions, and Political Order: Explaining Political Change." *American Political Science Review* 96 (4): 697–712.

Mahoney, James and Kathleen Thelen. 2009. "A General Theory of Institutional Change." In *Explaining Institutional Change: Ambiguity, Agency, and Power in Historical Institutionalism*, ed. James Mahoney and Kathleen Thelen. New York: Cambridge University Press, 1–37.

McDermott, Rose, James H. Fowler, and Oleg Smirnov. 2008. "On the Evolutionary Origin of Prospect Theory Preferences." *Journal of Politics* 70 (2): 335–350.

Morton, Rebecca and Kenneth Williams, eds. 2010. *From Nature to the Lab: Experimental Political Science and the Study of Causality*. Cambridge: Cambridge University Press.

Mettler, Suzanne. 2011. *The Submerged State*. Chicago: University of Chicago Press.

Mutz, Diana. 2011. *Population Based Survey Experiments:* Princeton, NJ: Princeton University Press.

North, Douglass. 1990. *Institutions, Institutional Change and Economic Performance*. Cambridge: Cambridge University Press.

Ostrom, Elinor. 2007. "Why Do We Need Laboratory Experiments in Political Science?" Paper Presented at the 2007 Annual Meeting of the American Political Science Association, Washington, D.C.

Peters, B. G. 1991. *The Politics of Taxation: A Comparative Perspective*, ed. G. Peele of *Comparative Politics*. Oxford: Basil Blackwell.

Peters, Guy. 1979. "Determinants of Tax Policy." *Policy Studies Journal* 7 (4): 787–793.

Pierson, Paul. 2000. "Increasing Returns, Path Dependence, and the Study of Politics." *American Political Science Review* 94 (2): 251–267.

PIPA. 2006. *20 Nation Poll Finds Strong Global Consensus: Support for Free Market System, But Also More Regulation of Large Companies: Selected Findings from GlobeScan Report on Issues and Reputation Questionaire and Methodology*. Washington, D.C.: Program on International Policy Attitudes.

Prasad, Monica. 2006. *The Politics of Free Markets: The Rise of Neoliberal Economic Policies in Britain, France, Germany, and the United States*. Chicago: University of Chicago Press.

Roth, Alvin. 2010. "Is Experimental Economics Living Up to Its Promise?" In *The Methods of Modern Experimental Economics*, ed. Giulluame Frechette and Andrew Shotter. Oxford: Oxford University Press.

Rothstein, Bo. 1998. *Just Institutions Matter: The Moral and Political Logic of the Universal Welfare State*. New York: Cambridge University Press.

Rothstein, Bo. 2005. *Social Traps and the Problem of Trust*. New York: Cambridge University Press.

Scholz, John and Mark Lubell. 1998. "Adaptive Political Attitudes: Duty, Trust and Fear as Monitors of Tax Policy." *American Journal of Political Science* 42: 398–417.

Skocpol, Theda, "Why I Am an Historical Institutionalist." *Polity* 28 (1) (Autumn 1995): 103–106.

Smith, Vernon. 2008. *Rationality in Economics: Constructivist and Ecological Forms*. New York: Cambridge University Press.

Steinmo, Sven. 1993. *Taxation and Democracy: Swedish, British and American Approaches to Financing the Modern State*. New Haven, CT: Yale University Press.

Steinmo, Sven. 2002. "Globalization and Taxation: Challenges to the Swedish Welfare State." *Comparative Political Studies* 35 (7): 839–862.

Steinmo, Sven. 2010. *The Evolution of Modern States: Sweden, Japan and the United States*. Cambridge Studies in Comparative Politics. New York: Cambridge University Press.

Streeck, Wolfgang. 2009. *Re-Forming Capitalism: Institutional Change in the German Political Economy*. New York: Oxford University Press.

Svallfors, Stefan. 1997. "Worlds of Welfare and Attitudes to Redistribution: A Comparison of Eight Western Nations." *European Journal of Sociology* 13: 283–304.

Svallfors, Stefan. 2011. "A Bedrock of Support? Trends in Welfare State Attitudes in Sweden, 1981–2010." *Social Policy and Administration* 45 (7): 806–825.

Taylor-Gooby, Peter. 1985. *Public Opinion, Ideology, and State Welfare*. London: Routledge & Kegan Paul.

Taylor-Gooby, Peter. 1995. *Who Wants the Welfare State?*", ed. Olli Kangas and Stefan Svallfors. Stockholm Umeå: Bank of Sweden Tercentenary Foundation, 11–51.

Thelen, Kathleen. 1999. "Historical Institutionalism in Comparative Politics." *Annual Reveiw of Political Science* 2: 369–404.

Thelen, Kathleen. 2003. "How Institutions Evolve: Insights from Comparative Historical Analysis." In *Comparative Historical Analysis in the Social Sciences*, ed. James Mahoney and Dietrich Rueschemeyer. New York: Cambridge University Press, 208–241.

Thelen, Kathleen A. 2004. *How Institutions Evolve: The Political Economy of Skills in Germany, Britain, the United States, and Japan.* of *Cambridge Studies in Comparative Politics.* Cambridge and New York: Cambridge University Press.

Torgler, Benno. 2002. "Speaking to Theorists and Searching for Facts: Tax Morale and Tax Compliance in Experiments." *Journal of Economic Surveys* 16 (5): 657–683.

Watts, Jon and Sven Steinmo. 1995. "It's the Institutions, Stupid! Why Comprehensive National Health Care Insurance Always Fails in America." *Journal of Health Politics, Policy and Law* 20 (2): 329–372.

Weingast, Barry. 2005. "Persuasion, Preference Change, and Critical Junctures: The Microfoundations of a Macroscopic Concept." In *Preferences and Situations*, ed. Barry Weingast and Ira Katznelson. New York: Cambridge University Press, 161–184.

Young, H. Peyton. 1998. *Individual Strategy and Social Structure: An Evolutionary Theory of Institutions.* Princeton, NJ: Princeton University Press.

CHAPTER 7

POWER IN HISTORICAL INSTITUTIONALISM

PAUL PIERSON*

THERE is a paradox at the heart of contemporary Political Science. On the one hand, there is increasing recognition of the growth of economic inequality in affluent democracies, along with substantial evidence that the distribution of political resources has shifted as well. On the other hand, empirical research has had a hard time demonstrating inequalities in political power. This paradox is especially pronounced in the field of American politics, which plays a leading role in shaping the contours of the discipline as a whole. For Americanists, power and influence remain elusive, unhelpful, and marginalized concepts. When Americanists have gone looking for "power"—decisive political advantages for those with more resources—they mostly haven't found it. There is very little evidence showing that campaign contributions or lobbying systematically effect roll call votes in Congress (Schlozman, Verba, and Brady 2012). Stephen Ansolabehere, John de Figueredo and James Snyder provocatively asked "why is there so little money in American politics?" They found that while this was partly because donating money to exert influence raised big collective action problems, it was equally because money seemed to make little difference for political results (Ansolabehere, de Figueredo, and Snyder 2003). A broad and sophisticated study of lobbying from some of the leading scholars of interest groups recently reported that it could "find virtually no linkage between [group] resources and outcomes" (Baumgartner et al. 2009). Of course, the inability to find power in empirical research is especially puzzling given the extraordinary increase in economic inequality in the United States over the past generation, which has been accompanied by growing and increasingly unequal campaign contributions and a massive expansion of lobbying.

Nor is the elusiveness of power just an empirical matter. More fundamentally, power doesn't really fit in the Downsian frameworks that have dominated the study of democratic politics for the past generation (Hacker and Pierson 2014). For these frameworks, "power" typically rests in the hands of the median voter—which means it hardly makes sense to talk about power at all. Politics changes as the preferences at the median of the electorate change. As a result, these frameworks typically depict politics as fluid or "plastic." Elections follow a Downsian logic; this cycle's loser adjusts and becomes next cycle's winner. Take out incumbency, David Mayhew observes, and presidential elections over the past century or so have been essentially a coin-toss between the two parties (Mayhew 2002). Legislatures are under the sway of Arrow's paradox of voting, so that losers in any legislative struggle are well-positioned to cycle back into the winner's position. The electorate, whose views are usually regarded as a strong constraint on policymakers, fluctuates back and forth over a moderate policy space. Voter preferences operate like a thermostat, bringing the political system back to the middle (Erikson, Mackuen, and Stimson 2002). Whether the focus is on voters, legislatures, or parties, temporary rather than durable advantages appear to be the rule. Jacob Hacker and I have suggested that the dominant frameworks treat politics like the movie *Groundhog Day*. Each morning, Bill Murray wakes again to find himself in Punxsutawney, nothing important has really changed, and all the participants just start over (Hacker and Pierson 2014).

If the striking juxtaposition between rapidly growing social inequality and a Political Science unable to detect inequalities of power is most evident in the study of American politics, it is not limited to that subfield. Recent developments in the field of comparative political economy reveal a similar tendency. In a trend that Peter Hall (Chapter 2, this volume) describes as "Schumpeterian," comparativists too have moved away from more "structured" frameworks toward ones that are more atomized and fluid. Comparative political economy has drifted from exploring systems of organized interest intermediation toward a behaviorist and electoralist focus on the links between voter preferences and policy outcomes. Like their Americanist counterparts, they now see the interface between politicians and voters, mediated by the structure of electoral and legislative institutions, as the heart of politics—indeed, almost its entirety.

Methodological trends have pushed strongly in the same direction. Part of the attractiveness of the "Downsian" framework to a whole generation of political scientists has been its compatibility with research in data-rich areas like voting behavior, public opinion, and legislative behavior. To this has now been added a new infatuation with experimental and quasi-experimental methods. Like the behavioral revolution that preceded it, the allure of experimentalism strongly orients research toward the investigation of a restricted set of immediately observable micro-level phenomena.

Unfortunately, both the theoretical and methodological approaches that are central to the research just described have great difficulty identifying inequalities of power. The reason is simple but the implications are profound: large inequalities of power are unlikely to generate open political struggles. The critics of pluralism were right on a crucial point: power is like an iceberg, with most of the mass lying below the waterline. It remains invisible unless one knows where and how to look for it (Pierson 2015).

The argument of this chapter is straightforward: unlike most of contemporary Political Science, historical institutionalism knows where to look. A systematic analysis of political power relationships in a society must have two central features: (1) it must be attentive to processes unfolding over time; and (2) it must focus on the ways in which core institutional arrangements—including policy arrangements—typically advance the interests of particular political coalitions. Given the need to combine these features, historical institutionalism has been well positioned to make core contributions to our understanding of political power, even as other prominent frameworks in the discipline have pushed the issue of power to the margins. In practice, the more structural and historical approach that has been at the heart of historical institutionalism has been much more likely to detect (and be able to account for) the more fundamental distribution of power in modern societies.

The Hidden Dimensions of Power

The old "community power" debate remains relevant. Pluralists limited the study of power to the study of open contestation. Anti-pluralists argued, rightly, that this was much too constricted (Bachrach and Baratz 1962; Crenson 1971; Lukes 1974). For the anti-pluralists open contestation was just the "first" dimension of power. They argued that there were other dimensions that were less visible but more significant. Crucially, a focus on open contestation will not just "miss" some aspects of power; it will produce fundamentally misleading results. Only a very restricted and distinctive set of power inequalities filter through into open conflict. Even those that do will be distorted by the need to pass through the filter. To see why this is, it is necessary to briefly introduce the other dimensions of power.

The "second dimension" refers to cases where competing interests are recognized (at least by the powerless) but open contestation does not occur because of power asymmetries. This dimension should in turn be divided into two distinct components, which involve quite different ways in which power can be at work without generating open conflict. The first is what can be termed *non-decisions*. It refers to the ways in which formal or informal decision rules may favor some actors' concerns over others. In coining the term Bachrach and Baratz follow E. E. Schattschneider's idea of "the mobilization of bias." Schattschneider's original formulation remains worth quoting:

> A conclusive way of checking the rise of conflict is simply to provide no arena for it or to create no public agency with power to do anything about it … All legislative procedure is loaded with devices for controlling the flow of explosive materials into the governmental apparatus. All forms of political organization have a bias in favor of the exploitation of some kinds of conflict and the suppression of others because *organization is the mobilization of bias*. Some issues are organized into politics while others are organized out. (Schattschneider 1960, 69)

Contemporary social scientists would say that this type of influence refers to agenda control. It is now well understood that this is one of the principal ways in which institutions may advantage particular actors. Work in formal theory clearly established the analytical foundations for this claim. McKelvey's path-breaking work demonstrated that given realistic assumptions about the distribution of preferences the structure of agenda control could determine the final outcome (McKelvey 1976). McKelvey's work catalyzed a rich literature. The allocation of agenda control can indeed effectively organize some issues (or groups) into politics while others are organized out. I will argue in the next section of this chapter that historical institutionalists have played a critical role in extending this insight, in particular through the exploration of how policy structures promote agenda control.

The other fundamental mechanism in the second dimension is that of anticipated reactions. Here too, potential issues are "organized out" of politics, but the way in which this happens is quite different. Open contestation does not occur because the weaker actor rationally chooses not to engage in light of her weak position. Contestation is costly, both because of the need to expend resources and, if you are weak, because of the prospect that the powerful will retaliate. To underscore what we are talking about, "retaliation" can mean the loss of a job, social ostracism, or physical violence against you, your family, or friends. Given these costs, choosing not to act may be completely reasonable if defeat seems likely.

The essential point is that the decision not to contest takes place in the shadow of power relationships. If a slave chooses not to rebel it would be absurd to treat the absence of open contestation as a sign that there is no power involved. Again, this dynamic is widely appreciated in some modern contexts. For instance, anticipated reactions feature prominently in standard game theoretic analyses, such as the study of presidential vetoes (Cameron 2000).

Still, the ways in which power relations can be obscured is not well integrated into core understandings of political influence in democratic polities. This is in part because dominant Downsian frameworks consider voters to be decisive. Voters rarely have an incentive to engage in the kind of strategic behavior that would lead to non-action in light of anticipated reactions. In a world where the electorate rules, voters face little constraint in expressing whatever preference they want. If, as the Downsian view of politics suggests, the median voters' preferences are decisive, then there is little need to worry about rational decisions not to engage in political conflict. As I will argue later, the role of anticipated reactions—of open conflict failing to emerge because of rationally chosen inactivity in light of power inequalities—makes much more sense when one is discussing a broader range of strategic interactions that occurs among groups beyond the political settings where individual choices are made at the ballot box.

There is, finally, what is typically termed the third dimension, which concerns ideational elements of power (Lukes 1974). Powerful actors can gain advantage by inculcating views in others that are to their advantage. In essence, this involves what Marx termed false consciousness. Those controlling the media, schools, churches, think tanks, or other key cultural institutions may promote beliefs in others (about what is desirable or possible) that serve the interests of the powerful. Again, what looks like consensus on the surface may reflect underlying inequalities of influence. Again, this kind of influence is likely to involve slow-moving processes that require a focus on group-based activity over a sustained period rather than concentration on the immediate effects of some stimulus on individual behavior.

The core theme of the anti-pluralists was that surface appearances were just that—appearances. If taken at face value they were likely to be highly misleading guides to the structure of power in a society. Articulation of the multiple dimensions of power represented a powerful assault on a narrow conception of influence. The force of the anti-pluralist critique rested on a critical insight: the exercise of power will often *not* take the form of open contestation. Indeed, the point can be put more strongly: on matters where the distribution of power is quite unequal we should expect to see *little or no open contestation*. Instead, some combination of agenda control, anticipated reactions and cultural manipulation mutes conflict and restricts it to a much narrower and less fundamental subset of potential issues. Most of the time open clashes will occur only on those matters, and between those political actors, where the balance of power is (believed to be) relatively even.

This characteristic of power relationships has a fundamental implication: examining the skewed subset of possible conflicts that actually produce open conflict should reveal no clear pattern of outcomes. As Walter Korpi (1985, 36) summarizes, "since the probability of manifest conflicts decreases with increasing differences in power resources between actors, to focus the study of power on situations involving manifest conflicts considerably increases the likelihood of discovering 'pluralist' power structures." Pluralists were, and their intellectual descendants still are, looking for power in all the wrong places. Their methodological insistence on studying open conflict systematically biases their results.

Returning to the earlier discussion of pluralist "non-findings" regarding unequal influence, we can place these results in a different light. Recall the paradox of power. Scholars of American politics observe an increasingly unequal distribution of resources (Schlozman, Verba, and Brady 2012), but when they go looking to see how that translates into unequal power they have a hard time finding it.[1] Mark Smith's careful study found that when the reputedly powerful business community was highly unified on a major policy issue, it had a very mixed record in achieving its preferred outcome (Smith 2000). Similarly, a team of leading interest group scholars (Baumgartner et al. 2009) could find no evidence that the side with greater resources had any discernible advantage in policy fights.

This is because the original critics of pluralism rightly insisted that most of the iceberg of power hides below the waterline. Smith is not examining *all* potential issues where other social actors might oppose the interests of a unified business community. He is looking only at the much more restricted set of issues that make it through the filters. Those are the issues on which (once anticipated reactions, tilted playing fields, and other obstacles are taken into account) other political actors believe they have a reasonable prospect for success and in fact manage to push their concerns onto the political agenda. In the absence of a big shock, which alters the balance of power in fundamental ways, we should expect high visibility political conflict to emerge *only* where the power resources of contending forces are relatively even. Examining only the smallish visible tip of the iceberg, we should *expect* to see no clear pattern.

Much to their credit, Baumgartner and colleagues recognize this limitation to their analysis. Just as economists say that the stock price of a company may embody all the information there is about the company's value, they suggest that the policy status quo may be said to embody the inherited distribution of power. If some groups have had greater influence over time, we should expect that the status quo *already reflects this*. We shouldn't expect that they will win a disproportionate share of the open conflicts going forward, among the select set of issues that make it through the second dimension of power. Existing policy is an equilibrium. They argue, in short, that their findings of little advantage stemming from the open deployment of greater political resources are consistent with a view of politics that sees underlying power resources as very unequally distributed.

The implication is that to get a handle on these power inequalities we need a different strategy. Theoretically, we must be cognizant of the "hidden" but fundamental dimensions of power. Methodologically, we need research designs that are geared to peer beneath open and immediate political conflict. In the next section I argue that political scientists have made considerable progress in developing theoretical frameworks and methodological tools for uncovering these power relationships.

A Structural and Historical Approach to Studying Power

When the anti-pluralists argued that a focus on open political conflict was likely to miss most of the story about power relations, pluralists' most effective response was methodological: you can't study what you can't see. It is worth noting at the outset that this is a pretty defensive posture. The pluralists didn't really deny that such subterranean inequalities might exist; they simply maintained that there was no way to know. Ironically, even as power has receded as a concern within the discipline we are actually in a much stronger position today to identify the kinds of influence explored by pluralism's original critics. Theoretical progress has made some of the claims of the anti-pluralists more tractable. Social scientists now have the capacity to see much more of what lurks below the waterline. Yet much of the discipline has failed to exploit these opportunities—precisely because the atomized and micro-orientations of contemporary research undercut social scientists' emerging capacity to study influence systematically.

The new opportunities to study power systematically are most likely to be seized if they draw heavily on insights derived from historical institutionalism. Indeed, during the discipline's long retreat from the study of power historical institutionalism has stood out as a crucial exception. Its defining features—an interest in substantive, high-stakes outcomes, its design of inquiry around the careful comparison of large-scale cases, and its concentration on historical process—have always been distinctly well-suited to the examination of deeply-rooted and highly consequential structures of power. Today, there are exciting opportunities to expand on its distinctive capacities to study power by combining it with increasingly sophisticated tools for investigating subterranean politics.

Why has influence become a more tractable problem? Some of the credit should go to rational choice institutionalism, which has succeeded in unpacking and investigating the two distinct dimensions of the second face of power (agenda control and anticipated reactions). It has given us a much richer appreciation for the importance of agenda control, and how particular rule structures allocate authority over agendas.

We now know that particular institutional arrangements will systematically favor the representation of certain views and interests. Consider two fundamental and well-researched examples:

- The construction of independent central banks is likely to durably shift monetary policy in predictable ways, by empowering particular sets of actors and reducing their vulnerability to particular kinds of political pressure (e.g., Franzese 1999).
- Legislative leaders can use their power of "negative agenda control" to keep items off the agenda that would divide their coalitions, obtaining outcomes that would not be sustainable otherwise (Cox and McCubbins 1993).

The same holds true for the idea of anticipated reactions. Recognition of the phenomenon obviously pre-dates the rise of rational choice institutionalism (Friedrich 1963). Still, game theory has given social scientists a more sophisticated understanding of the role of anticipated reactions in politics. This in turn has encouraged the development of techniques for studying bargaining power that treat "non-decisions" as a completely expected and researchable aspect of politics (Cameron 2000; Clark, Golder, and Golder 2007).

For the most part, however, these theoretical developments have failed to reinvigorate the study of power. Instead, they have uneasily co-existed with the broader turn toward an atomized, micro-oriented and power-free Political Science. They have been applied in a limited way to a limited set of problems, operating more or less at the margins of discussions emphasizing cooperation, responsiveness to citizen preferences, and the general fluidity of political arrangements (Hacker and Pierson 2014). There are two reasons historical institutionalism represents an exception: the first is its focus on the institutionalization of advantage, and the second is its understanding that this requires research attentive to the temporal dimensions of political processes. I consider each of these features in turn.

The Institutionalization of Advantage

The core claim historical institutionalists make regarding power is that winning coalitions will typically seek to institutionalize their advantages—that is, they will use their power to change "the rules of the game" to create further advantages down the road. These rules include both formal and informal institutions, as well as public policies. This claim is a theoretical one, but it has important methodological implications as well.

The idea that power in politics is generally about the institutionalization of advantage was the core of Terry Moe's broad critique of rational choice institutionalism (Moe 2005). He argued that the variant of institutionalism rational choice scholars imported from economics subordinated questions of power. Instead, they stressed how institutions facilitated coordination, enforced commitments, and enabled gains from trade. These frameworks rested on an assumption of *voluntary* exchanges. Although some might gain more than others, everyone was made better off (or at least not worse off) as a result of these arrangements. If individuals weren't better off, they would simply choose not to participate.

Moe countered that while these frameworks generated crucial insights about how institutions helped particular political coalitions, they ignored a crucial feature of politics. Unlike the case of market exchanges, in politics a winning coalition gets to use political authority, and it can use it to impose outcomes on losers. These losers often have no viable exit option. Ignoring (or downplaying) this crucial difference misses much that is at the heart of politics, and makes contestation look far more benign than it typically is.

The implications of Moe's insistence that in politics winners can exercise authority over losers run deep (Gruber 2000). Most fundamentally, it suggests the need to recognize that political contestation is *both* a battle to gain control over political authority *and* a struggle to use political authority to institutionalize advantage—that is, to lay the groundwork for future victories. In short, it calls for an appreciation of how political influence is often invested. The exercise of authority is not just an exercise of power; it is potentially a way of generating power.

In the field of comparative politics, the most famous of these institutional arrangements dictated by victors is democracy itself—a new configuration of authority that durably altered the rules for allocating political authority. New decision rules diminished the value of political resources based on the possession of property or coercive capacity and increased the value of resources based on sheer numbers (Rueschemeyer, Stephens, and Stephens 1992). Acemoglu and Robinson have recently developed a popular version of this argument, stressing the establishment of democratic institutions as the decisive "cut-point" in history, institutionalizing a set of durable advantages for ordinary citizens (Acemoglu and Robinson 2012).

Specific constitutional arrangements can have similar effects of durably advantaging particular actors, for instance by creating super-majority requirements for revision (Starr 2014). A large literature in comparative politics has developed around the crucial institutional divide between electoral institutions that enshrine majoritarian and proportional representation systems. Considerable research has demonstrated how particular coalitions chose to entrench one system or the other, depending on their prognostication of the long-term political effects (Iversen, Cusack, and Soskice 2007).

Yet as historical institutionalists have stressed, the basic point about institutionalizing advantage extends well beyond basic constitutional rules. In modern democracies the main mechanism for institutionalizing advantage is public policy. Winners get to impose their policy preferences on losers. Often, this means imposing arrangements to which losers must adjust *even if their side wins future elections*. Policies can create facts on the ground, durably altering resources and incentives. Policies can strengthen supporters and weaken losers. In extreme cases, policies can effectively eliminate the losers as a serious force altogether.

The establishment of new policy arrangements may constitute a kind of mini-constitution in a particular domain of social life. Eskridge and Ferejohn (2001) coined the term "super statutes" to distinguish extraordinary laws that exert a strong gravitational pull on jurisprudence and norms. When one looks more broadly at the capacity of policies to remake political circumstances the ranks of mini-constitutions expand dramatically (Pierson 2006). In Eric Patashnik's *After Reform*, for instance, airline deregulation was cemented in part by eliminating the Civil Aeronautics Board, the regulatory venue where the old-line airlines had their greatest leverage. At the same time, the new legislation unleashed market forces that induced a war of attrition, steadily removing the high-cost airlines (who were deregulation's strongest opponents) from the playing field (Patashnik 2008).

This basic insight about policy coalitions—once so deeply held that analysts felt little need to make it explicit—is at the heart of long traditions of historical institutionalist work, both in comparative politics and American political development (Gourevitch 1986; Skowronek 1993). Shifting coalitions of interests battle to exercise authority in order to impose their preferences through governance. The potential for policy trajectories to be highly path-dependent makes these efforts profoundly important. It is why comparativists can identify distinct "regimes" covering huge areas of public life like the welfare state and a nation's model of capitalism (Esping-Andersen 1985; Esping-Andersen 1990; Hall and Soskice 2001; Huber and Stephens 2001; Pierson 2004; Thelen 2004). These regimes are grounded in durable policy arrangements, resulting from fierce contestation among organized interests. Although often strongly connected to one party or another at the outset, these arrangements are sustained over time by supportive coalitions that have transcended and outlasted any specific electoral majority. Their endurance is testament to the capacity of long-lived political actors to use government authority to refashion economies and societies in enduring ways.

Studies that examine policymaking over time have been much more likely to appreciate this crucial dynamic than those focusing on the electoral see-saw. This research can explore the evolution of policy options, which groups favor particular outcomes, the conditions that allow particular alternatives to triumph, and the long-term effects of those policy enactments on the distribution of political resources and policy preferences. By considering multiple rounds of contestation it is possible to collect a variety of observations that help an analyst to evaluate alternative hypotheses about the underlying political processes, including those related to "non-decisions" and anticipated reactions.

Studies of this sort have been prevalent within the field of American Political Development, which has frequently focused on the efforts of political coalitions to institutionalize favored arrangements. I have already mentioned Patashnik's simple but telling example of how airline deregulation quickly drove its biggest opponents, the high-cost airlines, out of business. Moe's recent analysis of public sector collective bargaining has a similar dynamic (Moe 2011). Such processes operate on a grander scale as well. Jacob Hacker and I have sought to understand the neoliberal turn in American public policy since 1975 as a sequence of pitched battles, policy victories (and defeats) and downstream adaptations that have broadly favored the economically privileged (Hacker and Pierson 2010).

Similarly, research in American political development on race and ethnicity has repeatedly emphasized the role of institutionalized hierarchies, cemented through policy. These hierarchies proved stubbornly resistant to liberalizing developments in other domains of politics, precisely because they were deeply embedded in durable coalitions of organized actors hostile to emancipatory changes (King and Smith 2012). The collapse of Reconstruction after 1876 led to a series of statutory and constitutional changes, consolidating a Jim Crow regime that locked southern blacks (and many poor whites) out of politics for nearly a century (Keyssar 2000). Victory over core institutional arrangements tilted the playing field for future rounds of contestation, increasing the probability of victory (or the likely scale of victories) for one of the contending parties. The bargain of 1877 was critical in bringing Reconstruction to an end because it assured that future conflicts over the Southern political economy would occur in a different arena (the states), freed from federal intervention. This new venue was heavily slanted in favor of segregationists. While they did not achieve instantaneous victory, they steadily gained the upper hand.

Major policy enactments *are* the mobilization of bias. New institutions or policy regimes are often the main prizes awarded to the victors during critical junctures (Hacker and Pierson 2014). These new arrangements create advantages for certain actors over others, organizing some issues in and other issues out. They can often generate feedback effects that reinforce the advantages of winners over time, transferring resources, necessitating or underwriting social investments, and sending signals about likely outcomes that can encourage individuals to switch sides or adapt (Pierson 2015).

It is worth noting explicitly that this discussion of policy coalitions exerting (and building) power through control of governance shifts the focus of political analysis from voters to organized groups (Hacker and Pierson 2014). Most of those involved in politics in a sustained way participate because they care what government does. Again, politics is a contest where some gain the authority to make decisions of fundamental significance for others. This makes the exercise of authority a central object of political contestation. Yet effectively exercising political authority to remake the structures of opportunity is a daunting challenge. To do so requires the capacity to overcome collective action problems, mobilize resources, coordinate actions with others, develop extensive expertise, focus sustained attention, and operate flexibly across the multiple domains of political authority. Moreover, all of this must typically be done over long periods of time, across shifting partisan environments, despite considerable turnover of elected officials, and in the face of dogged resistance from other resourceful actors. These are not capacities we usually associate with voters. They are the comparative strength of organized interests.

Thus one can see why the shift in political scientists' focus from groups to voters has gone hand in hand with the subordination of an analysis of power. The subterranean character of power relationships means that it is simply impossible to see if one focuses primarily on elections and voting behavior. It is, instead, illuminated by the examination of group-based, long-term contestation over policy outcomes. As a result, historical institutionalism's sustained interest in group contestation over time, carried largely through efforts to institutionalize advantage, has been essential in keeping the subject of power alive in the discipline.

Consider one brief illustration from the field of comparative political economy. A central expectation of those studying the topic of inequality from a perspective that emphasizes the preferences and behavior of atomized voters is that of Meltzer and Richard (1981). Rising inequality skewed to the highest income groups should produce more egalitarian policies, as the median voter faces growing incentives to vote for redistribution. As Huber and Stephens have recently noted (Huber and Stephens 2012, 11), the logic may be elegant, but the empirics are "plain wrong." It is the *most egalitarian* societies that make the greatest efforts to equalize income. Moreover, as societies become more unequal they may decrease, rather than increase, their redistributive efforts. The reason, as Huber and Stephens emphasize, is that "a greater distance between the median and the mean income tends to be accompanied by a more skewed distribution of political power and thus lower responsiveness to demands for redistribution (11)."

Here Huber and Stephens draw on the central ideas of power resources theory, with its emphasis on what Korpi (1985, 36) calls " 'the Matthew effect' in exchange: to him that hath, shall be given." The example clarifies why historical institutionalists have typically emphasized the importance of distinctive policy regimes, which either enhance or discourage pressures for egalitarianism. More fundamentally, it points to the need to focus on how power is built into durable social structures, rather than operating exclusively at the level of open conflict. Only by explaining how outcomes at key junctures produce durable (but not permanent or unchanging) shifts in social arrangements can we make inequalities of influence visible. Indeed, arguably the most important contribution of historical institutionalism to social science is its commitment to understanding the ways in which inequalities of power are built deeply into the subterranean structures of modern societies.

Power Formation as a Historical Process

A second critical feature of historical institutionalism that has facilitated a sustained focus on power is its interest in examining unfolding historical processes. The examination of temporal process is central to the study of power, because *power is something that develops over time and simultaneously becomes less visible as it does so*. To see this, we can combine the preceding discussion of the institutionalization of advantage through policy structures with a brief review of John Gaventa's classic analysis of power (Gaventa 1982).

In *Power and Powerlessness: Quiescence and Rebellion in an Appalachian Valley*, Gaventa developed an astute defense of the anti-pluralist position, countering the pluralists' objection that you could not study what you could not see. He presented a careful empirical study of political conflict in a setting—a poor mining community simultaneously marked by ostensibly pluralist political institutions and vast economic inequalities—conducive to identifying how influence is deployed. Gaventa argued that one *could* study what wasn't visible, if one clearly explicated the mechanisms through which these dimensions of power should operate, and specified what the observable implications of power's exercise might be. Crucially, Gaventa highlighted that those implications had a clear temporal structure. We could uncover the "hidden" dimensions of power through historical analysis. Over time, open rebellion would give way to quiescence in predictable ways, and we could study that historical process systematically.

Unfortunately, Gaventa's incisive argument came too late to exert much influence among political scientists. The conversation had already shifted away from issues of power to the study of political behavior and a highly formalized analysis of institutions. Yet Gaventa's analysis provides the essential bridge between the community power debate—where critics of pluralism rightly insisted that political power is akin to an iceberg, with most of its mass lying under the waterline—and contemporary efforts to build theories more attentive to inequalities of influence.

Gaventa's analysis was partly a theoretical move. It stressed that major political conflicts involve repeated interactions among competing coalitions. The meaning of a particular conflict can only be seen by situating it within that larger process—a process through which many alternative outcomes are gradually removed from the agenda. At the same time, Gaventa noted that important forms of influence often became amplified over time. In the terminology of historical institutionalism, power was potentially subject to positive feedback or self-reinforcement (Pierson 2015).

Equally important, Gaventa's turn to historical analysis was a methodological move. He persuasively argued that we could *detect* political influence through historical process-tracing. Examining contestation over core institutional arrangements over an extended period of time could reveal the (often violent) suppression of alternatives, the ways in which new institutions mobilized bias, encouraged adaptations, and led to "quiescence" in a context of anticipated reactions. Historical institutionalist research has often followed this lead in designing historical inquiry to assemble indirect evidence about the distribution of power in this way. Carpenter (2001) uses this technique to make a persuasive case for the role of autonomous bureaucrats in imposing their preferences over congressional politicians during an important period of state-building in the early twentieth century. Two studies of American welfare state development (Hacker and Pierson 2002; Broockman 2012) have used similar methods to evaluate the political influence of employers. Broockman's study of Medicare's enactment draws on multiple forms of evidence to demonstrate that most employers only acquiesced to the establishment of Medicare once it became clear that the program's enactment was inevitable.

To study power effectively, you have to know where to look. Recent research highlights the exciting opportunities to build a new generation of systematic studies of influence. These opportunities stem in part from important theoretical developments in rational choice institutionalism. However, they will rely heavily on extensions of core frameworks of historical institutionalism. In contrast to work focused relentlessly on micro-behavior, historical institutionalism has always been extremely well-suited to the study of power. This is in part because of its emphasis on analyzing macro-level outcomes. The focus on highlighting and seeking to explain persistent structural differences in societies has led historical institutionalists to concentrate their research on efforts to institutionalize political advantage. Equally important has been historical institutionalism's interest in historical processes. It is through these processes that political advantage is built and sustained, and it is through the examination of politics over time that political influence is most likely to be detected.

A Research Agenda

In concluding this chapter I want to briefly discuss an issue central to the current agenda within historical institutionalism for thinking about the problem of power. What has traditionally been termed the "third" dimension of power occurs when actors deploy social resources to shift others' views of what is desirable or possible, to the benefit of those who promoted these ideational shifts. These social resources may shape the dissemination of information and argumentation in diverse arenas, including schools, the media, and religious organizations. Wuthnow (1989) argues that "communities of discourse" emerging during brief periods come to share, institutionalize, and reproduce ideologies. Berman (2003) has made a similar argument about the spread of radical Islam. Extremists gained control over key institutions of cultural production; they then used that control to foment a revolutionary transformation in citizens' worldviews. A recent report on new textbooks introduced in Hamas-controlled Gaza provides a contemporary example (Akram and Rudoren 2013). These textbooks describe Jerusalem's Western Wall as "Islamic property," do not recognize modern Israel, and fail to mention the Oslo Peace Accords.

By now, it will perhaps not be surprising to hear that the very concept of ideology has lost ground in the empirical study of politics with the rise of behaviorism and experimentalism. Since Converse (1964), behaviorists have emphasized the scarcity of ideological thinking within mass publics, stressing the inconsistency and shallowness of individual opinions. Yet many modes of thinking about political life and major public issues become more or less prevalent over time. Such shifts generally develop gradually, and bringing them about may require broad and durable mobilization. All of this is likely to be beyond the frameworks of behavioral research, which typically concentrate on observed individual attitudes. By the time broad changes in attitudes are widespread, the impact of resource mobilization is likely to be obscured—either lying in the past or deeply embedded in seemingly neutral or relatively apolitical structures. As Korpi (1985, 39) notes, "the analysis of the role of ideologies and beliefs in the context of power cannot be easily incorporated into the behavioral approach to the study of power."

Just as with the study of power's second dimension, efforts to study the transformation of beliefs requires a different strategy of inquiry. If power can operate through successful efforts to change beliefs about what is possible or about what is desirable it makes sense to refocus research. One important focus is elite discourse, which is an important source of mass opinion (Zaller 1992) and results in part from strategic interaction involving elites. A second focus concerns ideational mobilization nurtured by organized groups.

Noelle-Neumann's (1974) concept of "spirals of silence" illustrates the advantage of shifting from a focus on individual behavior to one of strategic interaction among elites. Noelle-Neumann's idea was that as actors see a particular viewpoint becoming marginalized, they are less willing to articulate that view. Her social psychological analysis emphasized the individual's desire for social conformity. However, there may be other incentive structures involving unequal power. Expression of particular views may become more costly as they become less prevalent. Such tendencies can "spiral" or become self-reinforcing as actors conclude that few people hold a particular view. The spreading silence generates a false consensus, which potentially can become "real" as particular arguments and viewpoints become increasingly rare in public discourse.

Micro-level evidence for this argument is, however, sketchy (Lang and Lang 2012)—polling and voting are private, individualized forms of expression in which participants should feel relatively free to express their authentic views rather than engaging in strategic behavior. Yet once one shifts away from individual voters, the context is fundamentally different. One can imagine a self-reinforcing dynamic working in important domains where participants in discourse make strategic decisions in the context of power relations. Politicians who see a particular argument become a political loser face strong incentives to drop that argument and join (or at least fail to challenge) the emerging consensus. Ellis and Stimson (2012) have recently suggested that this kind of dynamic among political elites may have played an important role in the decline of liberalism as a public philosophy in the United States after 1970.

Interest groups may make the same calculation. A striking characteristic of groups, however, is that they may have the capacity to discount immediate results in search of long-term benefits. In addition, unlike a politician, a group doesn't have to win elections to be successful—it just needs a niche where it can mobilize the resources it needs to flourish. Under the right conditions, a group or network of groups may be able to promote ideas over an extended period of time even if they are initially marginalized. The key point is that with respect to the expression and dissemination of ideas, both organized groups and political leaders face different incentives than ordinary citizens—incentives where power considerations are likely to be of great relevance.

A striking recent example in the United States that combines these elite and group dynamics in a self-reinforcing process of ideational change is the evolving discussion of the 2nd Amendment concerning "the right to bear arms" (Siegel 2008). The process involved both sustained organizational effort on behalf of initially marginal ideas and, eventually, a feedback loop of elite accommodation to an emerging consensus. Beginning in the 1970s, gun rights activists sought to overturn the long-standing consensus in American law that the 2nd Amendment (with its reference to "a well regulated militia") provided no protections for individual gun ownership. A key stage was gaining control of the National Rifle Association, which conservative activists transformed from an essentially apolitical organization into a powerful and well-resourced vehicle for changing public policy.

From this organizational base, gun-rights activists launched a multi-pronged and well-financed effort designed to first establish the doctrinal credibility of a contrary position, and then spread support for that stance among conservatives. This effort eventually yielded the 5–4 *Heller* decision of 2008, in which five conservative justices overturned 70 years of legal precedent. By then, the new view of gun rights had both a mass and elite base. A Google n-gram search reveals the phrase "second amendment rights" was virtually unheard of until the late 1970s. Its emergence between 1978 and 1982 closely followed with the takeover of the National Rifle Association by extreme conservatives. Then, between 1982 and 2000, frequency of use of "second amendment rights" grows 500 per cent. As the meme of "second amendment rights" gained force, politicians (including those who supported gun control) found it increasingly prudent to adopt the ascendant rhetoric. Their behavior reinforced a rapid shift in elite and mass discourse. Following sustained and substantial exertions of organized pressure, consensus understandings of a core constitutional issue had flipped completely.

The empirical challenges involved in studying this third dimension of power are severe. Yet the issue remains a cutting-edge one for the social sciences. Not only is the subject of obvious importance, but the "big data" revolution is creating exciting new opportunities to study the evolution of elite and mass discourse in much more systematic ways than would have been possible even a decade ago. Purely qualitative efforts to reconstruct the evolution of discourse are vulnerable to concerns about unrepresentative sampling, and they are in any event unable to make full use of the huge troves of data potentially available for the study of political ideas and culture. The digital revolution, however, makes it possible to examine huge quantities of text, increasing researchers' ability to accurately map mass and elite political expression over time (Bonikowski and Gidron n.d.; Noel 2013).

As the 2nd Amendment example suggests, however, any successful approach to the "third dimension" of power is likely to require attentiveness to the organized generation and reproduction of cultural power over extended time periods. And, indeed, historical institutional studies arguably have produced some of the most sustained efforts to explore these issues in Political Science (Blyth 2002; Hall 1989). In short, taking the third dimension of power seriously means looking beyond individual behavior and beyond open and short-term political conflict. Like the other aspects of power discussed in this chapter, it is a subject well-suited to the focus on big, substantive outcomes, group-based conflict, and temporal process that have long been central to historical institutionalist work in the social sciences.

NOTES

* This chapter draws in part on material in Pierson (2015). I am very grateful to Orfeo Fioretos for astute comments on an earlier draft, and to James Mahoney, Terry Moe, John Stephens, and Kathleen Thelen for ongoing discussions on the issues addressed here. My greatest debt is to Jacob Hacker, who deserves credit or blame for many of the ideas developed in this chapter.

1. I exaggerate. One place where Americanists are beginning to find some evidence is in research on legislators' responsiveness to public opinion (Bartels 2010; Gilens 2012; Gilens and Page 2014). But even here the research is better on revealing a disconnect between attitudes and outcomes than it is on explaining where the disconnect comes from. In other words, if voters don't govern, who does, and how?

REFERENCES

Acemoglu, Daron and James Robinson. 2012. *Why Nations Fail.* New York: Crown Books.

Akram, Fares and Jodi Rudoren. 2013. "To Shape Young Palestinians, Hamas Creates its Own Textbooks." *New York Times* November 4: A1.

Ansolabehere, Stephen, John de Figueredo, and James Snyder. 2003. "Why Is There So Little Money in American Politics?" *Journal of Economic Perspectives* 17, 105–130.

Bachrach Peter and Morton S. Baratz. 1962. "The Two Faces of Power." *American Political Science Review* 56: 947–952.

Bartels, Larry. 2010. *Unequal Democracy.* Princeton, NJ: Princeton University Press.

Baumgartner, Frank R., Jeffrey M. Berry, Marie Hojnacki, David C. Kimball, and Beth L. Leech. 2009. *Lobbying and Policy Change: Who Wins, Who Loses, and Why.* Chicago: University of Chicago Press.

Berman, Sheri. 2003. "Islamism, Revolution, and Civil Society." *Perspectives on Politics* 1 (2): 257–272.

Blyth, Mark. 2002. *Great Transformations: Economic Ideas and Institutional Change in the Twentieth Century.* Cambridge: Cambridge University Press.

Bonikowski, Bart and Noam Gidron. (nd). "Populist Claims-Making in U.S. Presidential Elections, 1952–1996." Unpublished manuscript.

Broockman, David. 2012. "The 'Problem of Preferences': Medicare and Business Support for the Welfare State." *Studies in American Political Development* October: 83–106.

Cameron, Charles. 2000. *Veto Bargaining.* Cambridge: Cambridge University Press.

Carpenter, Daniel P. 2001. *The Forging of Bureaucratic Autonomy: Reputations, Networks, and Policy Innovation in Executive Agencies, 1862–1928.* Princeton, NJ: Princeton University Press.

Clark, William Roberts, Matt Golder, and Sona N. Golder. 2007. "Power and Politics: Insights from an Exit, Voice and Loyalty Game." Unpublished manuscript.

Converse, Philip E. 1964. "The Nature of Belief Systems in Mass Publics." In *Ideology and Discontent*, ed. David E. Apter. New York: Free Press.

Cox, Gary W. and Mathew D. McCubbins. 1993. *Legislative Leviathan: Party Government in the House.* Berkeley: The University of California Press.

Crenson, Matthew A. 1971. *The Un-Politics of Air Pollution: A Study of Non-Decision-Making in the Cities.* Baltimore, MD: Johns Hopkins University Press.

Ellis, Christopher and James A. Stimson. 2012. *Ideology in America.* Cambridge: Cambridge University Press.

Erikson, Robert, Michael Mackuen, and James Stimson. 2002. *The Macro Polity.* Cambridge: Cambridge University Press.

Eskridge, William N. and John Ferejohn. 2001. "Super-Statutes." *Duke Law Journal* 50 (5): 1215–1276.

Esping-Andersen, Gosta. 1985. *States against Markets.* Princeton, NJ: Princeton University Press.

Esping-Anderson, Gosta. 1990. *The Three Worlds of Welfare Capitalism.* Cambridge: Polity Press.

Franzese, Robert J. 1999. "Partially Independent Central Banks, Politically Response Governments, and Inflation." *American Journal of Political Science* 7 (1): 681–706.

Friedrich, Carl. 1963. *Man and His Government: An Empirical Theory of Politics.* New York: McGraw Hill.

Gaventa, John. 1982. *Power and Powerlessness.* Champaign-Urbana, IL: University of Illinois Press.

Gilens, Martin. 2012. *Affluence and Influence: Economic Inequality and Political Power in America.* Princeton, NJ: Princeton University Press.

Gilens, Martin and Benjamin I. Page. 2014. "Testing Theories of American Political Elites, Interest Groups, and Average Citizens." *Perspectives on Politics* 12 (3): 564–581.

Gourevitch, Peter A. 1986. *Politics in Hard Times: Comparative Responses to International Economic Crises.* Ithaca, NY: Cornell University Press.

Gruber, Lloyd. 2000. *Ruling the World: Power Politics and the Rise of Supranational Institutions.* Princeton, NJ: Princeton University Press.

Hacker, Jacob and Paul Pierson. 2002. "Business Power and Social Policy: Employers and the Formation of the American Welfare State." *Politics and Society* 30: 277–325.

Hacker, Jacob and Paul Pierson. 2010. *Winner-Take-All Politics: How Washington Made the Rich Richer—and Turned Its Back on the Middle Class.* New York: Simon and Schuster.

Hacker, Jacob and Paul Pierson. 2014. "After the 'Master Theory': Downs, Schattschneider, and the Case for Policy-Focused Political Analysis." *Perspectives on Politics* 12(3): 643–662.

Hall, Peter A., ed. 1989. *The Political Power of Economic Ideas: Keynesianism across Nations* Princeton, NJ: Princeton University Press.

Hall, Peter A. and David Soskice, eds. 2001. *Varieties of Capitalism: The Institutional Foundations of Comparative Advantage.* London: Oxford University Press.

Huber, Evelyn and John Stephens. 2001. *Development and Crisis of the Welfare State.* Chicago: University of Chicago Press.

Huber, Evelyn and John Stephens. 2012. *Democracy and the Left: Social Policy and Inequality in Latin America.* Chicago: University of Chicago Press.

Iversen, Torben, Tom Cusack, and David Soskice. 2007. "Economic Interests and the Origins of Electoral Systems." *American Political Science Review* 101 (3): 373–391.

Keyssar, Alex. 2000. *The Right to Vote.* New York: Basic Books.

King, Desmond and Rogers Smith. 2012. *Still a House Divided: Race and Politics in Obama's America.* Princeton, NJ: Princeton University Press.

Korpi, Walter. 1985. "Power Resources Approach vs. Action and Conflict: On Causal and Intentional Explanations in the Study of Power." *Sociological Theory* 3 (2): 31–45.

Lang, Kurt and Gladys Engel Lang. 2012. "What Is This Thing We Call Public Opinion? Reflections on the Spiral of Silence." *International Journal of Public Opinion Research* 24 (3): 368–386.

Lukes, Stephen. 1974. *Power: A Radical View.* London: Macmillan.

McKelvey, Richard. 1976. "Insensitivities in Multidimensional Voting Models and Some Implications for Agenda Control." *Journal of Economic Theory* 12 (3): 472–482.

Mayhew, David. 2002. *Electoral Realignments: A Critique of an American Genre.* New Haven, CT: Yale University Press.

Meltzer, Allan H. and Scott F. Richard. 1981. "A Rational Theory of Government." *Journal of Political Economy* 89 (5): 914–927.

Moe, Terry M. 2005. "Power and Political Institutions." *Perspectives on Politics* 3: 215–233.

Moe, Terry M. 2011. *Special Interest: Teachers Unions and America's Public Schools.* Washington, D.C.: Brookings Institution Press.

Noel, Hans. 2013. *Political Ideologies and Political Parties in America.* Cambridge: Cambridge University Press.

Noelle-Neumann, Elisabeth 1974. "The Spiral of Silence: A Theory of Public Opinion." *Journal of Communication* 24 (2): 43–51.

Patashnik, Eric. 2008. *After Reform.* Princeton, NJ: Princeton University Press.

Pierson, Paul. 2004. *Politics in Time: History, Institutions and Social Analysis.* Princeton, NJ: Princeton University Press.

Pierson, Paul 2006. "Public Policies as Institutions." In *Rethinking Political Institutions: The Art of the State,* ed. Ian Shapiro, Steven Skowronek, and Daniel Galvin. New York: New York University Press, 114–131.

Pierson, Paul. 2015. "Power and Path Dependence." In *Advances in Comparative Historical Analysis,* ed. James Mahoney and Kathleen Thelen. Cambridge: Cambridge University Press.

Rueschemeyer, Dietrich, Evelyn Huber Stephens, and John D. Stephens. 1992. *Capitalism Development and Democracy.* Chicago: University of Chicago Press.

Schattschneider, Elmer Eric. 1960. *The Semisovereign People: A Realist's View of Democracy in America.* New York: Holt, Rinehart and Winston.

Schlozman, Sidney Verba and Henry Brady. 2012. *The Unheavenly Chorus: Unequal Political Voice and the Broken Promise of American Democracy.* Princeton, NJ: Princeton University Press.

Siegel, Reva B. (2008). "Dead or Alive: Originalism as Popular Constitutionalism in *Heller.*" *Harvard Law Review* 122: 191–245.

Skowronek, Stephen. 1993. *The Politics Presidents Make: Leadership from John Adams to Bill Clinton.* New York: Cambridge University Press.

Smith, Mark. 2000. *American Business and Political Power.* Chicago: University of Chicago Press.

Starr, Paul. 2014. "Three Degrees of Entrenchment: Power, Policy, Structure." Princeton University Department of Sociology. Unpublished Manuscript.

Thelen, Kathleen. 2004. *How Institutions Evolve: The Political Economy of Skills in Comparative-Historical Perspective.* New York: Cambridge University Press.

Wuthnow, Robert. 1989. *Communities of Discourse: Ideology and Social Structure in the Reformation, the Enlightenment, and European Socialism.* Cambridge, MA: Harvard University Press.

Zaller, John. 1992. *The Nature and Origins of Mass Opinion.* New York: Cambridge University Press.

CHAPTER 8

IDEAS AND HISTORICAL INSTITUTIONALISM

MARK BLYTH, ODDNÝ HELGADÓTTIR, AND WILLIAM KRING

WHY have a chapter on ideas and historical institutionalism in this handbook? The relationship between ideas as an analytical concept and historical institutionalism as a body of work is not as clear cut as it is between the concepts of power, critical junctures, and path dependence, all of which are central to the concerns of contemporary historical institutionalism and feature heavily in the chapters in this handbook. Instead, as this chapter demonstrates, ideas have a rather peculiar relationship to historical institutionalism that can perhaps be described as a case of "unconscious uncoupling."[1]

As we detail in the first part of this chapter, there was indeed an opening to ideas in historical institutionalism in the mid- to late 1990s. Yet despite this opening, ideas as core analytic variables in historical institutional scholarship, as Henry Farrell and Martha Finnemore (Chapter 34, this volume) put it, "largely withered away" by the turn of the millennium. The question is of course, why? We argue that a significant minority of the "ideational" scholars that appeared in the mid-1990s, especially in comparative politics, sought to situate their work within historical institutionalism, seeing their work as a progressive extension of it. Yet most historical institutionalist work around this same period chose not to incorporate the concerns of this literature into its research program for three reasons.

In brief, in the 1990s ideas, like culture, were seen by historical institutionalism theorists as rather suspicious variables for mainstream Political Science research. As such, turning to embrace them was a risky endeavor. Second, the materialist ontology employed by the majority of historical institutionalist scholars around this same period, coupled with the desire of those scholars to engage with rational choice scholars, further limited any potential engagement with ideas. Third, the nature of the intervention by ideational scholars themselves helped close the door from the other side of the engagement. The story of ideas and institutions is then one of "unconscious uncoupling" between ideationalists and materialists *and* one of a proposed relationship that could never really prosper, at least on the terms originally offered by the ideationalists.

These contentions are revealed by the pattern of citations analyzed and network-mapped in this chapter. This analysis of highly cited scholarship from both ideational and historical institutionalism scholars reveals two interrelated outcomes. First, early ideational scholars indeed sought to engage key historical institutionalist works. Second, early historical institutionalists chose to target key rational choice scholars rather than engage with ideational scholars. The network analysis reveals very little "backflow" in the citations: it is largely unidirectional across the map from ideationalists to historicists to rationalists.[2]

Despite this "unconscious uncoupling," this chapter details in its second section how interest in ideas did *not* in fact "largely wither away." Rather, the turn to ideas that this engagement was a part of had roots in many other areas, such as constructivism in international relations theory and economic sociology, which continued to grow. Meanwhile, an engagement with ideas, on the practical level of everyday scholarship, continued at the "frontier" of historical institutionalism research. Indeed, a close reading of historical institutionalism scholarship from this period shows that the break was never total. In what follows we show how more recent scholarship in historical institutionalism, and at the frontier of other fields, has increasingly turned to ideas, which suggests that a new and more "conscious re-coupling" between ideas and institutions may be on the cards for historical institutionalism.

The third and final section of this chapter reflects back on some key contributions to this volume to demonstrate the potential pay-off to such a rapprochement. This is especially apparent in what we term the "agency-problem" endemic in current work, a problem that becomes especially germane in an increasingly global and uncertain world characterized by multi-level governance problems and systemic crises. So while the conceptual and philosophical tensions that lay in bringing ideas and historical institutionalism together a decade or more ago may remain there today, this time around there is more reason to hope that the two strands of research inform each other.

Who Talks Ideas and Who Talks Institutions? And Do They Talk to Each Other?

One way to investigate the apparent neglect of ideas within historical institutionalism is to create a network map of citations between different scholarly communities. To do this we searched Google Scholar for the five most-cited self-identified historical institutionalists and the five most-cited self-identified ideas scholars. We then drew from each community their most highly cited contributions that had institutions, ideas and/or theory development of these issues as a core contribution. Finally we mapped citation patterns found in these publications.[3] We are particularly interested in "most-cited" pieces by "most-cited" scholars since they give us a data-driven picture of what the field of historical institutionalism considers its core concerns over time. Given that citation is in part a function of longevity, with earlier pieces garnering more cites, this criterion has the added advantage of focusing on pieces that continue to be cited as central to the historical institutionalism and ideas canon.

Network maps are composed of two parts: "nodes," which in our case represent individual scholars, and "ties" or "edges," which here represent one scholar citing another. In network maps, as Farrell and Quiggin have recently noted, "the most relevant features of network topology are the number of links between individuals, or nodes, within the network, the degree to which they are clustered into densely connected sub-networks, and variance in degree" (Farrell and Quiggin 2013, 8). Here the authors refer to a common measure of *network centrality*—degree—which is one way of helping us locate the most influential nodes in a network. Specifically, *degree* refers to the number of ties that any given node has to other nodes in the network.[4] The most cited actors, then, have the highest degree and determine the character of the network and thus the tenor and direction of the field of knowledge.

Figure 8.1 shows the overall map of citations in the historical institutionalism/ideas scholarship network. Historical institutionalists are grouped on the left (white) and ideational scholars are grouped on the right (light gray). As noted, historical intuitionalists cite rational choice theorists (dark gray) frequently. Conversely historical institutionalism scholars very rarely cite ideationalists. Ideationalists, on the other hand, cite both the other groups, though mainly historical institutionalism scholars. Scholars that do not fall into one of these three categories are grouped together in a final miscellaneous category (black). This map is directed, which means that the direction of the relationship matters—citing and being cited, after all, is not the same. Nodes in the network are weighted by in-degree, so that their size indicates the number of times the individual they represent is cited. Peter Hall has the highest in-degree, followed by Paul Pierson and Theda Skocpol who share the same score. Douglass North and Kathleen Thelen come next and also share the same score. Thus, out of the five most cited scholars in the network none are ideas scholars while four are historical intuitionalists and one is a rational choice theorist.[5]

Figure 8.2, which shows the citation flow between historical institutionalism and ideas scholars in a more simplified form, clarifies the relationship between the two camps by removing relationships of less than five citations. In the historical institutionalism group Kathleen Thelen, Paul Pierson, Peter Hall, and Sven Steinmo are all major nodes. Peter Hall is central to the entire network, which is not surprising given his continuing work on both ideas and institutions. Ideational scholars Mark Blyth, Colin Hay, and Vivien Schmidt cluster together on the right. John Campbell, an ideas scholar but a sociologist, is closely tied to nodes in both camps, but particularly to historical institutionalism. This simplified map of the most cited scholars shows once again that while ideas scholars regularly cite historical institutionalism literature, the reverse is not the case.[6]

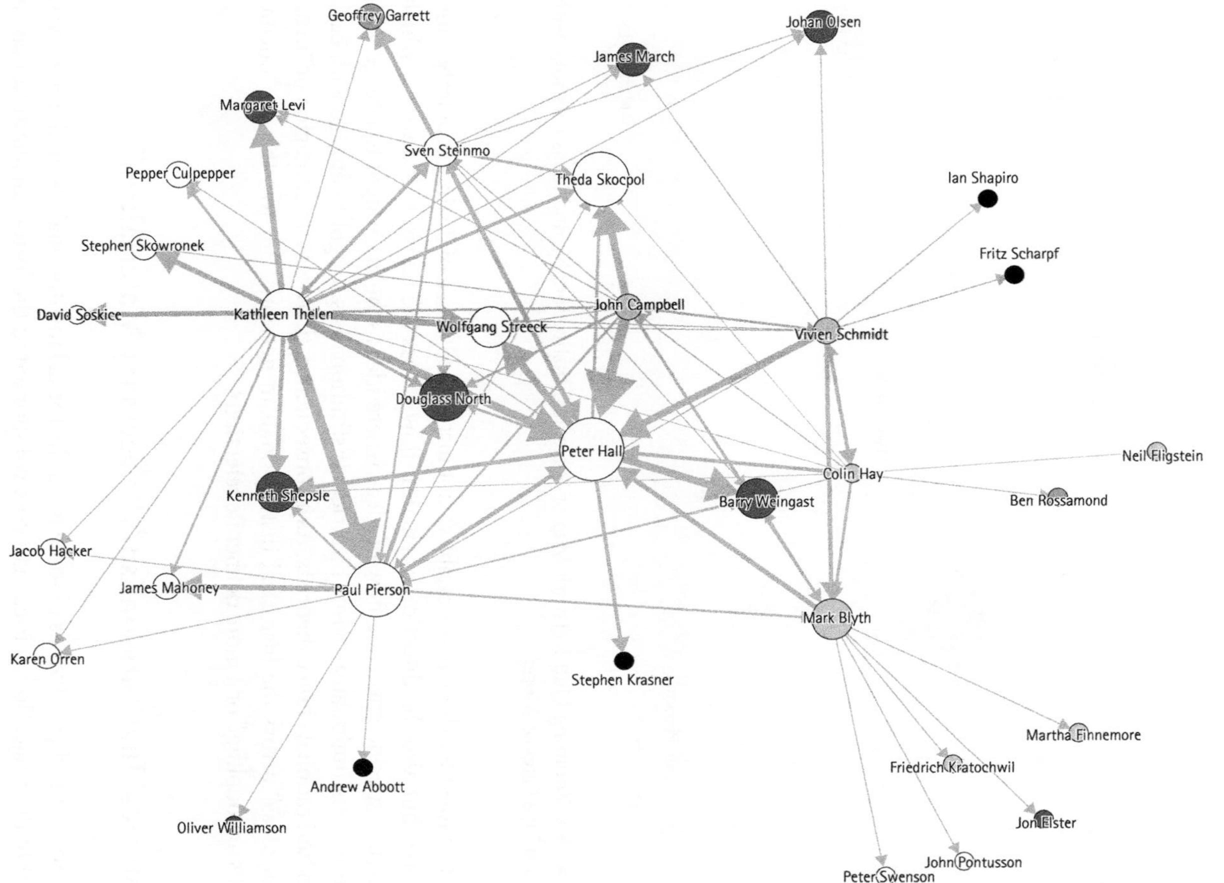

FIGURE 8.1 A Network Map of Historical Institutionalist and Ideas Citations

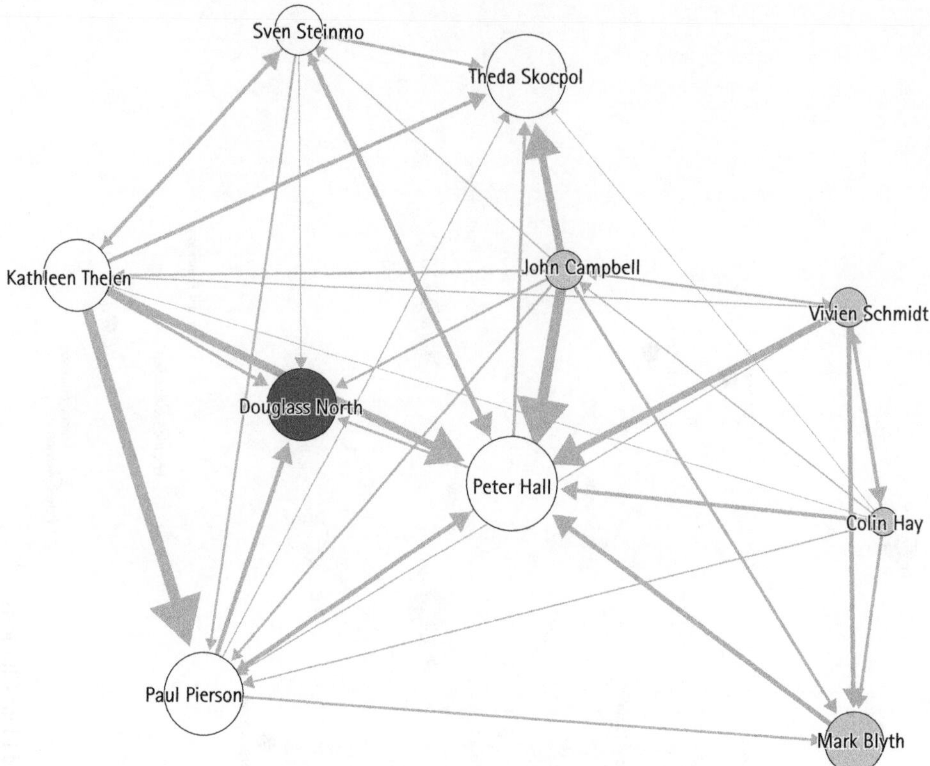

FIGURE 8.2 Zooming Out: Network Map of Historical Institutionalist and Ideas Citations with Edges of Five Cites or More:

Taken together these maps establish not just the existence of distinct scholarly communities but also the direction of citation-flow across the network as a whole, which suggests a specific epistemic flow of ideas where ideas scholars sought to engage with historical institutionalists while historical institutionalists sought to engage with each other and rational choice theorists. As a consequence, there was no contagion of "ideas about ideas" across the historical institutionalism network. But was this an "unconscious uncoupling," or a more deliberate rejection?

Historical Institutionalism's "Necessary Materialism"

The structuralist proclivities of some major historical institutionalists no doubt played a part in their rejection of ideas as a core component in the historical institutionalism toolbox. As the editors of this handbook note, emerging from the avowedly materialist school of "state theory" of the 1980s, early historical institutionalism scholars transplanted this ontology into historical institutionalism. As Theda Skocpol put it in 1995, "I do not think that institutions are ... systems of meaning or normative frameworks"

(105). Similarly, Kathleen Thelen's widely cited *Annual Review* piece from 1999 argued that, "the divide between rational choice and historical institutionalism is giving way to a divide between materialist-oriented analysis and norm-oriented analysis" (380). Emblematic of which side of the divide Thelen saw as representing the future of historical institutionalism, that same piece contains just one reference to ideas scholarship in the work of Vogel alongside nineteen references to the more materialist work of Pierson. More recently, but in the same vein, Streeck and Thelen argue that institutions are "formalized rules" and as a consequence they explicitly reject a view of institutions as "shared cognitive templates that some sociologists associate with institutions" (2005, 10–11).

One reason for this hewing to the materialist/structuralist ontology was the politics of the discipline in the 1990s. As Adcock, Bevir, and Stimson (2007, 86) note, the need to differentiate what was a then inchoate body of work in comparative politics as the effective opposition to the much-feared "hegemonic takeover" of the discipline of Political Science by rational choice theorists seemed to necessitate an equally no-nonsense materialist response. Ideas were then not seen to be a reliable weapon in this struggle and the citation flow from ideas to historical institutionalism to rational choice theorists seems to lend weight to this factor.

A second and perhaps more fundamental reason was that for institutions to have causal primacy over the individuals that occupy them at any moment, they had to be, logically, both anterior and ontologically prior to those individuals. In brief, if rational choice institutionalism was all about how agents (ontologically prior) chose structures, which resulted in a weak theory of institutions, then historical institutionalism, to have a strong theory of institutions, had to take the position where institutions (ontologically prior) structured choices independent of agent preferences. This necessitates taking institutions as both prior (structuralism) and as real (materialism). If historical institutionalism did not take that position then institutions could be anything, and therefore nothing.

Ideas scholars, whether constructivists concerned with norms or cognitivists concerned with frames, have no need to ground institutions in a material ontology. While they too see institutions as prior to the individuals that inhabit them, they instead view institutions as established norms, routines, practices, etc., rather than the formal rules that are the elaboration of those practices. To take one example, a central bank matters for historical institutionalism scholars because of how its constitution and agents' prior choices within those institutions limit possible future actions. In contrast, central banks matter for ideational scholars because of central bankers' belief in time inconsistency and the NAIRU, which in turn shapes its constitution, its institutions, and its subsequent choices. As the editors of this handbook note, early historical institutionalism had largely "structural and materialist features" (Fioretos, Falleti, and Sheingate, Chapter 1, this volume). Yet even in combination these two factors cannot explain all of the variation in which we are interested. To explain the residual we need to examine the content of ideational scholars' interventions and how they "unconsciously uncoupled" even as they thought they were becoming ever more engaged.

The Problem, the Proposal, and the Rejection

The literature on ideas that emerged in the mid- to late 1990s sought to be both a part of historical institutionalism and something quite apart from it. The first strand of this literature that directly engaged historical institutionalism came out of a broader engagement with the contending "new institutionalisms" of the period. Blyth (1997) identified the core problem, echoed today in James Conran and Kathleen Thelen (Chapter 3, this volume), that the two schools of institutional analysis that had emerged by the end of the 1980s, broadly, rational choice institutionalism and historical institutionalism, each had problems that were the inverse of the other.

For rational choice theorists, the lack of structure in their models, in particular, the problem of multiple equilibria in repeated games, suggested an endless cycling of choices that was quite at odds with the stability our world seemed to actually exhibit. The proposed solution, invoking institutions as "chosen structures" designed to minimize transaction costs, increase information flows, and facilitate Pareto-superior outcomes solved the problem, but at the cost of making these invoked institutions less than convincingly institutional. After all, if institutions are simply chosen structures, why choose to accept their dictates? Power, paths, and the weight of history, the "meat and potatoes" of historical institutionalism, were all conspicuous by their absence in such models.

Historical institutionalism instead took the position that institutions were much more than chosen structures. They were instead ontologically real (*qua* material) entities in their own right that "structured choices" in a more profound way, but how exactly? Early works seemed to operate with a kind of implicit socialization model, where actors' exposure to an institution's routines, plus its longevity, altered the preferences of the agents therein, which in turn explained cross-national variation in responses to common shocks (see for example Steinmo, Thelen, and Longstreth 1992; Hall 1986). As Steinmo put it in an early statement, "interests ... [do not] ... have substantive meaning if abstracted from the institutional context in which humans define them" (1989, 502). Interpretation (agents' *ideas* about their interests) and socialization looms large in this version of events. Yet while insightful, this position created a problem that was the mirror image of that encountered by rationalists. If institutions structure agents' choices so completely, why would the agents inside these institutions ever get the urge to change their environment? Both schools, in short, lacked an endogenous theory of change, which has remained the holy grail of institutional analysis ever since, and this is where ideas scholars entered into the frame.

Ideas scholars thought that they could supply that endogenous factor to historical institutionalism. They proposed, broadly, that if agents had different ideas about their environment, they could, as economist Dani Rodrik recently put it, change the "political transformation frontier" and alter the path of institutional development (2014). But to preserve the structuring role of institutions, ideas could only prove transformative in certain moments and under certain conditions. This of course begged the question as to the nature of those moments and conditions.

One answer was given by John Campbell (2004), who looked to the cognitive (micro) and normative (macro) dimensions of ideas and mapped those against forms of explicit argument and the types of background assumption present in policy debates in order to typologize when and where ideas become causally important. Mark Blyth (2002) and Kathleen McNamara (1998) looked to moments of institutional destabilization and uncertainty as the critical juncture when institutions lose their power and ideas come to the fore. But historical institutionalists were not in the main interested in buying what was on offer. Partly this was because of their already noted commitment to a more materialist ontology. After all, ideas could only be reflections of those underlying institutions, even in the moment of their failure. But the rejection was also due to the terms of the offer itself.

How Ideas Scholars Burned the Bridge They Built

Blyth (1997) cautioned that although invoking ideas as a mechanism of endogenous change in historical materialism was attractive, invoking ideas *only* to solve the problem of explaining endogenous change within institutional theory risked reducing ideas to a "helper-app" for institutionalism. He implored scholars to "take ideas seriously" as objects of investigation in their own right. However, in doing so he not so subtly elevated ideas above institutions as an explanatory concept and made them ontologically prior. What mattered were the ideas expressed in the moment of uncertainty, not the institutions themselves, except to the extent that they limited the set of possible ideas expressed in that moment. As a consequence, rather than expanding the space for ideas to play a role within historical institutionalism, his intervention may have served to reduce it.

Similarly, a critical exchange that further narrowed the space for synthesis between ideas scholars and historical institutionalists occurred between Peter Hall and Rosemary Taylor (1996), on the one hand, and Colin Hay and Daniel Wincott (1998), on the other. Hall and Taylor compared historical, rationalist, and sociological institutionalisms in order to ascertain what potential there was for integrating the insights of each literature. Hall and Taylor saw the real dividing line between approaches as a calculus approach (rational choice) and a cultural approach (historical and sociological) to institutions, with historical institutionalism more satisfactorily harmonizing both approaches. They further argued that as an approach historical institutionalism was more open to the influence of each of the other schools, including factors such as ideas and beliefs, thereby being best situated to benefit from the gains-in-trade of mutual engagement.

Hay and Wincott took strong issue with this stance, arguing that Hall and Taylor's desire to locate both calculus and culture within historical institutionalism confused distinct social ontologies that represented "an intractable divide" between "incompatible approaches to institutional analysis" (Hay and Wincott 1998, 953). Invoking what they saw as Steinmo and Thelen's original conception of historical institutionalism, Hay and Wincott argued that historical institutionalism has a distinctive dual ontology that sees institutions as both constraining and enabling of action (955).

Unfortunately, in placing this agency-structure problem at the heart of historical institutionalism, Hay and Wincott inadvertently replicated the original institutionalist dilemma noted above: if institutions constrain, how can they enable, and vice versa? Or, in this case, if institutions are resources, how can they also be constraints, and vice versa? Hay's answer, as seen in his later work, was to embrace ideas ever more fully and develop a distinct constructivist institutionalism as a way to resolve this structural dualism (see, e.g., Hay 2007). Doing so, which was implicit in both this piece and in Blyth's prior engagement, was however a step too far for most historical institutionalists and the door for engagement closed a little more.

A third set of interventions all but shut that door, again despite the ostensible intentions of the author, Vivien Schmidt (2002, 2010). Schmidt not only sought to take ideas seriously, she sought to bring "discourse" back in too—with all of the irrational angst that this supposedly "post-structuralist" term connotes in the American academy. Yet Schmidt's key theoretical claim was derived through a quite standard historical institutionalist comparison of policy reforms in the UK, France, and Germany. Where Schmidt differed was that she held exogenous shocks, institutional alignments, and path dependencies, the usual historical institutionalist toolbox, to be insufficient to explain actual reform trajectories in these states.

For Schmidt, policy and institutional reforms only worked when, given the institutions of the political system (single- or multi-actor), actors were able to develop specific communicative and coordinative discourses that enabled meaningful action within institutions. As such, single-actor polities, such as the UK, with majoritarian institutions, needed only a communicative discourse. More fragmented polities, such as Germany, needed a coordinative discourse as well as a communicative discourse to bring divergent players and institutions into line to affect reform by reshaping their preferences. In making these claims Schmidt still had institutions as central, and historical, but they were increasingly pushed into a secondary position behind the agency that ideas and discourse makes possible.

Perhaps all too quickly then, ideas, discourse, and processes of social construction had become the core problematique for the scholars that initially sought to engage with historical institutionalism. For such scholars supplying a theory of endogenous institutional change via ideas paradoxically suggested the necessity of transcending those institutions. As such, the space for a mutually rewarding relationship was narrowed from both sides—from the historical institutionalism materialists who felt uncomfortable with the notion of an ideational social science—and from the ideationalists who thought historical institutionalism should transcend its materialism to really be historical institutionalism.

Fruits of Engagement

By pressing their engagement with historical institutionalists, ideas scholars revealed deep philosophical problems in bringing ideas and institutions together such that the match, at least in the early stages, was set up to fail. Yet what both sets of theorists were trying to do was the same thing: to open up the space for an approach that can explain both political stasis and change simultaneously. Thankfully, as is usual in Political Science, it's the empirical work that goes on below the ostensibly higher register of theory that makes the most progress. So, despite this failure to couple at a theoretical level, work that combined ideas and institutions continued apace at a practical level. To show this we highlight examples from comparative politics, American political development (APD), and international relations that manage to do in practice what apparently could not be done in theory—that is, to bring ideas and institutions together under the auspices of historical institutionalism.

Ideas in Comparative Politics

Arguably, the first significant step in advancing the importance of ideas as causal variables in historical institutionalism analysis was Sheri Berman's *The Social Democratic Moment*. Berman employs both ideas and institutions to explain why the interwar German Social Democratic Party (SPD) did not even attempt to fight Germany's economic crisis through remedial policies when in government: a position that ended up handing power to the Nazis. The answer, argues Berman, was "each party's long held ideas and the distinct policy legacies [that] ideas helped to create," which acted as a cognitive mechanism for pathological path-dependent policymaking (1998, 7). In this work Berman implicitly reformulates path dependence to be less a material attribute of an institution, the typical historical institutionalism frame, and more a process of cognitive-locking driven by deeply held ideas. But those ideas, she is careful to note, are nonetheless engendered by particular institutional settings that change only slowly over time. As such, Berman is able to show us how ideas and institutions can usefully work in tandem rather than be served as mutually exclusive choices.

A few years later, Erik Bleich showed how policymaking in the area of race relations in the UK and France, where, for example, acts construed as racist were dealt with as either a civil or a criminal matter, or by non-governmental or governmental agencies, was best explained by the race frames operationalized in different national state bureaucracies. Here ideas appear as frames, defined as the "cognitive and moral maps that orient an actor within a policy sphere" (Bleich 2003, 26). Bleich notes that such frames serve political interests to be sure, but they also constitute them in an evolving policy space. As Bleich put it, "frames can have a causal effect on actions, but at the same time actors are free to maneuver within the structure of ideas and to attempt to manipulate them for their own purposes" (31). Bleich therefore does what Hay and Wincott warned was impossible within an historical institutionalism framework. He shows us that ideas are the medium that allows institutions to be both constraints and resources for agents as agents struggle over and with frames in a particular institutional context.

Building upon Vivien Schmidt's work, Mark Vail (2009) sought to explain the significant institutional changes that occurred in France and Germany in the 2000s despite these states being the archetypal "frozen" welfare states predicted by some historical institutionalism scholars. Vail finds instead a great deal of institutional change occurring as both states moved from dirigisme and corporatism respectively, to what he terms an agenda of "managed austerity." Key here once again is how ideas come into play, this time in locating how "shifts in political bargaining"—the basis of political coalitions and thus institutional transformations—"arise from … how actors *interpret* these interests" in moments of uncertainty over possible reform paths (Vail 2009, 18, author's emphasis). Highlighting how "the gradual redefinition of the narratives of the existing political-economic context" enables actors to produce major institutional shifts over time, Vail demonstrates how historical institutionalism's focus on gradualist political strategies such as layering and drift may have ideational micro-foundations. That is, actors have to have an idea as to what they want to residualize or layer, and why, with institutional reform not being predictable from the material context alone.

Ideas in American Politics

APD, which may be thought of as a "companion project" to historical institutionalism, emerged in the late 1980s and early 1990s as "an intellectual insurgency" (Bensel, quoted in Kersh 2005, 341) against the same kinds of rationalist strictures that Adcock, Bevir, and Stimson (2007) identified as a catalyst for historical institutionalism. From the outset the focus was decidedly substantive, rather than theoretical or methodological (Gerring 2003). Indeed, the pluralism of APD is such that Rogan Kersh argues that the fact of "multiple approaches to order and time" is one of three key characteristics of the subfield (2005, 336). Nevertheless, APD scholars have frequently employed both institutions and ideas to understand American politics.

For example, Rogers Smith (1999), countering the Hartzian notion that American politics are dominated by Lockean liberalism, posits instead that the central institutions of the American polity, including citizenship laws, the constitution, and political parties, were fundamentally shaped by two other ideas: republicanism and ascriptivism, with the latter including racism, sexism, class domination, and American nativism. Smith makes his case empirically, by combing through thousands of legal cases to show how these ideas buttressed the American political system through federal statutes and judicial decisions. While he sees both ideas and institutions as a function of the political needs of leaders that aspire to power, his empirical focus is nevertheless squarely on the interplay of ideas, identities and institutions.

Analyzing American nationalism, Desmond King (2006) argues that the American quest for "one people nationalism" in the face of racial and ethnic divisions gave rise to a strong state that pursued a host of contradictory policies and institutions, which further reified and reproduced group identities. Examples of the state reinforcing group identities, even as it pursued an inclusive nationhood, include "civilizing" missions for Native Americans, restrictive labor laws aimed at Chinese immigrants, the internment of Japanese Americans during World War II, and segregationist policies targeted at African Americans. King's work, like Smith's is more substantive than theoretical. Nevertheless the implicit co-constitution of identity, ideas and institutions is crucial to his argument.

The interplay of ideas and institutions is also clearly seen in the work of Robert Lieberman. Lieberman (2002) tackles how institutions can be understood both as resources for political change and the source of political stability. To address this he combines institutions and ideas into what he terms a distinct political order where "any political ... outcome is situated within a variety of ... institutional and ideological patterns" (2002, 701). For Lieberman, the layering together of these multiple institutional and ideological positions generates frictions for change when their elements embody contradictory logics. Upon such a view "at any given moment, politics is situated upon multiple paths," but it is only "When these paths are consonant ... the result may be stability; when they are not ... the result will more likely be instability and uncertainty" (Lieberman 2002, 701–702, 704).

Lieberman demonstrates his thesis empirically by showing us how the Equal Employment Opportunity Commission (EEOC), a weak set of actors, was positioned at the juncture of several institutional and ideological orders. Friction among these orders generated by electoral politics and the contradiction between color-blind and race-conscious affirmative action ideas coalesced to produce an outcome, the empowerment of the EEOC, that neither institutional nor ideational approaches alone could predict. Just as Berman in comparative politics shows how ideas and path dependence can be complementary concepts, Lieberman in APD shows us how ideas and intercurrence are together necessary and sufficient components of an historical institutionalism explanation.

Ideas in International and Comparative Political Economy

Crossing over to International Political Economy (IPE), Kathleen McNamara (1998) asked how states can have preferences over a set of monetary institutions with which they have no experience. After all, with no prior examples to draw upon, how can agents have a preference for *x* over *y* set of institutions? Applying this logic to European monetary cooperation, McNamara produced a three-step model that incorporates both institutions and ideas. First, the supply shocks and inflation of the 1970s destabilized existing institutions. Second, new monetarist and neoclassical ideas about policy credibility and inflation helped agents' expectations coalesce around more neoliberal ideas as to the appropriate role of the state in the economy. Third, European policy elites generalized from the experience of postwar Germany, whose positive outcomes were attributed to having an independent central bank, to the rest of Europe, with the end result being the euro and the European Central Bank. Here we see how the institutional destabilizations of the 1970s *plus* the new ideas of the period, together explain the path of institutional change.

In comparative political economy a similar tack is taken by Matthias Matthijs in his examination of postwar British economic policymaking (2012). Matthijs examines how Britain underwent two deep-seated institutional transformations when political elites successfully challenged the prevailing wisdom on how to govern the economy. UK Prime Ministers Clement Attlee and Margaret Thatcher were able to implement most of their political platforms while Edward Heath won the general election in 1970 promising radical change, only to fail in 1972. Similarly, Tony Blair's New Labour, winning a larger majority in 1997 than Attlee in 1945, failed to achieve a major break with the "Thatcherite" settlement. Matthijs combines Skowronek's notion of distinct political orders, Pierson's notion of path-dependence, and Blyth's notion of Knightian uncertainty to explain why, despite similar majorities and structural constraints, some British policymakers were able to effectively and convincingly "narrate" a crisis, which was critical in enabling them to make path-departing rather than path-dependent choices.

The now massive amount of work done in International Relations that falls under the rubric of constructivism originates from many of the shared concerns of those who identify more as ideational scholars. Indeed, while the line between the two has tended to grow less distinct over time they all still share a concern for institutions as critical components of their explanations. IPE scholars such as Nicolas Jabko have written to great effect about the "strategic constructivism" of the European Commission in what is otherwise a rather orthodox historical institutionalist framework (Jabko 2006). Similarly, Catherine Weaver (2007) analyzed the World Bank, where an internal organizational culture clashed with the imperatives of the bank's multiple external missions to produce an organizational culture characterized by a disconnect between what the bank says and what it does. Meanwhile, Michael Barnett and Martha Finnemore (1999) have blazed a trail with their pioneering work on the ideational power and pathologies of international organizations and of the importance of such variables in the study of global governance more generally.

Ideas beyond Political Science

Ideas scholarship that gives institutions and ideas co-equal billing now goes far beyond Political Science. The entire body of work known as economic sociology places ideas, frames, and other cognitive devices at the centre of their institutional analyses in studies as diverse as Jens Beckert's (2008) work on different national conceptions of intergenerational obligation *Inherited Wealth* and Marion Fourcade's (2009) path-breaking work showing how distinct national histories and consequent institutional cultures actually produce different, and differentially valued, forms of economic knowledge. Donald MacKenzie's (2005, 2006) work on derivatives pricing models, where the application of options pricing theory to the financial world changes the world of finance, gives us as clear an example—quantitatively measured—as one can get of ideas driving not just institutional change, but the institutional morphology of markets themselves.

In a somewhat ironic twist, some leading rational choice theorists (*qua* economists) have become the latest group of scholars eager to engage with ideas. As economics Nobel Laureate Douglass North put it, economics needs to be reformulated to understand how humans survive in an uncertain and non-ergodic world by sharing beliefs about how the world operates: "the 'reality' of a political-economic system is never known to anyone—but humans do construct elaborate beliefs about the nature of that 'reality' ... Th[ose] dominant beliefs ... overtime result in the accretion of an elaborate structure of institutions that determine economic and political performance" (North 2010, 2). Game theorist Avner Greif's analysis of the late medieval economic expansion takes a similar position, arguing that while "institutions are the engine of history" they take the form of ideational recombinative devices that "provide individuals with the cognitive, coordinative, normative, and informational micro-foundations ... [that] ... motivate them" (Greif 2006, 14, 399). Similarly, leading development economist Dani Rodrik has recently declared that it is only by "taking ideas into account ... [that we can] ... provide a more convincing account of political-economic life" (2014, 2). He argues such a move is vital since "the three components of the optimization problem [that lie at the heart of neoclassical economics]—preferences, constraints and choice variables—each rely on an implicit set of ideas" (Rodrik 2014, 4). Making an analogy between the production frontier of markets and politics, Rodrik models the elasticity of this frontier as shaped by the ability of agents to change other agents' perception of where the "political transformation frontier" lies through the strategic use of ideas. Again as Rodrik states, "the location and shape of the political transformation frontier depends upon the feasible set of elite actions—which is determined by the ideas that elites have about the range of strategies available to them" (Rodrik 2014, 15).

While these three theorists do not in any way represent the mainstream of the neoclassical tradition, they are nonetheless among the field's most prominent members. That they too are trying to tackle the relationship between ideas and institutions is indicative of an old line from John Steinbeck, "ideas are like rabbits. You get a couple and learn how to handle them and pretty soon you have a dozen." And, like rabbits, scholarship on ideas replicates and propagates across the frontier of historical institutionalism into a host of other fields. So where does all of this work on ideas and institutions in historical institutionalism and beyond leave the relationship between ideas and historical institutionalism today?

The Agency Problem and the Continuing Necessity of Ideas

Two reactions seem to typify the relationship between ideas and historical institutionalism today. The first suggests that despite a decade of mutual neglect, a closer engagement is possible, and warranted, as attested by the success of bringing ideas and institutions together within historical institutionalism and other areas. The second reaction is the default position of a continuing mutual disregard. Emblematic of this trend are recent moves on the ideas side to develop alternative conceptualizations of institutions, such as Schmidt's project of discursive institutionalism and Hay's constructivist institutionalism, both of which place primacy on ideas over institutions. Another version of this lies in recent attempts to define general frameworks for constructivist analyses in political economy that sidestep the concept of institutions in favor of the analysis of different mechanisms of social construction in complex systems, such as Abdelal et al. (2010). Such positions are sustainable, as the continuing growth of ideational scholarship make clear, but may also be regrettable. So, does it have to be this way? There is good cause to answer no, for two reasons.

First, as this volume demonstrates, despite major theoretical advances over the past decade or so, the core of contemporary historical institutionalism still struggles to explain endogenous change. In short, if there is only so far that materialist mechanisms can be invoked to generate determinate paths then something else has to be incorporated to do just that. This is why many of the historical institutionalism scholars take as the starting point of their research the fact that it is extremely difficult to explain change in complex systems without reference to the human capacity to create filters and frames to help them both understand their environment and build the institutions that simplify and stabilize that environment.

Second, as Farrell and Finnemore (Chapter 34, this volume) note, historical institutionalism has traditionally worked in bounded, relatively stable, national polities. In the twenty-first century such polities may become the global exception and not the global rule. An increasingly globalized world is an increasingly uncertain, volatile, interconnected, norm-governed, multi-level and multi-actor environment where the conditions that make historical institutionalism work in its classic cases may apply less and less.

In this regard recent work in historical institutionalism shows signs of such a shift becoming pronounced. In this volume, someone who has been central to both historical institutionalism and ideas scholarship, Peter Hall, clearly articulates such a position, arguing that it is quite reasonable to assume that "the ideas common to a community of discourse are likely to influence how an actor interprets the proposals she receives" (Hall, Chapter 2, this volume). Sven Steinmo (2010) makes an even stronger case for the centrality of ideas. He argues for an evolutionary approach where one does much more than just note the global macroeconomic context in which states operate and plug-in the institutions they have built to deal with external and internal pressures. What's missing for Steinmo is an analytic focus on actors that select ways to adapt to changing circumstances, with human agency, cognition and creativity being central. Lewis and Steinmo (2012) further this claim by stressing the fact that foregrounding human cognition as causal allows political actors to constantly generate new ideational variations that are then subjected to selection. This allows them to "bring human cognition and 'ideas' back into our understanding of change" (Lewis and Steinmo 2012, 316).

Alan Jacobs (2008) has also appealed to agency and cognition to explain institutional change. He focuses on the US Social Security program, an institution that imparted high short-term costs on a clearly defined group and only provided benefits in the long run, and should therefore have been politically contentious and potentially unstable from the outset. Yet the standard historical institutionalism model applied to this case sees continuity and not change due to path dependence and sunk costs as the key elements promoting stability. But Jacobs argues that the seeming stability of the program masks a lot of underlying volatility and endogenous change. He makes the case that agents within the institution who were disadvantaged by prevailing rules made changes. They exploited institutional ambiguities and challenged prevailing norms to advance their interests. Defenders of the status quo, forced to deal with such pressures, also reshaped the institution from the inside in reaction, again via rule changes and norm contests. The cumulative effect was a sometimes radical, if often difficult to discern, shift in the nature of the institution.

In a more recent monograph that compares pension systems across several cases, Jacobs (2011) fleshes this argument out in greater detail. A key claim therein is that since politicians, subject to bounded rationality and acting in a complex social world, cannot accurately predict the impact of their actions, their perceptions, ideas, and mental maps of policy cost and benefits are crucial to determining any course of action. Specifically, when they perceive pension plans as investments in future gains, rather than exorbitant current expenses, such plans are more likely to succeed.

But despite these interjections, historical institutionalism, especially in its understanding of mechanisms of change, remains resistant to such moves. For example, hewing to a materialist understanding of social processes, Conran and Thelen (Chapter 3, this volume) detail recent historical institutionalism work that posits stability and change as "two sides of the same coin," insofar as a theory of path dependence, for example, has within it an implicit theory of change. From this basis Conran and Thelen detail specific patterns of institutional layering, policy drift, and institutional conversion as historical institutionalism's major mechanisms of change, as does other work by Thelen and Mahoney that attempts to bring agency back in to explain change too (2008). All this is done without any explicit reference to ideas being necessary. But does this work nonetheless rest upon an unacknowledged ideational foundation? There are reasons to think that it does.

First of all, just as the inverse of theories of violence are not theories of peace, the absence of conditions that generate X outcomes does not mean X outcomes will in fact be generated given such absences. Omitted variable bias, compounding causes, non-linear dynamics caused by differential factor weighting due to changes in system dynamics and a host of other factors strongly suggest that it is highly likely that theories of change are not simply the inverse of theories of stasis. Indeed, and this is very important, the conditions of the former state cannot be simply translated to the conditions of the latter state if the major contention of historical institutionalism is actually correct, that causes are *historical* and vary over time. For the more materialist version of events to be true, time must in effect be reversible. If so, history, quite simply, cannot matter.

For history to matter the path forward has to be at least partially contingent, envisaged by real agents whose choices make such state-stable transformations quite unrealistic.[7] *Historical* causes mean that causes at T1 that occur change the system such that they cannot act as causes in the same way at T2. As such, a theory of stasis cannot also be a theory of change.

Second, as Hall notes in Chapter 2 in this volume, the idea that agents are constantly layering, creating drift, and transforming the very purposes of institutions makes it "difficult to understand why [institutions] should be seen as factors structuring behavior rather than simply as instruments in the hands of actors whose behavior is driven by something else." But if they are just that, such a position still begs what we term "the agency problem"—where one must always ask—"instruments to do what?" The material environment does not telegraph strategies into agents' heads, a point made by ideas scholars many years ago (Blyth 1997; Berman 1998). And as all of the work detailed above shows clearly, the choice to do X over Y in situation Z may be defined by and delimited to the institutional context—but it is never fully specified by it.

Tellingly however, when pushed, even more materialist versions of historical institutionalism have to go beyond materialism when they describe, for example, institutional conversion as a process that "occurs when rules on the books remain the same but are *interpreted* and *enacted* in new ways" (Conran and Thelen, Chapter 3, this volume, emphasis added). Or when "actors associated with an institution gradually change their *interpretation* of its rules ... without ... dismantling the formal institution itself" (Hall and Thelen 2009, 19). But surely interpretation is always and everywhere a mental event while enactment is always and everywhere a contingent event predicated on the former? If so, then references to processes of interpretation seem like smuggling a rather large ideational elephant into an otherwise neat materialist tent.

Rather than hiding the interpretive elephant in the classical historical institutionalism tent, let's admit that ideas need to be there to make the processes and mechanisms of gradual change into a deeper theory of ideas and institutions. Historical institutionalism may need to do this if it really is to continue as a leading research program. As Farrell and Finnemore argue in Chapter 34 in this volume, "historical institutionalism needs to engage more systematically with the role of norms and ideas" because the conditions that make historical institutionalism operationalizable, stable states with long lasting and slowly evolving complexes of institutions, may be a luxury for much of the world in the twenty-first century. Farrell and Finnemore, for example, note how much of the work that institutions do on the domestic level is in fact done by international governmental and non-governmental organizations through rather different, and much more obviously ideational processes, such as altering actors' preference functions through the shaping of policy ideas and expectations. Their studies of the behavior of the IMF and the thoroughly ideationally path dependent behavior of the ECB, which is busy fighting a crisis of inflation the middle of a policy-induced deflation, demonstrate how "ideas and expertise ... not only create power but discipline and direct it."

For historical institutionalism to grow, its practitioners may need to accept that ideational factors and mechanisms are coequal to those of layering, conversion, and the rest of the standard toolbox. If they do so, not only can they begin to engage a much broader literature that already does such work, and does it well, but they can finally build that endogenous theory of change they have been after for so long: yet this can only happen if they learn to embrace the elephant that is already present in the tent.

Conclusion

This chapter has argued that the relationship between ideas and historical institutionalism began as a story of "unconscious uncoupling," but that it does not have to end this way. Despite the initial engagement and subsequent break-up, a break-up that was caused by both sides, much hope remains for reconciliation. There are three reasons to be hopeful that a shift will take place from a "unconscious uncoupling" to a "friends with benefits" model. First, the growth of serious analyses within the broad tradition of historical institutionalism itself that takes both ideas and institutions equally seriously as explanatory complements provides evidence that the marriage can work. Second, among historical institutionalism scholars, the need to defend "the field" against rational choice has surely abated while, among ideas scholars, the need to maintain some kind of philosophical certainty as to the superiority of one variable over the other needs to be seen as the hindrance to learning and intellectual gains-in-trade that it actually is. As countless empirical works that use both concepts show, a little less philosophical certainty and more theoretical humility has a higher than average payoff.

Finally, and perhaps most important of all, even the most materialist of positions implicitly rests upon a theory of ideas or cognition to explain change. As Hall and Lamont (2013, 12) recently put it, any notion of sufficient explanation necessarily dispenses with the choice between "ideas or interests in the study of politics; rather, the contemporary condition is marked by the interaction between neoliberal ideas about states and markets and the material endowments of actors and groups." Replace the word "interests" above with the word "institutions" and Hall and Lamont have just summed up perfectly why the relationship discussed here needs to be strengthened. For that to happen, historical institutionalism scholars simply need to think that doing so is a good idea.

Notes

1. We thank Gwyneth Paltrow for this term.
2. This dynamic is not simply a function of time and "generational" differences between historical institutionalism and ideational scholarship. Although historical institutionalism took root earlier and ideational scholarship is to a great extent a reaction to it, the literature from each subgroup analyzed and network mapped here spreads out over roughly the same period. The earliest historical institutionalism work is from 1992 and

the most recent is from 2010, while the earliest ideas work is from 1997 and the most recent from 2010.

3. Self-identified in that these scholars either featured in this volume or have made distinct and highly cited theoretical contributions to this body of work. Those scholars are, in the historical institutionalism sample, Peter Hall, Kathleen Thelen, Paul Pierson, James Mahoney, and Sven Steinmo. In the ideas sample, Vivien Schmidt, Colin Hay, Mark Blyth, John Campbell, and Sheri Berman. All files and the underlying software used to generate the maps are available on request.
4. Citation networks, our target, are *directed networks* because the direction of the relationship—who does the citing, who is cited—matters. In directed networks it is important to differentiate between out-degree (the edges or relationships originating from any given node) and in-degree (the edges or relationships pointing to any given node). For citation analysis in-degree is usually a more telling indicator than out-degree as it reveals the number of other scholars citing the work of any given researcher.
5. Here we include five scholars rather than three because some scholars share the same score.
6. For this map only edges indicating five or more cites have been included to simplify the picture and underscore the division of these scholars into two distinct communities. The division of networks into different communities is important to observe because communities, tend to eliminate divergent opinions as actors have more ties within the community than outside it and interact mostly with likeminded individuals.
7. To take an example from the US civil rights movement, a structuralist can posit that eventually someone would have refused to give up their seat on the bus in Birmingham, but the fact that it was Rosa Parks that did it when she did it meant the path of change began at that moment, and not at any other, when the conditions of collective action would have been quite different.

References

Abdelal, Rawi, Mark Blyth, and Craig Parsons. 2010. *Constructing the International Political Economy*. Ithaca, NY: Cornell University Press.

Adcock, Robert, Mark Bevir, and Shannon C. Stimson. 2007. "Historicizing the New Institutionalism(s)." In *Modern Political Science: Anglo-American Exchanges Since 1880*, ed. Robert Adcock, Mark Bevir, and Shannon C. Stimson. Princeton, NJ: Princeton University Press, 259–289.

Barnett, Michael N. and Martha Finnemore. 1999. "The Politics, Power, and Pathologies of International Organizations." *International Organization* 53 (4): 699–732.

Beckert, Jens. 2008. *Inherited Wealth*. Princeton, NJ: Princeton University Press.

Berman, Sheri. 1998. *The Social Democratic Moment*. Cambridge, MA: Harvard University Press.

Bleich, Erik. 2003. *Race Politics in Britain and France: Ideas and Policymaking since the 1960s*. Cambridge and New York: Cambridge University Press.

Blyth, Mark M. 1997. "Any More Bright Ideas? The Ideational Turn of Comparative Political Economy." *Comparative Politics* 29 (2): 229–250.

Blyth, Mark M. 2002. *Great Transformations: Economic Ideas and Institutional Change in the Twentieth Century*. Cambridge: Cambridge University Press.

Blyth, Mark. 2006. "Great Punctuations: Prediction, Randomness, and the Evolution of Comparative Political Science." *American Political Science Review* 100 (04): 493–498.

Campbell, John L. 2004. *Institutional Change and Globalization*. Princeton, NJ: Princeton University Press.

Farrell, Henry and John Quiggin. 2013. "Consensus, Dissensus and Economic Ideas: The Rise and Fall of Keynesianism During the Economic Crisis." Unpublished Manuscript.

Fourcade, Marion. 2009. *Economists and Societies: Discipline and Profession in the United States, Britain, and France, 1890s to 1990s*. Princeton, NJ: Princeton University Press.

Gerring, John. 2003. "APD from a Methodological Point of View." *Studies in American Political Development* 17 (01): 82–102.

Greif, Avner. 2006. *Institutions and the Path to the Modern Economy: Lessons from Medieval Trade*. Cambridge and New York: Cambridge University Press.

Hall, Peter A. 1986. *Governing the Economy: The Politics of State Intervention in Britain and France*. New York: Oxford University Press.

Hall, Peter A. and Michelle Lamont. 2013. "Introduction." In *Social Resilience in the Neoliberal Era*, ed. Peter A. Hall and Michelle Lamont. Cambridge: Cambridge University Press, 1–34.

Hall, Peter A. and Rosemary C. R. Taylor. 1996. "Political Science and the Three New Institutionalisms." *Political Studies* 44 (5): 936–957.

Hall, Peter A. and Kathleen Thelen. 2009. "Institutional Change in Varieties of Capitalism." *Socio-Economic Review* 7: 19.

Hay, Colin. 2007. "Constructivist Institutionalism." In *The Oxford Handbook of Political Institutions*, ed. R. A. W. Rhodes, Sarah Binder, and Bert Rockman. Oxford: Oxford University Press, 56–74.

Hay, Colin and Daniel Wincott. 1998. "Structure, Agency and Historical Institutionalism." *Political Studies* 46 (5): 951–957.

Jabko, Nicolas. 2006. *Playing the Market: A Political Strategy for Uniting Europe, 1985–2005*. Ithaca, NY: Cornell University Press.

Jacobs, Alan M. 2008. "Policymaking as Political Constraint: Institutional Development in the U.S. Social Security Program." In *Explaining Institutional Change: Ambiguity, Agency, and Power*, ed. Kathleen Thelen and James Mahoney. Cambridge: Cambridge University Press, 94–131.

Jacobs, Alan. 2011. *Governing for the Long Term: Democracy and the Politics of Investment*. Cambridge: Cambridge University Press.

Kersh, Rogan. 2005. "The Growth of American Political Development: The View from the Classroom." *Perspectives on Politics* 3 (02): 335–345.

King, Desmond S. 2006. *The Liberty of Strangers: Making the American Nation*. New York: Oxford University Press.

Lewis, Orion A. and Sven Steinmo. 2012. "How Institutions Evolve: Evolutionary Theory and Institutional Change." *Polity* 44 (3): 314–339.

Lieberman, Robert C. 2002. "Ideas, Institutions, and Political Order: Explaining Political Change." *American Political Science Review* 96 (04): 697–712.

MacKenzie, Donald. 2005. "Opening the Black Boxes of Global Finance." *Review of International Political Economy* 12 (4): 555–576.

MacKenzie, Donald A. 2006. *An Engine, Not a Camera: How Financial Models Shape Markets*. Cambridge, MA: The MIT Press.

McNamara, Kathleen R. 1998. *The Currency of Ideas: Monetary Politics in the European Union*. Ithaca, NY: Cornell University Press.

Matthijs, Matthias M. 2012. *Ideas and Economic Crises in Britain from Attlee to Blair.* New York: Routledge.

North, Douglass C. 2010. *Understanding the Process of Economic Change.* Princeton, NJ: Princeton University Press.

Rodrik, Dani. 2014. "When Ideas Trump Interests: Preferences, Worldviews, and Policy Innovations." *Journal of Economic Perspectives* 28 (1): 189–208.

Schmidt, Vivien A. 2002. *The Futures of European Capitalism.* Oxford and New York: Oxford University Press.

Schmidt, Vivien A. 2010. "Taking Ideas and Discourse Seriously: Explaining Change through Discursive Institutionalism as the Fourth 'New Institutionalism.'" *European Political Science Review* 2 (01): 1–25.

Skocpol, Theda. 1995. "Why I Am a Historical Institutionalist." *Polity* 28 (1), 103–106.

Smith, Rogers M. 1999. *Civic Ideals: Conflicting Visions of Citizenship in U.S. History.* New Haven, CT: Yale University Press.

Steinmo, Sven. 1989. "Political Institutions and Tax Policy in the United States, Sweden, and Britain." *World Politics* 41 (04): 500–535.

Steinmo, Sven. 2010. *The Evolution of Modern States.* Cambridge: Cambridge Unveristy Press.

Steinmo, Sven, Kathleen Thelen, and Frank Longstreth, eds. 1992. *Structuring Politics: Historical Institutionalism in Comparative Analysis.* Cambridge: Cambridge University Press.

Streeck, Wolfgang and Kathleen Thelen. 2005. *Beyond Continuity: Institutional Change in Advanced Political Economies.* Oxford and New York: Oxford University Press.

Thelen, Kathleen. 1999. "Historical Institutionalism in Comparative Politics." *Annual Review of Political Science* 2 (1): 369–404.

Thelen, Kathleen R. 1999. *The Currency of Ideas: Monetary Politics in European Union.* Cornell Studies in Political Economy. Ithaca, NY: Cornell University Press.

Thelen, Kathleen and James Mahoney, eds. 2008. *Explaining Institutional Change: Ambiguity, Agency, and Power.* Cambridge: Cambridge University Press.

Vail, Mark. 2009. *Recasting Welfare Capitalism: Economic Adjustment in Contemporary France and Germany.* Philadelphia, PA: Temple University Press.

Weaver, Catherine. 2007. *Hypocrisy Trap: The World Bank and the Poverty of Reform.* Princeton, NJ: Princeton University Press.

PART III

COMPARATIVE POLITICS

Introduction

TULIA G. FALLETI

In Political Science, historical institutionalism developed first and foremost in the subfield of comparative politics. The chapters compiled by Steinmo, Thelen, and Longstreth in *Structuring Politics* (Cambridge University Press, 1992), a book that crystallized the historical institutional approach in the discipline, have their center in the comparative analysis of institutions, policies, and ideas across countries.

Several reasons explain the close affinity between historical institutionalism and comparative politics. First, the core political processes of comparative politics, such as state-building, democratization, or party system development, take a long time to unfold. The study of the historical record is thus essential to get the story right. Second, as Atul Kohli reminds us in the opening chapter in this part, institutions are wont to endure and historical institutionalism provides valuable analytical leverage to study them. The nation-state, political parties, constitutions, electoral systems, and corporatist institutions, among others, are created to last. Of course, not all do, but the study of institutions calls for a historical approach that can explain their origins, changes, and legacies. In fact, a historical institutional approach often unveils the social and political coalitions behind institutional formation and evolution, while at the same time specifying the multiple causal interactions between institutions and their relevant contexts. Third, the scholars of comparative politics study processes in which the sequence, timing, and pace of events are causally important. Temporality, in other words, is a key explanatory factor in most of the political processes that abound in comparative politics.

The chapters that follow nicely illustrate and elaborate upon this intimate relationship between the core topics and questions of comparative politics and historical institutionalism. With other sections focusing on the United States and Europe, this part's chapters center on the study of the developing world. The contributors combine expertise that spans Africa, Asia (including South Asia, Southeast Asia, and China), Latin America, and the Middle East.

The first two chapters elaborate on different aspects of the state. Atul Kohli studies the state's role as economic development promoter. He argues that the extent to which the state is successful at this task depends on colonial legacies and decolonization processes. Kohli's chapter combines an impressive breath of regional coverage with a sound and deep knowledge of the historical record. It opens by reviewing the role of the state in promoting economic development in the advanced industrial countries, a process that is then compared with the role of the state in countries of Africa, Latin America, and Asia.

Hillel David Soifer focuses on the building of state capacities and points to the explicit relationship between the studies of the state and historical institutionalism. Scholars of the state have used historical causes to explain state-building and applied concepts such as critical junctures and path dependence. Soifer argues there are missed opportunities, nonetheless. Scholars of historical institutionalism could, for example, provide better theories of state failure and conceptualizations and measurements of state strength. These are promising areas for future research on state capacities.

The chapter by Rodrigo Barrenechea, Edward L. Gibson, and Larkin Terrie demonstrates that while there is an intimate linkage between democratization studies and historical institutionalism, it has not been explicit. Democratization studies have applied the historical comparative method, considered institutions as key independent variables, and even used (explicitly or implicitly) the concepts of path dependence, critical junctures, and sequencing in their explanations. Yet, unlike the studies of the state, and with few exceptions, democratization studies have not made explicit use of the historical institutional framework. According to the authors, considerable room exists to advance the historical institutional approach in the study of democratization, particularly if future researchers adopt an episodic approach (as opposed to a transitology paradigm) and focus on the study of what they call *keystone institutions*, which are those with particularly important consequences for the long-term.

The chapter by Steven Levitsky and Lucan Way asks the flip-side question: Why are some party-based authoritarian regimes more durable than others? As in the case of Kohli's chapter, the historical record holds the key to the answer. Levitsky and Way argue that robust authoritarian institutions emerge out of periods of violent conflict, particularly social revolutions, which set regimes on one of two institutional paths (*revolutionary* or *counter-revolutionary*). Yet even durable party-based authoritarian regimes occasionally collapse. The founding institutional legacies may erode over time and a historical institutional approach can shed significant light on the mechanisms of reproduction that allow authoritarian regimes and parties to self-perpetuate and adapt or erode and collapse.

Focusing on political parties, Rachel Riedl shows the extraordinary leverage of the historical institutional approach. Citing numerous examples, Riedl analyzes the formation and institutionalization of party systems, the creation of parties in relation to social cleavages and coalitions, and the relationships between parties and other regime institutions such as the electoral system. In all these cases, she brings to the fore the contributions and insights of historical institutionalism and concludes with a number of intriguing and exciting questions and problems for future research on political parties.

Turning to social policies, Melanie Cammett and Aytuğ Şaşmaz offer an encompassing review of the literature on welfare provision in the developing world. Analyzing the relationships between welfare provision and social coalitions, production regimes, and state-building, Cammett and Şaşmaz stress the contributions of historical institutionalism and point to fruitful areas of future research. Finally, they highlight the importance of non-state welfare provision in the developing world.

Connected to the transformation of welfare regimes, the chapter by Teri Caraway zooms in on organized labor. Caraway reviews the foundational works of historical institutionalism in the studies of labor. Then, drawing from comparative and case studies spanning many countries of the Global South, she analyzes the role of organized labor in the adoption of neoliberal reforms, and their effects, in turn, on labor strength. Lastly, Caraway analyzes the role of unions during and after authoritarian regimes, proposing the concept of *legacy unions* (those state-sponsored unions created under authoritarianism that continue to operate under democracy). Like Levitsky and Way, Caraway prompts us to research the mechanisms of reproduction that explain when and why legacy unions adapt or perish.

Pushing the research agenda of historical institutionalism significantly forward, Kellee Tsai shows that the modalities of gradual institutional change recently conceptualized in historical institutionalism often take place through informal practices. Appealing to the mathematical image of the Möbius strip, Tsai argues that informal institutional aspects are present in all institutions, regardless of regime type, level of development, or state sanctioning of their legitimacy. Tsai proposes the concept of *adaptive informal institutions* and shows that informal institutions "comprise, subvert, and even facilitate reforms of formal institutions." Persuasively, Tsai incites historical institutionalist scholars to place informal institutions more straightforwardly in their research agendas.

These eight chapters provide readers with a comprehensive assessment of some of the most important topics and questions that historical institutionalism has addressed in comparative politics. Furthermore, the chapters point to new and promising questions and topics for future research. As these are tackled, our knowledge and theories in comparative politics and Political Science writ large will surely advance. At the same time, historical institutionalism will be further developed, sharpened, and strengthened.

CHAPTER 9

STATES AND ECONOMIC DEVELOPMENT

ATUL KOHLI

STATES influence rates and patterns of economic development everywhere. While how much a state should intervene is a subject of enduring debate, most scholars do not doubt that states matter—indeed, matter deeply—for the functioning and the development of an economy. This is because states make economic policy on the one hand and, on the other hand, provide the framework of laws and predictability within which economic actors operate. A puzzle of some intellectual significance then is this: Why are some states better at promoting economic development than other states? More specifically, we know that states in such late-developing countries as Japan, China, or South Korea have been relatively successful at generating industrialization, economic growth, and even, during some periods, equity. Contrasting cases of failed states and of state failure in economic development are to be found in a number of parts of the world, but especially in sub-Saharan Africa. Of course, most developing countries fall somewhere in between these extremes of success and failure. The question this chapter addresses is how best we understand such variations in state's economic performance. The answer revolves in part around what states do and in part around how well they pursue these goals. Since states are coercive institutions that acquire their specific ideologies and capacities only over time, a historical-institutional perspective is especially well suited for the study of this puzzle of the role and effectiveness of states in economic development.

Though the focus of this chapter is on late-developing countries—mainly countries of Asia, Africa, and Latin America that are still struggling to become modern, wealthy economies—a few historical comments on the state's role in the economic development of Western countries and of Japan may be useful at the outset. It is assumed by many that early industrialization in such countries as England in the eighteenth century or the United States in the nineteenth century was spearheaded mainly by private initiative and that states in such instances played a minimal role (North 1990). These views are more right than wrong but historical evidence also suggests that they need to be qualified. In the case of England, for example, the Navigation Acts of 1651 and 1660 created a trading monopoly that laid the foundation for the building of Britain's ship industry (Hill 1968, 123–143), banning of textile imports from India in 1700 helped facilitate the early Industrial Revolution in textiles, and then formal and informal imperialism opened markets for British textiles and railways, helping Britain's "first" and "second" industrial revolutions (Hobsbawm 1968). While there is no need to deny that these developments in Britain were moved by the rising influence of commercial groups, effective state intervention was also critical in shaping these important historical developments. The same was true in the United States during the nineteenth century, when tariffs and subsidies were used to promote rapid industrialization, especially toward the end of the century (Bensel 2000). In spite of liberal claims concerning the virtues of laissez faire and free trade then, states and state intervention were important even in the economic evolution of Britain and the United States.[1]

Late-developers within Europe—those who felt challenged by the rise of British economy and power—sought "defensive modernization." This often involved deliberate state intervention aimed at capital mobilization and tariff protection. In Germany, for example, rapid industrialization commenced only following state consolidation under Bismarck. A highly bureaucratized and nationalist state then partnered with big banks to support private industry (Pierenkemper and Tilly 2004, chapters 1 and 9). This experiment in "organized capitalism" succeeded in transforming Germany into a major industrial behemoth by the turn of the twentieth century, leading to serious power conflicts within Europe that culminated in the two world wars. Parallel efforts in Russia, by contrast, were less successful. Under the Czars, the Russian state remained more personalistic and the power of landed aristocracy hampered efforts toward industrialization. The weakness of indigenous capitalism remained a major stumbling block in Russia, not only then but even today. While a marriage of state initiative and foreign investment did succeed in generating some industry in late nineteenth-century Russia, progress was limited (Gerschenkron 1962) and Russia's rivals, including Japan, surpassed it during this period. When threatened militarily, the old regime in Russia withered, eventually giving rise to a revolutionary state, with considerable organizational and coercive capacities (Skocpol 1979). Without a robust private sector, however, even this communist state struggled for much of the twentieth century to put the Soviet Union on a self-sustaining route to a modern economy and eventually collapsed.

Japan remains a major example of a non-Western country that successfully fashioned its own path to a modern, industrial economy. Japan's pathway is thus of considerable relevance for those countries struggling to modernize in more recent periods. Unlike China, Japan resisted Western imperialism in the nineteenth century by reforming its state and economy. The Meiji Restoration brought to power a group of "nation-builders" in 1868—the Meiji oligarchs—who reformed the feudal system, centralized power, created a bureaucratized state, built a strong armed force, invested in literacy, and then used state propaganda to forge a strong Japanese national identity. The Japanese rulers then used this state power to both resist imperial encroachments and to borrow from the West, but on their own terms. Similar in some ways to the German experience during the same time period, the Meiji oligarchs used state power from 1870 onward to forge partnerships with large private firms to promote the building of infrastructure, railways, postal service, and of course, modern industry (Halliday 1975; Schumpeter 1940). As in the case of Germany, state-directed capitalism in Japan turned fascistic, leading to Japan's participation in World War II. It is noteworthy, however, that even after that war Japanese economic development remained state-led; institutions forged during an earlier period endured, as institutions are wont to do. Japan used a highly competent bureaucracy to both manage trade and to use industrial policy for the promotion of rapid economic growth (Johnson 1982). The long—and not always smooth—rise of Japan to the status of a modern industrial economy thus points to the importance of a national developmental coalition at the helm; important ingredients of this developmental state were economic nationalism, building of human capital, state competence, strategic state intervention, and a close partnership between state and business as facilitators of industrialization and economic growth.

Prior to World War II, then, liberal-capitalism, communism, and state-organized capitalism provided alternate pathways to a modern economy. Since World War II countries of Asia, Africa, and Latin America have also sought to emulate these (or some modified versions of these) pathways, with mixed results. A full "story" of why the results have been mixed will clearly be complex, involving more than the role of the state. Still, state actions and capacities have been one important determinant of relative success in late economic development (Evans 1995). Moreover, the answer to the question of why some states have been more effective developmentally than others often lies in the shape and form that state institutions acquired in the past (Kohli 2004). A look at some of the main regional variations across the developing world will now help put flesh on these bare-bone claims. While the main regions of the developing world—Asia, Africa, and Latin America—are complex places, with significant variation across both space and time, some regional generalizations are possible. Many countries of sub-Saharan Africa, for example, have recorded relatively poor economic performance since the mid-1960s. Ineffective states with roots in the colonial era have been largely responsible for this poor economic performance. Numerous Asian countries, by contrast, have industrialized and grown at rapid rates. Among the factors responsible for this outcome has been the role of nationalist developmental states. And finally, Latin America has tended to exhibit a boom and bust quality in their economic development, with continuing dependence on commodities. This I will propose is best understood as a function of ruling coalitions that prefer integration with the global economy over an autonomous path of creating complex, modern economies.

The scarcity of effective states is readily noticeable in parts of the developing world, especially in sub-Saharan Africa, but also elsewhere. Symptoms include short-lived governments, massive corruption, ethnic and class violence, and in a few cases, even civil wars. More extreme examples include the limited reach of the central government in such countries as the Congo or Afghanistan, ethnic violence in Sri Lanka, pogroms in Rwanda, and civil wars in El Salvador and the Sudan. Less dramatic but more common examples of ineffective states are what scholars of sub-Saharan Africa often refer to as neo-patrimonial states, that is, states that are ruled by personalistic and corrupt rulers who readily channel public resources for personal use (Callaghy and Ravenhill 1994; Van de Walle 2001). While such analyses of African failures have been criticized strongly in recent years (Mkandawire 2015) and growth performance of some African economies has improved (Radelet 2010), the theme of state ineffectiveness in the understanding of African economic failures continues to be important (Lewis 2007). Ineffective states hurt development. It is well understood by scholars of development that political instability discourages private investment and that personalistic rulers divert public investment away from productive uses. Beyond issues of capital accumulation and growth, ineffective states also hurt the societies they govern because they are often manned by less-than-professional armed forces, civil bureaucracies, and police. Instead of pursuing the public good, state agents in these settings use the power at their disposal to repress and exploit common citizens. These problems take on an especially ominous dimension when the rulers and the ruled are distinct in terms of ethnic or class divisions. Victims of state repression may, in turn, organize and arm themselves as a form of self-protection, opening up the prospect for long term violence. Ineffective states thus generally encourage social trends that development seeks to reverse, namely, economic stagnation, social insecurity, and lack of individual opportunities.

A few comments on the specific and important African case of Nigeria—that I analyzed in detail elsewhere (Kohli 2004)—might be helpful in understanding the broader problems of neo-patrimonial states. Nigeria represents a case of developmental failure. In spite of immense natural resource-based wealth, common Nigerians are probably not much better off in the early twenty-first century than they were at the time of independence in 1960. At the heart of this disappointing economic performance lies a poorly functioning state, a neo-patrimonial state characterized by a profound blurring of the private and the public realms. Behind the façade of a modern state, Nigeria has been ruled by personalistic and ethnically fragmented political elite on the one hand, and, on the other hand, by a bureaucracy and an army that not only shared these traits but was also not very competent and professional. These traits were inherited from the colonial period and the rulers of sovereign Nigeria failed to alter them. In spite of shifting development strategies—import substitution or export promotion—the results have included a recurring state failure to promote sustained economic growth.

In order to understand why the Nigerian state has been so developmentally ineffective, one has to understand how this state was formed; in other words, a historical-institutional perspective is essential. While this is no place for any detailed discussion of the political history of Nigeria (Crowder 1978), a few comments (and pointers to further reading) may be helpful. First, prior to British colonial imposition, there was no Nigeria. The rudimentary political units that the British carved into Nigeria lacked any such traditions of stateness as centralized authority over a sizable territory. Second, British colonial rule failed to create a cohesive, well-functioning state in Nigeria. British motives in colonizing Nigeria were minimal: keeping other European powers out and creating opportunities for trade and investment. The British thus ruled Nigeria as several separate administrative units via indirect rule. This led to a poorly formed state that reinforced a patrimonial, personalistic, and localized pattern of rule. It failed to centralize authority, to develop an effective civil service and to develop the capacity to tax the population directly (Nicolson 1969). And third, Nigerian political economy during the late colonial phase became quite distorted. In line with global currents, the Nigerian state became more involved in the economy but much more at encouraging control, extraction, and satisfying populist demands than at promoting national production. The framework of a weak colonial state also encouraged further fragmentation of what was already a divided nationalist movement (Coleman 1958). State power thus became further fragmented as it was pulled apart by particularistic and personalistic forces. The British then eventually ceded a poorly constructed state to a variety of indigenous forces that were divided along ethnic and tribal lines.

Sovereign Nigeria was off to a bad start at decolonization in 1960. With weak central authority and virtually no consensus on national purpose, the focus of the ruling elite was less on national development than on struggles over power and resources. A civil war soon followed (Diamond 1988). The post-civil war story of Nigeria's development efforts is a tragic story, a story of developmental failure of the state under military rule and of squandering of oil resources on a heroic scale (Joseph 1987; Forrest 1992; Lewis 2007). The Nigerian state since about 1970 has been dominated mainly by army officers and civilian bureaucrats, with a few periods of elected civilian politicians at the helm. Both the military and bureaucracy have internalized ethnic divisions, strong loyalties to kith and kin, and the shared belief of the Nigerian society that the main purpose of the state was to pursue personalistic and sectional interests. Fueled by oil revenues, the scale of corruption has been heroic. The state in Nigeria has thus been incapable of rising above the society it hoped to transform and of meeting that challenge. Whether ruled by civilians or by the military, and whether ruled more or less democratically, the main features of the Nigerian state have remained neo-patrimonial, contributing to Nigeria's long-term developmental failures.

Except for its oil resources, the Nigerian case is not unique. It helps underline the general proposition that ineffective states hurt development. As to why some parts of the developing world have ended up with more ineffective states than others, the Nigerian case again helps point to some historical and institutional variables. First, modern states emerged in Europe and spread from there to the non-West, often via colonial imposition. The fit between the state as a political form and indigenous political units was especially poor in some parts of the developing world, such as in sub-Saharan Africa, that lacked a tradition of large-scale, centralized political units. Second, and most important, the political impact of colonialism was especially pernicious in much of sub-Saharan Africa, leaving behind poorly functioning states. Third, revolutionary and nationalist movements proved to be important agents of state formation in the developing world; however, such movements emerged and succeeded only in some countries. And finally, well-organized militaries in power have at times succeeded in reforming developing country states; the problem, however, is not only that such militaries can readily become tyrannical, but also that well-organized militaries remain scarce, especially in ineffective states.

Leaving aside the group of states with relatively ineffective states, states in much of Asia and Latin America have provided more stability—though not always democratic stability—and made sustained efforts to modernize their respective economies. The regional patterns of development in Asia and Latin America, however, have varied, even varied sharply. Generalizing about regions that are quite varied internally—again, both over time and across space—it is still the case that Asian countries have on average grown faster than Latin American countries since World War II and with more modest inequalities.[2] This is because Asian countries have created economies with high domestic savings rates, careful channeling of foreign investment into priority areas, significant capacity to export manufactured goods, and limited foreign debt. These economic trends emerged from planned activities of effective national states and helped stimulate economic growth. By contrast, many countries in Latin America have remained more dependent on the global economy, with lower domestic savings rates, smaller roles for national capital, higher dependence on foreign capital to supplement limited mobilization of domestic resources, exports focused on lower value added commodities, and relatively high levels of foreign debt. These trends, too, resulted from policy choices of different types of states at the helm in Latin America, less effective, with sharp elite-mass gaps and more globally complicit.

The question for analysis is: Why, on balance, have Asian and Latin American countries pursued different models of development? What are the deeper determinants of these alternate pathways? Once again, a historical-institutional perspective is needed. Shorn of enormous complexities, my main suggestion here is that the origins of the differing pathways traversed by Asia and Latin America are political, rooted in differing patterns of state intervention, which in turn reflect the different processes of state formation in the two regions. Decolonization in Asia following World War II created significant political discontinuities, which in turn led to modified class relations, altered external relations, and more nationalist development choices. By contrast, there was no such discontinuity in Latin America in the post-World War II period; state and class formations modified of course, but only incrementally, continuing along the grooves of dependent development of a much earlier historical origin.

Following World War II, for example, China had a major communist revolution and the world's most significant non-communist nationalist movement captured state power in India. The Asian giants thus began their sovereign development experiments by focusing first and foremost on state consolidation. Once in power, the nationalistically inclined Chinese communists (Johnson 1962) minimized Western economic and political influence on China, eliminated China's comprador classes, and created a well-organized state that penetrated the Chinese society deeply (Schurmann 1968). While India's democratic state was less efficacious than the Chinese communist state, India's nationalist leaders also prioritized sovereignty and state consolidation. They too minimized the role of old landed classes that collaborated with the British, as well as keeping at bay new political and economic dependencies (Nayar 1989). The Asian giants then used the power of newly consolidated states to create nearly autarkic economies in the early decades, say, 1950 to 1980. While these experiments were hardly without costs, even serious costs in areas of state repression and state-led upheavals (China), slow and lingering poverty (India), and sluggish economic growth (both China and India), there is no denying that state consolidation laid the foundation for a nationalist model of development in both China and India, which is now paying off.

Decolonization created a variety of political outcomes in the rest of Asia, with one shared commonality, namely, the creation of sovereign, new, and, for the most part, effective states. For example, the Japanese lost World War II and, along with that, their power and investments in such colonies as Korea and Formosa; this led to a new political beginning in the partial countries of South Korea and Taiwan (Amsden 1989; Wade 1990). The Dutch were forced out of Indonesia, as were the British from Malaysia. Both the French and the Americans were eventually defeated militarily in Vietnam. While there were exceptions (e.g., the Philippines), well-organized mass nationalist and/or revolutionary forces consolidated power in most Asian countries following World War II. It might be objected that countries such as South Korea or Pakistan very quickly developed new dependencies, this time on the US. This is true but with one important qualification. These new dependencies were mainly a product of the Cold War and thus were security-oriented in nature. For the most part, countries like South Korea were left alone to pursue their economic development, even gaining preferential resources and treatment from the US as a quid pro quo for security arrangements (Hart-Landsberg 1993; Woo 1991).

In contrast to Asia, decolonization in Latin America was in the distant past. State consolidation occurred mainly in the interwar period. Unlike the Asian pattern of anti-colonial mass mobilization, the underlying processes leading to state consolidation in Latin America often involved struggles between rival elites, especially struggles between centralizing and regional elites. This was as true for a country like Brazil, where the process of gaining independence was relatively peaceful (Flynn 1978), as it was for Argentina, where post-independence decades were full of strife (Ferns 1971). Over time, of course, newer political formations emerged in many Latin American countries too, but there was more continuity than discontinuity in the social base of state power, in patterns of economic dependency, and in developmental choices (Cardoso and Faletto 1979). Most of these regimes readily embraced the emerging Western alliance, led by the United States. Consider, for example, the case of the most important Latin American country, Brazil. While a new democratic regime of sorts replaced an authoritarian regime following World War II, Skidmore (1967) skillfully demonstrated the elements of continuity in the pre- and the post-World War II political economy of Brazil. In Brazil, Vargas, the authoritarian leader of the prewar period, even came back to power, this time as a democratically elected president.

The Cuban revolution marked a moment of potential change in Latin American politics, in the direction of activist states supported by mass politics. From João Goulart to Salvador Allende, a variety of nationalists, populists, and social democrats emerged to give voice to new political forces of the region. The United States—the regional hegemon, committed to open economies, especially in its "backyard"—sought to co-opt the emerging political restlessness in a liberal direction via the Alliance for Progress.

When such efforts did not succeed, the US just as readily threw its weight behind more reactionary political forces that would provide favorable economic policies. This tilted the balance of power within Latin American societies, retarding the trend toward more nationalist and plebiscitary politics. Landed oligarchs, foreign investors, and militaries—often trained in the United States—felt threatened by the new direction. A variety of military coups that occurred in Latin American countries during the 1960s and the 1970s brought to power elites who were inclined to cooperate politically and economically with the US on the one hand and to pursue a highly elitist and a dependent model of development at home on the other hand. Scholars coined the term "associated-dependent development" to capture these new types of Latin American political economies (Cardoso 1973).

While anti-colonial mass movements consolidated power in many Asian countries during the 1950s and the 1960s, similar political forces were thwarted in Latin America. What emerged in the latter instead was a variety of narrower elitist arrangements under American tutelage. These contrasting political developments cast the die for a longer-term divergence in political and economic evolution of the two regions. Among the developmental changes in the two regions that can be traced back to these earlier contrasts in state construction are: land reforms and related patterns of inequalities; strategies toward dependence on foreign capital; and the role of national capital and indigenous technology, including trained manpower, in industrialization strategies. These contrasting policy choices in turn often reinforced the character of developmental states of the two regions, more nationalist in Asia and more dependent in Latin America.

Take, for example, the issue of land reforms. We know that land reforms were a lot more successful in Asia than in Latin America (Evans 1986). It is important to recall the strong political motivation in the pursuit of land reforms (Tai 1974). Traditional landowning elites not only limited the reach of the state into the countryside but comprador classes often had their roots in landed wealth. The process of consolidating nationalist states in Asian countries was thus aided by the elimination of a variety of "feudal" types of intermediate elites. Land reforms enhanced the reach of the state on the one hand, and moderated inequalities of wealth and power in the countryside on the other hand. Such developments were clearest in the communist cases of China and Vietnam. The threat of communism, in turn, also facilitated significant land redistribution in such other cases as South Korea and Taiwan. Even in an India—where land reforms were mostly a failure—the largest *zamindars* (traditional large land holders who had often cooperated with the British colonial government in India) were broken down and pressures of democracy mitigated the "urban bias" of the polity, leading to reasonable terms of trade between the city and the countryside. A similar outcome unfolded in Indonesia, where the mechanism was less democratic politics but more threats of peasant rebellion. Of course there were exceptions, such as the Philippines and Pakistan. These cases continued to resemble Latin American cases, where landed oligarchs survived well into the modern period, state consolidation remained incomplete, and dependence on the US was significant.

During the 1950s and the 1960s, the well-known import substitution industrialization (ISI) model of development was pursued in both Asia and Latin America. What is important to reiterate here are the significant differences across Asian and Latin American ISI strategies. On the whole, Latin American countries pursued ISI with foreign investors producing consumer goods for Latin American elites behind high tariff walls (O'Donnell 1988). By contrast—again, generalizing hugely—ISI policies in Asia focused on heavy industry that was promoted by domestic resources and for domestic markets. These contrasting policies both reflected the contrasting political preferences of more nationalist versus more dependent states on the one hand and further reinforced these tendencies, with future consequences, on the other hand.

In Communist China, for example, a heavy industrial base was laid down by public investments. This involved mobilization of domestic resources, often via brutal political mechanisms, and then borrowing and slowly but surely indigenizing technology. Public investments also played a crucial role in India's heavy industry-oriented ISI, but then so did indigenous capital. The Indian state also limited the role of foreign capital in India's development and prioritized training indigenous technical manpower to aid its industrial ambitions. When the dust of civil war and reconstruction settled in South Korea (say, around 1960), the government there pursued simultaneously heavy industry oriented ISI and a state-subsidized drive to promote light industry exports, both financed by domestic savings. Here too a direct role for foreign capital was minimized and spread of education helped rapid industrialization. Notice that none of these cases were cases of "easy ISI" that was pursued in Latin America, which I discuss below. Asian countries by contrast pursued "difficult ISI." Committed to creating modern but sovereign political economies, they initiated policies that helped mobilize domestic resources, limited foreign capital, and built indigenous technology and industry. Of course, a South Korea or a Taiwan grew much faster in this earlier period than an India or a China (for an analysis of why, see Kohli 2004), but in all of these cases foundations of more nationalist political economies were built by conscious political decisions of post-colonial states.

The Latin American version of ISI, by contrast, has been rightly characterized as "easy ISI." The term is apt because Latin American leaders seldom took the difficult decisions that might—say, over the medium term—enhance national savings, build national technology, and lay the foundation for heavy industry. One is tempted to impute fairly distinct developmental motivations to Latin American rulers: whereas many rulers in Asia were committed to creating strong and modern national political economies, development for Latin American rulers often meant enhancing national incomes so that a narrow ruling class could rapidly join the life styles of Europeans and Americans, with whom they identified. Be that as it may, the results are clearer. In Brazil, for example, the development strategy focused on inviting foreign investors to produce consumer goods for its upper and middle classes. To be fair, savings rates in Brazil did improve and some heavy industry did take root, but nothing in comparison with countries like South Korea, and then Brazil was an exception in Latin America.

Neoliberal scholars during the 1980s often blamed high tariffs in countries like Brazil as responsible for their lack of export prowess and debt crisis. What is often forgotten is the important role high tariffs played in attracting foreign capital to Brazil and elsewhere in Latin America in the first place. Foreign investors came to Latin America, not to take advantage of their cheap labor for export promotion, but to take advantage of their protected elite markets. This is what Fishlow (1987) probably had in mind when he brilliantly characterized East Asian integration into the world economy as more along the axis of trade and Latin America's integration more along the axis of foreign capital; while countries such as South Korea mobilized domestic resources and exported, Brazil and others invited foreign capital to produce for indigenous elites. The Latin American strategy worked as long as foreign capital kept coming in, and as long as a focus on enriching and catering industrialization to narrow elite tastes could be maintained politically, preconditions that have not always proven easy to sustain.

While there were many false starts, and a fair amount of learning occurred via trial and error, on the whole between 1950 and 1980, nationalist states consolidated power in most Asian countries, eliminating or mitigating the power of traditional intermediaries, minimizing the role of foreign capital, and laying the foundations for the development of indigenous technology and heavy industry. By contrast, the ruling elites in Latin America continued to rely heavily on foreign capital, failed to mitigate internal economic inequalities and the related elite-mass political gap, and constructed political economies that remained dependent on the outside world. Though the growth performance of many Latin American countries during this period was often impressive (again, notice Brazil), the fact is that this growth remained dependent on the availability of foreign capital. With growing foreign debt in the late 1970s and the early 1980s, foreign capital increasingly shied away from Latin America, leading to the "lost decade" of development. By contrast, most Asian economies surged ahead during the 1980s, especially the giants, China and India.

Over the last few decades, nationalist states of Asia have coped with globalization from a position of relative strength, making concessions when necessary, but also taking advantages of available opportunities. By contrast, indebted and dependent countries of Latin America have just as often confronted globalization on bended knees. When pressured by the US, the International Monetary Fund (IMF), and the World Bank, Latin American elites during the 1980s and the 1990s readily embraced policies based on the Washington Consensus on development. The results include higher rates of economic growth and lower inequalities in much of Asia since the mid-1980s than in Latin America. With democracy, political reactions in Latin America only seem to confirm these tendencies: considerable political rage against the Washington Consensus on the one hand but an uneven political capacity to mobilize this anger constructively on the other hand. At one extreme we notice that the Mexican elites have narrowed their own political room to maneuver via North American Free Trade Agreement. At the other extreme, states in Brazil and Argentina have reasserted their economic presence and also focused on redistributive issues, especially in Brazil. In yet other cases, angry neo-populism has resurfaced, as in a Bolivia or a Venezuela. While inequality has come down in several Latin American countries, the basic growth pattern continues to be characterized by commodity exports and heavy dependence on foreign investment.

Select Asian economies—China, India, Vietnam, South Korea—are now among the world's fastest growers. While the respective developmental approaches of these countries differ, they also share some commonalities, especially when juxtaposed with some typical tendencies in Latin America. China, for example, is undergoing a state controlled transition from socialism to capitalism. While the role of foreign direct investment (FDI) in this transition seems very large indeed, the accumulated stock of FDI in China is still relatively modest (some 10 percent of China's GDP in 2010, while that in Brazil is close to 22 percent, not to mention Chile's 67 percent; Kohli 2012). Second, timing and sequence matters; much of FDI in China has come in after the Chinese state was well consolidated, directing the process of economic modernization on its own terms. And finally, anywhere from half to two thirds of the so-called foreign investment going into China originates in Hong Kong and Taiwan. This diaspora investment is less foreign investment and more the revenge of the Chinese bourgeoisie that were once ousted by the communists, and who are now busy re-establishing a state-capital alliance that will manage the new, enlarged and powerful China in the future.

India's liberalizing reforms are partly real but partly a myth. FDI remains relatively limited in India and very recently India has even limited the inflow of the more speculative types of portfolio investments. The main model of development in India is a close alliance between state and indigenous capitalism. The Indian state has carefully calibrated external opening of the Indian economy, ensuring that indigenous capital does not bear the brunt of such an opening. The state–capital alliance has facilitated rapid growth and some reduction in poverty, but growing inequalities are also retarding the poverty alleviating impact of growth.

Besides the Giants, South Korea has of course been one of the world's fastest growing economies for a long time. The Asian financial crisis hit South Korea hard but what is remarkable is the relatively quick recovery of economic growth. The basic model of development has undergone some important changes in South Korea, but these are most evident in the financial sector. The core state–chaebol alliance for exports and growth remains intact. What is also noteworthy is the progress toward social democracy that is evident in South Korea (and in Taiwan) since democratization (Wong 2004). Democratic pressures from below are clearly more consequential in economies dominated by national than by foreign capital.

A nationalist state–capital alliance that presides over high economic growth rates and moderate inequalities is the main model of development in Asia. Of course, there are exceptions (Indonesia's recovery is slow, Malaysia is achieving good growth and distribution with heavy foreign investment, and Philippines and few other countries remain laggards) but, on the whole, Asian countries have pursued a nationalist capitalist model of development, and with considerable success.

By contrast, national political formations remain relatively weak in dependent Latin America, economic growth remains a function of availability of foreign capital and high commodity prices, and inequalities are proving to be very stubborn, as is the elite–mass political gap. Take, once again, the important case of Brazil. On the whole, Brazil is a well-governed country. However, development choices within it are highly constrained, constraints that reflect accumulation of past choices. The domestic rates of savings remain relatively low and, though the debt burden has declined, debt service burden (as a percentage of exports) remains very high. Brazil thus needs continuous inflows of foreign capital, both as a source of foreign exchange and economic growth. Wary of scaring away such investors, even left-leaning leaders such as Luiz Inácio Lula da Silva or Dilma Rousseff have shied away from policies—whether redistributive or growth promoting—that might involve the state in deficit spending and be held responsible for re-emergence of inflation. Modest economic growth has returned and inequalities have declined. All this is for the good; however, dependence on commodity exports—often to China—and on foreign capital continues. Without a strong developmental state, for now economic growth remains a function of steady foreign investment inflows and buoyant commodity demand.

To conclude, this chapter has provided a whirlwind tour of the state's role in late economic development. States are understood here as coercive institutions that both make economic policy and provide the setting in which economic actors operate. A historical understanding of the varying roles that states have played suggests that the debate on whether states should or should not intervene in the market is a false debate. In the modern era of sustained economic growth and industrialization states have intervened everywhere. Among late developers the role of the state has been that much more pronounced because of the felt need to "catch up" with the more advanced countries, as well as because of the related need to support national entrepreneurs compete with established firms elsewhere. The real issue for analysis then is why some states in late developing countries have been more effective at growth-promotion than other states. My suggestion here is that this variation is more a function of the quality than of degree of state intervention. Quality of state intervention, in turn, reflects the different types of states that govern developing countries.

In order to simplify a complex picture, I have in this chapter proposed some regional generalizations to highlight differing state types and their historical origins. Using a historical and institutional lens, I have suggested that neo-patrimonial states blur the distinction between the private and the public realm; in much of sub-Saharan Africa such states came into being during the colonial era and they have proved highly ineffective at promoting industrialization and growth. States in Latin America have been more effective economic actors but their performance has often been constrained, both by the commodity-dependent economies they have inherited, and by the nature of the ruling forces that tend to control the state in such economies; instead of sharply diversifying their economies, rulers of Latin America have often preferred an integration with the global economy, both as a source of investment to manufacture goods for domestic consumption and as markets for their commodity exports. Following decolonization, many Asian countries have sought instead to develop complex economies with significant national industry. In this important sense, such Asian countries as China, India, and South Korea—not to mention Japan—have sought to emulate the advanced industrial countries, and so far, with some success. Effective national states have been key actors in this difficult struggle to catch up with the advanced industrial West.

Notes

1. An important book that chastises international development agencies, as well as leading Western countries, for forgetting this history as they recommend open economies with minimal states to all developing countries is Chang (2003).
2. I am drawing much of the comparative analysis of Asia versus Latin America from Kohli (2012). Detailed data on economic performance and on other underlying variables are also available in this paper.

References

Amsden, Alice H. 1989. *Asia's Next Giant: South Korea and Late Industrialization.* New York: Oxford University Press.

Bensel, Richard. 2000. *The Political Economy of American Industrialization, 1877–1900.* Cambridge and New York: Cambridge University Press.

Callaghy, Thomas and John Ravenhill, eds. 1994. *Hemmed In: Responses to Africa's Economic Decline.* New York: Columbia University Press.

Cardoso, Fernando Henrique. 1973. "Associated-Dependent Development." In *Authoritarian Brazil: Origins, Policies, and Future*, ed. Alfred Stepan. New Haven, CT: Yale University Press: 142–178.

Cardoso, Fernando Henrique and Enzo Faletto. 1979. *Dependency and Development in Latin America.* Berkeley: University of California Press.

Chang, Ha-Joon. 2003. *Kicking Away the Ladder: Development Strategy in Historical Perspective.* London: Anthem Press.

Coleman, James S. 1958. *Nigeria: Background to Nationalism.* Berkeley: University of California Press.

Crowder, Michael. 1978. *The Story of Nigeria.* London: Faber and Faber.

Diamond, Larry Jay. 1988. *Class, Ethnicity, and Democracy in Nigeria: The Failure of the First Republic.* Syracuse, NY: Syracuse University Press.

Evans, Peter. 1986. "Class, State, and Dependence in East Asia: Some Lessons for Latin Americanists." In *The Political Economy of the New Asian Industrialism*, ed. Fredrick C. Deyo. Ithaca, NY: Cornell University Press, 203–226.

Evans, Peter. 1995. *Embedded Autonomy: State and Industrial Transformation.* Princeton, NJ: Princeton University Press.

Ferns, H. S. 1971. *The Argentine Republic.* New York: Barnes and Noble.

Fishlow, Albert. 1987. "Some Reflections on Comparative Latin American Economic Performance and Policy." *Wider Working Papers* 22 (August). Available at <http://econpapers.repec.org/paper/cdleconwp/qt205388wm.htm> (accessed September 1, 2015).

Flynn, Peter. 1978. *Brazil: A Political Analysis.* Boulder, CO: Westview.

Forrest, Tom. 1992. *Politics and Economic Development in Nigeria.* Boulder, CO: Westview.

Gerschenkron, Alexander. 1962. *Economic Backwardness in Historical Perspective.* Cambridge, MA: Harvard University Press.

Halliday, Jon. 1975. *A Political History of Japanese Capitalism.* New York: Pantheon.

Hart-Landsberg, Martin. 1993. *The Rush to Development: Economic Change and Political Struggle in South Korea.* New York: Monthly Review Press.

Hill, Christopher. 1968. *Reformation to Industrial Revolution: A Social and Economic History of Britain, 1530–1780*. London: Weidenfeld and Nicolson.

Hobsbawm, Eric. 1968. *Industry and Empire: The Birth of the Industrial Revolution*. New York: The New Press.

Johnson, Chalmers. 1962. *Peasant Nationalism and Communist Power: The Emergence of Revolutionary China*. Stanford, CA: Stanford University Press.

Johnson, Chalmers A. 1982. *MITI and the Japanese Miracle: The Growth of Industrial Policy, 1925–75*. Stanford, CA: Stanford University Press.

Joseph, Richard. 1987. *Democracy and Prebendal Politics in Nigeria*. Cambridge and New York: Cambridge University Press.

Kohli, Atul. 2004. *State-Directed Development: Political Power and Industrialization in the Global Periphery*. Cambridge and New York: Cambridge University Press.

Kohli, Atul. 2012. "Coping with Globalization: Asian versus Latin American Strategies of Development." *Brazilian Journal of Political Economy* 32 (4): 531–556.

Lewis, Peter M. 2007. *Growing Apart: Politics and Economic Development in Indonesia and Nigeria*. Ann Arbor: University of Michigan Press.

Mkandawire, Thandika. 2015. "Neopatrimonialism and the Political Economy of Economic Performance in Africa." *World Politics* 67 (3): 563–612.

Nayar, Baldev Raj. 1989. *India's Mixed Economy: The Role of Ideology and Interest in Its Development*. Bombay: Popular Prakashan.

Nicolson, I. F. 1969. *The Administration of Nigeria, 1900–1960*. Oxford: Clarendon.

North, Douglas. 1990. *Institutions, Institutional Change and Economic Performance*. Cambridge and New York: Cambridge University Press.

O'Donnell, Guillermo. 1988. *Bureaucratic Authoritarianism: Argentina, 1966–1973*. Berkeley: University of California Press.

Pierenkemper, Toni and Richard Tilly. 2004. *German Economy during the Nineteenth Century*. Oxford and New York: Bergham Books.

Radelet, Steven. 2010. *Emerging Africa: How 17 Countries Are Leading the Way*. Baltimore, MD: Fund for Global Development.

Schumpeter, E. B. 1940. *The Industrialization of Japan and Manchukuo*. New York: Macmillan.

Schurmann, Franz. 1968. *Ideology and Organization in Communist China*. Berkeley: University of California Press.

Skidmore, Thomas. 1967. *Politics in Brazil, 1930–1964: An Experiment in Democracy*. Oxford and New York: Oxford University Press.

Skocpol, Theda. 1979. *States and Social Revolutions: A Comparative Analysis of France, Russia and China*. New York: Cambridge University Press.

Tai, Hung-Chao. 1974. *Land Reform and Politics: A Comparative Analysis*. Berkeley: University of California Press.

Van de Walle, Nicolas. 2001. *African Economies and the Politics of Permanent Crisis, 1979–1991*. Cambridge and New York: Cambridge University Press.

Wade, Robert. 1990. *Governing the Market: Economic Theory and the Role of Government in East Asian Industrialization*. Princeton, NJ: Princeton University Press.

Wong, Joseph. 2004. *Healthy Democracies: Welfare Politics in Taiwan and South Korea*. Ithaca, NY: Cornell University Press.

Woo, Jung-en. 1991. *Race to the Swift: State and Finance in Korean Industrialization*. New York: Columbia University Press.

CHAPTER 10

THE DEVELOPMENT OF STATE CAPACITY

HILLEL DAVID SOIFER

A reasonable argument could be made for the claim that the historical institutionalist approach to social science first emerged as scholars sought to understand state-building (see the introductory chapter to this volume). Canonical studies of state development deployed concepts like path dependence and critical junctures in systematic ways. This is no accident: the processes underpinning the origin and evolution of state institutions, and the development of state capacity have strong affinities with the analytical core of historical institutionalism. In this chapter, I begin by exploring some of the ways in which the state development literature in both Political Science and sociology has drawn on key elements of the historical institutionalist approach. Drawing on studies of state-building in a variety of world regions, I show the central place of historical causation, critical junctures, and path dependence in the state-building literature.

Though the affinities between the state development literature and historical institutionalism are strong, however, my focus is on two opportunities for the state development literature to draw more fully on the insights of historical institutionalism. The first relates to failed state-building efforts: as I argue below, the state-building literature has only rarely explored this possibility. The consequence of this gap is a sort of creeping functionalism in the study of state development; I explore the few attempts to break out of this trap, and sketch a research agenda for the study of failed state-building and its theoretical and empirical implications. The second opportunity relates to the distinction made by Pierson (2004) between institutional *origins* and institutional *development*: much of the state-building literature has emphasized the former rather than the latter. Though it has accounted for why the broad *design* of state institutions persists, it has neglected to explore two elements of continuity: one is the steady growth of state scope over time, and the other is the persistence over time of the state's capacity to carry out core functions. Here, the questions of interest to scholars of state-building press historical institutionalists to think more broadly about assessing the institutions they study, and the ways in which they evolve over time, and press scholars of the state to better theorize the relationship between state capacity and the strength of its component institutions.

Historical Institutionalism and State Development

Many of the central elements of the historical institutionalist toolbox underpin the study of state development. Scholarship on state development grants a central place to historical causation, to critical junctures, and to path dependence.[1] Thus, the study of state-building in both Political Science and sociology has long found its core in the historical institutionalist tradition.[2] Perhaps the most fundamental way in which the conceptual core of historical institutionalism is echoed in the state-building literature is the nearly universal scholarly consensus that outcomes of state development are determined by what Stinchcombe (1968) called historical causes: causal factors that existed in the past but are no longer present. Only a few outlying accounts emphasize the role of constant causes to explain state development. Herbst (2000), for example, argues that the constant low population density of sub-Saharan Africa underlay the disinclination of both colonial and post-independence state leaders to extend authority outward over territory in the region.[3] Thies (2005) also makes a constant cause argument, claiming that long-lasting international rivalries have spurred a slow and steady accretion of state capacity over time in the developing world. More generally, a broad consensus about the importance of historical causes can be observed across the vast majority of studies of state-building. Scholars disagree, of course, on the specific historical causes at work, as they emphasize a wide range of alternatives including colonial rule (Kohli 2004; Lange 2009), internal contention (Hechter and Brustein 1980; Slater 2010), commodity booms (Karl 1997; Saylor 2014), the nature of domestic economic production (Spruyt 1994; Kurtz 2013), and war (Tilly 1975, 1992; Downing 1992; Ertman 1997; López-Alves 2000; Hui 2005).

Because there is such a broad consensus that state development is driven by historical causes, the historical institutionalist toolbox plays a central role in this body of scholarship. Historical causation, as Stinchcombe (1968) and Collier and Collier (1991) argued, immediately points to the importance of formative moments, and to at least a degree of institutional continuity over time. This implies that critical junctures and path dependence are central to the processes of state development; a view held in common by scholars who disagree sharply about the particular causes driving state-building.

In theorizing state development, scholars have emphasized the importance of critical junctures. Iterative waves of theorizing have refined these historical arguments to distinguish permissive from productive conditions, and thus move beyond the broad association of certain factors with state development outcomes to develop theoretically precise accounts of the causal structures that underpin state-building.[4] This theoretical precision can be seen in studies by Barnett (1992) and Saylor (2014) of how war and commodity booms, respectively, shape the development of state capacity.

In both of these works, the distinction between permissive and productive conditions is theoretically crucial. It points the way, in Barnett's case, to sharper analyses of the relationship between war and the state. Whereas Tilly's famous "states made war and war made states" only identified a relationship, Barnett develops a set of predictions about when this relationship will and will not hold. Barnett argues that war *created the conditions* for state-building, but did not always produce it. Instead, the strategy chosen in response to an external threat, not the threat itself, shaped the state power outcomes caused by war in Israel and Egypt. Saylor (2014) also sharpens our understanding of how commodity booms affect state capacity by distinguishing between the factors that make state-building possible, and the factors that produce it. He argues that commodity booms generate interest in new public goods among exporters, and thus act as a window of opportunity within which state-building is possible.[5] But exporter preferences are only translated into increased state capacity when they are represented in the ruling coalition, and this explains why in Chile, Argentina, and Mauritius, commodity booms led to increased public good provision, but similar commodity booms in Colombia, Ghana, and Nigeria had no such effect. By carefully elaborating critical juncture arguments, Barnett and Saylor uncover the precise nature of the conditional relationships tying war and commodity booms to state-building.

Scholars of state development also emphasize the importance of path dependence. Ertman (1997), for example, argues that the administrative institutions designed by state leaders as they responded to conflict in early modern Europe persisted for centuries after their initial creation. The result was that countries exposed to war earlier, whose leaders had no choice but to construct patrimonial institutions and rely on tax farming, were saddled with those institutions long thereafter even as more efficient alternatives came to be available. Change proved difficult "due to the power of vested interests with a material and ideological stake in already established institutions" (27). War not only increased pressure on state administrations, but it also strengthened the proprietary officeholders on which the central state depended. Reform was only possible after state collapse, and only then were France and Spain freed from the shackles of the institutional choices made centuries earlier. The reason that war can be said to have made the European state, then, is that initial institutional choices tend to persist over time.

In a different regional context, and with a very different line of argument, Kurtz (2013) also emphasizes the power of path dependence in the development of state capacity in Latin America. The institutions forged during the initial construction of political settlements among elites "launched a trajectory for Latin American states" (42) in terms of their development of the capacity to provide basic functions like taxation and property rights enforcement, and were "deflected" (43) in a second critical juncture when the middle and working classes emerged "into alternative long-term outcomes" in terms of the state's development of a broader range of state functions. In making his path dependent argument, Kurtz emphasizes mechanisms of the coordination of expectations around existing outcomes, and of "iterative cooperation" among elites from different factions

(228). The result is that "once a trajectory is laid in, it can be decidedly difficult to change long-term outcomes" (Kurtz 2013, 231).

Studies of state development overwhelmingly highlight the importance of "branching patterns of social development" (Pierson 2004, 21). Even as this type of argument is often criticized for overstating the distinction between periods of stability and change, and ignoring the possibility of gradual institutional change, most accounts claim that state development is marked by "long periods of stability punctuated by periods of change in specific critical moments" (Kurtz 2013, 34).[6] The fact that the historical record of state development is marked by critical junctures and path dependence raises several particularly promising research agendas for future scholarship on the evolution of the state. One relates to the failure of state-building efforts, and the second relates to striking stability in trajectories of state development. In developing these areas of research, opportunities for deeper engagement with historical institutionalist insights become clear, as do some ways in which the historical institutionalist conception of institutional change could be broadened.

Failed State-Building

One causal pathway to state weakness is the absence of the external shock that drives state leaders to opt for state-building. As Centeno (2002) argues, Latin American states are relatively weak because the kinds of wars that made European states never unfolded south of the Rio Grande. Similarly, Downing (1992) argues that isolation from the wars that swept early modern Europe prevented the emergence of absolutism in England. This is one of the two logical paths to the absence of an outcome in a critical juncture framework: in the absence of the permissive conditions, the status quo remains (Soifer 2012). But the causal structure of the critical juncture also identifies another logical possibility in accounting for state weakness. This second possible path is one in which the critical juncture opens but the productive conditions leading to the outcome are absent; it is a missed opportunity or a failed response to crisis.

The state-building literature has failed to allow for the possibility that state weakness might result from failed state-building projects. In the European context, despite Tilly's (1975) warning of the dangers of selection bias in considering only the political units that have survived centuries of warfare, scholars seem to see failed states as historical curiosities, the "vanished kingdoms" that have been erased from the map, and are irrelevant to long-term political development (Davies 2012). Outside Europe, where change in borders and the constituent political units in most regions has been more limited, weak states abound. Yet studies of weak states seem to nearly universally attribute that weakness not to the failure of state-building efforts but to their absence. Slater (2010) argues that the absence of existential threats from certain kinds of contentious politics meant that the protection pacts he sees as key to state-building failed to emerge in most Southeast Asian countries. Herbst (2000) argues that state weakness in sub-Saharan Africa results from the calculations of state leaders that the costs of extending authority would outstrip the potential gains. And Kurtz (2013) argues that state weakness in Peru resulted from the disinterest of its labor-repressive agricultural elites.

The one place where failed state-building efforts have received significant attention is in investigation of the failures of post-occupation reconstruction in Afghanistan and Iraq. Yet here, too, the lessons to be drawn from existing studies leave much to be desired. As Brownlee (2007) argues in a review of scholarship on these "nation-building" projects, the dominant explanation for failure is "volitional" (315), emphasizing insufficient resources, manpower, and time. As a result, the only policy prescription these studies can offer where state-building founders is unsatisfying: the need for more concerted, protracted, and costly efforts.

This suggests a sort of creeping functionalism among scholars of state-building, who nearly universally draw a direct line from structural conditions to outcomes without considering the possibility that state leaders might fail to implement their chosen initiatives. Here, a turn to historical institutionalism could provide some important insights. A key implication of the historical institutionalist approach, elaborated most clearly by Pierson (2004, chapters 4–5) is that functionalist explanations for political outcomes—those that explain outcomes by reference to the intentions and strategies of actors alone—are fundamentally lacking. The social world places many hurdles between intention and outcome, meaning that actors rarely are able to produce the institutions they intend. And the processes that create the sorts of macro-institutions that determine state capacity are often best traced back not to the intentional pursuit of chosen outcomes by powerful actors, but to complex interactions among multiple actors that produce enduring but unintended consequences.

Indeed, the few explorations of state-building failure that do exist resonate precisely with these insights from historical institutionalism. One set of accounts of state-building failure looks at the ability of societal actors to resist the impositions of state authority, with the result that outcomes do not reflect the intentions of state leaders. A second set of accounts highlights how tensions unfolding in the complex interactions among the multiplicity of actors within the state itself undermine state-building initiatives and produce their own enduring consequences.

Societal Resistance and State-Building Failure

A first set of accounts of state-building failure focus on the ability of non-state actors to disrupt state initiatives. As Barkey (1994, 9) writes, "social structure defines the ground in which states attempt to centralize."[7] This opposition may lead to retreat from state-building projects, or to what Migdal (1988, 254) calls "accommodation" between state leaders and societal actors.[8] Thus, state weakness may be the product of opposition that state leaders face when they try to centralize and extend authority, which causes those efforts to fail.

State-building efforts may fail because of the ability of locally powerful actors, who see the extension of state authority as a challenge to their own hegemony or local power, to resist and even overcome these initiatives. Migdal (1988) argues that the fate of state-building projects depends on the structure of social relations: only where social control is fragmented can state-building unfold successfully, but where "tenacious and resilient organizations" (32) are present, state-building efforts tend to "stall." The social power of strongmen—their ability to act collectively and induce the population to follow—accounts for their ability to stymie state-building.

Scholars have also argued that non-elite societal actors, who also see the extension of state authority as a threatening imposition, can pose an obstacle to state-building efforts. Most fully developed in the work of Scott (1998, 2009), this line of argument emphasizes the ways in which states disrupt the communities and ways of life of the (predominantly rural) poor, leading to resistance—whether covert or overt—against the extension of state authority, and causing state-building efforts to fall short of their goals of transforming space and society.

This scholarship makes an important contribution in explaining the origins of resistance to state expansion, and how that resistance can intervene between the intentions of state leaders and outcomes of state-building. Yet one suspects that other factors must be incorporated to paint a fuller picture of when and why state-building fails.

Indeed, the empirical record shows that societal actors welcome at least some elements of the state. As Slater (2008) points out, building electoral administration implies the same sorts of registration and data collection apparati implicated in conscription and taxation. Yet because it serves the purpose of representation, election administration does not generate the same sort of resistance, and may even be welcomed by mass actors (if not by local strongmen). Similarly, social policy and public goods like education and infrastructure are often demanded by societal actors. The politics of state expansion are not always as conflictual as the work discussed in this section might lead one to expect, and one should not assume that societal actors always resist state efforts to establish presence in their communities.

The Public Administration of State-Building

A few scholars have begun to explore what one might call the "public administration" of state-building as they look at how the outcomes of state-building are shaped within the state itself. This shifts the focus in explaining state-building from policy choice to its implementation. States are not unitary actors. Instead, they are composed of networks of administration that reach over territory and penetrate society, reaching from the central bureaucracy into areas where the state seeks control (Mann 1984). Officials within these networks have a degree of autonomy, which becomes important when local officials have interests that diverge from those of their superiors.

Thus, the uneven implementation of state policies can be shaped by the incentives of local administrators (Lipsky 1980; Callaghy 1984). One must ask, then, about the interests or incentives of those local administrators, and how they might generate intra-state obstacles to initiatives emanating from the center. Their interests might be shaped by the extent of reliance on patrimonialism (Ertman 1997), the importance of customary law (Young 1994; Lange 2009), the extent to which bureaucracies are professionalized (Evans and Rauch 1999), the nature of training and recruitment (Kaufman 1967), or other characteristics of institutional design.

Additionally, even when institutional design is held constant, variation in incentives can derive from the identity of administrators, since administrative positions can be delegated to local community members or filled through the deployment of outsiders to serve (Hechter 2000). Outsiders deployed into communities as state agents lack independent sources of income and wealth, and are therefore easier to sanction. By contrast, the appointment of local elites to bureaucratic posts, even in the absence of customary law, can undermine the implementation of state-building efforts, since these elites are likely less vulnerable to sanctions from their superiors, and therefore less likely to implement unpopular or costly policies (Hutchcroft 2000). As Matsuzaki writes, local elites charged with local governance in the Philippines during United States rule failed to respond to cholera epidemics, and undermined land reform efforts; when interests of the state and the Filipino elite diverged, policy implementation remained poor (Matsuzaki n.d., 19).

Thus we see that tensions *within* the state can underpin the failure of state-building projects even in the absence of societal resistance.[9] In addition to looking at relations between state and society to explain why state-building efforts are stymied, we must also take the institutions of the state seriously, and examine intra-institutional dynamics and incentives. Understanding failed state-building, then, requires a shift from studying the determinants of the incentives of state leaders to understanding state-building efforts as policies, where struggles over administration and implementation take center stage.

The Evolution of States

Historical institutionalists have increasingly called for a greater reorientation of the study of institutions away from exploring their origins and toward investigating their evolution over time (Mahoney and Thelen 2010). Some aspects of the evolution of state institutions are quite well understood. We know quite a bit about why the design of state institutions tends to be stable over time, even when it is sub-optimal and when more effective alternatives exist (North 1990; Ertman 1997). Scholars have also studied the rise and fall of state-building coalitions. Bensel (1990) shows that internal contradictions within the Republican party coalition in the aftermath of the United States civil war placed important limits on the extent of state-building during the postwar era. He argues that "the process of state expansion in any specific period can be self-limiting" because it creates "new groups and interests in the national political economy that retard further expansion" (10).

These are valuable insights about state institutions and the politics of state-building. But other aspects of the state's evolution over time remain relatively unexplored. In particular, scholars have paid fairly little attention to the evolution of state strength over time, whether in terms of its scope (the range of functions it performs),[10] or its capacity to perform the core functions it has long engaged in. At a very general level, stable trajectories have characterized the evolution of these aspects of state strength: the state's scope has tended to increase over time, and the state's core capacity, once forged, tends to persist. I close this chapter by sketching some opportunities for exploration of these aspects of the state's evolution, and identifying some of the hurdles that must be cleared for scholars of state-building to undertake this deeper engagement with the evolution of state institutions.

As the state-building literature has shifted from explaining institutional design to accounting for variation in state capacity, the historical institutionalist toolbox is pushed to ask new questions. In particular, a consideration of these questions highlights the need for a broader conception of institutional evolution among historical institutionalists. I also highlight the need for scholars of the state to refine our understanding of the relationship between state institutions and state capacity.

The Growth of State Scope

Over the course of time, the state has come to play an ever wider range of roles in the lives of its citizens. States that originally sought to tax, to mobilize manpower for war, and to manage economic activity in some very basic ways have come to undertake a wide variety of functions, including welfare provision, the regulation of labor markets, many forms of monitoring and data collection, and what Tilly calls (1992, 115) "the thousand other activities Europeans now take for granted as attributes of state power." There are, of course, many studies of the development of particular sets of state functions, such as the emergence of labor regulation or the welfare state, but this overall pattern of expanding state scope has not been explored in a holistic manner.

One of the few accounts of this phenomenon can be found in a brief discussion by Tilly (1992, 114–121). Tilly explains the steady increase in state scope with reference to three causal factors. First, he highlights the role of bargaining between states and their subject populations: as states pressed society to extract ever more resources, they faced demands in return, and pre-empted or responded to these by undertaking a wide variety of functions. Thus, many aspects of the state emerged as "unintended burdens" (117) taken on by rulers who were only interested in making war against external or internal rivals. Second, Tilly builds on the literature on state autonomy in arguing that bureaucratic organizations "developed interests, perquisites, needs, and demands requiring attention on their own" and bargained with state leaders for an expanded role in governance (117). The third part of Tilly's argument is an intersection of the first two: societal actors leveraged institutions for purposes other than those for which they were designed, and "in order to build the coalitions required to get their own work done, officials accepted the broadening of institutions" (118).

In two important ways, this account resonates with the advances made by Mahoney and Thelen (2010) in explaining gradual institutional change. First, Tilly's argument suggests that rather than being the product of intentional design, expansion of the scope of state functions resulted from complex negotiation and bargaining among multiple actors. This means that a functionalist account of the state's scope, or an attempt to draw a direct line between characteristics of the society or economy and the roles the state plays, will be only partially correct at best. Tilly's reference to "unintended burdens" suggests the possibility that important aspects of state activity emerged as unintended consequences; that the state acts in ways that no single actor intended or sought. Second, Tilly highlights the central role of actors within state institutions in shaping the functions it plays. This insight closely matches Mahoney and Thelen's call to move away from accounts of change based on exogenous factors to consider the ways actors within institutions drive change.

Tilly's proposed mechanisms, then, seem at first glance to set the stage for a historical institutionalist account of the growth of state scope. But this pattern is not well captured by existing typologies of institutional change, which focus instead on various ways in which old rules are altered and new ones introduced (Mahoney and Thelen 2010, 15–18). Rather than focusing on the content of institutional rules, Tilly guides us to consider the set of functions an institution (or in this case, a set of institutions—more on this issue below) performs. The expansion of the set of functions carried out by an institution could be the result of several of the different types of institutional change Mahoney and Thelen sketch, including layering (the introduction of new rules alongside old ones), drift (the changed impact of existing rules), or conversion (the changed enactment of existing rules). If one followed the gradual change research agenda, we would be pushed to investigate the circumstances under which actors within institutions pursued certain kinds of institutional change as they sought to expand state scope. And indeed, this variation is potentially grounds for a very fruitful research agenda. But alongside the exploration of changes in institutional rules, scholars might also consider the set of institutional *functions* as a site of stability and change. This would imply shifting the study of institutions from what they *are* to what they *do*.

The Persistence of State Capacity

State capacity is most often defined in terms of the state's ability to implement chosen policies, and to perform a set of core functions like extraction and security provision.[11] Yet most measures of this concept are output-based: they assess the extent to which a policy is implemented—for example, the level of taxation collected, the number of soldiers conscripted, or the amount of public services provided. This raises an important concern about measurement validity: the extent to which a policy is actually implemented may not fully reflect the state's capacity. For example, states do not necessarily tax to the full extent they are infrastructurally capable because political considerations lead state leaders to set lower tax rates. Output-based measurement strategies can only assess the strength of the state independent of the power it deploys when they be absolutely sure that they are choosing as proxies outputs that the state is seeking to maximize.[12]

Despite this concern, scholars taking this output-based approach have identified a second broad pattern about the evolution of the state. They have come to find that state strength—measured in terms of this output-based strategy—persists over time to a striking degree. For example, taxes, once raised during war, remain high rather than declining after conflict ends (Campbell 1993).[13] This pattern is especially striking given the degree of fluidity of governments, regimes, and economic conditions. And we have little explanation for it. This is exactly the sort of question for which a historical institutionalist framework would seem to be ideally suited, given its insights about institutional stability over time. Yet historical institutionalists have said strikingly little about institutional strength, and even the few insights that do exist fall short of shedding light on the persistence of state strength because they provide no guidance about how to aggregate the strength of individual state institutions into an overall measure of state strength.

Scholars have turned to output-based measures of state capacity, despite the problems noted above, because they solve a thorny measurement problem: the output-based strategy obviates the need to make causal claims about the relationship between the design of state institutions and the state's strength. This is especially advantageous to the extent that many different arrays of institutions can achieve the same level of performance of a particular function, and that states with similarly designed institutions can perform very differently. Moreover, the strength of individual state institutions has no direct and consistent effect on overall state strength. For example, a state's capacity to perform a particular function could remain consistent even as one institution in that functional realm is destroyed and replaced by another. Thus, scholars who study the strength of individual state institutions, like Dargent (2015), say little about how these might aggregate up into an overall measure of state strength. The relationship between the state's power and the strength of its constituent institutions is still not sufficiently well understood.

Historical institutionalists have made a great deal of progress in understanding why institutional forms tend to be stable. But arguably the most striking feature of stability about states is not the form of their institutions, but the continuity of their strength. Because state strength cannot be reduced to the sum of the strength of state institutions, and because we struggle to measure institutional strength independent of actual enforcement of rules, scholars have increasingly turned to non-institutional approaches to the state (Vu 2010). Thus, historical institutionalism's continued relevance for scholars of state-building will be heightened to the extent that it continues to build a theoretical toolbox for conceptualizing institutional strength and measuring it independent of institutional outputs, and continues to complement its study of the constituent institutions of the state with careful investigation of macro-institutions like the state itself.

Conclusion

Scholars of the state have always been in deep dialogue with historical institutionalists, as the first part of this chapter showed. Yet opportunities exist to deepen this dialogue, not for its own sake, but in order to develop more complete accounts of the evolution of states over time. I have sketched two such opportunities in this chapter. One relates to state-building failure. Scholars of the state can learn from historical institutionalists to identify the full set of conditions necessary for state-building by applying a precise critical juncture framework, and by shifting from theorizing the choice to construct states to seeing state-building as policy implementation unfolding over space and time. The second relates to stable trajectories of persistent state capacity and growing state scope.

Investigating these trajectories fits very well with the historical institutionalist turn to studying the evolution of institutions rather than their origins or outputs. To seize upon this affinity will require historical institutionalists to complement their current study of the evolution of institutional rules with the exploration of institutional strength as they continue to study how institutions evolve. It will also require more careful theorizing about the relationship between the state and its constituent institutions; between institutional strength and state capacity.

Notes

1. Other core elements of historical institutionalism that resonate well with the state-building literature include the importance of timing and sequence, and the ways in which institutions shape and constitute actors rather than just being an outcome of actors' interactions.
2. Other approaches have also been important in the study of state development. Of particular note are the valuable contributions of scholars working within the rational choice institutionalist tradition, including Barzel (2002), North (1990), and Levi (1988, 1997).
3. Not all geographic arguments take the form of constant causes. Geographic factors may instead act as historical causes, as in the Netherlands case study in Downing (1992), which argues that because Dutch geography favored defensive wars, it obviated the massive military mobilization that elsewhere led to the initial emergence of absolutism.
4. For a fuller discussion of permissive and productive conditions, see Soifer (2012, 1574–1576)
5. My discussion here focuses only on one part of Saylor's argument: he also traces a path from commodity booms to state capacity through institution-building.
6. On the periodization of state development, see Loveman (2005).
7. Note that this claim is distinct from the one made by scholars about how social structure shapes the choices of state leaders about *whether* (Kurtz 2013) and *how* (Boone 2003) to project power.
8. Barkey (1994) cautions against seeing state negotiation with non-state actors as evidence of state weakness, showing that confrontation is not the only strategy available to state leaders. This ambiguity about how to interpret accomodation suggests the need to measure state capacity independent of state-society relations or state strategies.

9. In a different argument about intra-state tensions as an obstacle to state projects, vom Hau (2008, 2009) shows that bureaucrats professionalized under one set of norms will resist state projects designed to change those norms.
10. This definition of state scope comes from Fukuyama (2004). For a different use of the term to describe the state's role in regulation of economic activity, see Barzel (2002).
11. This definition of state strength follows in the tradition of Mann (1984) and builds on his concept of infrastructural power (Soifer 2008).
12. For a critique of this measurement strategy, see Fukuyama (2013). Moreover, the few existing approaches to institutional strength suffer from the same problem in that they focus on enforcement rather than the *capacity* to enforce. They, too, define strength in terms of the degree to which power is exercised rather than measuring power itself. Levitsky and Murillo (2009), for example, identify two dimensions of strength along which institutions vary. One is stability, defined as the absence of abnormal institutional change. More relevant to state strength is the dimension of enforcement, which they define (117) as the level of routine compliance with an institution. But this measures the *extent* of enforcement, and not the extent of the *capacity* to enforce: this strategy of measuring institutional strength suffers from the same problem as the output-based measures of state strength discussed above. Indeed, Levitsky and Murillo acknowledge that pressure from "power holders" can lead institutional rules to be enforced less than they might be if "rule writers" had their way (122). And there are many other reasons why "rule writers" might choose not to fully enforce the rules they design. (Holland 2014) Thus, Levitsky and Murillo's definition of institutional strength, if applied to the state, captures the power that it exercises, rather than the full extent of the power it possesses. We lack an approach to institutional strength that captures the capacity to enforce rather than the actual degree of enforcement.
13. The fact that Campbell fails to find a satisfying causal account underpinning this regularity implies that the "ratchet effect" he identifies remains a label rather than an explanation.

References

Barkey, Karen. 1994. *Bandits and Bureaucrats: The Ottoman Route to State Centralization.* Ithaca, NY: Cornell University Press.

Barnett, Michael. 1992. *Confronting the Costs of War.* Princeton, NJ: Princeton University Press.

Barzel, Yoram. 2002. *A Theory of the State: Economic Rights, Legal Rights, and the Scope of the State.* Cambridge: Cambridge University Press.

Bensel, Richard Franklin. 1990. *Yankee Leviathan: The Origins of Central State Authority in America, 1859–1877.* Cambridge: Cambridge University Press.

Boone, Catherine. 2003. *Political Topographies of the African State.* Cambridge: Cambridge University Press.

Brownlee, Jason. 2007. "Can America Nation-Build?" *World Politics* 59 (2): 314–340.

Callaghy, Thomas M. 1984. *The State-Society Struggle: Zaire in Comparative Perspective.* New York: Columbia University Press.

Campbell, John L. 1993. "The State and Fiscal Sociology." *Annual Review of Sociology* 19: 163–185.

Centeno, Miguel Ángel. 2002. *Blood and Debt: War and the Nation State in Latin America.* University Park, PA: The Pennsylvania State University Press.

Collier, Ruth Berins and David Collier. 1991. *Shaping the Political Arena.* Princeton, NJ: Princeton University Press.

Dargent, Eduardo. 2015. *Technocracy and Democracy in Latin America: Experts Running the Government.* Cambridge: Cambridge University Press.

Davies, Norman. 2012. *Vanished Kingdoms: The Rise and Fall of States and Nations.* New York: Viking Penguin.

Downing, Brian. 1992. *The Military Revolution and Political Change.* Princeton, NJ: Princeton University Press.

Ertman, Thomas. 1997. *Birth of the Leviathan: Building States and Regimes in Medieval and Early Modern Europe.* Cambridge: Cambridge University Press.

Evans, Peter and James E. Rauch. 1999. "Bureaucracy and Growth: A Cross-National Analysis of the Effects of Weberian State Structures on Economic Growth." *American Sociological Review* 64 (5): 748–765.

Fukuyama, Francis. 2004. *State Building: Governance and World Order in the 21st Century.* Ithaca, NY: Cornell University Press.

Fukuyama, Francis. 2013. "What Is Governance?" *Governance* 26 (3): 347–368.

Hechter, Michael. 2000. *Containing Nationalism.* Oxford: Oxford University Press.

Hechter, Michael and William Brustein. 1980. "Modes of Production and Patterns of State Formation in Western Europe." *American Journal of Sociology* 85 (5): 1061–1094.

Herbst, Jeffrey. 2000. *States and Power in Africa: Comparative Lessons in Authority and Control.* Princeton, NJ: Princeton University Press.

Holland, Alisha. 2014. "The Distributive Politics of Enforcement." *American Journal of Political Science* 59 (2): 357–371.

Hui, Victoria Tin-bor. 2005. *War and State Formation in Ancient China and Early Modern Europe.* Cambridge: Cambridge University Press.

Hutchcroft, Paul D. 2000. "Colonial Masters, National Politicos, and Provincial Lords: Central Authority and Local Autonomy in the American Philippines, 1900–1913." *The Journal of Asian Studies* 59 (2): 277–306.

Karl, Terry Lynn. 1997. *The Paradox of Plenty: Oil Booms and Petro-States.* Berkeley: University of California Press.

Kaufman, Herbert. 1967. *The Forest Ranger: A Study in Administrative Behavior.* Washington, D.C.: Resources for the Future.

Kohli, Atul. 2004. *State-Directed Development: Political Power and Industrialization in the Global Periphery.* Cambridge: Cambridge University Press.

Kurtz, Marcus J. 2013. *Latin American State Building in Comparative Perspective: Social Foundations of Institutional Order.* Cambridge: Cambridge University Press.

Lange, Matthew. 2009. *Lineages of Despotism and Development: British Colonialism and State Power.* Chicago: University of Chicago Press.

Levi, Margaret. 1988. *Of Rule and Revenue.* Berkeley: University of California Press.

Levi, Margaret. 1997. *Consent, Dissent, and Patriotism.* Cambridge and New York: Cambridge University Press.

Levitsky, Steven and Maria Victoria Murillo. 2009. "Variation in Institutional Strength." *Annual Review of Political Science* 12: 115–133.

Lipsky, Michael. 1980. *Street-Level Bureaucracy: Dilemmas of the Individual in Public Services.* New York: Russell Sage Foundation.

López-Alves, Fernando. 2000. *State Formation and Democracy in Latin America, 1810–1900.* Durham, NC: Duke University Press.

Loveman, Mara. 2005. "The Modern State and the Primitive Accumulation of Symbolic Power." *American Journal of Sociology* 110 (May 6): 1651–1683.

Mahoney, James and Kathleen Thelen, eds. 2010. *Explaining Institutional Change.* Cambridge: Cambridge University Press.

Mann, Michael. 1984. "The Autonomous Power of the State: Its Origins, Mechanisms, and Results." *Archives Europeénes de Sociologie* 25 (2): 185–213.

Matsuzaki, Reo. n.d. "State-Building: A Problem of Political Authority." Unpublished Manuscript, Trinity College.

Migdal, Joel S. 1988. *Strong Societies and Weak States: State-Society Relations and State Capabilities in the Third World.* Cambridge: Cambridge University Press.

North, Douglass C. 1990. *Institutions, Institutional Change, and Economic Performance.* Cambridge: Cambridge University Press.

Pierson, Paul. 2004. *Politics in Time.* Princeton, NJ: Princeton University Press.

Saylor, Ryan. 2014. *State Building in Boom Times: Commodities and Coalitions in Latin America and Africa.* Oxford: Oxford University Press.

Scott, James C. 1998. *Seeing Like a State.* New Haven, CT: Yale University Press.

Scott, James C. 2009. *The Art of Not Being Governed.* New Haven, CT: Yale University Press.

Slater, Dan. 2008. "Can Leviathan Be Democratic? Competitive Elections, Robust Mass Politics, and State Infrastructural Power." *Studies in Comparative International Development* 43 (3–4): 252–272.

Slater, Dan. 2010. *Ordering Power: Contentious Politics and Authoritarian Leviathans in Southeast Asia.* Cambridge: Cambridge University Press.

Soifer, Hillel David. 2008. "State Infrastructural Power: Conceptualization and Measurement in Empirical Analysis." *Studies in Comparative International Development* 43 (3–4): 231–251.

Soifer, Hillel David. 2012. "The Causal Logic of Critical Junctures." *Comparative Political Studies* 45 (12): 1572–1597.

Spruyt, Hendrik. 1994. *The Sovereign State and Its Competitors.* Princeton, NJ: Princeton University Press.

Stinchcombe, Arthur L. 1968. *Constructing Social Theories.* Chicago: University of Chicago Press.

Thies, Cameron G. 2005. "War, Rivalry, and State-Building in Latin America." *American Journal of Political Science* 49 (3): 451–465.

Tilly, Charles. 1975. "Reflections on the History of European State-Making." In *The Formation of National States in Western Europe*, ed. Charles Tilly. Princeton, NJ: Princeton University Press, 3–83.

Tilly, Charles. 1992. *Coercion, Capital, and European States, AD 990–1992.* Cambridge, MA: Blackwell.

vom Hau, Matthias. 2008. "State Infrastructural Power and Nationalism: Comparative Lessons from Mexico and Argentina." *Studies in Comparative International Development* 43 (3–4): 334–354.

vom Hau, Matthias. 2009. "Unpacking the School: Textbooks, Teachers, and the Construction of Nationhood in Mexico, Argentina, and Peru." *Latin American Research Review* 44: 127–154.

Vu, Tuong. 2010. "Studying the State through State Formation." *World Politics* 62 (1): 148–175.

Young, Crawford. 1994. *The African Colonial State in Comparative Perspective.* New Haven, CT: Yale University Press.

CHAPTER 11

HISTORICAL INSTITUTIONALISM AND DEMOCRATIZATION STUDIES

RODRIGO BARRENECHEA, EDWARD L. GIBSON, AND LARKIN TERRIE

LINKAGES between democratization studies and historical institutionalism are as old as the field of democratization itself. Although not formalized, an historical institutional approach to the study of democratization can be traced back to some of the classics in the field, including Dankwart Rustow's 1970 article "Transitions to Democracy," and Robert Dahl's 1971 book *Polyarchy*. These authors revealed a sensitivity for timing considerations when assessing the effect of institutions on democratic transitions and the durability of democracy. Their works pre-dated the rise of historical institutionalism in the 1990s as a self-conscious and systematic approach to the study of politics. Only in recent years have democratization scholars begun to formally adopt the theoretical tools of historical institutionalism to study institutional continuity and change in authoritarian and democratic regimes.

In the first part of this chapter we develop a series of classifications of selected major works in democratization according to their relationship to historical institutionalist approaches. We do so for the purpose of illustration, to reveal different ways in which democratization studies have overlapped with historical institutionalism over time. First, we classify works in the democratization literature according to whether they possess two constitutive elements of a historical institutional approach: a consideration for timing in the causal model and the study of institutions as independent variables. Distinctions will then be made between authors using different theoretical tools of historical institutionalism, whether they do this self-consciously or not. A final set of classifications will be made according to how institutions are used in the analysis. In the case of institutions being used as independent variables we observe whether they have a central or supporting role in the causal model. In regard to the institutional outcomes being explained, we classify works as falling into one of the two broad outcomes addressed by democratization scholarship: the emergence or stability of democratic regimes as a whole and the emergence or transformation of specific democratic regime institutions.

In the second part of this chapter we suggest two potentially fruitful new directions for historical institutionalist democratization studies. First, we build on recent scholarship on "episodic" analysis by developing the concept of "keystone institutions." These are individual regime institutions that emerge from a particular episode of institutional change. The timing of their emergence has important and systematic consequences for subsequent development of other regime institutions, triggering alternative scenarios for the long-term development and durability of democratic regimes.

In the second part of the chapter we also propose transcending the "transitology" paradigm that emphasizes change from authoritarian to democratic regime in order to analyze democratization as a continuous process of institutional change that applies equally to new democracies and long-standing democratic regimes. Blurring the rigid distinctions that exist between the study of "developing" democracies and "advanced industrial" democracies is a promising avenue that the deeper integration of historical institutionalism and democratization studies offers the field of comparative politics.

Democratization and Historical Institutionalism: Intimate Strangers

The field of democratization studies is by definition a field whose focus is the study of institutional change. The institutions in question fall under the broad concept of "political regime," which includes a range of formal and informal institutions governing the relationship between individuals and the state as well as the behavior of those in government. The study of democratization involves regime change—its long-term determinants, the strategic dimensions of transitions from authoritarian to democratic regimes, as well as changes within democratic regimes themselves.

Surpisingly, given the intellectual affinities between the two research fields, historical institutionalism and democratization have tended to operate at arm's length. This situation persisted even after the 1990s when, despite the rise of historical institutionalism as an important field in Comparative Politics, the emphasis on transitology (which tended to focus on agency based analyses of transitions from authoritarian to democratic regimes) in democratization studies inhibited its integration with the rising historical institutionalist research field. Few democratization scholars structure their work self-consciously as "historical institutionalist" work. Similarly, relatively few theorists of historical institutionalism are democratization scholars.

Despite the relatively small number of explicitly historical institutionalist studies in democratization, the influence of historical and institutionalist *approaches* can be readily traced throughout the body of the democratization literature over the last half-century. Works belonging to the historical institutional tradition are generally seen as having certain core attributes. In particular, they treat institutions as independent variables and they incorporate issues of timing, or temporality, into the analysis in systematic ways. In order to assess the impact of historical institutionalism on comparative democratization studies, Figure 11.1 categorizes major works in the field according to whether they possess one or both (or none) of these characteristics. Those works that treat institutions as independent variables we label institutionalists, whereas those who have different types of concern for issues of timing we label comparative historical. At the intersection of these two groups, we locate comparative historical democratization studies.[1] "Agency-based" democratization studies, with their emphasis on specific agents and their decisions as causes of regime outcomes, lie outside the scope of these other two groups.

Even among the works at the intersection of the two top diagrams, which can be classified as historical institutional democratization studies in this scheme, only a small handful of authors can be seen as self-consciously historical institutionalist. Dankwart Rustow, with his famous 1970 article "Transitions to Democracy," is often referred to as a founding father of the "transitology" field. However, he might also well be viewed as the founding father of historical institutionalism in democratization studies. This by virtue of the fact that his article may be the first attempt to identify a clear sequence of

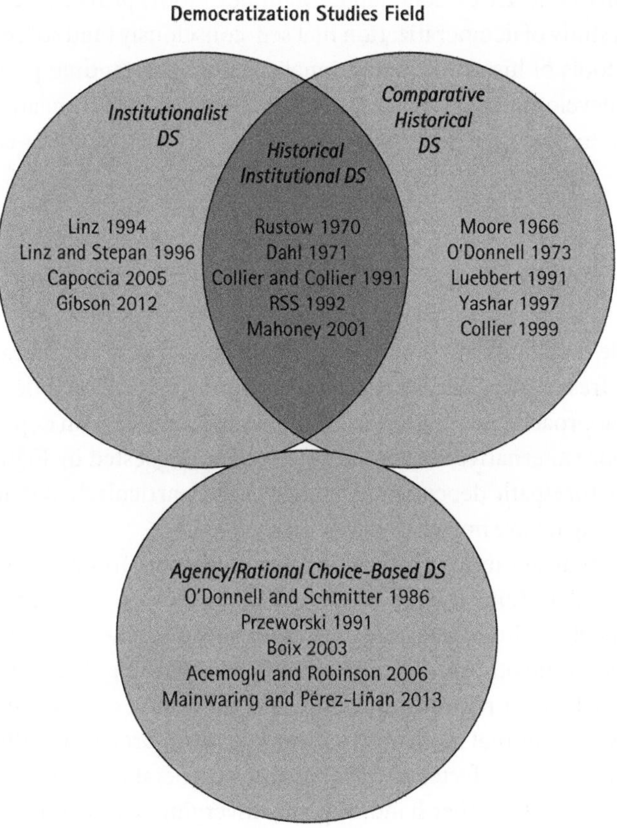

FIGURE 11.1 Classifying Democratization Studies

institutional formation and development and to specify the causal mechanisms linking the stages of this sequence to the consolidation of democratic regimes. Robert Dahl's *Polyarchy* (1971) applied varied approaches to his exploration of the determinants of democratic regimes. However, in one of the more cited chapters of the book Dahl proposed a nuanced sequential theory that bears a strong historical institutionalist imprint. He suggested that alternative sequential scenarios between the establishment of contestatory institutions and participatory institutions had different long-term effects on the stability of democratic regimes—namely that the initial establishment of institutions of contestation between elites set in motion sequential patterns that were more conducive to the establishment of stable polyarchies than situations where institutions of mass participation preceded those of contestation (see Dahl 1971, chapter 3).

However, historical institutionalism as a theoretical enterprise only began to become "self aware" in the early 1990s (the period of "crystallization" of historical institutionalism, as noted in this volume's introduction), and it was only as this field gradually developed over the course of the 1990s and 2000s that its present array of theoretical tools became available to scholars studying democratization. As such, many of the works in the upper-left quadrant of Figure 11.1, especially those published before the 2000s, treat issues of timing in a somewhat ad hoc manner, even though a concern with issues relating to temporality is clearly evident. James Mahoney (2001) provides perhaps the clearest example of a study of democratization that self-consciously (and successfully) applies the theoretical tools of historical institutionalism to understanding processes of democratic regime development, systematically using a critical juncture and path dependence framework to analyze regime outcomes in mid- to late twentieth-century Central America.

Timing and Sequencing in Democratization Studies

It is also possible to identify subgroups within the democratization literature according to how they address timing and sequencing of regime institutional development. The most common approaches are to use a critical juncture and/or path dependence framework or to explore alternative sequential patterns. As suggested by Figure 11.2, the use of a critical juncture/path dependence framework is particularly common (although many authors using it have not labeled it as such explicitly).

Among those that did make explicit use of critical junctures and path dependence in their causal models, Ruth Collier and David Collier (1991), and Mahoney (2001) are particularly important since they were the first to formalize these concepts. Collier and Collier identified the institutional incorporation of the working classes in Latin America as the critical juncture for regime development in the region during the mid-twentieth century. The institutions that mediated this incorporation process in different countries -state or political parties- affected the chances for democratic stability in the following decades. Mahoney, on the other hand, explains diverging regime outcomes in Central America based on the analysis of different policy choices (radical or moderate) in the

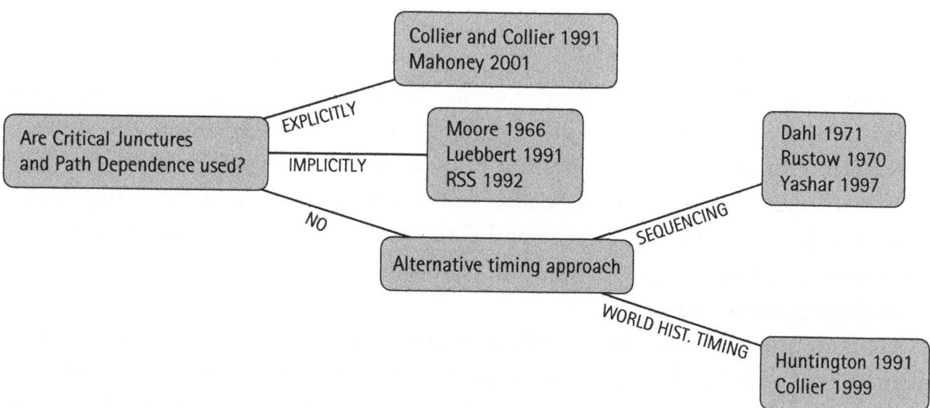

FIGURE 11.2 Timing in Democratization Studies

process of liberal economic reforms in the countryside put forward in the nineteenth century in these countries (see also Jones Luong 2008; Ertman 2010; Weyland 2010).

Barrington Moore (1966) and Gregory Luebbert (1991) are authors that make an implicit use of the critical juncture logic in their own explanations of regime outcomes. In Moore's classic account of the emergence of democracy in Europe and the United States, the moment of adoption of different allies by the bourgeoisie constitutes a critical juncture that determined whether a country would fall under a democratic, fascist, or communist regime. In Luebbert's case, the absence or presence of liberal and labor ("lib-lab") coalitions in the period previous to World War I would determine if liberal democracies persisted after the interwar crisis or if a new fascist or social democratic regimes emerged.[2]

The sequencing of institutional development is centrally important to Robert Dahl's work. Dahl suggests that the long-term "path" to democratic regimes (or "polyarchies") most conducive to regime stability was when institutions of political competition between elite sectors of society developed before the emergence of mass political participation. Where the latter preceded the former, or where both emerged simultaneously, the prospects for democratic regime stability were problematic (Dahl 1971, 33–40).[3] For other authors, specific historical periods determine the importance of different independent variables for democratic regime development. Samuel Huntington (1991), for example, identifies historical "waves" across two centuries, and stresses different variables as causes of transitions to democracy in each historical period.[4]

Institutions as Causes and Outcomes: Alternative Approaches

In regard to using institutions as independent variables, at least two different approaches can be identified. One group of authors treats specific regime institutions as factors that explain broader regime outcomes. Downing (1992) could be placed in this camp, since he argues that medieval representative assemblies constituted the basis for future liberal democracy in Europe. A particularly common approach is to treat characteristics of party systems as explanations of regime outcomes. For instance, Edward L. Gibson (1996) and Dietrich Rueschemeyer, Evelyne Stephens, and John Stephens (1992) see the presence of conservative parties as crucial to preventing democratic breakdown in Latin America, and Collier and Collier (1991) see the nature of the relationship between parties and unions in Chile and Brazil as driving democratic breakdown in these cases.[5]

Another group of authors combines institutional and socioeconomic variables in their explanations. This group focuses primarily on the socioeconomic determinants of democracy and tends to give institutions a smaller, supporting role in their analyses—treating parties and political coalitions not as independent variables in their own right but as the institutional means for expressing class interests. Deborah Yashar (1997), for example, expresses this approach when analyzing the class coalitional dynamics that favored transitions to democracy in Central America. Luebbert (1991) and Moore (1966) could be considered part of this group as well.

As seen in Figure 11.3, we can also distinguish authors according to whether a unitary conception of regime or a particular regime institution is treated as the dependent variable. The former group includes a large number of authors who examine Third Wave transitions. The late twentieth century in Latin America and Eastern Europe was characterized by movement from non-democratic regimes (e.g., military and communist dictatorships) to more or less democratic regimes. Earlier classics like Moore (1966) and Dahl (1971) also focused on a unitary concept of democratic regime.

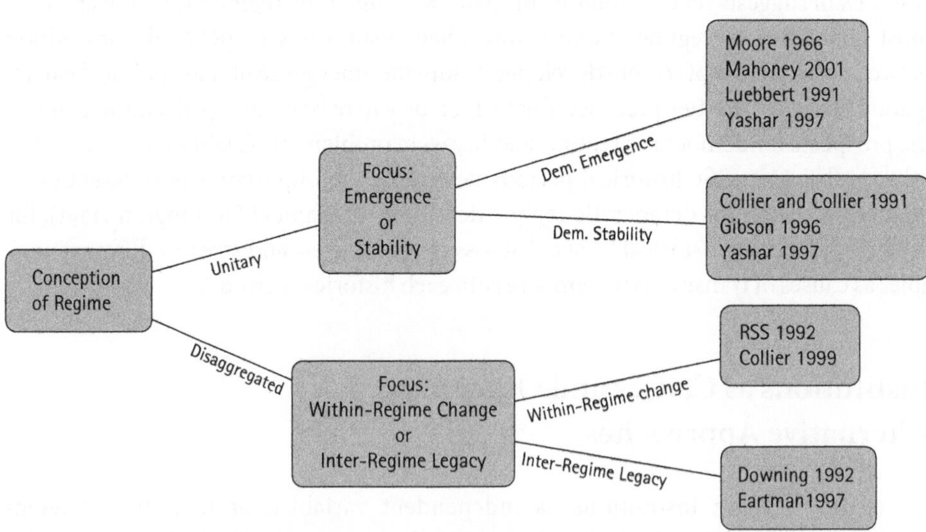

FIGURE 11.3 Institutional Outcomes in Historical Institutionalist Democratization Studies

A second group is composed of authors who have focused on specific regime institutions, whether in the form of changes within democratic regimes or inter-regime legacies, in which democratic institutions originated in a previous period. For example, in the context of existing democratic regimes, Collier (1999) and Rueschemeyer, Stephens, and Stephens (1992) focus on the expansion of suffrage in nineteenth century Europe and Latin America, while Ertman (1997) and Downing (1992) look at the development of parliamentary institutions in medieval and early modern Europe.

In sum, historical institutionalist democratization should be seen so far not as a coherent field of study, but rather as largely a collage of historical institutionalist approaches with different treatments of timing and institutions. The development of a systematic and relatively coherent field is still pending, although the classic literature and the most recent self-aware historical institutionalists have provide us with an important starting point. Given this state of affairs, and given the juncture at which the study of democratization finds itself in the 2010s, are there new promising avenues for building a more coherent and cumulative historical institutionalist body of work on democratization?

New Directions in Historical Institutionalism and Democratization Studies

From Long-Term Trajectories to Episodes ... and Back

A recent effort to develop new ways of analyzing institutional processes of democratization was advanced in 2010 by Giovani Capoccia and Daniel Ziblatt. The authors propose an approach for the "historically minded comparative analysis of democratization" (933) that analyzes democratization processes in terms of "key episodes of institutional change." Episodic analysis requires attention to multiple and specific instances of institutional change, which do not uniformly move toward democratization. The institutional outcomes result from conflicts across multiple lines of social and political cleavage across different moments in time, rather than a single coherent regime system created by one key factor. As Teri Caraway (2004, 454) suggested, "instead of thinking of democratization as a process that has a particular endpoint, the possibility of conceptualizing democratization as *episodes* of the expansion of suffrage to include new groups of people" will highlight the range of variables necessary to explain democracy's emergence as well as internal variations. This represents a departure from "trajectory-centered" analysis of prior historical comparative works, which analyzed democratic development as long-term regime trajectories. In a trajectory, each element or episode within the trajectory moves in the same direction, and is determined by previous events. In episodic analysis, each episode can be separate, not causally related, and potentially move in opposing directions.

Switching the temporal focus of the analysis from trajectories to episodes facilitates taking the "one institution at a time" pattern of European democratization into account. Europe's democratic regimes did not emerge fully formed at a specific historical moment but developed in fits and starts. Each regime institution was the product of particular struggles across a range of social and ideational conflicts.

Seeing democratic development in terms of episodes of institutional change leads us to see the process as a "chain of big and small events" (Capoccia and Ziblatt 2010, 941). Historical institutionalism is particularly well suited to analyzing these kinds of temporally ordered chains of events. Attention to issues of temporal ordering, and the identification of their causal significance, has traditionally been at the heart of historical institutionalist analysis. At the same time, episode analysis complements historical institutionalists' concern with critical junctures since, as Capoccia and Ziblatt point out, many key episodes of reform can be seen as critical junctures. Episode analysis can also lead to more careful examination of the politics of gradual institutional change, an issue historical institutionalist scholars have recently focused much attention on (Mahoney and Thelen 2010).

This analytical perspective is appropriate for the examination of either the adding *or subtracting* of elements from democratic regimes. A notable feature of the approach is that it is useful for examining change not only within countries that are struggling along the path to democracy but also in countries that have relatively well established democratic regimes. For example, Argentina's sweeping provincial constitutional reforms at the turn of the twenty-first century, or the US Supreme Court's recent overturning of key elements of the Voting Rights Act (each of these within particular causal sequences), can be analyzed as episodes of democratic reversal in established democracies (see Calvo and Miccozi 2005; Gibson 2012).

"Episodes" and "trajectories" can be distinguished conceptually, but analytically it is difficult to separate them as observable political processes if our purpose is to shed light on long-term institutional development patterns. An episode can be defined as "an event or a group of events occurring as part of a larger sequence; an incident or period considered in isolation" (*Oxford English Dictionary* n.d.). "Trajectory" is also a widely used, intersubjectively understood, but rarely defined term. In historical institutionalist literatures a "trajectory" tends to be understood as *an empirically observed long-term pattern of institutional development*. From these definitions it follows that episodes can be analyzed as pieces of a trajectory of institutional development, which raises the questions of how episodic analysis should be linked to the study of a larger trajectory and when it should remain a tool to study the emergence of institutions "one at a time." We also may want to explain why countries differ in regard to a wide variety of regime institutions (e.g., why was Costa Rica the only even remotely democratic country in Central America during most of the twentieth century?). It is certainly problematic to claim that there is such a thing as a fully democratic trajectory or a fully non-democratic trajectory, but it still might be the case that some trajectories are more democratic than others. Few would deny that England has experienced a more democratic path of development than, say, Paraguay or El Salvador. A full accounting of the development of democracy in England does require episode analysis—something that historians, if not political scientists, have long recognized—but what if we want to account for enduring differences across a variety of regime institutions between it and other countries?

Keystone Institutions as Links between Episode and Trajectory Analysis

Once we start disaggregating regimes into their constituent institutions, we begin to see that certain institutions can have particularly important consequences for long-term democratization processes.[6] Such institutions might be termed "keystone institutions," which are discrete regime institutions emerging from episodes of institutional change that trigger certain trajectories of regime institutional development. Some keystone institutions can spark long-term stabilizing or destabilizing regime development patterns. In addition, the emergence of a certain keystone institution may trigger or make more likely the subsequent emergence of particular regime institutions.

Regarding the first possibility, Dahl (1971) argues that early episodes of regime institutional development create a lock-in effect leading to the long-term endurance of a wider array of democratic institutions. When the emergence of institutions of competitive elections precede episodes of suffrage expansion, the whole cluster of democratic regime institutions is more likely to survive over the long term. Thus, episode analysis can shed light on the origins of a keystone institution that tends to stabilize long-term democratic regime development. Similarly, certain authors have suggested that conservative parties have been important for the survival of democratic regimes as the advent of mass politics creates episodes of lower-class political participation (Ertman 2010; Gibson 1996; Rueschemeyer, Stephens, and Stephens 1992).

A second effect of keystone institutions is to make the emergence of other regime institutions more likely. For example, scholars studying early modern political regimes in Europe have found that the successful assertion of parliamentary power in seventeenth-century England made possible the emergence of liberal democratic institutions in the eighteenth and nineteenth centuries (Downing 1992; Ertman 1997). Comparative research could further illuminate if the emergence of different regime institutions early in a democratizing process can spark the subsequent emergence of different sets of institutions in a democratizing trajectory.

Conclusion

Beyond Transitology Paradigms: Studying Gradual Change in Established Democracies

This chapter has explored interrelations between democratization studies and historical institutionalism. Basic tools and insights of this theoretical tradition have been part of the democratization field since its earliest contributions, although they were not acknowledged formally as part of the methodological toolbox of the democratization field. Recent works, however, have laid the foundations of a historical institutionalist agenda that could be central to the evolution of democratization studies.

The third wave is almost 40 years old. Most democracies in Latin America can be described as "established" democracies. Their problems and processes of institutional change are thus increasingly divorced from the problems and even legacies of the transitions that brought them into being. New approaches for the study of democratization that depart from transitology paradigms are thus needed. So is closer integration of approaches employed in the study of advanced and non-advanced democracies. Historical institutionalism can provide important theoretical and methodological supports to a new paradigm for the study of democratization.

Observation of struggles over political regimes in the United States, Europe, or other areas with long-standing democratic regimes indicates that "democracy" itself is a process rather than an end point (e.g., see Chapter 24, this volume). Established democracies are characterized by constant struggles over the structuring and restructuring of democratic institutions and over the expansion and contraction of democratic rights guaranteed to their citizens. These are battles over changes *within* democratic regimes rather than of democratic regimes (the latter being the focus of transitologists), and the stakes in these struggles, as we saw in the US civil rights struggles, can be very high.

The study of change within a democratic regime is precisely the study of change of its component institutions and the interaction between such institutions. Thus, an approach to democratization in established democracies that disaggregates regimes, focuses on episodes of creation or change in such institutions, and analyzes democratic development "one institution at a time" offers promising new agendas for democratization studies. It offers insights for studying how the timing and sequence in the creation of one regime institution affects the development of other regime institutions over time. Equally importantly, it offers possibilities for the mutual enrichment of democratization and historical institutionalism—by exposing historical institutionalists to new mechanisms of gradual institutional change and introducing democratization scholars to how such change shapes the evolution of democratic regimes.

NOTES

1. Ahmed (2010), Bunce (1999), Grzymala-Busse (2002), Jones Luong (2008), Gibson (1996), Riedl (2014), Ziblatt (2008), Bermeo (2010), Ertman (1997), Ertman (2010), Downing (1992), and Weyland (2010) are other examples within this same group.
2. Within the camp of authors making an implicit use of the critical juncture framework we could also place Downing (1992), Gibson (1996), Ertman (1997), Riedl (2014), and Ziblatt (2008), among others.
3. Grzymala-Busse (2002) could also be placed in this group.
4. A concern for the importance of historical timing to determine different causal variables for democratization processes can also be found in Bunce (1999) and O'Donnell (1973).
5. See Grzymala-Busse (2002), Bunce (1999), Mahoney (2001), Dahl (1971), Elkins (2010), Jones Luong (2008), Linz and Stepan (1996), Gibson (2012), and Scully (1992).
6. The scope of what one might label "regime institutions" is subject to various interpretations. For the time being we take a narrow view, focusing on such formal institutions of a democratic polity as legislatures, parties, courts, etc. One could reasonable take a wider view, incorporating other institutions (e.g., media, state bureaucracies, and such informal institutions as clientelism).

REFERENCES

Acemoglu, Daron and James Robinson. 2006. *Economic Origins of Dictatorship and Democracy*. New York: Cambridge University Press.

Ahmed, Amel. 2010. "Reading History Forward: The Origins of Electoral Systems in European Democracies." *Comparative Political Studies* 43 (8–9): 1059–1088.

Bermeo, Nancy. 2010. "Interests, Inequality, and Illusion in the Choice for Fair Elections." *Comparative Political Studies* 43 (8–9): 1119–1147.

Boix, Carles. 2003. *Democracy and Redistribution*. New York: Cambridge University Press.

Bunce, Valerie. 1999. *Subversive Institutions: The Design and the Destruction of Socialism and the State*. New York: Cambridge University Press.

Calvo, Ernesto and Juan P. Miccozi. 2005. "The Governor's Backyard: A Seat-Vote Model of Electoral Reform for Multiparty Races." *Journal of Politics* 67 (4): 1050–1074.

Capoccia, Giovanni. 2005. *Defending Democracy: Reactions to Extremism in Interwar Europe*. Baltimore, MD: Johns Hopkins University Press.

Capoccia, Giovanni and Daniel Ziblatt. 2010. "The Historical Turn in Democratization Studies: A New Research Agenda for Europe and Beyond." *Comparative Political Studies* 43 (8–9): 931–968.

Caraway, Teri. 2004. "Class, Gender, Race, and the Extension of Suffrage." *Comparative Politics* 36 (4): 443–460.

Collier, Ruth Berins. 1999. *Paths Toward Democracy: The Working Class and Elites in Western Europe and South America*. New York: Cambridge University Press.

Collier, Ruth Berins and David Collier. 1991. *Shaping the Political Arena: Critical Junctures, the Labor Movement, and Regime Dynamics in Latin America*. Princeton, NJ: Princeton University Press.

Dahl, Robert. 1971. *Polyarchy: Participation and Opposition*. New Haven, CT: Yale University Press.

Downing, Brian M. 1992. *The Military Revolution and Political Change: Origins of Democracy and Autocracy in Early Modern Europe*. Princeton, NJ: Princeton University Press.

Elkins, Zachary. 2010. "Diffusion and the Constitutionalization of Europe." *Comparative Political Studies* 43 (8–9): 969–999.

Ertman, Thomas. 1997. *Birth of the Leviathan: Building States and Regimes in Medieval and Early Modern Europe*. New York: Cambridge University Press.

Ertman, Thomas. 2010. "The Great Reform Act of 1832 and British Democratization." *Comparative Political Studies* 43 (8–9): 1000–1022.

Gibson, Edward L. 1996. *Class and Conservative Parties: Argentina in Comparative Perspective*. Baltimore, MD: Johns Hopkins University Press.

Gibson, Edward L. 2012. *Boundary Control: Subnational Authoritarianism in Federal Democracies*. New York: Cambridge University Press.

Grzymala-Busse, Anna. 2002. *Redeeming the Communist Past: The Regeneration of Communist Parties in East Central Europe*. Cambridge and New York: Cambridge University Press.

Huntington, Samuel. 1991. *The Third Wave: Democratization in the Late Twentieth Century*. Norman, OK: The University of Oklahoma Press.

Jones Luong, Pauline. 2008. *Institutional Change and Political Continuity in Post-Soviet Central Asia*. New York: Cambridge University Press.

Linz, Juan. 1994. "Presidential or Parliamentary Democracy: Does It Make a Difference." In *The Failure of Presidential Democracy*, ed. Juan Linz and Arturo Valenzuela. Baltimore, MD: John Hopkins University Press, 3–87

Linz, Juan and Alfred Stepan. 1996. *Problems of Democratic Transition and Consolidation*. Baltimore, MD: Johns Hopkins University Press.

Luebbert, Gregory M. 1991. *Liberalism, Fascism, or Social Democracy: Social Classes and the Political Origins of Regimes in Interwar Europe*. New York: Oxford University Press.

Mahoney, James. 2001. *The Legacies of Liberalism: Path Dependence and Political Regimes in Central America*. Baltimore, MD: Johns Hopkins University Press.

Mahoney, James and Kathleen Thelen. 2010. "A Gradual Theory of Institutional Change." In *Explaining Institutional Change: Ambiguity, Agency, and Power*, ed. James Mahoney and Kathleen Thelen. Cambridge: Cambridge University Press, 1–37

Mainwaring, Scott and Aníbal Pérez-Liñán. 2013. *Democracies and Dictatorships in Latin America: Emergence, Survival and Fall*. Cambridge: Cambridge University Press.

Moore, Barrington. 1966. *The Social Origins of Dictatorship and Democracy*. Boston, MA: Beacon Press.

O'Donnell, Guillermo. 1973. *Modernization and Bureaucratic Authoritarianism: Studies in South American Politics*. Berkeley: Institute of International Studies, University of California.

O'Donnell, Guillermo and Philippe C. Schmitter. 1986. *Tentative Conclusions about Uncertain Democracies*. Baltimore, MD: The Johns Hopkins University Press.

Oxford English Dictionary. n.d. *Episode*. Available at <http://www.oxforddictionaries.com/us/definition/american_english/episode> (accessed November 15, 2014).

Przeworski, Adam. 1991. *Democracy and the Market: Political and Economic Reform in Eastern Europe and Latin America*. New York: Cambridge University Press.

Riedl, Rachel Beatty. 2014. *Authoritarian Origins of Democratic Party Systems in Africa*. Cambridge: Cambridge University Press.

Rueschemeyer, Dietrich, Evelyne Huber Stephens, and John Stephens. 1992. *Capitalist Development and Democracy*. Chicago: University of Chicago Press.

Rustow, Dankwart. 1970. "Transitions to Democracy: Towards a Dynamic Model." *Comparative Politics* 2 (3): 337–363.

Scully, Timothy. 1992. *Rethinking the Center: Party Politics in Nineteenth and Twentieth Century Chile*. Stanford, CA: Stanford University Press.

Weyland, Kurt. 2010. "The Diffusion of Regime Contention in European Democratization, 1830–1940." *Comparative Political Studies* 43 (8–9): 1148–1176.

Yashar, Deborah J. 1997. *Demanding Democracy: Reform and Reaction in Costa Rica and Guatemala, 1870–1950s*. Stanford, CA: Stanford University Press.

Ziblatt, Daniel. 2008. "Does Landholding Inequality Block Democratization? A Test of the 'Bread and Democracy' Thesis and the Case of Prussia." *World Politics* 60 (4): 610–641.

CHAPTER 12

DURABLE AUTHORITARIANISM

STEVEN LEVITSKY AND LUCAN A. WAY

Authoritarianism remained alive and well in the early twenty-first century. Dictatorships in much of the Middle East emerged from the Third Wave of democratization largely unscathed. Communist regimes in China, Cuba, Laos, North Korea, and Vietnam survived the collapse of communism; regimes in Malaysia and Singapore remained intact despite high levels of socioeconomic modernization; and regimes in Cuba, Iran, Myanmar, North Korea, and Zimbabwe survived deep economic crises and intense international pressure.

The persistence of non-democracies in China, the Middle East, and much of the former Soviet Union gave rise to new efforts to theorize authoritarian durability (Herb 1999; Levitsky and Way 2010, 2012; Schedler 2002, 2013; Slater 2003, 2010; Fish 2005; Smith 2005; Greene 2007). Although scholars highlighted a range of causes, including economic performance (Przeworski et al. 2000), coalitions (Pepinsky 2009), and natural resource wealth (Ross 2001; Smith 2007), they placed particular emphasis on political institutions (Brownlee 2007; Gandhi and Przeworski 2007; Lust-Okar 2007; Gandhi 2008; Magaloni 2008; Blaydes 2010; Svolik 2012). Building on Barbara Geddes' (1999) finding that single party regimes are more stable than military regimes or personalistic dictatorships, for example, scholars pointed to the centrality of ruling parties (see also Huntington 1968, 1970). Many of these analyses focused on parties' role in managing intra-elite conflict. Ruling parties are said to provide institutional mechanisms to regulate access to the spoils of public office (Geddes 1999; Brownlee 2007). By offering future opportunities for career advancement, party machines lengthen time horizons and encourage elite cooperation, which can be critical to authoritarian stability (Geddes 1999; Brownlee 2007, 13; Magaloni 2008).

Yet authoritarian regimes with similar institutional arrangements vary markedly in their durability (Smith 2005). Whereas some ruling parties provide a foundation for decades of authoritarian stability, others collapse at the first sign of duress (Smith 2005; Levitsky and Way 2010, 2012). This variation was particularly manifest after the end of the Cold War. Whereas communist regimes collapsed throughout Eastern Europe in and after 1989, similar regimes in China, Cuba, Laos, North Korea, and Vietnam survived. Likewise, whereas many African single- or dominant-party regimes collapsed during the post-Cold War era (e.g., Kenya, Malawi, Senegal, Zambia), others proved strikingly durable in other states (e.g., Angola, Mozambique, Tanzania, Zimbabwe).

Efforts to explain this variation led scholars to move beyond the formal structure, or design, of authoritarian institutions and examine differences in institutional *strength*.[1] The question thus became a Huntingtonian one: "Where do strong parties, or single party regimes, come from?" (Smith 2005, 198). This is a question for which historical institutionalism is particularly well-suited.

This chapter examines historical institutionalist accounts of authoritarian durability. It argues that the "party-state complexes" that undergird many durable authoritarian regimes (Slater 2010) are rarely, if ever, a product of institutional design. Rather, as Samuel Huntington (1968, 1970) observed, their origins frequently lie in early periods of violent conflict and struggle. We identify two historical paths to durable authoritarianism: a revolutionary path and a counter-revolutionary path.

The Historical Roots of Durable Authoritarianism: Revolutionary and Counter-Revolutionary Paths

Institutions provide an important foundation for stable authoritarian rule, but not necessarily in the ways scholars have come to expect. Outside of dynastic monarchies (Herb 1999), most durable authoritarian regimes are based not on ruling parties per se, but rather on robust "party-state complexes" (Slater 2010), characterized by cohesive ruling party that is tightly wedded to an effective coercive apparatus. Cohesive ruling parties help limit elite defection, which is widely viewed as major cause of authoritarian breakdown (Geddes 1999; Brownlee 2007; Magaloni 2008; Levitsky and Way 2010, 2012; Svolik 2012). An effective coercive apparatus enables autocrats to systematically preempt opposition, nip protest in the bud, and, when necessary, crack down effectively on large-scale mobilization (Slater 2003, 2010; Bellin 2004; Levitsky and Way 2010). Yet because a powerful security apparatus may be turned against the government (another major source of authoritarian breakdown),[2] tight partisan control over the armed forces is an essential element of the party-state complex.

Robust party-state complexes are rarely, if ever, designed by far-sighted autocrats. Rather, most autocrats either inherit them or build them with resources (e.g., networks, identities) generated by circumstances over which they have little control.[3] Indeed, an examination of (non-monarchic) authoritarian regimes that survived for 50 years or more (e.g., China, Cuba, Malaysia, Mexico, Singapore, Soviet Union, Taiwan, Vietnam) reveals a striking pattern: nearly all of them were based on a party-state complex whose origins lie in periods of *extended and violent conflict*. As Huntington (1970, 13–14) noted decades ago, the most stable single party regimes have been a "product of struggle and violence."

Understanding the roots of durable authoritarianism thus requires an examination of historical processes of state- and party-building. Historical institutionalism is well -suited to such an endeavor. Indeed, research in the historical institutionalist tradition has identified two historical paths to durable authoritarianism: (1) a revolutionary path and (2) a counter-revolutionary path. Notwithstanding their many differences, these two paths share a key feature: origins in violent conflict. In each scenario, violent conflict (or the threat of conflict) during a regime's foundational period triggered a sequence of events that ultimately give rise to a cohesive party–state complex. These institutional legacies were not easily replicated in regimes with non-violent origins.

Revolution and counter-revolution are not the only paths to durable authoritarianism. Dynastic monarchies constitute a distinct path (see Herb 1999), and some party-based regimes have proven long-lasting in the absence of violent origins (e.g., Botswana, Tanzania). Nevertheless, it is striking how many of the world's most robust non-monarchic authoritarian regimes were born of violent conflict.

A Revolutionary Path

Revolutionary regimes may be defined as those which emerge out of sustained, ideological, and violent struggle from below, and whose establishment is accompanied by both mass mobilization and significant efforts to transform state structures and the existing social (i.e., class, racial, religious) order.[4]

The connection between revolution and durable authoritarianism can be traced back to Huntington (1968, 1970) and Skocpol (1979). Huntington famously argued that durable single party regimes were often "the product of nationalist or revolutionary movements from below which had to fight for power" (1968, 418). Revolutions, he argued, strengthen state and party structures, create disciplined ruling elites, and facilitate the elimination of political rivals (1968, 311–313, 328). Likewise, Skocpol (1979) argued that revolutions tend to produce states with far greater coercive capacity than the states they replace. Subsequent research leant some empirical support to Huntington's propositions on revolutions and state-building (Skocpol 1988; Gurr 1988; Walt 1996; Goodwin 2001; Taylor and Botea 2008), comparative communism (Adelman 1982), single party rule (Smith 2005; Levitsky and Way 2010, 2012), and civil-military relations (Perlmutter 1977; Nordlinger 1977; Adelman 1982). Drawing on this research, the following section argues that revolutions trigger sequences that, if not aborted by early military defeat, yield durable authoritarian regimes. Critical steps in the sequence are: (1) the seizure of power amid a prolonged, ideologically driven, and violent struggle, which gives rise to a cohesive ruling party and a new coercive apparatus that is rebuilt (and tightly controlled) by the party; and (2) a reaction, in the form of counter-revolutionary and/or external military conflict, which reinforces elite cohesion, strengthens the coercive apparatus, and facilitates the destruction of internal rivals and alternative power centers. Regimes that survive these initial sequences tend to be strikingly durable in their aftermath.

Revolutionary Struggle and the Seizure of Power

Revolutionary seizures of power lay a foundation for powerful party-state complexes. For one, revolutionary struggle produces strong ruling parties (Huntington 1968, 1970). Successful liberation struggles give rise to extensive mass organizations and, crucially, cohesive party structures (Levitsky and Way 2012). The exigencies of armed conflict compel revolutionary organizations to institutionalize military-style discipline—characteristics that often persist after the seizure of power. For example, in Zimbabwe, "military commandism" remained "deeply ingrained in ZANU-PF practice and political structures" (Tendi 2010, 151); and in Laos, decades of armed struggle against French and US-backed forces contributed to the "impressive cohesion" of the Lao Peoples Revolutionary Party (Brown and Zasloff 1986, 152).

Revolutionary struggle also enhances elite cohesion by strengthening partisan identities and hardening partisan boundaries. As Adrienne LeBas (2011) argues, intense polarization sharpens "us-them" distinctions, strengthens within-group ties, and fosters perceptions of a "linked fate" among cadres. Where cadres have participated in prolonged, violent struggle, they are more likely to view party membership in "moral" terms, and to frame choices about cooperation or defection in terms of loyalty rather than a simple material calculus (LeBas 2011, 44–47). The polarization generated by revolutionary wars often persists into the post-revolutionary era, effectively "trapping" potential defectors within the ruling party. When the opposition can be credibly linked to historic enemies against which the revolutionaries fought a life and death struggle, and where abandoning the ruling party can therefore be viewed as treason, the cost of defection will be high.

Revolutionary seizures of power thus produce unusually cohesive ruling parties. Ruling parties in China, Cuba, Mozambique, and Zimbabwe suffered strikingly few defections in the post-Cold War era, despite severe crises. In China, the Communist Party closed ranks in the face of the Tiananmen Square protests; in Mozambique, Frelimo suffered few defections despite the devastating civil war and economic collapse of the mid-1980s; and in Zimbabwe, ZANU-PF remained intact in the 2000s despite a serious opposition challenge, stolen elections, international isolation, and an extraordinary economic collapse.

Revolutionary seizures of power also give rise to cohesive security forces. Because revolutions are accompanied by state collapse, revolutionary elites frequently re-make the state. This entails either the creation of new revolutionary armies or a radical purge and reconstruction of existing ones (Adelman 1982; Skocpol 1988). As a result, the army and other security forces are almost invariably commanded by cadres from the liberation struggle and infused with a revolutionary ideology (Huntington 1968, 311–313; Adelman 1982; Gurr 1988). For example, in Cuba, the revolutionary regime was marked by "almost total overlap" between the ruling civilian and military elites (Dominguez 1982, 45–46, 54); in Vietnam, civilian and military roles were "blurred" during the revolutionary struggle, and post-revolutionary army commanders were "without exception … high-ranking party leaders" (Turley 1982, 66–68); in Mexico, all top military posts were filled by officers with revolutionary credentials into the 1950s (Camp 2005, 45).

Revolutionary armies are thus highly partisan. Government and military elites share a revolutionary identity and ideology (Huntington 1968, 311–313; Walt 1996, 24–30), and the security forces are "imbued with such extras as 'commitment,' 'dedication,' and 'purpose' " (Perlmutter 1977, 224). Thus, unlike military officials in other authoritarian regimes, who may view their interests as distinct from those in power, revolutionary army commanders view themselves "partner(s) in the revolutionary movement" and tend to be "unswervingly loyal to the revolution and its dogmas" (Perlmutter 1977, 15, 206). For example, Sandinista military officials were "possessed by a genuine sense of mission," which cast them as "defenders … of a revolutionary political project" (Cajina 1997, 125). Likewise, Iran's Revolutionary Guard viewed itself as the "principal bastion and perpetuator of revolutionary purity" (Katzman 1993, 23), and in Vietnam, the army's revolutionary origins ensured that its "loyalty to the party was above question" (Turley 1982, 66–68).

Partisan penetration enhances discipline and cohesion within the security forces. Security forces that are created by revolutionary forces, commanded by former revolutionary combatants, and infused with a revolutionary ideology are far less likely to suffer problems of insubordination and rebellion than are non-revolutionary ones. Indeed, remarkably few revolutionary regimes have fallen prey to military coups (Nordlinger 1977, 15–18; Adelman 1982). Because coups are the primary cause of authoritarian breakdown (Svolik 2012, 4–5), such invulnerability to coups is a major source of regime durability.

Counter-Revolution, War, and Authoritarian Consolidation

As important to regime durability is the process of state- and party-building that occurs in the *aftermath* of revolution (Skocpol 1979, 1988; Gurr 1988; Taylor and Botea 2008). Revolutions almost always trigger additional armed conflict, both civil and external (Skocpol 1988; Walt 1996). Most revolutions trigger armed counter-revolutionary movements that must be defeated if the new regime is to consolidate power (Huntington 1968, 269–270; Gurr 1988). Thus, as Jack Goldstone observes, "far more violence is committed by new revolutionary regimes after seizing power—in order to consolidate their control of society, or in civil wars between revolutionaries and counter-revolutionaries—than is committed by revolutionary actors against authorities before the latter are overthrown"

(2003, 53–54). Revolutions also frequently trigger *external* wars,[5] often with neighboring states whose governments feel threatened by the revolutionary regime and/or perceive a window of opportunity in the wake of state collapse (Skocpol 1988; Walt 1996).

Although revolutionary regimes may be weakened or destroyed by post-revolutionary military conflict (e.g., Cambodia, Nicaragua), surviving regimes tend to emerge strengthened, for at least three reasons. First, military conflict compels revolutionary elites to build up the state's coercive capacity. Revolutionary governments quickly find that an effective army is "a sine qua non for survival itself. Without such an army, physical extermination [is] inevitable" (Adelman 1982, 6). For this reason, most post-revolutionary states are transformed into "garrison states" (Gurr 1988, 57; Skocpol 1988). In Russia, for example, the civil war compelled the Bolshevik government to build a massive, "disciplined, efficient and versatile" political police (Leggett 1986, 121, 238). In Cuba and Nicaragua, security forces expanded tenfold in the aftermath of revolution (Dominguez 1982, 47). These expanded security forces are able to draw upon a large pool of experienced ex-combatants from the revolutionary struggle and subsequent civil or external wars. These former combatants may be formally incorporated into the security forces, as in the case of Iran's Revolutionary Guard, or mobilized into informal militias, as in the case of ZANU "war veterans" in Zimbabwe.

The "revolutionary garrison states" that emerge from post-revolutionary civil wars thus tend to be larger, more disciplined, and more experienced in violence than their predecessors (Gurr 1988, 57; Skocpol 1979, 1988; Walt 1996, 22; Taylor and Botea 2008). A ruling elite that has engaged in violent conflict is more likely to remain united behind coercive measures (Gurr 1988), and security officials who belong to that revolutionary elite are more likely to carry out orders to repress.[6]

Second, post-revolutionary conflict helps to consolidate ruling parties. In Russia, for example, the Bolshevik Party was marked by "anarchy and indiscipline" during the 1917 Revolution, but the "awesomeness of the struggle with the White armies" convinced party members that "truly iron party discipline ... was the only way to win the life and death struggle" (Service 1979, 92, 93, 95). Thus, the civil war generated a "siege mentality" that "would long remain the consciousness of the Bolsheviks, who drew no distinction between what they regarded as ubiquitous internal and external enemies" (Getty and Naumov 2008, 30). By the early 1920s, "discipline and obedience had become bywords of Bolshevik consciousness and behavior" (Service 1979, 133).

Third, post-revolutionary conflict enables governments to weaken or destroy alternative centers of power: institutions or social classes whose power, resources, or legitimacy can serve as a basis for mobilizing opposition to the regime. One such power center is the old army. In most revolutions, pre-existing armies either dissolved with the fall of the dictator (e.g., Cuba, Nicaragua) or were destroyed by civil war (e.g., China, Mexico, Russia). Revolutions also weaken or destroy traditional ruling and religious institutions whose "symbolic power" could be used to mobilize opposition to the regime (Slater 2009). Thus, the Russian, Vietnamese, Laotian, and Iranian revolutions destroyed pre-existing monarchic institutions. Likewise, the Cuban and Mexican revolutions weakened Catholic Churches, leaving them political emasculated for decades. In rural revolutions such as those in Mexico, Russia, China, and Vietnam, peasant rebellion and subsequent land reform destroyed once powerful agrarian elites.

Post-revolutionary conflict provides revolutionary elites with both a justification and the means to destroy other (often allied) political organizations with the potential to contest for power in the future. In Russia, for example, the 1918–1920 civil war allowed the Bolshevik government to "systematically eliminate" the Socialist Revolutionaries and other leftist parties that initially commanded greater popular support, thereby leaving the Bolsheviks as the "sole masters of the Soviet state" (Leggett 1986, 304–305). After the civil war, competing social forces in the country were "either exhausted and prostrate or pulverized" (Deutcher [1959] 2003, 5). In Iran, the Islamic government's "ruthless, brutal, and gruesome campaign" against the *Mojahedin-e-Khalq* and other insurgent groups in 1980–1982 resulted in the liquidation of virtually all effective opposition. (Bakhash 1990, 220)

The destruction of traditional rulers, established churches, landowning classes, and other organized political forces contributes to authoritarian durability by eliminating not only contemporary rivals but also the structural bases of future opposition. In the absence of independent sources of finance, infrastructure, and/or legitimacy, the organizational bases of opposition effectively disappear.

In sum, revolutions trigger a sequence of events that often culminate in powerful party-state complexes, which, in turn, provide a solid foundation for durable authoritarianism. Successful armed struggle engenders cohesive ruling parties that, upon seizing power, reconstruct and thoroughly penetrate the coercive apparatus. Moreover, post-revolutionary efforts to carry out radical change invariably threaten existing societal interests and institutions, triggering armed counter-revolutionary movements, civil wars, and in some cases, inter-state wars. Some revolutionary regimes (e.g., Cambodia, Nicaragua) do not survive such conflicts, but where they do, post-revolutionary violence facilitates the destruction of independent power centers and gives rise to a larger and far more powerful coercive apparatus. Such developments may limit the potential for opposition mobilization for decades to come. Post-revolutionary violence also deepens polarization and reinforces ruling party cohesion, which reduces the likelihood of regime-threatening elite defection. The result is a regime that is nearly invulnerable to military coups (Adelman 1982), less prone to elite defection (Levitsky and Way 2012), and well-equipped to survive economic crises and thwart opposition protest (Huntington 1968, 309–310).

The empirical record is striking. Several of the longest-surviving authoritarian regimes of the twentieth and early twenty-first centuries, including those in Mexico (83 years), the Soviet Union (74 years), China (65 years and counting), Vietnam (60 years and counting), and Cuba (55 years and counting), were born of violent revolution. Outside of Persian Gulf monarchies, few other modern dictatorships have survived as long. The durability of revolutionary regimes was made especially manifest after the end of the Cold War. After 1989, the loss of foreign patrons, unprecedented international democracy promotion, and economic crisis undermined authoritarian rule in much of the world. Yet ten of the twelve revolutionary authoritarian regimes that existed in

January 1989 survived through 2014, compared to barely a third (29 of 82) of the world's non-revolutionary authoritarian regimes.[7] Indeed, the only Communist regimes that persisted after the collapse of the Soviet Union—China, Cuba, Laos, North Korea, and Vietnam—were revolutionary. Likewise, in sub-Saharan Africa, among the handful of authoritarian regimes that remain intact 24 years after the fall of the Berlin Wall are three that were founded in violent liberation struggle: Angola, Mozambique, and Zimbabwe. And in the MENA region, the only non-monarchic regimes that were not seriously challenged during the Arab Spring were born of violent struggle: Algeria and Iran.

A Counter-Revolutionary Path

Durable authoritarianism may also be founded in violent struggle *against* revolution (Slater and Smith 2010; Slater 2010). Like Huntington (1968), Dan Slater (2010) traces the origins of durable authoritarianism to early periods of conflict. Yet he argues that the key to authoritarian durability is effective state-building, and that the main impetus for post-colonial state-building lay not in revolution but in counter-revolution.

For Slater (2010), the counter-revolutionary path to durable authoritarianism is rooted in early class and communal conflict. He argues that the emergence of powerful party-state complexes in Southeast Asia is rooted in elite "protection pacts" forged during regimes' founding periods. According to Slater, economic elites are only willing to pay the taxes necessary to sustain powerful state and party structures where they face "extreme duress," in the form of "endemic" and "unmanageable" contentious politics (2010, 13, 49). Thus, it is only where radical protest or insurgency afflicted urban areas and triggered communal violence during the post-colonial period that elites accede to "protection pacts" in which they pay higher taxes and finance ruling parties in exchange for order and security (2010, 13, 16). Timing and sequencing are critical to this outcome. Endemic and unmanageable contention gave rise to stable authoritarian Leviathans only when it occurred *prior to the consolidation of authoritarian rule* (Slater 2010, 14). It is only when fear struck the elite under relatively pluralistic regimes that emergent autocrats could credibly claim that authoritarian state-building is necessary to bring order (2010, 14).

For Slater, then, durable counter-revolutionary Leviathans emerged where endemic, unmanageable conflict threatened elites prior to the establishment of authoritarian rule. In Malaysia, Singapore, and Indonesia, and perhaps in Taiwan and South Africa (Slater 2010, 282–284), post-colonial elites confronted powerful class and/or communal threats in the form of communist or other radical movements. Faced with the prospect of losing everything, economic and communal elites turned to protection pacts, agreeing to cede authority, tax revenue, and other resources to emergent autocrats, who then provided order through the construction of powerful coercive and party structures.

Greater tax capacity enabled autocrats to finance a vast coercive apparatus while retaining fiscal health over the long haul, and business financed the construction of powerful party machines capable of sustaining hegemonic rule via elections. These early outcomes had important long-term regime consequences. Protection pacts generated "increasing returns to power," as greater tax revenue and political finance allowed autocrats to strengthen coercive and ruling party structures over time (Slater 2010, 18–19).

Where elites did not face the threat of endemic and unmanageable contention during the early post-colonial period, they were more likely to forge "provision pacts," in which autocrats maintained support via patronage distribution and public spending (Slater 2010, 19). The result was weaker states with more limited tax capacity, which undermined long-term authoritarian durability. Provision pacts suffered from "the political equivalent of a 'birth defect' " (2010, 19). Lacking tax capacity or elite cohesion, regimes based on provision pacts failed to build strong states or parties and instead grew "increasingly vulnerable to debilitating fiscal crises" (2010, 19).

Slater undertakes a comparative historical analysis of three cases that followed distinct regime trajectories: Malaysia, the Philippines, and Indonesia. In Malaysia, a potent class and communal threat by the (predominantly Chinese) Malayan Communist Party in the 1940s triggered the formation of the Malay-based UMNO and lay the initial bases for a protection pact (2010, 74–93). The pact was consolidated after the 1969 communal riots, which triggered an authoritarian turn, together with the enhancement of the state's coercive and tax capacity and a broadening of ruling coalition's communal and financial base (2010, 120–123, 146–163). The result was a robust regime capable of surviving economic crisis and a potent opposition challenge in the late 1990s (2010, 211–221). In the Philippines, by contrast, contentious class politics was less threatening to pre-authoritarian elites. Consequently, Filipino elites never acquiesced to a protection pact, and authoritarian rule was built upon a weaker state (Slater 2010, 94–105, 163–180). Ferdinand Marcos thus emerged as the "commander of an exceedingly weak authoritarian Leviathan" (2010, 200), and in the 1980s his personalistic regime collapsed in the face of fiscal crisis, elite defection, and large-scale popular mobilization (2010, 198–203). Indonesia followed a complex trajectory, beginning with a militarized response to postwar regional rebellion, followed in the 1960s by the construction of an authoritarian Leviathan in response to a class-based threat posed by large-scale communist mobilization (Slater 2010, 136–141, 180–188). However, the more militarized regime in Indonesia gradually gave way to a personalization of power once the communist threat was eliminated (2010, 188–196). Elite cohesion eroded, and in the late 1990s the regime collapsed amid economic crisis, internal conflict, and mass protest (2010, 203–210).

The case of South Vietnam demonstrates the importance of historical timing. Because postwar revolutionary contention was confined to the north and rural areas, South Vietnamese elites did not initially acquiesce to a protection pact, and consequently, the authoritarian regime that emerged under Diem resembled that of the Philippines under Marcos (Slater 2010, 253–260). The threat posed by the 1968 Tet Offensive unified elites and triggered significant state-building efforts, but given the weakness of state coercive and tax institutions, these efforts were largely a failure (2010, 260–263). The South Vietnamese case thus highlights the path dependent character of Slater's argument: only where an endemic, unmanageable threat led to a protection pact *before* the establishment of postwar authoritarian regimes do we see the development of the powerful party-state complex that underlies durable authoritarianism.

In Malaysia, Singapore, Taiwan, and to some degree Indonesia, then, protection pacts engendered powerful party-state complexes not unlike those found in revolutionary regimes. Well-organized and cohesive ruling parties attached to powerful coercive structures enabled counter-revolutionary elites to crush early opposition and consolidate hegemonic rule that would endure for decades. The KMT in Taiwan, UMNO in Malaysia, and the PAP in Singapore all remained in power for more than half a century, and the latter two regimes survive to this day.

Mechanisms of Authoritarian Reproduction

Historical institutionalist analyses thus highlight the importance of timing and sequencing in shaping long-term regime trajectories.[8] Institutions are central to these analyses, but unlike most contemporary institutionalist approaches, the key institutional structures underlying durable authoritarian rule tend to be inherited, rather than designed, by autocrats. Robust authoritarian institutions emerge out of a path dependent process. Foundational periods set in motion causally-linked sequences of events whose institution legacies cannot be easily replicated during subsequent periods, but which are of great consequence for regime durability.

No founding legacy is perpetual, however. Historical institutionalist accounts often treat founding legacies as self-perpetuating, and thus vulnerable to change only in the face of exogenous forces. Many of these analyses fail to adequately identify the mechanisms of reproduction sustaining founding legacies, or to consider when and why those legacies might (endogenously) end. As events such as the collapse of Soviet communism (or more recently, the fall of Mubarak in Egypt) remind us, there are few "infinite loops" in politics.[9]

A major challenge for historical institutionalist analyses of authoritarianism thus lies in specifying how and why party-state complexes persist and identifying the conditions under which they weaken or expire. Many founding legacies do, in fact, generate a self-reinforcing dynamic. As Slater (2010) argues, for example, tax capacity rooted in early protection pacts can enable autocrats to continually finance patronage machines and expand the coercive apparatus over time. Likewise, early electoral dominance may reinforce long-term regime stability by inducing existing regime opponents to abandon the political arena and discouraging potential opponents from entering it (Simpser 2013; Magaloni 2008).

Yet even powerful founding legacies are ultimately *bounded*, in the sense that their effects weaken over time—even in the absence of exogenous change. For example, the striking cohesion that characterizes many revolutionary regimes is, to a large extent, generated and sustained by the revolutionary generation—the leaders, cadres, and soldiers who participated in the violent struggle. Once the founding generation passes from the scene, revolutionary cohesion dissipates (Levitsky and Way 2013, 13–14). As a result, ruling parties tend to evolve into more standard, machine-like organizations (e.g., the Mexican PRI). These changes often leave ruling parties more vulnerable to elite defection (e.g., the PRI in the late 1980s; the KMT in the 1990s). They may erode governments' will and capacity to repress. In the Soviet Union, for example, high intensity coercion largely disappeared in the 1960s and proved impossible to carry out in 1990–1991 (Beissinger 2002). Hence, although revolutionary legacies may be quite powerful, they weaken with the departure of the founding generation.

The legacies of counter-revolutionary protection pacts may also be bounded. As Slater (2010) notes, protection pacts ultimately hinge on elite fear. If elites cease to perceive that mass unrest will re-emerge in the absence of authoritarian controls, they may become "attitudinally available" to the opposition (2010, 20). Thus, even powerful, well-financed party-state complexes do not guarantee authoritarian stability over the long haul. Regime elites must actively work to reproduce elite fears of unrest (Slater 2010, 20).

The boundedness of founding legacies has important implications for our understanding of the sources of authoritarian durability. If the effects of violent origins degrade over time, then elites in both revolutionary and counter-revolutionary regimes must eventually find new bases for regime stability. In China, Vietnam, Mozambique, and perhaps Laos, for example, economic growth and newly institutionalized mechanisms of leadership succession appear to have been critical to regime stability after the passage of the revolutionary generation. In North Korea and Zimbabwe, by contrast, governments appear to have sought out new sources of conflict in order to maintain elite cohesion and/or mass legitimacy. The question of regimes' capacity to adapt over time, and the potential sources of such adaptive capacity, is a crucial one for future research.[10]

Bounded legacies may thus constitute an endogenous source of regime change. As founding legacies weaken, authoritarian regimes may grow more vulnerable to collapse, even in the absence of exogenous change. If the effects of even the most powerful founding legacies are ultimately bounded, scholars must take more seriously the question of how and why these legacies weaken over time.

Conclusion

Recent research on authoritarian durability has highlighted the role of political institutions. Yet as this chapter has argued, ruling parties and other authoritarian institutions vary widely in their strength, and this variation is critical to explaining authoritarian durability. Thus, to understand why regimes in countries like China, Cuba, Iran, Malaysia, North Korea, Singapore, Vietnam, and Zimbabwe survived the end of the Cold War, scholars turned to historical causes.

Building upon the seminal work of Samuel Huntington (1968), we have argued that durable authoritarianism is often rooted in regime origins, and that the most robust authoritarian institutions tend to emerge out of violent conflict. Whether they are born of revolution or counter-revolution, regimes that are founded in protracted, violent, and ideationally-driven conflict engender cohesive party-state complexes that can sustain authoritarian regimes for decades—even in the face of economic crisis, opposition protest, and other conditions that are widely associated with authoritarian breakdown.

Notes

1. Huntington (1968), of course, stressed the centrality of institutional strength. More recently, see Levitsky and Murillo (2009).
2. Svolik finds that 68 percent of authoritarian breakdowns between 1946 and 2008 were caused by military coups (2012, 4–5; 10–12).
3. Slater and Fenner (2011, 16) make a similar argument.
4. This definition draws on Huntington (1968, 264) and Skocpol (1979, 4). We operationalize sustained violent struggle as one in which armed conflict persists for at least one year. Armed conflict may precede (e.g., China) or immediately follow (e.g., Russia) the seizure of power. Such a definition encompasses both classic social revolutions (e.g., China, Russia) and regimes founded in radical national liberation struggles (e.g., Angola, Mozambique, Vietnam, Zimbabwe). We treat armed struggle as ideological where it is aimed at the radical transformation of the existing social (e.g., economic, religious, or racial) order. It does not include regimes that emerge from violent independence struggles in which radical transformational goals do not predominate (e.g., Indonesia), cases of mass-based regime change in which state and social structures remain intact (e.g., Egypt 2011), or cases of radical change initiated by actors within the state itself (e.g., "revolutions from above" such as Egypt under Nassar, Peru under Velasco, or Ethiopia under Mengistu).
5. Walt (1996, 1) finds that revolutionary governments are more than twice as likely as non-revolutionary governments to be involved in war.
6. Revolutionary ties to security forces are said to have facilitated high intensity coercion in Mexico in 1968 (Camp 2005, 28–31, 47), China in 1989 (Nathan 2001), and Zimbabwe in 2000–2003 (Kriger 2003).
7. Revolutionary regimes that survived include Algeria, Angola, China, Cuba, Iran, Laos, Mozambique, North Korea, Vietnam, and Zimbabwe. Those that collapsed are Albania and Nicaragua. If we include post-revolutionary regimes, or cases in which the revolutionary generation had died off by 1989 (Mexico, USSR, Taiwan, Yugoslavia), the survival rate falls to 63 percent (10 of 16), which is still far greater than that of non-revolutionary regimes. Note that we exclude South Yemen, which ceased to exist after Yemeni unification in 1990. Calculations are based on data collected by Milan Svolik (n.d.)
8. Other path dependent arguments that seek to explain long-term regime outcomes include Collier and Collier (1991), Luebbert (1991), and Mahoney (2001).
9. "Infinite loop" is taken from Stinchcombe (1968, 103).
10. For example, see Heilmann and Perry (2011) on the adaptive capacity of the communist regime in China, and Stacher (2012) on the adaptive capacity of autocracies in Egypt and Syria.

References

Adelman, Jonathan, ed. 1982. *Communist Armies in Politics*. Boulder, CO: Westview.

Bakhash, Shaul. 1990. *The Reign of the Ayatollahs: Iran and the Islamic Revolution, Revised Edition*. New York: Basic Books.

Beissinger, Mark R. 2002. *Nationalist Mobilization and the Collapse of the Soviet State*. New York: Cambridge University Press.

Bellin, Eva. 2004. "The Robustness of Authoritarianism in the Middle East: Exceptionalism in Comparative Perspective." *Comparative Politics* 36 (2): 139–157.

Blaydes, Lisa. 2010. *Elections and Distributive Politics in Mubarak's Egypt*. New York: Cambridge University Press.

Brown, MacAlister and Joseph Zasloff. 1986. *Apprentice Revolutionaries: The Communist Movement in Laos, 1930–1985*. Stanford, CA: Stanford University Press.

Brownlee, Jason. 2007. *Durable Authoritarianism in an Age of Democratization*. New York: Cambridge University Press.

Cajina, Roberto J. 1997. *Transición política y reconversíon militar en Nicaragua, 1990–1995*. Managua: CRIES.

Camp, Roderic A. 2005. *Mexico's Military on the Democratic Stage*. Washington, D.C.: Center for Strategic and International Studies and Praeger Publishers.

Collier, Ruth Berins and David Collier. 1991. *Shaping the Political Arena*. Princeton, NJ: Princeton University Press.

Deutcher, Isaac [1959] 2003. *The Prophet Unarmed: Trotsky 1921–1929*. London: Verso.

Dominguez, Jorge I. 1982. "The Cuban Army." In *Communist Armies in Politics*, ed. Jonathan Adelman. Boulder, CO: Westview, 43–82.

Fish, M. Steven. 2005. *Democracy Derailed in Russia: The Failure of Open Politics*. New York: Cambridge University Press.

Gandhi, Jennifer. 2008. *Political Institutions under Dictatorship*. New York: Cambridge University Press.

Gandhi, Jennifer and Adam Przeworski. 2007. "Authoritarian Institutions and the Survival of Autocrats." *Comparative Political Studies* 40 (11): 1279–1301.

Geddes, Barbara. 1999. "What Do We Know About Democratization after Twenty Years?" *Annual Review of Political Science* 2: 115–144.

Getty, J. Arch and Oleg Naumov. 2008. *Yezhov: The Rise of Stalin's Iron Fist*. New Haven, CT: Yale University Press.

Goodwin, Jeff. 2001. *No Other Way Out: States and Revolutionary Movements, 1945–1991*. Cambridge, MA: Cambridge University Press.

Greene, Kenneth. 2007. *Why Dominant Parties Lose: Mexico's Democratization in Comparative Perspective*. New York: Cambridge University Press.

Gurr, Ted R. 1988. "War, Revolution, and the Growth of the Coercive State." *Comparative Political Studies* 21(1): 45–65.

Heilmann, Sebastian and Elizabeth J. Perry. 2011. "Embracing Uncertainty: Guerrilla Policy Style and Adaptive Governance in China." In *Mao's Invisible Hand: The Political Foundations of Adaptive Governance in China*, ed. Sebastian Heilmann and Elizabeth J. Perry. Cambridge, MA: Harvard University Press, 1–29.

Herb, Michael. 1999. *All in the Family: Absolutism, Revolution, and Democracy in the Middle Eastern Monarchies*. Albany, NY: State University of New York Press.

Huntington, Samuel P. 1968. *Political Order in Changing Societies*. New Haven, CT: Yale University Press.

Huntington, Samuel. 1970. "Social and Institutional Dynamics of One-Party Systems." In *Authoritarian Politics in Modern Society: The Dynamics of Established One-Party Systems*, ed. Samuel Huntington and Clement Moore. New York: Basic Books, 3–47.

Katzman, Kenneth. 1993. *The Warriors of Islam: Iran's Revolutionary Guard*. Boulder, CO: Westview Press.

Kriger, Norma J. 2003. *Guerrilla Veterans in Post-War Zimbabwe: Symbolic and Violent Politics, 1980–1987*. New York: Cambridge University Press.

LeBas, Adrienne. 2011. *From Protest to Parties: Party-Building and Democratization in Africa*. New York: Oxford University Press.

Leggett, George. 1986. *The Cheka: Lenin's Political Police*. Oxford: Clarendon Press.

Levitsky, Steven and María V. Murillo. 2009. "Variation in Institutional Strength." *The Annual Review of Political Science* 12: 115–133.

Levitsky, Steven and Lucan A. Way. 2010. *Competitive Authoritarianism: Hybrid Regimes after the Cold War*. New York: Cambridge University Press.

Levitsky, Steven and Lucan A. Way. 2012. "Beyond Patronage: Violent Struggle, Ruling Party Cohesion, and Authoritarian Durability." *Perspectives on Politics* 10 (4): 869–889.

Levitsky, Steven and Lucan A. Way. 2013. "The Durability of Revolutionary Regimes." *Journal of Democracy* (July): 5–17.

Luebbert, Gregory. 1991. *Liberalism, Fascism, or Social Democracy*. New York: Oxford University Press.

Lust-Okar, Ellen. 2007. *Structuring Conflict in the Arab World: Incumbents, Opponents, and Institutions*. New York: Cambridge University Press.

Magaloni, Beatriz. 2008. "Credible Power Sharing and the Longevity of Authoritarian Rule." *Comparative Political Studies* 41 (4–5): 715–741.

Mahoney, James. 2001. *The Legacies of Liberalism: Path Dependence and Political Regimes in Central America*. Baltimore, MD: Johns Hopkins University Press.

Nathan, Andrew J. 2001. "Introduction: The Documents and Their Significance." In *The Tiananmen Papers*, ed. Andrew Nathan and Perry Link. New York: Public Affairs, xxxv–lxv.

Nordlinger, Eric. 1977. *Soldiers in Politics: Military Coups and Governments*. London: Prentice Hall.

Pepinsky, Thomas B. 2009. *Economic Crisis and the Breakdown of Authoritarian Regimes: Indonesia and Malaysia in Comparative Perspective*. New York: Cambridge University Press.

Perlmutter, Amos. 1977. *The Military and Politics in Modern Times*. New Haven, CT: Yale University Press.

Przeworski, Adam, Michael E. Alvarez, José Antonio Cheibub, and Fernando Limongi. 2000. *Democracy and Development: Political Institutions and Well-Being in the World, 1950–1990*. New York: Cambridge University Press.

Ross, Michael L. 2001. "Does Oil Hinder Democracy?" *World Politics* 53 (3): 325–361.

Schedler, Andreas. 2002. "The Menu of Manipulation." *Journal of Democracy* 13 (2): 36–50.

Schedler, Andreas. 2013. *The Politics of Uncertainty: Sustaining and Subverting Electoral Authoritarianism*. Oxford: Oxford University Press.

Service, Robert. 1979. *The Bolshevik Party in Revolution 1917–1923: A Study in Organizational Change*. London: Macmillan Press.

Simpser, Alberto. 2013. *Why Governments and Parties Manipulate Elections: Theory, Practice, and Implication.* New York: Cambridge University Press.

Skocpol, Theda. 1979. *States and Social Revolutions.* New York: Cambridge University Press.

Skocpol, Theda. 1988. "Social Revolutions and Mass Military Mobilization." *World Politics* 40 (2): 147–168.

Slater, Dan. 2003. "Iron Cage in an Iron Fist: Authoritarian Institutions and the Personalization of Power in Malaysia." *Comparative Politics* 36 (1): 81–101.

Slater, Dan. 2009. "Revolutions, Crackdowns, and Quiescence: Communal Elites and Democratic Mobilization in Southeast Asia." *American Journal of Sociology* 115 (1): 203–254.

Slater, Dan. 2010. *Ordering Power: Contentious Politics, State-Building, and Authoritarian Durability in Southeast Asia.* New York: Cambridge University Press.

Slater, Dan and Sofia Fenner. 2011. "State Power and Staying Power: Infrastructural Mechanisms and Authoritarian Durability." *Journal of International Affairs* 65 (1): 15–29.

Slater, Dan and Nicholas Smith. 2010. "The Power of Counterrevolution: Contentious Origins of Dominant Party Durability in Asia and Africa." Paper presented at the Annual Meeting of the American Political Science Association, Washington, D.C.

Smith, Benjamin. 2005. "Life of the Party: The Origins of Regime Breakdown and Persistence under Single-Party Rule." *World Politics* 57 (3): 421–451.

Smith, Benjamin. 2007. *Hard Times in the Lands of Plenty: Oil Politics in Iran and Indonesia.* Ithaca, NY: Cornell University Press.

Stacher, Joshua. 2012. *Adaptable Autocrats: Regime Power in Egypt and Syria.* Stanford, CA: Stanford University Press.

Stinchcombe, Arthur. 1968. *Constructing Social Theories.* New York: Harcourt, Brace, and World.

Svolik, Milan W. n.d. *Regime Data, Leader and Ruling Coalition Data, Institutions Data.* Available at <http://publish.illinois.edu/msvolik/the-politics-of-authoritarian-rule/> (accessed May 15, 2014).

Svolik, Milan W. 2012. *The Politics of Authoritarian Rule.* Cambridge, MA: Cambridge University Press.

Taylor, Brian D. and Roxana Botea. 2008. "Tilly Tally: War-Making and State-Making in the Contemporary Third World." *International Studies Review* 10 (1): 27–56.

Tendi, Blessing-Miles. 2010. *Making History in Mugabe's Zimbabwe: Politics, Intellectuals and the Media.* Oxford: Peter Lang.

Turley, William. 1982. "The Vietnamese Army." In *Communist Armies in Politics,* ed. Jonathan Adelman. Boulder, CO: Westview, 63–82

Walt, Stephen M. 1996. *Revolution and War.* Ithaca, NY: Cornell University Press.

CHAPTER 13

POLITICAL PARTIES, REGIMES, AND SOCIAL CLEAVAGES

RACHEL BEATTY RIEDL*

HISTORICAL institutionalism is central to the study of political parties because party creation, competition, and adaptation are fundamentally processes structured over time. In these processes, time and sequence frequently are necessary components of causal arguments in understanding contemporary political outcomes. An historical approach to party politics highlights how, in particular moments, agency and contingency can generate long-term legacies, whereas in other moments party systems are resilient to elite attempts to reorder competition. Historical institutionalist arguments identify the mechanisms that sustain particular outcomes over time, and demonstrate when change occurs, according to which constraints, opportunities, and antecedent conditions.

Furthermore, the study of political parties illuminates how historical institutionalism is distinguished from other approaches. By analyzing parties' roles in contesting power and representing constituencies, historical institutional scholars show that preferences vary, and where change in preferences emerges from. Parties themselves are complex organizations that produce outcomes that are not determined by underlying structural conditions and are greater than the aggregate of atomized, individual preferences. Historical institutional approaches can interrogate which actors have the power to shape the agenda, influence preferences, and determine parties' roles as intermediaries of organized interests.[1] Historical institutional approaches are also beneficial for probing why certain cleavages are salient at a given time, and what role parties play in fundamentally *shaping* or *maintaining* the salient dimensions of competition over time, as other economic and social changes unfold. The process of party formation and competition increases the salience of some identities and decreases the salience of others (Torcal and Mainwaring 2003). As Steinmo suggests (Chapter 6, this volume), history matters not just because it provides different contexts in which rational actors make choices, but because history affects the beliefs, values and preferences of those actors. Parties' development make this process apparent: identities, beliefs, values, and preferences at a given point in time can become codified in organizations such as political parties. Once built, parties have enduring consequences as collective actors, crafting institutions (such as electoral systems or eligibility rules) in their struggles for short-term gain, further structuring the rules of the game in future rounds of contestation. These struggles can shape later possibilities for organizational adaptation, individual identification, and preference formation.

Three areas of scholarship demonstrate the critical role of historical institutionalism in studies of political parties in particular: (1) explaining characteristics of parties or the party system (such as organization, institutionalization, evolution, and demise); (2) understanding the relationship of the party system to social cleavages; and (3) differential party origins' effect on regime durability and institutions.

Political Parties and Party System Characteristics

First, historical institutionalism has been central to many studies that seek to explain the features of parties or party systems because parties are somewhat but not always fully responsive to changes in the external environment. Parties *may* be impacted by the relevant context at any given point in time, and yet parties are also conditioned by their own internal features and could be resistant to change and adaptation, based on the interests that become codified within the organization at an earlier point (Levitsky 2003). Historical institutionalism helps scholars to understand how and why parties form the way that they do in a certain moment, the importance of timing and sequence in party formation (Shefter 1977), and what pathways are available for adaptation and evolution as parties continue to exist in a changing world. In many instances, a shifting external environment makes party adaptation necessary, but the options available to parties for reform are truncated by the party's past organization, ideology, and skills that the party leaders and members have developed over time (Grzymala-Busse 2002; Przeworski and Sprague 1986). A party's past limits certain moves and makes other moves more feasible, given the sunk costs associated with building organizations according to a certain model, establishing particular linkage structures with citizens, and developing party reputations and policy platforms. Other approaches miss the interaction between exogenous catalysts and endogenous pressures for stasis on some fronts and adaptation on others based on each party's unique developmental trajectory, internal composition, and its previous relation to other parties within the system.

For example, when democracy is interrupted or re-established, the nature of new party formation and contestation can be significantly impacted by the legacies of party organizations and skills from an earlier democratic period. Prior experiences with democracy provide skills, resources, or networks that can be reconstructed or built upon in later party system formation. Completely new parties that form in the re-established democracy often form in relation to the pre-existing party organizations that endured through informal channels during the authoritarian period (Tsai, Chapter 16, this volume). Underground networks of party organization, partisan affiliations, behavioral routinization, and value infusion may endure despite autocratic repression (Levitsky 1998). For example, the dense collection of personal networks—unions, clubs, activists' gatherings, and civic organizations—were largely institutionally unconnected to the Peronist party bureaucracy in Argentina, yet helped sustain extensive linkages to working and lower-class society (Levitsky 2001). As an informal mass party, Peronism maintained powerful base-level infrastructure, a strong identity and loyalty link between civil society organizations and the Peronist party, and combined this base with party organizational fluidity, which allowed it to survive decades of proscription (1955–73), and adaptation to neoliberal economic reforms in the 1990s.

Authoritarian legacies can also impact the nature of democratic competition. The Muslim Brotherhood was able to build upon its religious social infrastructure established during decades of authoritarianism to defeat leftist parties and gain rapid support among poor voters when transitional elections were held in Egypt in 2011 (Masoud 2014). Whereas a purely sociological account would emphasize the importance of the religious-secular cleavage, and a rational-choice perspective would suggest voters' economic preference for radical redistribution, Masoud demonstrates that the party system that emerged in transitional Egypt reflected not the structure of basic conflict in that society, but rather the political opportunities developed over previous iterations of contestation, support-building, and organizational infrastructure.

Historical institutional approaches also provide a unique perspective on party and system change. Alternative approaches that focus on equilibrium outcomes of party positions and voter preferences suggest that parties can rapidly adjust to woo uncaptured constituencies or shift along with changes in the voting population. Yet the actual evolution of parties suggests that they are more responsive to some constituencies and less responsive to others because they are built historically from different social bases or particular elite coalitions. Therefore, parties, once formed along a particular dimension, are not credible to certain voters (Kalyvas 1996, 2000). Party credibility and capability is determined with reference to past party actions, constituencies built, and reputations established (Grzymala-Busse 2002). Parties cannot fully recalibrate due to reputations built over time, yet they can re-deploy their previously established organizations, leadership skills, and public service agendas to adapt within a historically circumscribed range of options. As Thachil (2014) demonstrates in the case of the Bharatiya Janata Party (BJP) in India, even where voters are structurally at odds with the party leadership's elite interests, a party's previous experience providing local services can build support among lower class constituencies. Attention to the historical development of partisan attachments can determine which dimensions the party can leverage in the face of external change. For example, in the recent history of Latin America and specifically in response to the hyperinflation faced in the 1980s and 1990s in many countries, major parties changed course profoundly and abruptly—yet the ability to do so and remain electorally viable is rooted in organizational strength and partisan attachments on dimensions *other* than policy positions previously constructed (Mainwaring, forthcoming). Future historical institutional research should establish which domains are more or less adaptive (policy positions, members and voter identities, core capacities, skills, or party organization), which contextual and structural conditions loosen the constraints and provide opportunities for greater change or encourage continuity, and through which mechanisms (Mahoney and Thelen 2009; Busemeyer and Trampusch 2012).

Given that a party's specific developmental trajectory offers unequal opportunities for adaptation, static typologies of party type frequently do not capture important features of party origin and evolution. What may appear to be similar contemporary parties may have important foundational differences that impact their ability to use either programmatic or patronage appeals (Shefter 1977; Kuhonta 2011), maintain dominance, or adapt to changing external conditions. For example, Smith (2005) demonstrates that early post-independence party building strategies in Africa and Asia were based on the access to rents and the nature of opposition, which shaped the elite coalition partners' willingness to invest in broad and deep organizations to unite the coalition in access to policymaking. Importantly, Smith demonstrates how ruling parties endured, but did not demonstrate stasis in the face of external crisis. Instead, endurance was based on simultaneous internal institutional changes (see also Huntington 1968). This account demonstrates a key contribution of historical institutionalism, by showing that institutions are *sometimes* pliable as instruments in the hands of actors, generally in periods of relative structural indeterminacy, or critical junctures (Capoccia, Chapter 5, this volume). Furthermore, how and when institutions structure the political world is dependent in part on their historically constructed social or political coalition (Hall, Chapter 2, this volume). Significant historical institutionalism contributions have focused on this congruence, understanding party origins, organization, and endurance as a function of the nature of ongoing processes of coalition formation and maintenance among elite actors.[2]

A focus related to party origins and development has been to examine the role of authoritarian successor parties, explaining when and why formerly authoritarian incumbents were able to transition into newly democratic regimes and successfully compete for power.[3] In this way, parties represent a prime example of institutional "conversion": [4] following democratization, former authoritarian parties operate in new ways through strategic redeployment in a new regime environment. Research on party systems in sub-Saharan Africa suggests that varied modes of authoritarian power accumulation that single party incumbents pursued during the decades of autocratic rule had direct implications for the incumbent's ability to maintain control over the democratic transition process, and ultimately create a more highly institutionalized party system (Riedl 2014). The diverse coalitions of support that authoritarian incumbents mobilized over decades meant that those ruling parties had unequal electoral bases to mobilize in support of their transition agenda when confronted with the necessity of organizing multi-party elections. The legacies of authoritarian rule shaped the construction of new democratic institutions, and ultimately the degree of party system institutionalization.

Historical institutionalist accounts demonstrate that authoritarian successor parties can survive transitions and regain power through distinctly different pathways, due to the context of the transition itself. In sub-Saharan Africa and much of Southeast Asia, incumbents intended to oversee transitions to multi-party elections that they could win in order to retain power (Hicken and Kuhonta 2014; Slater and Wong 2013). In contrast, the post-communist successor parties were confronted with a drastically different breakdown of their existing political world, and following the collapse of the communist regimes in 1989, these ruling communist parties were generally consigned to oblivion. Yet Grzymala-Busse (2002) demonstrates that communist successor parties could regenerate and successfully compete for power where they had previously prioritized internal organizational practices for that allowed rotation and selection of pragmatic elites. By converting skills and networks gained through the past structures and practices of the predemocratic organization, the parties were able to survive the external shocks, rebuild their reputations and capitalize upon the fluid institutional environment that follows such a crisis (2002, 279). Whereas post-communist parties faced a complete loss of power, and managed the transition through internal flexibility, pragmatism and adaptation in a period of institutional fluidity, African incumbents managed the transition through social mobilization and control over the new rule-making process, maintaining a great deal of the pre-existing institutional framework. These pathways then have distinct implications for democratic party competition (Grzymala-Busse 2006).

The preceding examples demonstrate how historical institutionalist approaches are particularly well suited to the study of political parties by identifying which legacies are critical in shaping party and party system characteristics, and how they vary by context. Using past reputation, organizational infrastructure, social linkages and elite coalitions as causal variables, historical institutionalism integrates parties' evolution into an encompassing explanation for institutional continuity and adaptability.

Parties and Social Cleavages

A second distinct area where historical institutional approaches have made significant contributions is in understanding the relationship between parties and social cleavages. In contrast to political economy and cultural approaches which do not take institutional development as central, historical institutionalism uses theoretical accounts for institutional formation and adaptation in particular contexts to identify the causal impact on other domains of political life. As Collier and Collier (1991) demonstrate, the question of which cleavages shape party competition and to what effect depends fundamentally upon the intersection in a particular moment when cleavages get encapsulated into a party system. Their historical institutional approach explains Latin American regime outcomes in the 1960s and 1970s as rooted in diverse forms of labor incorporation into the political and legal system during a period of expanding enfranchisement in Latin America. In this critical juncture, party systems formed as the institutional representation of new class coalitions, representing the newly formed working and middle classes in addition to peasants and landed elites. Variation in initial incorporation of labor produced distinctive patterns of reaction and counterreaction that were consequential for subsequent party structure and regime dynamics.

Historical institutional approaches problematize how, and if, cleavages shape the contours of competition, or if parties themselves make salient particular cleavages at specific moments in time. Without a sequential and historical approach, where we observe matching between party agendas and particular social divisions—such as class, race, religion, language, or ethnicity—we might assume that parties formed to represent those particular groups, and read the causal direction of the correlation as based in sociological origins. But historical institutionalism can demonstrate the ways that parties *shape* the salient cleavages as they struggle to remake society (de Leon, Desai, and Tugal, 2015). Studies of democratic representation and electoral politics in advanced industrial democracies have largely been dominated by voter-centered approaches, which focus on the interests and policy preferences of the electorate. However, the contextually specific and active role of parties to politicize particular social differences and identities at the expense of others suggests that parties influence the very preferences and salient identities of voters. The study of political parties in historical institutionalism exemplifies how "effect becomes cause" (Pierson 1993): political parties, formed in response to a particular context, then become independent institutions that can shape preferences, alter social cleavages, and influence the character of possible coalitions.

In this regard, one important advance in understanding the relationship between parties and social cleavages has been to differentiate historical periods, given that the process of party formation has occurred very differently across "waves" of democracy, and affected not only party organization but also has structured new lines of competition in society. In the first wave of democracy, Lipset and Rokkan emphasize the major societal cleavages present at the time of party formation for the Western European democracies and suggest that party system competition froze along these axes (1967). Working-class parties integrated workers into the political system and provided enduring and salient identities (Chalmers 1964). Pizzorno has suggested that ideologically strong parties that stabilize electoral cleavages and present clear alternatives in party programs are likely to emerge to control the access of the new masses into the political system (1981, 272). But these parties are only typical of the first "generative" phase following extension of suffrage, when "big collective actors are admitted to share power into a system of representation," as occurred in the first wave of democratization in Europe (Mair 1997, 40). This suggests that a particular type of strong party (ideologically oriented, focused on encadrement) emerges given the sequence of gradual enfranchisement following competition *and* contingent upon the timing of mass labor organization, developing within a class-based context that facilitated close party links with society (Mair 1990). The implication is that the labor-based mass parties that developed in Europe were rare because they required a particular sequence, domestic context, and world historical timing that made labor-based organization a powerful collective actor at that moment. And as the context changed, even these European parties gradually transitioned away from the mass party model (Kirchheimer 1966).

In contrast, when new parties were forming in third wave democracies, the era of mass media had fundamentally changed practical methods of party mobilization (Mainwaring and Torcal 2006). Candidates could reach out to voters directly, without the need for well-developed party organizations (Sartori 1989). This contributed to more personalistic voting and weaker partisan identities among citizens. Once parties have emerged that are weakly institutionalized, the contemporary technologies of media distribution and structural changes to the economy, such as the growth of the urban informal sector, limit their ability to rebuild. Levitsky and Cameron (2003) demonstrate that in post-Fujimori Peru, contemporary politicians lack both the incentive and capacity to build new party organizations in the wake of party breakdown. And yet other forms of mass parties have developed in other contexts, such as those based upon indigenous movements as in Bolivia (Anria 2013), in coordination with religious organization bases in Brazil (Trejo and Bizzarro Neto 2014), or revolutionary parties, as in South Africa and Zimbabwe (Levitsky and Way 2013). These contrasts in formation demonstrate that party development occurs in relation not only to existing social cleavages, but also in response to the contextual features of the contemporary social, economic, and political environment that encourage certain forms of organization, collective identification, and strategies of mobilization. Historical institutionalism is uniquely able to demonstrate how these factors of party development then have causal impact on the relevant cleavages in society, and can reshape existing lines of competition. Without a historical approach, the causal significance of the differences between waves of democracy (or other particular historical periods) is obscured because the context is often not theorized, and when different historical periods are lumped together the average effect misrepresents the actual causal pathways.

For example, historical institutional approaches can identify the processes by which collective actors self-identify, and become potential bases for mass party mobilization, which differs over time and space. In South Asia, on the eve of independence, social class provided not a cleavage per se but a set of possible coalition partners that the emerging national elites in India and Pakistan exploited differentially (Tudor 2013). As the colonial state shifted power toward and away from certain social groups, the dominant social classes constructed a particular type of party built to pursue their interests. The colonial legacies of institutionalized privilege for certain social groups ultimately influenced which class groups mobilized, how class interests became defined, and when mobilization happened. The perceptions of class interest, and the party organizations built to sustain them, are historically specific political interactions.

Parties can not only encapsulate social cleavages at a given point in time and project them into the future, but also potentially reshape relevant cleavages through the process of formation and contestation. This occurs quite clearly where a regime cleavage is established through the process of democratization: where the authoritarian successor party remains a player in the new regime and new opposition parties form as an alternative to the previous incumbent. This new cleavage is salient *because of* democratization: the campaign battle is pitched over preferences for stability versus reform. In creating this new divide, existing social cleavages such as class, religion, or ethnicity may be subsumed within elite coalitions represented on both sides of the new regime cleavage (Riedl 2014; Nalepa and Carroll 2014; Grzymala-Busse 2006; Loxton 2014. LeBas (2011) demonstrates that parties with their roots in opposition protest can transcend ethnic cleavages. Recent scholarship on Latin America demonstrates that political activists have incentives to build territorial, strong party organizations—and once built, these parties can connect previously disconnected social constituencies (Levitsky, Loxton, and Van Dyke, forthcoming). So whether parties are created out of decolonization struggles, revolution, civil wars, democratization protest movements, or intense left/right struggle, once they are created as organizations, they can further shape relevant cleavages by connecting some and realigning others along new lines of competition and contestation (Przeworski and Sprague 1986; Sartori 1969; Torcal and Mainwaring 2003). Parties can also reshape cleavages by powersharing, blocking resonant social themes from their articulation in the political sphere, and leaving previously significant social forces without party champions for their interests in national politics (Simmons and Slater 2013; Slater 2014). Rather than assuming preferences and interests, historical institutionalism demonstrates that the salience of particular dimensions of competition are shaped not only by competition *between* parties, but also by ongoing processes of coalition formation and maintenance that dictate processes *internal* to parties and *among* party elites, which can be significantly shaped by historical patterns of party formation and original coalition construction. The salient cleavages cannot be read off of the aggregate social landscape, because parties themselves are collective actors that can create new dimensions and mobilize around others, while letting others lie dormant, depending on the party's internal dynamics.

In all of these works a key contribution gained by viewing party development through a historical institutionalist lens is that the process of episodic party development is seen as a chain of big and small events, influenced by the context and what came prior. Capoccia and Ziblatt state that "democratic institutional arrangements at an earlier stage may constitute important resources for political actors in later struggles that lead to institutional change in other, connected arenas" (2010, 939). Research in the developing democracies adds that colonial and authoritarian legacies can be equally important for party development and later democratic representation. Parties often play autonomous roles and become key strategic actors in the process of democratization, and in upholding stable democracy. This is not because the parties themselves were necessarily democratic ideologically, but they organized coalitions of social groups seeking power into channeled patterns of contestation.

Whereas ahistorical accounts identify party formation and competition as mapping on to the sociological structure of the citizenry, and the accompanying costs and benefits of constituency mobilization, historical institutionalism makes a critical correction by demonstrating how identities are shaped, how collective actors are mobilized, and how cleavages are created or attempts to reorder society are thwarted. In the process, a host of issues become salient to the individual (and elite party agents) that do not reflect their original interests or goals. Identifying this progression requires attention to the opportunities created by the particular context, the agency of contending elites, and the legacies of the past that can be carried forward or redeployed to create either stasis or change in the party system landscape and social order.

Parties and Regime Institutions

Finally, parties are central to explaining a wide range of outcomes, and particularly regime type, durability, and institutions. Historical approaches have made significant contributions in these domains because the attention to the process by which regime institutions are constructed, contested, implemented, and changed over time focuses attention on the role of power and social coalitions, and how they are codified in party organizations. How rules are selected and implemented is an essential prior question to determining their causal effect.

Scholarship within the rational-choice institutionalist approach has usefully interrogated the endogeneity of electoral systems. Boix (1999), for example, argues that in developed democracies, ruling parties anticipate the effects of different electoral regimes on voters and candidates, and choose different sets of electoral rules to maximize their chances of securing executive and legislation representation. This attempts to answer the question of who has power to make the rules, and offers a strategic explanation for what they choose. But without interrogating the historical record, scholars mistakenly assume that the ruling parties that had discretion over electoral rulemaking understood the short-term (and possibly long-term) implications of their selection, and sought the institutional arrangements that would ensure their party's electoral success. Electoral rule crafting in Poland and Hungary in 1989–90 saw leading parties miscalculating their support bases and favoring compromise systems based upon party splits or attempts to forge a united front of disparate opposition (Bernhard 2000). Using historical data is useful to identify a certain set of players and outcomes to be explained, but only a historical *approach to causality* advances our understanding of the process of rule creation, by "reconstructing the path that led to institutional choice to determine what actors were actually fighting about" (Ahmed 2010, 1061; see also Rodden 2008). Actors' subjective understanding of their situation at a given moment and the choices made under uncertainty demonstrate the complexity of the decision-making process (Lupu and Riedl 2013).

Furthermore, this process can highlight the unintended consequences of institutional crafting. In hindsight, institutions such as electoral systems may look obvious as having privileged the winners, whereas at the time, the winners and losers may have been prioritizing other strategies, may not have self-identified as cohesive groups, or may have been pursuing other ends. Through an in-depth historical investigation in two paradigmatic cases, the United Kingdom and Belgium, Ahmed demonstrates that both proportional representation and single-member plurality were understood as functionally equivalent options, both meant to safeguard the position of right parties against the uncertain consequences of suffrage expansion. Furthermore, the fight over whether proportional representation or single-member plurality systems would be more effective as a safeguard took place not just between parties but also—decisively—within parties, as internal factions expressed different preferences (Ahmed 2010). Therefore, only in historically understanding the nature of internal party dynamics can we accurately trace their influence in shaping nascent democratic institutions. And, once in place, electoral institutions may reverberate back to have influence on the nature of the party itself, *creating* a match between contemporary party form and electoral system through a sequential feedback process. Given this possibility, analyzing the relationship between electoral law and the nature of the party system requires attention to sequence.

The party system can also evolve, given that parties are not monolithic organizations. Therefore, the explanation for political stability and voting alignments requires a historical causal analysis to first address the differential coordination capacity of elites and forms of party development across space and time.

Historical institutionalists have problematized these issues of party formation and maintenance in their explanations for regime type and durability in particular. Whereas the neo-modernization approach to democratization emphasizes structural factors, historical institutionalists have problematized the question of collective actors in particular, the role of global historical context and changing institutional configurations of democracy (Capoccia and Ziblatt 2010). Rather than assuming the primacy of class divisions between elites and masses, historical institutional approaches can identify the relevant cleavages and how they are identified, mobilized, and reshaped over time by political entrepreneurs and institutional incentives. For example, Grzymala-Busse highlights the aforementioned regime cleavage and demonstrates that the credibility and coherence of the former communist parties as viable democratic competitors can shape not only the nature of the democratic party system but also democratic stability more generally (2006). More coherent and competitive former communist parties help to stabilize party competition, and when they offer a credible governing alternative, it supports democracy over the long term. And the formation of coherent party coalitions has also been used to convincingly explain authoritarian durability (Smith 2005; Slater 2010; Brownlee 2007). Slater, for example, roots elite unification (and therefore, party strength) in the types of threats from below (2010). Where elites are challenged profoundly by a fusion of class and communal forces, demonstrated by contentious politics at the center, elites come together in protection pacts to safeguard their property and privilege. Challenges from below to elite interests create elite cohesion and party strength, and Slater demonstrates how this translates to state strength and capacity, as well as regime durability.

But, as mentioned earlier in this section, these authoritarian parties can also contribute to later democratic stability. When and why does democratization occur? Recent studies in the political-economy tradition have pointed to the importance of economic liberalization. Where reforms reduced the patronage available to the state and created the potential for a private business class to emerge, opposition parties had greater resources and incentive to cohere, and ultimately defeat the dominant party (Greene 2007; Arriola 2013). In many cases, however, the former authoritarian party is not defeated at the polls, but oversees democratizing reforms. Why would authoritarian ruling parties allow new parties to form and citizens to freely express their preferences at the polls, when they are still strong enough to win? In these cases, strong, well-institutionalized parties were durably authoritarian but could transfer their strength into a newly democratic era (Slater and Wong 2013; Riedl forthcoming; Loxton forthcoming). Whether the democratization process was implemented top-down by an authoritarian ruling party or emerged out of protest from below, the party systems that emerge from these fundamentally unequal origins offer disparate opportunities for participation, representation, and regime endurance.

Conclusion

The most significant contributions of historical institutionalism to the study of parties and party systems have been in understanding how formative periods of party origin, coalition building, and ongoing development shape the characteristics of the party and party system itself in enduring ways, and in turn, how those very processes of development determine the resulting effects of parties on other domains of the political system. Because party durability is often premised on internal evolution or external manipulation of the institutional arena, theoretical arguments of institutional endurance and change are necessarily combined. Historical institutionalism simultaneously explores party origins, continuity (of some elements) and evolution (of others) as a part of the causal framework, which provides crucial insight for understanding how parties act within and shape the political system. Moreover, historical institutionalism analyzes the historical evolution and temporal maintenance of constituencies, as collectivities shaped by party articulation, as opposed to individual aggregation. In doing so, multiple dimensions of power and influence, of collectivity and coherence are made apparent that would be missed by an atemporal or micro-level approach.

Due to specific historical developments, parties shape identities, bundle issues and groups into broader collectivities, and can determine which underlying social forces are organized to have national expression; for the individual, this can profoundly impact their worldviews beyond their particularistic interests. Electorates, therefore, are not simply made up of discrete individuals, but are articulated as groups that are historically identified, reified, and at times, challenged.

Because political parties are placed between individual agency, structural conditions and regime institutions, they are the perfect spotlight for what Sartori called "the autonomy of the political" (1973). For example, parties may be created to reflect certain social groups (such as labor or business), or they may be created by political entrepreneurs to advance their interests (Aldrich 1995), but the organizational resources they provide and coalitions they form can well outlast the initial conditions of their founding, and have unintended consequences for structuring new social cleavages through the process. Parties remind political scientists that power and organization mediate much of contemporary politics: focusing on individuals' preferences fails to account for the essential role of political parties in providing bundles of information to their constituencies, mediating the range of possible vote choices, and serving as intermediaries between local level contestations and national level resources and agendas. Political parties provide a complex web of formal and informal connections to power, and their strategies are often shaped by internal dynamics and forged over previous struggles. Parties are therefore a critical arena for historical institutionalism to complement and in many cases amend alternative approaches because historical institutionalism uses history not just as data points to be explained, but as a series of contexts, decisions and combinations of collective actors in contestation, rather than atomized individuals.

Future research could address the interaction of regime institutions and parties over time: When can parties set the rules and when are they constrained by and shaped by the existing rules? When does the process of parties acting to change the rules actually reinforce the significance of the rules themselves? The study of rules requires an explanation of how the rules came to be and when there are opportunities for change or not. This agenda overlaps with the recent work of Mahoney and Thelen to identify varied processes of institutional change (2009). Existing rules may well make parties adapt, but parties may also seek to implement the rules in different ways, exhibiting conversion. Parties can repurpose existing rules to achieve new or different ends, thus highlighting the agency of political parties to achieve their ends. And parties that win initial victories use them to generate more power, through agenda control and the distribution of resources. Thus, even as the constituencies that supported parties may shift in response to underlying structural changes, parties' power may appear to be self-reinforcing and can outlast its initial role of specific representation. Political parties' trajectories demonstrate the path dependent nature of power accumulation, and yet highlight opportunities for elite agency (through contention or colluding) and changing socioeconomic foundations to shift resources, identities, and interests. In the study of political parties, institutional erosion or unraveling is a process related to the replication of other elements of the party system or the creation of new features: understanding when and why these changes occur requires a historical institutionalist approach to connect evolution, transformation, and continuity of the component elements within the political system.

Future research should also address questions of causation by leveraging sequence and temporality to a greater extent to understand what the pace of change tells us about causal dynamics: When and why do parties change gradually, when do they experience punctuated equilibrium with rapid, transformative realignment, and what facilitates periods of "freezing?" How do electoral cycles overlap with long-term structural changes in society? When are new social groups seemingly emergent as important political players, in response to slow demographic changes or cataclysmic periods of mobilization and group identification? Parties are embedded in time and their gradual change demonstrates realignment. Parties are organizations that may be significantly influenced by agency (particularly in highly personalist systems) and ideology. Party competition is also simultaneously guided by long time horizons and shorter pre-determined cyclical elections, such that party activity is guided by cycles of feedback and mobilization. Electoral competition has fixed points of updating, given the cyclical nature of elections, which force organizational adaptation and provide opportunities for learning. Yet, *at some times,* parties are captive to their past, and change is difficult given embedded interests; at *other times in history,* parties have demonstrated fairly sweeping changes and have reordered society by creating new cleavages. Future research can further identify the tempo of party change, and theorize the causes of party system gradual adaptation, freezing, and rapid transformation (Grzymala-Busse 2011). Given their complex role in the political system, parties can provide lessons to advance historical institutionalism as well.

Notes

* The author would like to thank Rodrigo Barrenechea, Jaimie Bleck, Anna Grzymala-Busse, Alisha Holland, Erik Kuhonta, Scott Mainwaring, Monika Nalepa, Dan Slater, and Maya Tudor for helpful comments and suggestions, as well as the editors Tulia Falleti, Orfeo Fioretos, and Adam Sheingate.

1. See also Pierson (2004) on macro and temporal approaches to power.
2. Brownlee (2007), Bunce (1999), Collier and Collier (1991), LeBas (2011), Levitsky and Way (Chapter 12, this volume); Riedl (2014), Slater (2010), Smith (2005), Tudor (2013), Ziblatt (forthcoming).
3. These studies have been particularly prominent in the post-communist world (Grzymala-Busse 2002; Nalepa and Carroll 2014; Kitschelt et al. 1999, inter alia) but also in Asia (Hicken and Kuhonta 2014; Slater and Wong 2013), Latin America (Levitsky, Loxton, and Van Dyke forthcoming), Africa (Ferree 2011; LeBas 2011; Levitsky and Way 2012), and early twentieth century Europe (Ziblatt forthcoming).
4. See Mahoney and Thelen 2009.

References

Ahmed, Amel. 2010. "Reading History Forward: The Origins of Electoral Systems in European Democracies." *Comparative Political Studies* 43 (8–9): 1059–1088.

Aldrich, John. 1995. *Why Parties? The Origin and Transformation of Political Parties in America.* Chicago: University of Chicago Press.

Anria, Santiago. 2013. "Social Movements, Party Organization and Populism: Insights from the Bolivian MAS." *Latin American Politics and Society* 55 (3): 19–46.

Arriola, Leonardo. 2013. *Multiethnic Coalitions in Africa: Business Financing of Opposition Election Campaigns.* Cambridge and New York: Cambridge University Press.

Bernhard, Michael. 2000. "Institutional Choice after Communism: A Critique of Theory-Building in an Empirical Wasteland." *East European Politics & Societies* 14 (2): 316–347.

Boix, C. 1999. "Setting the Rules of the Game: The Choice of Electoral Systems in Advanced Democracies." *American Political Science Review* 93 (3): 609–624.

Brownlee, Jason. 2007. *Authoritarianism in an Age of Democratization*. New York: Cambridge University Press.

Bunce, Valerie. 1999. *Subversive Institutions: The Design and the Collapse of Socialism and the State*. Cambridge: Cambridge University Press.

Busemeyer, Marius and Christine Trampusch, eds. 2012. *The Political Economy of Collective Skill Formation*. Oxford: Oxford University Press.

Capoccia, Giovanni and Daniel Ziblatt. 2010. "The Historical Turn in Democratization Studies: A New Research Agenda for Europe and Beyond." *Comparative Political Studies* 43 (8–9): 931–968.

Chalmers, Douglas. 1964. *The Social Democratic Party of Germany, from Working-Class Movement to Modern Political Party*. New Haven, CT: Yale University Press.

Collier, Ruth Berins and David Collier. 1991. *Shaping the Political Arena: Critical Junctures, the Labor Movement, and Regime Dynamics in Latin America*. Princeton, NJ: Princeton University Press.

De Leon, Cedric, Manali Desai, and Cihan Tugal. 2015. *Building Blocs: How Parties Organize Society*. Stanford, CA: Stanford University Press.

Ferree, Karen. 2011. *Framing the Race in South Africa: The Political Origins of Racial-Census Elections*. New York: Cambridge University Press.

Greene, Kenneth. 2007. *Why Dominant Parties Lose: Mexico's Democratization in Comparative Perspective*. New York: Cambridge University Press.

Grzymala-Busse, A. M. 2002. *Redeeming the Communist Past: The Regeneration of Communist Parties in East Central Europe*. Cambridge and New York: Cambridge University Press.

Grzymala-Busse, Anna. 2006. "Authoritarian Determinants of Democratic Party Competition: The Communist Successor Parties in East Central Europe." *Party Politics* 12 (3): 415–437.

Grzymala-Busse, Anna. 2011. "Time Will Tell? Temporality and the Analysis of Causal Mechanisms and Processes." *Comparative Political Studies* 44 (9): 1267–1297.

Hicken, A. and E. Kuhonta, eds. 2014. *Party System Institutionalization in Asia: Democracies, Autocracies, and the Shadow of the Past*. Cambridge: Cambridge University Press.

Huntington, Samuel. 1968. *Political Order in Changing Societies*. New Haven, CT: Yale University Press.

Kalyvas, Stathis. 1996. *The Rise of Christian Democracy in Europe*. Ithaca, NY: Cornell University Press.

Kalyvas, Stathis. 2000. "Commitment Problems in Emerging Democracies: The Case of Religious Parties." *Comparative Politics* 32 (4): 379–398.

Kirchheimer, Otto. 1966. "The Transformation of the Western European Party Systems." In *Political Parties and Political Development*, ed. J. LaPalombara and M. Weiner. Princeton, NJ: Princeton University Press, 177–200.

Kitschelt, Herbert, Zdenka Mansfeldova, Radoslaw Markowski, and Gabor Toka. 1999. *Post-Communist Party Systems: Competition, Representation and Inter-Party Competition*. Cambridge: Cambridge University Press.

Kuhonta, Erik. 2011. *The Politics of Equitable Development in Southeast Asia: The Institutional Imperative*. Stanford, CA: Stanford University Press.

LeBas, Adrienne. 2011. *From Protest to Parties: Party Building and Democratization in Africa*. Oxford: Oxford University Press.

Levitsky, Steven. 1998. "Institutionalism and Peronism: The Concept, the Case and the Case for Unpacking the Concept." *Party Politics* 4 (1): 77–92.

Levitsky, Steven. 2001. "Informal Organisation and the Persistence of Local Party Structures in Argentine Peronism." *Journal of Latin American Studies* 33 (29): 29–65.

Levitsky, Steven. 2003. "From Labor Politics to Machine Politics: The Transformation of Party-Union Linkages in Argentine Peronism, 1983–99." *Latin American Research Review* 38 (3): 3–36.

Levitsky, Steven and Maxwell Cameron. 2003. "Democracy Without Parties? Political Parties and Regime Change in Fujimori's Peru." *Latin American Politics and Society* 45 (3): 1–33.

Levitsky, Steven, James Loxton, and Brandon Van Dyck. Forthcoming. "Introduction: Challenges of Party-Building in Latin America." In *Party-Building in Latin America.*

Levitsky, Steven and Lucan Way. 2012. "Beyond Patronage: Violent Struggle, Ruling Party Cohesion, and Authoritarian Durability." *Perspectives on Politics* 10 (4).

Levitsky, Steven and Lucan Way. 2013. "The Durability of Reovlutionary Regimes." *Journal of Democracy* 24 (3): 5–17.

Lipset, S. M. and S. Rokkan. 1967. *Party Systems and Voter Alignments: Cross-National Perspectives.* New York: Free Press.

Loxton, James Ivor. 2014. Authoritarian Inheritance and Conservative Party-Building in Latin America. Doctoral dissertation, Harvard University.

Lupu, Noam and Rachel Beatty Riedl. 2013. "Political Parties and Uncertainty in Developing Democracies." *Comparative Political Studies* 46 (11): 1339–1365.

Mahoney, James and Kathleen Thelen. 2009. *Explaining Institutional Change: Ambiguity, Agency and Power.* Cambridge: Cambridge University Press.

Mainwaring, S. and M. Torcal. 2006. "Party System Institutionalization and Party System Theory after the Third Wave of Democratization." In *Handbook of Party Politics,* ed. R. S. Katz and W. J. Crotty. London and Thousand Oaks, CA: Sage, 204–227.

Mainwaring, Scott. Forthcoming. *Party Systems in Latin America: Institutionalization, Decay and Collapse.* Cambridge University Press.

Mair, Peter. 1990. "Introduction." In *The West European Party System.* ed. Peter Mair. Oxford and New York: Oxford University Press, 1–22.

Masoud, Tarek. 2014. *Counting Islam: Religion, Class, and Elections in Egypt.* Cambridge: Cambridge University Press.

Nalepa, Monika and Royce Carroll. 2014. "Party Representation after Communism: Understanding the Emergence of Programmatic Parties through Parliamentary Behavior." Paper presented at Council of European Studies Panel.

Pierson, Paul. 1993. "When Effect Becomes Cause: Policy Feedback and Political Change." *World Politics* 45 (4): 595–628.

Pierson, Paul. 2004. *Politics in Time: History, Institutions and Social Analysis.* Princeton, NJ: Princeton University Press.

Pizzorno, Alessandro. 1981. "Interests and Parties in Pluralism." In *Organizing Interests in Western Europe: Pluralism, Corporatism, and the Transformation,* ed. Suzanne Berger, Albert Hirschman, and Charles Maier. New York: Cambridge University Press, 249–286.

Przeworski, Adam and John Sprague. 1986. *Paper Stones: A History of Electoral Socialism.* Chicago: University of Chicago Press.

Riedl, Rachel Beatty. Forthcoming. "Strong Parties, Weak Parties: Explaining Regime Outcomes in Sub-Saharan Africa." In *Parties, Movements and Democracy in the Developing World,* ed. Nancy Bermeo and Deborah Yashar. Cambridge University Press.

Riedl, Rachel Beatty. 2014. *Authoritarian Origins of Democratic Party Systems in Africa.* New York: Cambridge University Press.

Rodden, Jonathan. 2008. "Back to the Future: Endogenous Institutions and Comparative Politics." In *Comparative Politics: Rationality, Culture, and Structure*, ed. Mark Lichbach and Alan Zuckerman. 2nd Edition. Cambridge: Cambridge University Press, 333–357.

Sartori, Giovanni. 1969. "Politics, Ideology and Belief Systems." *American Political Science Review* 63 (2): 398–411.

Sartori, Giovanni. 1973. "What Is Politics." *Political Theory* 1 (1): 5–26.

Sartori, Giovanni. 1989. "Video-Power." *Government and Opposition* 24 (1): 39–53.

Shefter, Martin. 1977. "Party and Patronage: Germany, England and Italy." *Politics & Society* 7 (4): 403–451.

Simmons, Erica and Dan Slater. 2013. "Coping by Colluding: Political Uncertainty and Promiscuous Powersharing in Indonesia and Bolivia." *Comparative Political Studies* 46 (11): 1366–1393.

Slater, Dan. 2010. *Ordering Power: Contentious Politics and Authoritarian Leviathans in Southeast Asia*. New York: Cambridge University Press.

Slater, Dan. 2014. "Unbuilding Blocs: Indonesia's Accountability Deficit in Historical Perspective." *Critical Asian Studies* 46 (2): 287–315.

Slater, D. and J. Wong. 2013. "The Strength to Concede: Ruling Parties and Democratization in Developmental Asia." *Perspectives on Politics* 11: 3.

Smith, Benjamin. 2005. "Life of the Party: The Origins of Regime Breakdown and Persistence under Single Party Rule." *World Politics* 57 (3): 421–451.

Thachil, Tariq. 2014. *Elite Parties, Poor Voters: How Social Services Win Votes in India*. Cambridge: Cambridge University Press.

Torcal, Mariano and Scott Mainwaring. 2003. "The Political Recrafting of Social Bases of Party Competition: Childe, 1973–95." *British Journal of Political Science* 33 (01): 55–84.

Trejo, Guillermo and Fernando Bizzarro Neto. 2014. "Religious Competition and the Rise of the Workers' Party in Brazil: Why the Catholic Church Provided the Mass Base for the Democratic World's Largest Leftist Party." EDGS Working Paper No. 21.

Tudor, Maya. 2013. *The Promise of Power: The Origins of Democracy in India and Autocracy in Pakistan*. New York: Cambridge University Press.

Ziblatt, Daniel. Forthcoming. *Conservative Political Parties and the Birth of Modern Democracy in Europe, 1848–1950*. Cambridge: Cambridge University Press.

CHAPTER 14

SOCIAL POLICY IN DEVELOPING COUNTRIES

MELANI CAMMETT AND AYTUĞ ŞAŞMAZ*

RESEARCH on welfare states in the historical institutionalist tradition has largely centered on the advanced capitalist countries.[1] Alongside this work, a growing body of research focuses on welfare regimes in developing countries, some of which explicitly or implicitly draws on historical institutionalist approaches. As we argue in this chapter, however, a true appreciation of the origins and evolution of welfare regimes in developing countries calls for more extensive and systematic applications of the methods and approaches from the historical institutionalist toolbox to this expanding research program.

In this chapter, we review the findings of the limited, yet growing number of studies on the origins and transformation of social policies in developing countries, and explore their affinities with historical institutionalist approaches. We also emphasize the importance of including non-state welfare in this research agenda, whether in the industrialized or developing worlds. Non-state actors are an important part of all welfare regimes, but arguably are all the more critical in developing countries, where state capacity tends to be more limited than in wealthier, more industrialized countries.

HISTORICAL INSTITUTIONALISM AND THE WELFARE STATE RESEARCH PROGRAM

For decades, the vast majority of social science research on welfare states concentrated on advanced, industrialized countries and historical institutionalism has figured prominently in this work. Can this research program be productively extended to cases in developing regions? Can evidence be derived from developing countries generate new insights that will strengthen a broader research program on welfare regimes?

The predominant assumptions about the origins of welfare states in the scholarly literature are largely derived from the experiences of Organisation for Economic Co-operation and Development (OECD) countries, primarily in Europe or the United States. A precursor to historical institutionalist research on welfare regimes, one strand of scholarly literature emphasizes the role of the societal interests and groups in shaping welfare regimes. In this approach, which is known as the power resources model, social policies originate from labor-based mobilization within the context of class struggle in capitalist, industrialized societies (Korpi 1983). Yet this analytical framework is less appropriate for many less developed countries (LDCs), where industrialization is not as extensive and labor generally is not as powerful in the domestic political arena. Furthermore, many governments in LDCs enacted social policies, even if they were not triggered by labor demands from below.

A second variant of historical institutionalist research on welfare states in industrialized countries builds on some of the core insights of the power resource approach but points to a broader array of social actors and coalitions in explaining variation in social policies in industrialized countries (Esping-Andersen 1990). The presumption that welfare policies emerge through a demand-side dynamic, however, limits the applicability of this approach to the initial emergence of welfare policies in many developing countries, particularly where democracy is less consolidated or virtually absent. As we argue in this chapter, however, the approach is more useful in explaining the dynamics of change (or the limits to change) in such contexts.

Shaped by the power resources approach, a third strand of research stresses the effects of formal political institutions on welfare regimes (Huber and Stephens 2001). Despite its strong logical and empirical foundations, this argument is not as valuable for explaining variation in social policies in many developing countries. In these countries, formal political institutions are frequently not the main locus of policymaking, party politics and constitutions do not always constrain rulers, and political regimes are not democratic.

A fourth line of research in the historical institutionalist research program emphasizes the role of the state and state capacity in shaping welfare regimes (Skocpol 1992; Steinmo 1993). State actors can design and implement decisions autonomously, especially if they have developed a high level of administrative capacity, and can shape the identities, capacities, and goals of social groups that aim to affect state policies. Once in place, social policies form novel constituencies of support, and create strong incentives for politicians to expand or maintain social programs, although retrenchment can occur under some conditions (Hacker 2004, 2005; Mahoney and Thelen 2010; Pierson 1994, 2001; Streeck and Thelen 2005; Thelen 2004). Grounded in small-n, historical analyses, this line of research is at the core of the historical institutionalist research agenda (Thelen 1999).

These diverse perspectives on welfare regimes in industrialized countries share some presumptions about the origins of protective welfare policies. First, many (but not all) regard democracy as a prerequisite for the foundation of extensive social protection regimes, through which the class pressure of labor can be moderated and/or politicians gain the support of the masses. Yet some developing countries (and, of course, industrialized countries) have established and maintained social policies without democratic governance mechanisms in place.[2] Second, historical institutionalist research on welfare regimes tends to emphasize or presume the role of relatively strong and autonomous states in shaping the formulation of social policies, a condition that is often absent, or at least qualified, in developing countries. Third, until recently, most work on the welfare state in developed countries has downplayed the effects of the international setting and globalization on national social policies. For developing countries, these factors cannot be overlooked in analyzing the formulation and transformation of social policies, which are directly influenced by a variety of supranational factors such as the prescriptions of international financial institutions and the ramifications of global competition for labor and protective social policies.

The study of welfare regimes in developing countries is a relatively new frontier for the historical institutionalist research program. In the following sections, we review the current state of literature, focusing on work related to the origins and transformation of welfare regimes.[3] In so doing, we assess the extent to which historical institutionalism has been employed by scholars of welfare in developing countries.

Before proceeding, a quick note on the conceptual underpinnings of welfare policies is in order. Welfare policies are largely defined as public policies through which governments exercise responsibility for the "injury and dependency of their citizens on market exchanges" (Lowi 1986, 113, cited by Rudra 2008, 11). In advanced, industrialized countries relevant social policies generally include (1) social insurance systems that provide protection against dependency in the case of old age, temporary unemployment, and chronic sickness; (2) non-contributory social assistance mechanisms that provide protection in various cases of poverty; and (3) the provision of social services such as health, education, early childhood care, and elder care. In developing countries, however, the administrative and fiscal capacities of the state are often not sufficiently articulated to sustain an extensive mix of policies. Therefore, states in developing countries often use public sector employment, subsidies for basic foodstuffs and utilities including fuel, and input subsidies in a similar function to social protection.[4] As historical institutionalists would predict, once subsidies are instituted, it is very hard for political leaders to repeal them. Consumer subsidy programs for basic foodstuffs and utilities therefore tend to grow rapidly and become entrenched, especially in volatile economic environments. Thus, subsidies, public sector employment, and other features of welfare regimes in the developing world should be at the core of the expanding research agenda on welfare in the non-OECD countries.

The Origins of Welfare Regimes in Developing Countries

In the past decade, a number of scholars have proposed classifications of welfare regimes across developing regions and countries (Rudra 2008; Seekings 2008; Wood and Gough

2006; Haggard and Kaufman 2008). In this section, we review how these and other studies explain the origins of welfare regimes in developing countries: How and why have social policies emerged in developing countries? To what extent does historical institutionalism explicitly or implicitly inform these studies?

Social Coalitions or Authoritarian Strategies?

Reminiscent of Esping-Andersen's (1990) framework, Haggard and Kaufman (2008) emphasize the role of "critical realignments" at key historical moments in shaping welfare regimes across different global regions.[5] The origins of these diverse regional welfare regimes can be traced to the international setting in which countries found themselves in the aftermath of World War II, when new coalitions of domestic groups and political contenders had to form to remain in or secure power. In Eastern Europe and East Asia, political elites did not need to seek as much support from domestic forces because newly installed regimes enjoyed the backing of global powers. As a result, elites in these regions had more leeway to introduce their own political and economic projects without the support of the urban or rural classes. In Latin America, on the other hand, contenders for political power had to rely on the "support of cross-class coalitions that offered legal status and influence to segments of organized labor and, in some instances, to popularly based parties" (Haggard and Kaufman 2008, 8).

Beyond its emphasis on the geopolitical context, Haggard and Kaufman's framework of critical realignments is inspired (especially in the case of Latin America) by elements of Esping-Andersen's argument (1990), which highlights the distinct social foundations of varied welfare state configurations. Accordingly, as political contenders vied for the support of organized labor at a critical historical juncture, limited segments of the urban working class received benefits in the form of social insurance. By highlighting the social and political struggles underlying distinct social policy configurations, Haggard and Kaufman's explanation is consistent with the spirit of a sociologically grounded historical institutionalist approach.

By contrast, Mares and Carnes (2009) propose an argument based on the strategic actions of autocratic leaders who bargain with political influential components of society. Consistent with a rational choice historical institutionalist approach, they highlight the ways in which leaders can use social policies to secure their power, particularly in non-democratic developing countries. In their model, autocratic leaders maneuver in three distinct political scenarios. First, if the social groups or coalition which initially supported the autocratic leader falls apart or is sidelined, then the leader is likely to become a stationary bandit, who forms a predatory regime to extract economic surpluses and does not invest in social policies to shore up support from specific groups. Second, if these actors (i.e., military, political parties, etc.) are powerful, the dictator seeks to prevent potential coups by providing their leadership with a stream of rents in selected economic sectors, whether through the creation of de facto monopolies or other privileges such as trade tariffs. In this case, welfare regimes are characterized by restrictive social policies with narrow and general benefits for privileged sectors. Finally, if more than one organization pose potential threats, the dictator may adopt a strategy of "organizational multiplication" to diffuse political tensions and avoid further strengthening of organizations. In this case, the autocrat would confer economic rights to broader segments of the population, albeit in a selective, unequal, and piecemeal way. Although the coverage of social policies is broader under this scenario, it entails greater institutional fragmentation and inequality.[6]

Development Strategies and Production Regimes

A distinct explanation for the emergence of varied welfare regimes in developing countries emphasizes the macroeconomic context within which policies are adopted. Although this type of arguments differs from a historical institutionalist approach, it has implications for the latter research tradition: The policies adopted in response to macroeconomic circumstances create or consolidate actors which then develop vested interests in particularly welfare regimes. In addition to social coalitions, Haggard and Kaufman's (2008) critical realignments framework incorporates a second channel through which distinct welfare state configurations arise—the choice of development strategy. This explanation builds on the "varieties of capitalism" framework (Hall and Soskice 2001), an influential approach in the historical institutionalist tradition for explaining policy variation in developed country contexts. In this framework, the inter-linkages between production regimes and social policies explain differences in welfare systems across developing countries.

As Haggard and Kaufman (2008) argue, an additional by-product of struggles among political contenders in the mid-twentieth century was a reordering of the macro-level approaches to industrialization and development pursued by political elites. These broad developmental strategies are associated with distinct types of production regimes, which reinforce and perpetuate distinct types of social policy regime. For example, with the support of the Western powers, the East Asian countries opted for an export-led production regime in the aftermath of World War II. This externally-oriented development strategy fostered resistance to broad social insurance schemes while incentivizing governments to expand access to primary and secondary education in order to create more globally competitive workforces. In Eastern Europe, where planned industrialization was adopted in the context of communist systems, government provision of social insurance and basic services emerged as part and parcel of the socialization of the economy. In Latin America, the types of cross-class coalitions that emerged during the period of critical realignments were conducive to the adoption of import-substitution industrialization. This type of development strategy prioritized entitlements for the organized urban working classes while reducing the incentives for governments to invest in education.

Other approaches stress the importance of economic endowments in generating distinct developmental regimes, which in turn explain variation in social policy configurations in developing countries. According to Wibbels and Ahlquist (2011), the relative scarcity of factors in different national economies in the postwar closed international economy resulted in the selection of different industrial development strategies. In developing countries, where capital endowments were limited by definition, the relative scarcity of land and labor was pivotal. In labor scarce economies, particularly those with large domestic markets and high levels of inequality in rural land ownership, coalitions between protectionist capital and labor formed, which led to the adoption of inward-focused development strategies, notably import-substituting industrialization (ISI). Through this cross-factoral coalition, labor had the bargaining power to lobby governments to enact its policy preferences for employment guarantees and insurance policies. Over time, labor's interest in maintaining the policies further strengthened, which then evolved into an insurance-based social policy regime.

Wibbels and Ahlquist (2011) base their empirical claims on cross-national statistical analyses with little if any attention to the context in which political struggles over policy formulation and adoption unfold. As such, their approach differs from the analytical approaches at the core of historical institutionalism, which is better equipped to trace the dynamics of institutional formation and persistence. Furthermore, various conceptual and methodological concerns limit their contributions to studies of the origins and evolution of welfare regimes in developing countries. First, the dependent variable they used in the empirical tests does not capture the diverse tools developing countries use as welfare and social policies. Second, the explanatory variables they use are time variant and are themselves affected by the developmental policies of governments. Furthermore, by their own admission, their simplified conceptualization of politics assumes the near-automatic adoption and implementation of policies, while neglecting the motivations of the political elites or other actors. Their account also cannot explain why capitalists in countries that adopted ISI viewed education and health services as undesirable (Mares and Carnes 2009).

State-Building and Welfare Regimes in Developing Regions

In the research program on welfare regimes in industrialized countries, the historical development of institutions, the state and, especially, state capacity figure prominently. In the growing body of work on welfare in the developing world, however, state effectiveness has received less attention. This undoubtedly stems from the fact that state capacity is generally perceived to be lacking and at the root of development failures (Acemoglu and Robinson 2012; Evans 1995; Kohli 2004; Mahoney 2010). Yet scholarship on the varieties of welfare regimes in the developing world should pay more attention to this critical variable and, more generally, to the effects of state-building on the adoption and implementation of social policies.

In their typology of welfare regimes in developed and developing countries, Wood and Gough (2006) pay special attention to the role of institutional conditions in shaping the welfare mix of that country. The most important of these conditions include the pervasiveness and character of markets, the extent of societal integration, and the legitimacy and capabilities of state institutions. All of these institutional conditions can be seen as institutional subsystems shaped by their own histories. Given its emphasis on state capacity, this framework is in line with a classic historical institutionalist approach to welfare regimes. Unlike most accounts of welfare regimes in either industrialized or developing countries, however, Wood and Gough emphasize the importance of non-state actors, such as formal and informal community organizations and supranational institutions, in the welfare mixes of developing countries (also see Gough and Therborn 2010; Gough 2014). Using this framework and data from more than 60 developing countries, they identify four clusters of welfare (or "illfare") regimes in the developing world and order them in a moral hierarchy beginning with "formal security" regimes and descending to "dependent insecurity regimes."[7]

Research on the Middle East and North Africa, a neglected geographic region in the literature on welfare regimes, also suggests that distinct state-building histories accounts for some variation in social policies in the region (Cammett 2014). Theories linking the origins and variation of social policies to power resources, developmental strategies, or political regime type cannot adequately explain the diversity of welfare regimes across the Middle East. Autocratic leaders in the region introduced social policies with minimal pressure from below: organized labor and other mass-based social groups have been notoriously weak or fragmented, and the predominant post-independence development paradigms called for an interventionist state in promoting social mobility. Yet even countries following the same general development strategies adopted distinct welfare policy configurations in the Middle East.

As a first cut, a historical institutionalist approach attentive to the varied levels of bureaucratic capacity, understood as the product of distinct state-building histories, may explain why some rulers opted for and were able to implement more comprehensive systems of social protection than others. Analyses of welfare regime development in the non-oil economies of the Middle East, including Egypt, Jordan, Lebanon, Morocco, and Tunisia, helps to illustrate this point. These countries share similar resource profiles and significant budget constraints yet have adopted distinct welfare policies and responded to fiscal crises in varied ways. For example, the health systems of these non-oil Middle Eastern countries differ in their levels of government spending on this sector, the burden of out-of-pocket expenses on households, the extent of insurance coverage of the population, and health outcomes. The causes of each of these factors cannot be reduced to a single variable, but collectively they suggest that health systems in some of these countries are more effective at assuring access to medical care and well-being than in others. Despite problems in the quality of care and mounting health disparities, Tunisia and, especially, Jordan stand out for their comparatively well-developed capacities to meet population health needs in comparison with Egypt, Lebanon, and Morocco.

What explains the relatively effective Jordanian and Tunisian health sectors in comparison with other Middle Eastern non-oil countries? Whether measured by population or territorial expanse, country size does not provide a satisfying explanation. First, not all small countries have equally comprehensive and effective health infrastructure. The contrast between Lebanon, on the one hand, and Jordan and Tunisia, on the other hand, illustrates this point. Ethno-religious diversity provides another possible explanation for health system variation in the Middle East. A substantial literature holds that societal divisions have detrimental effects on public goods provision (Alesina, Baqir, and Easterly 1999; Easterly and Levine 1997; Habyarimana et al. 2009; Miguel 2004; Tsai 2007; but see Baldwin and Huber 2010; Gao 2011; and Gerring, Thacker, and Alfaro 2012 for partial critiques). Lebanon's comparatively poor performance with respect to health inputs and outputs seems to confirm this argument. By this logic, however, Jordan's superior health system is anomalous. First, Jordan is a colonial fabrication (Massad 2001), which lacked an organic or even imagined national political community to serve as the basis for solidaristic social programs. Second, the social cleavage between Jordanians of West and East Bank origins is politicized and, since the 1970s, Jordanians who initially came from the Palestinian Territories have been virtually excluded from coveted public sector and military jobs, which feature the most generous social benefits (Baylouny 2010).

Historical analyses of bureaucratic development are essential to trace the sources of variation in state capacity in the selected countries. Tunisia and Jordan emerged with more effective bureaucracies than their neighbors, albeit via distinct paths. New leaders in post-independence Tunisia inherited a relatively intact state bureaucracy from the French and even acquired valuable administrative and technical skills during the colonial period (Anderson 1986; Charrad 2001; Hermassi 1975). The dynamics of post-independence bureaucratic development differed in Jordan, which was a colonial creation established after World War I. British officials helped to run state agencies for the first few decades after Jordan gained independence in 1946 (Massad 2001).

Conversely, in Lebanon, the state is notoriously weak—not just with respect to providing physical security and protection from violence but also in assuring well-being. The fragmentation of the Lebanese state is a product of political institutions established during the Mandate period, which institutionalized power along sectarian lines. The power-sharing system was further cemented in independent Lebanon, in which politicians maintain tight control over patronage opportunities (Cammett 2014; Gates 1998; El-Khazen 2000; Makdisi 2000; Picard 2002).

State capacity is essential for the design and execution of public health measures and for proper "stewardship" of public and private health care providers (WHO 2000). In turn, variable levels of state capacity likely result from both colonial and post-independence institution-building in the region. With its emphasis on the historical processes of state-building and their linkages to the development of welfare regimes in the Middle East, this account adapts key insights from the historical institutionalist research program for developing country contexts.

The Transformation of Welfare Regimes in the Developing World

Theories of welfare regime formation should also be equipped to explain the evolution of social policies in subsequent periods. A major consensus holds that the 1980s ushered in broad transformations of economic and social policy across most developing regions (Haggard and Kaufman 2008; Huber and Niedzwiecki 2015, *inter alia*). The initial impetuses behind these changes range from state fiscal crises and democratization to pressures from international markets or international financial institutions, each of which are weighted differently in distinct accounts.

In response to economic crises beginning in the 1980s, an earlier wave of research on welfare reform in industrialized countries suggested that mobilized and organized labor, among other constituencies, could counterbalance the pressures of globalization (Garrett 1998) and pre-existing social and political institutions would prevent institutional "convergence" (Berger and Dore 1996). In developing countries, where welfare institutions were less developed and the beneficiaries of social programs were less equipped to block reform, global market integration was widely presumed to lead to a "race to the bottom" in welfare policies.

Rudra (2008) finds support for the race to the bottom hypothesis. Through a series of econometric analyses, she concludes that trade openness in interaction with weak labor power is associated with decreased spending on social security.[8] At the same time, her data indicate that global market integration may induce some increase in public education spending, as concerns about market competitiveness call for greater investment in education.[9] Rudra further contends that global market integration hurts the middle classes through its negative effects on social security spending. Yet strong legacies of protective social policies, which cultivated vested interest groups, particularly among the middle classes, ensures that these groups were less vulnerable to the effects of globalization than workers or the poor, who never benefited extensively from social policies in the first place. Case studies of India, Brazil, and South Korea support these arguments by showing how the middle classes in these countries were able to defend the policies and programs from which they benefited. Rudra's soft rational choice approach therefore borrows from institutionalist approaches to explain the path dependence of protective social policies.

Since the 1980s, the privatization of old-age pension systems has become a widespread policy prescription from international financial institutions for welfare reform in developing countries. The privatization of pensions presents an important puzzle for the institutionalist welfare state research because retrenchment in such an expansive and consolidated policy area should face serious resistance. In a study of 66 countries across the globe, however, Brooks (2008) finds that, between 1980 and 2002, 23 countries undertook structural reforms to add a private pillar to their old-age pension systems. Brooks argues that the extent of privatization (measured by private sector involvement in both premiums and pensions) depends both on the policy legacies of the public pension system and the capabilities of the government to pay the political and economic costs of the transition to a privatized pension system.

Through quantitative analyses and case studies of six Latin American countries, Brooks shows that the magnitude of the pension debt, or the cost of transitioning to a private pension system, can positively affect privatization up to a certain level, after which the depth and breadth of coverage in the previous public system prevents the government from bearing the cost of transition, especially in the context of globalized financial markets. The political legacies of the public pension system, too, affect the extent of privatization. If public coverage was already low and if citizens hold negative views of the system, then path-*departing* forces of institutional change can occur (Brooks 2008, 12). Governments may win support for reform, particularly if they are left-leaning and enjoy high credibility on issues of social justice. Brooks' emphasis on the ways in which prior institutional legacies either limit subsequent reform processes or create the possibility for reform is consistent with a historical institutionalist approach.[10]

Other scholars deploy frameworks grounded in the strategic interactions of social collectivities to explain the evolution of welfare regimes in developing countries. For Mares and Carnes (2009), the preferences of the middle class (and especially formal sector workers) are critical for explaining divergent patterns of social policy reform in developing countries. Perceived economic security, the legacies of previous policies, and the extractive capacity of the state shape middle class preferences. If the middle class perceives that its economic future is insecure, it is more likely to form an alliance with the lower class. In countries where the extractive capacity of the state is high, members of the middle class calculate favor universalistic social policies because taxation will be spread out more broadly across society. Conversely, if the extractive capacity of the state is underdeveloped, a middle class alliance with the lower class leads to means-tested, targeted social assistance programs. When the middle class expects a secure economic future, it tends to ally with the upper classes. In this scenario, perceptions of low state extractive capacity lead to a retrenchment of welfare policies. Elements of this explanatory framework build on some key insights of historical institutionalism because the perception of risk on the part of the middle classes depends on the legacies of former social policies and on policy feedback mechanisms. At the same time, the emphasis on strategic interactions among collective actors distinguishes it from classic historical institutionalist approaches and adheres more closely to rational choice institutionalism.

The configuration and actions of civil society, rather than explicitly class-based actors, are also invoked to explain the evolution of welfare regimes in developing countries. In a recent study of welfare state transformation in Latin America and East Asia, Lee (2012) contends that a well-structured "civil society" is a key agent militating for the universalistic expansion of welfare policies. Based on comparisons of Brazil, South Korea, Argentina, and Taiwan, Lee asks why the first two countries were able to enact more comprehensive social policies and expand their welfare states, despite the fact that they confronted similar challenges as the latter two countries. Using social network analysis techniques, Lee shows that distinct structures of civil society explain this variation. In

Brazil and South Korea, the formal political parties, unions, and professional organizations are cohesive (that is, they embody long-lasting social ties that facilitate coordination) and are embedded in the associational sector (i.e., formal sector organizations are tied to more informal networks of associations). Pressure from a more unified and effective civil society compels governments to launch expansionary programs toward universal welfare states, or, in the context of poor economic conditions, to at least resist pressures to retrench existing welfare programs.

This emphasis on civil society rather than the state as the dominant actor in driving social policy outcomes is a departure from much historical institutionalist research on welfare regimes. For developing countries, however, the emphasis on societal actors may be especially useful, particularly after democratic transitions. While class-based actors and organizations tend to be weak in many developing countries, other types of social actors such as issue-based NGOs, indigenous movements, and ethnoreligious groups are often more articulated.

Non-State Welfare Provision

Until the past decade, the research program on welfare states was dominated by specialists on the advanced, industrialized countries. As our preceding review shows, scholarship on welfare in developing countries has brought new insights to this research agenda by highlighting the ways in which distinct types of social coalitions, industrialization strategies, and authoritarian rule help to create distinct configurations of social policies. A new line of research on non-state welfare in developing countries adds critical dimensions to studies of welfare regimes, including in industrialized countries, but is only in its early stages. The types of non-state providers and their relationships with the state in a given national context affects the ways in which populations experience and access social welfare and shape, in a mutually constitutive fashion, the nature of welfare states (Cammett and MacLean 2014). These insights are just as applicable to industrialized countries, where non-profits play a major role in some countries (Salamon 1999; Allard 2009) and religious institutions affected the varieties of welfare regimes that emerged in twentieth-century Europe (van Kersbergen and Manow 2009).

Any study of social welfare in developing countries that neglects non-state providers (NSPs) misses important aspects of welfare regimes. In developing countries, NSPs encompass a wide array of actors, including international and national NGOs, community-based groups, multinational corporations, private domestic corporations, family and friendship networks, ethnic and sectarian organizations, faith-based organizations, and informal brokers. These distinct types of NSPs have varied implications for citizen access to social services, the accountability of providers to communities, and even for state capacity. The effects of non-state provision, however, vary depending on the type of NSP and its relationship with state institutions (Cammett and MacLean 2014).

Historical institutionalism offers a potentially valuable lens through which to study the origins and political consequences of non-state provision. For example, Lauren Morris MacLean (2010) contrasts the informal institutions of social reciprocity among extended families, friends, and village communities in neighboring regions of Ghana and Côte d'Ivoire. In response to the fiscal crises in the 1990s, fewer people were exchanging help in the Ghanaian region in comparison with the Ivoirian region, where greater numbers of village residents gave more significant amounts of help, albeit among narrower groups of immediate family members. MacLean argues that the distinct histories of the state's role in mediating risk in the two countries explain this variation. The local experience of state formation over time shaped both the extent and structure of the informal institutions of social reciprocity. In post-communist Russia, Linda Cook (2014) argues that the historical role of the Soviet state shaped the origins of non-state provision. The centralized, bureaucratized Soviet health care system left a dense legacy of statist institutions and interests that resisted the privatizing initiatives of neoliberal reformers and helped to foster a process of "spontaneous privatization" whereby service providers use their direct control over facilities to act as informal brokers of citizens' access to medical care. Cook therefore highlights the ways in which institutional legacies from the communist period shaped subsequent social policies, even after profound economic and political change.

These studies of non-state welfare in very different contexts implicitly draw on a historical institutionalist approach to show how long-term institutional legacies shape the nature and extent of distinct forms of non-state welfare in the contemporary period.[11] Ongoing research on welfare regimes—in developing and developed countries alike—should incorporate greater attention to non-state actors, which have potentially important ramifications for welfare outcomes, the political attitudes and behavior of beneficiaries and community members, and other important questions.

Conclusion

This chapter reviews the current literature on social welfare in developing countries and evaluates the extent to which the insights of historical institutionalism have shaped this area of inquiry. Especially during the foundation periods of welfare regimes, small-n, comparative historical analyses of developing countries—a key methodological hallmark of the historical institutionalist approach—help to identify the ways in which factors such as relative state capacity, the goals and behavior of political leaders, and the relationships between public and non-state actors affect the formation of social policies. The special focus of historical institutionalism on the state and different dimensions of state capacity is also essential to understand the origins and even the consequences of welfare state provision. In studying the transformation of welfare policies, a diverse array of scholars—even those who do not necessarily self-identify as historical institutionalists—employ the assumptions of policy feedback mechanisms in their work. Furthermore, as more and more scholars aim to identify and explain the varieties of welfare regimes across the Global South, their analyses have and will rely on core insights of historical institutionalism such as its emphasis on the ways in which diverse institutional configurations shape policy formation and the interests and behavior of key social actors. Ongoing work on welfare regimes should pay more attention to the role of informal institutions, non-state actors and civil society in shaping the formation and transformation of welfare regimes. These factors are increasingly highlighted in work on social welfare in developing countries but are equally relevant for industrialized countries, albeit in distinct institutional contexts.

Notes

* We thank Tulia Falleti for helpful comments on earlier versions of this chapter. All errors are our own.

1. For an in-depth treatment, see Julia Lynch and Martin Rhodes (Chapter 25, this volume).
2. Historically, this of course was also true for some Western European countries, such as Bismarck's Germany.
3. An important line of work, which we do not address in this chapter, examines social outcomes in the diverse welfare regimes of developing countries (see McGuire 2010).
4. Bril-Mascarenhas and Post (2012) report that the sums spent on consumer subsidies often approach and even exceed the amount spent on health or education in developing countries. Consumer subsidies serve as a key source of income support and as a tool to help populations to cope with price shocks. Similarly, product and input subsidies in agriculture can also be used widely as an income support and unemployment insurance mechanism, as documented by Eder (2010) in the Turkish context.
5. Critical realignments refer to new ruling coalitions and the social groups that sustain or support them.
6. Mares and Carnes (2009) further support this theoretical argument with examples of countries that would fit the second and third alternatives described above. Accordingly, the immigrant nationalist regime in Taiwan with its selective benefits to the leaders of the nationalist party, and the Institutional Revolutionary Party or Partido Revolucionario Institucional (PRI) regime in Mexico, where a highly fragmented social policy mix developed, are examples of these scenarios, respectively.
7. "Formal security" regimes are characterized by high state commitments and relatively high welfare outcomes. This cluster of "proto-welfare states" includes much of Eastern Europe, the southern cone of Latin America, some countries from Africa (i.e., Tunisia, Kenya, Algeria), and Thailand. The remaining two clusters are labeled as variants of "informal security regimes," in which developmental states attain relatively good welfare outcomes with lower levels of state social spending, suggesting that informal institutions and/or international remittances are important in the welfare mix. More effective informal security regimes include parts of Southeast Asia, Sri Lanka, the remaining countries of Latin America, and parts of the Middle East. Less effective informal security regimes, which are more dependent on international flows, include South Asia and certain countries in sub-Saharan Africa. The final cluster of "dependent insecurity regimes" comprises the bulk of sub-Saharan Africa (Wood and Gough 2006).

8. The effects of other indicators of globalization, including exposure to portfolio investment and foreign direct investment, are ambiguous, while the effects on health and education spending are not robust.
9. Rudra (2008) also conducts cluster analysis of the welfare policy mixes in developing countries to assess the degree to which globalization induces convergence toward minimalist welfare regimes. Her identification of three discernible welfare regimes in developing countries (productive, protective, dual) belies the extreme variant of the "race to the bottom" thesis. Nonetheless, it is difficult to draw definitive conclusions from her findings because her analysis is time-invariant and coincides with a period in which changes in global markets and country responses were occurring quickly.
10. It is worth noting that her arguments presuppose the willingness of governments to undertake retrenchment policies in the first place and pay limited attention to the role of societal actors in shaping reform processes.
11. For additional examples, see the contributions to the edited volume on non-state welfare by Cammett and MacLean (2014).

References

Acemoglu, Daron and James Robinson. 2012. *Why Nations Fail*. New York: Crown Publishers.

Alesina, Alberto, Reza Baqir, and William Easterly. 1999. "Public Goods and Ethnic Divisions." *Quarterly Journal of Economics* 114: 1243–1284.

Allard, Scott W. 2009. *Out of Reach: Place, Poverty, and the New American Welfare State*. New Haven, CT: Yale University Press.

Anderson, Lisa. 1986. *The State and Social Transformation in Tunisia and Libya, 1830–1980*. Princeton, NJ: Princeton University Press.

Baldwin, Kate and John D. Huber. 2010. "Economic versus Cultural Differences: Forms of Ethnic Diversity and Public Goods Provision." *American Political Science Review* 104 (4): 644–662.

Baylouny, Anne Marie. 2010. *Privatizing Welfare in the Middle East: Kin Mutual Aid Associations in Jordan and Lebanon*. Bloomington, IN: Indiana University Press.

Berger, Suzanne and Ronald Dore. 1996. *National Diversity and Global Capitalism*. Ithaca, NY: Cornell University Press.

Bril-Mascarenhas, Tomas and Alison E. Post. 2012. "Broad-Based Consumer Subsidies as 'Policy Traps': The Case of Utilities Subsidies in Post-Crisis Argentina." Paper Prepared for Delivery at the 2012 Annual Meeting of the American Political Science Association, August 30–September 2.

Brooks, Sarah. 2008. *Social Protection and the Market in Latin America: The Transformation of Social Security Institutions*. New York: Cambridge University Press.

Cammett, Melani. 2014. "State and Nation-Building Imperatives and Welfare Regime Formation: Health Systems in the Non-Oil Economies of the Middle East." Paper Presented at the Workshop on the Impact of Ethnicity on State Capacity Academy for International and Area Studies, Harvard University, October 25–26.

Cammett, Melani and Lauren M. MacLean, eds. 2014. *The Politics of Non-State Social Welfare*. Ithaca, NY: Cornell University Press.

Charrad, Mounira. 2001. *States and Women's Rights: The Making of Postcolonial Tunisia, Algeria, and Morocco*. Berkeley: University of California Press.

Cook, Linda. 2014. "'Spontaneous Privatization' and Its Political Consequences in Russia's Postcommunist Health Sector." In *The Politics of Non-State Social Welfare,* ed. Melani Cammett and Lauren Morris MacLean. Ithaca, NY: Cornell University Press, 217–236.

Easterly, William and R. Levine. 1997. "Africa's Growth Tragedy: Policies and Ethnic Divisions." *Quarterly Journal of Economics* 112 (4): 1203–1250.

Eder, Mine. 2010. "Retreating State? Political Economy of Welfare Regime Change in Turkey." *Middle East Law and Governance* 2 (2): 152–184.

El-Khazen, Farid. 2000. *The Breakdown of the State in Lebanon, 1967–1976.* Cambridge, MA: Harvard University Press.

Esping-Andersen, Gosta. 1990. *The Three Worlds of Welfare Capitalism.* Princeton, NJ: Princeton University Press.

Evans, Peter. 1995. *Embedded Autonomy: States and Industrial Transformation.* Princeton, NJ: Princeton University Press.

Gao, Eleanor. 2011. "Do the Buses Run on Time? Tribal Diversity and Public Goods in Jordan." Paper Presented at the Annual Meeting of the American Political Science Association.

Garrett, Geoffrey. 1998. *Partisan Politics in the Global Economy.* New York: Cambridge University Press.

Gates, Carolyn. 1998. *Merchant Republic of Lebanon: Rise of an Open Economy.* Oxford: Centre for Lebanese Studies in association with I.B. Tauris.

Gerring, John, Strom C. Thacker, and Rodrigo Alfaro. 2012. "Democracy and Human Development." *Journal of Politics* 74 (1): 1–17.

Gough, Ian. 2014. "Mapping Social Welfare Regimes beyond the OECD." *The Politics of Non-State Social Welfare,* ed. Melani Cammett and Lauren M. Maclean. Ithaca, NY: Cornell University Press, 17–30.

Gough, Ian and Goran Therborn. 2010. "The Global Future of Welfare States." In *The Oxford Handbook of Welfare State,* ed. Francis G. Castles, Stephan Leibfried, Jane Lewis, Herbert Obinger, and Christopher Pierson. Oxford: Oxford University Press, 741–758.

Habyarimana, James, Macartan Humphreys, Daniel N. Posner, and Jeremy M. Weinstein. 2009. *Coethnicity: Diversity and the Dilemmas of Collective Action.* New York: Russell Sage Foundation.

Hacker, Jacob. 2004. "Privatizing Risk Without Privatizing the Welfare State: The Hidden Politics of Social Policy Retrenchment in the United States." *American Political Science Review* 98 (2): 243–260.

Hacker, Jacob. 2005. *Off Center: The Republican Revolution and the Erosion of American Democracy.* New Haven, CT: Yale University Press.

Haggard, Stephen and Robert Kaufman. 2008. *Development, Democracy, and Welfare States: Latin America, East Asia, and Eastern Europe.* Princeton, NJ: Princeton University Press.

Hall, Peter and David Soskice. 2001. *Varieties of Capitalism: The Institutional Foundations of Comparative Advantage.* New York: Oxford University Press.

Hermassi, Elbaki. 1975. *Leadership and National Development in North Africa: A Comparative Study.* Berkeley: University of California Press.

Huber, Evelyne and Sara Niedzwiecki. 2015. "Emerging Welfare States in Latin America and East Asia." In *The Oxford Handbook of the Transformations of the State,* ed. Stephan Leibfried, Frank Nullmeier, Evelyne Huber, Matthew Lange, and John D. Stephens. Oxford: Oxford University Press, 796–814.

Huber, Evelyne and John D. Stephens. 2001. *Development and Crisis of the Welfare State: Parties and Policies in Global Markets.* Chicago: University of Chicago Press.

Kohli, Atul. 2004. *State-Directed Development: Political Power and Industrialization in the Global Periphery*. New York: Cambridge University Press.

Korpi, Walter. 1983. *Democratic Class Struggle*. Boston, MA: Routledge & Kegan Paul.

Lee, Cheol-Sung. 2012. "Associational Networks and Welfare States in Argentina, Brazil, South Korea, and Taiwan." *World Politics* 64 (3): 507–554.

Lowi, Theodore. 1986. "The Welfare State: Ethical Foundations and Constitutional Remedies." *Political Science Quarterly* 101 (2): 197–220.

McGuire, James. 2010. *Wealth, Health, and Democracy in East Asia and Latin America*. New York: Cambridge University Press.

MacLean, Lauren M. 2010. *Informal Institutions and Citizenship in Rural Africa: Risk and Reciprocity in Ghana and Cote d'Ivoire*. New York: Cambridge University Press.

Mahoney, James. 2010. *Colonialism and Postcolonial Development: Spanish America in Comparative Perspective*. New York: Cambridge University Press.

Mahoney, James and Kathleen Thelen. 2010. *Explaining Institutional Change: Ambiguity, Agency, and Power*. New York: Cambridge University Press.

Makdisi, Ussama. 2000. *The Culture of Sectarianism Community, History, and Violence in Nineteenth-Century Ottoman Lebanon*. Berkeley: University of California Press.

Mares, Isabela and Matthew E. Carnes. 2009. "Social Policy in Developing Countries." *Annual Review of Political Science* 12: 93–113.

Massad, Joseph Andoni. 2001. *Colonial Effects the Making of National Identity in Jordan*. New York: Columbia University Press.

Miguel, Edward. 2004. "Tribe or Nation?" *World Politics* 56: 327–362.

Picard, Elizabeth. 2002. *Lebanon, a Shattered Country: Myths and Realities of the Wars in Lebanon*. New York: Holmes & Meier.

Pierson, Paul. 1994. *Dismantling the Welfare State? Reagan, Thatcher, and the Politics of Retrenchment*. New York: Cambridge University Press.

Pierson, Paul. 2001. *The New Politics of the Welfare State*. New York: Oxford University Press.

Rudra, Nita. 2008. *Globalization and the Race to the Bottom in Developing Countries: Who Really Gets Hurt?* New York: Cambridge University Press.

Salamon, Lester M. 1999. "The Nonprofit Sector at a Crossroads: The Case of America." *Voluntas: International Journal of Voluntary and Nonprofit Organizations* 10 (1): 5–23.

Seekings, Jeremy. 2008. "Welfare Regimes and Redistribution in the South." In *Divide and Deal: The Politics of Distribution in Democracies*, ed. Ian Shapiro, Peter A. Swenson, and Daniela Donno Panayides. New York: New York University Press, 19–42.

Skocpol, Theda. 1992. *Protecting Soldiers and Mothers: The Political Origins of Social Policy in the United States*. Boston, MA: Belknap Press of Harvard University.

Steinmo, Sven. 1993. *Taxation and Democracy: Swedish, British and American Approaches to Financing the Modern State*. New Haven, CT: Yale University Press.

Streeck, Wolfgang and Kathleen Thelen. 2005. *Beyond Continuity: Institutional Change in Advanced Political Economies*. New York: Oxford University Press.

Thelen, Kathleen. 1999. "Historical Institutionalism in Comparative Politics." *Annual Review of Political Science* 2: 369–404.

Thelen, Kathleen. 2004. *How Institutions Evolve: The Political Economy of Skills in Germany, Britain, the United States, and Japan*. New York: Cambridge University Press.

Tsai, Lily. 2007. "Solidary Groups, Informal Accountability, and Local Public Goods Provision in Rural China." *American Political Science Review* 101 (2): 355–372.

Van Kersbergen, Kees and Philip Manow, eds. 2009. *Religion, Class Coalitions, and Welfare States*. New York: Cambridge University Press.

Wibbels, Erik and John S. Ahlquist. 2011. "Development, Trade, and Social Insurance." *International Studies Quarterly* 55: 125–149.

Wood, Geof and Ian Gough. 2006. "A Comparative Welfare Regime Approach to Global Social Policy." *World Development* 34 (10): 1696–1712.

World Health Organization (WHO). 2000. *World Health Report 2000: Health Systems—Improving Performance*. Geneva: WHO.

CHAPTER 15

LABOR IN DEVELOPING AND POST-COMMUNIST COUNTRIES

TERI L. CARAWAY

The late twentieth and early twenty-first centuries have presented enormous challenges and opportunities for unions. Transitions to democracy in much of the Global South and Eastern Europe heralded the recognition of rights denied to unions under authoritarianism, giving unions more freedom to act autonomously and increasing their opportunities to engage politically. At the same time, the transition to a market economy in Eastern Europe and neoliberal market reforms have increased the precarity of work, reduced union membership, and hampered new organizing efforts. These economic and political transformations have confronted organized labor in most of the world, but unions in some countries have faced the challenges of neoliberalism and seized the opportunities of democracy more successfully than in others.

Comparative labor politics scholarship has sought to explain this variation and in doing so has looked to the past to explain labor's present, linking unions' varying capacities to navigate their present to institutional legacies with deep historical roots. In this sense, comparative labor scholarship takes both history and institutions very seriously. But there are some important differences in approach between historical institutionalist scholarship and other historically informed institutional work that puts greater emphasis on strategic interaction within historically produced institutional configurations. Historical institutionalists do not ignore strategic interaction, but temporal processes figure more prominently. Institutions are therefore conceptualized not only as a strategic context that "holds together" a particular pattern of politics (Thelen 1999, 384). By problematizing institutional evolution and reproduction, historical institutionalist scholars embed institutions in broader political and social contexts, and as such, institutions may be dependent variables at one stage of the analysis and independent variables at a later stage; or, the same set of institutions may have quite distinct consequences depending on the temporal (and political and social) context in which they are situated (Pierson 2004).

This chapter analyzes these historically informed institutional approaches in comparative labor politics and assesses the contributions of the historical institutionalist literature to our understanding of contemporary labor politics, focusing on developing and post-communist countries, with an emphasis on labor in "new democracies." While there is some overlap in the literature on advanced democracies and the developing and post-communist world, most comparative work that concentrates on these regions addresses different questions, making the synthesis of these literatures in a short essay impractical. These differences in analytic focus arise from the distinctive histories of Eastern Europe and the developing world, where authoritarian regimes reigned for much of the late twentieth century and still rule in some. Authoritarian regimes incorporated workers in varying ways, but they shared important common features: a deeper state imprint on labor relations and greater levels of compulsion than typically found in postwar Western democracies. The context of late development also shaped the size and structure of the labor force differently than in advanced democracies, creating a smaller industrial working class, a larger informal sector, and a dominant role for the state, as opposed to the private sector, in industrialization.

The chapter proceeds by first analyzing Ruth Berins and David Collier's foundational works in comparative labor politics: *Shaping the Political Arena* (SPA) (1991) and "Inducements versus Constraints: Disaggregating 'Corporatism'" (IvC) (1979). The chapter then turns to a discussion of the literature on labor and the twin processes of political and economic liberalization, focusing specifically on neoliberal reforms and authoritarian legacies. Historical institutionalist scholarship has made contributions to our understanding of why unions in some countries have fared better than others by demonstrating the importance of timing and sequencing, and by problematizing the reproduction and evolution of founding institutions that later prove decisive in shaping the strategic context faced by unions. The chapter concludes with thoughts about directions for future research.

Foundational Works: SPA and IvC

The logical place to begin an exposition of historical institutionalist contributions to comparative labor politics is with a discussion of two foundational texts: Collier and Collier's SPA and IvC. SPA analyzed regime dynamics in eight Latin American countries, contributed to the development of the critical juncture framework, and established labor incorporation as a critical founding moment. IvC, while more modest in scope, outlined an approach for analyzing corporatist institutions comparatively that has arguably been just as important as SPA. These two works, though quite different in theoretical approach, have had a lasting impact on subsequent scholarship.

The Colliers are perhaps most recognized for their argument about the importance of initial labor incorporation for party systems and regime trajectories in Latin America. Indeed, in the updated edition, the authors observe that the lesson that most people draw from SPA is that "labor incorporation matters" (Collier and Collier 2002, xiv). The Colliers hypothesized that the period of labor incorporation—when unions became legitimate political actors and states began to rely less on repression and more on legalization and institutionalization to control the working class—was a critical juncture. The type of incorporation that took place during this critical juncture, whether party or state driven, produced reactive sequences that propelled countries down different pathways.

In Brazil and Chile, for example, state incorporation took place under uncompetitive authoritarian regimes. Unlike party incorporation, state incorporation aimed to control rather than to mobilize workers for electoral purposes. Authoritarianism, however, generated substantial popular opposition, and this popular *reaction* resulted in transitions to competitive electoral regimes. Unions, unchained to a political party, developed into radical and politically independent organizations. Although populist parties later emerged to garner working class votes, these parties never won a majority, which forced them to govern in coalitions with centrist parties. The accommodationist policies of these coalition governments, however, disappointed working class voters, leading to further radicalization. Increasingly polarized politics produced a *counterreaction*, resulting in military coups in the 1960s and 1970s.

By contrast, party incorporation mobilized the working class electorally and set off a different reactive sequence. In this case, the electoral mobilization of the working class provoked a conservative *reaction* that resulted in the marginalization or repression of the parties and unions from the incorporating period. These parties were later readmitted to the political game after conflict-limiting mechanisms were in placed that reduced the likelihood of further polarization of the party system.

Critical junctures and reactive sequences are at the heart of SPA's analytic framework. Despite this, scholars of comparative labor politics have largely neglected the Colliers's argument about reactive sequences and have rarely embraced their critical juncture framework. Instead, comparative labor scholars—and not only those consciously deploying historical institutionalist styles of argument—latched onto labor incorporation as a critical founding moment, treating the institutional legacies of incorporation as independent variables. In this sense, scholars have married SPA and its emphasis on links between unions and parties to the Colliers's (1979) work on corporatism in Latin America, IvC, in which the Colliers argued that labor law structured relations between unions and the state through sets of inducements and constraints. These institutions were central features of labor incorporation and had enduring consequences because they molded union interests, power, and resources, and gave states distinct sets of tools for managing unions.

The enduring legacy of the Colliers in the realm of comparative labor politics, then, is this marriage of founding moments—initial labor incorporation—with a configurational analysis of institutions. In scholarship that uses a configurational style of analysis, history matters because the institutions doing the causal work have historical roots.

But temporality, in the sense of analyzing processes unfolding over time, is not central to them. Temporality, of course, is integral to historical institutionalist analysis; some might say that temporality is its defining feature, more so than institutions. The historical institutionalist scholarship that has developed on the foundation established by the Colliers has branched out beyond critical junctures and reactive sequences to embrace more explicitly notions of institutional evolution, reproduction, path dependence, and sequencing. The next section, Neoliberal Reform, will illustrate these points through an analysis of the literatures addressing neoliberal reform and authoritarian legacies.

Neoliberal Reform

As many countries in Eastern Europe and the developing world rode the third wave of democratization, they also underwent traumatic economic restructuring. Debt and financial crises as well as the transition from a state to a market economy in Eastern Europe prompted austerity and structural adjustment programs that negatively affected many workers. Although scholarship on the politics of reform has typically framed labor as an obstruction to neoliberal reforms (Przeworski 1991; Haggard and Kaufman 1995), unions sometimes acceded to policies that had painful consequences for their members, and often did so despite partisan links to the governments enacting the reforms. Scholars of comparative labor politics therefore began to ponder the factors that determined how labor responded to neoliberal reform, what unions achieved through their political engagement, and why despite common pressures, unions in some countries fared better than others (Candland and Sil 2001). A common thread in the literature analyzing labor's role in economic reform is the role of historically rooted institutions—usually those connected to labor incorporation—in shaping the politics of market reform. Most importantly, scholars have highlighted the role of institutional legacies in molding union interests, power, and resources and therefore their ability to contest efforts by governments to impose market reforms.

Much of the most ambitious comparative scholarship on labor and neoliberal reform has closer affinities to rational choice accounts that stress strategic interactions within specific institutional settings than to historical institutionalist approaches. This scholarship carefully elucidates the historical roots of institutional variables and of historically constructed partisan loyalties. But issues of institutional reproduction and evolution, timing, and sequencing play little role in their causal stories. For example, Murillo's (2001) study of union responses to neoliberal reform in Argentina, Mexico, and Venezuela identified two institutional legacies, partisan competition and union competition, which mediated historically constructed partisan allegiances in shaping union responses to neoliberal reforms and union success in achieving their goals. Institutional legacies determined the power of unions and the strategic context in which parties, governments, and unions interacted. Similarly, Burgess (2004) highlighted the autonomy of parties from their governments and the comparative punishing power of union members versus parties on union leadership in influencing union responses to neoliberal reform. As with Murillo, these institutions shaped the strategic context in which labor leaders bargained with their partisan allies and hence also affected their strategies and even their success.[1]

Etchemendy (2011) adopted a similar historically rooted configurational notion of institutions in his analysis of varying adjustment paths in Argentina, Chile, and Spain, but also incorporated historical institutionalist elements by hypothesizing that the period of neoliberal reform was a critical juncture. Etchemendy argued that the antecedent condition of union strength, which was a product of prior historical developments under import-substitution industrialization, shaped the possibilities of reform in democratic countries during the critical juncture of neoliberal reform, resulting in different reform outcomes that produced path-dependent legacies.[2] Since historically produced antecedent conditions are doing the causal lifting, however, and since the subsequent path-dependent processes are hypothesized but not demonstrated, Etchemendy's work is in fact closer to Burgess and Murillo than to the historical institutionalist authors discussed in this section.[3] History comes into play primarily in the form of producing different values for the antecedent condition of union strength.

The historical institutionalist work on neoliberal reform complements these configurational analyses in part by problematizing the reproduction and evolution of founding institutions. Institutions are therefore not only independent variables but also dependent variables. In her study of labor responses to privatization in Czechoslovakia, Egypt, Mexico, and Poland, Paczyńska (2009) demonstrates that maintaining founding institutions is not a seamless process; it takes work, and periodic contentious encounters between labor and the state provide opportunities to renegotiate some features of founding institutions. In some cases, contentious encounters prompted states to make seemingly minor institutional concessions that gave labor more autonomy; in others states did not make such concessions. This evolution within the framework of founding institutions proved to be important when unions later confronted the state over neoliberal reforms. In Poland, for example, the contentious encounter between the state and Solidarity in the early 1980s not only prompted the internally divided communist regime to recognize Solidarity but also to institute self-management of enterprises. This procedural concession (and institutional change) at the firm level increased labor autonomy and gave unions the wherewithal to oppose partisan allies and reject the government's initial privatization program a decade later.[4] In Mexico, unlike in Poland, elites stuck together during contentious encounters with labor and did not placate unions with procedural concessions. One consequence of this was that the subordination of many official unions increased over time, leaving them in a weak position to oppose neoliberal reforms.[5] By opening up the black box of how founding institutions evolve, Paczyńska provides important insights into the conditions under which ruling parties acceded to changes in founding institutions that granted labor more autonomy and consequently offers deeper insight into why some unions opposed neoliberal reforms more effectively than others.

Aidi's (2009) comparative study of Egypt and Mexico, bears many similarities to Paczyńska's work, but he draws more heavily on the Colliers's distinction between party and state incorporation. The type of incorporation affected the state's capacity to effectively control workers at the grassroots level, and hence its ability to push through painful neoliberal reforms. In Mexico, party incorporation "actively included" unions for the purpose of electoral mobilization. Unions therefore had deeper connections to their members and to the ruling party than in cases of state corporatism. These same founding institutions, however, also allowed the state to undercut union leaders if they rebelled against state policies. Consequently, union leaders used their control over members to dampen their opposition to neoliberal reforms. In Mexico, then, founding institutions produced reinforcing dynamics that deepened state control over workers. In Egypt, by contrast, state incorporation established no institutions for bargaining between state, labor, and capital, which set in motion a process that loosened the state's grip on workers over time. Egypt's depoliticized unions were dependent on the state, but since the regime did not utilize unions to mobilize workers in support of the ruling party, the links between unions and the rank and file weakened over time. When the state tried to impose reforms, Egypt's state-backed union could not control its members, who revolted when the regime moved forward with privatization.[6] Aidi's analysis therefore demonstrates that different founding institutions create distinct dynamics that deepen or weaken state control over time. In this sense, even reinforcing processes have an evolutionary effect, as the formal institutions remain the same, but operate differently than when they were founded.

Historical institutionalist scholarship of neoliberal reform has also demonstrated the importance of timing and sequencing in explaining why some unions have been more successful than others in confronting market reforms. For example, Crowley and Stanojević (2011) show that the timing of protest—during a critical juncture—combined with the legacy of Yugoslavian communism, explain Slovenian exceptionalism. Like the rest of the region, the former Yugoslavia emerged from communism with high union densities. But Slovenia is unique in that it has neocorporatist institutions, experienced a less dramatic decline in unionization rates, and collective bargaining covers nearly all workers. One reason that Slovenia became exceptional is that the Yugoslavian legacy of worker self-management produced stronger ties between unions and their members than in the rest of Eastern Europe. But of the countries in the former Yugoslavia, only Slovenia emerged from the dual transition to democracy and the market with neocorporatist institutions. The reason for this is the *timing* of worker protest there. Unlike workers in the rest of the former Yugoslavia, Slovenian workers mobilized early in the transition process, when new institutions were being founded. The neocorporatist institutions established during this critical juncture have allowed Slovenian unions to weather the period of neoliberal reform better than in neighboring countries. So it is not the configuration of institutions that was most important but a relatively contingent factor—the timing of protest—that produced the institutions that put Slovenia on a distinct path.

Whereas Crowley and Stanojević highlight the importance of timing, Cook's (2007) account of labor reform in six Latin American countries demonstrates that the sequencing of political and flexibilizing reforms shaped labor law reform trajectories in the region. Where flexibilizing reforms preceded democratization, as in Chile, the authoritarian regime imposed flexibility on unions and enacted labor reforms that undercut union power. After democratization, Chile's unions were too weak to roll back many Pinochet era provisions. But where democratization preceded the period of neoliberal reform, as in Argentina, unions had greater capacity to resist reforms that weakened them. Although Argentine unions did not prevent all market reforms, they successfully defended provisions of the labor code crucial to their organizational power, which has put them in a stronger position going forward than in Chile.[7] The sequencing of reforms therefore had profound consequences for union power under democracy, and once again, countries split onto pathways of diminishing (Chile) and increasing (Argentina) returns. Cook's analysis also points to the importance of analyzing reform as a process that unfolds over time, with the outcomes of earlier rounds of reform having profound effects for what happens in later rounds.[8]

Historical institutionalist scholarship has made a number of important contributions to our understanding of labor and neoliberal reforms. It has shown that the sequencing of reforms has profound consequences for unions' capacities to resist such reforms and that mobilization during critical junctures may be necessary to lock in favorable outcomes. In addition, scholars have also added to our understanding of how founding institutions have evolved, both through reinforcing processes and through contentious encounters that introduce minor changes to these institutions that later prove to be tremendously important. While these studies do not necessarily contradict the configurational analyses of historically-rooted institutions, and in many ways they complement each other, the historical institutionalist scholarship has opened a broader discussion, one that it has only begun to tackle, of why some founding institutions prove to be stickier than others, and why some are more open to renegotiation than others. Rather than being merely the dead weight of the past, institutions and their reproduction and evolution over time have increasingly become the focus of analysis, as can be seen in the emerging literature on labor and authoritarian legacies.

Labor and Authoritarian Legacies

Historical institutionalism has profoundly shaped the emerging scholarship addressing the impact of authoritarian legacies on labor movements in new democracies. The intuition behind these analyses is that the web of institutions, ideologies, and actors passed onto new democracies shape the nature of union actors and the opportunities and constraints that they face. Since authoritarianism varied, so do its legacies (Caraway, Cook, and Crowley 2015). These legacies create different starting points or initial conditions for labor in new democracies. The historical institutionalist literature on authoritarian legacies grapples with two issues: research design challenges arising from regional variations in authoritarianism and the analytical problem of whether to conceptualize legacies as the mere dead weight of the past or as interacting with transition contexts to affect outcomes.

Regarding research design, the broad differences between regions and the family resemblances within regions have consequences for research design. If authoritarian legacies vary, then these variations should affect research design. Caraway, Cook, and Crowley (2015) observe broad family similarities in labor incorporation under authoritarianism in (capitalist) East and Southeast Asia, Eastern Europe, and Latin America, categorizing them respectively as exclusionary, state-paternalist, and inclusionary. These typologies capture important variations in the size of the unionized workforce, the extent to which states aimed to control or mobilize workers, and in party-union links.

In East and Southeast Asia, the Cold War bifurcated countries into communist and capitalist camps. In capitalist East and Southeast Asia, authoritarian regimes depoliticized labor through exclusionary corporatist institutions that granted state-backed unions special privileges but that constrained their capacity to represent workers (Deyo 1989; Hadiz 1997). Unions organized a small proportion of the workforce, were dependent on the state, and had weak links to their members and usually to political parties. Only in Taiwan was there a history of relatively robust ties between parties and unions.[9] Thus, a variable that has structured much of the work in Latin America has difficulty accounting for variations in labor outcomes in Asia.

In Latin America's inclusionary systems, the populist impulse was stronger than in Asia, perhaps due to the earlier timing of industrialization and its comparative distance from the most intense Cold War conflicts. Populism and the earlier formation of a working class resulted in forms of labor incorporation that, while putting some constraints on unions, also offered inducements that strengthened them. Unions typically organized more of the workforce than in East and Southeast Asia, often had strong links to political parties, and retained a greater capacity to mobilize their members. These partisan ties and labor institutions often survived the authoritarian backlashes of the 1960s and 1970s.

In Eastern Europe, communist regimes put in place state-paternalist systems in which unions were subordinated to but under the protection of the communist party (Crowley and Ost 2001). Virtually the entire workforce belonged to unions, which were integral in mobilizing workers to meet production targets. Unions emerged from communism dependent on state subsidies and with high densities but with no experience advocating for workers in a capitalist system. After the collapse of communism, unions there faced both a loss of official sponsorship and a traumatic transition to a market economy.

Different modes of labor incorporation under authoritarianism, then, mean that unions entered newly democratic settings from different starting points. In addition to these differences in starting points, unions also faced distinct transition contexts. Delineating precisely how authoritarian legacies affect labor in new democracies is therefore a challenging analytic task. Legacies may persist merely as the dead weight of the past, but it would be rather shocking if authoritarian institutions survived unchanged. Reproducing these legacies took work, so some legacies faded quickly while others persisted. For example, in Asia and Eastern Europe mono-unionism typically did not survive the transition to democracy. But labor law in inclusionary systems has proven far more resilient, and unions in Argentina, Brazil, and Mexico fought to defend state-corporatist labor codes after transitions to democracy (Bensusán and Cook 2015; Cardoso 2015). In other cases, labor law may be transformed, but authoritarian legacies, by creating distinct starting points or endowing some actors with greater power than others, shape the content of legal reforms (Crowley 2015; Caraway 2004).

This interaction between context and legacies is where much of the analytic work on authoritarian legacies is being done, and implicit in these analyses is that legacies exert their effects not by surviving as the dead weight of the past but through shaping pathways of change. In some cases, these changes may result in the formation of entirely new sets of institutions. For example, Crowley and Stanojević's work on Slovenia nicely shows how a specific authoritarian legacy interacted with a particular transition context to produce new neocorporatist institutions.[10] In the case of Slovenia, these new institutions empowered unions, but much of the scholarship on authoritarian legacies has demonstrated how they combine with transition contexts to weaken the labor movement (Hutchison 2015; Crowley 2015; Ost 2015).

One issue that has begun to receive attention from historical institutionalist scholars working on authoritarian legacies is the survival of legacy unions, former state-sponsored unions created under authoritarianism and inherited by newly democratic regimes (Caraway 2008, 2012). In many new democracies, legacy unions were, and often remained, the largest unions for many years after democratic transitions. Legacy unions were often poorly equipped to advocate for their members because their dependence on management and state sponsorship for sustenance resulted in tenuous links to their members. The transition to democracy imperiled legacy unions by displacing the regime that sponsored them and recognizing freedom of association, which introduced competition from other unions for membership. But legacy unions also inherited many advantages, which they could utilize to defend their turf. These resources depended greatly on how unions were incorporated under authoritarianism. Caraway analyzes how specific legacies interact with distinct transition contexts to produce distinct pathways of change. Through paired comparisons of legacy unions with similar pasts in former communist countries (Russia and Poland) and in exclusionary Asian countries (Indonesia and South Korea), Caraway shows how the interaction of these legacies with different transition contexts propelled legacy unions down different paths.

The big question arising from these studies of authoritarian legacies is which combinations of legacies and contexts have had the most beneficial (or most toxic) effects for labor's strength and effectiveness under democracy. Given that most of the work thus far has focused on a small number of cases, this line of research is still at the stage of documenting processes of change and generating hypotheses. Even in its infancy, however, this research has shown that comparative labor scholarship would benefit from more cross-regionally informed theorizing. The conclusion will reflect on future directions for the research on authoritarian legacies, and for historical institutionalist scholarship on labor in general, by putting the questions raised by this research in conversation with the Colliers's work on the lasting effects of initial incorporation.

Conclusion

Historical institutionalist research in comparative labor politics has advanced the study of contemporary labor politics by highlighting the processes through which institutional legacies persist and change within specific sociopolitical and temporal contexts and thereby later have profound impacts on the resources and capacities that unions bring to bear in confronting neoliberal reform and political change. The reproduction of these historically formed institutions become part of what must be explained rather than the mere gift of history. The challenge going forward is to think more systematically about why some authoritarian legacies and founding institutions are stickier than others, and the precise ways that that institutions interact with contextual variables to produce distinct pathways of institutional evolution and transformation.

The stickiness of institutions over long periods of time brings us back to the Colliers, in particular to the importance of initial incorporation for later developments. In some cases, these founding institutions have proven to be resilient across quite tumultuous political transformations. For example, Argentina's generals never refounded labor institutions as Pinochet did in Chile. Under certain conditions, then, founding institutions were overturned, but in others they were not. Historical institutionalist scholars have not grappled with this problem, and arguing that initial incorporation is most important simply because it came first is unpersuasive given that under certain conditions founding institutions are refounded.[11] Drawing on SPA, the rise of Pinochet could be understood as the end of the reactive sequence of initial incorporation, but Brazil's founding institutions were also state corporatist, yet Brazil's military did not refound labor institutions. Brazil seems to have more in common with Argentina in that founding institutions were reproduced over long periods of time and across multiple regimes. Under what conditions does initial incorporation come undone? Why are some founding institutions stickier than others and under what conditions do authoritarian regimes refound labor institutions?

Probing these questions may require historical institutionalists to consider more explicitly varying contexts—institutions in *contexts*—and insights from approaches that conceptualize institutions as strategic contexts. Caraway's (2008) work on legacy unions, for example, analyzes the varying evolutionary paths of legacy unions from a primarily historical institutionalist perspective, but in assessing why some legacy unions reform and others do not, she shifts to a more strategic notion of institutions, arguing that legacy unions only reform when they face fierce competition from rivals (context) and have inherited few resources with which to defend themselves (strategic institutions). Strategic conceptualizations of institutions analyzed in contexts can provide historical institutionalists with a means other than exogenous shocks to inject dynamism into stories of institutional reproduction and change.

Historical institutionalists have contributed to our understanding of labor's present through highlighting how historically produced institutions have endured and continued to shape contemporary labor politics in new democracies. One question that arises from the historical institutionalist literature is whether democratization was a critical juncture. In many countries a fairly radical reform of the institutions governing labor relations occurred, but in others, founding institutions from initial incorporation have remained resilient and/or authoritarian legacies have interacted with transition contexts to perpetuate authoritarian practices or to produce alternative sets of institutions. The scholarship on authoritarian legacies highlights historical continuities, suggesting that transformations may be more evolutionary than disruptive, yet at the same time, democratization created a context in which institutions could be renegotiated. Capoccia and Kelemen's (2007) notion of a critical juncture as being a moment of opportunity in which some cases may switch to another path and others not makes theoretical space for critical junctures to not be founding moments. Democracy, then, presented an opportunity, one that unions seized in varying ways depending in part on what they inherited from the past.[12] Reflecting on this question will be one of the major tasks for historical institutionalists as we continue to grapple with explaining the varying fates of unions in the face of the economic and political transformations of the late twentieth and early twenty-first century.

Notes

1. These authors also highlight the importance of historical legacies for labor reform outcomes. See Murillo (2005), Murillo and Schrank (2005), and Burgess (2010).
2. Antecedent conditions are not deployed in his exposition of the Chilean case, since Pinochet's authoritarian regime simply bypassed unions.
3. By taking contingency out of the critical juncture, questions of infinite regress also arise (Mahoney 2000). In Argentina, for example, was neoliberal reform a critical juncture that produced distinct legacies, or was the outcome of neoliberal reform simply part of a reinforcing pathway or reactive sequence produced by initial incorporation under Peron?
4. It is important to note, however, that privatization was the only area where Solidarity opposed market reform, and then only after facing a backlash from its membership. Ost (2005) argues labor's weak response to neoliberal reforms was a result of the ideological legacies of communism.
5. Paczyńska's analysis echoes Middlebrook's (1995) argument about the evolution of founding labor institutions in Mexico. Labor law provisions that facilitated unionization were double-edged, since they also gave the state enormous discretion, which the Institutional Revolutionary Party (Partido Revolucionario Institucional, PRI) increasingly used to discipline union leaders that resisted the party's policies and to protect those who cooperated with the regime from challenges from below.

6. Solinger (2009) makes a similar argument as Aidi for Mexico and an argument analogous to Egypt for China. The very weakness and ineffectiveness of China's official union, she argues, left workers free to take to the streets to demand compensation.
7. Etchemendy and Collier's (2007) analysis of the resurgence of Argentine unions in the twenty-first century nicely illustrates how this defense of organizational power was a necessary condition for its revival.
8. Caraway's (2004) study of labor reform in post-Suharto Indonesia also stresses the importance of analyzing reform as a process that unfolds over time, although she places more emphasis on how the strategic context changed dramatically from one round of reform to the next because developments in the first round caused political actors to change their strategies.
9. Lee's (2011) work is perhaps the first to explore the effects of partisan ties in the region. She traces the roots of labor militancy in South Korea and partisan cooperation in Taiwan to patterns of party-union relationships under authoritarianism. In South Korea, the absence of integrating institutions between parties and unions under authoritarianism facilitated the rise of a radical grass roots labor movement outside the official union structure. By contrast, local elections in Taiwan under authoritarianism led to different links between unions and parties and different patterns of mobilization after democratization. Lee (2015) has extended this analysis to show how these distinct legacies interacted with different transition contexts to produce varied partisan strategies.
10. See also Grdešić (2015).
11. Drawing on Pierson's (2004) work, Collier and Schipani (2015) make such an argument. See also Thelen (2000).
12. Slater and Simmons (2010) discussion of critical antecedents may be useful; that what unfolds during the moment of political transition depends in part on critical antecedents. Historical institutionalist case studies provide some insights into what these might be, but these hypotheses need to be fleshed out more carefully through systematic comparisons of multiple cases.

References

Aidi, Hishaam D. 2009. *Redeploying the State: Corporatism, Neoliberalism, and Coalition Politics*. New York: Palgrave Macmillan.

Bensusán, Graciela and Maria Lorena Cook. 2015. "State-Corporatist Legacies and Divergent Paths: Argentina and Mexico." In *Working Through the Past: Labor and Authoritarian Legacies in Comparative Perspective*, ed. Teri L. Caraway, Maria Lorena Cook, and Stephen Crowley. Ithaca, NY: ILR Press, 142–163.

Burgess, Katrina. 2004. *Parties and Unions in the New Global Economy*. Pittsburgh, PA: University of Pittsburgh Press.

Burgess, Katrina. 2010. "Global Pressures, National Policies, and Labor Rights in Latin America." *Studies in Comparative International Development* 45 (2): 198–224.

Candland, Christopher and Rudra Sil. 2001. *The Politics of Labor in a Global Age: Continuity and Change in Late-Industrializing and Post-Socialist Economies*. New York: Oxford University Press.

Capoccia, Giovanni and Daniel Kelemen. 2007. "The Study of Critical Junctures: Theory, Narrative, and Counterfactuals in Historical Institutionalism." *World Politics* 59 (3): 341–369.

Caraway, Teri L. 2004. "Protective Repression, International Pressure, and Institutional Design: Explaining Labor Reform in Indonesia." *Studies in Comparative International Development* 39 (3): 28–49.

Caraway, Teri L. 2008. "Explaining the Dominance of Legacy Unions in New Democracies: Insights from Indonesia." *Comparative Political Studies* 41 (10): 1371–1397.

Caraway, Teri L. 2012. "Pathways of Dominance and Displacement: The Varying Fates of Legacy Unions in New Democracies." *World Politics* 64 (2): 278–305.

Caraway, Teri L., Maria Lorena Cook, and Stephen Crowley, eds. 2015. *Working Through the Past: Labor and Authoritarian Legacies in Comparative Perspective*. Ithaca, NY: ILR Press.

Cardoso, Adalberto. 2015. "'Your Defensive Fortress': Workers and Vargas's Legacies in Brazil." In *Working Through the Past: Labor and Authoritarian Legacies in Comparative Perspective*, ed. Teri L. Caraway, Maria Lorena Cook, and Stephen Crowley. Ithaca, NY: ILR Press, 164–178.

Collier, Ruth Berins and Andres Schipani. 2015. "Conclusion: The Comparative Analysis of Regime Change and Labor Legacies." In *Working Through the Past: Labor and Authoritarian Legacies in Comparative Perspective*, ed. Teri L. Caraway, Maria Lorena Cook, and Stephen Crowley. Ithaca, NY: ILR Press, 217–234.

Collier, Ruth Berins and David Collier. 1979. "Inducements versus Constraints: Disaggregating 'Corporatism.'" *American Political Science Review* 73 (December): 967–986.

Collier, Ruth Berins and David Collier. 1991. *Shaping the Political Arena: Critical Junctures, the Labor Movement, and Regime Dynamics in Latin America*. Princeton, NJ: Princeton University Press.

Collier, Ruth Berins and David Collier. 2002. *Shaping the Political Arena: Critical Junctures, the Labor Movement, and Regime Dynamics in Latin America*. Notre Dame, IN: University of Notre Dame Press.

Cook, Maria Lorena. 2007. *The Politics of Labor Reform in Latin America: Between Flexibility and Rights*. University Park, PA: Pennsylvania State University Press.

Crowley, Stephen. 2015. "Russia's Labor Legacy." In *Working Through the Past: Labor and Authoritarian Legacies in Comparative Perspective*, ed. Teri L. Caraway, Maria Lorena Cook, and Stephen Crowley. Ithaca, NY: ILR Press, 122–141.

Crowley, Stephen and Davis Ost. 2001. *Workers after Workers' States: Labor and Politics in Postcommunist Eastern Europe*. Lanham, MD: Rowman & Littlefield.

Crowley, Stephen and Miroslavic Stanojević. 2011. "Varieties of Capitalism, Power Resources, and Historical Legacies: Explaining the Slovenian Exception." *Politics & Society* 39 (2): 268–295.

Deyo, Frederic C. 1989. *Beneath the Miracle: Labor Subordination in the New Asian Industrialism*. Berkeley: University of California.

Etchemendy, Sebastián. 2011. *Models of Economic Liberalization: Business, Workers, and Compensation in Latin America, Spain, and Portugal*. New York: Cambridge University Press.

Etchemendy, Sebastián and Ruth Berins Collier. 2007. "Down but Not Out: Union Resurgence and Segmented Neocorporatism in Argentina (2003–2007)." *Politics & Society* 35 (3): 363–401.

Grdešić, Marko. 2015. "Exceptionalism and Its Limits: The Legacy of Self-Management in the Former Yugoslavia." In *Working Through the Past: Labor and Authoritarian Legacies in Comparative Perspective*, ed. Teri L. Caraway, Maria Lorena Cook, and Stephen Crowley. Ithaca, NY: ILR Press, 103–121.

Hadiz, Vedi. 1997. *Workers and the State in New Order Indonesia*. London and New York: Routledge.

Haggard, Stephan and Robert R. Kaufman. 1995. *The Political Economy of Democratic Transitions*. Princeton, NJ: Princeton University Press.

Hutchison, Jane. 2015. "Authoritarian Labor Legacies in the Philippines." In *Working Through the Past: Labor and Authoritarian Legacies in Comparative Perspective*, ed. Teri L. Caraway, Maria Lorena Cook, and Stephen Crowley. Ithaca, NY: ILR Press, 64–81.

Lee, Yoonkyung. 2011. *Militants or Partisans: Labor Unions and Democratic Politics in Korea and Taiwan*. Stanford, CA: Stanford University Press.

Lee, Yoonkyung. 2015. "Labor's Political Representation: Divergent Paths in Korea and Taiwan." In *Working Through the Past: Labor and Authoritarian Legacies in Comparative Perspective*, ed. Teri L. Caraway, Maria Lorena Cook, and Stephen Crowley. Ithaca, NY: Cornell University/ILR Press, 44–63.

Mahoney, James. 2000. "Path Dependence in Historical Sociology." *Theory & Society* 29: 507–548.

Middlebrook, Kevin J. 1995. *The Paradox of Revolution: Labor, the State, and Authoritarianism in Mexico*. Baltimore, MD: Johns Hopkins University Press.

Murillo, María Victoria. 2001. *Labor Unions, Partisan Coalitions, and Market Reforms in Latin America*. New York: Cambridge University Press.

Murillo, María Victoria. 2005. "Partisanship amidst Convergence: Labor Market Reform in Latin America." *Comparative Politics* 37 (4): 441–458.

Murillo, María Victoria and Andrew Schrank. 2005. "With a Little Help from My Friends: Partisan Politics, Transnational Alliances, and Labor Rights in Latin America." *Comparative Political Studies* 38 (8): 971–999.

Ost, David. 2005. *The Defeat of Solidarity: Anger and Politics in Postcommunist Europe*. Ithaca, NY: Cornell University Press.

Ost, David. 2015. "The Peculiarities of Communism and the Emergence of Weak Unions in Polans." In *Working Through the Past: Labor and Authoritarian Legacies in Comparative Perspective*, ed. Teri L. Caraway, Maria Lorena Cook, and Stephen Crowley. Ithaca, NY: Cornell University/ILR Press, 82–102.

Paczyńska, Agnieszka. 2009. *State, Labor, and the Transition to a Market Economy: Egypt, Poland, Mexico, and the Czech Republic*. University Park, PA: Pennsylvania State University Press.

Pierson, Paul. 2004. *Politics in Time: History, Institutions, and Social Analysis*. Princeton, NJ: Princeton University Press.

Przeworski, Adam. 1991. *Democracy and the Market: Political and Economic Reforms in Eastern Europe and Latin America*. New York: Cambridge University Press.

Slater, Dan and Erica Simmons. 2010. "Informative Regress: Critical Antecedents in Comparative Politics." *Comparative Political Studies* 43 (7): 886–917.

Solinger, Dorothy J. 2009. *State's Gains, Labor's Losses: China, France, and Mexico Choose Global Liaisons, 1980–2000*. Ithaca, NY: Cornell University Press.

Thelen, Kathleen. 1999. "Historical Institutionalism in Comparative Politics." *Annual Review of Political Science* 2: 369–404.

Thelen, Kathleen. 2000. "Timing and Temporality in the Analysis of Institutional Evolution and Change." *Studies in American Political Development* 14 (1): 101–108.

CHAPTER 16

ADAPTIVE INFORMAL INSTITUTIONS

KELLEE S. TSAI*

ALTHOUGH historical institutionalism encompasses a variety of institutional dynamics, it has traditionally focused on the impact of *formal* institutions designed and enforced by official entities. The tendency to prioritize formal institutions reflects in part the fact that historical institutionalism grew out of the study of advanced industrial democracies. By contrast, efforts to take informal institutions seriously have derived primarily from research on developing countries and transitional economies where certain types of formal institutions may be less institutionalized than informal ones. An implicit division of analytic labor has thus emerged between scholars of established capitalist democracies who regard formal institutions as the normative barometer for institutional analysis, and comparativists who specialize in countries where key political economic processes occur beyond the scope of formal institutions. The reflexive association of formality with advanced industrial democracies and informality with incomplete development, however, is not only teleological, but misleading. Concepts developed from analyses of endogenous institutional change in varied political economic contexts reveal that the causal mechanisms of institutional transformation are often informal in character. Meanwhile, even though informal institutions have received more attention by comparativists studying developing and post-communist countries, an emerging second generation of historical institutionalists recognizes that even in advanced political economies, informal institutions are relevant in structuring political processes and economic performance. Going forward, direct theorization of informal institutions represents a fertile frontier for comparative politics, particularly when combined with insights from historical institutionalism about institutional stability and change.

This chapter develops these arguments in four main parts. The first two sections review key contributions in historical institutionalism, starting with now-classic contributions that concerned how institutions structure politics, followed by more recent efforts to explain institutional development over time. The latter studies continue to privilege formal institutions, but upon closer examination, present explanations that include dynamics generated by informal institutions. The second part discusses studies in comparative politics that explicitly engage informal politics, practices, and institutions—but are not necessarily identified with historical institutionalism. The third section proposes that informal institutions be analyzed in a manner that decouples institutional formality from functionality. The conclusion identifies promising directions for incorporating informal institutions into historical institutional analysis.

Historical Institutionalism 1.0: "Structuring Politics"

The term historical institutionalism emerged in the 1990s to describe research in comparative political economy that highlighted the importance of institutions in shaping political behavior and outcomes. As indicated in other chapters of this volume, historical institutionalism is self-described by its architects as *an approach to understanding politics*, rather than a particular methodology or theory (cf. Steinmo 2008, 118–138). The now-classic volume, *Structuring Politics: Historical Institutionalism in Comparative Analysis*, presented studies of advanced industrialized countries to demonstrate the value of taking historically contextualized institutions seriously (Steinmo, Thelen, and Longstreth 1992). Through narrative analysis, formal political institutions—rather than political culture or decontextualized rational actors—were found to explain cross-national variation in comparative political economy issues such as size of the welfare state, scope of the health care system, and levels of unionization. This initial focus on formal institutions is not surprising given that the contributions to *Structuring Politics* concerned comparative public policy, which reflects decisions taken by official entities (Pontussen 1995, 117–147).

Concurrently, the distinction of historical institutionalism from other variants of institutionalism (namely, economic and sociological) encouraged students of political economy to identify with one of the three institutionalisms (Hall and Taylor 1996, 936–957). Most comparativists straddled economic and/or historical institutionalism, including their accompanying emphasis on formal institutions. Those interested in informal institutions quietly borrowed concepts from sociological institutionalism such as taken-for-granted values, habits, and cultural scripts (Powell and DiMaggio 1991; Swidler 1986, 273–286). But few studies in comparative political economy overtly embraced sociological institutionalism as rationalist logic dominated the sub-field during the 1990s.

To the extent that first generation economic and historical institutionalists engaged "softer variables," such as ideas, norms, and culture, they were treated in either primordial or epiphenomenal terms (Bates 1988, 387–401). At the primordial end, Douglass North's influential reminder to neo-classical economists that formal institutions affect economic performance, ironically attributed third world poverty to "cultural constraints" "informal institutions," and "mental models" that inhibit the development of (western-style) property rights (North 1990). Other efforts to incorporate the role of ideas in comparative political economy tended to subsume them within a particular institutional setting in a residual manner (Blyth 1997, 229–250). For example, in a rationalist explanation of the European Community's move toward the single market in 1992, ideas about mutual recognition of goods and services instrumentally appeared as a focal point for facilitating cooperation (Garrett and Weingast 1993, 173–206). Rather than exercising independent causality, however, ideas merely served to coordinate actors' expectations under conditions of multiple equilibria (Blyth 1997, 242–244). Within historical institutionalism, economic ideas have received greater explanatory attention. Most notably, Peter Hall's account of the paradigmatic policy shift from Keynesianism to monetarism in Britain emphasized the role of economic ideas in influencing three sequential orders of policy change: overarching policy goals, the means to achieve the goals, and the details of policy instruments (Hall 1993, 275–296). From a more interpretive perspective, Kathryn Sikkink traced the divergence between Argentina and Brazil's postwar developmental strategies to differences in the extent to which ideas about import substitution were embedded in pre-existing state institutions (Sikkink 1991). Critical of the epiphenomenal handling of ideas in both economic and historical institutionalism, Mark Blyth placed economic ideas at the center of his work by conceptualizing them as "institutional blueprints during periods of uncertainty, as weapons in distributional struggles, and as 'cognitive locks' " (Blyth 2001, 1–26). When Sweden experienced economic downturn in the late 1970s, ideas provided substantive content for changing its economic model (Blyth 2002).

The ideational turn in comparative political economy and institutional analysis helped to demonstrate that especially during critical junctures, ideas matter as much as formal institutions. But in the end, ideas do not have direct causal impact. Although particular ideas may guide reforms of economic policies and institutions, they are still filtered through pre-existing institutions.[1] Moreover, as unwritten norms, rules, and practices, informal institutions encompass much more than ideas about the economy. The discussion of mechanisms of institutional change in the next section highlights the importance of informal institutional dynamics even in the absence of ideational signposts.

Historical Institutionalism 1.5: "Explaining Institutional Change"

While historical institutionalism provided convincing explanations for institutional stability, typically drawing on the logic of path dependency, the quest to explain institutional change within the same framework inspired new concepts to describe different modes of institutional transformation. These include *displacement, layering, drift, conversion*, and *exhaustion* (Streeck and Thelen 2005; Mahoney and Thelen 2010). What distinguishes these mechanisms of change from earlier historical institutional explanations of change is that they occur gradually over time, in a manner that is endogenous to the institutional environment. They identify the dynamics through which change may occur in the absence of crisis, exogenous shocks, or the critical junctures that characterize punctuated equilibrium models of institutional and policy change (Baumgartner and Jones 1993; Capoccia and Kelemen 2007, 341–369; Krasner 1984, 223–246). Although the geographic scope of James Mahoney and Kathleen Thelen's *Explaining Institutional Change* (2010) extends beyond advanced political economies—by including cases from Brazil, Indonesia, and Kenya—the framework remains focused on formal institutions. In particular, the latter volume "conceives institutions above all else as *distributional instruments* laden with power implications," emphasizing that "many formal institutions are specifically intended to distribute resources to particular kinds of actors and not to others" (Mahoney and Thelen 2010, 7–8). This does not preclude informal rules or expectations. Indeed, the five modalities of institutional change detailed in this literature entail critical shifts in institutional enforcement that are not articulated as informal institutions, but arguably, warrant such conceptual marking.

First, *displacement* occurs when the introduction of new institutions effectively replace pre-existing ones. Revolutions, external occupation/colonialism, regime change, and transitions from socialist to market economies are examples of institutional displacement. The trigger for institutional displacement may be exogenous or endogenous to a particular institutional environment. As will be elaborated in the next section (Informal Institutions in Comparative Politics), even though the movement goes from one set of formal institutions to another, adaptive informal institutions generated from the initial institutional context may facilitate the transition. But this intermediary channel has not been acknowledged within historical institutionalism.

Second, institutional *layering* entails incremental amendments to existing rules or the enactment of new rules without voiding others. The piecemeal accumulation of such amendments may inhibit the operation of existing institutions, and eventually undermine their original intent. In Eric Schickler's study of US congressional development, layering proved to be more politically feasible than dismantling institutions with strong supporters (Schickler 2001). In this respect, layering could be viewed as an informal strategy for reforming dominant institutions without challenging them directly. If widely practiced and repeated, as appears to be the case in the US Congress, then layering should be considered an informal institution in its own right.

The third mode of change, institutional *drift*, has a cognate similarity with layering in the sense that old rules remain untouched out of political (electoral) convenience. Instead of diluting the relevance of old rules with layers of additional rules, however, "policy drift" occurs when broader environmental conditions change in the absence of adjustments to ensure continuing vitality of the institution. In coining the term, Jacob Hacker observed that demographic shifts in the US population led, de facto, to retrenchment of social welfare coverage (Hacker 2004, 243–260). Policy inaction amidst growing need for protection of new groups eroded the substantive impact of the original policy. As with layering, drift may be consequentialist rather than reflecting benign neglect: drift "may be the result of active attempts to block adaptation of institutions to changing circumstances" (Hacker 2005, 41). Drift may be facilitated by external changes, but like layering, it can also be an informal political strategy.

Fourth, *conversion* refers to the redeployment of institutions for purposes that depart from their founding intentions. In organizational sociology, Philip Selznick's study of the Tennessee Valley Authority is a classic case of how local officials may redefine the goals of a public organization to serve alternative objectives (Selznick 1949). In a non-democratic setting, X. L. Ding noted that during the 1980s, the Institute for Marxism and Leninism in Beijing came to be populated with liberal intellectuals who advocated deepening reform of China's socialist system (Ding 1994, 293–318). Conversion enables reform-oriented entrepreneurs to introduce alternative missions within the confines of officially sanctioned institutions. The possibility of conversion suggests, however, that the original institution has already declined in relevance, effectiveness, and/or legitimacy. Not all institutions are equally vulnerable to appropriation by change agents. Changes in the broader social, political, or economic context facilitate conversion. Furthermore, as others have observed, layering may lay the foundation for conversion (Hacker 2004, 250).

Fifth and finally, *exhaustion* represents gradual institutional depletion. Certain institutions may become anachronistic due to changes in structural (demographic, political, economic) conditions. While the same changes could lead to institutional drift, in the case of exhaustion, institutions eventually cease to function. With institutional drift, the original institutions retain their authoritative essence, but may govern a more circumscribed population. Exhaustion, on the other hand, denotes institutional breakdown. As an example, Wolfgang Streeck and Kathleen Thelen point to Avner Greif and David Laitin's notion of "self-undermining" institutional dynamics over time.[2] Although Greif and Laitin present their argument in economistic terms—referring for example, to shifts in "quasi-parameters"—the causal logic of institutional self-destruction versus reproduction resonates with other strands of historical institutionalism.[3]

Even though all these modes of change concern formal institutions, a number of them would be more accurately categorized as "*adaptive* informal institutions," by which I mean, "regularized patterns of interaction that emerge as adaptive responses to the constraints and opportunities of formal institutions, that violate or transcend the scope of formal institutions, and that are widely practiced" (Tsai 2006, 125–126). Opportunistic actors can engage in layering, drift, and conversion when outright displacement is not a realistic option. Indeed, displacement is probably the least common mode of endogenous institutional change because it is typically preceded by an extreme event (e.g., war, economic crisis, regime change). During "normal times," layering and conversion provide a non-confrontational, *informal* means to introduce alternative rules. The third section of this chapter makes the case for viewing them as types of adaptive informal institutions that emerge in contexts where marked gaps exist between formal institutions and the aspirations of actors in the political economy.

Informal Institutions in Comparative Politics

In contrast to historical institutionalists focusing on advanced industrial democracies, comparativists studying transitional economies and the developing world have contributed more directly to the literature on informal institutions. In a key article in *Perspectives on Politics*, Gretchen Helmke and Steven Levitsky outlined a typology of informal institutions based on their functional relationship with formal institutions (Helmke and Levitsky 2004, 725–740). Specifically, informal institutions may be *complementary, accommodating, competing,* or *substitutive* vis-à-vis formal ones. They define institutions in general as "rules and procedures (both formal and informal) that structure social interaction by constraining and enabling actors' behavior," which is consistent with historical institutionalism (Helmke and Levitsky 2004, 727). Helmke and Levitsky further highlight that within the universe of institutions, informal institutions are "socially shared rules, usually unwritten, that are created, communicated, and enforced outside of officially sanctioned channels" (2004, 728). Both the typology and conscious definition of informal institutions have enhanced attention to the role of informal institutions in comparative politics. For ease of reference, Table 16.1 shows the resulting categories in their 2x2 matrix. As elaborated in the next section, however, relaxing the expectation that informal institutions be unwritten and "enforced outside of officially sanctioned channels" would expand the scope of activities and actors that could be fruitfully studied as informal institutions.

Building on Guillermo O'Donnell's earlier call for understanding "the actual rules that are being followed" rather than only "parchment institutions," the co-authors elaborate on the case for attending to informal political institutions in a volume on Latin America (O'Donnell 1996, 10, cited in Helmke and Levitsky 2006, 2). They start from the premise that "Informal rules coexist with formal democratic institutions throughout Latin America (O'Donnell 1996, 1)." Official parchment institutions include the constitution, which may specify whether the political system is unitary or federal, presidential or parliamentary; the electoral system; and institutional checks and balances. Much of the existing literature on Latin American politics has pointed to the competing influence of informal institutions such as clientelism, patrimonialism, and corruption.

Table 16.1 Helmke and Levitsky's Typology of Informal Institutions

Outcomes/Effectiveness	Effective Formal Institutions	Ineffective Formal Institutions
Convergent	Complementary	Substitutive
Divergent	Accommodating	Competing

Source: Helmke and Levitsky (2004, 728). Reprinted with permission from *Perspectives on Politics*.

Indeed, the subversive impact of informal institutions on formal ones dominates institutional analysis of emerging democracies in the developing and post-communist world. In other words, informal institutions are typically presented as *competing* with or undermining the intended functions of formal institutions. A few illustrative examples from this literature follow.

Defining informal institutions as "the patterns of patron-client relations by which power is also exercised," Michael Bratton finds that the three informal institutions of clientelism, corruption, and "Big Man" presidentialism play a greater role in shaping political processes in Africa than official state institutions (Bratton 2007, 97; cf Bratton 1994, 453–489). Data from the Afrobarometer survey reveals that overall, African citizens rely on informal patron-client ties because "all formal institutions systematically fall short of popular expectations" (Bratton 2007, 107). Due to the endurance of personal authority in shaping state-society relations, throughout sub-Saharan Africa political transitions from neopatrimonial rule have faced particular challenges in institutionalizing new rules of democratic accountability and participation (Bratton 1994, 453–489).

Studies of post-communist transitions have observed the revival of similar neopatrimonial institutions following the collapse of the Soviet Union. Kathleen Collins noted the re-emergence of *clans*—meaning, "informal identity networks based on kin or fictive kin bonds"—as key political actors in Central Asia (Collins 2004, 224–261). The resulting rise of clan politics, "the politics of informal competition and deal making between clans in pursuit of clan interests," has influenced post-Soviet political trajectories. Writing in 2004, Collins found that inter-clan rivalries led to violent regime collapse in Tajikistan, while deals struck between clans provided relative political stability during the initial political transitions of Uzbekistan, Kyrgystan, Kazakhstan, and Turkmenistan. But in hindsight, the mere continuity of autocracy in the latter republics belies continuing outbreaks of ethnic conflict throughout the 2000s (Kendzior 2013). As an informal institution, clans continue to compete with and undermine the efficacy of formal political institutions. The rise of "violent democracy" fueled by drug cartels in Mexico follows a similarly corrosive combination of what Andreas Schedler calls, "electoral authoritarianism" and the normalization of violence in Latin American politics (Schedler 2014, 5–18, 2006). Perhaps to an even greater extent than clans in Central Asia, drug cartels in Mexico represent coercive societal actors whose violent practices subvert the integrity of the country's formal institutions of electoral democracy.

Following Helmke and Levitsky's typology, in contexts with weak formal institutions, informal institutions may be *substitutive* rather than competing. The two types are distinguished by functionality: competing informal institutions subvert, while substitutive informal institutions make up for failures in the operations of formal institutions. Due to the ineffectiveness of Mexico's electoral courts, for example, "gentleman's agreements" (called *concertacesiones*) have served to resolve electoral disputes between government and opposition elites, albeit with decreasing effectiveness in recent years (Helmke and Levitsky 2006, 16; cf. Schedler 2014, 5–18). In a different context, Anna Grzymala-Busse observed that after the collapse of communism in Eastern Europe, "inherited informal institutions acted as substitutes for new formal rules" (Grzymala-Busse 2010,

311–333). Given the underdevelopment of formal institutions for monitoring and sanctioning incumbent politicians in Poland and Hungary, "press criticism [and] informal investigations ... rather than formal investigations launched by attorneys general or independent state investigators" exposed the rent-seeking activities of office holders (Grzymala-Busse 2010, 319). Through unofficial channels, informal institutions can sometimes deliver the political accountability that dysfunctional formal institutions are supposed to provide. Similarly, informal networks such as community solidary groups may be more effective in the provision of public goods and services than local governments (Tsai 2007).

In this regard, *complementary* informal institutions enhance the performance of generally functional formal institutions by reducing transaction costs and providing greater stability in the operations of the overall institutional environment. Complementary informal institutions reinforce rather than violate the spirit of formal institutions by "filling in the gaps" left by the latter. They are more likely to be found in contexts where there is congruence between formal political institutions and social norms and values. The US Supreme Court, for example, operates according to various judicial norms and customs for assigning opinions and reviewing cases (e.g., the "Rule of Four") (Helmke and Levitsky 2004, 728). Julia Azari and Jennifer Smith similarly point out numerous unwritten rules that complete, coordinate, and operate in parallel to formal rules in the US legislative and executive branches (Azari and Smith 2012, 37–55). Although complementary informal institutions also exist outside of well-established democracies, the literature has focused more on the shared expectations that support democratic governance.

Finally, *accommodating* informal institutions enable actors to work within the confines of official rules to pursue goals that deviate from, but do not undermine formal institutions. Informal power-sharing arrangements such as Dutch consociationalism exemplify this type of informal institution. Helmke and Levitsky also cite the example of personal networks (*blat*) in the Soviet Union as an accommodating informal institution that helped citizens meet both state-mandated production targets and individual needs without violating the letter of party-state regulations (Ledeneva 1998, cited in Azari and Smith 2012, 729). The same could be said of reliance on personal relations (*guanxi*) in urban China during the communist era (Walder 1988). Clientelism emerged in state work units as a means to access scarce resources (e.g., housing, cooking oil, soap) rationed by factory directors. As with the other three forms of informal institutions in this typology, accommodating institutions are labeled retrospectively based on their effects.[4]

In the end, whether a particular type of informal institution is complementary, accommodating, competing, or substitutive is contingent on its impact on formal institutions. As Hans-Joachim Lauth points out, common law is often perceived as complementing formal laws, but in the case of kangaroo or mafia courts, common law can also have deleterious effects on democracy (Lauth 2000, 21–50). Similarly, personal connections, whether called *blat* or *guanxi*, can facilitate transactions that are consistent with (*accommodate*) the broader mandates of official rules, while straying considerably from their spirit. Yet personalistic ties can also reinforce (*complement*), replace (*substitute*), or obstruct (*compete* with) parchment institutions—within the very same country. The boundaries between everyday shortcuts that support or erode a particular institution are contextually fluid. Therein lies the analytic limitation of categorizing informal institutions by functionality. We have no way of knowing a priori whether clans, gentlemen's agreements, patron–client ties, or undocumented judicial mores reinforce, impede, or overshadow formal institutions.

In this regard, a more fundamental concern is that formal institutions implicitly represent a normative baseline in both historical institutionalism and comparative politics. There is an unarticulated bias in the literature toward assuming that institutions sanctioned by official authority are "more important" than informal rules. This tendency is apparent even among students of authoritarian regimes who may privately question the desirability of non-liberal institutions, but in explanatory practice, accept them as a metric for assessing the degree of institutionalization or stability in the political economy. Because formal institutions are designed and enforced by the state, they are reflexively accepted as the reference point for empirical analysis. This is due in part to the sequential and overlapping rise of state-centric theorizing during the 1980s (Evans, Reuschemeyer, and Skocpol 1985), followed by the development of historical institutionalism in the 1990s. Both strands of literature employ the Weberian definition of the state, which equates legitimacy with state-sanctioned formal institutions.

As a result of this state-centric bias, informal institutions are defined as non-Weberian deviations from formal institutions, and viewed as residual "add ons" to an institutional context expected to embody legal rationality. Any widely practiced regularity in behavior that is not codified in writing becomes epiphenomenal, and therefore, is less likely to be studied in its own right. Helmke and Levitsky's four-part typology is productive in demonstrating that informal institutions have varying implications for the effectiveness of formal institutions. But as long as the conceptualization of informal institutions is tied to their functionality relative to formal ones, it is counterintuitive to trace their causal effects on behavior independent of official regulations.

Historical Institutionalism 2.0: Decoupling Formality and Functionality

In order to understand informal institutions on their own terms, explaining how they affect the political economy needs to be decoupled from their functionality relative to formal institutions. As Helmke and Levitsky advise,

> [M]oving beyond functionalist accounts entails identifying the relevant actors and interests behind informal institutions, specifying the process by which informal

> rules are created, and showing how those rules are communicated to other actors in such a manner that they evolve into sets of shared expectations. (Helmke and Levitsky 2004, 731)

In other words, we need to trace both the origins and the reproduction of informal institutions. This, in turn, provides a basis for identifying the sources of change in informal institutions. Implementing this recommendation is not intuitive for historical institutionalism, given its traditional emphasis on official rules and public policy. As suggested earlier, however, the modalities of endogenous institutional change delineated by historical institutionalists describe processes that are actually informal. Analytically, the logical next step is to theorize such processes as adaptive informal institutions when they recur in a patterned manner.

Operationally, this would be facilitated by a less restrictive definition of informal institutions than that provided by Helmke and Levitsky. Rather than limiting informal institutions to rules that are "usually unwritten ... created, communicated, and enforced" by non-official entities (Helmke and Levitsky 2004, 727), I propose to redefine informal institutions as socially shared values, norms, rules, and practices that are not officially proscribed. This alternative definition of informal institutions allows for the possibility of participation by state actors in the creation, communication, enforcement, and even (unofficial) documentation of regularized practices that are not legally codified.

Relatedly, I also propose a more inclusive ontology of institutions that accepts, and even expects the co-existence of formal and informal institutions within any given environment, even if one type may be more prevalent than the other. To borrow a mathematical visual metaphor, it would be more theoretically progressive to regard institutions as a single two-dimensional Möbius strip with both formal and informal components—regardless of regime type or level of economic development. While the empirical lens of historical institutionalism 1.0 and 1.5 remain focused on formal political institutions, as shown in Figure 16.1, the Möbius strip image reminds us that institutions are visibly double-sided. In contexts with dense layers of official institutions, the formal side may appear to be more robust, but they are simultaneously mediated by informal institutions that are highly relevant for explaining political and economic practices. By the same token, even environments seemingly dominated by informal institutions are governed, at least in principle, by formal institutions. Informal and formal institutions are co-terminous, as seen in the two sides of the Möbius strip.

This metaphoric move offers a less state-centric barometer of functionality and legitimacy. Rather than treating informal institutions as a departure from official regulations, it may well be that formal institutions obstruct informal practices preferred by both state and non-state actors. Informal institutions may provide greater efficiency and stability in the system than formal political institutions. When institutionalization is equated with state-enforced mandates, as is usually the case, unofficial sources of regulation are neglected. Yet the latter may be a more robust, if not predictable, basis for reading behavioral regularities, especially when official rules lack normative support. Clientelism may trump judicial independence. Informal financial institutions may be a

FIGURE 16.1 Möbius Strip

Note: Author's artwork

more reliable source of credit than registered banks. Anachronistic passages of a constitution may simply be ignored—by state and societal actors.

As such, it remains worthwhile to distinguish informal institutions that are deeply rooted—and therefore perceived as "cultural"—from more recently developed ones. The former are typically described as "indigenous" customs and beliefs that are taken-for-granted, unconsciously reproduced, and self-regulating. Informal institutions defined in these terms appear entrenched and resistant to change, though in reality, cultural endowments are rarely as static as depicted in accounts that view them as obstacles to (Western-style) formal institutions.[5] On the other hand, there is a universe of informal practices that emerge as a direct result of possibilities or deficiencies in the formal institutional environment. I have termed these innovative coping strategies, "adaptive informal institutions," to differentiate them from longer-standing practices that are apparently embedded in the cultural fabric of society.[6] As "regularized patterns of interaction that emerge as adaptive responses to the constraints and opportunities of formal institutions," adaptive informal *institutions* should also be distinguished from informal behavior that occurs in an ad hoc manner (Tsai 2006, 125–126). Ultimately, focusing on adaptive informal institutions encourages analysis of shifting norms and incentives that are endogenous to a particular institutional context.

The case of reform-era China illustrates how the emergence of adaptive informal institutions enabled reformers to overcome the institutional and political capital invested in a state-dominated economic system. Specifically, in the years following Mao Zedong's death in 1976, private entrepreneurs devised a creative repertoire of informal practices to circumvent socialist era regulatory and ideological constraints on for-profit activities.

For example, falsely registering as a collective enterprise, "wearing a red hat," enabled entrepreneurs and officials to run private businesses (with more than eight employees) with less hassle. The prevalence of this disguising strategy was well known to both party-state cadres and ordinary people, which eroded the legitimacy of official restrictions on capitalist activity. Similarly, due to limited access to credit from state banks, to date, private entrepreneurs have relied on various forms of informal finance, cleverly cloaked as other types of legitimate operations (Tsai 2002). Such obfuscating practices are so widespread and routinized that they may be regarded as adaptive informal *institutions*. Although these examples appear reactive to constraints in the formal institutional context, they can also be interpreted as proactive efforts by similarly situated entrepreneurial agents to get things done through non-official strategies—repeatedly.

There is both empirical and analytical value in recognizing when informal behavior becomes institutionalized for two main reasons: first, they may represent a more relevant reality for understanding the context of common coping strategies; and second, their popularity has potential effects on subsequent reforms of formal institutions. In terms of the latter, the emergence of widespread deviations from official mandates alerts the designers of formal institutions to repeated deficiencies in institutional enforcement. For informal practices to reach the point of being institutionalized indicates that the gatekeepers of formal institutions are complicit, if not supportive, of reiterated infractions. Political leadership then faces the question of whether to look the other way themselves, reassert the authority of formal institutions, or reform them. Passivity can be politically convenient, as seen in the "policy drift" channel for institutional change. Reinvigorating enforcement mechanisms is sensible when the informal practices entail criminal or other activities that adversely affect public welfare. But when adaptive informal institutions yield desired outcomes such as economic growth or political stability, they provide reform-oriented policy elites with practical evidence that can be marshaled to promote formalization of such practices. Adaptive informal institutions may serve as an indirect channel for newly emerging or underrepresented groups to affect policy change—even in the absence of such consequentialist ambitions. Quotidian coping strategies can have unintended policy effects.

More concretely, in the above examples from China, the adaptive informal institution of "wearing a red hat" facilitated the legalization of large private businesses, and later on, de facto privatization of small and medium state-owned enterprises; and the formal admission of private entrepreneurs into the Chinese Communist Party. In the absence of practical evidence that violations of existing rules were promoting economic growth and involving the staff of the party-state, it would have been much more challenging and politically costly for China's reformers to legalize private economic activities. By the same token, other dramatic departures from the People's Republic of China's founding mission—such as constitutional protection of private property rights, commercialization of print media (Fischer 2008, chapter 8), and development of land markets (Ho 2005)—evolved incrementally in response to local practices. Focusing solely on official policy changes and formal institutions would miss out on the informal dynamics that enabled near-revolutionary changes in formal institutions to occur in the absence of regime change.

A host of "fence-breaking activities" in Vietnam similarly paved the way for post-hoc legalization of private businesses, sale of land use rights, and market-based prices and wages (Tsai 2013; Kerkvliet 2005; Malesky 2004, 307–337; Arkadie and Mallon 2003). But to be sure, not all adaptive informal institutions become formalized. In Vietnam, informal decentralization in the provision of public order continues to compete with largely ineffective formal institutions (Vu, Zouikri, and Deffains 2014, 1–28). In China, many institutionalized forms of shadow banking remain banned or unregulated even as they literally enrich both state and non-state actors. Identifying the conditions under which adaptive informal institutions develop causal impact on institutional change requires analysis of specific political economies.[7] Depending on context, Grzymala-Busse finds that "informal institutions can replace, undermine, and reinforce formal institutions *irrespective of the latter's strength*" in the post-communist democracies of the Czech Republic, Hungary, Poland, and Slovakia (Grzymala-Busse 2010, 311–333).

These observations are not limited to post-socialist contexts where formal institutions may be expected to be in flux, and therefore, more susceptible to informal adaptations. In his study of the relationship between the European Parliament and the European Union's Council, for example, Henry Farrell identifies a "*recursive relationship* between formal and informal institutions" such that (adaptive) informal institutions created in response to formal rules may influence subsequent adjustments to formal institutions (Farrell and Hertier 2003, 577–600). Even in the United States, an established democracy known for its formal political institutions, unwritten rules perform critical mediating functions by supplementing and clarifying ambiguities in parchment institutions (Azari and Smith 2012, 37–55). They are fundamental components of political processes in the US rather than distracting aberrations. Azari and Smith further suggest, "that the interface between formal and informal institutions is itself dynamic, and that written and unwritten rules can each promote change in the other" (Azari and Smith 2012, 43). As mentioned earlier, common law can have similar dynamic effects vis-à-vis formal institutions, with varying consequences for democratic governance.

Conclusion

Historical institutionalism has contributed significantly to our understanding of institutional development, but avoided direct theorization of informal institutions, even while specifying modalities of endogenous institutional change that occur through distinctly informal pathways and practices. This hesitance derives from a division of labor—segmented by regional/developmental expertise—that evokes Gabriel Almond's concern about the rise of "various schools and sects ... [sitting] at separate tables" in the discipline of Political Science (Almond 1989, 13). His reflection may be extended to the rise of institutional analysis in recent decades. Even within the sub-field of comparative politics, we have tended to study separate institutions. Fortunately, there is emergent recognition that formal institutions should not be analyzed in isolation from informal ones, and that informal institutions merit dedicated attention without presuming them to be pathological. As Scott Radnitz explains, "The persistence of informality in an otherwise 'formalized' world challenges basic assumptions about the evolution and organization of society, and must be dealt with on its own terms" (Radnitz 2011, 362).

Future research should thus start from the Möbius strip-informed premise that all institutional eco-systems include both formal and informal components, irrespective of regime type, level of development, or geographic region. Such a stance would encourage students to interrogate the origins, the reproduction, and the evolution of informal institutions in interaction with the dynamics derived from the study of formal institutions in historical institutionalism. In particular, certain modes of endogenous institutional transformation already point to informal practices and processes. Conversion describes informal means of reappropriating formal institutions for new purposes. Layering need not exclude informal institutions. As seen in the sub-category of adaptive informal institutions, the broader institutional context may be multi-tiered, such that formal institutions articulate the formal rules of the game, giving rise to adaptive informal institutions (including conversion and layering) that compromise, subvert, and even facilitate reforms of formal institutions. The concept of "institutional bricolage" from sociological institutionalism and anthropology captures the patchwork of possibilities for identifying potential sources of recombinant change (Cleaver 2002, 11–30). Dennis Galvin refers to the mutually transforming synthesis of formal and informal institutions as "institutional syncretism" (Galvin 2004). In contrast to situations where formal institutions co-opt informal ones, or vice versa, syncretic institutions represent wholly novel institutions fashioned out of changes in both their formal and informal components. Such processes may lead to institutional drift, as new policies are prioritized to the neglect of those supporting earlier priorities. Even institutional displacement may occur through syncretic re-engineering of formal and informal institutions over time.

Adopting a more holistic approach to institutional analysis has implications for the manner in which political scientists, including historical institutionalists, conceive of political development and governance. Rather than equating modernization with the elimination of informality, informal institutions should be incorporated when evaluating the extent of "institutionalization" in a political economy. In practice, this entails a departure from the state-centric theorizing that intersected with the rise of historical institutionalism. Formal institutions are more likely to be documented and enforced by the state, yet not all institutions are subject to official third party enforcement (e.g., clientelism). Indeed, in many of the examples reviewed in this chapter, state agents also abide by unwritten rules and allow informal institutions to flourish, either directly or indirectly. Moreover, these informal institutions may be competing or substitutive, rather than merely complementary or accommodating. Even though the modern Weberian state monopolizes the legitimate use of force, individual state institutions do not necessarily monopolize legitimacy. Different sections, levels, and policies of the state are subject to contestation by both state and non-state actors. Informal institutions that pose challenges to one part of the state may be valued in others. The possibility of incongruence in inter-bureaucratic and central-local priorities provides clues into the circumstances under which informal institutions could become formalized. Internal inconsistencies in formal rules, coupled with gaps between formal institutions and ground-level realities provide inviting opportunities for entrepreneurial actors to create adaptive informal institutions. Such adaptive coping strategies become part of an institutional context that is susceptible to endogenous transformation. In short, future scholarship in historical institutionalism would be enriched by recognizing that a host of informal institutions structure political governance and the distribution of resources even in societies with well-established formal institutions. Ample opportunity remains for detailing and theorizing the dynamics of informal institutions in their own right.

Notes

* The author gratefully acknowledges constructive feedback from Tulia Falleti and the APSA 2014 meeting audience, and assistance from Xiaoxiao Sheng.

1. Even when these ideas are fully formed *ideologies*—comprising both causal beliefs and normative prescriptions—they regulate behavior through institutions.
2. Streeck and Thelen (2005) cite a working paper, but the more developed argument was published as Greif and Laitin (2004, 633–652).
3. In particular, James Mahoney (2000, 507–548) distinguishes between "self-reinforcing" and "reactive" sequences.
4. Hence, clientelism in Maoist China could be viewed as accommodating in urban work units, but closer to competing or substitutive in the context of local rural politics (Oi 1989).
5. For example, see North (1990).
6. This is more of an analytic distinction than an empirical one. In reality, there may well be adaptive informal institutions that represent a revival of more "traditional" practices. An excellent example is Sarigil and Ozdemir's (2014) paper.
7. Four propositions on the conditions under which adaptive informal institutions are likely to contribute to formal institutional change are outlined in Tsai (2015).

References

Almond, Gabriel A. 1989. *A Discipline Divided: Schools and Sects in Political Science.* New York: Sage Publications.

Arkadie, Brian Van and Raymond Mallon. 2003. *Vietnam: A Transition Tiger?* Canberra: Asia Pacific Press at Australian National University.

Azari, Julia R. and K. Jennifer Smith. 2012. "Unwritten Rules: Informal Institutions in Established Democracies." *Perspectives on Politics* 10 (1): 37–55.

Bates, Robert. 1988. "Contra Contractarianism: Some Reflections on the New Institutionalism." *Politics and Society* 16 (2–3): 387–401.

Baumgartner, Frank and D. Bryan Jones. 1993. *Agendas and Instability in American Politics.* Chicago: University of Chicago Press.

Blyth, Mark M. 1997. "Any More Bright Ideas? The Ideational Turn of Comparative Political Economy (Review Article)." *Comparative Politics* 29 (2): 229–250.

Blyth, Mark M. 2001. "The Transformation of the Swedish Model: Economic Ideas, Distributional Conflict, and Institutional Change." *World Politics* 54 (1): 1–26.

Blyth, Mark M. 2002. *Great Transformations: Economic Ideas and Institutional Change in the Twentieth Century*. New York: Cambridge University Press.

Bratton, Michael. 1994. "Neopatrimonial Regimes and Political Transitions in Africa." *World Politics* 46 (4): 453–489.

Bratton, Michael. 2007. "Formal versus Informal Institutions in Africa." *Journal of Democracy* 18 (3): 96–110.

Capoccia, Giovanni and R. Daniel Kelemen. 2007. "The Study of Critical Junctures: Theory, Narrative and Counterfactuals in Historical Institutionalism." *World Politics* 59 (3): 341–369.

Cleaver, Frances. 2002. "Reinventing Institutions: Bricolage and the Social Embeddedness of Natural Resource Management." *The European Journal of Development Research* 14 (2): 11–30.

Collins, Kathleen. 2004. "The Logic of Clan Politics: Evidence from the Central Asian Trajectories." *World Politics* 56 (2): 224–261.

Ding, X. L. 1994. "Institutional Amphibiousness and the Transition from Communism." *British Journal of Political Science* 24 (3): 293–318.

Evans, Peter B., Dietrich Reuschemeyer, and Theda Skocpol, eds. 1985. *Bringing the State Back In*. New York: Cambridge University Press.

Farrell, Henry and Adrienne Hertier. 2003. "Formal and Informal Institutions under Codecision: Continuous Constitution-Building in Europe." *Governance: An International Journal of Policy, Administration, and Institutions* 16 (4): 577–600.

Fischer, Doris. 2008. "Censorship and Marketization: Institutional Change within China's Media." In *Regime Legitimacy in Contemporary China*, ed. Thomas Heberer and Gunter Schubert. New York: Routledge, 175–196.

Galvin, Dennis. 2004. *The State Must Be Our Master of Fire: How Peasants Craft Culturally Sustainable Development in Senegal*. Berkeley: University of California Press.

Garrett, Geoffrey and R. Barry Weingast. 1993. "Ideas, Interests, and Institutions: Constructing the European Communities' Internal Market." In *Ideas and Foreign Policy: Beliefs, Institutions and Political Change*, ed. Judith Goldstein and Robert Keohane. Ithaca, NY: Cornell University Press, 173–206.

Greif, Avner and D. David Laitin. 2004. "A Theory of Endogenous Institutional Change." *American Political Science Review* 98 (4): 633–652.

Grzymala-Busse, Anna. 2010. "The Best Laid Plans: The Impact of Informal Rules on Formal Institutions in Transitional Regimes." *Studies in Comparative International Development* 45 (3): 311–333.

Hacker, Jacob. 2004. "Privatizing Risk without Privatizing the Welfare State: The Hidden Politics of Social Policy Retrenchment in the United States." *American Political Science Review* 98 (2): 243–260.

Hacker, Jacob. 2005. "Policy Drift: The Hidden Politics of US Welfare State Retrenchment." In *Beyond Continuity: Institutional Change in Advanced Political Economics*, ed. Wolfgang Streeck and Kathleen Thelen. New York: Cambridge University Press, 40–82.

Hall, Peter A. 1993. "Policy Paradigms, Social Learning, and the State." *Comparative Politics* 25: 275–296.

Hall, Peter and Rosemary Taylor. 1996. "Political Science and the Three Institutionalisms." *Political Studies* 44 (5): 936–957.

Helmke, Gretchen and Steven Levitsky. 2004. "Informal Institutions and Comparative Politics: A Research Agenda." *Perspectives on Politics* 2 (4): 725–740.

Helmke, Gretchen and Steven Levitsky. 2006. "Introduction." In *Informal Institutions and Democracy: Lessons from Latin America*, ed. Gretchen Helmke and Steven Levitsky. Baltimore, MD: John Hopkins University Press, 1–30.

Ho, Peter, ed. 2005. *Developmental Dilemmas: Land Reform and Institutional Change in China*. New York: Routledge.

Kendzior, Sarah. 2013. "The Curse of Stability in Central Asia." *Foreign Policy*. Available at <http://www.foreignpolicy.com/articles/2013/02/19/the_curse_of_stability_in_central_asia> (accessed February 19, 2013).

Kerkvliet, Benedict J. Tria. 2005. *The Power of Everyday Politics: How Vietnamese Peasants Transformed National Policy*. Ithaca, NY: Cornell University Press.

Krasner, Stephen D. 1984. "Approaches to the State: Alternative Conceptions and Historical Dynamics." *Comparative Politics* 16 (2): 223–246.

Lauth, Hans-Joachim. 2000. "Informal Institutions and Democracy." *Democratization* 7 (4): 21–50.

Ledeneva, Alena. 1998. *Russia's Economy of Favors: Blat, Networking, and Informal Exchange*. New York: Cambridge University Press.

Mahoney, James. 2000. "Path Dependence in Historical Sociology." *Theory and Society* 29 (4): 507–548.

Mahoney, James and Kathleen Thelen. 2010. "A Theory of Gradual Institutinal Change." In *Explaining Institutional Change: Ambiguity, Agency, and Power*, ed. James Mahoney and Kathleen Thelen. New York: Cambridge University Press, 1–37.

Malesky, Edmund. 2004. "Leveled Mountains and Broken Fences: Measuring and Analyzing De Facto Decentralization in Vietnam." *European Journal of Southeast Asian Studies* 3 (2): 307–337.

North, Douglass. 1990. *Institutions, Institutional Change, and Economic Performance*. New York: Cambridge University Press.

O'Donnell, Guillermo. 1996. "Another Institutionalization: Latin America and Elsewhere." *Kellogg Institute Working Paper No. 222*. Notre Dame, IN: University of Notre Dame.

Oi, Jean C. 1989. *State and Peasant in Contemporary China: The Political Economy of Village Government*. Berkeley: University of California Press.

Pontussen, Jonas. 1995. "From Comparative Public Policy to Political Economy: Putting Political Institutions in Their Place and Taking Interests Seriously." *Comparative Political Studies* 28 (1): 117–147.

Powell, Walter W. and J. Paul DiMaggio, eds. 1991. *The New Institutionalism in Organizational Analysis*. Chicago: University of Chicago Press.

Radnitz, Scott. 2011. "Informal Politics and the State (Review Article)." *Comparative Politics* 43 (3): 351–371.

Sarigil, Zeki and Burcu Ozdemir. 2014. "Informal Institutions in Dispute Resolution: 'Cem Courts.'" Paper Presented at the 72nd Annual National Conference of the Midwest Political Science Association (MPSA), Chicago.

Schedler, Andreas, ed. 2006. *Electoral Authoritarianism: The Dynamics of Unfree Competition*. Boulder, CO: Lynne Rienner.

Schedler, Andreas. 2014. "The Criminal Subversion of Mexican Democracy." *Journal of Democracy* 25 (1): 5–18.

Schickler, Eric. 2001. *Disjointed Pluralism: Institutional Innovation and the Development of the U.S. Congress*. Princeton, NJ: Princeton University Press.

Selznick, Philip. 1949. *TVA and the Grass Roots: A Study in the Sociology of Formal Organization*. Berkeley: University of California Press.

Sikkink, Kathryn. 1991. *Ideas and Institutions: Developmentalism in Argentina and Brazil*. Ithaca, NY: Cornell University Press.

Steinmo, Sven. 2008. "What Is Historical Institutionalism?" In *Approaches and Methodologies in the Social Sciences*, ed. Donatella Della Porta and Michael Keating. New York: Cambridge University Press, 118–138.

Steinmo, Sven, Kathleen Thelen, and Frank Longstreth, eds. 1992. *Structuring Politics: Historical Institutionalism in Comparative Analysis*. New York: Cambridge University Press.

Streeck, Wolfgang and Kathleen Thelen. 2005. "Introduction." In *Beyond Continuity: Institutional Change in Advanced Political Economics*, ed. Wolfgang Streeck and Kathleen Thelen. New York: Cambridge University Press, 1–39.

Swidler, Ann. 1986. "Culture in Action: Symbols and Strategies." *American Sociological Review* 52 (2): 273–286.

Tsai, Kellee S. 2002. *Back-Alley Banking: Private Entrepreneurs in China*. Ithaca, NY: Cornell University Press.

Tsai, Kellee S. 2006. "Adaptive Informal Institutions and Endogenous Institutional Change in China." *World Politics* 59 (1): 125–126.

Tsai, Kellee S. 2013. "Cause or Consequence? Private-Sector Development and Communist Resilience in China." In *Why Communism Did Not Collapse*, ed. Martin Dmitrov. New York: Cambridge University Press, 205–234.

Tsai, Kellee S. 2015. "China: Economic Liberalization, Adaptive Informal Institutions, and Party-State Resilience." In *Oxford Handbook of Transformations of the State*, ed. Stephan Leibfried, Frank Nullmeier, Evelyne Huber, Matthew Lange, Jonah Levy, and John Stephens. New York: Oxford University Press.

Tsai, Lily L. 2007. *Accountability Without Democracy: Solidary Groups and Public Goods Provision in Rural China*. New York: Cambridge University Press.

Vu, Thanh Thuy, Messaoud Zouikri, and Bruno Deffains. 2014. "The Interrelationship between Formal and Informal Decentralization and Its Impact on Subcentral Governance Performance: The Case of Vietnam." *CESifo Economic Studies*. Available at <http://cesifo.oxfordjournals.org/content/early/2014/02/20/cesifo.ifu003> (accessed September 1, 2015).

Walder, Andrew G. 1988. *Communist Neo-Traditionalism: Work and Authority in Chinese Industry*. Berkeley: University of California Press.

PART IV

AMERICAN POLITICS

Introduction

ADAM SHEINGATE

HISTORICAL institutionalism has long informed, and been informed by, the study of the United States. Particularly within the field of American political development, historical institutionalism has helped scholars shed light on the elusive character of the American state and the legacy of struggles over race and citizenship that continue to animate much of American politics. At the same time, core concepts like path dependence and feedback effects figure prominently in historical-institutionalist explanations of American politics, such as the distinctive character of US social policy and the heavy reliance on private, arms-length instruments for the provision of health care and other government benefits. The study of American politics has also been central to the development and elaboration of theories of gradual institutional change such as layering, conversion, and drift. Finally, attention to the intercurrent character of institutional arrangements is also a common feature of work in American politics, perhaps because of the fragmentation of the American political system. Partial, overlapping patterns of authority illuminate the contradictory tendencies and impulses in American politics, such as the coexistence of surprisingly robust anti-discrimination policies alongside a sprawling criminal justice system that disproportionately incarcerates racial minorities.

The chapters in this section illustrate the ongoing vibrancy of research on historical institutionalism and American political development. Desmond King sets the stage by exploring the enduring connections between American state-building and the politics of race. King shows that to fully appreciate the origin and evolution of the American state one must account for the racially-inflected struggles over the construction of national political authority. This struggle shaped the design of American political institutions and established an enduring dynamic in which states and localities often frustrated national efforts to guarantee political rights for African Americans. However, this frustration also fueled state-building achievements. This is a subject taken up by Paul Frymer, who also sees racial conflict as central to American political development. However, Frymer also points out that contrary to perceptions of a weak American state, the growth of federal power in the twentieth century came about as a result of nationally enforced social and political rights. Frymer shows how legal institutions and actors played a central role in this state-building process. The important role of legal institutions is addressed further in the chapter by Sarah Staszak. One of the distinctive, and sometimes misunderstood, features of the American state is the role of the judiciary in the process of American political development. Recently, however, scholars have moved away from a near-exclusive focus on the Supreme Court in order to examine the broader institutional development of the federal judiciary as well as the key role private litigation has played in the extension and enforcement of national political authority.

Each of the chapters in this section explores how historical institutionalism offers a particular set of tools and concepts with which to approach the study of American politics. As noted in the introduction to the volume, historical institutionalism is much more than simply the truism that "history matters." In the study of American politics, scholars working within the tradition of historical institutionalism provide distinct explanations for political phenomena that differ in important ways from other approaches. For example, Daniel Galvin contrasts historical instituitonalist approaches to the study of American political parties with functionalist explanations that begin from the assumption that political organizations are designed with the electoral interests of politicians in mind. In this view, party structures change when they no longer address political needs. As Galvin points out, this yields a rather thin conception of institutions and an incomplete account of the changes in the character of American political parties that have taken place over the last fifty years. Rather than assume form follows function, Galvin describes how the evolution of the Democratic and Republican parties traced distinct paths. These differences reflected the way leaders in the respective parties acquired new resources and adapted existing ones in order to enhance their role in national elections. Organizational capacity, in other words, is an outcome to be explained rather than an institutional feature to be assumed.

Providing explanations for political phenomena other approaches take as fixed or given is also a characteristic feature of historical institutionalist scholarship on the distinctive character of US social policy. Unsatisfied with accounts that contrasted the minimal American welfare state with more generous forms of social provision in Europe, historical institutionalist scholars uncovered a precocious social spending regime in the nineteenth century as well as a robust if "hidden" welfare state in the twentieth century that delivered health and pension benefits through private insurance linked to the employment contract. As Alan Jacobs explores in his chapter, these considerable insights into the distinctive character of US social policy included important theoretical advances into the nature of institutional development and the dynamics of policy change. Scholars developed concepts such as path dependence, feedback effects, and gradual institutional change (e.g., conversion, layering, and drift) as a way to explain the origins and evolution of the American welfare state. As Jacobs concludes, however, these concepts do not provide clear propositions about when policy change is likely to occur. Going forward, Jacobs argues, historical institutionalism is well placed to address such questions by paying particular attention to the power resources of key stakeholders, the shifting coalitions that support specific policies, and the tendency for stable policies to sow the seeds for their own, gradual demise.

Ultimately, historical institutionalism is particularly well-suited to study the contingent nature of political authority in the United States. Lacking a tradition of a centralized bureaucracy, the exercise of public power has varied considerably across time and place. As a result, the American state can sometimes display an elusive quality that belies an extensive apparatus of coercive capacity. This is illustrated vividly, and tragically, in the expansive reach of the US criminal justice system. As Marie Gottschalk explores in the concluding chapter of the section, the extraordinary growth of the prison population and its disproportionate effect on African American men has deep historical and institutional roots. To understand the retributive turn in penal policy and its effects, as Gottschalk does, one must grapple with multiple and complex causes that defy parsimonious explanation. As Gottschalk warns, historical institutionalism risks losing more than just its distinctive character by succumbing to disciplinary pressures; it will also lose its comparative advantage addressing important questions about pressing issues in American politics that mainstream approaches are sometimes ill equipped to handle.

CHAPTER 17

THE AMERICAN STATE AND THE ENDURING POLITICS OF RACE

DESMOND KING*

THE most important scholarly finding about the American state is how the politics of race and racial inequality have shaped all aspects of the state's structure and policy outcomes. Such research overcomes the neglect of race in the "bringing the state back in" revival. This engagement (Katznelson 2005; King 2007) continues to expand and to drive new research agendas (for example, Francis 2014; Jung and Kwon 2013; Kato 2012). The American state performs and combines the standard functions of maintaining order, delivering public policy, monopolizing the legitimate use of violence, and maintaining revenues, all with an appreciation of the politics of race: this "weak" state was capable of both long disregarding the outrage of lynching and designing policy to advantage white workers over African Americans in the new social security system of the 1930s. Although efforts to enforce racial equality has commonly evoked inadequate policy (Rugh and Massey 2013), the rapid escalation of disproportionately racial incarceration patterns from the 1980s implies no lack of national state capacity to function (Alexander 2010). These nuances become clear from a discussion of how the American state has democratized (Gibson 2012; Mickey 2008, 2015) and its comparative distinctness in how the American state has classified its citizens by race since such census work commenced (Hattam 2009; Nobles 2000).

If the enduring politics of race is the primary finding of Political Science analyses of the American state, two other, not unrelated, findings follow closely. First, the state's institutions from their inception have been permeated by arrangements to obfuscate policy outputs (for example, through the "submerged state" of tax expenditures or the significant role of private actors in delivering policy fostering equality of opportunity). In large part this pattern has been driven by the need of state officials (policy makers, courts, and administrators) to camouflage activism in a political culture hostile to government because government is believed to benefit the "undeserving," a category which predominantly includes African Americans (Bartels 2008; Gilens 1999). As historical institutional analysis would anticipate, this fragmentary structure has shaped the way in which the American state operates. Scholarly research reveals two particular patterns—resort to the surreptitious and to the dramatic, each of which is discussed below.

Second, state-building in the US has been decisively affected by processes of nationalization. Because racial inequality was made constitutionally fundamental to the founding of the US, major periods of disruptive public disorder and conflict have ensued to democratize America. These disruptions provoke national level policy responses. Examples of the latter factor include the near break-up of the US averted by Civil War (with emancipation granted eventually during the conflict) and the passage of civil and voting rights laws in the 1960s (Gibson 2012). The politics of race has been a key dynamic of state expansion and struggles over state capacity to address enduring material racial inequalities.

As these findings imply, the scholarly literature on the American state is now too important to be dismissed by purists un-persuaded of the concept's theoretical or empirical relevance. Following the behavioral-centered research of the half century to the 1970s, American political development scholars took the lead in constructing a body of original scholarship focused on this concept, led by Stephen Skowronek in his seminal *Building a New American State* (Carpenter 2005; Galambos 1987; Johnson 2007; Nordlinger 1981; Poggi 1978; Rohr 1986; Skowronek 1982). Twentieth-century processes of administrative enlargement, military organization, and a social-regulatory apparatus built a state despite itself. These developments put flesh on what Skowronek characterized as the "absence of a sense of the state" in nineteenth-century America despite the fact that "the state was essential to social order and social development" in that hundred years (1982, 19; and see Balogh 2009; Adler and Polsky 2010; Moore 2011). Paul Pierson (2007) uses more traditional language but, with his notion of an "activist state" to describe the rapid expansion in spending, regulating, and taxing by the state since the 1940s, gets at the same phenomenon of expansion and enlarged intervention in society.

So the modern American state has evolved into a set of extensive bureaucratic and administrative resources available to new presidential administrations. For historical institutional scholars this set of resources, rooted in inherited yet changing institutions and structures, set the context within which change occurs or implodes, almost invariably driven by or responding to the politics of racial inequality (Frymer 2008a). Institutions—that is, agencies, programs, and rules (formal laws and informal norms)—are products of historical struggles. Consequently, the American state, because of fragmentation across government, federalism, and fluctuations of state contraction versus expansion, often assumes contradictory roles.

Fragmentation versus Capacity in the American State

A common theme across many of these studies of the American state is the difficulty of policy delivery because of fragmentation within the state. Fragmentation includes both the familiar separation of powers at the national level and the conflicts this calibration induces for instance between the executive and the legislature, or between the judiciary and policy administrators; and the variety and conflicts introduced through the competing ambitions of different actors in the federal system. Because the American state is undoubtedly fragmentary and amorphous, the production of public policy outcomes is necessarily circuitous. The executive on occasion may seize initiatives and seek to impose presidential authority on a policy goal, galvanizing supporters and appointing his personnel to senior bureaucratic posts to deliver the articulated change.

But other American state policy outputs arrive without such national fanfare or direction, through amendments on bills passed by Congress or in the myriad of key regulations and rules formulated by civil servants in federal departments and agencies as they place precision and substance on laws and enabling legislation or in judicial decisions (Frymer 2008b). How bureaucrats resolve to pursue or not to pursue particular issues is crucial to state policy outcomes. For instance, the way in which officials at the Department of Housing and Urban Development opted to implement the obligation to desegregate and promote anti-discrimination in housing markets under Title VIII of the Civil Rights Act of 1968 (the Fair Housing Act) led to no improvements until the law was amended and strengthened in 1988 (Goering 1986; King and Smith 2011, chapter 5), though critics argued a much more aggressive stance to mirror that of the EEOC's efforts in the labour market should have been developed.

The Submerged State as Policy Design

Suzanne Mettler (2011a, 2011b) coined the term "submerged state" to describe the way in which significant government programs are implemented unobtrusively, so discreetly that voters often don't associate particular programs with the state. As argued also by Christopher Howard (1997), the raft of government programs which give tax relief to citizens—such as relief on retirement savings schemes or mortgages—constitute major American state policy interventions that few voters recognize as part of the state. The purposeful design of policies either to connect taxpayers' contribution and final benefit directly as in social security pensions or to make them costs to the Inland Revenue in such tax expenditures as relief on mortgages (Home Mortgage Interest Deduction) results in many American voters believing state activism to be far less than it is *and* to be something consumed by others but not themselves. These latter programs and others such as the exemption from taxes on employer-provided health and retirement savings accounts constitute the submerged state.

Submerged state programs differ from other types where direct interaction between the individual and the state is high—for instance, an income support program such as TANF or housing assistance and disability payments if the scheme requires a meeting with a "street level bureaucrat" to determine a supplicant's eligibility. Experience of the state is physical, transparent and often continuing. Many of these income assistance programs are perceived as consumed disproportionately by African Americans. Access to publicly subsidized programs such as government underwritten mortgage insurance or student grants under the Pell scheme or means tested Medicare prescription drugs have less visibility than income support programs but are commonly perceived as reasonable activities which don't drain fiscal resources and present as entitlements for average taxpaying households. A Tea Party town hall meeting in the summer of 2009 included one irate man famously warning his congressional representative to "keep your government hands off my Medicare." Because twenty-four per cent of Medicare payments (covering 11.1 million recipients) are made through private insurance companies (a form of delegation in Morgan and Campbell's (2011) terms), the failure to misconstrue the American state origin of such benefits was less peculiar than it seemed at first. The town hall agitator demonstrates how successful the submerged state policy is in camouflaging the government sources of selective programs.

Because the submerged state effectively hides American state activity (Sheingate 2009), it encourages Americans to believe that they have no need for the kind of legitimate expression of public authority associated with state power. It strengthens the populist view of the US as a stateless society.

Furthermore, the submerged state is partial in respect to the politics of racial inequality. The host of policies propped up by the submerged state through tax expenditures give few benefits to African American households since, historically, fewer of them have participated in mortgages or secured retirement accounts with tax relief. Of course the federal government has a long-standing record of direct discrimination in housing policy as mortgage insurance underwriting rested on a racial classification of properties' desirability—redlining. By benefitting high income earners and those with household assets, the submerged state deepened the subprime mortgage crisis when it occurred, helping to push many African American households into further debt and loss of their primary asset, their home. Mettler's remark that "the policies of the submerged state have aided and abetted the upward distribution of riches, with more and more of the largesse accrued to those at the very top" (2011a, 26), applies most grimly for African American workers and households because of the entrenched unequal distribution of material wealth and opportunities.

Administering a Submerged State and the Paradox of "Weakness"

Because of racial inequality this submerged state is also administrative. Several scholars document how extensively the American state relies upon working with private sector actors to deliver policy as a way of shielding the state from voter scrutiny and direct accountability. The legitimation of state activity—a perennial challenge to an American state located in a society which prides itself on being anti-statist, anti "big government" but in which activism has grown—is partially avoided by making the private actor an arm of state policy, either through delegation, indirect control, or public-private associations. This pattern is pronounced in respect to the policies designed to promote racial equality.

Dobbin (2009) described one variant of this subtle configuration in his analysis of how the threat of legal action against corporations failing to comply with civil rights law produced radical change in private employment practices. This discreet and unanticipated "strength of a weak state" (Dobbin and Sutton 1998) stands as one of the major instances of American state policy efficacy. The way in which personnel officers and HR departments in large firms complied with equal opportunity and anti-discrimination law exploited the view held by Americans of "their social institutions and national culture as originating in the community rather than in the state." Consequently Dobbin finds that in the implementation of anti-discrimination law "the link between most compliance programs and the law has been deliberately severed," because "in a nation that has long defined government regulation as illegitimate, this was perhaps the surest way to guarantee the survival of compliance measures" (Dobbin 2009, 20). But to underline, this policy and its forms of implementation exist only because of the politics of race at heart of the American state.

Not only do voters view "government regulation as illegitimate" but any support they had for regulatory policy as a means of enforcing civil rights evaporated amongst white voters from the mid-1970s. The "strength of the weak state" is yet another consequence of the politics of racial inequality at the core of the American state (Jung and Kwon 2013). In this context political scientist Paul Frymer (2008b) advances the category of the "legal state" to describe the way in which judges in the 1970s enforced civil rights to desegregate and integrate labor unions. Courts produced dramatic change toward integration by confronting segregated unions with huge damages in their judgments. Expensive litigation had "direct impact on [unions'] racial demographics" (2008b, 92). He adds that "civil rights lawyers besieged unions with lawsuits, and judges compelled compliance with the use of special masters and by ordering unions to pay significant financial fees for back pay, attorneys and damages. In turn courts created new institutional incentives for employers to follow." This latter meant that despite employers' own racial preferences, employers faced "structural reasons to follow civil rights law, recognizing the potential costs" (2008b, 94). Extending the "legal state" perspective, Sean Farhang argues that the fragmentary state created by enduring institutional conflicts between congress and the president encourages enactment of laws which "incentivize private lawsuits" (2010, 5). Farhang's empirical focus is the way federal job discrimination lawsuits are prosecuted, again as policy for racial equality. Congress wrote the Civil Rights Act of 1964 purposefully to create a private enforcement regime in the CRA. Thus in Farhang's analysis it is "America's fragmented state structures" which drove "legislative enactment of private enforcement regimes," (2010, 5) with the example of the 1964 Act's Title VII to the fore. The fragmentary aspect of the American State upon which Farhang dwells is the institutional struggle to control and direct the federal bureaucracy—the core of the state—waged between the executive and legislature. But what Farhang underlines is that private enforcement is a dimension of American state capacity beyond the curtilage of the standard instruments theorized from an overly executive centered and Weberian formulation of stateness. The institutional complexity—expressed in conflicts between defining elements of the state—and the fragmentary structures of policy delivery mechanisms—the ability to opt for private or public regulation—draws attention to capacity, and works to refute the conventional claim about state weakness (a refutation pioneered by Novak 2008). Private enforcement systems, Farhang finds from his study, are a central feature of the American state, but in contrast with administrative state capacity enforcement resides in the sphere of private litigation. His larger claim, germane to historical institutionalist analysis, is to show how the fragmentary system of the American state does not simply generate an inadequate administrative enforcement capacity but stimulates distinct methods of enforcement. This view is consistent with King and Lieberman's (2009) claim that rather than bemoaning the weak Weberian framework of the American state scholars should probe its distinctness. Farhang (2010, 214, emphasis in original) terms the private enforcement regime "*a different form of state-building*."

Delegating the delivery of American state policy directly to private sector actors is another version of the administrative submerged state, the "delegated welfare state" in Morgan and Campbell's terms, which they define as "the delegation of responsibility for publicly funded social welfare programs to non-state actors" (2011, 4). Their empirical case study is legislation enacted in 2003 which made prescription drug benefits part of Medicare, the Medicare Modernization Act. The new law delegates delivery of the program to competing, private insurance companies enhancing the power of such commercial providers. Morgan and Campbell explain the adoption of delegated governance by American state actors for three reasons. First, it hides the visibility of government activism, a pattern consistent with Mettler's submerged state. Second, the private actors benefitting from delegation powers lobby for such a role and to maintain it once granted: "across the forms of delegated governance, private interests have not only stymied the growth of direct federal administration but have enriched themselves by delivering publicly funded benefits and services" (2011, 7). Third, complementing Farhang's "litigation state," Morgan and Campbell find that the institutional tensions intrinsic to the American state—again at the executive-legislative level—create incentives for law makers to enact delegated governance arrangements. Delegation to private actors cements the sort of public-private linkages necessary to sustain a social program they argue.

Delegated governance helps scholars to understand how the American state-building process has occurred distinctly—compared to other industrial democracies—yet in a way which still demonstrates capacity as a measurable dimension of stateness. Morgan and Campbell coin the felicitous description "anti-bureaucratic statebuilding" (2011, 19).

The President's State: Grandiloquent Strategies and Racial Equality

Holders of key offices in the American state also have institutional incentives to engage periodically in policy strategies which are the obverse of the discreet world of the submerged state. In this style executives articulate concentrated, focused policy agendas using a "shock and awe" or war-like focus on an inanimate target (King 2013). Mimicking warfare at home galvanizes and renews national administration to set a focused policy agenda. The language of "wars on" is a recurring one in modern American state usage. It has been common in respect to racial inequalities as illustrated by the War on Poverty, the creation of the Kerner Commission and the war on illegal drugs. Richard Nixon told Americans that illegal drugs posed "public enemy number one" while Lyndon Johnson went after poverty (declaring an "unconditional war on poverty in America" in his January 1964 State of the Union address) and Ronald Reagan came down on illegal drug use and culture. As two legal scholars argue recently despite measures such as the Administrative Procedures Act of 1946, intended to ringfence the civil service more precisely, executive control and deployment of the American state has soared (Posner and Vermeule 2011). They write that "in the administrative state, it is not the case that legislatures govern, even subject to constraints and the need for cooperation with other branches. Rather the executive governs, in the sense that it drives the policy agenda, even where the cooperation of other branches is needed for political reasons" (2011, 11).

These sorts of policy strategies—submerged versus concentrated—differ significantly in design and process but each is explicable as responses to the institutional structures constraining the American state and its officeholders. This is a key insight for comparativists incorporating the American case into theories of state power. Fragmentation of powers, the fluctuating autonomy of bureaucrats, and challenges to executive authority judicially or politically incentivise the president to engage in American state policy initiatives which set agendas and dominate the political landscape. Most of them get attention but implementation and outcome rest on continuing complicated and institutionally constrained processes within the state. Furthermore, crisis—often a prompt to dramatic style policy plans—is rarely objectively defined (King 2013). The school desegregation crisis in Little Rock, Arkansas in 1957 compelled President Eisenhower to intervene but America's levels of segregated residential housing—measured on standard dissimilarity and isolation criteria—does not attain the status of a crisis requiring state action (Charles 2003; Sharkey 2013).

The Dangers of Associational Ties

The role of the American state in sustaining America's segregationist racialist order (Katznelson 2005, 2013; King 2007; Kryder 2000; Lieberman 1998; Patler 2004; Sparrow 2011) and in the incomplete efforts to dismantle segregation since the 1960s is unique

(King 2013; King and Smith 2011). The historical and post-1960s eras have been documented extensively.

The key issue for this chapter is the enduring legacies of moving from an era of segregated race relations (1896–1964), in which the American state was not merely complicit in but an agent of segregation (King 2007; Patler 2004; Yellin 2013) to one unfolding since the 1960s when passage of voting and civil rights laws ended *de jure* racial discrimination and established voting laws (Valelly 2004). The resulting transformation has been partial. Voting rights are much more secure than before the 1965 act though subject to continuing struggles: for instance, there is a significant difference in attending to state level voting violations and abuses by the Civil Rights Division of the Justice Department under the Obama administration compared with that of his predecessor, and in a 2013 decision, *Shelby County, Alabama v. Holder*, the Supreme Court diluted rigorous American state enforcement of federal laws requiring new strategies from the federal Justice Department. This pre-clearance system is one of the major instances of how the need to create and enforce national standards for equality has played a role in building the American state as a set of interventionist institutions. But in other spheres of the American state's legacy of racial inequality, the dismantling of entrenched patterns of segregation—in housing, labor markets, and education—has been far more tepid, and some new areas of inequality have emerged—notably in criminal justice and household wealth (King 2014; Rugh and Massey 2013).

The depth of associational ties between state and society ensured a pernicious interlocking of racial hierarchy in both spheres. This pattern historically was no mere functionalist reflection of one sphere in the other—that is, society pushing its preferences onto the state. Rather it was a co-existing and sutured associational world in which the American state worked *de facto* and *de jure* as a segregated state. This complex inter relationship continues. Legislation has desegregated American state employment patterns (black-white wage inequalities remain in the public sector but have lower ratios than in the private sector) and integrated the Armed Forces. But the engagement of the American state in delivering desegregated cities, measured in levels of integrated housing or schools, has faltered. Since the 1960s the American state has shifted from focused and systematic busing measures to integrate and balance racial ratios in schools (disallowed by the Supreme Court) to tightly fought legal battles about the mildest change in school districting or zoning density rulings which have significant effects on housing patterns.

Varieties of American State Bureaucratic Autonomy

Bureaucratic autonomy is a defining component of any state and specifying its extent and significance animates assessments of the strength of stateness or organizational capacity (Evans, Rueschemeyer, and Skocpol 1985; Hooks 1990; Katznelson 2002; Weir and Skocpol 1985). In the American state, bureaucratic autonomy is additionally calibrated by the range of types of bureaucratic agencies and bureaus within the state's own purview. Furthermore, there are important agencies in the American state with enhanced autonomy resulting from their design which seals them off from electoral pressures. Examples include the Federal Reserve System, about which more below, and port authorities.

Conventional Bureaucratic Autonomy

Daniel Carpenter (2001) has decisively advanced understanding of the evolution and content of American state autonomy. For him this is the absolute center of the American state as an institution intervening to deliver policy in society: "bureaucratic policy making is the hallmark of modern American government. Our agencies write regulations and draft legislation based on this information ... They administer with considerable discretion the resulting rules and statutes, in accordance with their own standardized routines and procedures ... The brute fact of modern politics is that myriad national programs begin and end in the hands of federal agencies" (2001, 5–6). This is a conventional view of how bureaucratic autonomy works in a quasi Weberian account of the state: civil servants plan, innovate, and deliver policy whether in terms of regulations, building, or service provision. Such activities grew in tandem with expansion of government activism from the middle of the twentieth century.

Carpenter reaches this argument from meticulous empirical research. In his cross case study of three departments' development between 1862 and 1928, Carpenter argues that historically some bureaucrats developed such strength on some occasions as to outflank politicians. He identifies common Progressive era narratives consisting of "bureaucrats building reputations for their agencies, erecting coalitions behind their favoured policies, and securing the policies that they favour despite the opposition of the most powerful politicians" (2001, 34). A key issue is to determine why some agencies are successful in advancing autonomous goals and others not. The departments of Agriculture and the Post Office worked but not the Interior Department. In explanation Carpenter develops a calibrated concept of autonomy. He argues that "bureaucratic autonomy lies less in fiat than in leverage. Autonomy prevails when agencies can establish political legitimacy—a reputation for expertise, efficiency, or moral protection and a uniquely diverse complex of ties to organized interests and the media—and induce politicians to defer to the wishes of the agency even when they prefer otherwise" (2001, 4). Within the institutional constraints and opportunities of the American state administrative leaders at the Post Office Department and US Department of Agriculture proved adroit in establishing the legitimacy upon which leverage could be maximized unlike their colleagues in the Interior Department. Consistent with historical institutionalist arguments, Carpenter emphasizes the "rigid confines" set by the US polity's institutional configuration, expressed in the "primacy of elected officials, the constraints of

American political culture, and the dominance of parties" (2001, 6). Success depended on policy outcomes which, if perceived as successful helped make a tentative trajectory more embedded in the state and allowed forms of institutional inertia to build up. This process always proceeded within the context of a complex American state Carpenter demonstrates. He writes about the Post Office and Agriculture programs that "at almost every step in the development of these programs, the institutional authorities of the American order—Congress, the president, the parties, the courts, and organized interests—assented to greater and greater administrative innovation." Hence, "through reputation building, federal agencies won the capacity to innovate. In American political development, bureaucratic autonomy was not captured but earned" (2001, 6). The role of these agencies as discriminatory employers and enforcers in shaping the politics of race is crucial (King 2007; Yellin 2013).

Carpenter's work helped generate studies about delegation and invisible programs since his analysis of bureaucratic autonomy directed attention to policy outcomes in addition to accounts of the processes of agency creation and development (and see his own subsequent work: Carpenter 2010, 2011). Carpenter's analysis also throws light on the evolutionary theory of state development articulated by Sven Steinmo (2010), since in the "forging of bureaucratic autonomy" Carpenter explicates, the development of American state capacity, was an "evolutionary outcome" (Carpenter 2001, 359) rather than a process of deliberate organizational design and reform. Steinmo finds internal coherence in the way in which, once institutionalized, certain values and ideas evolve to adapt to change. His analysis rests in a detailed reading of the origin of the US polity, and particularly of the distinct interaction between resource richness and egalitarian ideas at the nation's founding. Like others he stresses the fragmentation of institutions and the consequences of this fragmentation for political power. The draining of natural resources but especially the conclusion of land allocation shaped institutional design and policy makers: "the result has been to create a political system that divides public decisions so that elected officials can take maximum credit for the minimum amount of spending" (Steinmo 2010, 204).

That bureaucrats have engaged in policy planning and delivery is illustrated in Margot Canaday's (2009) historical study of how federal laws about homosexuality developed. Through historical analysis of policies and regulations from the Bureau of Immigration, the military and welfare benefits federal agencies, Canady demonstrates how federal state-building in this policy area developed gradually from the nineteenth century and received robust institutionalization during World War II and particularly in the McCarthy early Cold War years. While federal bureaucrats responded to sex and gender nonconformity at a "sluggish" pace until the 1930s, drawing on "regulatory devices aimed at broader problems" such as disorder or crime, from the 1940s state-building efforts became policy focused and much clearer about "what it sought to regular." Canaday explains that "after the Second World War, an increasingly powerful state wrote this new knowledge into federal policy, hoping to produce the category of homosexuality through regulation" (2009, 3). Its success made the straight state. The latter's framework included policies delineating who could explicitly immigrate and naturalize, eligibility for state benefits, and eligibility to enrol in the Armed Services. Canaday describes the legal and administrative procedures used to construct and imply these rules about citizenship rights as the "*bureaucratization* of homosexuality" (2009, 4, emphasis in original). The last decade and a half have seen fundamental reforms of these laws, even for institutions such as the Armed Services.

Canaday's account of federal bureaucrats' diligent categorizing and defining of homosexuality complements studies of the census as an arm of the American state categorizing members and citizens (Hattam 2009; Nobles 2000), a practice embedding racial hierarchy in the American state; and James Sparrow's (2011) broad stroke account of the American state's wartime construction of a consensus for government of the scale necessitated by nationwide mobilization. War mobilization, Sparrow observes in quasi-Gramscian terms, placed millions of Americans "in new contact with the federal government, whose ideological guarantees suddenly had concrete ramifications in their everyday lives" (2011, 113). Through the use of propaganda, peer pressure, volunteerism and deliberate regulatory activities the American state created a consensus about this scale of commitment and the intrusions into micro aspects of American life required by the state for the mobilization to be fit for purpose presented by the wartime challenge.

The consensus came at a price—for African Americans the war did not lead to much change in policy though with the planned March on Washington harbingers of the unsustainability of legalized segregationist racism were set out (Kryder 2000; Katznelson 2013). For veterans the implication of wartime propaganda and cushioning was that the state would not permit a return to the economic miseries of the 1930s when the conflict ended. For Sparrow the various "meanings of fiscal citizenship, war work, or military service" were shaped by Americans' new relationship to the national state (2011, 117). But these new relationships were shaped by the state's differential treatment of citizens by race, including the prevailing de jure segregationist framework.

The American State in Comparative Historical Institutionalism

One core characteristic of the American state and two resulting implications stand out as distinct and important points of reference for scholars of comparative historical institutionalism writing about state theory.

No other democratic state has a foundation and trajectory so rooted in racial inequality. The American state has variously fostered, defended, and implanted racial hierarchy at different historical points; alternatively at other times, the state has attacked discrimination, enforced standards of equal rights of citizenship, and attempted to remedy legacies of profound racial inequality. The American state continues to be both a forum in which the politics of racial inequality is integrated and contested about; and the dominant political institution in a polity seared through with racial inequality. No state in

Europe comes close to having this intimate relationship racial inequality. Settler states such as Canada or Australia confront continuing legacies of their mistreatment of indigenous peoples and operated whites only immigration regimes, which comes closest to the American state pattern. Neither Brazil nor South Africa—often linked in comparative studies with the US—present the same depth of racial inequality in a democratic regime developed in the American polity.

This primary feature of the American state has two consequences bearing on research about the role of states in comparative historical analysis.

First, because the American state's origins and evolution was deeply infected by racial inequality the struggles about its constitution's content and design centered on accommodating this inegalitarianism (Smith 1997). Slavery was in the Constitution ratified in 1787 and both the design of representation in the US Senate and the role of judicial activism stemmed from this unseemly accommodation. The settlement was inherently unstable, blowing up after *Dred Scott* in the Civil War (1861–65), then reconfigured until the 1960s and contemporaneously expressed in the legacies of racial inequality (Francis 2014; King and Smith 2011). The constricted and undemocratic institutional design enacted in 1787 set the trajectory for the contemporary American state, whose many institutions coalesce into a greater number of veto points than in any comparable democracy as Stepan and Linz (2011) document. As designed in the Constitution federalism is a purposeful impediment to change. The American state faces an entrenched difficulty to galvanize state and local cooperation with its initiatives, a point Margaret Weir (2005) underscores in respect to the New Deal era and which helps explains inadequate momentum on housing and school desegregation.

Second, a state permeated with racial inequality is exceptionally vulnerable to exogenous shocks and crises, though what is a crisis is sorely contested. Crises occur regularly and drive policy changes—or at least fulsome statements of intended reform by political leaders of the American state. Most of the literature on change in historical institutionalism concentrates on endogenous sources of reform—that is, how a policy initiative reinforces, often through policy feedback mechanisms, an existing institutional configuration because of path dependence (Pierson 2000) or policy feedback (Hacker 2002), or is layered onto existing institutional configurations. Even challenges on the scale of natural disasters fit, according to historian Michele Landis Dauber (2013, 12) with this largely linear model of change: "the history of disaster relief appropriations and the institutional structures, politics, narratives, legal briefs, and discourses surrounding them created ... a set of 'policy feedbacks' that exerted a continuing influence on the structure and shape of the eventual welfare state that emerged." In this sphere of quite dramatic and visible events stimulating American state responses and initiatives, Dauber maintains, a process of path dependence shaping the policy trajectory best characterizes what occurs. If accurate, Dauber's argument is testimony to the strength of the historical institutional framework.

Other crises seem to generate responses of a more fundamental kind. The deployment of troops to Little Rock in Arkansas in 1957 to force school integration was an exogenous shock to the placid if potentially explosive world of America's racial hierarchy.

This hierarchy could not be sustained especially as the American state's dithering with civil rights garnered global attention (Dudziak 2000). Little Rock closed its school for a year in response to the crisis but in Virginia's Prince Edward County school district officers opted to close the public schools for five years rather than desegregate, and made no provision at all for the harmed African American children (Bonastia 2012). These crises shook the system but did not merely produce institutional persistence or radical reform—rather a debilitating mixture of weakly enforced (or not enforced) national directives which dragged the segregation crisis into the next decade and eventually new laws, often in the wake of political violence including assassinations. Desegregation of schools proceeded for a decade with significant changes in the South but then stalled (Clotfelter 2004).

The deeper effect of this reluctant American state to shift from upholder and fosterer of segregation to agent of integration and desegregation was to affect a crisis. Even with the passage of civil and voting rights laws, urban disorder erupted and a national commission on public order famously conceded that the US had reached two societies. In this context change looks more substantial than merely institutional reconfiguration. Frances Fox Piven offers an explanation for such a scale of "big bang" changes which over ride institutional constraints: "if features of American political institutions inhibited policy development, those features were nevertheless at least partly overridden during the big bangs of social policy creation. And once initiated, new policies obviously change institutional arrangements. The big bang led to enormous growth in national government capacity as a result of the enlargement of its policy and spending authority." She concludes that, "none of this could easily have been predicted as a simple outgrowth of earlier policies" (Piven 2006, 91). Without the civil rights movement first but then specifically black insurgency the reforms of the 1960s would have been timid.

The emphasis here on the centrality of the politics of race for the American state and the implications of this pivotal place for how its institutions were designed and how hard it is achieve fundamental change are not intended to promote a version of American exceptionalism. Indeed, quite the contrary is intended. The American state, as most comparativists now understand, is distinct. But this distinctiveness—measurable for instance in the proliferation of veto points, development of agency specific autonomy absent the core Weberian centralized elite overseeing all executive departments, the capacity of federal levels to stymie reform, and the difficulty of executive-led change—and expressed fundamentally in the American state's embrace of the politics of racial inequality—mark it out as a key case in comparative studies offering major points of reference to researchers developing and testing arguments formulated about other democratic states with complex histories and enigmatic institutional arrangements (Rose 2005).

Note

* The author would like to express his gratitude to the editors of this handbook for very helpful comments on earlier versions of this chapter.

References

Adler, William and Andrew Polsky. 2010. "Building the New American Nation: Economic Development, Public Goods and the Early U.S. Army." *Political Science Quarterly* 125: 87–110.

Alexander, Michelle. 2010. *The New Jim Crow*. New York: Free Press.

Balogh, Brian. 2009. *A Government Out of Sight*. New York: Cambridge University Press.

Bartels, Larry. 2008. *Unequal Democracy*. Princeton, NJ: Princeton University Press.

Bonastia, Christopher. 2012. *Southern Stalemate: Five Years without Public Education in Prince Edward County, Virginia*. Chicago: University of Chicago Press.

Canaday, Margot. 2009. *The Straight State: Sexuality and Citizenship in Twentieth-Century America*. Princeton, NJ: Princeton University Press.

Carpenter, Daniel P. 2001. *The Forging of Bureaucratic Autonomy: Reputations, Networks, and Policy Innovation in Executive Agencies, 1862–1928*. Princeton, NJ: Princeton University Press.

Carpenter, Daniel P. 2005. "The Evolution of National Bureaucracy in the United States." In *The Executive Branch*, ed. Joel Aberbach and Mark Peterson. New York: Oxford University Press, 41–71.

Carpenter, Daniel. 2010. *Reputation and Power: Organizational Image and Pharmaceutical Regulation at the FDA*. Princeton, NJ: Princeton University Press.

Carpenter, Daniel. 2011. "Institutional Empowerment and Strangulation: Bureaucratic Politics and Financial Reform in the Obama Administration." In *Obama at the Crossroads*, ed. Lawrence Jacobs and Desmond King. New York: Oxford University Press, 62–83.

Charles, Camille Zubrinsky. 2003. "The Dynamics of Racial Residential Segregation." *Annual Review of Sociology* 29: 167–207.

Clotfelter, Charles T. 2004. *After Brown: The Rise and Retreat of School Desegregation*. Princeton, NJ: Princeton University Press.

Dauber, Michele Landis. 2013. *The Sympathetic State: Disaster Relief and the Origins of the American Welfare State*. Chicago: University of Chicago Press.

Dobbin, Frank. 2009. *Inventing Equal Opportunity*. Princeton, NJ: Princeton University Press.

Dobbin, Frank and John R. Sutton. 1998. "The Strength of a Weak State: The Employment Rights Revolution and the Rise of Human Resources Management Division." *American Journal of Sociology* 104: 441–476.

Dudziak, Mary L. 2000. *Civil Rights, Cold War*. Princeton, NJ: Princeton University Press.

Evans, Peter B, Dietrich Rueschemeyer, and Theda Skocpol, eds. 1985. *Bringing the State Back In*. New York: Cambridge University Press.

Farhang, Sean. 2010. *The Litigation State: Public Regulation and Private Lawsuits in the United States*. Princeton, NJ: Princeton University Press.

Fioretos, Orfeo, Tulia Falleti, and Adam Sheingate, eds. 2016. "Historical Institutionalism in Political Science." In this volume, 3–28.

Francis, Megan Ming. 2014. *Civil Rights and the Making of the Modern American State*. New York: Cambridge University Press.

Frymer, Paul. 2008a. "Law and American Political Development." *Law & Social Inquiry* 33: 779–803.

Frymer, Paul. 2008b. *Black and Blue: African Americans, the Labor Movement and the Decline of the Democratic State*. Princeton, NJ: Princeton University Press.

Galambos, Louis, ed. 1987. *The New American State: Bureaucracies and Policies Since World War II*. Baltimore, MD: Johns Hopkins University Press.

Gibson, Edward L. 2012. *Boundary Control: Subnational Authoritarianism in Federal Democracies*. New York: Cambridge University Press.

Gilens, Martin. 1999. *Why Americans Hate Welfare*. Princeton, NJ: Princeton University Press.

Gilens, Martin. 2012. *Affluence and Influence*. Princeton, NJ: Princeton University Press.

Goering, John M. 1986. *Housing Desegregation and Federal Policy*. Chapel Hill, NC: University of North Carolina Press.

Hacker, Jacob. 2002. *The Divided Welfare State*. Cambridge: Cambridge University Press.

Hansen, Randall and Desmond King. 2013. *Sterilized by the State: Eugenics, Race, and the Population Scare in Twentieth-Century North America*. New York: Cambridge University Press.

Hattam, Victoria. 2009. *In the Shadow of Race*. Chicago: University of Chicago Press.

Hooks, Gregory. 1990. "From an Autonomous to a Captured State Agency: The Decline of the New Deal in Agriculture." *American Sociological Review* 55: 29–43.

Howard, Christopher. 1997. *The Hidden Welfare State: Tax Expenditures and Social Policy in the United States*. Princeton, NJ: Princeton University Press.

Johnson, Kimberley S. 2007. *Governing the American State*. Princeton, NJ: Princeton University Press.

Jung, Moon-Kie and Yejoon Kwon. 2013. "Theorizing the US Racial State: Sociology Since Racial Formation." *Sociology Compass* 7: 927–940.

Kato, Daniel. 2012. "Strengthening the Weak State: Politicizing the American State's 'Weakness' on Racial Violence." *Du Bois Review* 9 (2): 457–480.

Katznelson, Ira. 2002. "Flexible Capacity: The Military and Early American Statebuilding." In *Shaped by War and Trade: International Influences on American Political Development*, ed. Ira Katznelson and Bruce Pietrykowski. Princeton, NJ: Princeton University Press, 58–71.

Katznelson, Ira. 2005. *When Affirmative Action Was White*. New York: Norton.

Katznelson, Ira. 2013. *Fear Itself: The New Deal and the Origins of Our Time*. New York: Norton.

Katznelson, Ira and Bruce Pietrykowski. 1991. "Rebuilding the American State: Evidence from the 1940s." *Studies in American Political Development* 5: 301–339.

Katznelson, Ira and Martin Shefter, eds. 2002. *Shaped by War and Trade: International Influences on American Political Development*. Princeton, NJ: Princeton University Press.

King, Desmond. 2007. *Separate and Unequal: African Americans and the US Federal Government*. New York: Oxford University Press.

King, Desmond. 2013. "The American State as an Agent of Race Equity: The Systemic Limits of Shock and Awe in Domestic Policy." In *Beyond Discrimination: Racial Inequality in a Post-Racial Era*, ed. Fredrick Harris and Robert C. Lieberman. New York: Russell Sage Foundation, 73–104.

King, Desmond. 2014. "America's Civil Rights State: Amelioration, Stagnation or Failure?" In *Developments in American Politics 7*, ed. Gillian Peele and B. Guy Peters. London: Palgrave, 263–283.

King, Desmond and Robert C. Lieberman. 2009. "Ironies of State Building: A Comparative Perspective on the American State." *World Politics* 61: 547–588.

King, Desmond and Rogers M. Smith. 2011. *Still a House Divided: Race and Politics in Obama's America*. Princeton, NJ: Princeton University Press.

Krasner, Stephen. 1978. *Defending the National Interest: Raw Materials Investment and U.S. Foreign Policy*. Stanford, CA: Stanford University Press.

Kryder, Daniel. 2000. *Divided Arsenal*. New York: Cambridge University Press.

Lieberman, Robert C. 1998. *Shifting the Color Line*. Cambridge, MA: Harvard University Press.

Light, Jennifer S. 2003. *From Warfare to Welfare: Defense Intellectuals and Urban Problems in Cold War America*. Baltimore, MD: Johns Hopkins University Press.

McCarty, Nolan, Keith T. Poole, and Howard Rosenthal. 2006. *Polarized America*. Cambridge, MA: MIT Press.

Mettler, Suzanne. 2011a. *The Submerged State*. Chicago: University of Chicago Press.

Mettler, Suzanne. 2011b. "Reconstituting the Submerged State: The Challenges of Social Policy Reform in the Obama Era." In *Obama at the Crossroads*, ed. Lawrence Jacobs and Desmond King. New York: Oxford University Press, 33–52.

Mickey, Robert. 2008. "The Beginning of the End for Authoritarian Rule in America: *Smith v. Allwright* and the Abolition of the White Primary in the Deep South, 1944–1948." *Studies in American Political Development* 22: 143–182.

Mickey, Robert. 2015. *Paths Out of Dixie: The Democratization of Authoritarian Enclaves in America's Deep South, 1944–1972*. Princeton: Princeton University Press.

Moore, Colin D. 2011. "State Building through Partnerships: Delegation, Public–Private Partnerships and the Political Development of American Imperialism, 1898–1916." *Studies in American Political Development* 25: 27–55.

Morgan, Kimberley and Andrea Campbell. 2011. *The Delegated Welfare State*. New York: Oxford University Press.

Nobles, Milessa. 2000. *Shades of Citizenship*. Stanford, CA: Stanford University Press.

Nordlinger, Eric A. 1981. *On the Autonomy of the Democratic State*. Cambridge, MA: Harvard University Press.

Novak, William. 2008. "The Myth of the Weak State." *American Historical Review* 113: 752–772.

Patler, Nicholas. 2004. *Jim Crow and the Wilson Administration: Protecting Segregation in the Early Twentieth Century*. Boulder, CO: University Press of Colorado.

Pierson, Paul. 2000. "Increasing Returns, Path Dependence, and the Study of Politics." *American Political Science Review* 94: 251–267.

Pierson, Paul. 2007. "The Rise and Reconfiguration of Activist Government." In *The Transformation of American Politics*, ed. Paul Pierson and Theda Skocpol. Princeton, NJ: Princeton University Press, 42–62.

Piven, Frances Fox. 2006. *Challenging Authority: How Ordinary People Change America*. Lanham: Rowman & Littlefield Publishers.

Poggi, Granfranco. 1978. *The Development of the Modern State*. Stanford, CA: Stanford University Press.

Posner, Eric A. and Adrian Vermeule. 2011. *The Executive Unbound: After the Madisonian Republic*. New York: Oxford University Press.

Rohr, John A. 1986. *To Run a Constitution: The Legitimacy of the Administrative State*. Lawrence, KS: University Press of Kansas.

Rose, Richard. 2005. "Giving Direction to Government in Comparative Perspectives." In *The Executive Branch*, ed. Joel Aberbach and Mark Peterson. New York: Oxford University Press, 93–112.

Rugh, Jacob S. and Douglas C Massey. 2013. "Segregation in Post-Civil Rights America: Stalled Segregation or End of the Segregated Century." *Du Bois Review* 11: 1–28.

Sharkey, Patrick. 2013. *Stuck in Place: Urban Neighborhoods and the End of Progress toward Racial Progress*. Chicago: University of Chicago Press.

Sheingate, Adam. 2009. "Why Can't Americans See the State?" *The Forum* 7: 4.

Skowronek, Stephen. 1982. *Building a New American State: The Expansion of National Administrative Capacities, 1877–1920*. Cambridge: Cambridge University Press.

Smith, Rogers M. 1997. *Civic Ideals*. New Haven, CT: Yale University Press.

Sparrow, James T. 2011. *Warfare State: World War II and the Age of Big Government*. New York: Oxford University Press.

Steinmo, Sven. 2010. *The Evolution of Modern States*. New York: Cambridge University Press.

Stepan, Alfred and Juan J. Linz. 2011. "Comparative Perspectives on Inequalities and the Quality of Democracy in the United States." *Perspectives on Politics* 9: 841–856.

Valelly, Richard M. 2004. *The Two Reconstructions*. Chicago: University of Chicago Press.

Weir, Margaret. 2005. "States, Race and the Decline of New Deal Liberalism." *Studies in American Political Development* 19: 157–172.

Weir, Margaret and Theda Skocpol. 1985. "State Structures and the Possibilities for 'Keynesian' Responses to the Great Depression in Sweden, Britain and the United States." In *Bringing the State Back In*, ed. Peter B. Evans, Dietrich Rueschemeyer, and Theda Skocpol. Cambridge: Cambridge University Press, 234–264.

Yellin, Eric S. 2013. *Racism in the Nation's Service*. Chapel Hill, NC: University of North Carolina Press.

CHAPTER 18

POLITICAL PARTIES IN AMERICAN POLITICS

DANIEL J. GALVIN*

SCHOLARS have long observed that the most pivotal turning points in American political development have involved significant changes in the political parties and what they do. Changes in party composition and operation have been linked to the rise and fall of partisan regimes, to the formation and preservation of durable policy coalitions, and to the changing terms of "organizational combat" that define American politics (Hacker and Pierson 2010). Surprisingly little effort, however, has been devoted to understanding the processes and mechanisms through which the parties, themselves, actually change.

One reason for this oversight involves the pervasive influence of functionalism in the study of American political parties. Functionalist premises appear in different guises: sometimes parties are understood to be reflections of actors' preferences (Aldrich 1995), socioeconomic conditions (Burnham 1970), or the structure of the political system (Lowi 1967). In each case, parties are presumed to change automatically or reflexively when their broader environment changes, with changes in their forms following changes in their functions. Eliding the complex organizational logic (and oftentimes laborious work) through which parties are actually reconfigured and redirected to new purposes over time, functionalist approaches obscure underlying processes of party change.

The historical institutional approach thus offers a particularly attractive alternative in this area of study. Refusing to accept that party development can be reduced to changes in actors' preferences or environmental conditions, it argues that what parties *do* is fundamentally shaped by what they *are*—specifically, how they are *structured*. It thus begins with an inquiry into the parties' component parts—their institutional arrangements, coalitional structures, and group alliances—and then examines the mechanisms and processes through which those arrangements change. Only then does it move to consider the relationship between those changes and observed shifts in the parties' functions. Inverting the functionalist paradigm in this way, the historical institutional approach treats party change as structurally delimited and historically constrained. It views party change as both an organizational *problem* and a political *process*—and both require explanation.

This chapter begins with a brief overview of functionalist perspectives in American parties scholarship and then discusses historical institutional alternatives for studying the two most common conceptualizations of parties: (1) parties as formal organizations and (2) parties as networks or "long coalitions" of groups. Finally, it considers how these alternative approaches can help to illuminate broader patterns of order and change in American political development.

Varieties of Functionalism in American Parties Scholarship

From the normative perspective that parties *should* serve particular democratic functions for the American polity (Wilson 1908; Merriam 1923; Schattschneider 1942; American Political Science Association 1950; Ranney 1954; Broder 1972) to the structural-functional view of parties as constitutive of, and *selected for*, the peculiarities of the American constitutional system (Banfield 1961; Lowi 1967; Epstein 1986), scholars have long evaluated parties with reference to the "roles" they are said to play in American politics. At issue is the perceived utility of political parties for the political system: Are they fulfilling their democratic, integrative, or constituent purposes? If not, why not?

Those older varieties of functionalism have lost much of their appeal in contemporary Political Science, but two more modern variants—what Pierson (2004) has termed "societal functionalism" and "actor-centered functionalism"—remain widely influential. These perspectives, though more empirically grounded and theoretically explicit than their predecessors, still treat parties as solutions to, or reflections of, the problems faced by society or by the actors who design them. The main challenge is to specify those problems and ascertain the parties' relationship to them. Both sidestep the question of whether the structural arrangements of the parties might, themselves, be integral to the processes through which they change.

Consider realignment theory, perhaps the most influential conceptual framework in the history of US parties scholarship (Burnham 1970; Clubb, Flanigan, and Zingale 1980; Sundquist 1983). The theory holds that growing tensions between socioeconomic changes, on one hand, and non-adaptive political institutions, on the other, serve as a driving force of American political development. When those tensions escalate to a breaking point, citizens express their discontent in "critical" elections that usher in durable new partisan alignments. Parties, in this framework, are not engines of change, but forces of inertia. They are constitutive of "normal" periods, in which "systematically patterned" political activities, institutional relationships, and policy structures have "obvious functional utility in fulfilling dominant system and elite needs," writes the best-known proponent of realignment theory (Burnham 1970, 185). Far from "action instrumentalities," parties are passive and serve as obstacles to change. Their routines are "disturbed not by adaptive change within the party-policy system, but by the application of overwhelming external force" (1970, 183).

This perspective offers a subtle variation of the societal-functionalist conceit that "a particular institution *X* exists because it constitutes an effective response to some kind of societal problem" (Pierson 2004, 105). If and when parties change, it is because their environment—the societal problem—has changed. The structural form of the party does not make much of an appearance—nor do the relationships between party organizations, interest groups, political activists, and elected officials. Whether those party structures, networks, and relationships might make a difference in how and when they change is left unexamined.

Whereas "societal functionalism" treats parties as reflections of broad social forces, the "actor-centered functionalism" that has risen to prominence in recent years treats parties as reflections or instantiations of actors' preferences (Schlesinger 1985, 1991; Aldrich 1995; Cox 1997). Consistent with traditional rational choice theory, this perspective conceptualizes parties as "endogenous institutions" that exist to solve the problems of the politicians who create them (Aldrich 1995, 19). The explanation for party change is thus relatively straightforward: when actors' problems change, so too will the parties' forms.

Actor-centered accounts are more attuned to the importance of the parties' institutional forms than societal-functional perspectives, but they still treat changes in those forms as far too easy. When actors find that existing party structures have become inadequate to address the new problems they are facing, they simply choose new institutional forms to replace the old ones. Which forms they pick are wholly contingent on actors' preferences: theoretically, all institutional possibilities are on the table, so long as they promise to solve the actors' new problems. The primary obstacle to change is therefore not institutional, but behavioral: it is the difficult task of mobilizing and aligning the interests of a diverse lot of ambitious actors in favor of party change (Aldrich 1995, 284–285). The new party forms that eventually emerge are presumed to reflect the preferences of the politicians who use them. This proposition, of course, is difficult—if not impossible—to refute, since politicians always seem to get what they want from their parties (at least, they always want what they can get from them).

The problem, therefore, is not what goes into the model, but what it leaves out: the institutional attributes of the parties. By making politicians' problems and preferences the main object of inquiry, the actor-centered functionalist account is unable to make all but the most basic observations about the how parties are structured or the processes through which they change.

Beyond Functionalism: Historical-Institutional Approach

Both societal and actor-centered functionalist accounts treat parties as highly susceptible to change when their environment changes. The implicit suggestion is that structural change in the parties is easy—either automatic or inevitable—and peripheral to the main action, which is external to the party itself. But what if the internal process of change in the parties is not so seamless or inconsequential? What if the parties' institutional attributes are, themselves, important factors in their own development?

If the institutional arrangements of the parties are, in fact, important omitted variables, then functionalist accounts may be systematically overestimating the power of societal forces and actors' preferences to produce party change. By assuming that exogenous variables are the primary catalysts for party change, they may also be failing to capture important endogenous changes in the parties that occur during "normal" periods, such as incremental and cumulative changes that might, over time, amount to major transformations in party form and function.

The process of party change, I wish to argue, needs to be explained, not assumed. This is where a historical institutional approach is uniquely well positioned to add value. By examining how parties are arranged and investigating the mechanisms through which their structures and operations change over time, it aims to identify internal processes of development and specify conditions under which different types of change may occur. It does not jettison the functionalists' motivating concerns about whether, when, and how parties perform (or do not perform) particular functions—it simply flips the analysis around, arguing that the best way to get an empirical handle on those questions is to begin with the parties' institutional attributes. As Frank Sorauf (1975) has written:

> A meaningful approach to political parties must be concerned with parties as organizations or structures performing activities, processes, roles, or functions... The logical intellectual and analytical point of reference is the party as a structure. Activity (or function) is certainly important, but *one must begin by knowing who or what is acting*. (38, italics added)

The historical institutional approach thus tends to emphasize internal processes of party change. While exogenous forces are expected to push for or inhibit party change, it is assumed that their effects will be mediated by the parties' internal attributes. But while we already know a great deal about the former, there is still much to learn about the latter. This is precisely the point made by comparativists Panebianco (1988) and Harmel and Janda (1994) in their agenda-setting work on the subject, as well as by comparative politics scholars including Koelble (1992), Kitschelt (1994), Murillo (2001), Grzymala-Busse (2002), Levitsky (2003), and Burgess (2004), and others, who have shown that pre-existing, inherited party arrangements interact with environmental pressures to narrow or widen the possibilities for party change.

The following two sections consider the two most prominent conceptualizations of parties in the US setting—(1) parties as formal organizations and (2) parties as "networks" or "long coalitions" of groups—and discuss how a historical institutional approach can provide new insights and open new lines of inquiry in both areas of research. In the first section, I discuss how the investments actors make in their formal parties' institutional *resources* can generate gradual, incremental change over long stretches of time, expanding the parties' organizational capacities and altering their institutional "functions." In the second section, I consider how modifications made to the *links* connecting groups, activists, and party organizations—that is, reconfigurations of the broader party network—can produce significant changes in party goals and activities. Both types of inquiries are shown to offer promising paths forward for historical institutional research.

Investments in Party Resources

The largest and most traditional area of scholarship on US parties treats the Democratic and Republican parties as formal, "quasi-public institutions" that are comprised of national, state, and local committees and other "official" party structures (Epstein 1986; Bibby and Shaffner 2008). One of the key findings of this literature is that both parties have become increasingly institutionalized and nationalized over the last hundred years or so, turning into primarily campaign-service vendors for party candidates. Through a gradual process of adaptation, adoption of new technologies, and development of new organizational capacities, the formal party organizations have undergone a dramatic transformation in their forms and functions (Cotter and Bibby 1980; Cotter et al. 1984; Kayden and Mahe 1985; Schlesinger 1985; Aldrich 1995; Shea 1999; Herrnson 2002; Galvin 2012).

One way to explain these changes is to emphasize environmental shifts and changed actor preferences. Actor-centered functionalist accounts, for example, posit that both parties were transformed from "mass parties" to "parties in service" to their candidates in and around the "critical era of the 1960s," when a series of "sweeping and fundamental" changes in public opinion and electoral behavior created new problems for ambitious politicians that existing party arrangements were ill-equipped to solve (Schlesinger 1985; Aldrich 1995; Aldrich and Niemi 1996). In an increasingly fractious, candidate-centered era, "mass" parties could no longer control campaigns or satisfy their candidates' needs. This "mismatch between form and problem" prompted party actors to dismantle old party forms and create new ones that better served their purposes—and "parties in service" were the result (Aldrich 1995, 286).

Closer consultation of the historical record, however, reveals that precisely the same forms and functions said to characterize the modern "party in service" began to emerge three decades earlier in the Republican Party (in the 1930s) and two decades later in the Democratic Party (in the 1980s) than the actor-centered punctuated-equilibrium model allows (Galvin 2012). Indeed, the 1960s did not represent a critical breakpoint in either party's institutional development.

This temporal discrepancy might be shrugged off as a mere historical oversight if it did not so clearly expose the main theoretical fault line between functionalist and historical institutional approaches. Consider how the issue is investigated. The actor-centered functionalist model begins with new observed party functions (e.g., services to candidates), and then works backward to attribute those new functions to observed changes in the environment (e.g., the tumultuous 1960s), which are presumed to have presented political actors with new problems they needed to solve. New party forms are thus said to have emerged *because* they solved those new problems, irrespective of whether they actually did, or whether they were created for those purposes in the first place.

The historical institutional approach, in contrast, begins with a close examination of party structures, examines how they change over time, and only then moves to consider the relationship between those changes and new party activities ("functions"). Moving from form to function enables the researcher to stay true to the historical record while allowing potentially new findings to turn up and new mechanisms of change to come to light.

In a recent study of structural change in the two national party committees, for example, I find that the parties' accumulation, renovation, and conversion of their institutional *resources*—meaning their money, information assets, technology, human resources, and the like—helps to explain how each evolved into a modern "service" party and why each made its transition on such different timetables (Galvin 2012). Resource investments had multiplying effects on party activities, opening the door to unexpected changes in what each party did and how it did it. For example, investments in human resources—in party personnel and their knowledge and skills—enhanced each party's adaptive capacities, enabling it to solve new problems, pursue new purposes, and engage in myriad activities. Likewise, investments in information assets—proprietary information like voter data, or any other intellectual resource of value—multiplied the range of political activities each party could undertake in the future.

Rather than "lock in" specific patterns of behavior or "remove certain options from the menu of political possibilities" as in path-dependent processes (Pierson 2004, 12), the development of party resources gradually *expanded* the menu of options facing party actors in the future. As new party actors inherited existing institutional resources, added to them, altered them, and deployed them in pursuit of new and oftentimes unexpected purposes, they contributed to a gradual process of party change. This process may be understood as a variant of what Kathleen Thelen has termed "institutional conversion," whereby old institutions remain in place but are directed to new purposes (2004, 36–37; see also Mahoney and Thelen 2010). The two national parties were not dismantled, but their primary functions were altered over time.

Aldrich (1995) is thus correct that the primary functions of formal party organizations in America changed dramatically over time. But *how* did those changes come about? And what does that tell us about the overarching theory of parties and party change? The historical institutional approach suggests these changes were not reflexive responses to new actor preferences or to changed environmental conditions: rather, the emergence of new "service" functions in both parties resulted from long, drawn-out processes of gradual institutional development involving the dynamic interplay of both structure and agency. The range of activities the parties could undertake and the extensiveness of the services they could provide—and the ways in which those capacities were exploited by ambitious actors—expanded only slowly as their institutional resources became increasingly operational, effective, and technologically sophisticated over time.

Thus, it is simply not possible to specify a date—or even a short span of years (e.g., Aldrich's "critical era" of the 1960s)—when the national committees can be said to have been functionally transformed. Not only did each party follow its own distinct timetable, but different candidate-service capacities emerged within each party at different times: some appeared immediately, some were more fully realized in the medium-term, and some developed over the "longue durée," as the utility of specific institutional resources spilled into new realms of activity and gradually expanded the range of the national committees' campaign service offerings.

Empirically, then, it makes little sense to begin the inquiry with a search for new party functions. Rather, one must begin with changes in specific party forms, and only then consider changes in party functions. Proceeding in that fashion enables the researcher to identify the discrete mechanisms of change at work. Of course, this approach need not only apply to the study of formal party structures. Other potentially fruitful areas of investigation might include the influence of institutional resource investments on (1) levels of grassroots activism; (2) party rules, nomination processes, and other decision-making activities; (3) coordination and collective action across party units; and (4) relationships between formal and informal party structures, including interest groups, nonprofits, and other party-like organizations.

Directing attention to endogenous mechanisms of change in the parties thus gives extra weight to the "internal" side of the story and helps to counterbalance studies that focus exclusively on "external" factors. But it also has a substantive payoff: it helps us to recognize forward-moving trajectories *as they happen* and develop a better understanding of where a party might be headed. The alternative requires us to wait for exogenous shocks to disrupt the status quo while we remain agnostic about the shape the new equilibrium will take.

Change in the Party Network

Parties, however, consist of more than just the Democratic and Republican national committees, state parties, and other formal party structures. As a growing body of scholarship has demonstrated, parties may also be fruitfully envisioned as informal "networks" or "long coalitions" of interest groups, activists, campaign professionals, non-profit organizations, social movement groups, media outlets, formal party organizations, and other various groups working toward common purposes (Bernstein and Dominguez 2003; Cohen et al. 2008; Koger, Masket, and Noel 2009; Masket 2009; Bawn et al. 2012). Most effort, thus far, has been put toward defining these networks and establishing their existence. Partly because of this careful work—and partly because recent changes in the campaign finance system have thrust party networks into the political spotlight—the value of this more expansive definition of party is no longer seriously questioned. Parties *are* usefully conceptualized as networks, and when viewed as such, they can illuminate a great deal about the workings of American politics.

A number of paths for future research have opened up along these lines, including deeper engagement with, and wider application of, social network analysis (Fowler et al. 2011; Heaney et al. 2012; Noel 2012b; Sinclair 2012). For historical institutional researchers, however, perhaps the most promising path forward involves comparative case studies of how different party networks—in different temporal or spatial settings—change over time, through what mechanisms, and with what downstream consequences for party activities, institutional arrangements, and political development.

As Peter Hall (2014) has suggested, studying how coalitions form, persist, and change over time can generate key insights into broader processes of institutional change. Indeed, to the extent that institutions are "creatures of coalitions," getting a better handle on the underlying coalitional dynamics of party networks should illuminate how American party politics is structured across time and place. Comparative-historical studies of party networks in the US—across states, for example, or over time—can thus bolster our understanding of party networks and their significance in American political development.

Research along these lines begins with the structural arrangements of party network. Which groups and actors are "in" the network, which are on the boundaries, and which are "outside"? How do groups move in and out of the network? How do they relate to one another? How should we conceptualize and identify the "ties" or "links" that bind them together?[1] Changes in the broader party network—in *what* it does, *how* it does it, *when* it changes, and *why*—should register in those connections, alliances, and other structural features. Studies of these ties are still in their infancy, and the data are notoriously difficult to get. Even the mechanisms of collaboration around candidate nominations are admittedly "hard to study and poorly documented" (Bawn et al. 2012, 572; see also Cohen et al. 2008). But we know enough, at present, to say with confidence that network ties at the activist, elite, and organizational levels do exist and are of central importance to what networks actually do.

Recent scholarship has documented several points of contact, overlap, and exchange among diverse groups, and begun to flesh out their effects. Heaney et al. (2012), for example, find that formal party organizations, policy-focused interest groups, and social movement organizations share robust, overlapping activist membership bases that are distinct for each party network. Those shared membership ties appear to help build solidarity and facilitate collaboration across the network while reinforcing partisan polarization. Likewise, Skinner, Masket, and Dulio (2012) show that there is a revolving door of sorts between parties, non-profit groups, and candidates' campaigns, as professional staff members regularly move between organizations. And as Koger, Masket, and Noel (2009, 2010) have demonstrated, parties, interest groups, and myriad non-profit and for-profit organizations regularly share valuable information assets across organizational boundaries, suggesting significant inter-group cooperation despite the sometimes very different goals pursued by each group.

Learning more about these ties is important because they lend the party network *organizational capacity*—they determine what it is able to do. For example, to the extent that "policy demanding" groups are able to coordinate their endorsements and collectively mobilize other sources of support, they can influence candidate selection and nomination processes and exert influence over policy outcomes (Masket 2007, 2009, 2011; Cohen et al. 2008; Dominguez and Grossman 2009). Indeed, some see coordination around nominations as the *sine qua non* of party activity (Bawn et al. 2012). *Changes* to those ties, therefore, should affect the party's capacity to carry out its essential activities.

Particularly illuminating extensions of this idea include Karol (2009), which shows that changes in group alliances and coalitional arrangements can prompt elected officials to adopt new issue positions, and Noel (2012a), which shows how the ideologies crafted by intellectuals can help to shape and reshape party coalitions. These studies strongly suggest that the configuration of groups in the network and the nature and extent of their coordination are major factors that shape what parties do, what purposes they pursue, and how they interact with other political institutions (also see Allern and Bale 2012).

Numerous questions emerge from these findings. Perhaps most importantly, how does coordination and collaboration actually occur within party networks? How institutionalized or routinized are the links between network participants? How susceptible are those links to change? How do groups enter and exit the network? What effects do changes in the composition of the network have on the politicization of existing groups' identities, the creation of new politically relevant groups, or on the party's aggregate organizational capacities and the goals it pursues? How is collective responsibility fostered among diverse groups? These questions suggest only a few of the many research opportunities for historical institutional scholarship in this area. They also suggest a research strategy: begin with the configuration of a given party network, examine its mechanisms of change, then seek to explain the variation in effects observed over time and across cases.

Consider, for example, inquiries into the relative *resilience* of party networks. What factors influence the party's capacity to adapt to environmental change? What kinds of network ties make a difference, and how? Numerous comparative studies have found, for example, that industrial labor unions tend to act as a "drag" on party adaptation efforts in the context of globalization and deindustrialization. The more central industrial labor unions are to the broader party network—the more power union officials wield over party nominations and policy positions—the more likely the party is to suffer electoral decline. Kitschelt (1994) finds confirmation of this dynamic in his extensive study of left-of-center parties in Europe, where adaptation was more difficult for parties dominated by labor unions. The same logic is also on display in Levitsky's (2003) study of the Argentine PJ party, in which party adaptation was easier in no small part because labor unions were only loosely integrated in the party. Swapping out labor organizations for new clientelist mechanisms at the local level, the party was able to maintain its mass base while freeing itself to shift dramatically to the right.

Although one might expect a different pattern to adhere in the US two-party system, the same kinds of assumptions animate the ongoing debate over the relationship between organized labor and the Democratic Party. Centrist "third way" Democrats have long attributed the party's electoral challenges since the late 1970s to the outsized influence of organized labor in the party (Galston and Kamarck 1989; Baer 2000; From 2013). Those on the other side tend to lament labor's *diminished* influence within the Democratic Party and argue that its decline has contributed to the party's rightward drift, abandonment of core values, and loss of enthusiasm at the grassroots (Meyerson 1986; Kuttner 1987; Dreyfuss 2000; Francia 2006). Both sides thus agree that a negative relationship exists between the party's ties to organized labor and its adaptive capacities: they differ only in how much of the former they are willing to trade for the latter.

Theory-building is a collective enterprise. One study at a time, historical institutional scholars can begin to flesh out the differential effects produced by:

(1) links of different *kinds* (e.g., financial ties vs. personnel overlap vs. separate organizations engaged in joint operations);
(2) links of different *strength* (e.g., deeply rooted cultural ties between groups vs. short-term policy-specific alliances vs. more contentious relationships; different degrees of institutionalization, routinization, and susceptibility to change)
(3) different *types of groups* in a network (e.g., labor unions vs. issue advocacy groups vs. social movement groups; and differences within group-type—e.g., UAW vs. SEIU vs. public sector unions).

By examining the variation along each of these dimensions—and by developing stronger and more dynamic theories of how network links are formed, reinforced, and fragmented over time—one can develop a deeper appreciation for how party networks operate internally, as well as how they impinge upon their broader environment. Clarifying how these processes unfold over time promises shed light on the underlying dynamics of American political development.

Conclusion: Parties in American Political Development

Whether parties are conceptualized as formal organizations or networks, studying them from a historical institutional perspective directs attention to the mechanisms and processes through which they change over time. It also promises to elucidate the relationship between *party* change and *political* change more broadly.

Several key organizing principles in the study of American political development, for example, imply the existence—and central political significance—of parties as networks of groups. These conceptual frameworks are particularly amenable to further historical institutional study. Consider the concept of *partisan regimes* (Skowronek 1993; Plotke 1996; Polsky 2012). According to Andrew Polsky, political coalitions drive the formation of partisan regimes and are responsible for their subsequent maintenance and breakdown over time. Treating those coalitions as party networks structured by various links and mechanisms of coordination would tackle the question of regime formation and dissolution from a theoretically fresh and rigorously empirical angle.

The related concept of *policy regimes* can be approached in a like manner. As Patashnik (2008) has shown, without the support and buy-in of broad coalitions of interest groups, party actors, and activists, major policy reforms tend to be more susceptible to dismantlement or drift. How those coalitions are constructed, reinforced, and weakened over time thus emerges as a pressing question (see also Hall 2014). Hacker and Pierson (2010, 2012) have gone so far as to depict such "durable policy coalitions" as the key players in the main drama of American politics, which they term "politics of organized combat." Examining the mechanisms of change in those networks over long stretches of time can thus illuminate critical shifts in American politics, including the rise and fall of policy regimes, the restructuring of the American economy, and the dramatic rise of income inequality since the 1970s.

Party networks and policy coalitions also figure prominently in studies of how leaders and entrepreneurs seek to alter their structural confines and reshape the political landscape. Presidents, congressional leaders, and other political actors who seek to reinforce, exploit, or undermine partisan regimes, for example, often target existing party networks for strategic reconfiguration (Ginsberg and Shefter 1988; Skowronek 1993; Sheingate 2003; Karol 2009; Galvin 2010; DiSalvo 2012; Krimmel 2013). Paying more attention to the structure and process of change in those networks thus promises to illuminate both the causes and effects of entrepreneurial innovation in politics.

Party organizations and party networks, in sum, are constitutive of American political development. They are integral to partisan regime cycles, coalition-formation processes, policy regimes, and major structural arrangements in American politics. They are, in short, inseparable from "durable shifts in governing authority" (Orren and Skowronek 2004). Examining what makes them more or less resilient and capable of operating forcefully on the broader political environment thus offers an exciting path forward for historical institutional scholarship in this area.

Notes

* The author wishes to thank Adam Sheingate and participants at the Political Parties Working Group at Northwestern University for helpful comments.

1. These links are also called "ties," "lines," or "edges" in social network analysis terminology. See Noel (2012b).

References

Aldrich, John. 1995. *Why Parties? The Origin and Transformation of Political Parties in America*. Chicago: University of Chicago Press.

Aldrich, John H. and Richard G. Niemi. 1996. "The Sixth American Party System: Electoral Change, 1952–1992." In *Broken Contract? Changing Relationships between Americans and Their Government*, ed. Stephen C. Craig. Boulder, CO: Westview Press, 87–109.

Allern, E. H. and T. Bale. 2012. "Political Parties and Interest Groups: Disentangling Complex Relationships." *Party Politics* 18 (1):7–25.

American Political Science Association, A Report of the Committee on Political Parties. 1950. "Toward a More Responsible Two-Party System." *American Political Science Review* 44 (3): 1–100, Part 2, Supplement.

Baer, Kenneth S. 2000. *Reinventing Democrats*. Lawrence, KS: University Press of Kansas.

Banfield, Edward C. 1961. "In Defense of the American Party System." In *Political Parties U.S.A.*, ed. Robert A. Godwin. Chicago: Rand McNally, 21–39.

Bawn, Kathleen, Martin Cohen, David Karol, Seth Masket, Hans Noel, and John Zaller. 2012. "A Theory of Political Parties: Groups, Policy Demands and Nominations in American Politics." *Perspectives on Politics* 10 (3): 571–597.

Bernstein, Jonathan J. and Casey B. K. Dominguez. 2003. "Candidates and Candidacies in the Expanded Party." *PS: Political Science & Politics* 36 (2):165–169.

Bibby, John F. and Brian F. Shaffner. 2008. *Politics, Parties, and Elections in America*. 6th Edition. Boston, MA: Thomson/Wadsworth.

Broder, David. 1972. *The Party's Over*. New York: Harper & Row.

Burgess, Katrina. 2004. *Parties and Unions in the New Global Economy*. Pittsburgh, PA: University of Pittsburgh Press.

Burnham, Walter Dean. 1970. *Critical Elections and the Mainsprings of American Politics*. New York: W.W. Norton & Co.

Clubb, Jerome M., William H. Flanigan, and Nancy H. Zingale. 1980. *Partisan Realignment: Voters, Parties and Government in American History, Sage Library of Social Research*. Beverly Hills, CA: Sage Publications.

Cohen, Marty, David Karol, Hans Noel, and John Zaller. 2008. *The Party Decides: Presidential Nominations Before and After Reform*. Chicago: University of Chicago Press.

Cotter, Cornelius P., James L. Gibson, John F. Bibby, and Robert J. Huckshorn. 1984. *Party Organizations in American Politics*. New York: Praeger.

Cotter, Cornelius and John F. Bibby. 1980. "Institutional Development of Parties and the Thesis of Party Decline." *Political Science Quarterly* 95 (1): 1–27.

Cox, Gary W. 1997. *Making Votes Count: Strategic Coordination in the World's Electoral Systems*. New York: Cambridge University Press.

DiSalvo, Daniel. 2012. *Engines of Change: Party Factions in American Politics, 1868–2010, Oxford Studies in Postwar American Political Development*. New York: Oxford University Press.

Dominguez, Casey B. K. and Matt Grossman. 2009. "Party Coalitions and Interest Group Networks." *American Politics Research* 37 (5): 767–800.

Dreyfuss, Robert. 2000. "Rousing the Democratic Base." *The American Prospect*, November 6, 20–23.

Epstein, Leon D. 1986. *Political parties in the American mold*. Madison, WI: University of Wisconsin Press.

Fowler, James, Michael Heaney, David Nickerson, John Padgett, and Betsy Sinclair. 2011. "Causality in Political Networks." *American Politics Research* 39 (2): 437–480.

Francia, Peter L. 2006. *The Future of Organized Labor in American Politics*. New York: Columbia University Press.

From, Al. 2013. *The New Democrats and the Return to Power*. New York: Palgrave Macmillan.

Galston, William A. and Elaine C. Kamarck. 1989. *The Politics of Evasion: Democrats and the Presidency*. Washington D.C.: Progressive Policy Institute.

Galvin, Daniel J. 2010. *Presidential Party Building: Dwight D. Eisenhower to George W. Bush*. Princeton, NJ: Princeton University Press.

Galvin, Daniel J. 2012. "The Transformation of Political Institutions: Investments in Institutional Resources and Gradual Change in the National Party Committees." *Studies in American Political Development* 26 (1): 50–70.

Ginsberg, Benjamin and Martin Shefter. 1988. "The Presidency and the Organization of Interests." In *The Presidency and the Political System*, ed. Michael Nelson. Washington, D.C.: Congressional Quarterly Press, 311–330.

Grzymala-Busse, Anna Maria. 2002. *Redeeming the Communist Past: The Regeneration of Communist Parties in East Central Europe*. Cambridge: Cambridge University Press.

Hacker, Jacob S. and Paul Pierson. 2010. *Winner-Take-All Politics: How Washington Made the Rich Richer and Turned Its Back on the Middle Class*. 1st Simon & Schuster Hardcover Edition. New York: Simon & Schuster.

Hacker, Jacob S. and Paul Pierson. 2012. "Presidents and the Political Economy: The Coalitional Foundations of Presidential Power." *Presidential Studies Quarterly* 42 (1): 101–131.

Hall, Peter A. 2016. "Politics as a Process Structured in Space and Time." In *Oxford Handbook of Historical Institutionalism*, ed. Orfeo Fioretos, Tulia Falleti, and Adam Sheingate. New York: Oxford University Press, 31–50.

Harmel, Robert and Kenneth Janda. 1994. "An Integrated Theory of Party Goals and Party Change." *Journal of Theoretical Politics* 6 (3): 259–287.

Heaney, Michael, Seth E. Masket, Joanne M. Miller, and Dara Z. Strolovitch. 2012. "Polarized Networks: The Organizational Affiliations of National Party Convention Delegates." *American Behavioral Scientist* 56 (12): 23.

Herrnson, Paul S. 2002. "National Party Organizations at the Dawn of the Twenty-First Century." In *The Parties Respond: Changes in the American Parties and Campaigns*, ed. L. Sandy Maisel. Boulder, CO: Westview, 47–78.

Karol, David. 2009. *Party Position Change in American Politics: Coalition Management*. Cambridge: Cambridge University Press.

Kayden, Xandra and Eddie Mahe. 1985. *The Party Goes On: the Persistence of the Two-Party System in the United States*. New York: Basic Books.

Kitschelt, Herbert. 1994. *The Transformation of European Social Democracy, Cambridge Studies in Comparative Politics*. Cambridge and New York: Cambridge University Press.

Koelble, T. A. 1992. "Recasting Social-Democracy in Europe: A Nested Games Explanation of Strategic Adjustment in Political-Parties." *Politics & Society* 20 (1): 51–70.

Koger, Gregory, Seth Masket, and Hans Noel. 2009. "Partisan Webs: Information Exchange and Party Networks." *British Journal of Political Science* 39: 633–653.

Koger, Gregory, Seth Masket, and Hans Noel. 2010. "Cooperative Party Factions in American Politics." *American Politics Research* 38 (1): 33–53.

Krimmel, Katherine. 2013. "Special Interest Partisanship: The Transformation of American Political Parties." Unpublished Ph.D. Dissertation, Columbia University Department of Political Science.

Kuttner, Robert. 1987. *The Life of the Party: Democratic Prospects in 1988 and Beyond*. New York: Viking.

Levitsky, Steven. 2003. *Transforming Labor-Based Parties in Latin America: Argentine Peronism in Comparative Perspective*. Cambridge and New York: Cambridge University Press.

Lowi, Theodore J. 1967. "Party, Policy, and Constitution in America." In *The American Party Systems: Stages of Political Development*, ed. Walter Dean Burnham and William Nisbet Chambers. New York: Oxford University Press, xi, 321.

Mahoney, James and Kathleen Thelen. 2010. "A Theory of Gradual Institutional Change." In *Explaining Institutional Change: Ambiguity, Agency, and Power in Historical Institutionalism*, ed. James Mahoney and Kathleen Thelen. Cambridge: Cambridge University Press, 1–37.

Masket, Seth E. 2007. "It Takes an Outsider: Extralegislative Organization and Partisanship in the California Assembly, 1849–2006." *American Journal of Political Science* 51 (3): 482–497.

Masket, Seth E. 2009. *No Middle Ground: How Informal Party Organizations Control Nominations and Polarize Legislatures*. Ann Arbor: University of Michigan Press.

Masket, Seth E. 2011. "The Circus that Wasn't: The Republican Party's Quest for Order in California's 2003 Gubernatorial Recall Election." *State Politics & Policy Quarterly* 11 (2): 123–147.

Merriam, Charles E. 1923. *The American Party System*. New York: Macmillan.

Meyerson, Harold. 1986. "Why the Democrats Need Labor." *The Nation*, February 22, 193–210.

Murillo, Maria Victoria. 2001. *Labor Unions, Partisan Coalitions and Market Reforms in Latin America, Cambridge Studies in Comparative Politics*. Cambridge and New York: Cambridge University Press.

Noel, Hans. 2012a. "The Coalition Merchants: The Ideological Roots of the Civil Rights Realignment." *Journal of Politics* 74 (1): 156–173.

Noel, Hans. 2012b. "Towards a Networks Theory of Political Parties: A Social Networks Analysis of Internal Party Cleavages in Presidential Nominations, 1972–2008." Paper Read at American Political Parties: Past, Present, and Future, October 8–9, 2012, at Charlottesville, VA.

Orren, Karenand Stephen Skowronek. 2004. *The Search for American Political Development*. New York: Cambridge University Press.

Panebianco, Angelo. 1988. *Political Parties: Organization and Power, Cambridge Studies in Modern Political Economies*. Cambridge: Cambridge University Press.

Patashnik, Eric M. 2008. *Reforms at Risk, Princeton Studies in American Politics*. Princeton, NJ: Princeton University Press.

Pierson, Paul. 2004. *Politics in Time: History, Institutions, and Social Analysis*. Princeton, NJ: Princeton University Press.

Plotke, David. 1996. *Building a Democratic Political Order: Reshaping American Liberalism in the 1930s and 1940s*. Cambridge and New York: Cambridge University Press.

Polsky, Andrew J. 2012. "Partisan Regimes in American Politics." *Polity* 44 (1): 30.

Ranney, Austin. 1954. *The Doctrine of Responsible Party Government: Its Origins and Present State*. Urbana: University of Illinois Press.

Schattschneider, E. E. 1942. *Party Government*. New York: Rinehart and Winston.

Schlesinger, Joseph A. 1985. "The New American Political Party." *American Political Science Review* 79 (4): 1152–1169.

Schlesinger, Joseph A. 1991. *Political Parties and the Winning of Office*. Ann Arbor: University of Michigan Press.

Shea, Daniel M. 1999. "The Passing of Realignment and the Advent of the 'Base-less' Party System." *American Politics Quarterly* 27 (1): 33–57.

Sheingate, Adam D. 2003. "Political Entrepreneurship, Institutional Change, and American Political Development." *Studies in American Political Development* 17 (2): 185–203.

Sinclair, Betsy. 2012. *The Social Citizen: Peer Networks and Political Behavior, Chicago Studies in American Politics*. Chicago and London: The University of Chicago Press.

Skinner, Richard M., Seth E. Masket, and David A. Dulio. 2012. "527 Committees and the Political Party Network." *American Politics Research* 40 (1): 60–84.

Skowronek, Stephen. 1993. *The Politics Presidents Make: Leadership from John Adams to George Bush*. Cambridge, MA: Harvard University Press.

Sorauf, Frank J. 1975. "Political Parties and Political Analysis." In *The American Party Systems: Stages of Political Development*, ed. William Nisbet Chambers and Walter Dean Burnham. New York: Oxford University Press, 33–55.

Sundquist, James L. 1983. *Dynamics of the Party System*. Washington, D.C.: The Brookings Institution.

Thelen, Kathleen. 2004. *How Institutions Evolve: the Political Economy of Skills in Germany, Britain, the United States, and Japan*. New York: Cambridge University Press.

Wilson, Woodrow. 1908. *Constitutional Government in the United States*. 1961. New York: The Columbia University Press.

CHAPTER 19

LAW AND COURTS

SARAH STASZAK*

With a few exceptions, courts have received relatively little attention from comparative historical institutionalist (HI) scholars interested in processes of state formation and the development of the welfare state. Early works employing HI approaches to the study of the United States paid attention to courts, but often considered the judicial branch an obstacle to further state development, notably as courts fought elected officials over the establishment of economic regulating institutions (see, e.g., Orren 1992; Skocpol 1995; Skowronek 1982). The passage and implementation of civil rights measures in the 1950s and 1960s, however, thrust courts to the center of modern American political development. When the Supreme Court handed down its landmark 1954 decision in *Brown v. Board of Education* it asserted itself as a promoter of state activism, working hand in hand with elected officials (and even going much further) to enforce and implement the political and legal developments of the rights revolution.

The "rights revolution"—an era defined by a series of foundational courtroom victories for activists of civil rights and liberties in the mid-twentieth century—transformed both the American political landscape and the role that law and courts played in American state-building. Judges gained and asserted a range of new powers that they used to expand rights, and they also became active administrators, implementing public policy and managing government institutions in areas as diverse as environmental protection, welfare administration, and prison reform. Congress created judicial administrative bodies empowered to revise legal rules and procedures in order to manage the flood of litigants at the courthouse door. As demand for legal redress grew, the supply of lawyers, mediators, and administrative law judges grew exponentially as well, as the federal government increasingly funded and supported legal services. The result—a vastly broadened and empowered institutional judiciary—has led many scholars to argue that the judiciary is now a centerpiece of the modern American state, essential for resolving issues of politics and policy when the elected branches fail to address them (Epp 2010; Farhang 2010; Feeley and Rubin 1998; Frymer 2008b; Melnick 1994; Silverstein 2009; Skrentny 2006).

The rights revolution also had a major impact on public law scholarship, as scholars confronted the pervasive notion that courts primarily served as a roadblock (or at best, an appendage) to state development, shifting academic debates to the legacies of the civil rights era where the judicial branch fully took form as a protectorate of rights. With profound institutional and political barriers written into our Constitution that motivated political actors (ranging from private citizens to Congress) to turn to courts to address an array of political, social, and policy issues, it became necessary that individuals and social movements embrace the legal realm once a broader sense of "rights consciousness" manifested itself. Transforming a cause into a legal one went a long way in unifying disparate groups and creating social movements, and the value of having a court (as opposed to the legislature) act in one's favor came with an increased and enduring sense of legitimacy (McCann 1994). Coupled with a growing support structure (Epp 1998) that rapidly expanded who could access the courts (and for what), the legal strategy for enforcing policy quickly developed a cross-party appeal as lawyers, rights organizations, judges, and judicially-appointed administrators took the lead in enforcing political matters ranging from civil rights and liberties to massive bureaucratic reformation. With the effect of entrenching a system of "adversarial legalism" (Kagan 2003) where "law and politics cannot be disentangled in the United States" (Silverstein 2009), it is no surprise that this historic moment would come to define the work of those who study public law in American politics.

In response to this "juridification" of American politics (Silverstein 2009), legal scholars have employed many of the core contributions of HI in their analyses, primarily by engaging with the field of American Political Development (APD) and creating what has been called a "Law and APD" approach to studying law (Brandwein 2006; Kahn and Kersch 2006.) These scholars highlight the role of courts and judges as active participants in American state-building and argue that political outcomes can only be understood within a broad historical and institutional context, as at any point in time the political landscape is built of multiple institutions, created at different historical moments, acting according to their own institutional rhythms and mandates (Orren and Skowronek 2004; Pierson 2004; Skowronek 1982). Judicial authority is both meaningfully independent and continuously shaped by interactions with other institutions. For example, given that the judicial branch arguably lacks a clear constitutional grant of independent authority to intervene in policy, those who study law in the field of Political Science are mindful that studies of court behavior must include the role that elected officials play in enabling or constraining judicial activism (Rosenberg 1991; Whittington 2000).

As such, the study of law and APD has both benefited from historical institutional concepts like path dependence and intercurrence and continues to push HI scholars to confront the independent institutional authority of courts. But as the field moves forward, law and APD scholars should look to expand further their conception of courts as multi-faceted institutions. A "regime politics" approach to understanding law and courts has dominated, emphasizing the ways in which courts are enabled and empowered by dominant political coalitions driven by their own strategic imperatives (Gillman

2002; Graber 1993; Tushnet 2006; Whittington 2007). But as a growing group of scholars that study judicial development and reform have increasingly demonstrated, the regime politics approach does not account for or fully explain the range of institutional change (and stasis) observed in the judiciary over time. Because of a focus on Supreme Court decision-making and negotiations with the political branches, law and APD scholars sometimes overlook the range of rules, procedures, incentives, and actors that constitute the judiciary as an *institution*, consisting of more than judges and courts. While it is undoubtedly true that political parties seek to entrench and enable their ideological and policy interests through judicial appointments, for example, the explanatory power of this scholarship is limited by overlooking the institutional features and dynamics of the judicial branch that are often the sites of change, as well as the ways in which the judiciary is an autonomous institution, operating more broadly in the American political process with its own incentives.

Related, this tendency to focus on grand acts of politics (whether from the Supreme Court or Congress) limits the types of institutional change that are addressed in the literature (Engel 2011; Lovell 2003). This is further complicated by the propensity to view change in the judiciary as primarily the product of partisan politics (as with the current conservative legal movement, for example), and by the field's focus on institutional development. The APD canon emphasizes important dynamics of institutional change; but "change" typically tends toward a narrative of more "state" and more institutional development, "thickening," and entrenchment, not less. By extension, APD scholars view the potential for changes in judicial authority in a similar way; once legal reforms are enacted, they create interests and institutions that become entrenched, making significant change unlikely. These insights are heavily influenced by historical institutionalism and are indispensable to the study of state development over time, but they also obscure the ways in which politics can promote genuine reversals (of institutional authority and policy) and the political and institutional variables that affect retrenchment and reform. As such, historical institutionalism has had much to offer the study of law and courts when it comes to the development of the "legal state;" but now more than four decades into a sustained conservative backlash against the developments of the rights revolution, law and APD scholars have struggled to integrate the anti-litigation agenda in a narrative of institutional change.

However, institutional change scholars in dialogue with APD have begun to employ a more robust historical institutional perspective when studying law and courts. Whether by focusing on the role that legal actors play in the processes of policy implementation and reform, the ways in which private litigation is used in lieu of traditional bureaucratic enforcement, or utilizing the concept of intercurrence to develop a more nuanced sense of the relevant parties to legal change, at their core, these efforts have involved conceiving of the judiciary as an institution that has developed its own institutional incentives over time; recognizing that the judicial branch is an autonomous institution in American politics, not simply an agent of the elected branches; and integrating the possibility of genuine reform into theories of legal development and change. I proceed in the sections that follow by tracing these scholarly developments—as well as their core achievements and limitations—through a consideration of the literature on law and APD, the role that the judiciary plays in the American state, and theories of judicial institutional change. I conclude with an examination of the impact of this literature and raise possibilities for future work.

Law and American Political Development

In the immediate aftermath of the Supreme Court's landmark civil rights decisions, the legal academy initially seemed little concerned with the politics of the implementation process, tending to focus on doctrinal developments even as the Court increasingly met with a firestorm of political and cultural opposition. This focus shifted dramatically when Gerald Rosenberg (1991) provocatively called the *Brown* decision, and the Warren Court era more broadly, a "hollow hope" that had provided negligible benefits for civil rights reform. Rosenberg argued that when courts act without the support of another branch of government (as the Supreme Court seemingly did in *Brown*) their lack of a constitutional mandate to implement policy changes on the ground would lead to institutional over-reaching and failure, a claim that was consistent with the view that courts struggle with effectiveness when acting outside the preferences of the nation's elected branches (see, e.g., Dahl 1957). But Rosenberg himself acknowledged that courts could be meaningfully important under certain conditions, and subsequent scholarship examined the conditions and mechanisms by which courts can act authoritatively in the policy arena.

Influenced by these critical questions regarding the capacity of courts to affect politics and policy, the partisan/regime politics approach to studying judicial power provided an HI account of why elected officials often find it in their best interest to grant policymaking authority to the judiciary. Law and APD scholars have examined how party leaders seek to entrench their policy agendas through court appointments (Gillman 2002); how courts are encouraged to be active (particularly through judicial review) when a dominant political party wishes to avoid a political issue that might upset their coalition (Graber 1993); how the Supreme Court is most powerful when elites across government share a commitment to policymaking (Tushnet 2006); and how judicial authority—even judicial supremacy—is a product of our democratic system, where historically situated presidents have found it expedient to legitimate and even expand judicial power for their own interests (Whittington 2007). Subsequently, an even wider group of scholars ascribing to this approach have extended this analysis outward to include U.S./foreign affairs and judicial activism in specific policy areas (Lovell 2003; McMahon 2004; Novkov 2008; Silverstein 2009).

The regime politics approach has been highly successful in its pursuits, and it provides for an HI model that importantly supplements judicial politics models premised on strategic decision-making. But as a smaller group of scholars who study judicial institutional development and reform have begun to argue, this approach does not fully explain the range of institutional change observed in the judiciary over time or the independent force that judicial activism can play in American state-building. While political parties have undoubtedly sought to entrench and enable their ideological positions and policy interests (through court appointments and by legitimating broad "warrants" for judicial activity and power, respectively), such enhancements of authority have often stemmed from cross-party coalitions as well. Robert Kagan (2003), for example, has written extensively about the cross-party appeal of "adversarial legalism," ascribing the phenomenon to cultural and structural features of American democracy. In terms of the development of judicial authority and access to courts in specific policy areas, Sean Farhang (2010) has argued that, due to their intense suspicion of bureaucracy, the Republican Party established a system of private litigation to handle the problem of job discrimination around the time of the 1964 Civil Rights Act, despite the fact that such a system would ultimately be effective in promoting causes near and dear to the Democratic Party.

Thus, although the regime politics approach importantly situates courts within a historical institutional context, law and APD scholars could go further in examining the ways that institutional dynamics incentivize behaviors that defy party combat. In contrast to HI scholars who study the legislative branch, administrative agencies, and political parties (which stress the importance of rules, practices, and procedures) many law and APD scholars have limited their institutional analysis to the justices of the Supreme Court. But as an institution, the judiciary is far more complex, including lawyers, judicial policymaking bodies, administrators, mediators, professional associations, public interest law firms, private groups that support litigation, and a vast, fluctuating array of interest groups. These actors directly influence judicial activities that bear on state authority and the implementation of national policies; perhaps most importantly, they shape rules and procedures critical to courtroom access. Lawyers and other judicial actors influence major fluctuations in institutional incentives for bringing certain types of cases (e.g., constrictions on attorneys' fees, class action reform, and caps on punitive damages), and can enhance or detract from the legitimacy of judicial activity. If we ignore the role of interest groups in legal change, we miss the ways in which legal reform can be made through "stealth" insider strategies that skirt the courtroom entirely (Epp 1999; Haltom and McCann 2004). Leaving government bodies like the Judicial Conference (the primary policy-setting body for the US courts) out of the analysis leads us to forget entire sites of judicial reform, and therefore entire forums where a vast array of groups lobby for judicial change (Crowe 2007; Staszak 2010). Losing sight of the ways in which the growth of *other* political institutions (most prominently the administrative state) can cause a shift in venue for where legal determinations are made (from the traditional courtroom to the quasi-judicial realm of administrative adjudication) significantly detracts from our analyses of access to courts and due process, as does ignoring the range of private foundations and donors that fueled, professionalized, and sustained "alternative dispute resolution" in the US. In short, a focus on partisan politics and judges—and usually Supreme Court justices, at that—misses much of the action in legal politics. A more robust conception of the judiciary as an institution, then, is essential for a true historical institutional treatment of law and courts.

The Judiciary and the American State

With an expanding sense of judicial authority has come a new scholarly interest in the private enforcement of public policy through litigation (as opposed to classic bureaucratic enforcement), with an eye toward how this private enforcement contributes to our understanding of public power. This interest in private enforcement is just one piece—albeit a crucial one—of two broader stories that have developed in the HI literature on the judiciary, the first regarding the changing role of law and the legal establishment over the course of the twentieth century, and the second involving a revised understanding of the American state and the scope of public authority. The first story engages the frequency with which Congress has expressly incorporated judges and lawyers as part of the policymaking and enforcement process—a critical component of what Robert Kagan (2003) terms "adversarial legalism" and Gordon Silverstein (2009) labels the "juridification" of American politics in which courts are increasingly called upon to supplement state power. This trend is, of course, not entirely new; as Alexis de Tocqueville (1969, 270) famously wrote nearly two centuries ago, lawyers and judges "constitute a power which is little dreaded and hardly noticed," enwrapping "the whole of society." But what remains remarkable today is that while many other nations in the time since Tocqueville have created vast government bureaucracies to respond to a range of politically charged regulatory matters, in the United States, "lawyers, legal rights, judges, and lawsuits are the functional equivalent of the large central bureaucracies that dominate governance in high-tax, activist welfare states" (Kagan 2003, 16).

This trend has sometimes been ascribed to a propensity for Americans to be especially litigious. As the workload of the state and federal judiciaries grew heavy from the 1960s onward, a public quest for justice through litigation was certainly a narrative embraced by the national media in order to explain the apparent "litigation explosion." A more persuasive explanation, developed by scholars largely in response to this cultural narrative, asserts that the choice to rely on courts (whether to enforce policy or simply to hold someone liable for their injurious actions) is in many ways a natural byproduct of our very constitutional structure (e.g., Burke 2002; Kagan 2003; Kelemen 2004; Silverstein 2009). In a system of simultaneously separated and shared powers created by individuals intensely skeptical of government power, we have inherited a policymaking process that is fraught with veto points and that creates incentives that can get in the way of making (or later implementing and enforcing) policy. It seems nearly inevitable, then, that legislators would develop tools for navigating this institutional arrangement over time, whether in order to avoid blame for unpopular legislative choices or to protect their victories from future legislatures hostile to a particular policy accomplishment.

Private enforcement is one such tool. Congress increasingly chose (by the 1960s in particular) to provide statutory provisions for private civil actions as the presumed best option for enforcing certain policies (Farhang 2010; Melnick 1994). As Congress opened the door to private lawsuits even further—not only through private enforcement provisions, but also in the form of fee-shifting statutes and damages enhancements—there was a marked acceleration in the number of private suits actually *filed* to enforce policy implementation as well (Farhang 2010).

The second story of the American state provided by scholars in recent years involves the ways in which policymakers have harnessed and promoted the activity of private actors—not just lawyers, but a range of business and political entrepreneurs—to serve public goals, whether by incentivizing certain types of behavior or providing market space for business entrepreneurs to engage in activities beneficial to government interests. John Fabian Witt's (2004) work on late nineteenth century innovations by courts in response to tort litigation illustrates the use of common law development in the face of failed federal and state efforts to respond to the increasing dangers of the workplace, and a number of scholars have charted the ways in which private and public actors were brought together to construct public welfare and health care laws during the New Deal and Great Society (see, e.g., Hacker 2002; King and Lieberman 2009). These scholars seek to revise earlier understandings of policymaking and state authority in which public and private actors are considered to work in opposition. They do not reject the juxtaposition, but rather push us to think in a more complex way about how we understand the relationship between public and private power.

This relationship, in turn, forces scholars to rethink their definition of what constitutes state authority with regard to the judiciary specifically. There has long been a narrative of the American administrative state stressing its weakness in authority and capacity—at least in comparison to the other industrialized welfare states that developed over the course of the nineteenth and twentieth centuries (see, e.g., Orren and Skowronek 2004). Within this narrative, as William Novak (2003) notes, the judicial branch has often been cast as a structural roadblock to the growth of an administrative state. From this executive-centered understanding of state regulatory capacity, courts serve more often than not to "check" the exercise of centralized state power and to inhibit the ability of the state to implement new policies. The relationship between the burgeoning regulatory state of the early twentieth century and the Supreme Court is illustrative; only once the Court backed down in its famous 1937 confrontation with Franklin Roosevelt could the regulatory state fulfill its mission (see, e.g., Orren 1992).

Public law scholars have increasingly challenged this understanding of state incapacity and have illuminated the role of courts in contributing to state development. The alternate story that they have produced has come by examining whether and how the claims asserted by citizens and movements during the rights revolution era have been satisfied, and if so, by what mechanisms. Far from taking for granted that doctrinal developments have automatic direct effects for citizens, these scholars moved beyond detailing the rise and decline of civil rights era jurisprudence to studying the origins and effects of private litigation as a means of enforcing policy. By using litigation as a policy instrument, legislators explicitly empower the courts as a vehicle for buttressing state power, particularly when political leaders either cannot agree or are heavily confined by a variety of veto points. This leads to a different form of state-building in which courts and judges—sometimes even the mere existence or threat of their involvement—play a crucial role in policy implementation. The end result is a "litigation state" where the courts are central players not only in interpreting the law, but also in enforcing policy. From this perspective, what at first appears to be the pervasive weakness of the American state becomes its strength.

Research in this area has become quite extensive in the last decades, with much of it centered specifically on the legal and political expansion of Title VII of the Civil Rights Act of 1964. The Civil Rights Act created a new federal agency, the Equal Employment Opportunity Commission (EEOC), which was designed without much in the way of enforcement powers. Without clear authority to carry out the anti-discrimination mandate, bureaucrats in the EEOC were entrepreneurial in their ability to create that authority (see, e.g., Dobbin and Sutton 1998; Lieberman 2002; Skrentny 2002). These bureaucrats also benefited from the actions of private lawyers—themselves empowered in Title VII of the act—to help them in this task. Private lawyers seized the opportunity and took charge of mass of disputes by taking them directly to federal court (Frymer 2008a; Pedriana and Stryker 2004). The massive amount of litigation that came from Title VII disputes (and its surprising success) has therefore been a popular subject for scholars, and for good reason; the statues offers a classic example of a successful policy arising from a weak statutory mandate (Lieberman 2002).

But private litigation as a vital enforcement mechanism in other policy areas is also ripe for HI scholarship. Whether in the realm of welfare policy, education, prison reform, police brutality, vaccine and playground safety, or mass tobacco, asbestos, and lead pigment litigation, scholars writing in this area have situated the propensity to rely on law to enforce policy in an inter-branch context, where institutional actors interact in complex ways and weigh in on the important question of whether to rely on litigation to enforce policy (see, e.g., Barnes 2008). At its best, this literature has shown how law can change even the self-conception of bureaucrats and become part of the bureaucratic state. For example, in a recent study on rights implementation at the local level, Charles Epp (2010) illustrates how bureaucratic reform can arise when activists seeking to implement rights bearing statutes exploit the divisions inherent in most administrative agencies—between career bureaucrats and those open to reform—in such a way that "the law" is absorbed into the mission, function, and self-definition of that agency. In this way, law may even *become* the state.

Law, Courts, and Institutional Change

Most APD models of institutional change emphasize development, reconstitutions of political authority, and the "intercurrence" of political and institutional orders

(Orren and Skowronek 2004; Pierson 2004). Even when institutions are confronted and defeated, individual instances of retrenchment tend to be theoretically subsumed within a broader narrative of state development (see, e.g., Skowronek 1982). The New Deal retrenchment of courts, for example, became in the literature a reconfiguration of institutional authorities that enabled courts to expand alongside the administrative state in the 1950s and 1960s, as the courts gained authority over additional policy areas (Kersch 2006; McMahon 2004). While this is undoubtedly true, the successful attacks on the Supreme Court by the late nineteenth century also marked a moment where judicial institutional decline had notable consequences for the politics of the time—and down the road as well.

Here too, HI scholarship has much to offer models of change that can account for a wider variation in judicial activism over time. Scholars continue to grapple with the task of understanding the relationship between institutional stability and change (see, e.g., Clemens and Cook 1999); but even here the emphasis in APD remains largely on state-building, and institutional "change" is most often understood as part of ongoing "institutional development" (Pierson 2004). This is not to say that stasis, incremental change, or failed reforms go unnoticed in the literature; in fact, recognizing these has led scholars to amend the assumption of linearity (punctuated by "critical junctures") to include the role that path dependence plays in creating self-reinforcing institutions that shape the prospects for later change (see, e.g., Hacker 2004). But while entrenchment is a historical reality, it is not the whole story. Reform efforts do sometimes succeed. From Andrew Jackson's war against the national bank onward, retrenchment examples range from the successful elements of the New Deal and Reagan Revolution to legislative constriction of court jurisdiction and informal changes to interpretations of statutes that limit the range of their application. As these examples show, even when institutional orders are shattered, authority is not always simply transferred to other sectors of the state. Reforms often seek to fundamentally reduce state capacity as a whole—even if informally, through chipping away at the margins—or to transfer state power to nongovernmental actors. Further, some institutions may be subject to retrenchment while we continue to see broader growth in others, and even the same institution can constrict in one regard and expand in another.

But subsuming these examples within a broader narrative of growth hinders our understanding of institutional reform; and now, well into an era characterized by an anti-court, anti-"activist judge" political and legal movement, it is increasingly essential that we account for legal reform within broader theories of institutional change. If we focus only on the fact that growth and expansion has continued, in broad strokes, to characterize institutional change in the judiciary, we obscure effectual instances of retrenchment. We run the risk, for example, of missing the fact that certain groups of citizens find access to justice increasingly difficult. As innumerable legal scholars have noted, the jurisprudence of the Rehnquist and Roberts Courts has been defined by an anti-litigation sentiment; and whether or not that sentiment has definitively turned the tides away from judicial development is in many ways irrelevant to the practical consequences that it has wrought for the protection of rights (Burke 2002; Dodd 2007; Galanter 2004; Keck 2004; Teles 2008).

The HI literature on institutional change and retrenchment, therefore, has much to offer our understanding of legal change. Scholarship on policy feedback and retrenchment is of special importance, as we cannot make causal or predictive arguments about the potential for the success of judicial reform without also delving into the distinctive politics of and strategies for counter mobilization. As Paul Pierson argues, policy feedback—"the ways in which previous choices influence present political processes"—is highly important for understanding the political goals and context of actors pursuing retrenchment. Policy feedback shapes the distribution of political resources, alters the mindset and goals of political elites, creates incentives for both reform (usually due to unintended consequences) *and* defense of the status quo (through policy "lock-in"), and often broadens the range of pertinent actors. The creation of positive policy feedback is not automatic (and negative feedback creates its own complications); but if a reform successfully reconfigures the actors and groups invested in a new institutional arrangement, retrenchment becomes an especially difficult prospect (Pierson 2004). Because retrenchment generally requires imposing concentrated costs for diffuse gains, the popularity of social programs create powerful constituencies well positioned to fight it, requiring that political actors turn from strategies of credit claiming to blame avoidance (Hacker 2004; Sheingate 2003). This is especially true when individual and group actors have adapted and made extensive commitments to a new institutional arrangement, thereby increasing the costs of change (Patashnik 2008). Where judicial retrenchment is concerned, the creation of a "legal state" (much like the welfare state) effectively restructured the political landscape and created dense networks of interest groups for whom imposing losses for diffuse gains (namely a more efficient judiciary) is a highly problematic enterprise. Coupled with a more expansive sense of the judiciary as an institution, this perspective provides for a more thorough analysis of judicial institutional change.

Conclusion

The growth, development, and entrenchment of the judiciary over the course of the twentieth century prompted a transformational moment in public law scholarship. In confronting an entrenched narrative of courts and judges as antithetical to the state, public law scholars embraced several core precepts of HI in order to account for the role that the judicial branch has played in realizing the promises of the rights revolution. The role that law and courts have come to play in the modern American state represents a meaningful shift in the structure and manner of governing authority in America (Orren and Skowronek 2004), a complex shift in many ways authorized by a variety of institutional actors across all three branches of government. For example, judicial administrative bodies (like the Judicial Conference) themselves opened the courthouse door by establishing the class action; presidents and members of Congress promoted government-sponsored programs aimed to give more citizens better access to the courts (the Great Society-era creation of Legal Services Corporation for the poor is a clear example); and Congress itself began to write "litigious" policies authorizing "private attorneys general." Viewed in this way, there is more than first meets the eye when characterizing law as an integral part of the state, and turning our attention to the complex institutional relationships that develop in the midst of these "shifts" in authority illuminates several questions deserving more attention from HI scholars.

First, in order to get the most out of exploring whether and how the promises of the rights revolution have been "realized" or otherwise encroached upon, a broad conception of "the state" is crucial. But this also requires recognizing not just the expansive array of involved actors, but also the different institutions that influence the ability of legal actors to operate. Situating the effects of the rights revolution's legacies in the context of a "shift" in governing authority broadens the potential universe of actors and institutions involved in that conversation. Where it is otherwise easy to cast the leading roles in the rights revolution solely to the Warren Court justices, public law scholars who take a historical institutional approach can continue to draw our attention to the role that lawyers, private citizens, legislators, activists, policy experts, and bureaucrats play in the modern American state. Further, in a complex governing arrangement where institutions, each with their own entrenched interests, have to negotiate over how best to govern, it only seems possible to explain institutional change in an inter-branch context—even legal change.

Second, so long as private enforcement remains an attractive option for Congress, and the availability of lawsuits generally proliferates, litigation will continue to exert its force on bureaucratic change. However, in an era when reformers have sought to retrench the rights revolution, scholars must be alert to the temporality of these claims, as well as to ask whether these techniques can be blunted or used on behalf of different political agendas. Running through the work on law, courts, and the American state are a variety of legal, procedural mechanisms (of which private enforcement is just one) that serve to complement or enhance state authority. However, these very same tools—whether in the form of attorneys' fees or punitive damages, changes to the rules governing pleading and settlement, or the promotion of binding arbitration or other alternatives to litigation—can be used for the retrenchment of both civil rights laws and the state (see, e.g., Staszak 2010). The private weapons of the strong state, then, can serve multiple purposes and can be used by actors with different agendas—some promoting the enhancement of the state, and others promoting its retrenchment. We should be careful, then, not to make too broad of claims about certain practices as part of the development of institutions, absent the specific historical and political context in which they are leveraged.

In total, this suggests that the HI literature on change may prove essential for shaping this narrative. The development of American political and institutional capacity, as well as the expansion of the rights revolution, has not amounted to a linear expansion of democracy, state authority, and rights. By recognizing that there are always multiple agendas in contest with each other and maneuvering within our complex institutional universe, we can also be mindful that the institutional processes that transformed the American state may also be the tools for its constriction, or at least for a chipping away at the edges of the rights revolution—and subsequently at the role that law and courts play in the modern American state.

Note

* The author thanks Adam Sheingate for inviting her to contribute to the volume, and for his thoughtful comments and guidance.

References

Barnes, Jeb. 2008. "Courts and the Puzzle of Institutional Stability and Change: Administrative Drift and Judicial Innovation in the Case of Asbestos." *Political Research Quarterly* 61; 636–648.

Brandwein, Pamela. 2006. "Law and American Political Development." *Annual Review of Law and Social Science* 7: 187–216.

Burke, Thomas F. 2002. *Lawyers, Lawsuits, and Legal Rights: The Battle Over Litigation in American Society.* Berkeley: University of California Press.

Clemens, Elisabeth S. and James M. Cook. 1999. "Politics and Institutionalism: Explaining Durability and Change." *Annual Review of Sociology* 25: 441–495.

Crowe, Justin. 2007. "The Forging of Judicial Autonomy: Political Entrepreneurship and the Reforms of William Howard Taft." *Journal of Politics* 69: 73–87.

Dahl, Robert A. 1957. "Decision-Making in a Democracy: The Supreme Court as National-Policymaker." *Journal of Public Law* 6: 279–295.

De Tocqueville, Alexis. 1969. *Democracy in America*, ed. J. P. Mayer. New York: Knopf Publishing Group.

Dobbin, Frank and John Sutton. 1998. "The Strength of a Weak State: The Employment Rights Revolution and the Rise of Human Resources Management Divisions." *American Journal of Sociology* 104: 441–476.

Dodd, Lynda. 2007. "*DeShaney v. Winnebago County*: Governmental Neglect and the 'Blessings of Liberty.'" In *Civil Rights Stories*, ed. Myriam Gilles and Risa Golubuff. New York: Foundation Press, 185–210.

Engel, Stephen M. 2011. *American Politicians Confront the Court: Opposition Politics and Changing Responses to Judicial Power.* New York: Cambridge University Press.

Epp, Charles R. 1998. *The Rights Revolution: Lawyers, Activists, and Supreme Courts in Comparative Perspective*. Chicago: University of Chicago Press.

Epp, Charles R. 2010. *Making Rights Real: Activists, Bureaucrats, and the Creation of the Legalistic State*. Chicago: University of Chicago Press.

Farhang, Sean, 2010. *The Litigation State: Public Regulation and Private Lawsuits in the U.S.* Princeton, NJ: Princeton University Press.

Feeley, Malcolm M. and Edward L. Rubin. 1998. *Judicial Policy Making and the Modern State: How the Courts Reformed America's Prisons.* New York: Cambridge University Press.

Frymer, Paul. 2008a. *Black and Blue: African Americans, Labor Unions, and the Decline of the Democratic Party.* Princeton, NJ: Princeton University Press.

Frymer, Paul. 2008b. "Law and American Political Development." *Law and Social Inquiry* 33: 779–803.

Galanter, Marc. 2004. "The Vanishing Trial: An Examination of Trials and Related Matters in Federal and State Courts." *Journal of Empirical Legal Studies* 1: 459–470.

Gillman, Howard. 2002. "How Political Parties Can Use the Courts to Advance Their Agendas: Federal Courts in the United States, 1875–1891." *American Political Science Review* 96: 11–24.

Graber, Mark A. 1993. "The Non-Majoritarian Difficulty: Legislative Deference to the Judiciary." *Studies in American Political Development* 7: 35–72.

Hacker, Jacob S. 2002. *The Divided Welfare State: The Battle over Public and Private Social Benefits in the United States.* New York: Cambridge University Press.

Hacker, Jacob S. 2004. "Privatizing Risk without Privatizing the Welfare State: The Hidden Politics of Social Policy Retrenchment in the United States." *American Political Science Review* 98: 243–260.

Haltom, William and Michael McCann. 2004. *Distorting the Law: Politics, Media, and the Litigation Crisis.* Chicago: University of Chicago Press.

Kagan, Robert A. 2003. *Adversarial Legalism: The American Way of Law.* Cambridge, MA: Harvard University Press.

Kahn, Ronald and Ken I. Kersch, eds. 2006. *The Supreme Court and American Political Development.* Lawrence, KS: University of Kansas Press.

Keck, Thomas M. 2004. *The Most Activist Supreme Court in History: The Road to Modern Judicial Conservatism.* Chicago: University of Chicago Press.

Kelemen, R. Daniel. 2004. *The Rules of Federalism: Institutions and Regulatory Politics in the EU and Beyond.* Cambridge, MA: Harvard University Press.

Kersch, Ken I. 2006. "The New Deal Triumph as the End of History? The Judicial Negotiation of Labor Rights and Civil Rights." In *The Supreme Court and American Political Development*, ed. Ronald Kahn and Ken Kersch. Lawrence, KS: University of Kansas Press.

King, Desmond and Robert C. Lieberman. 2009. "Ironies of State Building: A Comparative Perspective on the American State." *World Politics* 61: 547–588.

Lieberman, Robert C. 2002. "Ideas, Institutions, and Political Order: Explaining Political Change." *American Political Science Review* 96: 697–712.

Lovell, George I. 2003. *Legislative Deferrals: Statutory Ambiguity, Judicial Power, and American Democracy.* New York: Cambridge University Press.

McCann, Michael W. 1994. *Rights at Work.* Chicago: University of Chicago Press.

McMahon, Kevin. 2004. *Reconsidering Roosevelt on Race: How the Presidency Paved the Road to Brown.* Chicago: University of Chicago Press.

Melnick, R. Shep. 1994. *Between the Lines: Interpreting Welfare Rights.* Washington, D.C.: Brookings Institution.

Novak, William. 2003. "The Legal Origins of the Modern American State." In *Looking Back on Law's Century*, ed. Byrant Garth, Robert Kagan, and Austin Sarat. Ithaca, NY: Cornell University Press, 249–286.

Novkov, Julie. 2008. *Racial Union: Law, Intimacy, and the White State in Alabama, 1865–1954.* Ann Arbor, MI: University of Michigan Press.

Orren, Karen. 1992. *Belated Feudalism: Labor, the Law, and Liberal Development in the United States.* New York: Cambridge University Press.

Orren, Karen and Stephen Skowronek. 2004. *The Search for American Political Development.* New York: Cambridge University Press.

Patashnik, Eric M. 2008. *Reforms at Risk: What Happens After Major Policy Changes Are Enacted*. Princeton, NJ: Princeton University Press.

Pedriana, Nicholas and Robin Stryker. 2004. "The Strength of a Weak Agency: Enforcement of Title VII of the Civil Rights Act and the Expansion of State Capacity, 1965–1971." *American Journal of Sociology* 110: 709–760.

Pierson, Paul. 2004. *Politics in Time: History, Institutions, and Social Analysis*. Princeton, NJ: Princeton University Press.

Rosenberg, Gerald N. 1991. *The Hollow Hope: Can Courts Bring About Social Change?* Chicago: University of Chicago Press.

Sheingate, Adam. 2003. "Political Entrepreneurship, Institutional Change, and American Political Development." *Studies in American Political Development* 17: 185–203.

Silverstein, Gordon. 2009. *Law's Allure: How Law Shapes, Constrains, Saves, and Kills Politics*. New York: Cambridge University Press.

Skocpol, Theda. 1995. *Protecting Soldiers and Mothers: The Political Origins of Social Policy in the United States*. New York: Cambridge University Press.

Skowronek, Stephen. 1982. *Building a New American State: The Expansion of National Administrative Capacities, 1877–1920*. New York: Cambridge University Press.

Skrentny, John D. 2002. *The Minority Rights Revolution*. Cambridge, MA: Harvard University Press.

Skrentny, John D. 2006. "Law and the American State." *Annual Review of Sociology* 32: 213–244.

Staszak, Sarah. 2010. "Institutions, Rulemaking, and the Politics of Judicial Retrenchment." *Studies in American Political Development* 24: 168–189.

Teles, Steven M. 2008. *The Rise of the Conservative Legal Movement: The Battle for Control of the Law*. Princeton, NJ: Princeton University Press.

Tushnet, Mark. 2006. "The Supreme Court and the National Political Order: Collaboration and Confrontation." In *The Supreme Court and American Political Development*, ed. Ronald Kahn and Ken I. Kersch. Lawrence, KS: University of Kansas Press, 117–137.

Whittington, Keith E. 2000. "Once More Unto the Breach: Post-Behavioralist Approaches to Judicial Politics." *Law and Social Inquiry* 25: 601–634.

Whittington, Keith E. 2007. *Political Foundations of Judicial Supremacy: The Presidency, the Supreme Court, and Constitutional Leadership in U.S. History*. Princeton, NJ: Princeton University Press.

Witt, John Fabian. 2004. *The Accidental Republic: Crippled Workingmen, Destitute Widows, and the Remaking of American Law*. Cambridge, MA: Harvard University Press.

CHAPTER 20

SOCIAL POLICY DYNAMICS

ALAN M. JACOBS*

The study of American social policy has been one of the most important incubators of historical institutionalist argumentation. It is in seeking to explain the development and resilience of US social programs, for instance, that scholars first devoted sustained attention to concepts such as policy feedback and path dependence (Skocpol 1992; Pierson 1994)—concepts that would become central to historical institutionalist lines of explanation across many substantive domains. As I will argue in this chapter, an historical institutionalist approach has also made vital contributions to our understanding of US social politics.

Substantively, historical institutionalist (HI) inquiry in the domain of American social policy has addressed itself to a set of tightly interconnected and comparatively informed questions. Why does the United States, compared to other rich democracies, spend so little on public social programs? Why has the US fashioned such distinctive forms of social protection, relying so heavily on tax instruments and private-sector actors, rather than direct spending and service-provision? How has the peculiar design of America's institutions of social protection shaped the politics of social policy over time? And what have been the consequences for the US political economy of the substantial rightward shift in the political center of gravity since the 1970s?

This chapter seeks to assess the contributions of historical institutionalism to the study of American social politics by tracing four distinct analytical "moves" that HI scholars have made over the last three decades. These are (1) a move from accounts of policy as a straightforward reflection of societal preferences and groups' political capacities to the examination of institutions as structuring groups' opportunities to achieve their policy goals; (2) a shift toward a longer-term analysis of how institutions shape the very demands and capacities that groups bring to the political arena; (3) the study of policies themselves as key institutions shaping—and, especially, stabilizing—social politics over time; and (4) a richer assessment of the processes through which policies, and the distributive contours of the American political economy, have changed over time.

In tracing these intellectual shifts, I will argue that the most distinctive and important achievement of historical institutionalist scholarship on the American welfare state has been the increasing *endogenization* of the causes of policy development. By this I mean that successive analytical moves have, by providing more deeply historical accounts, increasingly provided *explanations* of central features of welfare-state politics that prior frameworks had taken as fixed and given—including basic power relations in the American political system. The chapter also considers a key challenge confronting historically oriented welfare-state scholarship: identifying the causes of, and conditions conducive to, policy change. In closing, I point to a number of lines of analysis that may offer a fruitful way forward in devising more variegated explanations of social policy development over time.

Reframing the Puzzle of "American Exceptionalism"

The puzzle of American welfare-state "exceptionalism" has long occupied students of political economy. Early approaches to comparative social policy viewed the welfare state as a basic functional response to the risks and dislocations generated by industrial development (e.g., Wilensky 1974). Against this universalizing logic of industrialism, the United States appeared to be a stark outlier. The American state spent a far smaller proportion of national income on social programs like pensions, social assistance, unemployment insurance, and health care. Where it offered benefits, those benefits were typically meager and often means-tested, rather than provided universally as in many peer nations. And, perhaps most striking of all, the United States was by the 1980s alone among advanced industrialized democracies in not providing its citizens with some form of universal medical insurance.

Early welfare-state scholars sought to resolve this puzzle by pointing to a number of distinctive and enduring features of American society. These included, most prominently, the character of American political culture and values (e.g., Rimlinger 1971) and the organizational weakness of labor and the political left in the United States (e.g., Korpi 1983).

As historical institutionalist scholarship on the American welfare state began taking shape, HI scholars drew attention to two sorts of problems with cultural and power-resource explanations. First were a set of empirical puzzles: comparative and historical mismatches between proposed cause and observed effect. Any explanation centered on cultural values, for instance, had difficulty accounting for striking policy differences between the United States and other nations with similar, Anglo-liberal political cultures, including Canada and Britain itself (Hacker 1998). Nor could a culturalist account explain why social policy ideas broadly popular with the American public—such as universal health coverage—never emerged (Hacker 1998). Power-resource explanations, for their part, confronted historical quandaries. These included the fact that US trade unions had been, in the early decades of the twentieth century, as strong and as radicalized as worker organizations in many peer nations (Hattam 1993). Why had similar levels of labor organization not been met by comparable extensions of social protection?

Further, as HI scholars more systematically unpacked the structure of social provision in the United States, the original puzzle of "exceptionalism"—understood as the United States' unusually small welfare state—began to look poorly specified. The inherited portrait of the American welfare state derived from a European model of welfare provision characterized by a strong role for direct public insurance of male breadwinners. One limitation of this model was its gendered assumptions. Slow to establish broad insurance programs for male workers, the United States set up a raft of social policies designed to protect women well before the New Deal (Skocpol 1992). The European model also provided a misleading yardstick in its emphasis on direct public spending. Combined public and private spending on social benefits in the US in fact approximate those in continental Europe (Hacker 2002). But as Christopher Howard's (1997) and Jacob Hacker's (2002) work have brought to the fore, a great deal of social protection in the United States is neither public in form nor expenditure in the classic sense. The US federal government "spends" hundreds of millions of dollars each year, for instance, in tax deductions to subsidize pension and health benefits that are provided by private employers. Historical-institutionalist reframings of the outcome of interest have generated new puzzles of American exceptionalism, focused as much on the distinctive *structure* of the American welfare state—considered in greater detail in the sections that follow—as on its size.

Institutions and Social Policymaking: "Synchronic" Effects

Political institutions have been central to HI scholars' attempts to explain America's distinctive social policy arrangements. We can usefully distinguish between two types of HI arguments about institutions, which I will term *synchronic* arguments and *diachronic* arguments. A synchronic institutional argument identifies a short-run effect of prevailing political-institutional arrangements on the relative influence of political actors. Arguments about synchronic institutional effects—to which I turn first—take actors' political capacities and policy demands as given and then assess the ways in which the "rules of the game" favor or disadvantage particular types of actors and demands over others.

Synchronic arguments have focused on the ways in which American political institutions have tended to privilege certain types of group interests, in the making of social policy, over others. Central to most synchronic analyses has been the extreme fragmentation of authority in the American polity. National policymaking in the US is dispersed *horizontally* across three branches of the federal government and within each chamber of Congress. Relatively weak party discipline, attributable in part to the logic of presidentialism, prevents anything like party government from emerging. Weak discipline has tended to combine with Congress's internal rules to empower small factions and even individual legislators to amend, delay, or obstruct new legislation. At the same time, federalism disperses policymaking authority *vertically* between the national government and subnational units.

The result is a policymaking process riddled with "veto points": opportunities for actors opposed to policy change to block its enactment (Immergut 1992; Tsebelis 1995). Crucially, however, these opportunities are not equally distributed. A key theme of HI scholarship has been the *asymmetrical* implications of the fragmentation of authority for group influence. In particular, veto points in the policymaking process tend to create disproportionate lobbying opportunities for the best-organized interests in a policy domain (Steinmo 1996; Patashnik 2003; see also contributions in Weaver and Rockman 1993). American institutional arrangements thus raise high hurdles to the enactment of social policies that would inflict concentrated pain on mobilized groups, even when those policies would deliver benefits to a broad swathe of society. Steinmo and Watts (1995), for instance, demonstrate how national health insurance (NHI) reform efforts—despite broad public support—have faced an uphill battle on an institutional playing field tilted in favor of the well-organized groups that stood to lose from an expansion of public coverage. America's policymaking institutions have also generated regional asymmetries in influence. Seniority rules in Congress interacted with one-party rule in the South to give disproportionate power to conservative Southern whites, who successfully resisted many welfare initiatives that would have threatened the region's low-wage, paternalistic labor system (Lieberman 1998; Katznelson 2013; Quadagno 1994).

Thus, synchronic institutional arguments have helped explain why even broadly popular social-policy initiatives have often failed to emerge in the United States. Equally, however, arguments focused on the fragmentation of authority have gone a long way toward explaining why those programs that have emerged have taken the distinctive forms that they have. In a high veto-point environment, reformers have had to engineer policy designs that could draw together unusually broad legislative coalitions. Social protection initiatives had to be crafted in ways that could placate the best-organized interests; overcome conservative suspicion of federal power; and offer tangible benefits to identifiable constituencies across most or all congressional districts. The result has been a social protection regime with several cross-nationally distinctive features, including:

(1) *Targeting.* US social policy expansions have often been targeted at, or away from, beneficiary groups in ways designed to placate organized or conservative opposition. Whereas other advanced democracies first extended social insurance to (male) workers, American social policy development has tended to favor demographic groups excluded from existing labor-market and insurance arrangements. For instance, expansions of public health coverage in the 1960s extended benefits only to groups that were of little interest to the private insurance industry: seniors and the poor (Hacker 1998). Likewise, to appease powerful Southern interests in the Senate, the 1935 Social Security Act excluded agricultural and domestic workers, mostly African-Americans, from most benefits (Quadagno 1994; Lieberman 1998).

(2) *"Pork-barrel" social spending.* Fragmentation of authority in Congress has eased the way for social programs that distribute localized gains to constituents across a large share of congressional districts. For instance, while national health insurance proposals faced fierce opposition from doctors and the private insurance industry, Congress found the politics of hospital construction much simpler, repeatedly passing large appropriations to finance medical infrastructure across the country (Hacker 1998). Repeated expansions of Civil War veterans' pensions similarly provided an opportunity for Congress to deliver visible rewards to beneficiaries spread across all legislative districts (Skocpol 1992).

(3) *Avoidance of direct spending.* The United States's heavy reliance on tax deductions and subsidies, rather than direct spending, as tools of social policy has also been eased and encouraged by institutional arrangements. Like pork-barrel spending, the costs of tax expenditures are of low salience, spread thinly across the federal budget. Their intrinsic ambiguity—as both governmental largesse and reductions in tax burdens—also makes tax expenditures less likely to face opposition from conservative politicians and voters. Moreover, Congressional rules give more concentrated legislative authority to Congress's revenue committees than to its spending bodies, effectively reducing the number of veto points in the domain of tax policy (Howard 1997). Equally important, once enacted, socially oriented tax expenditures tend to be championed by well-organized intermediary groups—those whose market activities are being subsidized—that have a vested interest in their expansion.

(4) *Delegated delivery.* Especially discernible in the field of health care is a form of arm's length delivery that Morgan and Campbell (2011) call "delegated governance": the use of private actors or lower levels of government to provide services. Delegating responsibility helps build broad legislative coalitions in at least two ways. First, like tax expenditures, delegated governance constitutes a less obtrusive form of state intervention, curbing conservative opposition to welfare expansion (see also Mettler 2011). Second, delegating delivery turns potential foes of social protection into allies by creating new business opportunities for well-organized market actors. Expansions of health coverage in the 2000s, for instance, granted private insurers a central—and lucrative—role in providing the new benefits.

Institutions and Social Policymaking: "Diachronic" Effects

Synchronic arguments have excelled at explaining the outcomes of welfare-state conflict among differently resourced groups with diverse social-policy preferences. Yet synchronic arguments leave group resources and policy demands themselves unexplained.

Why, for instance, have battles for welfare-state expansion in the United States not been led by a robust workers' movement or a viable social democratic party? And why have the groups doing battle over the American welfare state tended to organize themselves around quite narrow, particularistic goals rather than—as in much of continental Europe—the collective interests of capital and labor?

This is where *diachronic* institutional arguments come in. Central to diachronic institutional analysis is a fundamentally historical analytical move: the examination of how political structures have, over time, shaped the political capacities and the policy demands that actors bring to the political battlefield. As Julia Lynch and Martin Rhodes argue in their contribution to this handbook, the long-term effects of institutions on actors' identities, capacities, and goals have also been a central historical-institutionalist concern in the comparative analysis of welfare-state politics (Lynch and Roberts, Chapter 25, this volume). The move to diachronic explanation is a move to endogenize features of social-policy conflict that earlier arguments had largely taken as given.

Among the most important of these features is the political weakness of the American left and working class. Consider, for instance, Victoria Hattam's (1993) comparative study of trade unions in the US and Britain. Hattam seeks to explain why the American Federation of Labor (AFL) has pursued a "voluntarist" strategy centered around collective bargaining and industrial action while British unions have spent most of the twentieth century deeply engaged in electoral politics and in advancing an agenda of social reform. Hattam's explanation charts the responses of these two labor movements over time to differing institutional opportunity structures and patterns of success and failure. While unions in both countries began pursuing broad political strategies in the late nineteenth century, American labor faced a more forbidding institutional landscape featuring an unusually powerful judiciary, which routinely sided with business interests and slowed the progress of worker-protection legislation. After decades of frustrated effort, AFL leaders decided largely to withdraw from the political sphere and concentrate their efforts on shop-floor organization and collective bargaining. As a result, labor unions in the United States failed to develop many of the mobilizational capacities and party-organizational linkages that would characterize labor movements in most other developed democracies; and organized labor in the US would be a muted voice in many of the key social policy debates of the twentieth century. Antonia Maioni (1998) has, likewise, employed a diachronic comparative-institutional logic to trace the differing long-term of effects of Canadian and US institutions on the prospects of a nationally viable socialist party.

Historical institutionalists have also illuminated the ways in which the fragmentation of authority in the US political system has spawned a particular form of interest-group politics. Sven Steinmo's (1996) comparative study of tax policy in Britain, Sweden, and the United States provides a compelling illustration of this dynamic. In the Swedish political system—characterized by relatively centralized authority and disciplined, programmatic parties—social groups have had to form broad interest coalitions and formulate demands on behalf of broad segments of society if they were to exercise policy influence. In contrast, broad policy change is exceedingly difficult to realize in an American institutional environment riddled with veto points—but that very same fragmentation of authority makes it easy for groups to win narrowly targeted benefits. The result has been a disjointed pattern of interest representation, marked by narrowly organized groups pressing particularistic policy demands. Thus, in the domain of tax policy, individual industries and corporations in the United States have tended to work independently to win targeted exemptions, rather than coordinating to achieve a broadly capital-friendly tax regime. A fragmentation of political *authority* has thus generated fragmented political *mobilization*. Narrow organization, Steinmo points out, has also made certain kinds of policy bargains impossible to achieve in the US context. It has precluded the kinds of grand social compromise that have underwritten welfare-state development in much of continental Europe, such as a pact between labor and capital marrying relatively regressive taxation with generous social protection. In the United States, no organized business or labor group has either the motive or the capacity to commit to such an encompassing policy bargain.

Reversing the Causal Arrow: Policies as Institutions

HI scholars have identified myriad mechanisms, synchronic and diachronic, through which the "rules of the game" have impeded the creation of broad-based policies of state social protection in the US. Yet an account of American social politics as institutionally biased against pro-welfare forces has proved incomplete as an explanation of the development of social-insurance arrangements over time, once they have been established. In battles over America's largest welfare-state programs, pro-welfare forces have held and, in some instances, gained ground in recent decades—even amidst a withering of organized labor and massive conservative mobilization. If the enactment of universal social programs confronts such immense hurdles, how then can we explain the extreme difficulty of dismantling them?

Historical institutionalists have gone a long way toward unraveling this puzzle by taking diachronic analysis a step further. In a particularly fruitful analytical move, HI scholars have turned to conceptualizing public policies themselves as causally important institutions that, once established, structure downstream political dynamics. In a range of contexts, historical institutionalists have demonstrated that public policies exert powerful "feedback" effects on future politics, configuring the options available to individuals and organizations, modifying the costs and benefits associated with different kinds of behavior, structuring the information available to citizens, and altering the distribution of resources and capacities across social groups. Policy feedback arguments represent a further step toward endogenizing the basic parameters of social-policy conflict.

Pierson's (1994) analysis of retrenchment politics in the 1980s features one of the earliest and most-cited examples of a policy-feedback logic. Employing the economic concept of "increasing returns," Pierson points out that certain types of social policies generate mounting benefits for citizens as they remain in place for longer periods of time. For instance, every year that a contributory pension system like Social Security remains in place, workers will have accumulated a larger and larger entitlement to benefits and, in turn, made less private provision for retirement. Over time, the material costs of scaling back the program's benefits—and, in turn, the electoral risk to politicians seeking to do so—grows sharply. Against the organizational decline of labor—a traditional welfare-state ally—Social Security itself has generated its own fiercely protective constituency among the broad middle class, and the program survived the Reagan years largely intact.

Scholars have also identified cognitive effects of social-policy structures on citizen preferences: ways in which policy designs enacted at t_1 shape mass preferences over reform at t_2 by altering the informational environment in which reform choices will be made. In comparing the efforts of Reagan and Thatcher to roll back welfare provision, Pierson (1994) shows that program structures in the two countries differently conditioned citizens' (anticipated) reactions to retrenchment by determining how easy it was for conservatives to craft reforms that would minimize the salience of losses. Eric Patashnik (2000), in a study of the politics of trust funds, similarly demonstrates how segregated program-financing structures can impede retrenchment by making cutbacks more readily detectable to the average voter.

In other feedback accounts, policy choices at one point in time reshape patterns of group mobilization and coalition-formation that then influence the possibilities for social policy development at later points in time. As Skocpol (1992) demonstrates, for instance, the creation of Civil War pensions helped provoke the mobilization of veterans as a political force pressing for ever more generous benefits. Likewise, Andrea Campbell's (2003) study of the mass politics of Social Security traces how the retirement program provoked far greater political activism by senior citizens—both sheltering the program from political attack and fostering its incremental expansion.

HI scholars have also illuminated important feedback effects of social policies on the political activities of market actors. Studies by Howard (1997), Hacker (2002), and Morgan and Campbell (2011) have demonstrated how the distinctive delegated and subsidy-based structure of many US social programs has given rise to armies of private-sector intermediaries—who, in turn, frequently become influential advocates for the maintenance or expansion of the programs that they help to implement. The logic of market feedback, however, has also run against welfare-state expansion. As Hacker (1998) details, the non-adoption of national health insurance during the New Deal led to the rapid growth of a profitable private insurance industry, which would become one of the fiercest political foes of efforts to socialize health care financing in the postwar era.

Explaining Social Policy Change: An Emerging Agenda

One striking feature of most arguments about social-policy feedback is their emphasis on *self-reinforcing* feedback effects.[1] By far the most significant contributions of feedback arguments have been the explanation of relatively long-standing features of American social policy, including the persistence or incremental growth of major social-insurance schemes through an era of conservative political ascendance. Yet the logic of self-reinforcing feedback is less well suited to explaining other important forms of policy development: in particular, policy changes that entail a reversal of past policy movements or a major shift in the distribution of policy costs and benefits. How might policy rollbacks and reorientations arise in a policy domain characterized by such strong positive feedback effects? And, notwithstanding the resilience of America's largest public welfare-state programs, how has its regime of social protection, taken as a whole, held up in recent decades?

Early studies of welfare-state retrenchment, including Pierson's (1994) seminal account, defined their object of analysis as formal, authoritative cutbacks to social programs. And major cutbacks to state social programs were indeed found to be relatively rare. More recently, however, HI scholars have developed a far more variegated conceptualization of the forms that policy and institutional change can take (Thelen 2004; Streeck and Thelen 2005; Mahoney and Thelen 2010a; Hacker 2004; Schickler 2001). Discussed in greater detail elsewhere in this volume, these modes of change include:

- *conversion*, a repurposing of existing policy structures to serve new functions
- *layering*, the superimposition of new policy structures atop old, and
- *drift*, a change in social consequences as exogenous conditions change while policy structures remain fixed.

This conceptual refinement has yielded a substantial reconsideration of the American welfare state's postwar developmental trajectory. Most importantly, it has allowed scholars to correct a somewhat misleading portrait of social policy resilience since the 1970s. Two examples outlined by Hacker (2004) illustrate the implications. As in most industrialized democracies, America's postwar welfare-state arrangements had been largely premised on a male-breadwinner model of employment. However, changes in family structures and rising female labor-force participation since the 1960s gradually created a disconnect between institutions of social protection and the risks faced by families. In a classic instance of drift, however, conservatives successfully resisted policy innovations—such as an expansion of childcare provision or meaningful parental-leave policies—that would have adapted the American welfare state to the new social environment. As Hacker also details, the field of pension policy has seen a striking individualization of risk via processes of layering. Unable to dismantle Social Security or the rules covering defined-benefit occupational pensions, conservatives created and gradually expanded opportunities for firms and their workers to invest in a range of individualized savings vehicles. Over time, this initially supplementary retirement system came to displace traditional arrangements as employers shifted the bulk of their workforce into defined-contribution schemes. The result has been a massive shift of financial risk from firms onto American workers—without the enactment of any explicit policy decision to scale back social protection.

HI scholars have further enhanced our understanding of policy change by expanding the object of analysis. In their work on the political sources of economic inequality, Hacker and Pierson (2010) have argued that many of the most important distributional changes in the American economy have occurred outside the bounds of the formal welfare state. To capture these changes, Hacker and Pierson examine developments in the broader institutional framework undergirding the US political economy. While conservatives in the US have found it difficult to roll back core public social programs like Social Security and Medicare, they have achieved substantial changes in other domains—including cuts to top marginal tax rates and the dilution of financial-sector regulations—that have dramatically reduced the state's redistributive role and redirected a large share of national income toward the extremely rich. Drift in the broad parameters of economic policy has also been crucial, including a stagnant federal minimum wage and the non-enforcement of labor laws amidst aggressive anti-union tactics by employers. While the largest social-insurance programs remain intact, Hacker and Pierson demonstrate that American social policy, writ large, has in fact undergone massive change over the last four decades.

My own research has, along a different dimension, expanded the conceptual space for mapping policy development. In studying the politics of the long term (Jacobs 2011), I observe that most scholarship on policymaking has focused tightly on the problem of cross-sectional distribution: on how policies distribute gains and losses across social groups. Most important policy decisions, however, also involve choices about how resources should be distributed over *time:* choices about intertemporal allocation between present and future. My analysis demonstrates, moreover, that policy decisions that appear to maintain the status quo in cross-sectional terms sometimes involve a major reallocation of benefits and burdens intertemporally. Clear cases in point are the 1977 and 1983 reforms to Social Security. Scholars have typically classified these reform episodes as cases of policy stasis because program benefits were largely preserved (e.g., Pierson 1994). Viewed from an intertemporal angle, however, the two reforms effected major transfers over time. By raising payroll taxes and trimming benefits in the short run, these policies imposed enormous costs on current contributors (and, to a lesser extent, seniors) but generated decades of trust fund surpluses to the benefit of future workers, employers, and retirees. In fact, cross-sectional stability—preserving long-run retiree benefits at close-to-current levels—*required* intertemporal reallocation: a costly investment in a buildup of future reserves.

Together with arguments about policy drift, this analysis also suggests a more general lesson for the study of policy change: that, in a changing social environment, continuity and change are often best understood as complements. Maintaining substantive outcomes over long periods of time often requires policy adjustment; and long-run policy stasis will frequently generate considerable distributional change (see also Mahoney and Thelen 2010a; Jacobs 2010).

HI scholarship has given us a far better understanding of the nature and extent of changes in the American political economy since the late 1970s. Yet it would be fair to say that a richer conceptualization of change has not been matched by an abundance of crisp propositions about the *conditions* under which change is most likely to emerge. Nonetheless, significant advances are worth noting. One effective approach has been to turn the logic of positive policy feedback on its head. If programs that generate increasing returns tend to be more resilient, then change should be more likely when policies do not spawn self-reinforcing feedback processes. For instance, in his study of the sustainability of general-interest policy reforms, Patashnik (2008) shows that those initiatives that did not reshape group identities and alliances or encourage actors to make costly new investments were far more likely to be eroded or reversed over time. Similarly, scholars analyzing the arm's length and hidden character of much American social provision have pointed to the failure of "submerged" social programs to generate self-reinforcing dynamics. Drawing on survey experimental evidence, Mettler (2011) finds that the indirect and low-visibility character of much social provision makes it difficult for citizens to perceive the state's role in advancing their material welfare, thus undercutting public support for state intervention. Mettler's data also drive home a central developmental irony of American social politics: that the social-policy designs most likely to win enactment in the US institutional context happen to be those most likely to undermine the long-term political support base for public social protection.

Scholars have also begun to advance plausible hypotheses about the conditions under which particular forms of change are most likely to occur. Hacker (2004), for instance, proposes that the type of policy change we observe should depend, jointly, on the number of veto points in the policymaking process and on the degree of discretion involved in policy implementation. Where the number of veto points is high and policy implementation involves broad discretion, conversion is a likely outcome. On the other hand, low discretion and fewer veto players will tend to make layering a more feasible strategy for those seeking policy revision (see also Mahoney and Thelen 2010a). And, in analyzing tradeoffs over time, I have argued that a dispersion of veto power makes it more difficult for groups to advance their long-term welfare by redistributing resources cross-sectionally, thus enhancing the likelihood of intertemporal solutions that reallocate consumption from present to future (Jacobs 2011).

Future Directions

Though scholarship on the American welfare state has yet to generate a large number of well-specified claims about the causes of policy change, several promising lines of analysis are beginning to emerge. First, recent work on the new politics of inequality suggests that the study of social-policy change may benefit from renewed attention to a core insight of an earlier literature: that, in struggles over distribution, *power resources matter*. Hacker and Pierson (2010), for instance, persuasively attribute the unraveling of the postwar "mixed economy" to a massive political mobilization of American capitalists and the steep decline of organized labor since the 1970s. This kind of long-run shift in the underlying balance of political capacities has received surprisingly little attention in the broad field of American politics. Yet I expect that HI scholars will gain substantial explanatory purchase on the evolution of the American political economy by exploring linkages between policy development over time and the dynamics of organized group struggle.

Second, efforts to explain change could usefully focus on the *coalitional structure* of group politics. Even where organizational resources remain relatively stable, policy change can arise from a reconfiguration of the lines of battle. Silja Häusermann's (2010) masterful study of social-policy reform in Europe offers an illustration of the promise of coalitional analysis. Häusermann demonstrates how fluctuating, issue-by-issue group alliances have generated substantial policy change in continental welfare regimes characterized by powerful positive feedback effects, and she advances testable propositions about the organizational and institutional conditions that generate greater or lesser coalitional flexibility. Likewise, accounts of the passage of landmark health-reform legislation in the US in 2010 make clear the importance of movement over time in the configuration of positions taken by key stakeholders, including large employers, medical providers, and insurers (Hacker 2010; Starr 2011; Jacobs and Skocpol 2010). Scholars seeking to explain both continuity and change in US social-policy arrangements might gain traction by more systematically analyzing the rigidity and fluidity of group coalitions, and identifying the conditions that make coalitional realignments in American politics more or less likely to emerge (see also Mahoney and Thelen 2010a).

Third, the analysis of policy feedback—focused, to date, largely on self-reinforcing processes—could profit from systematic attention to long-run *negative* feedback effects: to the ways in which social policies may undermine their political support bases over time (Jacobs and Weaver 2015; Weaver 2010; Greif and Laitin 2004). HI scholars across substantive domains have become increasingly interested in endogenous sources of institutional change, including the processes through which institutions provoke their own opposition and enable challengers (see, e.g., contributions in Mahoney and Thelen 2010b). In light of the complex and incoherent designs that litter the US policy landscape (Teles 2013; Clemens 2006), American social politics ought to be an especially promising site for the unfolding of self-undermining institutional dynamics, or what Streeck and Thelen (2005) term "institutional exhaustion." Consider, again, the enactment of major health care reform in the United States in 2010. It would be difficult to explain the passage of the Affordable Care Act without reference to the ways in which the pre-existing policy patchwork—which had worked well for the best-organized stakeholders for much of the postwar era—engendered social consequences that gradually expanded the coalition for policy change, and diminished the ranks of reform opponents (Hacker 2010; Starr 2011; Jacobs and Skocpol 2010). Indeed, the ACA is perhaps best understood as a consequence of the simultaneous operation of powerful positive *and* negative feedback effects, resulting in a reform that blended strong continuity—a preservation of most existing arrangements for financing and providing health care—with important change (Jacobs and Weaver 2015). Explanations of social policy development could gain considerable traction from systematic attention to the ways in which social-protection arrangements both build their own bases of political support and sow the seeds of their own revision over time.

Notes

* The author thanks the volume's editors and participants at the New Perspectives on Historical Institutionalism Conference at Temple University and the University of Pennsylvania for their helpful comments on earlier versions of this chapter.

1. Though see Skocpol's (1992) account of the self-undermining consequences of the entanglement of Civil War pensions with patronage politics.

References

Campbell, Andrea Louise. 2003. *How Policies Make Citizens: Senior Political Activism and the American Welfare State*. Princeton, NJ: Princeton University Press.

Clemens, Elizabeth. 2006. "Lineages of the Rube Goldberg State: Building and Blurring Public Programs, 1900–1940." In *Rethinking Political Institutions: The Art of the State*, ed. I. Shapiro, S. Skowronek, and D. Galvin. New York: New York University Press, 380–443.

Greif, Avner and David D. Laitin. 2004. "A Theory of Endogenous Institutional Change." *American Political Science Review* 98 (4): 633–652.

Hacker, Jacob S. 1998. "The Historical Logic of National Health Insurance: Structure and Sequence in the Development of British, Canadian, and U.S. Medical Policy." *Studies in American Political Development* 12 (1): 57–130.

Hacker, Jacob S. 2002. *The Divided Welfare State: The Battle over Public and Private Social Benefits in the United States*. New York: Cambridge University Press.

Hacker, Jacob S. 2004. "Privatizing Risk without Privatizing the Welfare State: The Hidden Politics of Social Policy Retrenchment in the United States." *American Political Science Review* 98 (2): 243–260.

Hacker, Jacob S. 2010. "The Road to Somewhere: Why Health Reform Happened." *Perspectives on Politics* 8 (3): 861–876.

Hacker, Jacob S. and Paul Pierson. 2010. "Winner-Take-All Politics: Public Policy, Political Organization, and the Precipitous Rise of Top Incomes in the United States." *Politics and Society* 38 (2): 152–204.

Hattam, Victoria C. 1993. *Labor Visions and State Power: The Origins of Business Unionism in the United States*. Princeton, NJ: Princeton University Press.

Häusermann, Silja. 2010. *The Politics of Welfare State Reform in Continental Europe: Modernization in Hard Times*. New York: Cambridge University Press.

Howard, Christopher. 1997. *The Hidden Welfare State: Tax Expenditures and Social Policy in the United States*. Princeton, NJ: Princeton University Press.

Immergut, Ellen M. 1992. *Health Politics: Interests and Institutions in Western Europe*. New York: Cambridge University Press.

Jacobs, Alan M. 2010. "Policymaking as Political Constraint: Institutional Development in the U.S. Social Security Program." In *Explaining Institutional Change: Ambiguity, Agency, and Power*, ed. J. Mahoney and K. Thelen. New York: Cambridge University Press, 94–131.

Jacobs, Alan M. 2011. *Governing for the Long Term: Democracy and the Politics of Investment*. New York: Cambridge University Press.

Jacobs, Alan M. and R. Kent Weaver. 2015. "When Policies Undo Themselves: Self-Undermining Feedback as a Source of Policy Change." *Governance* 28 (4): 441–457.

Jacobs, Lawrence R. and Theda Skocpol. 2010. *Health Care Reform and American Politics: What Everyone Needs to Know*. New York: Oxford University Press.

Katznelson, Ira. 2013. *Fear Itself: The New Deal and the Origins of Our Time*. 1st Edition. New York: Liveright.

Korpi, Walter. 1983. *The Democratic Class Struggle*. Boston, MA: Routledge & K. Paul.

Lieberman, Robert C. 1998. *Shifting the Color Line: Race and the American Welfare State*. Cambridge, MA: Harvard University Press.

Mahoney, James and Kathleen Thelen. 2010a. "A Theory of Gradual Institutional Change." In *Explaining Institutional Change: Ambiguity, Agency, and Power*, ed. J. Mahoney and K. Thelen. New York: Cambridge University Press, 1–37.

Mahoney, James and Kathleen Thelen, eds. 2010b. *Explaining Institutional Change: Ambiguity, Agency, and Power*. New York: Cambridge University Press.

Maioni, Antonia. 1998. *Parting at the Crossroads: The Emergence of Health Insurance in the United States and Canada*. Princeton, NJ: Princeton University Press.

Mettler, Suzanne. 2011. *The Submerged State: How Invisible Government Policies Undermine American Democracy*. Chicago: University of Chicago Press.

Morgan, Kimberly J. and Andrea Louise Campbell. 2011. *The Delegated Welfare State: Medicare, Markets, and the Governance of Social Policy*. New York: Oxford University Press.

Patashnik, Eric. 2000. *Putting Trust in the U.S. Budget: Federal Trust Funds and the Politics of Commitment*. New York: Cambridge University Press.

Patashnik, Eric. 2003. "After the Public Interest Prevails: The Political Sustainability of Policy Reform." *Governance* 16 (2): 203–234.

Patashnik, Eric M. 2008. *Reforms at Risk: What Happens After Major Policy Changes Are Enacted*. Princeton, NJ: Princeton University Press.

Pierson, Paul. 1994. *Dismantling the Welfare State? Reagan, Thatcher, and the Politics of Retrenchment*. New York: Cambridge University Press.

Quadagno, Jill S. 1994. *The Color of Welfare: How Racism Undermined the War on Poverty*. New York: Oxford University Press.

Rimlinger, Gaston V. 1971. *Welfare Policy and Industrialization in Europe, America, and Russia*. New York: Wiley.

Schickler, Eric. 2001. *Disjointed Pluralism: Institutional Innovation and the Development of the U.S. Congress*. Princeton, NJ: Princeton University Press.

Skocpol, Theda. 1992. *Protecting Soldiers and Mothers: The Political Origins of Social Policy in the United States*. Cambridge, MA: Belknap Press of Harvard University Press.

Starr, Paul. 2011. *Remedy and Reaction: The Peculiar American Struggle Over Health Care Reform*. New Haven, CT: Yale University Press.

Steinmo, Sven. 1996. *Taxation and Democracy: Swedish, British, and American Approaches to Financing the Modern State*. New Haven, CT: Yale University Press.

Steinmo, Sven and Jon Watts. 1995. "It's the Institutions, Stupid! Why Comprehensive National Health Insurance Always Fails in America." *Journal of Health Politics, Policy and Law* 20 (2): 329–372.

Streeck, Wolfgang and Kathleen Thelen. 2005. "Introduction: Institutional Change in Advanced Political Economies." In *Beyond Continuity: Institutional Change in Advanced Political Economies*, ed. Wolfgang Streeck and Kathleen Ann Thelen. New York: Oxford University Press, 1–39.

Teles, Steven. 2013. "Kludgeocracy in America." *National Affairs* (17): 97–114.

Thelen, Kathleen. 2004. *How Institutions Evolve: The Political Economy of Skills in Germany, Britain, the United States, and Japan*. New York: Cambridge University Press.

Tsebelis, George. 1995. *Veto Players: How Political Institutions Work*. Princeton, NJ: Princeton University Press.

Weaver, R. Kent. 2010. "Paths and Forks or Chutes and Ladders? Negative Feedbacks and Policy Regime Change." *Journal of Public Policy* 30 (2): 137–162.

Weaver, R. Kent and Bert A. Rockman, eds. 1993. *Do Institutions Matter? Government Capabilities in the United States and Abroad*. Washington, D.C.: The Brookings Institution.

Wilensky, Harold L. 1974. *The Welfare State and Equality: Structural and Ideological Roots of Public Expenditures*. Berkeley: University of California Press.

CHAPTER 21

CITIZENSHIP AND RACE

PAUL FRYMER*

BENEDICT Anderson (1983) has famously argued that nation-states are "imagined communities," and the United States is no exception. What constitutes an "American"—whether it is defined legally, ideologically, or geographically—has evolved dramatically over the nation's history and over the course of a territorial expansion whereby thirteen Atlantic-side states became fifty states crossing a continent and an ocean. One of the most notable ways in which the definition of an American has changed is with regard to the perceived racial boundaries of citizenship and rights. Although the United States has never officially declared itself a nation exclusively built of one racial or ethnic group, for much of its history it nonetheless restricted citizenship and related rights on racial grounds. Under the Naturalization Act of 1790, only people of European ancestry were allowed to naturalize as citizens. Most opportunities in early America for settlement, property rights, and naturalization were restricted to either existing American citizens or immigrants of European descent.

Along the way, critical extensions were made, most notably with the passage of the Fourteenth Amendment and Naturalization Act of 1870 that extended citizenship and naturalization rights to African Americans that followed the Civil War. Decades later, the Dawes Act of 1887 began the process of granting citizenship rights to Native Americans, a process that was formalized in 1924. Important legal and bureaucratic decisions continued to fine tune citizenship opportunities along racial and ethnic lines, though often in seemingly arbitrary and racially biased ways (Hochschild and Powell 2008; Jacobson 1998; Skrentny 2002). In the middle of the twentieth century, Congress finally intervened formally with the Immigration and Nationality Act of 1952 that abolished the use of gender and racial categories in making naturalization restrictions, and in 1965 with the Hart-Celler Act that ended national origins quotas.

The Hart-Celler legislation was passed in the midst of a dramatic decade that witnessed a series of foundational civil rights measures, most notably the 1964 Civil Rights Act and the Voting Rights Act of 1965. At the time, many believed that the United States was on the precipice of achieving the long-standing aspiration of a color-blind society that privileged and legally mandated individual rights and toleration. Today, a half-century later, there are many important trajectories that suggest significant progress toward racial equality in our nation's schools, businesses, and government, with the election of President Barack Obama providing a critical, if largely symbolic, milestone on these possibilities and achievements. But the United States also continues to confront racial inequality in many different forms, some that stem from continuing individual and societal racism, some that derive from institutional dynamics that continue to promote racial inequities, and some resulting from long-standing legacies of inequality and prejudice that have not been sufficiently removed. Furthermore, there are trends that have developed in the post-civil rights era that reflect new and frequently profound forms of inequality, with perhaps no trend more alarming than the massive rise of black male incarceration in the post-civil rights era.

Thus, expanding equality in the areas of both citizenship rights and civil rights has very much been an "unsteady march" with defeats and renewed exclusionary politics frequently following and even paralleling moments of progress and inclusion (Klinkner and Smith 1999). Such unsteadiness challenges many of the conventional understandings for why race and racism have been surprisingly relevant in a nation that espouses individual rights and toleration. Scholars had long believed that racism was something that existed because of irrational prejudices that "lingered" within individuals, and as such would eventually disappear as people became more educated and integrated and better equipped to confront their own irrational beliefs in the face of their more rational and long-standing ideological predispositions toward liberal equality of opportunity. A consequence of this understanding is that it has led political scientists to see race itself as "irrational" and thus outside of the broader dynamics of American politics, worthy of an important footnote or final week of a course syllabus, but unnecessary for further integration into institutional and ideological models and theoretical understandings.

In recent decades, historical institutional (HI) scholars have done much to counter this long-standing narrative, arguing that institutional dynamics, particularly those temporally impacted by racial cleavages, both embed racial inequality and frequently incentivize political actors to maintain certain divisions and hierarchies, even as societal attitudes appear to be changing. Equally important, this scholarship has provocatively argued that we cannot understand American politics and institutions without incorporating race and racial cleavages into our definitional models. In this chapter, I begin then with a discussion of how race is most conventionally understood within the American political tradition, and then focus on different ways in which historical institutional approaches contradict this tradition by emphasizing how quite normal and every day politics of American state-building and institutional dynamics work to shape the development of racial conflict and broader conceptions of race. I also explore how racial conflict has importantly impacted the development of the state, with attention both to how race and racial conflict have *impeded* state institutional growth and critically *enhanced* state authority, enabling surprising institutional strengths that may well have otherwise defied a nation-state built on political foundations emphasizing weakness. Indeed, one of the real insights of historical institutional research has been to show how important political and welfare provisions and societally accepted "rights"—many of the foundations of the nation's modern state—have only become legitimated and politically entrenched because of the state's initial and often enduring need to intervene to confront racial divisions and conflict.

Understanding the Existence of Race within the American Liberal Tradition

Although few scholars of American politics would disagree that race was and remains important to American politics and institutional development, there is much confusion as to how to incorporate the concept into broader understandings of the dynamics of American government. To discuss racial distinctions in the United States necessarily involves examining a range of features and events that lie in contradiction with a polity celebrated for its liberal-democratic institutions. Indeed, leading democratic thinkers have long struggled to make sense of these incongruities. Thomas Jefferson (1780 [1999]) arguably never made sense of them, nor did Alexis de Tocqueville (1832 [2001]) who relegated his discussion of slavery and Indian removal to the final chapter of *Democracy in America*, a chapter that though sharply incompatible with much of the rest of the book, did not lead him to compromise his broader conclusions about the nation's foundations in liberalism and egalitarianism. Frederick Douglass (1852) both celebrated the substance of American ideals and denounced them as ironic and a sham, while W. E. B. Du Bois (1903 [1994]) talked of African Americans experiencing an ever-present feeling of "two-ness" or double consciousness that separates their understanding of individuality, race, and nation. Gunnar Myrdal's (1944) *The American Dilemma* emphasized that racism and liberalism were sharply at odds, with the former on its way out and the latter poised (at the time of his writing) to triumph. In all of these accounts, racism is portrayed as a regrettable exception to an otherwise foundational liberal tradition, a phenomenon rooted in irrational prejudice among individuals but not necessarily consequential for the nation's established democratic ideologies and institutions. Attitudes and behaviors of individuals are the problem, and progress would only occur if white Americans shed such prejudices and aligned their attitudes with their professed values.

This view continues to influence contemporary Political Science scholarship, motivating a research agenda dominated by behavioral scholars interested in political psychology, individual attitudes, and the priming of irrational prejudice (see, e.g., Huddy and Feldman 2009; Hutchings and Jardina 2009; Sears, Sidanius, and Bobo 2000). Such a view also impacts the way many institutional scholars handle the concept; because race is irrational and exceptional, it by and large stands outside of institutional dynamics with only the rare occasion in which it flares up to such a degree that otherwise racially-neutral institutions must of necessity respond (e.g., Carmines and Stimson 1989; Poole and Rosenthal 2007). But race's consequence is always relatively short-term—it can emerge for a series of years to capture a political party, dominate a legislative session, and even lead to widespread violence and civil war. But what is critical in these accounts is that its impact for institutions is not considered as lasting; race is not foundational nor embedded in institutional dynamics in any meaningful way and such institutions are thought to respond to incentives and ideal points that exist independently of racial hierarchies and history.

This view of irrationality and exceptionality is not without important merits and fits with our quite correct understanding that race is a constructed category, with perceived differences in society the result of societal intervention, not a product of genetic makeup (Appiah 1996). It also offers important rhetorical power for those seeking to promote change in America, as it allows activists from Douglass to Martin Luther King to Barack Obama to make powerful political critiques that challenge Americans to at least make personal changes that fulfill national ideals.

But even an irrational and artificial concept such as race becomes normalized and rationalized when embedded within nation-state-building and institutional development. As Paul Gilroy (1991, 11) argues, treating racism as an exception is "akin to a coat of paint on the external structures of social relations which can be scraped off if the right ideological tools and political elbow grease are consciously applied to the task." Race is not just socially constructed but politically constructed and in a nation that has been divided along racial lines from its founding, it cannot help but become intrinsic to national politics and state-building. We cannot understand either political development or modern politics without understanding how race importantly participated in creating and structurally maintaining political and societal cleavages. As Anthony Marx (1998, 5–6) has written, states make race, as they "play a central role in imposing the terms of official domination, with unintended consequences. Official exclusion, as by race, legitimates these categories as a form of social identity" which in the long run entrenches such identities by mobilizing and institutionalizing these identities into long-standing functions of the government. In the United States, national institutions from the Constitution to the two-party system to the policymaking process have been critical in constituting and reifying racial categories, structuring how people of different races are treated by privileging certain populations over others, and alternately creating and reinforcing economic, social, and geographical differences that become marked by racial categorization (Goldberg 2001; Lieberman 1998; Omi and Winant 1994).

Of course, the race exceptionalism thesis is by no means ubiquitous, and an important list of scholars over time have engaged in rich and complicated debates over the roots and political meanings of race and racism, with a frequent emphasis on more structural forces in society that sees inequality as enduring and embedded in political institutions (e.g., Bobo 1988; Bunche 1936; Dawson 2001; Katznelson 1976; Pinderhughes 1987; Reed 1999; Thompson 2005; Walton and Smith 2000). Historical institutional scholars have importantly contributed to this exchange by specifying the way that ideological, coalitional, and institutional forces continue to renegotiate our understandings of race with consequences for public policy, societal relationships, and individual identity. Much of this research has relied on imaginative uses of the "the state," a term with a meaning that varies across disciplines—critical race theorists, for instance, have tended to use the term more expansively, seeing the state involved in the production of cultural-capital (e.g., Gilroy 1991; Goldberg 2001; Harris 1993; Omi and Winant 1994)—but allows political scientists to show how a range of institutional rules and actors develop in ways that are importantly divergent from society, following temporally and path-dependent models that enable entrenched actors to shape policy and political agendas often well after there is an active public mobilized in support of certain mandates. By focusing on the politics of "development" and including a greater array of political behavior, including the significance of non-behavior, historical institutional scholars have been able to incorporate racial divisions and the politics of racial formation in ways missed by more straightforwardly positivist and formal discussions of legislatures and elections. Understanding structures that have developed temporally in response to varying mobilizations and both endogenous and exogenous forces enables us to see the important ways in which social conflicts of yester-year continue to impact current day politics, often without the recognition or conscious intent of public officials.

The Impact of National Institutions and the State on Racial Formation

Broadly, there are two important categories of historical institutional research interested in race and racial formation. First is a group of scholars interested in understanding the ideological dimensions of race, both in the ways they intersect and contradict with dominant national ideologies grounded in liberal language, and in the ways that these ideologies are in turn institutionalized in national politics. These scholars are broadly in dialogue with the likes of Tocqueville, Myrdal, and Louis Hartz (1955), whose work in the middle of the twentieth century has in particular cast a powerful shadow over APD understandings of American development because of his provocative claim that the nation is both fundamentally and importantly bounded by "liberal" thought. The claim has led respondents to be in fierce disagreement over whether he defined the boundaries in terms that are inclusive or exclusive of racial hierarchies, with some arguing that liberalism and racial hierarchies are importantly intertwined or even necessarily connected (Hattam 2007; HoSang 2010; Kim 2000; Mehta 1999; Reed 1999; Rogin 1987; Sawyer 2006; Tillery 2009), and others claiming that liberalism is more separable and better understood as an ideology in constant conflict with an equally established and powerful ideology rooted in hierarchies and racial difference (King and Smith 2005; Smith 1997). Certainly, both sides agree that American political development has been fundamentally driven by racial conflict, with a rather constant fight over the meaning of American-ness being driven by a sense throughout much of the nation's history among both political elites and the public that the nation is both liberal *and* white, with the resulting contradictions fought over in ways that continuously alter and negotiate our understandings of the nation's most fundamental precepts.

What is in turn critical to all of this work is that, regardless of how they define liberalism, the polity is infused with multiple racial orders that are layered, often intersecting, and reignite in different historical moments to continually shape state-building and policymaking (King and Smith 2005). Embracing complexity instead of being confounded by it, this scholarship nicely employs the many tools of APD—such as intercurrence and patchwork (Orren and Skowronek 2004)—to show a multi-layered political project that is open to different paths and trajectories all the while being importantly confined by earlier historical acts (Pierson 2004). Indeed, only through this approach can we truly understand the politics of racial formation because we need to be aware of both the ways in which race is denied salience and the historical variations in the way it is manifested in order to truly encompass its scope and implications (Omi and Winant 1994).

A second group of scholars has focused more directly on the ways that these ideologies have impacted national policymaking through institutional mechanisms. Institutions, in these accounts, are thought to incentivize certain types of behaviors and enable certain types of inequalities. Structures and institutions are the hallmarks of power—they provide a place for power to lie, provide it with advantageous rules and weapons, and create a separation and protection for those with power from those without it. Powerful actors, in turn, construct reality with the weapons at their disposal, and race is both one of the many weapons and a byproduct of this construction. Moreover, because of their attention to the role that institutions and politics play in identity construction, political representation and power, as well as to the temporal dimensions by which ideas and ideologies fluctuate through different eras and regimes, historical institutional scholars offer unique resources in uncovering why race continues to structure so much of society's inequalities. This research illuminates that the confluence of institutions, power, and interests shape politics in ways that cannot simply be explained through ideology, prejudice, or even hegemony.

This literature tends to be separable by their focus on different historical eras in which institution building would have critical long-term consequences for racial formation and the longevity of inequality. The impact of race's exclusion from New Deal policies of the 1930s and 1940s has been particularly fruitful (Brown 1999; Katznelson 2005; King 1995; Lieberman 1998; Kryder 2001; McMahon 2004; Mettler 1998; Quadagno 1996). Political coalitions and institutional forms at the time of the creation of important welfare policies created patterns of opportunity and exclusion. In different ways, this scholarship argues that a racially divided New Deal era, with the Democratic Party encompassing northern liberals, southern segregrationists, and a labor movement dominated by white men resistant to racial and gender equity, had important consequences in the creation of national policies designed to remedy social and economic inequality. These policies frequently created bifurcated possibilities and further entrenched racial inequities in work spheres left untouched by the New Dealers. This era was also marked by striking tension between national and state institutions over implementation, and instructively illuminates how federal structures became the terrain in which civil rights advocates and opponents fought, and the way in which states were able to importantly bifurcate otherwise "universal" government policies so as the enforcement practices were alternatively race neutral and race specific dependent on the sovereign location of the implementation.

Although the New Deal period, one that encompasses the long development between the Progressive Era and the culmination of the Roosevelt Administration's implementation of an extensive federal bureaucracy, has dominated historical institutional work among American politics scholars, there has also been important and increasing attention to other time periods, including the institutional politics of slavery both at the time of the Founding and in the aftermath of the Civil War (e.g., Brandwein 2000, 2011; Graber 2006; Marx 1998; Smith 1997), as well as Indian Removal and the politics of US expansion (e.g., Bruyneel 2007; Rogin 1987), whereby scholars have shown how early institutional developments shaped not just racial politics but the later functioning and trajectory of the New Deal welfare state. At each period, state-building was directly impacted by political elites responding to perceived threats coming from racial cleavages and hierarchies. Our Constitution was profoundly shaped by the need to respond to perceived threats from Indian nations and the national divisions over slavery. The nation perceived itself from an early stage as simultaneously liberal, expansionist, exclusionary, and colonial, with foundational policies such as the Northwest Ordinance designed to promote all of these seemingly contradictory visions simultaneously, and politicians used the threats of Indian nations to gather the necessary warrants needed to strengthen institutional apparatuses otherwise weakened by postwar fears of a strong state. Slavery also impacted state-building, both in ways that created weakness and strength as politicians negotiated how to best balance north versus south while simultaneously prohibiting slavery's expansion and defending the property rights of southern slave owners. Many of the institutions that developed out of this period were designed to check the power of both sides in the slavery debate—federalist principles provided important autonomy to individual states, the national party system incentivized campaign politics that would focus on national medians that would moderate the louder advocates and opponents of slavery. At the same time, other institutions that became critical weapons for later national government exertions, such as the commerce clause, would develop in direct interaction to these political divides, intervening at the time to preserve the institution of slavery and control people of African descent, but setting the precedents for future national authority on behalf of quite different goals.

Scholars have also turned their attention to more recent periods. One area of focus has been on the politics of the rights revolution and Civil Rights Era both in terms of the development of civil rights policies, the new forms of institutional power and state capacity, and the important consequences of these developments for current day racial inequality. Much of this work has a long historical view, typically beginning with the earliest ground-level mobilizations around civil rights in the 1930s and 1940s and showing how they importantly began the work of forming what would become a powerful intersection between the civil rights movement and the Democratic Party of the 1960s (Lee 2002; Parker 2009; Schickler 2013). But this work has also been particularly insightful in emphasizing how the Civil Rights Act and the Voting Rights Act reshaped both federal and local politics and provided the American state with new capacities that were frequently fused from public and private conglomerations. The creation of employment rights and affirmative action policies provided new actors with authority to intervene in the workplace and more broad-standing cultural inequities, but in a manner that also importantly limited future efforts to remedy inequalities in the workplace (Chen 2009; Dobbin and Sutton 1998; Skrentny 2002). Legal actors—not just the judges who importantly jumpstarted the rights revolution with cases such as *Brown v. Board of Education*, but a broader legal community of lawyers and private administrators—moved to the center of state implementation. To enforce this new set of laws, legislators frequently incentivized private lawyers to implement an array of civil rights laws that were otherwise provided with few formal enforcement powers (Farhang 2010; Frymer 2008; Goluboff 2010; Pedriana and Stryker 2004). Still others, such as Robert Mickey (2008) and Richard Valelly (2005), have examined the importance of historical trajectories in the rise of voting rights reforms driven both by courts and electoral branches; here the varying capacity of state institutions looms large in understanding why certain features of voting rights had success and others led to shake ups more than results.

In light of politically provocative changes by the US Census Bureau to its definitions of racial categories, historical institutionalists have begun to look at the consequences that the institutional act of counting those residing on US soil necessarily provides for racial formation. The political evolution of the Census illuminates how government agencies not only mirror, but create imprints on American society by creating racial categories at the exclusion of others (Hochschild and Powell 2008; Williams 2008), and by providing government benefits to certain groups simply because they fit within more politically acceptable definitions. Similarly, scholars have given attention to the rising incarceration of African Americans, and particularly black men, in the post-civil rights era, with important emphasis on how changes to drug and crime laws were part a long-standing political-institutional process of an American state responding to the reconfiguration of racial hierarchies in the mid-twentieth century (Alexander 2012; Gottschalk 2006; Murakawa 2008; Weaver 2007). Each of these literatures emphasize how modern snapshots of public policy cannot be understood without attention to how evolving institutions are shaping current events because they are responding to differing and sometimes inconsistent logics and transformations of prior eras.

Moving Forward: Race and the Formation of the American State

A leading claim of American historical institutional scholarship is that national institutions gained notable authority and capacity as it responded to the late nineteenth-century Industrial Revolution and its exacerbations on the economy and society, culminating in the New Deal welfare state of the 1930s. Much of the scholarship discussed here uses this claim as a launching point for understanding the contribution of race. For many of these scholars, the major consequence of race for American political development has been to *deny* or *bifurcate* or *slow down* important features of an otherwise developing welfare state. Race, as W. E. B. Du Bois (1935 [1998]) famously argued, divided class coalitions, weakening the labor movement and hindering Progressive efforts to bring about major welfare reform. But overlooked in this narrative is the way in which race, akin to class and economic industrialization, has critically enhanced state capacity. Many of the most singularly important and successful policy creations promoting substantive rights for Americans—not just for African Americans and other racial minorities but all Americans—have come about because of powers granted to the state in the midst of battles over race and civil rights.

I have made reference throughout this chapter to a number of institutional features that the US government has used to promote further centralization and national authority that were developed very much in the midst of national debates over race—constitutional provisions such as the commerce clause, extra-constitutional institutions such as a strong two-party system, and non-government institutions incentivized by the state such as litigators and legal administrators. Of course, the most profound institutional weapon was provided with the passage of the Fourteenth Amendment, an Amendment that would eventually become a centerpiece for rights that have extended well beyond the politics of race. Passed shortly after the Civil War to protect the rights of newly freed slaves entering into a society deeply resistant to racial equality, the Fourteenth Amendment has been used to assert individual rights in an era where capitalism was still widely contested and later promoted the rights of numerous minority groups in the middle of the twentieth century. The Civil Rights Act of 1964 and Voting Rights Act of 1965 are yet further examples of state-building as a product of racial conflict. Both statutes provided a powerful institutional resource, intersecting with the Fourteenth Amendment, and providing further substantive rights for Americans that have remained importantly entrenched even in an era of hyper-retrenching policy agendas.

What is important to recognize from the workings and interpretations of these enactments is that it has provided rights for Americans in places they otherwise would not—voting, the work place, the home—by using a far more expansive notion of substantive rights that are otherwise hard to locate within other areas of the Constitution. Current day employment law is just one example of this: with the exception of a dwindling unionized workforce, only the Civil Rights Act and related statutes provide substantive protections for American workers; most Americans have few rights (and certainly not drawn from statutes) and are labeled as "at will" and subject to the whims of their employers. The principles of the Civil Rights Act has been expanded by courts and legislators to provide rights that extend far beyond its initially quite narrow scope, an expansion that was otherwise unlikely. The Voting Rights Act, similarly, provides protections against partisan gerrymandering and other political gamesmanship that are otherwise completely acceptable outside the act's legislated boundaries, but in turn which have provided important legitimacy for reconceptualizing voting and electoral rights for all Americans.

The American state is a different state than existed at the nation's founding. To the important degree that race played a role in this transformation, it is not simply a result of racism and prejudice being removed from an otherwise democratic polity, but is also a byproduct of ongoing interaction between politically and societally driven racial cleavages and national institutional dynamics. The intersection of race and the American state has harnessed opportunities for institutional growth, a reconceptualization of state weapons, and a profound altering of the nation's ideological range and boundaries.

Note

* The author thanks Adam Sheingate for very helpful suggestions and revisions to an earlier draft of this chapter.

References

Alexander, Michelle. 2012. *The New Jim Crow: Mass Incarceration in the Age of Colorblindness*. New York: New Press.

Anderson, Benedict. 1983. *Imagined Communities: Reflections on the Origins and Spread of Nationalism*. New York: Verso.

Appiah, Anthony K. 1996. "Race, Culture, Identity: Misunderstood Connections." In *Color Conscious: The Political Morality of Race*, ed. Anthony Appiah and Amy Gutmann. Princeton, NJ: Princeton University Press, 30–106.

Bobo, Lawrence. 1988. "Group Conflict, Prejudice, and the Paradox of Contemporary Racial Attitudes." In *Eliminating Racism: Profiles in Controversy*, ed. Phyllis Katz and Dalmas A. Taylor. New York: Plenum Press, 85–114.

Brandwein, Pamela. 2000. "Slavery as an Interpretive Issue in the Reconstruction Debates." *Law and Society Review* 30 (2): 315–366.

Brandwein, Pamela. 2011. *Rethinking the Judicial Settlement of Reconstruction*. New York: Cambridge University.

Brown, Michael K. 1999. *Race, Money, and the American Welfare State*. Ithaca, NY: Cornell University Press.

Bruyneel, Kevin. 2007. *The Third Space of Sovereignty: The Post-Colonial Politics of U.S.-Indigenous Relations*. Minneapolis, MN: University of Minnesota Press.

Bunche, Ralph J. 1936. *A World View of Race*. Washington, D.C.: Associates in Negro Education.

Carmines, Edward G. and James A. Stimson. 1989. *Issue Evolution: Race and the Transformation of American Politics*. Princeton, NJ: Princeton University Press.

Chen, Anthony S. 2009. *The Fifth Freedom: Jobs, Politics, and Civil Rights in the United States*. Princeton, NJ: Princeton University Press.

Dawson, Michael. 2001. *Black Visions: The Roots of Contemporary African-American Political Ideologies*. Chicago: University of Chicago Press.

Dobbin, Frank and John R. Sutton. 1998. "The Strength of a Weak State: The Rights Revolution and the Rise of Human Resource Management Divisions." *American Journal of Sociology* 104 (2): 441–476.

Douglass, Frederick. 1976 [1852]. "What to the Slave is the Fourth of July." *The Black Scholar* 7 (10): 32–37.
Du Bois, W. E. B. 1903 [1994]. *The Souls of Black Folk*. New York: Dover.
Du Bois, W. E. B. 1935[1998]. *Black Reconstruction*. New York: Free Press.
Farhang, Sean. 2010. *The Litigation State: Public Regulation and Private Lawsuits in the United States*. Princeton, NJ: Princeton University Press.
Frymer, Paul. 2008. *Black and Blue: African Americans, the Labor Movement, and the Decline of the Democratic Party*. Princeton, NJ: Princeton University Press.
Gilroy, Paul. 1991. *"There Ain't no Black in the Union Jack": The Cultural Politics of Race and Nation*. Chicago: University of Chicago Press.
Goldberg, David Theo. 2001. *The Racial State*. New York: Wiley-Blackwell.
Goluboff, Risa. 2010. *The Lost Promise of Civil Rights*. Cambridge, MA: Harvard University Press.
Gottschalk, Marie. 2006. *The Prison and the Gallows: The Politics of Mass Incarceration in America*. New York: Cambridge.
Graber, Mark A. 2006. *Dred Scott and the Problem of Constitutional Evil*. New York: Cambridge University Press.
Harris, Cheryl. 1993. "Whiteness as Property." *Harvard Law Review* 106 (8): 1707–1791.
Hartz, Louis. 1955. *The Liberal Tradition in America*. New York: Harcourt, Brace, and World.
Hattam, Victoria. 2007. *In the Shadow of Race: Jews, Latinos, and Immigrant Politics in the United States*. Chicago: University of Chicago Press.
Hochschild, Jennifer and Brenna Marea Powell. 2008. "Racial Reorganization and the United States Census 1850–1930: Mulattoes, Half-Breeds, Mixed Parentage, Hindoos, and the Mexican Race." *Studies in American Political Development* 22 (1): 59–96.
HoSang, Daniel Martinez. 2010. *Racial Propositions: Ballot Initiatives and the Making of Postwar California*. Berkeley: University of California Press.
Huddy, Leonie and Stanley Feldman. 2009. "On Assessing the Political Effects of Racial Prejudice." *Annual Review of Political Science* 12: 423–447.
Hutchings, Vincent L. and Ashley E. Jardina. 2009. "Experiments on Racial Priming in Political Campaigns." *Annual Review of Political Science* 12: 397–402.
Jacobson, Matthew Frye. 1998. *Whiteness of a Different Color: European Immigrants and the Alchemy of Race*. Cambridge, MA: Harvard University Press.
Jefferson, Thomas. 1780 [1999]. *Notes on the State of Virginia*. New York: Penguin.
Katznelson, Ira. 1976. *Black Men, White Cities: Race, Politics, and Migration in the United States, 1900–1930, and Britain, 1948–1968*. Chicago: University of Chicago Press.
Katznelson, Ira. 2005. *When Affirmative Action Was White: An Untold Story of Racial Inequality in Twentieth-Century America*. New York: W.W. Norton.
Kim, Claire Jean. 2000. *Bitter Fruit: The Politics of Black-Korean Conflict in New York City*. New Haven, CT: Yale University Press.
King, Desmond. 1995. *Separate and Unequal: Black Americans and the U.S. Federal Government*. New York: Oxford University Press.
King, Desmond S. and Rogers M. Smith. 2005. "Racial Orders in American Political Development." *American Political Science Review* 99: 75–92.
Klinkner, Philip A. and Rogers M. Smith. 1999. *The Unsteady March: The Rise and Decline of Racial Equality in America*. Chicago: University of Chicago Press.
Kryder, Daniel. 2001. *Divided Arsenal: Race and the American State During World War II*. New York: Cambridge University Press.

Lee, Taeku. 2002. *Mobilizing Public Opinion*. Chicago: University of Chicago Press.
Lieberman, Robert C. 1998. *Shifting the Color Line: Race and the American Welfare State*. Princeton, NJ: Princeton University Press.
McMahon, Kevin. 2004. *Reconsidering Roosevelt on Race: How the Presidency Paved the Road to Brown*. Chicago: University of Chicago Press.
Marx, Anthony. 1998. *Making Race and Nation: A Comparison of the United States, South Africa, and Brazil*. New York: Cambridge University Press.
Mehta, Uday Singh. 1999. *Liberalism and Empire: A Study in Nineteenth-Century British Liberal Thought*. Chicago: University of Chicago Press.
Mettler, Suzanne. 1998. *Dividing Citizens: Gender and Federalism in New Deal Public Policy*. Ithaca, NY: Cornell University Press.
Mickey, Robert. 2008. "The Beginning of the End for Authoritarian Rule in America: *Smith v. Allwright* and the Abolition of the White Primary in the Deep South, 1944–1948." *Studies in American Political Development* 22 (2): 143–182.
Murakawa, Naomi. 2008. "The Origins of the Carceral Crisis: Racial Order as 'Law and Order' in Postwar American Politics." In *Race and American Political Development*, ed. Joseph Lowndes, Julie Novkov, and Dorian T. Warren. New York: Routledge, 234–255.
Myrdal, Gunnar. 1944. *An American Dilemma*. New York: Harper Brothers Publishing.
Omi, Michael and Howard Winant. 1994. *Racial Formation in the United States: From the 1960s to the 1990s*. New York: Routledge.
Orren, Karen and Stephen Skowronek. 2004. *The Search for American Political Development*. New York: Cambridge University Press.
Parker, Christopher. 2009. *Fighting for Democracy: Black Veterans and the Struggle against White Supremacy in the Postwar South*. Princeton, NJ: Princeton University Press.
Pedriana, Nicholas and Robin Stryker. 2004. "The Strength of a Weak Agency: Enforcement of Title VII of the 1964 Civil Rights Act and the Expansion of State Capacity, 1965–1971." *American Journal of Sociology* 110 (3): 709–760.
Pierson, Paul. 2004. *Politics in Time: History, Institutions, and Social Analysis*. Princeton, NJ: Princeton University Press.
Pinderhughes, Dianne. 1987. *Race and Ethnicity in Chicago Politics*. Urbana: University of Illinois Press.
Poole, Keith T. and Howard Rosenthal. 2007. *Ideology and Congress*. New York: Transaction.
Quadagno, Jill. 1996. *The Color of Welfare: How Racism Undermined the War on Poverty*. New York: Oxford University Press.
Reed, Adolph, Jr. 1999. *Stirrings in the Jug: Black Politics in the Post-Segregation Era*. Minneapolis, MT: University of Minnesota Press.
Rogin, Michael. 1987. *Ronald Reagan the Movie: And Other Episodes in Political Demonology*. Berkeley: University of California Press.
Sawyer, Mark Q. 2006. *Racial Politics in Post-Revolutionary Cuba*. New York: Cambridge University Press.
Schickler, Eric. 2013. "New Deal Liberalism and Racial Liberalism in the Mass Public, 1937–1968." *Perspectives on Politics* 11: 75–98.
Sears, David O., Jim Sidanius, and Lawrence Bobo, eds. 2000. *Racialized Politics: The Debate About Racism in America*. Chicago: University of Chicago Press.
Skrentny, John D. 2002. *The Minority Rights Revolution*. Cambridge, MA: Belknap Press.
Smith, Rogers M. 1997. *Civic Ideals: Conflicting Visions of Citizenship in U.S. History*. New Haven, CT: Yale University Press.

Thompson, Phillip J. 2005. *Double Trouble: Black Mayors, Black Communities, and the Call for Deep Democracy*. New York: Oxford University Press.

Tillery, Alvin B., Jr. 2009. "Tocqueville as Critical Race Theorist: The Perverse Effects of Whiteness as Property in Jacksonian America." *Political Research Quarterly* 62 (4): 639–652.

Tocqueville, Alexis de. 1832 [2001]. *Democracy in America*. New York: Signet.

Valelly, Richard M. 2005. *The Two Reconstructions: The Struggle for Black Enfranchisement*. Chicago: University of Chicago Press.

Walton, H. and Smith, C. 2000. *American Politics and the African American Quest for Universal Freedom*. New York: Longman.

Weaver, Vesla. 2007. "Frontlash: Race and the Development of Punitive Crime Policy." *Studies in American Political Development* 21 (Fall): 230–265.

Williams, Kim M. 2008. *Mark One or More: Civil Rights in Multiracial America*. Ann Arbor, MI: University of Michigan Press.

CHAPTER 22

INEQUALITY AND THE CARCERAL STATE

MARIE GOTTSCHALK*

THROUGHOUT American history, politicians and public officials have exploited public anxieties about crime and disorder for political gain. Over the last half-century, these political strategies and public anxieties have come together in the perfect storm. They have radically transformed US penal policies, spurring an enormous prison boom. Since the 1970s, the United States has built a carceral state that is unprecedented among Western countries and in US history. Today the United States is the world's warden, incarcerating a higher proportion of its people than any other country.

The carceral state has become a key governing institution in the United States and a major source of political, social, and economic inequalities. Its construction has deep historical and institutional roots. Struggles over penal policy and punishment have had "important and lasting consequences" for "the structure and legitimating fictions of American social order more generally" (McLennan 2008, 3).

The emergence and consolidation of the carceral state is a major milestone in American political development that arguably rivals in significance the expansion and contraction of the welfare state in the postwar period. What we have witnessed is a "durable shift in governing authority," to use Karen Orren and Stephen Skowronek's elegant definition of what constitutes political development (2004, 123). The state now exercises vast new controls over millions of people, resulting in a remarkable change in the distribution of authority in favor of law enforcement and corrections at the local, state, and federal levels. More than 8 million people—or in 1 in 23 adults—are under some form of state control through the criminal justice system (Pew Center on the States 2009).[1] These figures understate the enormous and disproportionate impact that this bold social experiment has had on certain groups in US society. If current trends continue, one in three black men and one in six Hispanic men are expected to spend some time in prison during their lives (Bonczar 2003).[2] The criminal justice system is increasingly serving as a gateway to a much larger system of stigmatization and permanent marginalization (Alexander 2010, 12). Evidence is mounting that the carceral state fundamentally impedes not only the political advancement of the most disadvantaged people in the United States, but also their economic advancement (Western 2006).

The carceral state is no longer just a problem largely confined to the prison cell and prison yard and to poor urban communities and minority groups—if it ever was. The US penal system has grown so extensive that it has begun to metastasize. It has altered how key governing and public institutions operate, everything from elections to schools to social programs like public housing and food stamps. Furthermore, it is bluntly and subtly remaking conceptions of citizenship as it condemns millions of people in the United States to "civil death"—the denial of core civil liberties and social benefits because of a criminal conviction—and creates a large and permanent group of political, economic, and social outcasts. In short, the country's penal system is no longer just the creation of the larger political, social, and economic forces that shape US society. It has become "one of those causal or shaping forces" (Haney 2008, 90).

The explosion in the size of the prison population and the retributive turn in US penal policy are now well documented. But the underlying political causes and wider political consequences of this massive expansion have not been well understood. This is beginning to change. Some of the most promising new research in this area explicitly or implicitly uses a historical institutional lens to understand the origins and development of the carceral state and the political possibilities for dismantling it. Just as the carceral state casts an ever-wider net, so does this new research.

This body of research has many of the hallmarks of what I identify as the exceptional niche that scholars associated with historical institutionalism originally carved out a generation ago: a willingness to tackle big, important political questions that often have enormous public policy and normative implications and that cannot be neatly sliced and diced; a high tolerance for answers that are sometimes messy and often not parsimonious; a healthy skepticism toward the neat and conventional periodizations that bookend political moments like the Progressive era or the "law-and-order" era; use of some basic analytical tools and frameworks from history, politics, and sociology in order to illuminate an important political phenomenon or problem but not necessarily to develop a grand theory of politics; a reflexive skepticism toward claims of American exceptionalism; a foregrounding of substance over methodology; a willingness to treat regional and state-level exceptions to the established national narrative as important problems that need to be explained in their own right and not just dismissed with an asterisk or footnote; and finally, a greater willingness to tackle what Ira Katznelson once described as the silences in the study of politics and public policy, especially the complex and intersecting ways in which race, class, ethnicity, and gender have altered the course of American political development (Katznelson 1986).

The emergence of the carceral state is cause to reconsider some fundamental issues in American politics. This chapter first discusses the deeper political, institutional, and historical origins of the carceral state at the national level. It then examines race and the development of the carceral state; state-level variations in the development of the carceral state; the relationship between the carceral state and the transformation of the welfare state; and explanations of cross-national differences in penal policy. It concludes with some musings on the state of historical institutional scholarship today, especially its capacity to illuminate pressing political problems related to growing political, economic, and social inequalities in the United States.

The Deeper Historical and Institutional Origins of the Carceral State

Until recently, analyses of the carceral state generally adopted a truncated timeframe to explain what changed in the United States beginning in the 1960s to disrupt its generally stable and unexceptional incarceration rate and to bolster the retributive model of punishment at the cost of the "rehabilitative ideal." The main political explanations included: an escalating crime rate and related shifts in public opinion, the war on drugs, the emergence of the profitable prison-industrial complex, structural changes in American culture and society with the coming of late modernity, politicians playing the "race card" as part of a public backlash against the civil rights movement and the political upheavals of the 1960s, and the collapse of the urban labor market for unskilled men due to deindustrialization and globalization.

These factors are critical to understanding the origins of the carceral state. But accounts that stress relatively recent developments seem to suggest that this major expansion of the state and radical shift in public policy have shallow roots. Yet contemporary penal policy actually has deep historical and institutional roots. Both state capacity to incarcerate and the legitimacy of the federal government to handle more criminal matters were built up slowly but surely well before the incarceration boom that began in the 1970s.

Political elites in the United States have a long history of raising law-and-order concerns in an attempt to further their own political fortunes. And Americans have a long history of periodic intense anxiety about crime and disorder. Yet only recently have these concerns and anxieties resulted in such a dramatic and unprecedented transformation of penal policies in a more punitive direction. By understanding the subtleties of this institutional and political context, we can begin to grasp why elite political preferences for a war on crime had such profound consequences for penal policies despite contemporary public opinion polls showing that Americans can be quite ambivalent about the crime issue.

Law and order was a recurrent and major theme in American politics long before the 1960s and long before the modern Republican Party strategically wielded this issue to achieve national political domination (Gottschalk 2006, chapter 3). The United States had an early identity as a convict nation. Penal concerns informed broader debates about republicanism, utilitarianism, and law and order during the founding decades.

Disagreements over the establishment of the penitentiary were deeply entangled with disputes over slavery and abolition in the antebellum years. After the Civil War, the convict-lease system was pivotal in the politics of Populism, Progressivism, race relations, and the economic development of the South. Penal labor was a leading issue for organized labor and a central feature in electoral politics from the late nineteenth century to the 1930s. During the New Deal, Franklin D. Roosevelt and Attorney General Homer Cummings shrewdly and quite successfully exploited sensational crimes, most notably the Lindbergh kidnapping, to advance their broader agenda of extending federal jurisdiction into crime control.

A number of historically embedded institutional developments that pre-date the 1960s laid the foundation for the construction of the carceral state (Gottschalk 2006). These include the historical underdevelopment of the US welfare state; the early establishment of an extensive network of rights-based and other public interest groups stretching back to the 1920s that helped lodge capital punishment in the courts, not the legislature; the exceptional nature of the origins and development of the public prosecutor in the United States; and the country's long history of morally charged crusades that helped build up the law enforcement apparatus by fits and starts.

In addition to these early institutional developments, a variety of other factors with deep historical roots help explain the emergence of the carceral state. For example, the much-heralded "liberal" features of American political culture and American institutions likely have contributed to rendering the US penal system harsher, more degrading, and less forgiving. As Whitman (2003) explains, in the absence or rejection of an aristocratic political culture and society, prisons in the United States historically have been rooted in extending a brute egalitarianism that subjects all prisoners, regardless of their social or political status, to "low status," dehumanizing treatment. By contrast, waves of penal reform in Germany and France often entailed "leveling up," or extending the penal and legal privileges enjoyed by political prisoners and incarcerated aristocrats to other offenders.

Race and the Development of the Carceral State

The construction of the carceral state complicates understandings of the role of race in American political development. The establishment of the carceral state was not merely the latest chapter in a book that began with slavery and moved on to convict leasing, Jim Crow, and the ghetto to control African Americans and other "dangerous classes." Although there are similarities between these social control institutions, it is important not to flatten out their differences and the differences in the political, institutional, and economic context that created and sustained them. Treating these institutions as one and the same minimizes the unprecedented nature of the incarceration boom in the United States since the 1970s.

Furthermore, racial explanations that are too narrowly constructed tend to keep the focus on the role of whites—especially elite politicians and other public figures—in the construction and defense of the carceral state. This has come at the cost of short shifting the varied roles that members of other racial and ethnic groups have played in challenging and bolstering the carceral state. It also slights other important political and institutional factors that built the carceral state and now stand in the way of devising successful political strategies to dismantle it. These other factors help explain substantial differences at the state level in the mechanisms, political actors, and timing of the prison boom.

Early work on the role of political elites in mass incarceration tended to center on how leading white politicians from Barry Goldwater to George Wallace to Richard Nixon to George H. W. Bush to Bill Clinton sought to refashion their political bases in the wake of the seismic political shifts set in motion by the civil rights movement. The conventional view is that the mid-1960s escalation in crime rates prompted national leaders, most notably presidential candidates, to exploit the issue of street crime by invoking the law-and-order card, which was really a thinly veiled race card. This provided an opening for the Republican Party to unsettle the New Deal liberal coalition by deploying the Southern strategy. This entailed courting whites disaffected from the Democratic Party by making appeals to law and order that were really thinly disguised racial appeals.

A new wave of historians and historically oriented political scientists and sociologists has complicated this story. These scholars have identified key developments dating back to the Progressive era and the early years of the civil rights movement that are pivotal in explaining the relationship between race and the development of the carceral state. This work has helped illuminate how and why the carceral state became so entrenched after incarceration rates began their decades-long ascent in 1973; why blacks were disproportionately affected; and why the carceral state has not faced more organized political opposition, especially from the groups that have been most directly affected by its growth. Some of this new historically oriented work also shifts the focus from the South to the North and identifies the central role that black Southern migrants to urban centers in the North played as political actors, political symbols, and political foils in the politics of crime and punishment (see, e.g., Murch 2010 and McLennan 2008).

In his magisterial study of what he calls the "biography of the idea of black criminality in the making of modern urban America," Khalil Gibran Muhammad (2010) excavates the varied and changing set of claims about black criminality that were constructed in the half-century leading up to World War II. He singles out the Progressive era as a formative moment in the development of the carceral state. Muhammad provocatively challenges the conventional wisdom that the Jim Crow South was the primary cauldron of racial criminalization that laid the foundations for the punitive turn that gave birth to the carceral state. He artfully shows how Progressive-era academics, journalists, politicians, and public figures located primarily in the North refashioned blackness through crime statistics. In the process, "white criminality gradually lost its fearsomeness" as Irish, Italian, Polish, and other white immigrant groups were "able to shed their criminal identities," but blacks were not (Muhammad 2010, 5). White criminality in urban areas with high concentrations of immigrants was increasingly viewed as largely a symptom of industrial capitalism and urban life. This fostered the widespread belief that white criminality could be ameliorated though greater public and private investment in education, social services, social programs, and public infrastructure. By contrast, blacks were increasingly viewed as heralding from an inferior culture, one so scarred by centuries of slavery that government intervention would be of little help until blacks uplifted their own race on their own (Muhammad 2010, 76).

The Strange Career of Law and Order

Naomi Murakawa picks up the story where Muhammad leaves off—the 1940s and 1950s, which she identifies as a formative period in the development of the carceral state (Murakawa 2014). She contends that race liberals associated with Harry Truman in the 1940s and 1950s, not race conservatives like Goldwater, Wallace, and Nixon in the 1960s, were the ones who first made "law and order" a national issue. For a time, the meaning of the phrase "law and order" was politically indeterminate and thus hotly contested. In the 1940s, race liberals invoked "law and order" as a rallying point to push for measures to protect blacks from interpersonal and state violence directed at them by white citizens and law enforcement officials. In the 1950s, conservative Southern Democrats opposed to desegregation and civil rights challenged race liberals by formulating their own association between civil rights, criminality, and blackness (Murakawa 2014; Weaver 2007). These race conservatives began strategically wielding the street crime issue well before national crime rates began to escalate and well before leading Republicans took up the law-and-order charge. By the late 1960s, calls for more law and order were widely understood to be calls for tougher laws, tougher sanctions, and tougher police and prosecutors to protect whites from street crime and from disorderly protests by blacks and their allies. Murakawa argues that the ways in which Truman and other race liberals formulated the law-and-order issue made it ultimately vulnerable to capture by race conservatives.

Many urban white voters in the North initially maintained a delicate balancing act on the civil rights issue. While they opposed racial integration at the local level, they supported national candidates who were pro-civil rights. This split political personality became less tenable as crime and disorder "became the fulcrum points at which the local and national intersected," thus weakening the New Deal coalition (Flamm 2005, 10). Leading strategists of the Republican Party sought to exploit this new political context. As part of the Southern strategy, they sought to appeal to whites' anxieties about the rising crime rate, which were entangled with other anxieties about their "loss of stature and privileges as economic opportunities narrowed and traditionally marginalized groups gained new rights" in a time of vast social, political, and cultural changes (Hohler-Hausmann 2010, 73).

The Republican Party was well situated to exploit these fears for political and electoral gain if it chose to do so. As the Democratic Party sundered over civil rights issues, the South became politically competitive for the first time since the end of Reconstruction a century earlier. This ushered in a major political realignment. Furthermore, exceptional features of the institutional structure of the United States—most notably the widespread use of elections to select judges and prosecutors—made it especially vulnerable to politicians seeking to stoke the public's fears of crime and to politicize law-and-order issues. We now know that some key social movements and liberal interest groups, including the victims' rights movement, women's movement, prisoners' rights movement, and the anti-death penalty movement, developed in ways that reinforced the punitive turn in penal policy (Gottschalk 2006; Bumiller 2008; Ritchie 2012).

The Carceral State and the State of Black Politics

Although black leaders, politicians, and advocacy groups were clearly not the main instigators of the punitive turn, their actions also contributed to the consolidation of the carceral state, in many cases unwittingly. The developments discussed so far coincided with the emergence of new patterns of racial inequality that would have important consequences for the politics of crime and punishment and the development of the carceral state. Until the civil rights era, the predominant pattern was one based largely on the exclusion of blacks. The pattern that emerged subsequently was rooted in selective incorporation in the context of widening education and income gaps amongst blacks and greater residential mobility for more affluent blacks (Wilson 1980; Katz, Stern, and Fader 2005; Gottschalk 2015, chapters 6 and 7).

The disincentives to represent the poor and disadvantaged have always been enormous (Paden 2011, 2). The disincentives to represent poor people who have run afoul of the law are even higher. In the immediate decades after World War II, competition from more radical organizations was key in prodding mainstream identity-based civil rights organizations to make the cause of the truly disadvantaged truly part of their mission and not just a rhetorical flourish. As Catherine Paden shows, even during the War on Poverty in the 1960s, aggressive advocacy on behalf of poverty alleviation was intermittent among older mainstream civil rights organizations like the National Association for the Advancement of Colored People (NAACP) and the National Urban League. When some mainstream organizations did act, it was often because younger organizations that aggressively challenged the status quo posed a competitive threat to their funding and membership bases. With the demise of the black power movement and the atrophy of groups like the Southern Christian Leadership Conference (SCLC), the Student Nonviolent Coordinating Committee (SNCC), and the Congress of Racial Equality (CORE), mainstream civil rights organizations faced less political pressure to embrace issues such as poverty alleviation and prisoners' rights. Furthermore, their priorities and strategies shifted substantially as they, like many interest groups, became professionally managed organizations that emphasized mass membership rather than mass mobilization (Paden 2011, 3; Skocpol 2003). As social, political, and economic inequalities have widened within historically disadvantaged groups in recent decades, some advocacy organizations have been increasingly unable or unwilling to give meaningful attention to the needs and interests of the most marginalized people within their more complex constituencies (Strolovitch 2007; Gottschalk 2015).

With the onset of the war on drugs in the 1970s, fissures began to open up among African Americans on the crime and punishment issue. Some leading black officials and public figures began to distance themselves from the cause of prisoners' rights and to abandon their earlier focus on prisons as key sites of state violence. They also started backing, at times quite enthusiastically, some of the signature punitive measures that helped build the carceral state.

The conventional wisdom is that the Republicans launched the war on drugs in the 1970s, and Democrats, including leading black politicians, became belated conscripts in the 1980s in the face of what they perceived to be electoral Armageddon if they did not wrest the crime issue back from Republicans. New historical research, however, suggests that some leading African Americans supported aspects of the war on drugs and other get-tough measures from much earlier on. They did so for a complex set of reasons, including rising fears of crime and rampant substance abuse, widening class inequalities among African Americans, growing fears among middle-class blacks of the black underclass, and changing electoral incentives for the post-civil rights generation of black politicians (Barker 2009, 150–151; Fortner 2013; Forman 2013).

Just as the political and organizational incentives and constituency base changed for civil rights organizations, they also changed for African American politicians (see, for example, Tate 2010). The downfall of the Jim Crow regime transformed electoral incentives and institutional arrangements in ways that have been consequential for the carceral state. These transformations help explain considerable local and state-level differences in the punitive turn. They also complicate explanations about the role of race in the construction and maintenance of the carceral state. For example, Schoenfeld (2009) persuasively shows how the political and institutional remedies to address racial disparities in electoral representation—notably the forced reapportionment of the state legislature and the opening up of the voting booth to more blacks—paradoxically were catalysts for a political realignment that ultimately ushered in a new era of punitiveness in Florida.

Scholars of black politics have identified the emergence of a new generation of "post-racial" or post-civil rights black politicians who have sought to catapult into higher office in majority-white jurisdictions by pursuing "deracialization" strategies. These post-racial politicians have sought to defuse racial issues by generally avoiding talking directly about race, especially the persistence of racism (Harris 2012, 174; Cohen 2010; Dawson 2011). However, this new generation of post-racial black politicians has not remained silent about the law-and-order issue. As the urban crisis worsened, some leading black politicians and public figures endorsed a causal story that focused on individual flaws, not structural problems, and that singled out the addict, the drug pusher, and the street criminal as part of the "undeserving poor" that posed the primary threat to working and middle-class African Americans. In addressing issues of crime and urban decay, they increasingly emphasized individual explanations and solutions rather than structural ones that highlighted racial and economic factors. They burnished their post-racial credentials by lecturing those who had run afoul of the law, many of whom happened to be African American. This new generation of black leaders has contributed to a wider moral panic in which young black Americans have been "increasingly vilified," according to Cohen (2010, 19).

Gender and the Origins of the Carceral State

The significance of race in unsettling the New Deal coalition and building the carceral state has long been recognized, if not always well understood. The role of gender in the construction of the carceral state remains comparatively understudied. We now know that politicians of all stripes, including Goldwater, Wallace, Lyndon Johnson, Nixon, George H. W. Bush, and Clinton, strategically used highly gendered appeals related to crime and punishment to further their political and electoral agendas (Flamm 2005, 42, 45, 51, 178; Bosworth 2010). They promulgated the politically potent—but highly misleading—image of white women, preyed on by strangers, as the most likely victims of violent crime. But leading politicians were not the only culprits in feminizing the crime issue.

Women's groups and feminists in the United States have a long and conflicted history on issues related to crime, punishment, and law and order. Periodically, they have played central roles in defining violence as a threat to the social order and pushing for enhanced policing powers to address law-and-order concerns. The women's reform movements and waves of feminist agitation that have appeared off and on since the nineteenth century in the United States helped to construct institutions and establish practices that bolstered stridently conservative tendencies in penal policy. For example, because of stark differences in the historical and institutional context, demands by the US women's groups in the 1970s and 1980s to address the issues of rape and domestic violence had more far-reaching penal consequences in the United States than other countries where burgeoning women's movements also identified these two issues as central concerns (Gottschalk 2006, chapters 5 and 6). As a consequence, the women's movement helped facilitate conservative law-and-order politics in the United States but not in much of Western Europe.

The Carceral State at the State and Local Levels

Among the many political questions about what propelled the construction of the carceral state, one in particular remains central: Why were law-and-order conservatives able to launch an expensive prison-building spree that spanned decades even though the burgeoning conservative movement they spearheaded was premised on fiscal conservatism and rolling back the public sector? Case studies of the development of penal policy at the state level, much of it produced by scholars outside of Political Science using key tools of historical institutional analysis either explicitly or implicitly, are beginning to unravel this puzzle (see, for example, Lynch 2010; Gilmore 2007; Page 2011; Campbell 2011; Barker 2009; Schoenfeld 2009; Garland 2010). This research identifies some common factors that help explain what propelled the prison boom at the state level, as well as some differences that account for variations in the timing, extent, and nature of the punitive turn amongst the states.

The construction of such an expansive and unforgiving carceral state in the United States is a national phenomenon that has left no state untouched. All fifty states have seen their incarceration rates explode since the 1970s. But the state-level variation in incarceration rates is still enormous, far greater than what exists across the countries of Western Europe. This great variation and the fact that crime control in the United States is primarily a local and state function, not a federal one, suggest that differences in historical and institutional developments at the local, state, and perhaps regional levels might help explain differences in US penal policies. Trying to unravel why the carceral state has been more extensive, abusive, and degrading in some states than others is a growing and promising area of research. So is work on the political and institutional factors that have propelled some countries and jurisdictions to drastically cut their incarceration rates or otherwise pursue less punitive policies (Lappi-Seppälä 2007; Gartner, Doob, and Zimring 2011; Campbell 2007).

Much of the recent state-level scholarship has focused on the South and the Southwest (Perkinson 2010; Lynch 2010; Schoenfeld 2009; Campbell 2011; Chase 2009; Gilmore 2007; Page 2011). This work has upended the conventional narrative of the rise of the US penal system, with its emphasis on the northeast, notably New York and Pennsylvania. In the standard account, the foreboding penitentiaries of the nineteenth century, meant to restore wayward citizens to virtue through penitent solitude, evolved by fits and starts into the modern correctional bureaucracies of the twentieth century that, at least for a time, viewed rehabilitating prisoners as a central part of their mission. More recent scholarship suggests that the history of punishment in the United States is a more Southern story than has been generally recognized. Notably, in much of the South and southwest, the commitment to the "rehabilitative ideal" appears to have been fragile and fleeting (Lynch 2010).

In California and some other western and Southern states, the postwar establishment of statewide departments of corrections to oversee their penal facilities, which had been run largely as independent, patronage-ridden fiefdoms, was a critical institutional and political development. It gave states the capacity for the first time to develop integrated penal systems, pursue large-scale prison construction schemes, and respond to national trends in penal policy, if lawmakers chose to do so. When legislators sought to build up their penal capacity, they often enacted measures that exempted their departments of corrections from key oversight, budgeting, and financial rules that applied to other state agencies (Gilmore 2007; Edgerton 2004; Lynch 2010; Schoenfeld 2009). Furthermore, state officials, working closely with the financial sector, devised innovative financing mechanisms that obscured the true fiscal costs of the prison boom, thus helping to inoculate this massive and expensive expansion of the public sector from the public's anti-tax wrath.

Differences in the structure of state governance and in the practice of civic engagement also help explain why some states were more vulnerable to the siren call of law-and-order politics than others. In her three-state study of the punitive turn, Barker (2009) argues that California's neopopulist political culture and institutions, most notably its ballot initiatives and its relatively low levels of civic engagement, help explain why it pursued penal policies that were comparatively more punitive than those of New York State or Washington State. Lynch (2010) examines the case of Arizona, which was Barry Goldwater's home state and a cauldron of the conservative movement premised on anti-tax fever and disdain for the public sector. She explicates how Arizona nonetheless embarked on a huge, costly penal expansion that transformed its department of corrections into one of the largest and most politically influential state agencies in Arizona (Lynch 2010, 172).

Until the 1950s, Arizona looked like a traditional one-party Southern state dominated by conservative Democrats. Beginning in the 1960s, the state became more politically competitive as right-leaning Republicans made serious electoral inroads and pockets of progressive Democrats challenged the party's old guard (especially in more urbanized areas as the Democratic Party fractured on the shoals of the civil rights movement). This new political competition resulted in the hyper-politicization of penal policy, as the "practical, collaborative" style of lawmaking yielded to more "symbolic, partisan-based" legislating (Lynch 2010, 113).

A similar story unfolded in Texas, which today operates the country's largest state prison system, imprisoning more people than Germany, France, Belgium, and the Netherlands combined (Campbell 2011; Perkinson 2010). Penal hard-liners in Texas faced little political resistance. They operated in a political culture characterized by low levels of political participation by the groups most likely to be ensnared in the state's widening dragnet. African Americans, low-income people, and Mexican Americans voted in low numbers and did not forge powerful statewide civic associations. Campbell (2011) attributes the low level of civic involvement to the state's deep-seated patriarchal political culture. He also singles out several institutional factors, including Texas's frequent elections, its off-year gubernatorial contests, and numerous constitutional amendments related to trivial aspects of government (Campbell 2011).

Recent state-level analyses of the origins and development of the carceral state are a sober reminder that the growing expectations that the United States will begin closing many of its jails and prisons because it can no longer afford to be the world's warden may be unwarranted.[3] Gaping budget deficits will not necessarily reverse the prison boom because a penal system is not only deeply embedded in a state's budget but also in its political, cultural, institutional, and social fabric. In order to understand the political possibilities for dismantling the carceral state, we need a fine-grained understanding of how electoral, party, and other institutional developments at the local and state levels helped to consolidate the carceral state. We can infer from the state-level case studies discussed here that some states might be better able than others to reduce their prison populations in the future.

The Carceral State and the American State

The emergence of the carceral state is cause to rethink how we conceptualize the US state, especially characterizations of the US state as weak. The United States has developed an awesome power and an extensive apparatus to monitor, incarcerate, and execute its citizens that is unprecedented in modern US history and among other Western countries. This development raises deeply troubling questions about the health of democratic institutions in the United States and the character of the liberal state.

A new civil and political order based on "governing through crime" has been in the making for decades (Simon 2007). The war on crime has fundamentally recast both governmental and nongovernmental institutions in the United States as the "technologies, discourses, and metaphors of crime and criminal justice" have been migrating to all kinds of institutions and public policies that seem far afield from crime fighting (Simon 2007, 4). In the new regime, criminal analogies are wielded in many diverse settings, from homes to schools to the workplace to the political arena.

This war on crime has created imbalances in the political system. The US Department of Justice and the office of the attorney general have swollen at the expense of other parts of the federal government. The power of the prosecutor has expanded at the expense of judges, defense attorneys, and other actors in the criminal justice system. Perhaps even more significantly, the all-powerful, largely unaccountable prosecutor has become the new model for exercising executive authority in the United States. In word and deed, mayors, governors, and presidents increasingly fashion themselves as "prosecutors-in-chief" (Simon 2007, 35). Moreover, serving as an attorney general or district attorney has become a major launching pad to higher political office.

The Carceral State and the Welfare State

The emergence of the carceral state is also cause to rethink our understanding of the US welfare state. For example, Western's portrait in *Punishment and Inequality* of the deteriorating labor-market position of poor, unskilled blacks is at odds with the conventional view that the US labor market outperforms the labor markets of Western Europe. His account challenges the widespread claim that the United States, with its relatively unregulated labor market, weak unions, and stingy welfare benefits, is better at reducing unemployment, especially for low-skilled workers, than "nanny states" like France, Italy, and Germany. Moreover, state regulation of the poor did not recede in the United States in the 1990s, it merely shifted course. The government significantly increased its role in regulating the lives of poor, uneducated men and women by sweeping more and more of them up into the criminal justice system's growing dragnet (Western 2006, 105).

As Wacquant (2009), Beckett and Western (2001), and others have documented, the carceral state has expanded at the expense of the welfare state. By a number of measures—expenditures, personnel, congressional hearings, and legislation—the law enforcement and penal apparatus has been growing while social welfare provision has been contracting. Some states have experienced a direct dollar-for-dollar tradeoff as budgets for higher education shrank and corrections budgets grew. States and countries that spend more on social welfare tend to have relatively lower incarceration rates (Sutton 2004; Downes and Hansen 2006). Communities and countries vexed with large economic and racial stratifications tend to have higher crime rates, especially for violent crime (Peterson and Krivo 2010; Currie 2008, 48–117).

What we may be witnessing is not so much the contraction of the welfare as its absorption by the carceral state, which has become the primary regulator of the poor and a main conduit of social services for the poor and disadvantaged. Jails and prisons in the United States are now responsible for the largest number of mentally ill people in the country. Drug courts, domestic violence courts, and parole and probation officers not only monitor the behavior of offenders but also provide key links to dwindling social services and employment and educational opportunities. Wacquant contends that social and penal policy cannot be analyzed in isolation from one another because they are so enmeshed today and have been for a long time (2009, 13).

The Comparative Politics of Penal Policy

Mass imprisonment within a democratic polity and the hyper-incarceration of certain groups are unprecedented developments. The consolidation of this new model in the

United States has spurred interest in comparative penal policy, in particular whether the other countries will follow the United States down such a punitive path. An underlying theme of much of this work is that the persistence of relatively stable incarceration rates and penal policies in other countries cannot be taken for granted (Tonry 2007).

Some scholars have identified a number of deep-seated cultural differences to explain US exceptionalism in criminal justice policy, including an abiding mistrust of the government (Whitman 2003; Zimring 2003; Zimring, Hawkins, and Kamin 2001; Tonry 2011), a history of vigilantism (Zimring 2003), an enduring attachment to liberal egalitarianism (Whitman 2003), and the impact of centuries of white supremacy on American political development (Kaplan 2006). Others have focused on more recent cultural and social changes to explain American exceptionalism, most notably the arrival of late modernity in the postwar era and the onset of a new "culture of control" (Garland 2001). Institutional and political factors are not incidental to these accounts of American exceptionalism in penal policy, but they do not predominate.

The issue of American exceptionalism in penal policy has spurred greater interest in comparative work on crime control and, in particular, on how exceptional institutional, political, and economic factors create exceptional penal policies (Lacey 2008; Cavadino and Dignan 2006; Garland 2010; Tonry 2007). Scholars have identified several institutional factors as pivotal. Conflict-style political systems based on two dominant parties, first-past-the-post electoral systems, and single-member electoral districts are more likely to enact harsher measures than consensual, multiparty systems with proportional representation, coalition governments, and greater policy continuity. Not surprisingly, conflict-style political systems (like those in the United States and England) tend to produce conflict-style political cultures with lower levels of public trust and lower levels of government legitimacy—two important contributors to law-and-order politics. Other important institutional variables include the level of party discipline, whether the political economy leans more toward neoliberalism, corporatism, or social democracy; differences in the organization of the media (Green 2007); and the varied ways that industrialized countries have responded to the decline of the Fordist model of production and the emergence of a more contingent workforce and a less regulated global market (De Giorgi 2006). Another important institutional factor is sharp differences in the organization, selection, and training of judges and prosecutors. The United States is the only major Western country where judges and prosecutors are either elected or selected according to partisan criteria, making these officials highly susceptible to public opinion and emotions.

Whither Historical Institutionalism?

For all the recent advances in our understanding of the contemporary politics of crime and punishment, this remains an emerging field in which historical institutionalist scholars across a range of disciplines have been pioneers. The discipline of Political

Science is belatedly beginning to recognize the carceral state as a critical area in the study of American and comparative politics.[4]

I once thought the subfield of American political development was particularly well situated to take up some of the analytical and political challenges of the carceral state because of its emphasis on historical and comparative approaches to understanding public policy; its sensitivity to how institutions, social movements, political coalitions, and ideological communities develop over time, often in unanticipated ways with unanticipated consequences; and its growing appreciation of how cross-national and international developments affect public policy (Bensel 2003).

Perhaps most importantly, historical institutional scholars and the subfield of American political development appeared to be more receptive to Mr. Perestroika's exhortation 15 years ago to pursue research that has broad political and policy relevance and to produce scholarly work that is aimed at real-world problems and is accessible to a non-scholarly audience (Mr. Perestroika 2000; Monroe 2005). I also once thought that scholarly activity around political questions related to the carceral state could serve as a catalyst to help establish and legitimize a "public political science" to match the movement within sociology for a "public sociology," which seeks to transport sociology to a wider audience and engage in public discussions of pressing issues (Burawoy et al. 2004, 104; Clawson et al. 2007). Today, I am not so sure.

As a graduate student two decades ago, I was initially drawn to historical institutionalism because it was not primarily defined by methodology but rather by certain tendencies and sensibilities. Historical institutionalism was attractive to me because it attracted an eclectic group of scholars who did not fit neatly into the other subfields of American politics, which tended to be defined foremost by privileging the science of politics and not the politics of politics. For me, historical institutionalism was an invitation to think big on pressing political questions and problems that have enormous normative implications. It was hospitable to asking big questions and seeking answers to complex problems using a methodological toolbox that was often elegant in its soak-and-poke simplicity.

It is not obvious to me that historical institutionalism has aged well in Political Science in the years since I was a graduate student. In the case of the carceral state, with a few shining exceptions (see, e.g., Murakawa 2014; Fortner 2013; Miller 2008; Weaver 2007), some of the best work on the origins, development, and political causes and political consequences of the carceral state is being produced by scholars trained in other disciplines—sociology, history, law, and criminology—not Political Science. The defensive crouch that some historical institutionalists in Political Science took when faced with scholars zealously promoting rational choice, political behavior, and now the experimentation wave is partly to blame. So is the intensified department ratings race that has endowed an ever-smaller number of elite universities with disproportionate power to define what matters in Political Science in increasingly narrow ways. Furthermore, demonstration of competency in mixed methods has in many instances become the price of professional admission for scholars of historical institutionalism and American political development in particular. This has meant sacrificing what had been so distinctive about historical institutionalism and its comparative advantage. It has entailed sliding down the slippery slope of posing smaller questions that can be nailed with methodological rigor but that yield neat but "so what" conclusions.

As they say on *The Wire*, you cannot lose if you do not play. With a few exceptions, scholars of historical institutionalism will never produce the sophisticated methodological breakthroughs or grand theories of politics or parsimonious explanations that scholars of rational choice, political behavior, or experiments revere. In aiming to do so, they risk sacrificing what made historical institutionalism so attractive and compelling in the first place—its audacity to ask big, compelling political questions, its high tolerance for complex answers, and its deep substantive understanding of the subject or issue at hand. All this raises the question of whether this is the moment to celebrate the achievements of historical institutionalism over the past few decades or to ponder what's been lost along the way.

Notes

* A special thank you to my editor, Adam Sheingate, whose attentive reading and incisive comments made this a much better chapter.

1. This figure was calculated from Pew Center on the States 2009, 10. It includes people confined to jail and prison, those serving probation, parole, and community sanctions, people under the supervision of pretrial authorities, drug courts, and other specialized programs, and people detained in Immigration and Customs Enforcement facilities.
2. These ratios would be even more alarming if they also included the likelihood of spending time in jail, not just prison.
3. For a skeptical view of the claim that fiscal pressures in the wake of the Great Recession mark the beginning of the end of mass incarceration, see Gottschalk (2015, chapter 2).
4. See, for example, Burch (2013), Weaver and Lerman (2010), Lerman (2013), and Owens (2014).

References

Alexander, Michelle. 2010. *The New Jim Crow: Mass Incarceration in the Age of Colorblindness*. New York: The New Press.

Barker, Vanessa. 2009. *The Politics of Imprisonment: How the Democratic Process Shapes the Way America Punishes Offenders*. New York: Oxford University Press.

Beckett, Katherine and Bruce Western. 2001. "Governing Social Marginality: Welfare, Incarceration, and the Transformation of State Policy." *Punishment & Society* 3 (1): 43–59.

Bensel, Richard. 2003. "The Tension between American Political Development as a Research Community and as a Disciplinary Subfield." *Studies in American Political Development* 17 (1): 103–106.

Bonczar, Thomas O. 2003. "Prevalence of Imprisonment in the U.S. Population, 1974–2001." U.S. Department of Justice, Bureau of Justice Statistics.

Bosworth, Mary. 2010. *Explaining U.S. Imprisonment*. Thousand Oaks, CA: Sage.

Bumiller, Kristin. 2008. *In an Abusive State: How Neoliberalism Appropriated the Feminist Movement against Domestic Violence*. Durham, NC: Duke University Press.

Burawoy Michael, William Gamson, Charlotte Ryan, Stephen Pfohl, Diane Vaughan, Charles Derber, and Juliet Schor. 2004. "Public Sociologies: A Symposium from Boston College." *Social Problems* 51 (1): 103–130.

Burch, Traci. 2013. *Trading Democracy for Justice: Criminal Convictions and the Decline of Neighborhood Political Participation*. Chicago: University of Chicago Press.

Campbell, Michael. 2011. "Politics, Prisons, and Law Enforcement: An Examination of 'Law and Order' Politics in Texas." *Law & Society Review* 45 (3): 631–666.

Campbell, Michael C. 2007. "Criminal Disenfranchisement Reform in California: A Deviant Case Study." *Punishment & Society* 9 (2): 177–199.

Cavadino, Michael and James Dignan. 2006. *Penal Systems: A Comparative Approach*. 4th Edition. London: Sage.

Chase, Robert. 2009. "Civil Rights on the Cell Block: Race, Reform, and Violence in Texas Prisons and the Nation, 1945–1990." Ph.D. Dissertation, University of Maryland.

Clawson, Dan, Robert Zussman, Joya Misra, Naomi Gerstel, Randall Stokes, Douglas L. Anderton, and Michael Burawoy, eds. 2007. *Public Sociology: Fifteen Eminent Sociologists Debate Politics and the Profession in the Twenty-first Century*. Berkeley: University of California Press.

Cohen, Cathy J. 2010. *Democracy Remixed: Black Youth and the Future of American Politics*. New York: Oxford University Press.

Currie, Elliot. 2008. *The Roots of Danger: Violent Crime in Global Perspective*. Upper Saddle River, NJ: Prentice Hall.

Dawson, Michael C. 2011. *Not in Our Lifetimes: The Future of Black Politics*. Chicago: University of Chicago Press.

De Giorgi, Alessandro. 2006. *Re-Thinking the Political Economy of Punishment: Perspectives on Post-Fordism and Penal Politics*. Aldershot: Ashgate.

Downes, David and Kirstine Hansen. 2006. "Welfare and Punishment in Comparative Context." In *Perspectives on Punishment: The Contours of Control*, ed. Sarah Armstrong and Lesley McAra. Oxford: Oxford University Press, 33–54.

Edgerton, Keith. 2004. *Montana Justice: Power, Punishment, and the Penitentiary*. Seattle, WA: University of Washington Press.

Flamm, Michael W. 2005. *Law and Order: Street Crime, Civil Unrest, and the Crisis of Liberalism in the 1960s*. New York: Columbia University Press.

Forman, James, Jr. 2013. "Race, Crime, Punishment and Local Democracy in America." Paper Presented at the Robina Conference, University of Minnesota Law School, April 25.

Fortner, Michael Javen. 2013. "The Carceral State and the Crucible of Black Politics: An Urban History of the Rockefeller Drug Laws." *Studies in American Political Development* 27 (1): 14–35.

Garland, David. 2001. *The Culture of Control: Crime and Social Order in Contemporary Society*. Chicago: University of Chicago Press.

Garland, David. 2010. *Peculiar Institution: America's Death Penalty in an Age of Abolition*. Cambridge, MA: Belknap Press of Harvard University Press.

Gartner, Rosemary, Anthony N. Doob, and Franklin E. Zimring. 2011. "The Past as Prologue? Decarceration in California Then and Now." *Criminology & Public Policy* 10 (2): 291–325.

Gilmore, Ruth W. 2007. *The Golden Gulag: Prisons, Surplus, Crisis, and Opposition in Globalizing California*. Berkeley, CA: University of California Press.

Gottschalk, Marie. 2006. *The Prison and the Gallows: The Politics of Mass Incarceration in America*. New York: Cambridge University Press.

Gottschalk, Marie. 2015. *Caught: The Prison State and the Lockdown of American Politics*. Princeton, NJ: Princeton University Press.

Green, David. 2007. "Comparing Penal Cultures: Child-On-Child Homicide in England and Norway." In *Crime, Punishment, and Politics in Comparative Politics*, vol. 36, ed. Michael Tonry. *Crime and Justice: A Review of Research*. Chicago: University of Chicago Press, 591–643.

Haney, Craig. 2008. "Counting Casualties in the War on Prisoners." *University of San Francisco Law Review* 43 (1): 87–138.

Harris, Fredrick C. 2012. *The Price of the Ticket*. New York: Oxford University Press.

Hohler-Hausmann, Julilly. 2010. " 'The Attila the Hun Law': New York's Rockefeller Drug Laws and the Making of a Punitive State." *Journal of Social History* 44 (1): 71–95.

Kaplan, Paul J. 2006. "American Exceptionalism and Racialized Inequality in American Capital Punishment: The Contradictions of American Capital Punishment." *Law & Social Inquiry* 31 (1): 149–175.

Katz, Michael B., Mark J. Stern, and Jamie J. Fader. 2005. "The New African American Inequality." *The Journal of American History* 92 (1): 75–108.

Katznelson, Ira. 1986. "Rethinking the Silences of Social and Economic Policy." *Political Science Quarterly* 101 (2): 307–325.

Lacey, Nicola. 2008. *The Prisoners' Dilemma: Political Economy and Punishment in Contemporary Democracies*. Cambridge: Cambridge University Press.

Lappi-Seppälä, Tapio. 2007. "Penal Policy in Scandinavia." In *Crime, Punishment, and Politics in Comparative Politics*, vol. 36, ed. Michael Tonry. *Crime and Justice: A Review of Research*. Chicago: University of Chicago Press, 217–295.

Lerman, Amy E. 2013. *The Modern Prison Paradox: Politics, Punishment, and Social Community*. New York: Cambridge University Press.

Lynch, Mona. 2010. *Sunbelt Justice: Arizona and the Transformation of American Punishment*. Stanford, CA: Stanford University Press.

McLennan, Rebecca. 2008. *The Crisis of Imprisonment: Protest, Politics, and the Making of the American Penal State, 1818–1938*. New York: Cambridge University Press.

Miller, Lisa L. 2008. *The Perils of Federalism: Race, Poverty and the Politics of Crime Control*. New York: Oxford University Press.

Monroe, Kristen Renwick, ed. 2005. *Perestroika! The Raucous Rebellion in Political Science*. New Haven, CT: Yale University Press.

Mr. Perestroika. 2000. "On the Irrelevance of APSA and APSR to the Study of Political Science." October 17. Available at <https://archive.org/stream/OnTheIrrelevanceOfApsaAndApsrToTheStudyOfPoliticalScience/mrperestroika#page/no/mode/2up> (accessed December 6, 2013).

Muhammad, Khalil Gibran. 2010. *The Condemnation of Blackness: Race, Crime, and the Making of Modern America*. Cambridge, MA: Harvard University Press.

Murakawa, Naomi. 2014. *The First Civil Right: How Liberals Built Prison America*. New York: Oxford University Press.

Murch, Donna. 2010. *Living for the City: Migration, Education, and the Rise of the Black Panther Party in Oakland, California*. Chapel Hill, NC: University of North Carolina Press.

Orren, Karen and Stephen Skowronek. 2004. *The Search for American Political Development*. Cambridge: Cambridge University Press.

Owens, Michael Lee. 2014. "Ex-Felons' Organization-Based Political Work for Carceral Reforms." *The ANNALS of the American Academy of Political and Social Science* 651 (1): 256–265.

Paden, Catherine M. 2011. *Civil Rights Advocacy on Behalf of the Poor.* Philadelphia, PA: University of Pennsylvania Press.

Page, Joshua. 2011. *The Toughest Beat: Politics, Punishment, and the Prison Officers Union in California.* New York: Oxford University Press.

Perkinson, Robert. 2010. *Texas Tough: The Rise of America's Prison Empire.* New York: Metropolitan Books.

Peterson, Ruth D. and Lauren J. Krivo. 2010. *Divergent Social Worlds: Neighborhood Crime and the Racial-Spatial Divide.* New York: Russell Sage Foundation.

Pew Center on the States. 2009. *One in 31: Behind Bars in America 2008.* Washington, D.C.: Pew Center on the States.

Ritchie, Beth. 2012. *Arrested Justice: Black Women, Violence, and America's Prison Nation.* New York: NYU Press.

Schoenfeld, Heather. 2009. "The Politics of Prison Growth: From Chain Gangs to Work Release Centers and Supermax Prisons, Florida, 1955–2000." Ph.D. Dissertation, Northwestern University.

Simon, Jonathan. 2007. *Governing Through Crime: How the War on Crime Transformed American Democracy and Created a Culture of Fear.* New York: Oxford University Press.

Skocpol, Theda. 2003. *Diminished Democracy: From Membership to Management in American Civic Life.* Norman, OK: University of Oklahoma Press.

Strolovitch, Dara. 2007. *Affirmative Advocacy: Race, Class, and Gender in Interest Group Politics.* Chicago: University of Chicago Press.

Sutton, John R. 2004. "The Political Economy of Imprisonment in Affluent Western Democracies, 1960–1990." *American Sociological Review* 69 (2): 170–189.

Tate, Katherine. 2010. *What's Going On? Political Incorporation and the Transformation of Black Public Opinion.* Washington, D.C.: Georgetown University Press.

Tonry, Michael, ed. 2007. *Crime, Punishment, and Politics in Comparative Politics*, vol. 36. *Crime and Justice: A Review of Research.* Chicago: University of Chicago Press.

Tonry, Michael. 2011. *Punishing Race: A Continuing American Dilemma.* New York: Oxford University Press.

Wacquant, Löic. 2009. *Punishing the Poor: The Neoliberal Government of Social Insecurity.* Durham, NC: Duke University Press.

Weaver, Vesla M. 2007. "Frontlash: Race and the Development of Punitive Crime Policy." *Studies in American Political Development* 21 (2): 230–265.

Weaver, Vesla and Amy E. Lerman. 2010. "Political Consequences of the Carceral State." *American Political Science Review* 104 (4): 817–833.

Western, Bruce. 2006. *Punishment and Inequality in America.* New York: Russell Sage Foundation.

Whitman, James Q. 2003. *Harsh Justice: Criminal Punishment and the Widening Divide between America and Europe.* Oxford: Oxford University Press.

Wilson, William Julius. 1980. *The Truly Disadvantaged: The Inner City, the Underclass, and Public Policy.* Chicago: University of Chicago Press.

Zimring, Franklin E. 2003. *The Contradictions of American Capital Punishment.* New York: Oxford University Press.

Zimring, Franklin E., Gordon Hawkins, and Sam Kamin. 2001. *Punishment and Democracy: Three Strikes and You're Out in California.* Oxford: Oxford University Press.

PART V

EUROPEAN POLITICS

Introduction

ORFEO FIORETOS AND TULIA G. FALLETI

ANY stocktaking of historical institutionalism is incomplete without considering the study of Europe, just as any stocktaking of the study of Europe would be incomplete without considering the contributions of historical institutionalism. Chapters in this section illustrate the wide scope of historical institutionalism research on Europe and how that research has informed historical institutionalism over time. From classic areas of study such as the state and democracy, the welfare state, business, and finance, as well as more recent areas such as religion in politics, and the emergence of new forms of supranationalism and transnational regulation, the chapters in this Part take stock of the findings in extant contributions and share suggestions for future research. They detail how attention to the consequences of critical junctures, positive feedback effects, intercurrence, and the sources of a wide variety of incremental change help scholars answer why patterns of institutional durability and change vary at national and international levels of governance.

In the opening chapter, R. Daniel Kelemen provides a panoramic view of historical institutionalism's contributions to the study of the European state. Home to an unusually large number of states living in close proximity, Europe has served as a particularly fruitful place to study the sources for the enduring and changing features of the modern state, including rules governing authorities to tax, police, and provide security. Kelemen underscores that even after 50 years of steady additions to the supranational structures of the European Union (EU), European states remain characterized by diversity due to legacies of early state formation and the prevalence of incremental over radical changes in how states have been reformed over time.

Unlike the state, which has existed in various permutations for centuries, the widespread consolidation of liberal democracy is a phenomenon reserved for the post-1945 period. In her chapter, Sheri Berman explains why liberal representative democracy was consolidated after World War II. Pointing to conditions shortly after the war that contributed to the emergence of new ideas on appropriative forms of political governance and the empowerment of new social coalitions, Berman concludes that the conditions that consolidated democracy in Western Europe are not easily replicated elsewhere. For this reason, she concludes that opportunities to emulate the lessons from Europe are limited; the stability of democracy in other regions may require a different set of ideas and institutions than those that are so closely linked to the durability of liberal democracy in Europe.

Few areas of research have had as symbiotic a relationship to historical institutionalism as has the study of European welfare states. Julia Lynch and Martin Rhodes's chapter documents that research on the welfare state has served as an analytical incubator for historical institutionalism. From early work exploring critical junctures and path dependence in contributing to diverse welfare states, to later work identifying positive feedback effects as the major reason why retrenchment in welfare states was limited during moments of crises, scholars have employed and expanded the tradition's toolbox. In the process, they have created a vibrant historical institutionalism research program that remains a major theoretical anchor for studies of modern welfare states inside and outside Europe, and that at the same time has inspired research in areas only remotely related to institutions of social insurance.

The comparative study of capitalism has parallels to the study of the welfare state in that it too has been both heavily informed by and contributed to historical institutionalism. While Richard Deeg and Elliot Posner detail the tradition's central position in a large literature on comparative financial systems, Pepper Culpepper documents its contributions to the study of business preferences and organization. Surveying a large literature on national and EU institutions of financial regulation, Deeg and Posner argue that careful attention to the timing and sequence of national reforms enables scholars to explain both why countries have persisted in using diverse institutional blueprints to secure domestic economic objectives, as well as why European financial cooperation has largely changed in incremental fashion along with the gradual introduction of novel forms of international cooperation. Meanwhile, Culpepper encourages future researchers to further refine the tradition's analytical toolbox and devote more attention to how the power of business and variations in the political salience of economic issues impact economic policy across time and space.

Over time, historical institutionalists have moved beyond the classic focus on the state, democracy, welfare states, and political economy with a strong focus on Western

Europe, to explore other areas and parts of the continent. The transition from communism after 1989 in East and Central Europe, for example, is at the center of a large literature that simultaneously examines the effects of major historical turning points and the legacies of past institutions for democratic practice, market regulation, and social incorporation. In her chapter, Anna Grzymala-Busse explores the role of religious doctrine in European politics. The populations of many European countries have long been known for strong preferences for secular society and post-materialist priorities. Yet, as Grzymala-Busse shows, religion has continuously influenced the political landscape of Europe, including transitions to capitalism and democracy in the 1990s and core EU commitments.

As European societies became more deeply integrated economically and politically, scholars have expanded the purview of historical institutionalism to include extensive attention to the origins, evolution, and effects of international cooperation through the EU. While some international relations scholars debated the evolution of integration using adaptations of realist and (neo-)functionalist theories that carried overtones of rational choice and sociological institutionalism, others probed the contributions of historical institutionalism. The latter underscore the presence of European institutions that generated positive and negative feedback effects that respectively served to strengthen and undermine long-established national practices, including how markets are regulated, social risks are insured, and political voices are represented. Part V concludes with two chapters exploring the contributions of historical institutionalism to the study of European integration, including the evolving relationship between domestic and supranational political authority.

Pointing to European and national-level institutions in shaping the constraints on and opportunities for political action, Tim Büthe argues that historical institutionalism is particularly well placed to explain the preferences and strategies of subnational, national, and supranational change agents. With its emphasis on contextual factors and endogenous logics of institutional change, Büthe argues that the tradition provides the means to explain the sources for the steady expansion in the authority vested in supranational legislative and judicial bodies within the EU. Mark Thatcher and Cornelia Woll continue the exploration of historical institutionalism's contributions to the study of European integration in a survey of the European regulatory landscape. Detailing the evolutionary logic of European regulation and how the EU's regulatory landscape become characterized by a patchwork of overlapping national and European-level institutions, Thatcher and Woll document the value of historical institutionalism's analytical toolbox in providing nuanced answers to how the world's largest internal market has been structured over time.

CHAPTER 23

EUROPEAN STATES IN COMPARATIVE PERSPECTIVE

R. DANIEL KELEMEN

MOST political scientists will be familiar with a fairy tale about European states that goes something like this: Once upon a time, medieval Europe was full of a rich mixture of forms of political organization including the Holy Roman Empire, kingdoms, duchies, principalities, city states, city leagues, confederations, and Papal States. These bodies often overlapped—some owing allegiance to others through feudal bonds, others having universal ambitions, and some not defining themselves territorially. Legal pluralism also prevailed with multiple legal systems applying in the same territories. Then in 1648 came the Peace of Westphalia, which put an end to the Thirty Years' War and introduced the modern state system, based on sovereign territorial states. Europe was then divided into independent, sovereign states, each of which exercised ultimate legal authority with in its own borders and each of which enjoyed equal legal status in the international system as the representative of its domestic society. Though borders and number of states have changed over the centuries through conquest and secession, the sovereign state system has proved incredibly resilient, even in the face of contemporary pressures emanating from globalization and European integration.

This is a nice story, but the reality is very different and far more interesting. The sovereign state system did not emerge all at once, and certainly not at Westphalia. State-building in Europe has been incremental, unfolding over centuries. While some approximations of modern states emerged in Europe between the eleventh and thirteenth centuries, other states are very recent creations. Though the state has been the dominant form of political organization for centuries, alternative forms of political organization—from the Austro-Hungarian Monarchy, to the Union of Sweden and Norway, to city-states such as the Free City of Danzig, Monaco, and San Marino—continued to coexist with sovereign states, some even up to the present. The norm of sovereignty—both its internal and international dimensions—has been regularly violated through both voluntary and involuntary means (Krasner 2001). Even after the Treaty of Versailles, when the principle of national self-determination reached its apogee, minority rights treaties constrained the authority of governments within their borders (i.e., constrained their "domestic sovereignty"). Even into the twentieth and twenty-first centuries, nominally sovereign states have been subject to varying degrees of foreign domination—from the East European states subject to Soviet control, to Germany which was rendered a "semi-sovereign state" (Katzenstein 1987) in the postwar years by the victorious Allied powers, to Greece whose finances have repeatedly been subject to control by foreign creditors from its independence in the 1830s to the present (Levandis 1944; Krasner 1999, 132–135). With the deepening of the process of European integration, twenty-eight European states have in practice voluntarily surrendered—or at least "loaned"—much of their sovereignty to a quasi- federation, the European Union (EU). EU member states remain sovereign in that they are free to leave the European Union,[1] but so long as they remain members, the EU is the ultimate governing authority in many spheres and EU law has supremacy over national law in the areas it covers.

The character of European states—their approaches to governance, the extent to which they penetrate and shape their societies—has changed radically over centuries. European states continue to vary from one another across many fundamental dimensions. Some are nation-states—meaning that they are legitimized in part by the claim that they represent a community of people who share, or at least imagine that they share (Anderson 1991), a common ethnic or cultural heritage. Other states are openly multinational. Some are unitary, others federal. Some command strong bureaucratic capacities including the capacity to collect revenue. Others struggle to collect taxes and keep roads paved. Some states operate impartial and effective systems of justice, while in others judicial systems are either plagued by corruption or hobbled by inefficiency. Some states intervene heavily to shape the operation of their "coordinated market economies," while others support the operation of "liberal market economies" subject to less state intervention (Hall and Soskice 2001).

Historical institutionalism offers important insights into the varied origins, evolution, and impact of European states. It is hardly an exaggeration to say that most of what we know about the origins, evolution, and impact of the state in Europe comes from works that take an historical institutionalist approach. However, few of these works have applied to themselves the label "historical institutionalism"—indeed, that would have been rather unlikely as many of them were written long before the term was coined in the early 1990s. Nevertheless, decades of research on the European state have been guided by a historical institutionalist approach *avant la lettre*. The emergence of historical institutionalism in the 1990s was part of the broader movement in American Political Science to "bring the state back in"; however, the state as a conceptual variable (Nettl 1968) had never really left the study of European states—and hence didn't need to be brought back in (Immergut 1998). As Sven Steinmo (2008) explains, many classic works on the European state by scholars including Max Weber (see Gerth and Mills 1946), Stein Rokkan (1975), Karl Polanyi (1944), and Alexander Gerschenkron (1962), would be identified as historical institutionalist were they published today.

These classic works may not share the vocabulary of contemporary historical institutionalism or focus on all of the same causal mechanisms, but they do share a common approach to the study of politics that emphasizes the importance of timing and sequencing in institutional development and emphasizes how multiple constellations of institutions—from electoral systems, to bureaucratic structures, to the state itself—jointly influence politics and policy outcomes (Pierson and Skocpol 2002; Steinmo 2008; Immergut 1998; Thelen 1999). Classical works on the European state and works of contemporary historical institutionalists also share a focus on a number of causal mechanisms (sometimes under different labels) that can explain institutional durability and change including, critical junctures, path dependence, and mechanisms of gradual institutional change including displacement, layering, drift, and conversion (Fioretos, Falleti, and Sheingate, Chapter 1, this volume).

This chapter provides an overview of the contributions that historical institutionalist scholarship has made to our understanding of the origins, evolution, and impact of the state in Europe. It begins with a brief discussion of the concept of the state as it emerged in Western Europe. The chapter then discusses historical institutionalist literature on the origins and evolution of the state in Europe. Next it explores the impact of the state with a particular focus on how it shaped the European economy and what role European integration has played in shaping the state over time. The final section concludes.

What Is the State?

As Max Weber defines it in his 1921 essay "Politics as a Vocation," "a state is a human community that (successfully) claims the *monopoly of the legitimate use of physical force* within a given territory" (Gerth and Mills 1946, 78, italics in original). For Weber, a state's legitimacy could derive from tradition, charisma of the ruler, or law. However, if we consider contemporary European states, law provides the only acceptable basis for the legitimate use of force. The modern state is a legal construct and it is legal concepts—rather than practical questions about the capacity to govern a territory effectively that many political scientists emphasize—that distinguish the state from other forms of political organization.[2] Sovereignty is the central legal concept that underpins statehood. Indeed, the state and sovereignty exist in "a reciprocal relationship" (Loughlin 2013).

Two dimensions of sovereignty are particularly essential; one domestic, one international. First, a sovereign state is an entity that has the ultimate legal right to exercise governing authority (including the use of force) within its territory. That authority need not be vested in a person (such as a king or president) or a particular branch of government (such as the executive), but can be situated in the collective governing authority of the state, which may be subdivided between various (i.e., judicial, executive and legislative) institutions. Second, the sovereign state is an entity that is recognized by other states and by the international legal system as having the ultimate authority to enter into treaties and other agreements on behalf of its domestic polity. The state may even enter into treaties whereby it delegates some control of its internal or external affairs to a supranational body—but that delegation is voluntary and can be retracted. Sovereignty, then, means that, "there is no legal superior to the state in its internal or external affairs" (Caporaso 1996, 35).

Beyond this very minimalist definition of characteristics a polity must possess to be considered a state, there is scope for enormous variation in the forms a state may take. To be sure, there are a set of core powers or functions traditionally associated with the sovereign state that include defense, policing, taxation, public administration, and justice (Genschel and Jachtenfuchs 2014), but how extensive a role the central state plays in each of these domains and how it subdivides them with other levels of government (i.e., in federal systems) can vary tremendously (Kelemen 2014). In addition to variations concerning core state powers, the functions performed by European states and the roles they have played in their economies and societies have varied profoundly. Indeed, the political landscape of Europe has seen everything from predatory states, to totalitarian states, to night-watchman states, to welfare states, to regulatory states. In the economic sphere, the state may take a more laissez-faire approach, focusing simply on establishing uniform weights and measures, ensuring that private property is protected and contracts are enforced. Or the state may play a highly interventionist role, directing investment, training workers, steering or even owning industry (Hall 1986; Hall and Soskice 2001). Likewise, the state may construct a social welfare system to provide for cradle to grave protection of its citizens, or it may provide only much more limited forms of poverty relief (Esping-Andersen 1990). In the realm of interest group politics, the state may act more as simply an institutional arena in which pluralist forces struggle for influence, or it may actively intervene in structuring societal interests in a corporatist fashion (Schmitter 1985).

Origins and Evolution

Europe was not home to the first state. States emerged in China and India centuries before they did in Europe. But it was in Europe beginning in the late Middle Ages that states became "synonymous with sovereign territorial rule" (Spruyt 2002). It was also in Europe that a particular form of state emerged for the first time—one which combined sovereign statehood with the rule of law and some form of accountability of state leaders to (at least some of) their citizens (Fukuyama 2012). And today, it is in Europe that we see the emergence of a quasi-federal union that presents the most profound challenge to the sovereign state model as a form of political organization.

What explains the emergence of the state in Europe and its eventual emergence as the dominant form of political organization on the continent? One school of thought on the origins of the state in Europe emphasizes the role of the military environment and military technology in the rise of European states. In short, changes in military technology began to favor mass infantries, which put pressure on kings to assemble larger armies and diminished the importance (and hence the leverage) of vassals in the feudal system. These technological changes, coupled with persistent military threats, pressured rulers to come up with revenue to fund larger and larger mass infantries. This led rulers to expand their systems of administration and tax collection (Tilly 1975). Other scholars place more emphasis on economic factors, suggesting that the rise of an urban commercial class, increases in trade, and other structural changes undermined the feudal economy and advantaged rulers who could provide secure property rights in larger jurisdictions and thereby stimulate growth (and collect taxes from) the emerging capitalist economy (North 1981). In its simplest form, the state is depicted as a kind of protection racket that provides security in exchange for taxes (Tilly 1985; Levi 1988). But these are not actually rival interpretations because economic and military factors encouraging the emergence of the modern state were inextricably linked: a chief reason that rulers had an incentive to take commercial interests into account and to work to facilitate trade and commerce was that a larger economy could serve as a larger base from which to collect revenue for military purposes.

Other historical accounts emphasize the impact of the ideational and institutional context—in particular that of legal ideas and legal institutions—on the origins and evolution of European states (Berman 1983; Padoa-Schioppa 1997; Strayer 1970; Fukuyama 2012). This perspective emphasizes that the European state was born in an environment of legal pluralism and that much of the early work of state-building consisted of, "a progressive appropriation of the task of administering the law in it various manifestations" (Padoa-Schioppa 1997, 337). With the papal revolution of the eleventh and twelfth centuries, the papacy asserted supremacy over the Church and the independence of the Church from secular control. This move in turn pushed secular political rulers to develop their own systems of law to govern the internal affairs of their kingdoms. As Francis Fukuyama explains, "one of the peculiar features of European state-building was its heavy early dependence on law as both the motive and the process by which state institutions grew" (2012, 271; see also Strayer 1970, 26–31). State builders sought to supplant the mishmash of legal norms and judicial institutions that existed within their territories with uniform systems of law, and they largely succeeded. As Harold Berman (1983, 406) explains, "In the various kingdoms of Europe the common law of the king and of the king's courts gradually replaced most of the disparate features of tribal, local and regional law within the territory." However, rulers of early European states never fully succeeded in establishing their primacy; despite the concerted efforts of some monarchs, they never extinguished the notion that the Church had a universal jurisdiction and that its canon law drew on an authority higher than any monarch—namely God. This notion of a "higher law" formed the basis for the concept of the rule of law in Europe—the notion that there was a source of law above any ruler and that no ruler was above the law. With the democratization of European states and growing secularization, the people replaced God as the ultimate sovereign and the constitution replaced natural law or canon law as sources of "higher law" to constrain leaders. More recently, new sources of "higher law" have emerged to constrain national leaders in the form of the laws of the European Union and Council of Europe.[3]

These macro-historical accounts of the emergence of the state in Europe paint in broad brushstrokes but leave many crucial questions unanswered. While these accounts may explain the underlying reasons why the state emerged, they tell us little about variations in the nature of the states that emerged or their institutional structures. Historical institutionalist work on the origins and evolution of the state in Europe has emphasized that to answer such questions we must go beyond the macro-structural factors identified in the earlier literature and explore in more detail the role of institutional legacies, ideas, historical contexts, timing, and the agency of key actors in shaping the emergence and evolution of particular states.

Just as Europe's great cities are built on layers or archaeological ruins, so too are modern European states "built on top of and with the half-collapsed, half-standing institutions of the past" (Berger 1973, 334). And those institutional artifacts influence the ongoing evolution of European states. Recent historical institutionalist works take this to heart and are contributing to a more nuanced understanding of the origins and evolution of European states. For instance, Ertman (1997) asks why some European states became absolutist and others constitutional and why they developed either patrimonial or bureaucratic administrations. He explains that variations in the pre-existing structures of local governance, the existence of national representative institutions, and differences in the timing of the onset of geopolitical competition explain why European states developed along such different lines. Roeder (2007) argues that nation-state-building projects are successful where they are built upon existing "segment states"—territorial jurisdictions that, while not independent states, already possessed institutional capacity and a common identity. Ziblatt (2006) traces how variations in the development of subnational institutions prior to national unification explain why Germany was formed as a federation while Italy emerged as a more unitary state.

In the post-World War II era, the evolution of states in Western (and after 1989 Eastern) Europe has been inextricably linked to the process of European integration. Alan Milward (1992) has famously argued that the process of European integration "recued" the nation-state in postwar Western Europe and allowed it to reach its apogee as a form of political organization by the late 1960s. He argued against the widespread belief that the growing power of the supranational European Community (later European Union) undermined the authority of the nation-state. Instead, he argued that the postwar rescue and economic reconstruction of states that the war had brought to the brink of collapse (or in some cases to outright collapse) was only possible because it took place within the economic and political framework provided by the European Community.

Milward is surely correct that the process of European integration facilitated the economic and political redevelopment of European states after World War II. Nevertheless, we cannot so readily dismiss the notion that there is tension between the growing authority of the EU and the authority of the national state. Today, the growing power of the EU raises questions about whether the process of European integration threatens to eclipse the sovereign state, or at least to assume responsibility for some of the powers that have been traditionally viewed as exclusive competences of the state. Some scholars have compared the process of European integration to the historic process of state-building in Europe and elsewhere (Bartolini 2005; Marks 1997). The EU is not a state in a strict sense because it is not sovereign. Though EU law has primacy over national law in many fields and though the EU has the exclusive power to sign international treaties in some fields (such as trade), member states remain sovereign in that their participation in the EU is voluntary and they retain the legal authority to exit. Moreover, the EU still plays a relatively limited role in the areas of "core state powers" (Genschel and Jachtenfuchs 2014; Wallace 1994) traditionally reserved to sovereign states, such as policing, defense, taxation, and the operation of the state administration. However, it is important to recognize that the EU continues to accrue powers in all of these fields, gaining more and more influence over member states' activities concerning policing, defense, taxation, and public administration (Genschel and Jachtenfuchs 2014; Kelemen 2014).

The EU should be understood as a "coming-together federal system" (Stepan 1999)—a federal polity formed through the voluntary union of previously independent states. If we apply a strict definition, there have been only two other such systems in modern history—the US and Switzerland—and even these two were not entirely voluntary (Forsyth 1981).[4] Nearly all historic state-building projects in Europe involved a strong element of coercion from the state builders. What is so remarkable about the construction of the European Union and its steady accrual of greater powers is precisely the fact that it has been voluntary. To be sure, many member states have not anticipated the assertions of power made by EU institutions such as the Commission and Court of Justice. But, the member states have all acquiesced in them, for reasons to do with path dependence, increasing returns, and institutional lock-in that historical institutionalist scholarship on the EU has elucidated (Pierson 1996; Alter 1998). Member states have repeatedly signed treaties that reaffirm and extend EU powers, and despite the fact that they are free to leave the union, none have done so. Instead, neighboring states have lined up to join. The EU does not yet qualify as a state in the strict sense and perhaps it never will. But its construction can be understood as a form of a state-building project. And it is a project that can only be understood as a process unfolding over time and in which factors identified by historical institutionalism—such as the unintended consequences of choices taken during critical junctures, path dependence, and opening caused by leaders' preoccupation with short term concerns—have played a crucial role.

Impact

Historical institutionalists have not only examined the state as a phenomenon to be explained or as a dependent variable, they have also treated it as a crucial independent variable influencing a range of political outcomes. The scope of activities states were involved in, their administrative capacities, and the degree to which they could penetrate their societies grew dramatically over the nineteenth and twentieth centuries.

Where early European states focused primarily on the provision of security and justice, in the nineteenth and twentieth centuries states came to play central roles in the provision of all manner of social welfare and public goods. While states had played a role in economic governance for centuries, they came to play a central role in the rise of the modern capitalist economy (Polanyi 1944). Scholars working from a historical institutionalist perspective have demonstrated how earlier decisions about state intervention in the economy, some of them taken during critical junctures, gave rise to historical trajectories that reinforced the varieties of European capitalism and welfare state models that are with us to this day (Shonfield 1965; Schmitter and Lehmbruch 1982; Katzenstein 1985; Hall 1986; Esping-Andersen 1990; Berger and Dore 1996; Hall and Soskice 2001; Streeck 2001; Thelen 2004). Indeed, most of the academic subfield of the comparative political economy of Europe is built on an historical institutionalist perspective; as Immergut and Anderson (2008, 350) explain, "only historical-comparative analysis sensitive to the contextual particularities of Western Europe as a unique region could meet the challenge of understanding patterns of continuity and change in these embedded economies, including tendencies of dualism and discontinuous development." As European states sought to liberalize their economies and roll back some aspects of their welfare states, historical institutionalists again demonstrated how institutional choices made in the past and entrenched in the structures of European states influenced—and sometimes blocked—efforts at reform. For instance, Pierson (1994) deployed historical institutionalist analysis to explain the impediments faced by those who pursued welfare state retrenchment in the 1980s. He showed that social welfare policies were highly path dependent in large part because social programs create constituencies of beneficiaries who then mobilize to resist any efforts at retrenchment. Levy (1999) deploys historical institutionalist insights on the impact of sequencings, showing how the social legacies of postwar dirigisme in France (which had severely weakened civil society organizations) undermined subsequent efforts to decentralize and reduce the state's role in economic policy in the 1980s and 1990s.

Though the most extensive historical institutionalist literature on the impact of European states focuses on political economy, many other fields have been influenced by this approach as well. Skocpol (1979) famously demonstrated the impact of the state on social revolutions in Europe (and elsewhere). Scholars of social movements (Kitschelt 1986) and neocorporatist interest group politics (Schmitter 1985) in Europe have treated the state as a central factor explaining variations in the patterns of mobilization and outcomes achieved by social movements and interest groups. Scholars of national identity formation have shown that European states—through public education, military conscription, and other policies—promoted the emergence of the national identities, or the "imagined communities," that emerged in European states in the nineteenth and early twentieth centuries (Weber 1976; Anderson 1991). Variations across these historic national identity models have enduring implications for contemporary issues ranging from citizenship regimes and immigrant incorporation (Howard 2009) to efforts to construct a common European identity (Risse et al. 1999). Recently, scholars have applied the lens of historical institutionalism to examine how state structures influenced the process of democratization in Europe (Capoccia and Ziblatt 2010; Berman 2007). These disparate studies are united in their attention to the enduring impact of pre-existing state institutions and to the importance of timing and historical sequences in influencing paths of institutional development.

Conclusion

It is hard to think of a subject of interest to political scientists that is more freighted with and shaped by the weight of history than the European state. Historical institutionalism provides a powerful set of analytic tools with which to study the origins, evolution, and impact of the state in Europe. One great irony in this literature is that scholars doing "historical institutionalist" work talked about "the state" more before they called themselves historical institutionalists. In other words, the state was a central analytic concept—treated both as a phenomenon to be explained and as an important causal factor—in much of the historically oriented research on European politics conducted in the postwar era. However, after the rise of the label "historical institutionalism" since the 1990s and the conscious effort to establish it as a distinctive analytic perspective, the use of the concept of "the state" actually decreased—to be replaced with more fine grained discussions of the origins and impact of particular state-related institutions, such as electoral rules, labor market institutions, worker training institutions, monetary and fiscal institutions and federalism, to name but a few. While early historical institutionalists were trying to "bring the state back in," it seems more recent contributions may have actually reduced discussion of the state as a conceptual variable in its own right. There were likely good reasons to move away from the broad concept of "the state" in order to focus on particular institutional elements of the state that were more tractable for institutional analysis. The benefits of this move are obvious, in that the analytic tools of contemporary historical institutionalism have shed light on the reproduction and change of a wide variety of political institutions in Europe. But, in downplaying the state as a central conceptual variable in its own right, historical institutionalists may be missing some profound changes in the fundamental characteristics of European states—in particular those resulting from the growing power of the EU in fields traditionally thought of as exclusive competences of sovereign states. Perhaps it is now time for scholars of European politics to look back to their intellectual traditions and to bring "the state" back in to historical institutionalism.

Notes

1. This was formalized in Article 50 of the Lisbon Treaty.
2. The modern conception of the state emerged over centuries, but it was certainly firmly in place by the mid-eighteenth century. For an overview of the history of the concept of the state, see Skinner (1989, 2009).

3. Like early European state builders, the EU leaders today seeking to construct a European polity are placing a great emphasis on constructing a common system of law and justice (Kelemen 2011).
4. Though the US initially came together voluntarily, the process of asserting federal supremacy involved use of coercive force in the form of the Civil War. Switzerland too only took the leap from a loose confederation to a federal state after a brief civil war in 1847 (the *Sonderbundskrieg*).

References

Alter, Karen. 1998. "Who Are the 'Masters of the Treaty'? European Governments and the European Court of Justice." *International Organization* 52 (1): 121–147.

Anderson, Benedict. 1991. *Imagined Communities*. London: Verso.

Bartolini, Stefano. 2005. *Restructuring Europe*. Oxford: Oxford University Press.

Berger, Suzanne. 1973. "The French Political System." In *Patterns of Government*, ed. Samuel H. Beer and Adam B. Ulam. 3rd Edition. New York: Random House, 333–463.

Berger, Suzanne and Ronald Dore, eds. 1996. *National Diversity and Global Capitalism*. New York: Cornell University Press.

Berman, Harold. 1983. *Law and Revolution: The Formation of the Western Legal Tradition*. Cambridge, MA: Harvard University Press.

Berman, Sheri. 2007. "How Democracies Emerge: Lessons from Europe." *Journal of Democracy* 18 (1):28–41.

Capoccia, Giovanni and Daniel Ziblatt. 2010. "The Historical Turn in Democratization Studies: A New Research Agenda for Europe and Beyond." *Comparative Political Studies* 43 (8–9): 931–968.

Caporaso, James. 1996. "The European Union and Forms of State: Westphalian, Regulatory or Post-Modern?" *Journal of Common Market Studies* 34 (1): 29–52.

Ertman, Thomas. 1997. *The Birth of the Leviathan: Building States and Regimes in Early Modern Europe*. New York: Cambridge University Press.

Esping-Andersen, Gøsta. 1990. *The Three Worlds of Welfare Capitalism*. Cambridge: Polity Press.

Fioretos, Orfeo, Tulia Falleti, and Adam Sheingate. 2016. "Historical Institutionalism in Political Science." In *The Oxford Handbook of Historical Institutionalism*, ed. Orfeo Fioretos, Tulia Falleti, and Adam Sheingate. New York: Oxford University Press, 3–28.

Forsyth, Murray. 1981. *Unions of States*. New York: Leicester University Press/Homes & Meier Publishers, Inc.

Fukuyama, Francis. 2012. *The Origins of Political Order*. New York: Farrar, Straus and Giroux.

Genschel, Philip and Markus Jachtenfuchs. 2014. *Beyond the Regulatory Polity: The European Integration of Core State Powers*. Oxford: Oxford University Press.

Gerschenkron, Alexander 1962. *Economic Backwardness in Historical Perspective*. Cambridge, MA: Belknap Press of Harvard University.

Gerth, H. H. and C. Wright Mills, eds. 1946. *Max Weber: Essays in Sociology*. New York: Oxford University Press.

Hall, Peter. 1986. *Governing the Economy: the Politics of State Intervention in Britain and France*. Oxford: Oxford University Press.

Hall, Peter and David Soskice. 2001. *Varieties of Capitalism*. Oxford: Oxford University Press.

Howard, Marc Morje. 2009. *The Politics of Citizenship in Europe*. New York: Cambridge University Press.

Immergut, Ellen. 1998. "The Theoretical Core of New Institutionalism." *Politics & Society* 26 (1): 5–34.

Immergut, Ellen and Karen Anderson. 2008. "Historical Institutionalism and West European Politics." *West European Politics* 31 (1): 345–369.

Katzenstein, Peter J. 1985. *Small States in World Markets: Industrial Policy in Europe*. Ithaca, NY: Cornell University Press.

Katzenstein, Peter J. 1987. *Policy and Politics in West Germany: The Growth of a Semisovereign State*. Philadelphia, PA: Temple University Press.

Kelemen, R. Daniel. 2011. *Eurolegalism: The Transformation of Law and Regulation in the European Union*. Cambridge, MA: Harvard University Press.

Kelemen, R. Daniel. 2014. "Building the New European State? Federalism, Core State Powers and European Integration." In *Beyond the Regulatory Polity? The European Integration of Core State Powers*, ed. Philip Genschel and Markus Jachtenfuchs. Oxford: Oxford University Press.

Kitschelt, Herbert. 1986. "Political Opportunity Structures and Political Protest: Anti-Nuclear Movements in Four Democracies." *British Journal of Political Science*, 16 (1): 57–85.

Krasner, Stephen. 1999. *Sovereignty: Organized Hypocrisy*. Princeton, NJ: Princeton University Press.

Krasner, Stephen. 2001. "Rethinking the Sovereign State Model." *Review of International Studies* 27: 17–42.

Levandis, John A. 1944. *The Greek Foreign Debt and the Great Powers, 1821–1898*. New York: Columbia University Press.

Levi, M. 1988. *Of Rule and Revenue*. Berkeley: University of California Press.

Levy, Jonah. 1999. *Tocqueville's Revenge: State, Society and Economy in Contemporary France*. Cambridge, MA: Harvard University Press.

Loughlin, Martin. 2013. "Why Sovereignty?" In *Sovereignty and the Law: Domestic, European and International Perspectives*, ed. Richard Rawlings, Peter Leyland, and Alison Young. Oxford: Oxford University Press, 34–49.

Marks, Gary. 1997. "A Third Lens: Comparing European Integration and State Building." In *European Integration in Social and Historical Perspective: 1850 to the Present*, ed. Jytte Klausen and Louise Tilly. Lanham, MD: Rowman and Littlefield.

Milward, Alan. 1992. *The European Rescue of the Nation State*. London: Routledge.

Nettl, J. P. 1968. "The State as a Conceptual Variable." *World Politics* 20: 559–592.

North, Douglass C. 1981. *Structure and Change in Economic History*. New York: Norton.

Padoa-Schioppa, Antonio. 1997. *Legislation and Justice*. Oxford: Clarendon Press.

Pierson, Paul. 1994. *Dismantling the Welfare State? Reagan, Thatcher and the Politics of Retrenchment*. Cambridge: Cambridge University Press.

Pierson, Paul. 1996. "The Path to European Integration: A Historical Institutional Analysis." *Comparative Political Studies* 29 (2): 123–163.

Pierson, Paul and Theda Skocpol. 2002. "Historical Institutionalism in Contemporary Political Science." In *Political Science: State of the Discipline*, ed. Ira Katznelson and Helen Milner. New York: W.W. Norton, 693–721.

Polanyi, Karl. 1944. *The Great Transformation: The Political and Economic Origins of Our Times*. 2nd Edition. Boston, MA: Beacon Press.

Risse, Thomas, Daniela Engelmann-Martin, Hans Joachim Knopf, and Klaus Roscher. 1999. "Constructing Europe? The Evolution of French, British and German Nation State Identities." *Journal of European Public Policy* 6 (4): 614–633.

Roeder, Philip. 2007. *Where Nation-States Come From: Institutional Change in the Age of Nationalism*. Princeton, NJ: Princeton University Press.

Rokkan, Stein. 1975. "Dimensions of State Formation and Nation-Building: A Possible Paradigm for Research on Variations within Europe." In *The Formation of National States in Western Europe*, ed. Charles Tilly. Princeton, NJ: Princeton University Press, 562–600.

Schmitter, Philippe. 1985. "Neo-corporatism and the State." In *The Political Economy of Corporatism*, ed. W. Grant. London: Macmillan, 58.

Schmitter, Philippe and Gerhard Lehmbruch, eds. 1982. *Patterns of Corporatist Policy-Making*. Beverly Hills, CA: Sage.

Shonfield, Andrew. 1965. *Modern Capitalism*. New York: Oxford University Press.

Skinner, Quentin. 1989. "The State." In *Political Innovation and Conceptual Change*, ed. Terence Ball, James Farr, and Russell Hanson. Cambridge: Cambridge University Press, 90–131.

Skinner, Quentin. 2009. "A Genealogy of the Modern State." *Proceedings of the British Academy* 162: 325–370.

Skocpol, Theda. 1979. *States and Social Revolutions*. New York: Cambridge University Press.

Spruyt, Hendrik. 2002. "The Origins, Development and Possible Decline of the Modern State." *Annual Review of Political Science* 5: 127–149.

Steinmo, Sven. 2008. "Historical Institutionalism." In *Approaches and Methodologies in the Social Sciences*, ed. Donatella Della Porta and Michael Keating. Cambridge: Cambridge University Press, 118–138.

Stepan, Al. 1999. "Federalism and Democracy: Beyond the US Model." *Journal of Democracy* 10 (4): 19–34.

Strayer, J. 1970. *On the Medieval Origins of the Modern State*. Princeton, NJ: Princeton University Press.

Streeck, Wolfgang and K ō z ō Yamamura. 2001. *The Origins of Nonliberal Capitalism: Germany and Japan*. Ithaca, NY, and London: Cornell University Press.

Thelen, Kathleen. 1999. "Historical Institutionalism in Comparative Politics." *Annual Review of Political Science* 2: 369–404.

Thelen, Kathleen. 2004. *How Institutions Evolve*. Cambridge: Cambridge University Press.

Tilly, Charles. 1975. *The Formation of National States in Western Europe*. Princeton, NJ: Princeton University Press.

Tilly, Charles. 1985. "War Making and State Making as Organized Crime." In *Bringing the State Back In*, ed. Peter Evans, Dieter Rueschemeyer, and Theda Skocpol. Cambridge: Cambridge University Press, 169–191.

Wallace, William. 1994. "Rescue or Retreat? The Nation State in Western Europe, 1945–93." *Political Studies* 42: 52–76.

Weber, Eugen. 1976. *Peasants into Frenchmen*. Stanford, CA: Stanford University Press.

Ziblatt, Daniel. 2006. *Structuring the State: The Formation of Italy and Germany and the Puzzle of Federalism*. Princeton, NJ: Princeton University Press

CHAPTER 24

INSTITUTIONS AND THE CONSOLIDATION OF DEMOCRACY IN WESTERN EUROPE

SHERI BERMAN

EUROPE's contemporary crisis has once more brought debates about democracy to the forefront of the continent's political agenda. Indeed, one reason the crisis has appeared so shocking to Europeans and outside observers alike is that for the second half of the twentieth century European politics was remarkably stable. The reality, of course, is that this period was an historical anomaly. During the nineteenth and first half of the twentieth century Europe was the most turbulent region on earth, convulsed by war, economic crises, and social and political conflict. Yet after 1945 Western Europe became among the most stable, a study in democracy, social harmony, and prosperity. How can we understand this remarkable transformation?

The answer lies in changes that occurred after 1945. Among the most important of these were a series of domestic and regional institutional changes. On the domestic level, postwar political economies were rebuilt after the war in a "social democratic" way, designed to foster the economic growth, social peace, and political moderation that would allow for the consolidation of democracy. European integration was meant to be the regional counterpart to this domestic shift, with institutions at the European level working together with those at the national level to make certain that Western Europe would not fall back into the destructive domestic and international conflicts that had led to economic and political collapse as well as world war. In short, if we want to understand why democracy was able to consolidate in Western Europe after World War II but not before we need an historical institutionalist analysis of the continent's political development in general and of the critical juncture that occurred in 1945 in particular, that is, one that focuses on the role played by institutions in reshaping social and economic life and political dynamics and views institutions as products of the historical contexts within which they evolve (Steinmo, Thelen, and Longstreth 1992; Rothstein 1996; Immergut and Anderson 2008; Thelen 1999). Indeed, as we will see, an historical institutionalist analysis can help us explain not only the puzzle of democratic consolidation in Western Europe after 1945, but also help us understand the problems democracy is facing in Europe today.

The Background

Before the early twentieth century Europe had undergone several democratic waves, all of which had been failures. Europe's first democratic experiment came with the French Revolution.[1] After the overthrow of what had hitherto seemed Europe's most powerful monarchical dictatorship, various groups in French society proved unable to agree on precisely what type of regime should follow it. The first attempt to create a new political order out of the ashes of the old was in 1791 when a form of constitutional monarchy was proposed. This fairly moderate regime received little support, and conflict between more radical and conservative forces continued, until by 1793 the radicals emerged triumphant. The king, Louis XVI, was sent to the gallows and a republic with universal suffrage declared. Europe's first experiment with democracy did not, however, last long and quickly led to chaos, terror, and an eventual transition back to dictatorship, first of the military populist and then eventually back to a new version of the monarchical variety. Between 1789 and 1814 France had thus moved from an absolutist dictatorship to a constitutional monarchy to democracy to war and domestic chaos, and then back to dictatorship again.

Europe's next attempt at democracy came in 1848. During the early nineteenth century the Industrial Revolution had begun sweeping across Europe, increasing the size of the working and middle classes and generating new forms of economic dislocation (Sperber 2005; Stearns 1974). One result was a growing frustration on the part of these groups with political regimes that were not responding to their needs nor allowing them influence commensurate with their growing numbers and economic power. As Eric Hobsbawm put it, by 1848 European politics was "out of balance":

> the forces of economic, technical, and social change released in the past half-century were unprecedented, and, even to the most superficial observer, irresistible. Their institutional consequences, on the other hand, were as yet modest . . . It was inevitable that landed aristocracies and absolute monarchies must retreat in all countries in which a strong bourgeoisie was developing, whatever the political compromises or formula found for retaining status, influence, and even political power. Moreover, it was inevitable that the injection of political consciousness and permanent political activity among the masses, which was the great legacy of the French revolution, must sooner or later mean that these masses were allowed to play a formal part in politics. (Hobsbawm 1996, 356)

As in 1789, in 1848 it was once again events in France that got the ball rolling. When an increasingly reactionary government attempted to squash popular meetings and then responded to protests with force, barricades began to appear in the streets and soon another French political regime was headed to the dustbin of history. These events sent shock waves across Europe: from north to south, east to west, Europeans took to the streets demanding an end to the dictatorships that ruled their lands. At first, these uprisings were remarkably effective. Dictatorships began to totter even in what had seemed to be some of the continent's most sturdy regimes (e.g., Austria and Germany).

But almost as soon as the old order began to crumble, fissures began to open up in the oppositional camp. In country after country it became clear that although there was often massive discontent with existing dictatorships, there was also massive disagreement about the nature of the political regime that should replace them. In particular two divisions that appeared first in 1789 returned to shape the outcome of the democratic wave in 1848. The first was between what we might broadly call liberals and democrats—that is, between people who wanted to reform the old regime while also ensuring safeguards against unchecked mass participation and those who insisted that nothing less than a transition to full democracy would be acceptable. To some degree, this was a class division, with middle class groups largely in the former camp and the emerging working class in the latter (Langer 1969a, 1969b; Jones 1991; Stearns 1974; Kranzberg 1959).

Alongside political/class divisions, the second division that shaped the fate of the 1848 wave, especially the further east one traveled, involved national and communal issues. Nationalism had appeared as a powerful political force with the French revolution and spread across Europe with Napoleon's armies. Since then, economic development, along with the social discontent, political mobilization, and new forms of communication that it brought in its wake, helped bring identity issues further to the forefront of many people's consciousness. Thus as the old order began to weaken in 1848 not only did frustration with unrepresentative and unresponsive regimes explode, suppressed national, ethnic, and linguistic conflicts also came to the fore. These conflicts, in turn, made it difficult to keep the opposition to the old order unified.

Largely as a result of these divisions, by 1851 there was little left of the democratic wave that had swept Europe in 1848. In retrospect there are several striking things about what happened in Europe during this time. First: how rapid the emergence and how extensive the reach of the democratic wave was. Second: how quickly and completely many long-standing dictatorships collapsed in the face of the mass pressures that produced the wave.[2] And third: how soon thereafter divisions within European societies appeared—over national/communal issues and regime type—and how difficult it was to maintain momentum once these disagreements appeared. As a result of such divisions, 1848 became—in the words of the great historian G. M. Trevelyan—"the turning point at which modern history failed to turn."

Despite the failure of democracy in 1848 the issues that had defined this period—rising class conflict, growing nationalist mobilization, and increasing political instability—continued to drive European political development during the late nineteenth and early twentieth centuries. Returning to France, for example, the country underwent another transition to democracy in 1871, but not before having to endure another revolutionary uprising (the Paris Commune) that cost perhaps 20,000 French citizens their lives. (Reflecting the frequency of political upheaval in France, a long-standing joke had it that the National Library kept its copies of the constitution in the "periodicals" section (Bell 2010, 32).) The Third Republic that emerged from this chaos was the only real democracy that existed in Europe at the time. Although it achieved many important successes, in today's terms we would probably not consider it fully consolidated since significant groups on both the left and right rejected the democratic "rules of the game" (Linz and Stepan 1996), with the nationalist right growing particularly rejectionist, anti-semitic and even violent over the course of time. The divisions that weakened the Third Republic were, of course, nothing new, but had become so deep that many wondered whether France would ever be able to achieve political stability. The historian Augustin Thierry, for example, mused: "We think we are one nation, yet we are two nations in the same land; two nations, hostile in their recollections of the past, irreconcilable in their projects for the future" (Bell 2010, 32; Thierry 1856, xiii).

Thus by the eve of World War I, Europe already had behind it several decades of rising political instability, mobilization, and conflict. The end of the war unleashed yet another democratic wave, bringing political change to places as diverse as Germany, Austria, Sweden, and Poland. Many of these new democracies were, however, burdened with a huge number of problems generated by the war, including economic devastation, high debt, inflation, and in those countries on the losing side (like Germany), a sense of national humiliation. In addition, the war and its aftermath worsened many problems inherited from the prewar period. Class conflict, for example, increased during the interwar period as a result of economic difficulties and the rise of communism. Communist parties not only fed off and exacerbated existing class resentments and divisions; they also injected into European polities powerful anti-democratic actors, able and willing to use terrorism and other forms of insurrectionary activity to achieve their goals.

Another problem inherited from the prewar period was nationalism. After 1918 a number of new countries were created in Central and Eastern Europe out of the wreckage of the Habsburg Empire. Many of these new countries had deeply divided and very mixed populations, with borders that did not correspond to their citizens' sense of identity or history. These new democratic, multi-ethnic states were beset by ethnic and social conflict almost from the moment of their birth; many experienced significant amounts of violence during the interwar years; none survived the interwar years and the Nazi onslaught. Nationalism was not, however, a degenerative force only in Europe's new states. The continent's older nations had to deal with nationalist movements carried over from the prewar period that grew even more violent and popular after the war; many of these groups provided the foundation upon which fascist and national socialist parties were built during the interwar years. These parties were much stronger and more dangerous than their predecessors, mobilizing large, cross-class constituencies around an anti-democratic but mass mobilizing ideology that mixed elements from both the left and right and directly targeted the growing number of Europeans who felt frustrated and alienated by the rapidly changing world around them (Berman 2007; Sternhell 1995a, 1995b).

Thus by the time of the Great Depression, many of Europe's young democracies were already in serious trouble, weakened by deep divisions in their societies and attacked by extremists on the left and right. The economic suffering and social chaos generated by the Depression simply pushed many of these regimes over the edge. By 1940 the democratic wave of 1918 was but a dim memory across much of the continent and Britain was standing alone against the Nazi dictatorship. Not only had democracy once again failed in Europe, this time failure led to the rise of possibly the most brutal regime and the most destructive war the world had ever known. If there was ever a time and place where democracy seemed to be a lost cause, Europe in 1940 was it.

The Postwar Era

It was only after the most destructive war in history that Western Europe was finally able to achieve widespread, consolidated democracy despite myriad attempts at democracy since 1789. How did this remarkable transformation happen?

There were, of course, many factors that shaped this transformation, including World War II itself. The radical right was discredited by the collapse of the interwar years and the war that followed, and many anti-democratic groups and movements were eliminated by the chaos and destruction of the 1940s. This was particularly true in Germany, where old social hierarchies were shattered by the Nazis (Dahrendorf 1969; Kogan 1968; Schoenbaum 1967) and the old conservative and Junker elite were disproportionately killed off in large numbers during the war (and then dispossessed by the communist regime in the East after it). In addition the war and its aftermath resulted in massive ethnic cleansing and population transfers which rendered many of the countries of central and Eastern Europe in particular more ethnically homogenous. (Historians estimate that between 1939 and 1943 perhaps 30 million people were uprooted, expelled, or dispersed (Hitchcock 2008; Wimmer 2002; Naimark 2002). As Mark Mazower put it, "war, violence and massive social dislocation had turned Versailles's dream of national homogeneity into realities" (2000, 218). Also important in promoting democratic consolidation in Western Europe after 1945 was the changed international situation and role of the United States. A relatively long-term occupation helped set the continent's most problematic country—Germany—firmly on the path to democracy. And with the Soviet Union and the developing Cold War prodding it forward, the United States, the world's strongest democracy, made a firm commitment to ensuring that Western Europe would be both a political and economic success.

However important these factors (and others), without socioeconomic stability, democratic consolidation could not have succeeded. As we have seen, class, social, and communal conflicts had been an ongoing source of political instability and violence throughout modern European history. In addition, the experience of the Great Depression—where the collapse of capitalism had led to social chaos, disillusionment with democracy, and a widespread embrace of extremism—led many to recognize that finding a way to ensure both economic prosperity and social peace was absolutely necessary if democracy were to succeed in Europe after 1945. On top of all this, the condition the continent found itself in after war—economically devastated, politically exhausted and with a powerful Soviet Union just outside its borders and revitalized communist parties within them—heightened fears that socioeconomic instability might quickly return and scuttle democratic experiments.

And yet, despite a history of failure and initially inauspicious conditions, democratic experiments did succeed in Western Europe after 1945. 1945 turned out to be, in other words, a crucial juncture in European political development and a key reason for this lies in the institutions reconstructed at both the domestic and regional levels after World War II. After 1945 actors across the political spectrum came to recognize that if democracy was finally going to work in Europe, not merely a change in political institutions but also a restructuring of social and economic ones would be necessary as well. In particular, democratic states would have to assert greater authority over the market (and key economic actors) and take responsibility for ensuring social peace so as to avoid the economic meltdowns, social chaos, and political extremism that had scuttled democratic experiments in the past. Such views had long been championed by many parties on the democratic left; what changed after 1945 is that they were embraced by other key groups as well. The 1947 program of the German Christian Democrats, for example, declared that, "The new structure of the German economy must start from the realization that the period of uncurtailed rule by private capitalism is over." In France, meanwhile, the Catholic Mouvement Républican Populaire declared in its first manifesto in 1944 that it supported a "revolution" to create a state "liberated from the power of those who possess wealth" (Sassoon 1998, 140). Even the United States, least affected by the war and most committed to the restoration of a global free-trade order, recognized that its commitment to stability and democracy in Europe meant that there was no going back to the socioeconomic *status quo ante* (Ikenberry 1992, 1996).

After 1945, accordingly, West European nations began constructing a new order, one that could ensure economic growth while at the same time protecting societies from capitalism's destructive and destabilizing consequences (Armstrong, Glyn, and Harrison 1991; Marglin and Schor 1991). This order represented a decisive break with the past: states would not be limited to ensuring that markets could grow and flourish nor would economic interests be given the widest possible leeway. This shift to a "social democratic" understanding of the relationship between states, markets, and societies (Berman 2007) was based on recognition that for democratic consolidation to finally succeed in Western Europe institutions capable of eradicating or at least tempering the social conflict and divisions that had helped scuttle democratic experiments in the past would have to be constructed.

The two most oft noted manifestations of this were Keynesianism and the welfare state. Keynesianism's significance lay in its rejection of the view that markets operated best when left to themselves and its recognition that substantial state intervention might be necessary in economic affairs. Keynes argued that state action was often necessary to help avoid economic crises that could threaten both democracy and the capitalist system itself. Having experienced the rise of the Soviet Union and the Great Depression, Keynes understood that unchecked markets could be socially and politically dangerous. As his biographer Robert Skidelsky has noted, "Keynes was quite conscious in seeking an alternative to dictatorship … a programme on which to fight back against facism and communism" (Skidelsky 1989, 35–36). Keynes hoped that by designing a "system that held out the prospect that the state could reconcile the private ownership of the means of production with democratic management of the economy" (Przeworski 1985, 207) he could convince people that there was a democratic solution to capitalism's problems.

Like Keynesianism, the welfare state helped transform the relationship among states, markets, and societies during the postwar era in ways that helped promote democratic consolidation. As C. A. R. Crosland noted, after 1945, "it was increasingly regarded as a proper function and indeed obligation of Government to ward off distress and strain not only among the poor but almost all classes of society" (Crosland 1967, 98). Western European welfare states were significant not only because they protected individuals from economic distress—they were also critical because they gave renewed importance to membership in a national community, since they both required and fostered a sense of kinship and solidarity among citizens: welfare states could only be sustained if individuals believed that ensuring a basic level of well-being for all citizens was a worthy goal. This move toward expanding welfare states after the war was thus not merely a reflection of a desire to rectify past mistakes, but it was also a deliberate attempt to undercut the support of extremist ideologies on the left and right that had played off anomie, dislocation, and atomization in the past in order to undermine support for democracy.

Of course, Keynesianism and welfare states were not the only ways in which postwar European political economies changed. Each European nation developed its own set of institutions that used the power of the state to protect societies from capitalism's most destructive effects and promote social solidarity and stability. In France, for example, planning became a key feature of the country's reconstructed political economy, while in Germany a number of innovative institutions including codetermination helped workers and management come to view themselves as "social partners" rather than adversaries, thus breaking a pattern that had contributed to economic, social, and political instability in the past. These institutional innovations probably went furthest in Sweden, where more generous and universal welfare state policies helped not only stabilize democracy, but also the dominance of the social democratic party.

Across Europe, in short, a variety of institutional innovations after 1945 helped transform European political economies in a social democratic way. These were, of course, still capitalist, but in a very different way than before the war—institutions now tempered or limited capitalism and explicitly tried to reconcile it with the goals of social stability and solidarity. As we know, these social democratic institutions worked remarkably well: despite fears after the war that it would perhaps take decades for Europe to recover economically,[3] by the early 1950s most of Europe had easily surpassed interwar economic figures and the 30 years after 1945 were Europe's fastest period of growth ever. The restructured political economies of the postwar era were able not only to foster growth, but also offer benefits to a wide variety of groups; this diminished the "zero-sum" nature of socioeconomic conflict during the interwar years (Maier 1981) and helped eliminate the belief—long held by liberals, Marxists, and others—that democratic states could not or would not protect particular groups' interests. As a result, both workers and employers (and the organizations and parties that catered to them) underwent a remarkable de-radicalization after 1945 and became more willing to work together to achieve what came to be seen as many common interests. As Claus Offe noted,

> What was at issue in class conflicts [after 1945] was no longer the mode of production, but the volume of distribution, not control but growth, and this type of conflict was particularly suited for being processed on the political plan through party competition because it does not involve 'either/or' questions, but questions of a 'more or less' or 'sooner or later' nature. Overarching this limited type of conflict, there was a consensus concerning basic priorities, desirabilities and values of the political economy, namely economic growth and social . . . security. (Offe 1983, 237)

The impact of postwar socioeconomic changes on European party systems was also striking. From the late nineteenth century through the interwar years, European politics had been increasingly driven by both right and left wing extremism. World War II largely discredited the radical right, but not the radical left—since its foreign champion was among the victors rather than the vanquished and since many communists had resisted rather than collaborated. In the decades after 1945, the success of the postwar order undercut the support for communist radicalism as well, helping to explain why these parties moderated, making clear their commitment to democracy and rejection of insurrectionary methods and slowly distancing themselves from the Soviet Union. So in place of the centrifugal political dynamics of the interwar years, during which tough times drove parties and voters to the extremes of the spectrum, the postwar years saw a reverse movement, with good times bringing parties and voters back toward the political middle (Kirchheimer 1996).

The social democratic institutions embedded in Western Europe's domestic political economies were, in short, a key factor in facilitating economic prosperity, social peace, political de-radicalization and hence the consolidation of democracy during the postwar period. But the architects of this transformation understood that domestic changes would have be matched by regional ones for everything to work out well. Postwar economic reconstruction, for example, was recognized as being too large a task to be accomplished by the uncoordinated efforts of individual governments. As Robert Schumann put it, if "Europe" were "to exist … It will be a Europe where the standard of living will rise and [France and Germany] work together for common goals."[4] Reconstruction had to be complemented by peace, moreover, which meant finding a way to reconcile Germany with Europe and vice versa. In Churchill's words, "to bring [Europe's horrible history] to an end, it would be necessary to re-create the European family ... and provide it with a structure under which it can dwell in peace, safety and freedom." The goal had to be the creation of a "continent so integrated, so connected that war would be impossible" (Churchill 1946).

And so alongside the transformation of Western European domestic political economies after 1945, a new set of regional institutions binding the countries together transformed the relationship among them as well. Ironically, however, despite European integration originating in a desire to promote economic development, prevent war and hence consolidate democracy, the institutional infrastructure of integration is weakening rather than strengthening democracy today. This is because the integration process developed a complex set of economic institutions that promoted economic interdependence, but neglected to develop a set of political institutions that could promote corresponding political interdependence or legitimacy. This disjuncture was based not on ignorance of the problem but rather on a false hope that it would eventually be solved—that somehow the continent's politics would evolve and catch up to the continent's economics.[5] But it proved pernicious nonetheless, because such evolution never really occurred.

A political deficit appeared during the earliest stages of the integration process. The very foundation of the European project—the 1951 European Coal and Steel Community (ECSC)—set a pattern whereby economic integration far outpaced the development of corresponding political institutions. The goals of the ECSC were explicitly political—ensuring peace and stability in Europe by binding France and Germany so closely together so as to make conflict between them unthinkable. But the means chosen to achieve these ends were economic—the creation of a common market for coal and steel. As Europe's common market expanded to include more countries and more sectors of the economy, the pattern continued. In the 1957 Treaty of Rome, for example, France, Germany, Italy, Belgium, Luxembourg, and the Netherlands agreed to remove all restrictions on trade, institute common external tariffs, reduce barriers to the free movement of people, services, and capital, and develop common agricultural policies, but did little to integrate political decision-making. The result was that by the 1960s, European economic integration had gone further than even early architects of the process could have hoped while political integration and the development of regional political institutions lagged further and further behind.

The bills started to come due in the 1970s. After 30 years of growth and progress, the European political economies that had been functioning so well sank into a noxious bog of unemployment and inflation. Partially in response, the United States decided to abandon the gold standard, throwing the postwar monetary order into chaos. European governments responded to these developments with various policies, none of which worked well and some of which, like floating currencies, threatened to lead to conflict among them. In response, European leaders decided to move forward with monetary cooperation and, eventually, integration (McNamara 1998).

At the time, this was seen by many as merely the next logical step in the process of economic integration. But with hindsight we can see now that it sowed the seeds of contemporary problems. It furthered and deepened the political deficit already embedded in the European project, even more so than might have been expected thanks to the spread of neoliberal thinking from the 1970s on. Neoliberalism's central goal was to unshackle markets from "interference" from political authorities and institutions (Blyth 2002). Not fully achievable on the domestic level thanks to the deeply rooted social democratic institutions put in place during the postwar period, this impulse gained freer reign in regional matters, as the development of European monetary union deprived national governments of a critical economic policy tool and shifted authority to central bank free from all political, let alone democratic, oversight. The results, as we know, were economic and political catastrophe.

The economic consequences are well known and horrific—record unemployment and poverty and declines in GDP not seen since the Great Depression. Politically, the consequences are almost as bad. The lack of authoritative, democratic political institutions at the regional level has robbed the European Union of the ability to respond forcefully to the crisis, thereby fanning the flames of nationalism and extremism and creating a backlash against the European project itself. Such worrisome trends have emerged even in countries that have done relatively well during the crisis, not merely the ones suffering through Great Depression-level meltdowns. Given Europe's past and the strides that have been made in overcoming it over the last two generations, such movement backward is both tragic and scary.

Democracy and Historical Institutionalism in Europe

Understanding why 1945 turned out to be a critical juncture in European political development requires examining institutional changes that occurred at both the domestic and regional levels during the postwar period. A crucial lesson European elites and publics learned from generations of democratic failure and the collapse of the interwar period in particular was that socioeconomic stability was a necessary prerequisite for democratic consolidation. After World War II a fairly broad consensus reigned in Western Europe that the continent needed to rebuild not merely its political instiutions, but its social and economic ones as well in order to achieve socioeconomic stability and hence democratic consolidation.

At the domestic level, a new understanding of democracy developed in Western Europe, one that went beyond what we think of today as "electoral" or even "liberal" democracy (Schumpeter 1954; Diamond 1999, 2009; Collier and Levitsky 1997) to what is best understood as "social" democracy. This order was characterized by the development of a variety of social and economic institutions designed to avoid the social divisions and conflicts that had scuttled democratic experiments in the past. Although every country and each era is different, one lesson an examination of postwar Western European history makes clear is that political stability in general and democracy in particular requires dealing forthrightly with the social divisions and conflict generated by economic development. All scholars recognize that guaranteeing free and fair elections is a necessary component of democracy; increasing numbers have come to accept that a state willing and able to ensure civil liberties and human rights is fundamental to democracy too. What the European experience seems to suggest is that especially in countries prone to deep social divisions and conflicts, institutions capable of dealing with the destabilizing social consequences of economic development in particular and modernity in general may be a prerequisite for a consolidated, well-functioning democracy as well. The social democratic institutions embedded in postwar West European political economies were an attempt to do just this—to come up with a form of democracy explicitly focused on dealing with the social and economic conflicts that had scuttled democratic experiments in the past.

Ironically, perhaps, this fundamental insight ended up being partially contradicted by developments at the regional level in Europe. Although the continent's economic integration went very far, its political integration did not. Europe never developed the regional level institutions capable of promoting and protecting the socioeconomic stability that is a necessary prerequisite for political stability in general and well-functioning democracy in particular. The contemporary crisis has shown that Europe as a whole lacks the tools to respond effectively to economic problems or protect it citizens from the vicissitudes of life under global capitalism. Citizens in southern Europe in particular wonder whether outside creditors or unelected elites have more power over their lives than their own governments; the result, not surprisingly, has been growing political apathy and extremism. Political-insitutional underdevelopment at the regional level, in other words, is a large part of the reason why Europe is in such a mess today.

An examination of institutions, in short, is absolutely necessary to understand the development of democracy in Western Europe after 1945 as well as the state of democracy in Europe today. And, in order to understand these institutions, an examination of their historical background and development is also necessary. Both the postwar social democratic domestic order and the European Union grew out of the political failures of the prewar period; both were designed to correct problems that had scuttled democracy in the past. But both sets of institutions—domestic and regional—are in trouble today, a clear example that institutions that can help solve problems in one period, may be less functional or efficient as the contexts they are embedded in change (Hall and Taylor 1996; Pierson 2000; Eichengreen 2008). Institutions are, as historical institutionalism teaches us, "sticky"—once they are in place, political coalitions, social expectations and other institutions develop around them, making them very costly and difficult to change. However, change they must, if Europe as a whole as well as many of its constituent countries is to progress and flourish. Europe's last period of institutional innovation happened after the bloodiest, most destructive war in the continent's history. Let us hope that a similar level of tragedy is not necessary for institutional renovation today.

Notes

1. This may not be entirely true if one considers the Commonwealth produced by the English civil war Europe's first major try at democracy; nonetheless, the outcome of this democratic experiment was more or less the same as that of the French first republic.
2. As Eric Hobsbawm put it, "There have been plenty of greater revolutions in the history of the modern world, and certainly plenty more successful ones. Yet there has been none which spread more rapidly and widely, running like a brushfire across frontiers, countries and even oceans ... [All these revolutions] succeeded and failed rapidly, and in most cases totally. During the first few months all governments in the revolutionary zone were swept away or reduced to impotence. All collapsed or retreated virtually without resistance. Yet within a relatively short period the evolution had lost the initiative almost everywhere ... 1848 appears as the one revolution in the modern history of Europe which combines the greatest promise, the widest scope, and the most immediate initial success, with the most unqualified and rapid failure (1979, 4, 8, 10).
3. German residents polled in the American zone after World War II expected that it would take at least twenty years for the country to recover. De Gaulle had similarly informed French citizens that would take twenty-five years of "furious work" before France would be back on its feet again (Judt 2005, 89).
4. The Schuman Declaration, Speech May 5, 1950. Available at <http://www.schuman.info/9May1950.htm> (accessed August 4, 2015).
5. E.g., the following quote is often attributed to Jean Monnet but in fact it is a paraphrase of Monnet's intentions by British Conservative Adrian Hilton: "Europe's nations should be guided towards a super state without their people understanding what is happening. This can be accomplished by successive steps each disguised as having an economic purpose, but which will eventually and irreversibly lead to federation." Available at <http://europa.hs-pforzheim.de/jeanmonnet_biography.html> (accessed August 4, 2015).

References

Armstrong, Philip, Andrew Glyn, and John Harrison. 1991. *Capitalism Since 1945*. New York: Basil Blackwell.

Bell, Daniel. 2010. "Pogroms of Words." *The New Republic* June 24.

Berman, Sheri. 2007. *The Primacy of Politics: Social Democracy and the Making of Europe's Twentieth Century*. New York: Cambridge University Press.

Blyth, Mark. 2002. *Great Transformations*. New York: Cambridge University Press.

Churchill, Winston. 1946. "I Wish to Speak to You Today About the Tragedy of Europe." Zurich.

Collier, David and Steven Levitsky. 1997. "Democracy with Adjectives." *World Politics* 49 (3): 430–451.

Crosland, C. A. R. 1967. *The Future of Socialism*. London: Fletcher and Son.

Dahrendorf, Ralf. 1969. *Society and Democracy in Germany*. New York: Anchor.

Diamond, Larry. 1999. *Developing Democracy*. Baltimore, MD: Johns Hopkins.

Diamond, Larry. 2009. *The Spirit of Democracy*. New York: St. Martin's.

Eichengreen, Barry. 2008. *The European Economy Since 1945*. Princeton, NJ: Princeton University Press.

Hall, Peter and Rosemary Taylor (1996) "Political Science and the Three New Institutionalisms." *Political Studies* 44: 936–957.
Hitchcock, William. 2008. *The Bitter Road to Freedom*. New York: Free Press.
Hobsbawm, Eric. 1979. *The Age of Capital, 1848–1875*. New York: Meridian.
Hobsbawm, Eric. 1996. *The Age of Revolution: 1789–1848*. New York: Vintage Books.
Ikenberry, G. John. 1992. "A World Economy Restored." *International Organization* 46 (1): 289–321.
Ikenberry, G. John. 1996. "Workers and the World Economy." *Foreign Affairs* May/June.
Immergut, Ellen and Karen Anderson. 2008. "Historical Institutionalism and West European Politics." *West European Politics* 31 (1–2): 345–369.
Jones, Peter. 1991. *The 1848 Revolutions*. New York: Longman.
Judt, Tony. 2005. *Postwar*. New York: Penguin.
Kapstein, Ethan. 1996. "Workers and the World Economy." *Foreign Affairs* May/June: 16–37.
Kirchheimer, Otto. 1966. "The Transformation of West European Party Systems." In *Political Parties and Political Development*, ed. Joseph LaPolombara and Myron Weiner. Princeton, NJ: Princeton University Press.
Kogan, Nancy. 1968. "Fascism as a Political System." In *The Nature of Fascism*, ed. S. J. Woolf. London: George Weidenfeld & Nicolson, Ltd.
Kranzberg, Melvin. 1959. *1848: A Turning Point?* Boston, MA: D.C. Heath and Company.
Langer, William. 1969a. *Political and Social Upheaval, 1832–1852*. New York: Harper and Row.
Langer, William. 1969b. *The Revolutions of 1848*. New York: Harper and Row.
Linz, Juan and Alfred Stepan. 1996. "Toward Consolidated Democracies." *Journal of Democracy* 7 (2): 14–33.
McNamara, Kathleen. 1998. *The Currency of Ideas: Monetary Politics in the European Union*. Ithaca, NY: Cornell University Press.
Maier, Charles. 1981. "The Two Postwar Eras." *American Historical Review* 6 (2): 327–352.
Marglin, Stephen and Juliet Schor. 1991. *The Golden Age of Capitalism*. New York: Oxford University Press.
Mazower, Mark. 2000. *Dark Continent*. New York: Vintage.
Naimark, Norman. 2002. *Fires of Hatred: Ethnic Cleansing in Twentieth Century Europe*. Cambridge, MA: Harvard University Press.
Offe, Claus. 1983. "Competitive Party Democracy and the Keynesian Welfare State: Factors of Stability and Disorganization." *Policy Sciences* 15: 225–246.
Pierson, Paul. 2000. "The Limits of Design: Explaining Institutional Origins and Change." *Governance* 13 (4): 475–489.
Przeworski, Adam. 1985. *Capitalism and Social Democracy*. New York: Cambridge University Press.
Rothstein, Bo. 1996. "Political Institutions." In *A New Handbook of Political Science*, ed. R. Goodin and H.-D. Klingemann. New York: Oxford University Press.
Sassoon, Donald. 1998. *One Hundred Years of Socialism*. New York: New Press.
Schoenbaum, David. 1967. *Hitler's Social Revolution*. New York: W.W. Norton & Co.
Schumpeter, Joseph. 1954. *Capitalism, Socialism and Democracy*. New York: Harper and Row.
Skidelsky, Robert. 1989. "The Political Meaning of Keynesianism." In *The Political Power of Economic Ideas*, ed. Peter Hall. Princeton, NJ: Princeton University Press.
Sperber, Jonathan. 2005. *The European Revolutions*. New York: Cambridge University Press.
Stearns, Peter. 1974. *1848: The Revolutionary Tide in Europe*. New York: WW Norton & Co.

Steinmo, Sven, Kathleeen Thelen, and Frank Longstreth, eds. 1992. *Structuring Politics: Historical Institutionalism in Comparative Politics*. New York: Cambridge University Press.

Sternhell, Zeev. 1995a. *The Birth of Fascist Ideology*. Princeton, NJ: Princeton University Press.

Sternhell, Zeev. 1995b. *Neither Right Nor Left: Fascist Ideology in France*. Princeton, NJ: Princeton University Press.

Thelen, Kathleen. 1999. "Historical Institutionalism in Comparative Politics." *Annual Review* of Political Science 2: 369–404.

Thierry, Augustin. 1856. *History of the Conquest of England by the Normans; Its Causes, and Its Consequences, in England, Scotland, Ireland, and on the Continent*, translated from the seventh Paris edition by William Hazlitt. London: H.G. Bohn, 1856.

Wimmer, Andreas. 2002. *Nationalist Exclusion and Ethnic Conflict*. New York: Cambridge University Press.

CHAPTER 25

HISTORICAL INSTITUTIONALISM AND THE WELFARE STATE

JULIA LYNCH AND MARTIN RHODES*

Historical institutionalism and the analysis of welfare states (including the ancillary policy domain of the labor market) overlap significantly. More than elsewhere in Political Science and public policy, much single-country, program, and comparative analysis of the welfare state since the 1980s has taken an historical approach (Amenta 2003). Relatedly, some of the major welfare state scholars have also been major historical institutionalism theorists and proponents—most prominently, but not only, Theda Skocpol, Paul Pierson, and Kathleen Thelen. Those scholars and their colleagues have set the agenda for much (though not all) contemporary welfare state analysis. Indeed, the nexus between historical institutionalism and welfare state studies has become something of an "institution" itself, with a strong, path-dependent core of actors (academic path- and boundary-setters), rules (methodology and methods), and norms (ontological and epistemological assumptions). Using a framework derived from the philosophy of science, we analyze this institution as a "scientific research program" to better understand its intellectual history and characteristics.

Together, the actors, rules, and norms of historical institutionalism in welfare state analysis constitute what Imre Lakatos (1970, 132–138) called a distinctive "scientific research program." As he defined it, a scientific research program consists of a stubbornly defended "hard core" (or "negative heuristic") of rules, norms, and core hypotheses; a more flexible "protective belt" (or "positive heuristic") of more modest and specific "auxiliary" hypotheses,[1] that can be modified or discarded in response to empirical discoveries; and an elaborate array of problem-solving mechanisms. We also use Lakatos's notion of "progressive" versus "degenerative" scientific research programs as a guide to assessing the development of the historical institutionalist–welfare state nexus (hereafter HIWS) over time. In a progressive research program, the productive development of auxiliary hypotheses will increase and strengthen its predictive and analytical power in the face of new evidence and rival theories, allowing an extension to new cases—indicating what Lakatos calls the program's "heuristic power" (1970, 137). But a degenerative research program will produce only ad hoc auxiliary hypotheses that give way in the face of new evidence, thereby exposing and weakening the theoretical core.

Using Lakatos's framework as a heuristic facilitates an intellectual history and sociology of the HIWS. In true historical institutionalist fashion, it allows us to process trace the dynamics of developments across time, and to determine the relationships between contributors to different areas of the program. As Elman and Elman (2002, 253) argue, one of the most useful aspects of Lakatos's methodology is that it "insists on explicit program descriptions . . . that clearly delineate the connections and continuities between associated research." That is precisely our aim. Our framework also helps us explain why some critiques of the program's core (such as its early neglect of power, agency, and change) are more successfully accommodated than others (the ideational critique in particular).

Our exploration and assessment of the HIWS research program reveal the following characteristics: a robust and well-defended theoretical core, reinforced over time through conceptual elaboration and deepening; a rich "protective belt" of evolving and productive auxiliary hypotheses that have strengthened the program in the face of new evidence and rival theories and hypotheses; and a productive extension of the program to new cases by many authors who, adopting the program's rules and norms, engage with and enrich its auxiliary hypotheses with empirical investigations. The latter, in turn, contribute to the program's "positive heuristic" strength.

As with historical institutionalism in general, there are multiple positions and preferences in HIWS regarding core analytical issues. These include the relative emphasis on order and stability versus innovation; on how institutions structure action through regulative, normative, and cognitive constraints versus creative action; and on the importance of material resources versus human cognition in institutional emergence, durability, and change. We suggest that this flexibility derives from the enrichment and adaptability of the program's auxiliary hypotheses.

Similarly, far from weakening HIWS research, the scope for theoretical and methodological cross-fertilization with other research programs (rational choice, sociological institutionalism, and constructivism) has given it new dimensions. Positive engagement between rival approaches in welfare state analysis, including the addition of novel methodologies to the historical institutionalist repertoire, has been facilitated by some core historical institutionalists (e.g., Hall 2010) as well as those seeking to import institutional analysis into rival schools or seek bridges between them (e.g., Moe 2005; Katznelson and Weingast 2005).

Yet, precisely because of the strength of its core theoretical and methodological rules and norms, there is clear resistance in HIWS to absorbing too much from these rival programs, and we see strong boundary limitations in certain areas. While ideas and cognition have always been part of the historical institutionalist "core," there is a clear standoff in welfare state analysis (as elsewhere in historical institutionalism) between the institutionalist ontology and epistemology and that of strongly values- or identity-oriented research, especially in its cultural/semiotic form (see Orloff 2005). Early "openings" to ideas and cognition in historical institutionalism have been less well exploited by historical institutionalism (and by core participants in HIWS) than those with in rational choice (Hall and Lamont 2013).

At the same time, the methodological boundary with rational choice has to be carefully negotiated (e.g., Katznelson and Weingast 2005). There are similar barriers, which must be bridged via strategies of triangulation, to linking HIWS research with other forms of comparative political research or with large-N statistical work (Hall 2003; Skocpol 2003). Nevertheless, as we conclude, those links must be made if some of the most important claims of HIWS are to be subjected, as they should be, to the harsh light of empirical analysis using the multiple (and fine-grained) methods now available to researchers.

The Core of the Historical-Institutionalist Welfare State (HIWS) Scientific Research Program and Its Critics

In this section we first set out the rules (methodology and methods), and norms (ontological and epistemological assumptions) of the HIWS research program's "hard core" and its key builders and defenders. In a second step we look at a series of assaults on that core.

The "Hard Core" of the HIWS Research Program

The "hard core" of the HIWS research program has its origins with Hugh Heclo's *Modern Social Politics in Britain and Sweden* (1976) which first demonstrated the extent to which "policy creates politics" by shaping actors interests and positions over time. Theda Skocpol (and various co-authors) brought this perspective into US welfare state research in the early 1980s, initially via a vigorous debate with neo-Marxist analysts of early American social policy who, in Skocpol's view, had grossly neglected state institutions and political parties (Skocpol 1980; Skocpol and Ikenberry 1983).

As the 1980s wore on, the debates became more intense—for example, the clash between Jill Quadagno and Skocpol and Edwin Amenta over the use of neo-Marxist state theory to explain the passage of the US Social Security Act of 1935 (Quadagno 1984; Skocpol and Amenta 1985)—and the historical institutionalist approach became more analytically sophisticated. In joint work with Amenta, John Ikenberry, Ann Orloff, and Margaret Weir, the notion of states as actors and structures was further developed by

Skocpol, and the concept of "policy feedback" first introduced, and applied to both US and comparative social policy studies (Skocpol and Ikenberry 1983; Orloff and Skocpol 1984; Skocpol and Amenta 1986; Weir, Orloff, and Skocpol 1988). Orloff and Skocpol (1984) was a pioneering analysis that compared the origins of the British and US welfare states through a "state-centered frame of reference" while also critiquing reigning explanatory approaches, including logic of industrialism, working-class strength, and cultural/values-based arguments.

The approach was consolidated in three important books that appeared almost simultaneously in the early 1990s: Weir's *Politics and Jobs* (1992), Skocpol's *Protecting Soldiers and Mothers* (1993)—both focusing on the US—and Orloff's monumental comparative historical study, *The Politics of Pensions* (1993). All three emphasize the centrality of political institutions in mediating social pressures and socioeconomic processes, the role of policy initiatives in "setting boundaries" that restrict the scope of future innovation (Weir 1992, 5), and the relationship between policy feedbacks and coalition formation. Although not strictly part of the same school, and linked to the "working-class strength" approach that they rejected, Skocpol and her colleagues embraced Gøsta Esping-Andersen's seminal *Three Worlds of Welfare Capitalism* (1990) because of its historical explanation of welfare state emergence and development.

Skocpol's *Protecting Soldiers and Mothers* made the strongest analytical statement demarcating historical institutionalist analysis from competing perspectives. Dismissing a series of explanations for the distinctiveness of US social policy—as the by-product of industrialization, national values, working-class weakness (power resources theory), business hegemony, and the gender perspective—Skocpol presents her "structured polity perspective" as the basis for understanding the "patterns and tempos" of US social policy provision. The analysis focused on four kinds of processes: the establishment and transformation of state and party organizations; the effects of political institutions and procedures on the identities, capacities, and goals of social groups; the "fit"—or lack thereof—between the goals and capacities of politically active groups and the changing points of access and leverage allowed by political institutions; and the ways in which previously established social policies affect subsequent politics. With these works, the basic foundations of HIWS had been put in place.

In the mid-1990s, HIWS was further consolidated by three publications: Skocpol's *Social Policy in the United States* (1995a), Finegold and Skocpol's *State and Party in America's New Deal* (1995), and Paul Pierson's *Dismantling the Welfare State?* (1995). The second and third of these were especially important in advancing the critique of rival approaches (pluralism and elite theories, Marxism and rational choice) and in providing empirical support for two core historical-institutionalists concepts: policy feedback and path dependence.

Skocpol's "Why I am a Historical Institutionalist" (1995b) summarized and explicitly defined the approach's core principles. Skocpol views institutions as formal organizations or informal networks, with shared meanings and stable bundles of resources and patterns of communication and activity. A "realist," neo-positivist position underlies this view: the interpretivist notion of institutions as systems of meaning or normative frameworks is roundly rejected—"It is not enough just to explore how people talk or think" (Skocpol 1995b, 105)—and causal analysis and hypothesis testing strongly endorsed. Moreover, although a dialogue between historical institutionalism and "institutionally embedded rational choice" was to be encouraged (see also Hall and Taylor 1996; Moe 2005; Hall 2010), the methodological individualism and formal deductive modeling of rational choice was beyond the pale. Marxist or *marxisant* approaches were not even mentioned in Skocpol's statement: apparently their time had passed. Some clear boundaries (and for the approach's critics, limitations) had now been set. Similar points were made by Steinmo, Thelen, and Longstreth (1992), three of whose chapters focused on welfare state issues.

Skocpol and Pierson (2002) further embellished these core precepts, emphasizing the importance in HIWS of tackling big, real-world questions, tracing processes through time, and analyzing institutional configurations and contexts. This work also paid particular attention to certain theories of causation, principally "path dependence" (effectuated via dynamic processes of positive feedback or "increasing returns") and slow-moving causal processes in which structural preconditions are established for particular outcomes (see also Mahoney, Mohamedali, and Nguyen, Chapter 4, this volume). In so doing, it marked as erroneous the search for explanations based on "idiosyncratic or precipitating factors" rather than "deeper causes." This resulted in subsequent accusations of "institutional determinism" and was a source of much dispute over where the focus of welfare state analysis should lie. But Pierson (2003, also 2004) argued for "the need for social scientists to be attentive to the Braudelian focus on the *longue durée*" and not succumb to the temptation to focus on "snapshots of a single moment in time." On this issue see also Thelen (1999).

Both Pierson and Skocpol developed their historical institutionalism by building on conceptual observations and concepts from other theorists and, occasionally, disciplines (e.g., "increasing returns" is borrowed from economics); but they also took direct lessons from their own research into social policies and welfare states. If Skocpol developed her notion of policy legacies from the evolution of US social policy—policies "flow from prior institutions and politics, making some developments more likely, and hindering the possibilities for others" (Skocpol 1993, 531)—Pierson's contributions to the "hard core" came from his comparative analysis of British and US welfare reform in the 1980s (1995) and from the broader comparative analysis contained in *New Politics of the Welfare State* (Pierson 2001). If *Dismantling the Welfare State?* sought explanations for the apparent timidity of welfare retrenchment under neoliberal governments in the "stickiness" of institutions, political vetoes, and the electoral coalitions that mobilize in defense of existing entitlements, *New Politics* developed the notion of post-industrial welfare states as "immovable objects" confronting "irresistible forces" under conditions of "permanent fiscal austerity."

But contrary to an oft-made criticism, this was not a conception of welfare states as "frozen" or completely resistant to reform. Rather, Pierson argued that the core of welfare states would remain largely intact, and that "recalibration" (cost containment, rationalization and updating), rather than a radical retrenchment of welfare programs, would occur. The *longue durée* would end up revealing a degree of institutional and programmatic persistence greater than that posited by a focus on the *courte durée* of policy battles and reforms. This did not prevent an explosion of analysis that focused precisely on the latter and sought to explain why, regardless of institutional resilience, welfare state retrenchment and change occurs (for a useful survey, see Giger 2011, chapter 1).

Perhaps the strongest recent statement of this core argument comes from Pierson's "The Welfare State over the Very Long Run" (2011). In this paper, Pierson restates the need to explain not the variation in welfare state programs over time (for there is often very little variation to explain, he argues), but rather their relative stability in a context of sometimes dramatic socioeconomic change. He links this argument with Esping-Andersen's (1996, 24) notion of a welfare state that cannot respond adequately to "new social risks" because of the weight of existing institutional commitments to old ones.

In highly influential parallel work with Stephan Leibfried and others (Leibfried and Pierson 1995), Pierson extended to European social policy his interests in the role of previous policy commitments and their institutional "lock-in" effects for actors (and governments)—spurring a new generation of historical institutionalism-oriented analysis of EU-level policymaking and its impact on EU members states in the welfare state arena (e.g., Leibfried and Pierson 2000; Rhodes 2010).

In sum, the "hard core" of the HIWS research program includes key areas of analysis (the centrality of state and political party institutions; the effects of those institutions and their procedures on of the actions and goals of interest groups); a series of characteristic methods (process tracing, attention to the *longue durée* and to relations among institutions and between institutions and their contexts); and privileged theories of causation (path dependence, increasing returns, feedback mechanisms, slow-moving causal processes).

In turn, the "hard core" *excludes* certain possibilities. First, it rejects the notion of welfare states as unchangeable institutions, frozen in time. It focuses instead on their institutional resilience and incremental recalibration in the face of dramatic changes in political, social, economic, and demographic contexts. Methodologically, the hard core claims that reforms to the welfare state cannot be understood by examining the *courte durée* of policy battles. It claims causal process analysis as its key methodology, and at an epistemological level is essentially neo-positivist, using historical narrative for hypothesis testing and for the most part eschewing both formal deductive modeling and strongly interpretivist epistemologies and methods.

For critics of what we can fairly call the "Skocpol-Pierson school" of HIWS analysis, such as Ira Katznelson, the approach so defined demanded "too high a price for entry to historical institutionalism's house". It insisted, he claimed, that other theories be left behind as irremediably flawed (Katznelson 1998, 196), and succeeded only in replacing "a Marxist materialism with a more static and cross-sectional organizational materialism" (Katznelson 2009, 100). But that was, perhaps, the price to be paid for creating the irrefutable "hard core" of a distinct, underivative, and non-eclectic research program.

Critiques of the HIWS Core

Disagreement with the core precepts of HIWS can be broken down into four categories of criticism: of the scope and definition of the welfare state; of the limited consideration given to power and conflict; of the neglect of actors and "mechanisms"; and of the restricted conception of "change" in the perspective of the *longue durée*. Some of these have amounted to "friendly sparring" with proponents of the hard core's precepts, in which opponents seek to strengthen rather than undermine the HIWS core. Other critiques are more adamantly opposed to the HIWS core, and come from quite different ontological/epistemological and methodological traditions. We identify six such controversies:

The WS dependent variable "problem." This criticism has appeared in two quite different forms. The first, found in numerous reviews of work by Skocpol, Orloff, and Weir in the 1980s and 1990s, yearned for the parsimony of a more positivist political or sociological science from which Skocpol et al.'s form of institutionalism clearly departed. Alber (1994, 545), for example, argued that given the complexity of Orloff's historical argument in *The Politics of Pensions* (1993), "it is difficult to specify the dependent variables precisely and the reader occasionally wonders what exactly the author is attempting to explain." For Orloff, the "dependent variable" was quite broad—the system of pensions provision—rather than something quantifiable or a single event.[2] A second form of criticism ten years on argued that the dependent variable in HIWS was now being too narrowly defined, as articulated in several publications by Jacob Hacker (e.g., 2004, 2005), beginning with a *critique raisonnée* of Pierson's (1995) *Dismantling the Welfare State.*

Hacker identified three core problems in Pierson's account. First, like the pluralists, Pierson analyzed observable decisions and paid little attention to agenda setting by powerful actors in the welfare state domain. Second, Pierson ignored "social context," that is, how policy changes in the welfare state interact with the fortunes and lives of citizens, and failed to acknowledge the evolving nature of social risk. Finally, Hacker argued, Pierson had adopted a too-narrow conception of the welfare state, ignoring what Christopher Howard (1999) has labeled "the hidden welfare state," and neglecting to analyze, in particular, two very important overlapping policy realms in US social policy: tax expenditures with social welfare aims, and regulatory and tax policies governing privately-provided social welfare benefits. In making this critique, which could have been applied to much of the HIWS canon, Hacker was arguing that not only was the dependent variable mis-specified, but that the analysis was also methodologically blinkered. The critique was to have a major impact on Pierson's subsequent intellectual development.

Neglect of contestation and conflict. This criticism comes in two main forms. First, "power resources" analysts like Alexander Hicks (1999), Walter Korpi (2001, 2003, 2006), and Evelyne Huber and John Stephens (e.g., 2001) have argued that HIWS is insufficiently attentive to the class and power dynamics underlying welfare state formation and reform (also Culpepper, Chapter 27, this volume). Going back to the work of earlier exponents of HIWS (e.g., Orloff 1993), one sees a much greater attention then to what is now called "power resources" or class conflict than in the newer "new politics" form of HIWS. Korpi (2003, 2006) addressed the issue of employers' class-based power, and criticized the "new politics" approach of Pierson quite centrally for its neglect of class-based analysis in its understanding of the politics of retrenchment. Korpi in fact sidelined historical institutionalism and identifies Rational-Choice Institutionalism (RCI) as his favored partner in linking a power-resources approach with a new institutionalism (2001).

Second, and from sources often within the HIWS tradition, has come the critique that an excessive focus on critical junctures and positive feedback mechanisms can obscure the role of power politics. For example, Immergut (2008, 355) argues that in historical institutionalism "the focus on pinning down history has resulted in the neglect of two basic features of both politics and history: political contestation and actor reflexivity." Orloff (2005) points out that the earliest works in the HIWS tradition conceived of policy feedbacks as having multivalent consequences, including contestation, quite differently from the "lock in" or "increasing returns" notions that a newer version of HIWS inspired by Pierson (2000) had embraced. In seeking to account for changes in labor market institutions and their outputs, Thelen (2004) eschews the contemporary strain of HIWS that pays obeisance to critical junctures and path dependence in favor of a more conflict-oriented analysis of power-distributional and political coalitions.

Insufficient attention to actors and mechanisms of change. Relatedly, numerous works critique the tendency in HIWS research for submerging the role of actors within structural arguments. This leaves little scope for institutional contradictions that actors can exploit (e.g., Clemens and Cook 1999; Ebbinghaus 2005), or for creativity in innovating, recrafting or recombining institutions (e.g., Campbell 2004; Crouch 2005, 2007). If Crouch disagrees with some of the core conceptual and methodological precepts of HIWS, Cerami (2006, 2008) seeks to "rescue historical institutionalism" from "institutional determinism" in his work on the emergence and adaptation of post-communist Central and East European welfare states, identifying several "mechanism-based models of institutional change" (ideational, communicative, and coordinative) in addition to the "recombinant transformation" and "institutional bricolage" concepts found in Campbell and Crouch.

Difficulty explaining change. Perhaps the most common criticism of historical institutionalism work in general is an alleged bias toward stability and difficulty in explaining change. Peters, Pierre, and King (2005) present a broad summary of this critique. In HIWS, the major contributions responding to this critique have come from Hacker and Thelen independently and from the contributions to both Mahoney and Thelen (2009) and Streeck and Thelen (2005).

An unclear and limited role for ideas, values, and attitudes. This critique has come from many directions—including from mainstream political scientists, historical sociologists, and more radical constructivists. Seymour Martin Lipset (1996, 340) argued that Skocpol's account of US social policy history was deficient due to its neglect "of the larger value context within which American politics takes place." Daniel Béland (2007) argued similarly but more completely that historical institutionalism needs a systematic analysis of ideational processes for a full understanding of institutional change. Movement toward that position was already apparent in the extended use of Hall's (1993) policy paradigm concept in Béland and Hacker (2004). Robert Lieberman (2002) provides another important contribution theorizing the connection between ideas and institutions, focusing on what he calls "friction" among mismatched institutional and ideational patterns' in explaining important episodes of institutional change.

Additional critiques regarding ideas and culture that are essentially compatible with the HIWS core, but somewhat more radical, have come from other scholars. Thus Larsen (2008), for example, seeks to escape what he calls the "dead end" of the institutional line of reasoning regarding public opinion (which he argues is mechanistic and lacks micro-foundations), and explores the links between the macro-institutional level of welfare state regimes and micro-level of public attitudes (for a similar critique see Giger 2011). An important critique of the lack of attention to culture and the social construction of identities and goals comes from an historical sociology perspective, as in Orloff's depiction of the HIWS mainstream's "weakly utilitarian understanding of actors," which she would like to see "discarded for a more fully culturally situated conception of selves" (2005, 214)—including a more complete engagement with feminist scholars on issues of gender (Adams, Clemens, and Orloff 2005).

There is undoubtedly room for some accommodation of the ideational and cultural critiques within HIWS (see below). However, the HIWS core research program is not infinitely malleable. Works by Herrigel (2005), Rothstein (1998), and Schmidt (2003, 2008), for example, move into a social constructivist terrain that allows much more space for norms in the definition of institutions than would the HIWS core (also Blyth, Helgadóttir, and Kring, Chapter 8, this volume). Schmidt (2008) argues for the importance of a fourth institutionalism—"discursive institutionalism"—alongside the traditional three institutions (historical, rational-choice, and sociological) as set out in Hall and Taylor (1996), an attempted innovation that has gained little traction in HIWS, except in the work of Cerami (2008) mentioned above.

Methodological Problems. Historical institutionalism generally, and especially theory based on path dependence, has been subject to the critique that it routinely generates hypotheses that are not easily testable or falsifiable—or if they are testable, then HIWS's macro-institutional focus is incapable, on its own, of doing so due to the frequent absence of micro-foundations or readily-identified causal connections (e.g., Giger 2011). Many critics (e.g., Alber 1994) argue that HIWS is not even interested in testing hypotheses and is essentially an (historically) interpretative approach—a label which many historical institutionalists would be happy to accept. Even Ellen Immergut, the author of a key historical institutionalist analysis of comparative health systems (1992) worries that "it is difficult to see how... historical narratives can ever be proved wrong" (Immergut 1998). Drezner (2010) asks "Is Historical Institutionalism Bunk?" for similar reasons, while Peters, Pierre, and King (2005) argue that if historical institutionalism often generates compelling historical narratives, it has trouble generating real explanations for political and policy change. Although scholars such as Hall (2003) and Brady and Collier (2010) have mounted a spirited methodological defense of historical institutionalism, some of its fiercest critics (e.g., Schwartz 2005; Drezner 2010) complain that historical institutionalism is under-theorized and suffers from serious problems in establishing causality and elaborating plausible causal mechanisms.

The "Protective Belt": Auxiliary Hypotheses and "Progressive Adaptation"

Flexible Responses to Rival Hypotheses

The HIWS research program has been remarkably successful in responding to many of these critiques. Contributions by Hacker, Pierson, and Thelen, in particular, have both critiqued and then adapted and enriched the program. They have built into the approach a greater attention to and theorization of different modes of institutional change, as well as to the agency, power, and conflict dynamics that lie behind them. Especially noteworthy are Hacker's *The Divided Welfare State* (2002), Thelen's *How Institutions Evolve* (2004), Streeck and Thelen's *Beyond Continuity* (2005), and the work of Hacker and Pierson on business power and welfare state formation (e.g., 2002, 2004). Thelen, and especially Pierson, are interesting in that their intellectual trajectories mark them as original members of the HIWS core, but also active participants in the adaptation of the research program's protective belt.

To the "dependent variable problem," Hacker (2002) in particular responded by shining a light on private as well as public provision and on the "hidden welfare state" consisting of government regulation and taxation of private benefits. In subsequent work (*The Great Risk Shift*, 2006), Hacker moved to further expand the definition of the welfare state to include responsibility for the distribution of risk in society. Relatedly, Hacker's (2002) focus on non-decisions as key drivers of welfare state change in the US—in the form of "policy drift" caused by not updating policies to keep up with changing social realities—also helped to reveal the asymmetric power held by opponents of expanding social provision. More recently, Pierson has joined forces with Hacker in applying this argument to US industrial relations, taxation, financial deregulation, and corporate governance in their study of "winner-take-all" politics (Hacker and Pierson 2010).

Hacker and Pierson's work on the role of employers in the emergence of the US welfare state (2002), and their related vigorous debate with Peter Swenson on the nature of business power (Hacker and Pierson 2004; Swenson 2004a, 2004b), effectively "brings power back in" to HIWS, explicitly criticizing the early HIWS neglect of class and especially business power in the work of Skocpol and Ikenberry (1983), Orloff and Skocpol

(1984), Weir, Orloff, and Skocpol (1988), and Skocpol (1993). In that and related later work (Hacker and Pierson 2006, 2010), Pierson has been influenced not just by Hacker's notion of "policy drift" (i.e., the incapacity of welfare state institutions and programs to adapt to changing socioeconomic conditions) but also by the "power resources" analysis of Huber and Stephens (2001) and Korpi (2001, 2003, 2006). The result has been a shift of attention to the broader political economy rather than the formal welfare state as the relevant analytical terrain. Pierson now sees his work with Hacker as "a hybrid of institutional and power resource elements, and the focus is on the evolution of the mixed economy rather than the welfare state narrowly defined."[3] Although she criticizes the ongoing principal focus on political economy, Orloff sees this "filling out" of the HIWS agenda in the newer work of Pierson and others as exploiting the analytical potential of her earlier HIWS work with Weir and Skocpol.[4]

Kathleen Thelen arguably made a similar shift at around the same time. In *How Institutions Evolve* (2004), she used her analysis of incremental changes within the German training regime to illuminate how shifting coalitions within institutions work to determine the ends to which these institutions are put—and who benefits. Thelen's documentation of how training systems created in the nineteenth century against the opposition of organized labor were converted into a key resource for unions also highlights the importance of agents working within institutions to make incremental changes with important consequences. Streeck and Thelen (2005), in turn, fleshed out and systematized Hacker's and Thelen's observations of the importance of incremental change for HIWS. Chapters in that edited collection by Streeck and Thelen, Hacker, Levy, Palier, and Trampusch, in particular, illustrated clearly a series of mechanisms—drift, conversion, layering, displacement, and exhaustion—by which the decisions of political actors, working within and upon institutions, could produce change in the absence of critical junctures or large exogenous shocks. In so doing, they laid the foundations for a more change-oriented, "agentic" version of the HIWS approach, as the role of political actors becomes woven into the fabric of institutions. Thelen (2014) extends her comparative work on persistence and change in labor market institutions by emphasizing the importance of focusing on their political-coalitional bases.

Taken together, these works have expanded the scope of HIWS and emphasized that the outputs of institutions can and do change, even when the institutions themselves are apparently static; and that institutions are not rigid shells but the product of active manipulation and adaptation performed by political actors with real agency. The "auxiliary hypotheses" and theories developed in these works and others have not sought to develop a new theoretical core to rival that of the HIWS. They have in fact enhanced rather than undermined the core of the HIWS approach and hence "protected" it from the potentially eroding effects of rival arguments and hypotheses. At the same time, this literature is much more attentive than work in the HIWS core to actors, preferences, behavior and strategies, and as a result it is sometimes referred to as "second-generation" or "second wave" institutionalism (see Hall, Chapter 2, this volume). The development of this second generation of analysis is evidence of the program's capacity for flexible responses to rival hypotheses.

But reflecting on the extent to which the HIWS core has embraced rival hypotheses, as in its greater attention to agency, power, and change in the work of Pierson, Thelen, and others referred to above, it is also clear that ideas and culture remain marginal to the mainstream of this tradition. We would argue that this is related to the "sociology" of the research program and the epistemological priorities of its "protective belt." When major figures *within* historical institutionalism and HIWS innovate, providing an intellectual stamp of authority, it is more likely that others will follow. Thus, Vivien Schmidt's plea from *outside* the historical institutionalism/HIWS research program, and from a quite different epistemological perspective, for a distinct "discursive institutionalism," has not impacted the HIWS core and has provoked little reaction from its "protective belt." We suspect that Peter Hall's more active recent embrace of the notion of institutions as being "cultural artifacts" as well as "matrices of sanctions and incentives" (Hall and Lamont 2013) will not only spur but also *legitimize* a shift toward a deeper engagement with cultural sociology, and promote a greater attention to culture and social relations in future HIWS research.

Building Out the Program: New Evidence, New Cases, and New Arguments

At the same time, a number of important new contributions have built on the precepts of the core by extending the analysis to new cases, and have allowed the HIWS research program to adapt progressively to the demands of analyzing complex institutional settings. Four studies of the welfare state provide examples of the "progressive adaptation" of the research program and demonstrate its vitality: Morgan's *Working Mothers and the Welfare State* (2006); Fleckenstein's *Institutions, Ideas and Learning in Welfare State Change* (2011); Lynch's *Age in the Welfare State* (2006); and Häusermann's *The Politics of Welfare State Reform in Continental Europe* (2010).

Morgan (2006) is in part a standard HIWS narrative that explains cross-national variation—in this instance, variation in policies geared toward working mothers—by showing how early policy decisions become incarnate in institutional forms that then shape subsequent policy directions. But if Morgan shows that the religious *organization* of society in the nineteenth century has institutional consequences that affect future work-family policy arrangements, it is an *idea*—the social conservative "male-breadwinner" ideology—whose persistence over time among key actors has the real motive force in her argument.

Lynch (2006) also sets up her study in the classic HIWS vein, explaining contemporary cross-national variation in the relative emphasis in social policies on the elderly versus working-aged adults and children today by process-tracing a century's worth of political and institutional developments. Lynch's explanation for the long-term evolution of the different age-orientation of welfare regimes hinges, though, on the largely unintended consequences of the mismatch between political actors' purposive behavior and the wider demographic and economic environments that surround welfare state policies. Lynch's analysis is thus compatible with second-generation institutionalism's more agent-centered view, but also hints at some of its limitations. Thus, while Hacker (in Streeck and Thelen 2005) defines policy drift as a choice that political actors make, Lynch's analysis of policy drift focuses more on *longue durée* changes in the surrounding environment of which policymakers may be only vaguely aware, but that can constrain future choices, and have a profound influence on policy outputs.

Silja Häusermann (2010) focuses on the interplay of social structure, welfare state and party institutions, and actors' preferences and strategies to analyze hard-to-achieve pension reform in Western Europe. In some regards this analysis is more structuralist than institutionalist, since it takes public individuals' preferences as given by their position in the social structure. On the other hand, Häusermann, unlike many authors writing on "new social risks," also shows that different welfare state setups generate different sets of interests in society. And in a neat twist, the politics of accommodating those interests are constrained by the longer-term development of the welfare state, which provides nationally-specific opportunities for reform.

Most recently, Fleckenstein (2011) takes up the ideational critique, seeking to integrate an institutional approach to policy learning into new institutionalism as a mechanism for knowledge-based institutional change. Like much second-generation HIWS research, Fleckenstein pays attention to the incoherence of institutional settings and the diversity of policy legacies, but gives more causal significance to ideas and ascribes even more discretion to agency in his study of German labor market reform policy than is the case in more recent HIWS research. Yet Fleckenstein remains firmly within the HIWS tradition. We provide an example of a more "constructivist" departure from it at the end of the next section.

These works, along with other progressive adaptations, add to the "hard core" of HIWS by (1) testing the original propositions on a new range of policy and country cases; (2) constructing stronger links between welfare state policy development and underlying systems of political contestation; (3) giving more weight and systematic attention to ideational factors (e.g., religion, knowledge, and policy learning); and (4) being more attentive to both the unintended consequences of policy actions and to the interaction between welfare state institutions and the larger context. None of these innovations has constituted a challenge to the core of the HIWS paradigm as such; but they extend and modify the research program so that it can be applied fruitfully to a range of cases in ways that had not been fully considered in the HIWS "core."

Challenges—Methodological and Theoretical

In this final section we look at welfare state studies and criticism that are less easily accommodated by the HIWS research program and are therefore, strictly speaking, outside it.

The first of these are not necessarily inimical to the research program, but find the HIWS focus on macro-institutional variables and methodological bias toward historical process tracing too limited for addressing the numerous questions it raises. They therefore complement or substitute HIWS with rival theoretical angles and methodological approaches.

Nathalie Giger's *The Risk of Social Policy?* (2011) investigates the Piersonian argument about the risks for governments of engaging in policies of retrenchment, but uses theoretical modeling, regression analysis of social attitudes and voting behavior, and the simulation of different counterfactual scenarios to do so. Her key motivation is the absence in the HIWS literature of any serious empirical analysis of the core claim that welfare state retrenchment is politically unpopular and electorally treacherous. She fills that gap by focusing on the voter's perspective and by engaging with the literature on issue voting. Her findings weaken some of the key assumptions in the "New Politics" argument: social policy reform is rarely risky for governments, and much less painful to incumbents than alienating the electorate in other policy areas, while social policy attitudes rarely alter government composition or transfer directly into policies. Giger's study reveals the limits to a purely macro-institutional approach when seeking to understand the relationship between micro-variables (voters and their electoral behavior) and macro-outcomes.

Barbara Vis uses prospect theory (a psychological approach) and fuzzy-set QCA in the *Politics of Risk-Taking* (2010) to interrogate the same Piersonian claim that welfare state reform politics is "risky," leading to reform evasion or blame avoidance. Vis shows that under certain circumstances governments that want to stay in, or return to power do indeed engage in risky behavior and embrace unpopular policy reforms. Understanding why, Vis argues, requires methodological innovation that complements rather than replaces the HI approach. Her findings nuance considerably our understanding of the conditions under which governments tackle unpopular and not unpopular reform. Thus, only when governments face losses in the form of a deteriorating socioeconomic and/or deteriorating political situation are they willing to run the electoral risk of launching unpopular reform; and only when a government's political position is solid and the socioeconomic situation improving is it likely to engage in popular reform.

Both Giger and Vis use investigative tools from outside of historical institutionalism to "test" some of the core propositions of the HIWS research program. In doing so, they enrich the historical institutionalism approach, first by "triangulating" it with methods less frequently used in comparative historical analyses, and (consequently) also by making it scientifically more robust. Avdagic, Rhodes, and Visser seek to do something similar in *Social Pacts in Europe* (2011), which triangulates process tracing, a rational-choice based heuristic bargaining model, and fuzzy-set QCA to investigate when and how social actors contract to engage in negotiated reforms of social and labor market policies. These techniques allow for insights that a macro-institutional approach on its own cannot provide. Like Vis, the authors can explain the broad contours of cross-national variation in social pacting by using fuzzy-set QCA; they can illuminate real-world negotiations between actors through a "bounded rationality" model of bargaining; and they draw on functionalist, utilitarian, normative, and power-distributional perspectives to focus and structure their use of historical narrative.

Finally, it is worth considering how far historical institutionalism can be stretched before it becomes something else. As noted above, although ideas and cognition have always been part of the historical institutionalist "core," there is a clear standoff in HIWS between the institutionalist ontology and epistemology and that of strongly values- or identity-oriented research. Skocpol (1995b) explicitly rejected the notion of institutions as systems of meaning or normative frameworks. But Van Oorschot, Opielka, and Pfau-Effinger use precisely that notion in *Culture and the Welfare State* (2008): Pfau Effinger (185–186) defines culture as "a system of collective constructions of meaning by which human beings define reality." Yet they also attempt, at certain points, to reconcile culture, so defined, with more standard institutionalist analysis.

Thus, Van Oorschot, Opielka and Pfau Effinger seek to identify a dimension of "values and beliefs" underpinning Esping-Andersen's (1990) "worlds of welfare capitalism," while sidelining the class-conflict that is central to his "power resources" approach. Pfau Effinger, in an analysis of family policies in Germany and Austria, attempts to add a cultural dimension to Pierson's use of "increasing returns," arguing that policy change can only be explained by including "the role of cultural factors outside the specific institutions of the welfare state" (2008, 185). More generally in the book, shared values, norms, perceptions, and beliefs assume the character of meta-phenomena that sometimes have causal effect, as in Pfau-Effinger's argument where "cultural change" produces "path breaks" in welfare state development, cutting through the "stickiness" of institutional mechanisms. Here we are clearly moving beyond the outer boundaries of the HIWS research program (which after all has strong rationalist foundations) into the orbit of a rival constructivist tradition.

Conclusions

We began this chapter by likening historical institutionalism to an "institution" itself, with a path-dependent core of actors, rules, and norms. We then used Imre Lakatos's conception of a "scientific research program" to help us classify the literature that has constructed the HIWS research project over time (its core as well as its protective belt), and to assess its capacity to sustain itself over time. Referencing Lakatos's notion of "progressive" versus "degenerative" scientific research programs, we conclude that the HIWS program is "progressive" in that it has promoted, and continues to promote, the development of auxiliary research and hypotheses that have strengthened its analytical power in the face of new evidence and rival theories.

The "core" of the program and its principles are strongly defended, but it is important to recognize that there has been a remarkable fluidity of exchanges and evolution of the conversation over time. Pierson and Thelen, in particular, have refined and enriched the program's core, the first by accommodating and rearticulating the "power critique" within the HIWS tradition, and the second by making institutional change a central preoccupation of historical institutionalism research. Their work, and that of others in the HIWS core, continues to inspire a remarkable proliferation of welfare state studies in the "protective belt," with no evidence of a mass-migration of scholars to rival research programs. "Triangulation"—the use by a new generation of scholars of research methods less favored in the core of HIWS, which have been critical, we argue, for giving greater scientific validity to historical institutionalism propositions and hypotheses—might in principle lead to that outcome. But because borrowings from rational choice or psychological theory have been used largely to investigate institutionalist hypotheses rather than to negate the precepts of institutionalism as such, the core of the program remains protected, and quite distinctive from those of its rivals—including alternative approaches that place causal emphasis on actors' rational choices or on culture and ideas.

Notes

* We would like to thank Peter Hall, Ann Orloff, and Paul Pierson for their comments and advice.

1. The term "negative heuristic" indicates the "irrefutable" nature of the program's core principles that its protagonists adhere to. "Positive heuristic" refers to the "refutable variants" of the program and its capacity for modification and adaptation to new evidence and challenges (Lakatos 1970, 134–135).
2. We are indebted to Ann Orloff for this observation.
3. Personal communication between Pierson and the authors.
4. Personal communication between Orloff and the authors.

References

Adams, Julia, Elizabeth S. Clemens, and Ann Shola Orloff, eds. 2005. *Remaking Modernity: Politics, History, and Sociology*. Durham, NC, and London: Duke University Press.

Alber, Jens. 1994. Review of Ann Shola Orloff, "The Politics of Pensions: A Comparative Analysis of Britain, Canada and the United States 1880–1940." *American Journal of Sociology* 100 (2): 545–547.

Amenta, Edwin. 2003. "What We Know About the Development of Social Policy: Comparative and Historical Research in Comparative and Historical Perspective." In *Comparative Historical Analysis in the Social Sciences*, ed. James Mahoney and Dietrich Rueschemeyer. Cambridge: Cambridge University Press, 91–130.

Avdagic, Sabina, Martin Rhodes, and Jelle Visser. 2011. *Social Pacts in Europe: Emergence, Evolution and Institutionalization*. Oxford: Oxford University Press.

Béland, Daniel. 2007. "Ideas and Institutional Change in Social Security: Conversion, Layering, and Policy Drift." *Social Science Quarterly* 88 (1): 20–38.

Béland, Daniel and Jacob Hacker. 2004. "Ideas, Private Institutions and American Welfare State 'Exceptionalism': The Case of Health and Old-Age Insurance, 1915–1965." *International Journal of Social Welfare* 13 (1): 42–54.

Brady, Henry and David Collier. 2010. *Rethinking Social Inquiry: Diverse Tools, Shared Standard.* Lanham, MD: Rowman and Littlefield Publishers, Inc.

Campbell, John. 2004. *Institutional Change and Globalization.* Princeton, NJ: Princeton University Press.

Cerami, Alfio. 2006. *Social Policy in Central and Eastern Europe: The Emergence of a New European Welfare Regime.* Berlin: LIT Verlag.

Cerami, Alfio. 2008. "Mechanisms of Institutional Change in Central and Eastern Europe: Welfare State Restructuring." In *Post-Communist Welfare Pathways: Theorizing Social Policy Transformations in Central and Eastern Europe*, ed. A. Cerami and P. Vanhuysse. Basingstoke: Palgrave Macmillan, 35–52.

Clemens, Elizabeth and James Cook. 1999. "Politics and Institutionalism: Explaining Durability and Change." *Annual Review of Sociology* 25 (1): 441–466.

Crouch, Colin. 2005. *Capitalist Diversity and Change: Recombinant Governance and Institutional Entrepreneurs.* Oxford: Oxford University Press.

Crouch, Colin. 2007. "How to 'Do' Post-Determinist Institutional Analysis." *Socio-Economic Review* 5 (3): 527–567.

Drezner, Daniel. 2010. "Is Historical Institutionalism Bunk?" *Review of International Political Economy* 17 (4): 791–804.

Ebbinghaus, Bernhard. 2005. "Can Path Dependence Explain Institutional Change? Two Approaches Applied to Welfare State Reform." Max-Planck Cologne Discussion Paper 05/2.

Elman, Colin and Miriam Fendius Elman. 2002. "How Not to Be Lakatos Intolerant: Appraising Progress in IR Research." *International Studies Quarterly* 46 (2): 231–262.

Esping-Andersen, Gøsta. 1990. *The Three Worlds of Welfare Capitalism.* Cambridge: Polity Press.

Esping-Andersen, Gøsta. 1996. "After the Golden Age? Welfare State Dilemmas in a Global Economy." In *Welfare States in Transition: National Adaptations in Global Economies*, ed. Gøsta Esping-Andersen. London: Sage, 1–31.

Finegold, Kenneth and Theda Skocpol. 1995. *State and Party in America's New Deal.* Madison, WI: The University of Wisconsin Press.

Fleckenstein, Timo. 2011. *Institutions, Ideas and Learning in Welfare State Change: Labour Market Reforms in Germany.* Basingstoke: Palgrave Macmillan.

Giger, Nathalie. 2011. *The Risk of Social Policy? The Electoral Consequences of Welfare State Retrenchment and Social Policy Performance on OECD Countries.* London and New York: Routledge.

Hacker, Jacob S. 2002. *The Divided Welfare State: The Battle over Public and Private Social Benefits in the United States.* New York: Cambridge University Press.

Hacker, Jacob S. 2004. "Privatizing Risk without Privatizing the Welfare State: The Hidden Politics of Social Policy Retrenchment in the United States."*American Political Science Review* 98 (2): 243–260.

Hacker, Jacob S. 2005. "Policy Drift: The Hidden Politics of US Welfare State Retrenchment." In *Beyond Continuity: Institutional Change in Advanced Political Economies*, ed. Wolfgang Streeck and Kathleen Thelen. Oxford: Oxford University Press, 40–81.

Hacker, Jacob S. 2006. *The Great Risk Shift: The Assault on American Jobs, Families, Health Care, and Retirement and How You Can Fight Back.* New York: Oxford University Press.

Hacker, Jacob S. and Paul Pierson. 2002. "Business Power and Social Policy: Employers and the Formation of the American Welfare State." *Politics and Society* 30 (2): 277–325.

Hacker, Jacob S. and Paul Pierson. 2004. "Varieties of Capitalist Interests *and* Capitalist Power: A Response to Swenson." *Studies in American Political Development* 18 (2): 186–195.

Hacker, Jacob S. and Paul Pierson. 2006. *Off Center: The Republican Revolution and the Erosion of American Democracy*. New Haven, CT: Yale University Press.

Hacker, Jacob S. and Paul Pierson. 2010. *Winner-Take-All Politics: How Washington Made the Rich Richer—and Abandoned the Middle Class*. New York: Simon and Schuster.

Hall, Peter. 1993. "Policy Paradigms, Social Learning, and the State: The Case of Economic Policymaking in Britain." *Comparative Politics* 25 (3): 275–296.

Hall, Peter. 2003. "Aligning Ontology and Methodology in Comparative Research." In *Comparative Historical Analysis in the Social Sciences*, ed. James Mahoney and Dietrich Rueschemeyer. Cambridge and New York: Cambridge University Press, 373–404.

Hall, Peter. 2010. "Historical Institutionalism in Rationalist and Sociological Perspective." In *Explaining Institutional Change: Ambiguity, Agency and Power*, ed. James Mahoney and Kathleen Thelen. New York: Cambridge University Press, 204–224.

Hall, Peter and Michèle Lamont. 2013. "Why Social Relations Matter for Politics and Successful Societies." *Annual Review of Political Science* 16: 49–71.

Hall, Peter and Rosemary Taylor. 1996. "Political Science and the Three New Institutionalisms." *Political Studies* 44 (5): 936–957.

Häusermann, Silja. 2010. *The Politics of Welfare State Reform in Continental Europe: Modernization in Hard Times*. Cambridge: Cambridge University Press.

Heclo, Hugh. 1976. *Modern Social Politics in Britain and Sweden: From Relief to Income Maintenance*. New Haven, CT, and London: Yale University Press.

Herrigel, Gary. 2005. "Institutionalists at the Limits of Institutionalism: A Constructivist Critique of Wolfgang Streeck and Kozo Yamamura." *Socio-Economic Review* 3 (3): 559–567.

Hicks, Alexander. 1999. *Social Democracy and Welfare Capitalism*. Ithaca, NY: Cornell University Press.

Howard, Christopher. 1999. *The Hidden Welfare State: Tax Expenditures and Social Policy in the United States*. Princeton, NJ: Princeton University Press.

Huber, Evelyne and John Stephens. 2001. *Development and Crisis of the Welfare State: Parties and Policies in Global Markets*. Chicago: University of Chicago Press.

Immergut, Ellen. 1992. *Health Politics: Interest and Institutions in Western Europe*. Cambridge and New York: Cambridge University Press.

Immergut, Ellen. 1998. "The Theoretical Core of the New Institutionalism." *Politics and Society* 26 (1): 5–34.

Immergut, Ellen. 2008. "Historical Institutionalism in West European Politics." *West European Politics* 31 (1–2): 354–369.

Katznelson, Ira. 1998. "The Doleful Dance of Politics and Policy: Can Historical Institutionalism Make a Difference?" *American Political Science Review* 92 (1): 191–197.

Katznelson, Ira. 2009. "Strong Theory, Complex History: Structure and Configuration in Comparative Politics Revisited." In *Comparative Politics: Rationality, Culture and Structure*, ed. Mark Irving Lichbach and Alan S. Zuckerman. 2nd Edition. Cambridge and New York: Cambridge University Press, 96–116.

Katznelson, Ira and Barry Weingast. 2005. *Preferences and Situations: Points of Intersection Between Historical and Rational Choice Institutionalism*. New York: Russell Sage Foundation,

Korpi, Walter. 2001. "Contentious Institutions: An Augmented Rational-Action Analysis of the Origins and Path Dependency of Welfare State Institutions in Western Countries." *Rationality and Society* 13 (2): 235–283.

Korpi, Walter. 2003. "Welfare State Regress in Western Europe." *Annual Review of Sociology* 29: 589–609.

Korpi, Walter. 2006. "Power Resources and Employer-Centered Approaches." *World Politics* 58 (2): 167–206.

Lakatos, Imre. 1970. "Falsification and the Methodology of Scientific Research Programmes." In *Criticism and the Growth of Knowledge*, ed. Imre Lakatos and Alan Musgrave. Cambridge and New York: Cambridge University Press, 91–196.

Larsen, Christian Albrekt. 2008. "The Institutional Logic of Welfare Attitudes." *Comparative Political Studies* 41 (2): 145–169.

Lieberman, Robert. 2002. "Ideas, Institutions, and Political Order: Explaining Political Change." *American Political Science Review* 96 (4): 697–712.

Leibfried, Stephan and Paul Pierson, eds. 1995. *European Social Policy: Between Fragmentation and Integration*. Washington, D.C.: The Brookings Institution.

Leibfried, Stephan and Paul Pierson. 2000. "Social Policy: Left to the Courts and Markets?" In *Policy-Making in the European Union*, ed. Helen Wallace and William Wallace. 4th Edition. Oxford: Oxford University Press, 297–292.

Lipset, Seymour Martin. 1996. "Comment on Skocpol's 'The Politics of American Social Policy, Past and Future.'" In *Individual and Social Responsibility: Child Care, Education, Medical Care, and Long-Term Care in America*, ed. Victor R. Fuchs. Chicago: University of Chicago Press, 336–340.

Lynch, Julia. 2006. *Age in the Welfare State: The Origins of Social Spending on Pensioners, Workers and Children*. Cambridge and New York: Cambridge University Press.

Mahoney, James and Kathleen Thelen. 2009. *Explaining Institutional Change: Ambiguity, Agency, and Power.* Cambridge and New York: Cambridge University Press.

Moe, Terry M. 2005. "Power and Political Institutions." *Perspectives on Politics* 3 (2): 215–233.

Morgan, Kimberly. 2006. *Working Mothers and the Welfare State: Religion and the Politics of Work-Family Policies in Western Europe and the United States*. Stanford, CA: Stanford University Press.

Orloff, Ann Shola. 1993. *The Politics of Pensions: A Comparative Analysis of Britain, Canada and the United States 1880–1940*. Madison, WI: University of Wisconsin Press.

Orloff, Ann Shola. 2005. "Social Provision and Regulation: Theories of States, Social Policies and Modernity." In *Remaking Modernity: Politics, History, and Sociology*, ed. Julia Adams, Elizabeth S. Clemens, and Ann Shola Orloff. Durham, NC, and London: Duke University Press, 190–224.

Orloff, Ann Shola and Theda Skocpol. 1984. "Why Not Equal Protection? Explaining the Politics of Public Social Spending in Britain, 1900–1911, and the United States, 1880s–1920." *American Sociological Review* 49 (6): 726–750.

Peters, Guy B., Jon Pierre, and Desmond King. 2005. "The Politics of Path Dependency in Historical Institutionalism." *The Journal of Politics* 67 (4): 1275–1300.

Pierson, Paul. 1995. *Dismantling the Welfare State? Reagan, Thatcher and the Politics of Retrenchment*. Cambridge and New York: Cambridge University Press

Pierson, Paul. 2000. "Increasing Returns, Path Dependence and the Study of Politics." *American Political Science Review* 94 (2): 251–267.

Pierson, Paul, ed. 2001. *New Politics of the Welfare State*. Oxford: Oxford University Press.

Pierson, Paul. 2003. "Big, Slow-Moving, and … Invisible: Macro-Social Processes in the Study of Comparative Politics." In *Comparative Historical Analysis in the Social Sciences*, ed. Dietrich Rueschemeyer and James Mahoney. Cambridge and New York: Cambridge University Press, 177–207.

Pierson, Paul. 2004. *Politics in Time: History, Institutions and Social Analysis*. Princeton, NJ: Princeton University Press.
Pierson, Paul. 2011. "The Welfare State over the Very Long Run." University of Bremen, Centre for Social Policy Research ZeS-Arbeitspapier, No. 02/2011. Available at <http://hdl.handle.net/10419/46215> (accessed September 1, 2015).
Quadagno, Jill S. 1984. "Welfare Capitalism and the Social Security Act of 1935." *American Sociological Review* 49 (5): 632–647.
Rhodes, Martin. 2010. "Employment Policy: Between Efficacy and Experimentation." In *Policy-Making in the European Union*, eds. Helen Wallace, Mark A. Pollack, and Alasdair R. Young. 6th Edition. Oxford: Oxford University Press, 283–306.
Rothstein, Bo. 1998. *Just Institutions Matter: The Moral and Political Logic of the Universal Welfare State*. Cambridge and New York: Cambridge University Press.
Schmidt, Vivien. 2003. "How, Where and When does Discourse Matter in Small States' Welfare State Adjustment." *New Political Economy* 8 (1): 127–146.
Schmidt, Vivien. 2008. "Discursive Institutionalism: The Explanatory Power of Ideas and Discourse." *Annual Review of Political Science* 11: 303–326.
Schwartz, Herman. 2005. "Down the Wrong Path: Path Dependence, Increasing Returns, and Historical Institutionalism." Available at <http://people.virginia.edu/~hms2f/Path.pdf> (accessed September 15, 2013).
Skocpol, Theda. 1980. "Political Response to Capitalist Crisis: Neo-Marxist Theories of the State and the Case of the New Deal." *Politics and Society* 10 (2): 155–201.
Skocpol, Theda. 1993. *Protecting Soldiers and Mothers: The Political Origins of Social Policy in the United States*. Cambridge, MA: Harvard University Press.
Skocpol, Theda. 1995a. *Social Policy in the United States: Future Possibilities in Historical Perspective*. Princeton, NJ: Princeton University Press.
Skocpol, Theda. 1995b. "Why I am a Historical Institutionalist." *Polity* 28 (1): 103–106.
Skocpol, Theda. 2003. "Doubly Engaged Social Science: The Promise of Comparative Historical Analysis." In *Comparative Historical Analysis in the Social Sciences*, ed. James Mahoney and Dietrich Rueschemeyer. Cambridge: Cambridge University Press, 407–427.
Skocpol, Theda and Edwin Amenta. 1985. "Did Capitalists Shape Social Security?" *American Sociological Review* 50 (4): 572–575.
Skocpol, Theda and Edwin Amenta. 1986. "States and Social Policies." *Annual Review of Sociology* 12: 131–157.
Skocpol, Theda and John Ikenberry. 1983. "The Political Formation of the American Welfare State in Historical and Comparative Perspective." *Comparative Social Research* 6: 87–147.
Skocpol, Theda and Paul Pierson. 2002. "Historical Institutionalism in Political Science." In *Political Science: State of the Discipline*, ed. I. Katznelson and H. V. Milner. New York: Norton, 693–721.
Steinmo, Sven, Kathleen Thelen, and Frank Longstreth. 1992. *Structuring Politics: Historical Institutionalism in Comparative Analysis*. Cambridge: Cambridge University Press.
Streeck, Wolfgang and Kathleen Thelen, eds. 2005. *Beyond Continuity: Institutional Change in Advanced Political Economies*. Oxford and New York: Oxford University Press.
Swenson, Peter A. 2004a. "Varieties of Capitalist Interests: Power, Institutions, and the Regulatory Welfare State in the United States and Sweden." *Studies in American Political Development* 18 (1): 196–200.
Swenson, Peter A. 2004b. "Yes, and Comparative Analysis Too: Rejoinder to Hacker and Pierson." *Studies in American Political Development* 18 (2): 1–29.

Thelen, Kathleen. 1999. "Historical Institutionalism in Comparative Politics." *Annual Review of Political Science* 2: 369–404.

Thelen, Kathleen. 2004. *How Institutions Evolve: The Political Economy of Skills in Germany, Britain, the United States, and Japan*. Oxford: Oxford University Press.

Thelen, Kathleen. 2014. *Varieties of Liberalization and the New Politics of Social Solidarity*. Cambridge and New York: Cambridge University Press.

Van Oorschot, Wim, Michael Opielka, and Birgit Pfau Effinger. 2008. *Culture and the Welfare State: Values and Social Policy in Comparative Perspective*. Cheltenham: Edward Elgar.

Vis, Barbara. 2010. *Politics of Risk-Taking: Welfare State Reform in Advanced Democracies*. Amsterdam: Amsterdam University Press.

Weir, Margaret. 1992. *Politics and Jobs: The Boundaries of Employment Policy in the United States*. Princeton, NJ: Princeton University Press.

Weir, Margaret, Ann Shola Orloff, and Theda Skocpol, eds. 1988. *The Politics of Social Policy in the United States*. Princeton, NJ: Princeton University Press.

CHAPTER 26

DURABILITY AND CHANGE IN FINANCIAL SYSTEMS

RICHARD DEEG AND ELLIOT POSNER*

Historical institutionalism (HI) features extensively in the study of banking and financial regulation in Europe. This chapter reviews scholarship that explicitly, implicitly, or inadvertently draws heavily on that tradition's central tenets. We find that historical institutionalism can help explain the emergence, persistence, and evolution of distinct kinds of financial systems in Europe, as well as the pattern and effects of European financial integration. In Europe, for example, with "free" capital mobility since the early 1980s one would expect market incentives to produce significant change and convergence. While this has occurred, the patterns of domestic institutional change, the remaining extent of divergence in regulations, financial market structure, actor preferences (both across and within EU member states), and the path of financial market integration reveal much resilience, as well as the continued importance of institutions in constituting national interests and in embedding finance in broader economic and political systems.

Our survey finds a rich literature on *domestic* European financial systems and regulation that has explicit historical institutionalist characteristics. This literature includes classic and more recent works that use the timing and sequence of events, critical junctures, path dependence, and other concepts to account for the origins and persistence of distinct types of financial systems. It also includes considerable work analyzing change during the 1990s and 2000s, with explanations drawing on historical institutionalist themes such path dependence, processes of intercurrence, and modes of incremental change through the mechanisms of layering, displacement, conversion, and drift. In contrast, while there is a rich and growing literature on EU financial regulation and market integration efforts, only a small portion of this literature explicitly adopts historical institutionalism to analyze regulatory developments at the European level. In the second part of the survey we examine the development and impact of the European (EU) regulatory framework in finance and discuss the extent to which HI has informed this literature. We conclude that there is considerable untapped potential for historical institutionalism as an analytical approach for studying European financial market integration and regulation and discuss ideas for future research in the final section.

The Emergence and Evolution of Domestic European Financial Systems

One of the longest running interests in the literature on financial systems is the emergence and evolution of alternative types. While there are a variety of typologies, the most common one divides financial systems into bank-based and market-based. The comparative capitalisms literature associates distinct financial systems with complementary institutional arrangements, such as labor markets, welfare states, and corporate governance regimes (e.g., Roe 2003; Hall and Soskice 2001). Financial systems are also associated with distinct paths of industrial development, comparative (or competitive) advantage in global markets, and diverse strategies for state intervention (Shonfield 1965; Zysman 1983).

Arguably one of the best-known works on the historical and institutional origins of diverse financial system is that of Alexander Gerschenkron (1962). Like other business and economic historians, his work focused on explaining the emergence of universal versus segmented (or specialized) banking systems that roughly map onto more contemporary distinctions between bank and market-based finance. Gerschenkron argued that the *timing* and *sequence* of a state's industrialization relative to other states largely determined the kind of financial system that emerged. For example, middle-late industrializers such as Germany developed universal (bank-based) banking in order to mobilize finance on an appropriately large scale. Verdier (2003) revises Gerschenkron, and proposes an alternative causal explanation that is also consistent with HI principles: rather than the timing of industrialization, Verdier argues that alternative financial systems reflect differences in state structure and the incentives and preferences these impart to political and market actors. Though the logic is somewhat different, both Gerschenkron and Verdier find that the institutional roots of national financial systems kept them on distinct evolutionary paths throughout the twentieth century.

The legal origins theory of financial systems also includes features of historical institutional analysis (LaPorta, Lopez de Silanes, and Shleifer 2000). This theory holds that common law systems led to market-based financial systems because more extensive contract law and private property norms facilitated the arm's length exchanges characteristic of markets. Relying explicitly on rational choice institutionalism, but also sociological theories of the embeddedness of norms, legal origins theory sees financial systems as Piersonian "deep equilibria" (Pierson 2004, 157–160).

The predominant conceptualization of postwar financial systems envisioned three primary forms—bank-based, market-based, and state-led. The addition of a state-led category reflected the emergence during the 1930s and postwar years of banking systems in which direct or indirect state control of banks became common, particularly in southern Europe. The work of Shonfield (1965) and Zysman (1983) presages some important analytical arguments that later became part of the historical institutionalism canon, perhaps most notably the argument that *institutional complementarities* across financial systems, corporate strategy, and state industrial policy generated *increasing returns* to a particular model or path of economic development. Thus, when confronted with periodic economic crises or new challenges, each system responded in distinct but predictable ways (e.g., Deeg 1999).

Not long after the publication of Zysman's seminal work, however, the foundation of relatively stable postwar national financial systems in Europe began to change—slowly at first, but then at an accelerating pace. This change in European financial systems was driven by a combination of technological developments, policy decisions (especially by the US and UK), financial market innovations, and eventually by the relaunch of the European integration project in the 1980s. Consequently, in the 1990s a new wave of literature—a good part of it consistent with historical institutionalism—emerged to explain the visible and accelerating changes in domestic financial market structure and regulation.

Financial System Change

The broad trend in financial market structure and regulation in Europe since the late 1980s has been a shift in financial transactions out of banks as hierarchical organizations and into markets. These developments led many to argue that continental bank-based models would converge on the market-based finance model (Rajan and Zingales 2003). The reality has turned out to be more complicated: financial markets have indeed become bigger and more important throughout Europe, but there has not been wholesale convergence in national financial systems (Lütz 2004). Many accounts employ a path dependency argument in highlighting banks' continued central role in traditionally bank-based systems (Deeg 2010). That said, the business models of banks and their connections to the broader economy have changed quite substantially. Banks, especially large ones, have become more directly dependent on market transactions to finance themselves and have increasingly turned to securitization, securities trading, and the development of structured financial products to generate profits (Hardie et al. 2013). Across most financial systems there has also been a de-segmentation or "universalization" of banks (i.e., regulatory restrictions on their market activities being lifted), as well as a rise of non-banking financial institutions such as hedge, equity, and money market funds. In short, these common trends have resulted in no less diverse but even more complex financial systems. Meanwhile, in the push for European financial market integration based on liberalized finance, state-led finance has virtually disappeared in Europe.

Prominent structural-functional accounts like those of Eichengreen (2006) and Rajan and Zingales (2003) see increasing convergence as a result of the maturation of European economies: bank-based systems were better for extensive growth in more traditional sectors (incremental change and innovation); while market-based financial systems are better for risk finance and radical innovation (knowledge-intensive growth). There are also a variety of systemic theories (liberal and realist variants) that see financial system convergence in Europe as driven by the demands of global financial investors and market-oriented states, such as the US and UK, who are advancing the interests of global financial investors. Within this literature one common argument emphasizes the increased mobility of capital under current conditions of globalization (open capital markets and deregulated finance) as the structural force driving regulatory change and convergence (e.g., Goodman and Pauly 1993; Moran 1991; Helleiner 1994; Laurence 2001).

While acknowledging considerable change and elements of convergence, research inspired by historical institutionalism sees greater institutional resilience in financial systems. In this literature, many of the bank-based systems—notably Germany, Spain and Italy—are seen as having retained their largely bank-based character (Vitols 2004; Lütz 2004; Deeg 2005; Culpepper 2005). Most see a mixture of convergence and divergence that reflects path-dependent effects of domestic institutions, such as the institutions protecting non-profit financial organizations in many countries. To date there has been no clear resolution of the convergence debate and the bank- versus market-based typology of banking systems in Europe appears outdated. This has led some to advance the concept of market-based banking to indicate the degree to which a nation's banks have become dependent on financial markets for their own funds, thus blending the distinction between banks and markets and raising questions about whether such banks are still in a position to support continental coordinated market economies through the provision of "patient capital" (Hardie and Howarth 2013; Hardie et al. 2013).

The natural corollary to the discussion over the *extent* and *character* of change are efforts to identify their *causes*. Most historical institutional analyses of change fall along what Sobel (1994) labels "inside-out" or "outside-in" approaches. Research from the "inside-out" perspective views changes in European financial regulation as mostly originating in domestic politics, typically shifts in state policy preferences or shifts in the preferences of banks (Deeg and Pérez 2000; Pérez and Westrup 2010; Rosenbluth and Schaap 2003; Pérez 1998; O'Sullivan 2007). These works argue that endogenous processes—either shifts in relative political power, shifts in preferences of powerful actors, or some combination of both—led to processes of institutional (including regulatory) change that were constrained by previous paths. Research from the "outside-in" perspective gives greater explanatory weight to global (and European) market pressures in explaining domestic institutional change (Laurence 2001), but acknowledges that domestic institutions shaped responses to external pressures and contributed to evolutionary change along previous paths (Busch 2009; Lütz 2004; Deeg and Lütz 2000).

Since the late 1990s much historical institutionalist work has moved toward understanding financial system changes as a process of intercurrence in which multiple, overlapping processes of institutional change occur at different levels (see Fioretos, Falleti, and Sheingate, Chapter 1, this volume; Story and Walter 1997). Some of the more influential finance literature took its framing from the varieties of capitalism approach (Hall and Soskice 2001) by emphasizing how institutional complementarities between finance and other elements of national capitalist models defined and limited the pattern of change in financial market regulation in a manner consistent with established coordinated and liberal market economies (e.g., Callaghan and Höpner 2005; Fioretos 2001; Vitols 2004). While this work is very useful in identifying sources of institutional durability and seeing broad similarities and difference, the varieties of capitalism approach is less helpful in explaining why diverse patterns of change take place *within* national models or why countries respond in different ways to banking crises (e.g., Woll 2014; Hardie et al. 2013).

The historical institutionalism literature has given much attention to the mechanisms of institutional change. Nearly all the finance literature emphasizes gradual change rather than punctuated equilibriums in which an exogenous shock produces dramatic institutional changes. Slow-moving change over a longer period of time is viewed as accumulating into transformational change, as studies of France among others illustrate (Culpepper 2005; O'Sullivan 2007). While there is not a lot of research that *explicitly* addresses how radical change in financial systems might take place, the existing literature identifies many potential mechanisms by which gradual change may become transformative. A number of studies see institutional change occurring through a process of *layering*; including the emergence of new securities markets (Posner 2005, 2009b) and corporate governance systems (Vitols 2004). Other studies point to processes of *displacement* (Deeg 2005), such as in the adoption of new international accounting and financial reporting rules by the EU (Leblond 2011). An example of *conversion* can be found in the transformation of stock exchanges from private clubs and appendages of the state to private, for-profit entities (Lütz 2004). Processes of incremental change through institutional *drift* are also at work in Europe: for example, the rise of non-banking financial organizations and new technologies have produced major innovations in financial products such as derivatives, often without any changes in regulation. Gradual change through these mechanisms detailed in historical institutional studies have both undermined the effectiveness of historic forms of regulation and produced new ideas for how to regulate financial markets.

The Uneven Development of the EU's Regulatory Framework

The integration of diverse national financial systems was an early goal of regional cooperation in Europe. Yet, for most of the European Union's history, disagreements over core issues prevented governments from advancing toward even the most minimalist vision of an integrated European financial market. Even in the wake of the 1985 Single European Act (SEA), when Brussels introduced "mutual recognition" as a principle for accommodating national diversity, a wave of new legislation had too many loopholes to make significant headway toward cross-national regulatory compatibility, let alone harmonization. Instead, many analyses considered the existence of alternative national financial systems as a source of competition and conflict among member states over EU regulation—what Story and Walter (1997) referred to as "the battle of the systems."

With few exceptions, then, scholars interested in the evolution of European finance saw little reason to focus on regional developments or to treat them as possible explanatory factors driving domestic outcomes (Story and Walter 1997; Coleman and Underhill 1995). That view began to subside with deepening European cooperation and especially after the advent of the euro (Mügge 2010; Quaglia 2010; Posner 2007, 2009b). Consequently, scholars rethinking the EU's impact on European as well as international finance have raised a range of new questions including ontological ones about the consequences of omitting EU variables in analytical models (Jabko 2006; Posner 2005).

The Evolution of the EU's Regulatory Framework

Three periods of rapid legislative activity shaped the evolution of EU financial regulation. The first occurred after the SEA's passage, culminating in 1993 with a directive governing cross-border competition of investment services and trading, including stock exchanges (Mügge 2010, 51–68). On the whole this period produced a batch of weak legal experiments with the notable exception of the agreement to liberalize capital controls (Jabko 2006). Nonetheless, the legislation of this period established legal foundations for later market integration efforts, helped some domestic elites advance a market-oriented reform agenda (Spain, Italy, Germany, and France are all good examples), and paradoxically facilitated public and private actors in France, Germany, and other continental countries to reform financial centers and regain capital market trading lost to London.

Spurred largely by prospects of financial integration from a single currency, a second period of legislative activity began in the late 1990s. Several scholars consider this legislative program to be a turning point in the legal development of the EU financial framework (Donnelly 2010; Mügge 2010; Quaglia 2010; Posner 2007). The regulatory overhaul had multiple dimensions. First, deeper cooperation rested on political bargains that included inter-institutional agreements about the relative powers of the European Parliament and the European Commission; an explicit deal among finance ministers to include the UK (in contrast to monetary union) and keep on-the-ground financial supervision away from the European Central Bank (ECB) and in the hands of national authorities; and an elaborate new rule-making and rule-coordinating architecture introduced in 2001 (Lamfalussy Process). The latter marked a shift of governing authority, albeit with clear limits, to the EU-level and created new political actors comprised of national regulators (Eberlein and Newman 2008; Posner 2010b). Second, the Financial Services Action Plan of 1999 included 40-plus pieces of legislation that built on previous laws and frequently reflected international best practice as determined by transnational standard-setting bodies such as the International Accounting Standards Board and the Basel Committee on Banking Supervision. Even though each piece of EU legislation reflected a separate (often complex) political compromise between national regulatory and financial models (and preferences), the overall framework looked more British (that is, neoliberal) than German or French (Posner and Véron 2010; Quaglia 2010).

In reaction to the great financial crisis of 2008, EU policymakers launched a third round of regulatory reform. Many of these measures have again been incremental additions, that is, layering, to existing legislation. For example, policymakers gave the "Lamfalussy Committees" of national supervisors greater power vis-à-vis national governments and revised existing laws to bring the EU into line with fast-changing international standards and US rules (Ferran 2012; Quaglia 2013). Despite their incremental nature, many of these reforms (and those still in discussion) have initiated a process leading to substantial change in the balance of regulatory power between Brussels (including the ECB) and national governments and in the content of financial rules.

The initiatives spurred by the financial crisis would have been unimaginable before 2008. As in the US, the EU has moved away from self-regulatory models and now directly regulates credit rating agencies, hedge funds, and derivatives and central counterparties (Pagliari 2013). EU leaders also introduced fiscal-federalist mechanisms with the potential to bail out banks and sovereigns (Gocaj and Meunier 2013). And as part of the so-called "banking union," they agreed to give the ECB supervisory authority over many of Europe's largest banks (Véron 2012) and are bargaining over the form of a joint banking resolution scheme (Barker and Spiegel 2013). These far-reaching measures unraveled the political bargains of the late 1990s that separated financial and monetary arrangements and defined the relationship between the EU and member governments (Posner and Véron 2013).

Scholars responded to the deepening of EU financial regulation by addressing a range of new questions and incorporating regional-level factors into existing approaches (Mügge 2013). Some of this work is HI-informed, yet remarkably little of it is explicitly so. One set of questions concerns the character and degree of EU financial regulatory integration. For example, some research contemplates the emergence of a fortress EU (Pagliari 2012) and European-supported "managed globalization" of finance (Abdelal 2007). Yet, like the earlier literature (Coleman and Underhill 1995), recent scholarship finds the EU regime highly compatible and intertwined with international finance and analysts frequently use the neoliberal label to characterize it (Macartney 2011; Posner and Véron 2010; Mügge 2011a; Dür 2011). In fact, few dispute that an increased intermingling has taken place between the national and European levels of financial regulation, but debate remains over how extensively and evenly formal and informal institutional developments in Brussels have trickled down to national-level regulation and market structures. Echoing the convergence debates discussed earlier, on one side Grossman and Leblond (2011) argue from a perspective informed by historical institutionalism that cross-border financial market integration lags regulatory integration largely because of persistent differences in domestic market structures and preferences. The widely noted retreat of capital and financial services to home countries after the sovereign debt crisis lends some support to this view. On the other side, Mügge (2010) maintains in a modified structural materialist analysis that regional market integration came first, prompting a preference shift among the major financial firms toward EU regulation and thereby enabling deepened legal integration.

Explaining the Evolution of EU Financial Regulation

Mügge's explanation for European integration thus contends that EU policy entrepreneurs were only able to carry out a financial regulatory overhaul in the late 1990s because they aligned with the changed material interests of leading financial firms. By contrast, much of the literature has drawn from historical institutionalism's toolbox to account for EU financial regulatory outcomes. Newman and Posner (2013) attribute the turn-of-millennium cooperation in Europe to feedbacks from transnational financial regulatory soft law. Moreover, the "clash of capitalisms" perspective, used to explain persistence in national-level financial systems, also offers credible explanations of some EU-level outcomes, including legislation on takeovers, hedge funds, and capital reserves (Fioretos 2010, 2011; Zimmermann 2009; Howarth and Quaglia 2013). The latter line of argument follows in the tradition of Story and Walter (1997), tracing the limits and contours of cooperation to path-dependent differences in domestic financial arrangements and structures. In this vein, Quaglia (2010, 2012) attributes FSAP legislation to the outcomes of contests between two broad coalitions of aggregated national preferences—which are themselves reflections of domestic arrangements. Donnelly's (2010) more constructivist account also has affinities to the clash of capitalisms perspective, in that EU financial regulatory ideas are seen as an amalgam of national ones that have strong historical legacies.

These examples belong to the broader challenge to rational institutionalist accounts of international cooperation in general and in particular to Moravcsik's liberal intergovernmentalism (1998). Like the rationalist arguments, the clash of capitalism approaches treat EU outcomes as bargains based on relative power and preferences of the largest member governments. Yet the HI-informed work, which emphasizes path-dependence from complementarities of domestic institutions, offers richer and empirically more robust explanations of national preferences. However, its statist ontology makes it difficult to assess the extent to which prior EU-level decisions and processes, supranational actors and other regional-level factors affect later EU outcomes. The strongest HI-informed scholarship of this type is careful to claim not to explain outcomes (i.e., EU legislation), rather only the preferences of leading countries. Thus, if deepening of regulatory integration in finance has the kinds of effects—that is, setting off its own path-dependent processes that structure future politics—that it has had in other policy areas, such as competition policy (Büthe 2007), a failure to incorporate EU-level factors leaves a potential gap in our understanding of important outcomes.

We are aware of only a few scholars who have taken up this challenge. Building on supranationalist approaches to the European Union (Haas 2004 [1958]; Stone Sweet, Sandholtz, and Fligstein 2001) and the Europeanization literature (Cowles, Caporaso, and Risse-Kappen 2001), recent studies have explored the possibility that the deepening of financial regulatory integration produces independent effects on national and firm preferences and the context structuring negotiations, and suggests that this process gives rise to new ideational frames and political actors (such as transnational bodies of national regulators). This work has close affinities to historical institutionalism as exemplified in Pierson (1996), which spells out how regional bargains at one point in time give rise to endogenous processes that shape subsequent outcomes. Jabko (2006), for example, fuses historical institutionalist insights with systemic and ideational variables in an approach reminiscent of the Streeck and Thelen (2005) view of how actors try to change rules via enactment/implementation. Moschella (2011) highlights the impact of previous regional governance institutions on the EU's financial regulatory policy agenda. Posner (2007), in an explicit historical institutionalism application of the supranationalist approach, argues that early regional legislation and the presence of supranational actors set off slow-moving, endogenous processes that account for the late 1990s burst of EU legal and market-making activity. Moreover, Posner (2010b) and Maggetti and Gilardi (2011) have shown that EU regulatory bodies (of national officials) with delegated responsibilities, once created, have converted into key political actors with important degrees of relative autonomy from their "principals" and behave as collective units greater than the sum of their members.

The International Effects of EU Regulatory Integration

Scholars have recently begun to explore the impact of EU financial regulatory integration beyond Europe's borders (Leblond 2011; Dür 2011; Posner 2009a, 2010a; Mügge 2011a, 2011b; Quaglia 2014). A theme of this literature is that deepening legal integration in Europe turned the EU into a global financial rule-maker, roughly on par with the US. Much of this research is closely associated with the "HI in IR" literature (Fioretos 2011; Büthe and Mattli 2011; Farrell and Newman 2010; Meunier and McNamara 2007), especially in terms of the attention given to contingent sequences, timing of regulatory capacity building, and availability of transnational soft law. For example, Posner (2009a) attributes changes in transatlantic regulatory cooperation to the largely unintended but patterned consequences of prior EU institutional reform. Applying Mahoney's (2000) notion of a path-dependent reactive sequence to highlight the gradual effects of EU's deepening integration on transatlantic regulatory relations, Posner (2010a) explains changes in the international politics of accounting standards. Quaglia (2014) extends these themes to explain the content of transnational soft law, again illuminating the patterned international spillovers of internal EU processes and highlighting that the order by which polities develop regulatory capacities affects their abilities to influence international rules. Similarly, in Mügge (2011b), prior EU financial arrangements shape later EU influence at the international level.

Future Research on European Finance

One way to advance historical institutional research on European financial regulation is to start from the question of how this approach might help us understand developments in the aftermath of the recent financial market, banking, and sovereign debt crises. We see three promising research programs. The first is to apply critical juncture and contingent event analysis, not only to the recent crisis but also to earlier episodes that appear to be such events. For example, the agreement on Economic and Monetary Union or the Financial Services Action Plan could be fruitfully analyzed as a "critical juncture" that set in motion a new path toward market liberalization, ending in 2008. Critical juncture analysis forces us to confront what are often implicit path dependency arguments and may identify factors that are causally more important than they originally appeared to be.

Second, research could explore more systematically the mechanisms that are reinforcing (or undermining) the regulatory development paths of the EU and national regimes. This kind of analysis might help to explain why the EU financial project and especially the monetary union did not collapse in the wake of the recent crisis but elicited concerted salvation efforts, as well as why governments responded differently in the face of similar problems. Investigations of this kind may focus on identifying the presence or absence of different reinforcement mechanisms—such as complementarities, network effects, learning effects—that buttress and regenerate existing paths.

Third, there is much potential for understanding regulatory change through the study of mechanisms highlighted in recent historical institutionalism literature, notably layering, conversion, drift, and intercurrence. For instance, in addressing the vexing question of how national paths are combining or intermingling with EU and global ones, Europeanists have used concepts such as Europeanization and goodness of fit and depicted the EU as an opportunity structure. There may be analytical gains from instead conceiving EU legislation and architectures as examples of layering with potentially disruptive effects at the domestic level. Examples might include EU legislation concerning auditing, accounting and banking, and processes such as peer review in the new EU financial authorities. Also the concept of conversion might capture processes of EU financial change, such as ECB's new role of banking supervisor and the transformation of the Lamfalussy committees into EU authorities. Likewise, the concept of drift might be useful for understanding EU regulatory evolution after banking union, were British–Eurozone differences to make future legislative agreement difficult. Finally, the concept of intercurrence may help reveal the potential effects on European financial regulation of the diverse matrix of interacting causal forces. For example, Germany's Landesbanks were fundamentally impacted by the Commission's successful application of competition policy rather than by EU financial regulation.

In sum, while historical institutional analysis has been fruitfully applied to explain the emergence and evolution of national financial systems and regulation, we see considerable—as yet untapped—prospects for applying HI analysis to European finance. EU integration efforts stand out, in particular, for being potentially central to understanding domestic and regional finance and remain largely unexplored by historical institutionalist researchers.

Note

* The authors thank the participants of the October 2013 Historical Institutionalism in Political Science workshop, especially Orfeo Fioretos, for comments on previous drafts of this chapter.

References

Abdelal, Rawi. 2007. *Capital Rules: The Construction of Global Finance*. Cambridge, MA: Harvard University Press.

Barker, Alex and Peter Spiegel. 2013. "Europe Agrees to Pool Control of Bank Wind-Ups." *FT.com* December 18. Available at <http://www.ft.com/intl/cms/s/0/ed8cc406-681d-11e3-8ada-00144feabdc0.html?siteedition=intl#axzz3ipoP9rrG> (accessed September 1, 2015).

Busch, Andreas. 2009. *Banking Regulation and Globalization*. Oxford: Oxford University Press.

Büthe, Tim. 2007. "The Politics of Competition in the European Union: The First Fifty Years." In *Making History: European Integration and Institutional Change at Fifty*, ed. Sophie Meunier and Kathleen R. McNamara. Oxford: Oxford University Press, 175–194.

Büthe, Tim and Walter Mattli. 2011. *The New Global Rules: The Privatization of Regulation in the World Economy*. Princeton, NJ: Princeton University Press.

Callaghan, Helen and Martin Höpner. 2005. "European Integration and the Clash of Capitalisms: Political Cleavages over Takeover Liberalization." *Comparative European Politics* 3 (3): 307–332.

Coleman, William D. and Geoffrey R. D. Underhill. 1995. "Globalization, Regionalism and the Regulation of Securities Markets." *Journal of European Public Policy* 2 (3): 488–513.

Cowles, Maria Green, James. A Caporaso, and Thomas Risse-Kappen, eds. 2001. *Transforming Europe: Europeanization and Domestic Change*. Ithaca, NY: Cornell University Press.

Culpepper, Pepper. 2005. "Institutional Change in Contemporary Capitalism: Coordinated Financial Systems since 1990." *World Politics* 57: 173–199.

Deeg, Richard. 1999. *Finance Capital Unveiled: Banks and the German Political Economy*. Ann Arbor: University of Michigan Press.

Deeg, Richard. 2005. "Change from within: German and Italian finance in the 1990s." In *Beyond Continuity: Institutional Change in Advanced Political Economies*, ed. Wolfgang Streeck and Kathleen Thelen. Oxford: Oxford University Press, 169–202.

Deeg, Richard. 2010. "Institutional Change in National Financial Systems." In *Oxford Handbook of Comparative Institutional Analysis*, ed. Glenn Morgan, John Campbell, Colin

Crouch, Peer Hull Kristensen, Ove Kai Pedersen, and Richard Whitley. Oxford: Oxford University Press, 309–334.

Deeg, Richard and Sofia Pérez. 2000. "International Capital Mobility and Domestic Institutions: Corporate Finance and Governance in Four European Cases." *Governance: An International Journal of Policy and Administration* 13 (2): 119–154.

Deeg, Richard and Susanne Lütz. 2000. "Internationalization and Regulatory Federalism in Financial Systems: The United States and Germany at the Crossroads?" *Comparative Political Studies* 33 (3): 374–405.

Donnelly, Shawn. 2010. *The Regimes of European Integration: Constructing Governance of the Single Market.* Oxford: Oxford University Press.

Dür, Andreas. 2011. "Fortress Europe or Open Door Europe? The External Impact of the EU's Single Market in Financial Services." *Journal of European Public Policy* 18 (5): 619–635.

Eberlein, Burkard and Abraham L. Newman. 2008. "Escaping the International Governance Dilemma? Incorporated Transgovernmental Networks in the European Union." *Governance* 21 (1): 25–52.

Eichengreen, Barry J. 2006. *The European Economy Since 1945: Coordinated Capitalism and Beyond.* Princeton, NJ: Princeton University Press.

Farrell, Henry and Abraham L. Newman. 2010. "Making Global Markets: Historical Institutionalism in International Political Economy." *Review of International Political Economy* 17 (4): 609–638.

Ferran, Eilis. 2012. "Understanding the New Institutional Architecture of EU Financial Market Supervision." In *Financial Regulation and Supervision: A Post-Crisis Analysis*, ed. Eddy Wymeersch, Klaus J. Hopt, and Guido Ferrarini. Oxford: Oxford University Press.

Fioretos, Orfeo. 2001. "The Domestic Sources of Multilateral Preferences: Varieties of Capitalism in the European Community." In *Varieties of Capitalism*, ed. Peter A. Hall and David Soskice. Oxford: Oxford University Press, 213–244.

Fioretos, Orfeo. 2010. "Capitalist Diversity and the International Regulation of Hedge Funds." *Review of International Political Economy* 17 (4): 696–723.

Fioretos, Orfeo. 2011. *Creative Reconstructions: Multilateralism and European Varieties of Capitalism after 1950.* Ithaca, NY: Cornell University Press.

Gerschenkron, Alexander. 1962. *Economic Backwardness in Historical Perspective.* New York: Praeger.

Gocaj, Ledina and Meunier, Sophie. 2013. "Time Will Tell: The EFSF, the ESM, and the Euro Crisis." *Journal of European Integration* 35 (3): 239–253.

Goodman, John B. and Louis W. Pauly. 1993. "The Obsolescence of Capital Controls? Economic Management in an Age of Global Markets." *World Politics* 46 (1): 50–82.

Grossman, Emiliano and Patrick Leblond. 2011. "European Financial Integration: Finally the Great Leap Forward?" *Journal of Common Market Studies* 49 (2): 413–435.

Haas, Ernst B. 2004 [1958]. *The Uniting of Europe: Political, Social, and Economic Forces, 1950–1957.* Notre Dame, IN: University of Notre Dame Press.

Hall, Peter A. and David Soskice, eds. 2001. *Varieties of Capitalism: the Institutional Foundations of Comparative Advantage.* Oxford: Oxford University Press.

Hardie, Iain and David Howarth, eds. 2013. *Market-Based Banking and the International Financial Crisis.* Oxford: Oxford University Press.

Hardie, Iain, David Howarth, Sylvia Maxfield, and Amy Verdun. 2013. "Banks and the False Dichotomy in the Comparative Political Economy of Finance." *World Politics* 65 (4) (October): 691–728.

Helleiner, Eric. 1994. *States and the Reemergence of Global Finance: From Bretton Woods to the 1990s*. Ithaca, NY: Cornell University Press.

Howarth, David and Lucia Quaglia. 2013. "Banking on Stability: The Political Economy of New Capital Requirements in the European Union." *Journal of European Integration* 35 (3): 333–346.

Jabko, Nicolas. 2006. *Playing the Market: A Political Strategy for Uniting Europe, 1985–2005*. Ithaca, NY: Cornell University Press.

LaPorta, Rafael, Florencio Lopez de Silanes, and Andrei Shleifer. 2000. "Investor Protection and Corporate Governance." *Journal of Financial Economics* 58: 3–27.

Laurence, Henry. 2001. *Money Rules: The New Politics of Finance in Britain and Japan*. Ithaca, NY: Cornell University Press.

Leblond, Patrick. 2011. "EU, US and International Accounting Standards: A Delicate Balancing Act in Governing Global Finance." *Journal of European Public Policy* 18 (3): 443–461.

Lütz, Susanne. 2004. "Convergence within National Diversity: The Regulatory State in Finance." *Journal of Public Policy* 24 (2): 169–197.

Macartney, Huw. 2011. *Variegated Neoliberalism: EU Varieties of Capitalism and International Political Economy*. London: Routledge.

Maggetti, Martino and Fabrizio Gilardi. 2011. "The Policy-Making Structure of European Regulatory Networks and the Domestic Adoption of Standards." *Journal of European Public Policy* 18 (6): 830–847.

Mahoney, James. 2000. Path Dependence in Historical Sociology. *Theory and Society* 29 (4): 507–548.

Meunier, Sophie and Kathleen R. McNamara, eds. 2007. *Making History: European Integration and Institutional Change at Fifty*. Oxford: Oxford University Press.

Moran, Michael. 1991. *The Politics of the Financial Services Revolution: The USA, UK, and Japan*. New York: St. Martins Press.

Moravcsik, Andrew. 1998. *The Choice for Europe: Social Purpose and State Power from Messina to Maastricht*. Ithaca, NY: Cornell University Press.

Moschella, Manuela. 2011. "Getting Hedge Fund Regulation into the EU Agenda: The Constraints of Agenda Dynamics." *Journal of European Integration* 33 (3): 251–266.

Mügge, Daniel. 2010. *Widen the Market, Narrow the Competition: Banker Interests and the Making of a European Capital Market*. Colchester: ECPR Press.

Mügge, Daniel. 2011a. "From Pragmatism to Dogmatism: European Union Governance: Policy Paradigms and Financial Meltdown." *New Political Economy* 16 (2): 185–206.

Mügge, Daniel. 2011b. "The European Presence in Global Financial Governance: A Principal–Agent Perspective." *Journal of European Public Policy* 18 (3): 383–402.

Mügge, Daniel. 2013. "The Political Economy of Europeanized Financial Regulation." *Journal of European Public Policy* 20 (3): 458–470.

Newman, Abraham and Elliot Posner. 2013. "Transnational Feedbacks and the Sources of Preferences in Global Financial Regulation." Paper Presented at the Annual Conference of the International Studies Association, San Francisco.

O'Sullivan, Mary. 2007. "Acting Out Institutional Change: Understanding the Recent Transformation of the French Financial System." *Socio-Economic Review* 5 (3): 389–436.

Pagliari, Stefano. 2012. "A Wall around Europe? The European Regulatory Response to the Global Financial Crisis and the Turn in Transatlantic Relations." *Journal of European Integration* 35 (4): 1–18.

Pagliari, Stefano. 2013. "Public Salience and International Financial Regulation: Explaining the International Regulation of OTC Derivatives, Rating Agencies, and Hedge Funds." Dissertation, University of Waterloo.

Pérez, Sophia. 1998. "Systemic Explanations, Divergent Outcomes: The Politics of Financial Liberalization in France and Spain." *International Studies Quarterly* 42 (4): 755–784.

Pérez, Sofia and Jonathan Westrup. 2010. "Finance and the Macroeconomy: The Politics of Regulatory Reform in Europe." *Journal of European Public Policy* 17 (8): 1171–1192.

Pierson, Paul. 1996. "The Path to European Integration: A Historical Institutionalist Analysis." *Comparative Political Studies* 29 (2) (April): 123–163.

Pierson, Paul. 2004. *Politics in Time: History, Institutions, and Social Analysis.* Princeton, NJ: Princeton University Press.

Posner, Elliot. 2005. "Sources of Institutional Change: The Supranational Origins of Europe's New Stock Markets." *World Politics* 58 (1): 1–40.

Posner, Elliot. 2007. "Financial Transformation in the European Union." In *Making History: European Integration and Institutional Change at Fifty*, ed. Sophie Meunier and Kathleen R. McNamara. Oxford: Oxford University Press, 139–155.

Posner, Elliot. 2009a. "Making Rules for Global Finance: Transatlantic Regulatory Cooperation at the Turn of the Millennium." *International Organization* 63 (4): 665–699.

Posner, Elliot. 2009b. *The Origins of Europe's New Stock Markets.* Cambridge, MA: Harvard University Press.

Posner, Elliot. 2010a. "Sequence as Explanation: The International Politics of Accounting Standards. *Review of International Political Economy* 17 (4): 639–664.

Posner, Elliot. 2010b. "The Lamfalussy Process: The Polyarchic Origins of Networked Financial Rule-Making in the EU." In *Experimentalist Governance in the European Union: Towards a New Architecture*, ed. Charles F. Sabel and Jonathan Zeitlin. Oxford: Oxford University Press, 43–60.

Posner, Elliot and Nicolas Véron. 2010. "The EU and Financial Regulation: Power Without Purpose? *Journal of European Public Policy* 17 (3): 400–415.

Posner, Elliot and Nicolas Véron. 2013. "The End of EU Financial Regulatory Internationalism?" Paper Presented at the Annual Meeting of the International Studies Association, San Francisco.

Quaglia, Lucia. 2010. *Governing Financial Services in the European Union: Banking, Securities and Post-Trading.* New York: Routledge.

Quaglia, Lucia. 2012. "The 'Old' and the 'New' Political Economy of Hedge Funds Regulation in the European Union." *West European Politics* 34 (4): 665–682.

Quaglia, Lucia. 2013. "Financial Services Governance in The European Union after the Global Financial Crisis: Incremental Changes or Path-Breaking Reform?" In *Great Expectations, Slow Transformations: Incremental Change in Post-Crisis Regulation*, ed. Manuela Moschella and Eleni Tsingou. Wivenhoe Park: ECPR Press, 57–76.

Quaglia, Lucia. 2014. "The European Union, the USA and International Standard Setting in International Fora in Finance." *New Political Economy* 19 (3): 427–444.

Rajan, Raghuram and Luigi Zingales. 2003. "Banks and Markets: The Changing Character of European Finance." CEPR Discussion Paper No. 3868, London.

Roe, Mark J. 2003. *Political Determinants of Corporate Governance: Political Context, Corporate Impact.* Oxford and New York: Oxford University Press.

Rosenbluth, Frances and Ross Schaap. 2003. "The Domestic Politics of Banking Regulation." *International Organization* 57 (2): 307–336.

Shonfield, Andrew. 1965. *Modern Capitalism: the Changing Balance of Public and Private Power*. Oxford: Oxford University Press.

Sobel, Andrew C. 1994. *Domestic Choices, International Markets*. Chicago: University of Chicago Press.

Stone Sweet, Alec, Wayne Sandholtz, and Neil Fligstein. 2001. *The Institutionalization of Europe*. Oxford: Oxford University Press.

Story, Jonathon and Ingo Walter. 1997. *Political Economy of Financial Integration in Europe: The Battle of the Systems*. Cambridge, MA: The MIT Press.

Streeck, Wolfgang and Kathleen Thelen, eds. 2005. *Beyond Continuity: Institutional Change in Advanced Political Economies*. Oxford: Oxford University Press.

Verdier, Daniel. 2003. *Moving Money: Banking and Finance in the Industrialized World*. Cambridge: Cambridge University Press.

Véron, Nicolas. 2012. *Europe's Single Supervisory Mechanism and the Long Journey towards Banking Union*. Washington D.C.: Peterson Institute for International Economics.

Vitols, Sigurt. 2004. *Changes in Germany's Bank-Based Financial System: A Varieties of Capitalism Perspective (Discussion Paper SP II 2004–03)*. Berlin: Wissenschaftszentrum Berlin.

Woll, Cornelia. 2014. *The Power of Inaction: Bank Bailouts in Comparison*. Ithaca, NY: Cornell University Press.

Zimmermann, Hubert. 2009. "Varieties of Global Financial Governanc? British and German Approaches to Financial Market Regulation." In *Global Finance in Crisis: The Politics of International Regulatory Change*, ed. Eric Helleiner, Stefano Pagliari, and Hubert Zimmermann. New York: Routledge, 121–136.

Zysman, John. 1983. *Governments, Markets, and Growth: Financial Systems and the Politics of Industrial Change*. Ithaca, NY: Cornell University Press.

CHAPTER 27

CAPITALISM, INSTITUTIONS, AND POWER IN THE STUDY OF BUSINESS

PEPPER D. CULPEPPER*

HAROLD Lasswell defined politics as who gets what, when, and how. In studying the role of business in capitalism, historical institutionalist (HI) scholarship has made substantial strides in understanding the "what" and, especially, the "when" of politics; but it has been less attentive to the "how." HI research has shed substantial light on the determinants of, and cross-national variation in, employer preferences over policy and institutions (the "what"). It has also underscored the role of temporal processes in politics, and the ways in which the strength of winning coalitions at times of institutional change gets built in to sticky institutions, which in turn influence the future preferences of employers and their political opponents (the "when"). These advances, however, pushed into the analytical background the "how" question foregrounded by an earlier generation of scholars of political economy: How does the concentration of economic power that occurs in capitalism translate into the political power of capitalists in democratic institutions, which are putatively built on the principle of one-person, one-vote?

This chapter explores the contributions of HI scholarship to understanding preference formation in business, which would be difficult to overstate, as they have substantially altered the field of political economy. Yet it also critiques the HI drift away from some of the conceptual sites of real political action in democratic capitalism: issues of power, common trends across capitalist countries, and the role of voters in structuring the character of political conflict among interest groups and political parties. Recent scholarship has tried to overcome these lacunae. Building on this work, I explore a framework for incorporating the HI concern with institutional context into an investigation of the evolution of business power in different issue areas.

Contributions of Historical Institutionalism

Historical institutionalist scholarship has transformed the way in which political scientists conceptualize the interests of business in politics. This dramatic change resulted from three related insights into the character of business preferences. The first was the recognition that the interests of business organizations in the advanced industrial countries are a product both of material economic characteristics and of past patterns of interaction with labor and the state. The theoretical awareness that employer preferences did not result solely from their structural economic position grew out of an empirical observation, which constituted the second major insight of this literature: business groups in different countries have in fact pursued different objectives with respect to economic policy. Employers do not always push for the rollback of state regulation and the weakening of trade unions. Finally, clarity about the political preferences of employer groups led to an important revisionist trend in highlighting the cross-class coalitions that lay behind many welfare state institutions.

Notable contributions from HI scholars showed that the preferences of organized business were products of historical developments of the state and of strategies of industrialization. Peter Katzenstein's edited volume *Between Power and Plenty* was an influential early statement. For Katzenstein, business preferences were not just a product of their struggles with labor, but also with the bureaucracy and political parties. Industrializing early and facing only a weak state and a weak political left, US business developed "hostility to all forms of business or state organization," while the late-industrializing Japanese business community developed a centralized structure as part of its close relationship to a state that guided economic development (1978, 325). Peter Hall (1986) similarly wrote about the decisive differences between the collective preferences of business in Britain, dominated by an internationally oriented financial sector, and a French business community in which banks and industry worked closely together. Katzenstein (1985) also traced the historical divergence in strategies of small European states between the international orientation and centralized organizational structure of the business community in liberal corporatist countries and the more domestically oriented business communities in social corporatist countries. In each of these contributions, the interests of business developed in interaction with the state and society, and these institutionalized compromises durably influenced the way in which employers collectively defined their interests.

The emphasis on the cross-country variation in business interests underscored that firms in some cases favored collectivist or government-led solutions, rather than intrinsically preferring market regulation. This led to a new appreciation of the different ways in which countries organized their internal economic policy and responded to shocks from the international economy.[1] While the literature on corporatism had already drawn attention to the extensive involvement of employers in systems of wage bargaining (Goldthorpe 1984), other work in this vein showed how employers were involved in different sets of relationships for procuring finance (Zysman 1983; Deeg 1999) or for providing local collective goods for smaller firms (Herrigel 1996). Indeed, the importance of organizations as meditators of internal divisions led to renewed attention to the organizational characteristics of business associations themselves and how this influenced their input into politics (Schmitter and Streeck 1999; Culpepper 2003, 2007).

No group of employers has been under the microscope of historical institutional scholarship more than those of Germany. Scholars working on the (West) German political economy observed that business associations were involved in intricate arrangements for delivering collective goods, notably in the area of vocational training, which underlay the strategy of diversified quality production (Streeck 1991). Such commitments gave German employers considerable motivation to work together with unions to support the institutions that underpinned collective good provision in this field, as well as in that of wage-setting. The efflorescence of interest in employers and vocational training in Germany (Culpepper and Finegold 1999; Culpepper 2003; Thelen 2004), managed to obscure an important difference in this literature over the interests of German employers. On the one side were those scholars, typically associated with the "varieties of capitalism" literature, for whom the incentives of German employers to support this set of institutional endowments were so powerful that any rational analysis would expect these firms to continue to support the institutions almost regardless of union strength (Hall and Soskice 2001). On the other side were those scholars who spoke of the "beneficial constraints" that ensnared German employers and gave them incentive to support collective institutions, but only so long as their relative political strength did not offer the possibility of exit from these institutions (Streeck 1997). I will return to this tension later in the chapter, as it now animates one of the new frontiers on which scholars are doing research to understand the interaction of employer preferences and contemporary capitalism.

The debate on German employers is part of the third key contribution of HI research on business: arguing for the importance of cross-class coalitions between employers and unions in building, or tearing down, modern arrangements of economic governance and welfare provision. Peter Swenson (1991) identified the key elements of the cross-class alliance model, in which differences between the interests of employers in the exposed and sheltered sectors led the former to fight for the centralization of industrial relations institutions.[2] Isabela Mares (2003) found cross-class alliances between employers and workers in the same sectors to account for major extensions of social policy in unemployment, old age, and disability provision in France and Germany. While this revisionist history of the welfare has provoked strong challenge from defenders of conventional class analysis in welfare state research (Hacker and Pierson 2002; Korpi 2006), the focus on cross-class alliances has proved one of the enduring insights of HI scholarship.

Shortcomings of Historical Institutionalism

HI placed employer interests, and the variation therein, at the forefront of political economy research. In so doing, however, the success of this scholarship shouldered aside other ways of thinking about capitalist politics, which would have consequences for the way that comparative and international political economy were studied. In this chapter I focus on three neglected phenomena: power, common trends in capitalism, and voters.

Perhaps no subject was more central to debates about political economy in the 1960s and 1970s than that of power: who has it, who does not, and how is it exercised in capitalist democracies (Dahl 1961; Bachrach and Baratz 1962; Lindblom 1977). The productive theoretical debate over the instrumental and structural power of business in advanced capitalism (Miliband 1969; Block 1980; Przeworski and Wallerstein 1986) ran into the stubborn objections of scholars whose empirical work showed that no matter what the odds, business was capable of losing political battles, and thus was simply one interest group among others (Vogel 1987; Smith 2000). Over time, HI scholarship became less concerned with the systematic advantages that accrue to business in capitalist democracies, and more concentrated on the complex determinants of how business came to want what it wants, and which coalitional partners it found. Kathleen Thelen, in her celebrated comparative inquiry into the politics of skill formation, concisely summarized this development in her own work, in which she acknowledged avoiding "the language of 'power' in favor of identifying the interests and coalitions on which institutions are founded [because], unlike power, actors and their interests are more tractable empirically" (2004, 32–33).

While such research has produced a rich catalogue of the determinants of employer's political preferences and the coalitions they build in pursuit of them, it leads scholars to downplay what used to be the central question of political economists: does the commanding economic power of business in capitalism convert into an equally commanding role for capitalists in capitalist democracies? Research on business power, and the community power debate that preceded it (Schulze 1958; Dahl 1961), acknowledged that there was prima facie evidence to think business owners and the managers of large enterprises had privileged access to policymakers. The contrast with labor, which had to organize in order to have any political impact, was stark, and it was structural (Offe and Wiesenthal 1980). HI research is often attentive to the way in which institutional configurations favor the interests of one group over another, but its openness to contingency and the possibility of "institutional conversion" to a different set of interests (Thelen 2004; Streeck and Thelen 2005), disposes it to say less about the structural advantage of business in democratic capitalism.

Similarly, the focus of HI research on the cross-national variation in the interests of business associations led to a neglect of common trends within the different varieties of capitalism. A good deal of research during the 1990s asked the question, are models of capitalism converging, given the openness of international trade and financial flows? Heavily informed by the HI research program, much of that work came to the conclusion that, in fact, national models were robustly following their distinct, institutionally determined paths of adjustment (e.g., Berger and Dore 1996; Kitschelt et al. 1999; Hall and Soskice 2001). And indeed, a host of empirical indicators that scholars had used to measure degrees of coordination in industrial relations and finance showed that these institutions were remarkably resilient in many countries, and that beyond this resilience lay organized employers who favored institutional continuity (Golden, Wallerstein, and Lange 1999; Kenworthy 2001; Culpepper 2005).

Viewed through the lens of HI, the continued variation of institutions across the capitalist countries appears as evidence of the robustness of variety in capitalism itself. Yet some scholars who were themselves prominent contributors to the HI research program have in more recent years begun to focus on non-institutional outcomes, such as strike behavior or the character of collective contracts. They conclude from this evidence that the reorganization of capitalist activity is in fact moving in a single neoliberal direction, redistributing power from workers to employers, despite the vitality of different institutional forums for negotiating this transfer of power (Streeck 2009; Baccaro and Howell 2011).

A final critique of the HI research program's treatment of employers is that its great concentration on interest groups has brought with it an unfortunate inattention to voters. Prominent HI scholars Jacob Hacker and Paul Pierson have decried the fact that scholars of American politics build models with an almost exclusive attention to voters (2010). If this is a sin, it is one of which HI scholars are certainly innocent. Interest groups rule in the analysis of sources of institutional stability and change. Whereas early practitioners of HI blended the ways in which vote-seeking political parties and policy-seeking interest groups battled through different institutional forums, later work has tilted the balance decisively in favor of interest groups. This is consistent with the broader time frame often adopted in HI research, in which elections are merely episodic battles in the broad and ongoing conflict over policy and institution-building, often in non-legislative forums.

And yet this has meant that the mainstream of HI research has left unexploited two important determinants of institutional change: the preferences of the electorate (the core concern of most behavioral political scientists—e.g., Bartels 2008; Gilens 2012) and the dynamics of change in public opinion, which policy research has shown to play a dramatic role in determining when radical policy change takes place (Baumgartner and Jones 1993; Jones and Baumgartner 2005). Indeed, one of the most important findings of research on business power in politics is that business influence weakens when the electorate is interested in an issue and monitoring it, and that employers enjoy great success under these conditions only when a substantial portion of the public shares their views on particular issues (Smith 2000; Culpepper 2011).

Synthesis and Research Frontiers

Some of the most exciting current research on employers in politics involves work at the frontiers of these areas that past HI research has underemphasized. In each case, new avenues of inquiry combine insights associated with the HI research program and a return to the questions of power that animated previous generations of research on business and political economy.

One such strand focuses on the character of incremental and transformative change in institutions of the political economy, particularly in industrial relations systems. This work, led by Wolfgang Streeck's *Re-Forming Capitalism* (2009), maintains its institutionalist focus, but renews interest in institutions of advanced capitalism as a forum for ongoing conflict between labor and capital. If the varieties of capitalism literature emphasized the coordinating features of institutions, and other HI research illuminated the way in which institutionalization of conflicts permitted low-voltage politics (Katzenstein 1985), Streeck's research returns to the idea of capitalism as crisis-ridden and conflictual, characterized by sharp disagreements between the two parties to the wage bargain. Change and conflict, rather than stability and coordination, are the watchwords of this new strand of research.

Lucio Baccaro and Chris Howell (2011) have pursued this insight empirically with respect to the variable of power. They find that across different varieties of capitalism, empirical indicators all point to movement in a neoliberal direction. Although the institutions across these countries remain widely divergent, these movements have resulted in a concrete change in employer discretion over the rules governing workplace relations or negotiations with labor. That is, they have answered Thelen's call to make power an empirically tractable variable. And their conclusion is unsettling for HI:

> continuing divergence of institutional form is perfectly compatible with convergence in institutional functioning, which . . . raises questions about the centrality accorded institutions by scholars in the field of comparative political economy in explaining the functioning of capitalist political economies. (Thelen 2011: 527)

Not only can power be measured empirically, but the findings of these measurements show some potential to undermine insights generated by institutional variables, as exemplified by Baccaro and Howell's finding that employer discretion (which is a form of power in the workplace) is increasing in the presence of institutional stability. If the rules governing workplace negotiation—which are the centerpiece in many exhibits of capitalist variety—are themselves being undermined by actual practices that have increased employer power and weakened that of workers, it may well be the case that many cases of institutional stability mask substantial transfers of economic power over time.

Recent research has also returned to debates about the relationship between the instrumental and structural power of business. Instrumental power includes lobbying and campaign donations: the political instruments that business deploys in order to get its way. Structural power, by contrast, denotes influence that accrues to the firm solely by virtue of its position in the economy as an engine of economic activity, typically anticipated by policymakers and automatically built into policy. Attention to this distinction was first revived in an article by Jacob Hacker and Paul Pierson (2002), in which they challenged Peter Swenson's (2002) claim that American business was an active supporter of the American Social Security Act (SSA) in the 1930s. Hacker and Pierson claimed that any support business showed for SSA was simply a strategic accommodation to its loss of *structural* power, because the Great Depression shifted social policymaking away from the states to the federal level, thus depriving business of its ability to exit one state for another. While business continued to enjoy access to policymakers through lobbying—*instrumental* power—this power was outweighed by the loss of *structural* power. Thus, the cross-class coalitions that Swenson had analyzed were, for Hacker and Pierson, merely a shotgun wedding, in which labor and the left were holding the shotgun.

Following the financial crisis and Great Recession, the question of business power is once again returning to the forefront of debates in political economy, a theoretical move made by several scholars associated with HI analysis. The various aspects of corporate governance law—long ignored by political scientists—have become the locus of some of the strongest debates about the character of the power of business in politics. Inspired by work on the varieties of capitalism, this research has gone from talking about cross-class coalitions in finance (Gourevitch and Shinn 2005) to asking questions about how left parties came to work with financial interests, and how these financial interests were able to exercise disproportionate sway in democratic politics (Cioffi and Höpner 2006). Others have looked at the politics leading up to and following the financial crisis, shifting emphasis from the institutional roots of political equilibria to the power resources of business and their exercise in politics (Hacker and Pierson 2010; Culpepper and Reinke 2014; Woll 2014). In each case, this research manifests a greater attention to the resources available to employers as actors in the political process.

Beyond renewing attention to business power, the insights of HI research would be improved through a greater dialogue with the policy agendas work of Frank Baumgartner and Bryan Jones on institutional change in public policy (Baumgartner and Jones 1993; Jones and Baumgartner 2005). In parallel to HI scholarship, this research program has found that policy subsystems are sticky, as the balance of power between vested interests is slow to change. Yet in the few places where they do find change, it is overwhelmingly of the radical, transformative nature, pushed by explosions of public interest in new policy areas. HI research has focused on gradual, transformative change (Streeck and Thelen 2005). Increased dialogue between these literatures could redound to the benefit of both. And from the HI perspective, it would provide a way to return a largely absent figure—the voter—to models of institutional change and stability.

In the remainder of the chapter I draw on some of my own recent work to suggest one way to push forward the research agenda on the role of employers in politics. This approach combines an institutionalist concern for the rules of the game in politics with an attentiveness to the political salience of different issue areas and how salience affects business power, returning the voting public to inquiry into political conflict between interest groups.

The Governance Space

As Theodore Lowi (1964) first pointed out, different policy regimes can create their own sort of politics. We should therefore expect power resources of different groups to vary in systematic ways across these regimes. What are the most important dimensions along which they vary? Culpepper (2011) prioritizes two dimensions of variation that define different regimes of governance. The first is political salience. Do voters on average care about issues and vote based on them? The second is the character of rules governing the regime: are institutions formal (i.e., the product of legislatures or public bureaucracies), or are they instead informal, meaning they are devised and maintained by non-state actors (such as employers' associations or labor unions)? One salutary product of the HI research program has been a renewed emphasis on the importance of moving the focus beyond the formal rules to those informal rules that structure political and policy conflict (Helmke and Levitsky 2004; Culpepper 2005).

Table 27.1 depicts the intersection of these two dimensions and the sort of politics to which they characteristically give rise. In the quadrant entitled partisan contestation, rulemaking is primarily formal and voters are highly interested in the outcomes. Tax reform, for example, generally lies in this quadrant: parties compete on their positions over tax policy to attract voters, who are paying attention to this pocketbook issue. In such a domain, business needs allies in order to convince broad swathes of public opinion, because the parties that have to pass policies also want to get re-elected. It is in such policy areas that business has endured many defeats, despite its formidable lobbying capacity (Smith 2000).[3] Much of the rulemaking in capitalist democracies happens in the other quadrants however, and these other quadrants of the governance space privilege different political resources.

Table 27.1 The Governance Space

	Informal Rules Primary	Formal Rules Primary
High Salience	Social partner bargaining	Partisan contestation
Low Salience	Private interest governance	Bureaucratic network negotiation

Source: Culpepper (2011): 181. Table reprinted with permission of Cambridge University Press.

It is in the quadrant furthest from partisan contestation—labeled private interest governance in Table 27.1—in which we expect business power to be disproportionately high. These are issues in which the voting public evinces little sustained interest, and in which rulemaking is primarily private. In areas such as corporate governance regulation, non-legislative codes of conduct established by experts are often endorsed by government without being codified, reinforcing deference to business. Keeping the rules out of the legislative and regulatory domains means that business can rely less on its lobbying capacity, except to convince government not to intervene in a policy area. These are conditions in which business domination is the rule, partly because of the absence of partisan political incentives to bring the preferences of large portions of the voting public into policymaking.

The other two quadrants of the governance space stand midway between the two poles of private interest governance and partisan contestation. Bureaucratic network negotiation denotes rulemaking involving state actors, but the lack of public attention suggests that political parties and legislatures are unlikely to be relevant players. Because rules are formal in policies governed in this quadrant, business cannot simply impose its will; influence must be exercised through networks established around regulators, where expertise is the coin of the realm, and where civil servants have some discretion about which interests to include.

The opposing quadrant, that of high salience and informal rules, is dominated by social partner bargaining under the shadow of the state (Scharpf 1997). The public is paying attention, but governments either hesitate to enter this area because of delicately constructed private governance systems, or (as in the case of German wage bargaining), because they are constitutionally prevented from doing so. The ability to create economic or political dislocation constitutes the most effective form of resources here (Culpepper and Regan 2014). Strikes or lockouts betoken economic power, which is useful in informal governance, and the ability to raise public awareness in by bringing large number of protesters into the streets can lengthen of the shadow of the state over private bargaining. Typically the political actors in this quadrant are employers' associations and trade unions, but in principle they can be any associations representing a functionally defined interest group in the economy.

For expository purposes, this discussion has associated policies with a single quadrant, which is sometimes the case. But in the real world, a single policy area may involve contestation in different quadrants of the governance space. Consistent with the broad thrust of HI scholarship, this sort of context matters, and the actors know it. Sometimes they try to move contestation from one area in which their resources are weaker to another, in which their resources are stronger; other times the shift may happen for reasons that are contingent, such as a sudden scandal catching public attention and transforming an area from low salience to high salience. These sorts of shifts can lead to sudden institutional changes, as the balance of power among actors flows from significant changes in the two underlying dimensions of salience and institutional formality.

The governance space illuminates how the political power of business organizations rises and falls depending on the involvement of the public. Take for example the issue of executive compensation, whose recent rise to high salience across the world's rich countries has led to dramatic new forms of regulation of what was previously a privately governed issue: how much public companies can pay their CEOs. In research on these policies in Britain and the United States, I have shown that if voters are not paying attention to an issue of great concern to business leaders, then business leaders will almost always get their way.[4] And getting their way means having no constraints on the prerogatives of boards of directors as to how they set pay.

Rising political salience is not a sufficient condition to lead to institutional change, however. It must be transformed into political effect through interest group or political party action. In regulating executive pay, a government of the right may be able to limit the effect of public outrage on legislative output, as happened in the United Kingdom in 1995. Even a partisan change in government in 1997 was not enough to effect institutional change in this area, given the deference of the Labour government to organized business as the salience of the issue was in decline after the election. It required interest group action on the part of institutional investors and sustained high salience with the public to convince the left government to adopt formal laws governing executive pay-setting in Britain in 2002.

Similar dynamics were observed in the passage of initial restrictions related to executive compensation in the Sarbanes-Oxley bill in the US in 2002, in the wake of the Enron scandal, and then later with the outbreak of the financial crisis in the US in 2008. In each case, public attention shifted the balance of power between business and other actors by concentrating the attention of politicians on what voters wanted. Business does not always lose in high salience environments, when voters are paying attention and have clear preferences, but it will lose if it does not have strong allies in government or the interest group environment. In noisy political conflicts, the lobbying tools of "quiet politics" are generally insufficient to convert business preferences into public policy.

Conclusion

The challenge of future research on employers is to build on the insights of HI scholarship on the construction of business preferences while reinforcing attention to the "how" of Lasswell's politics: what are the mechanisms of employer power in the advanced capitalist democracies? How do democratic institutions and decision-making rules interact with the concentration of economic power that is inherent in capitalist development?

Exciting avenues of current inquiry build on HI insights while placing business power closer to the center of analysis. There remains much to be done in thinking about the most appropriate ways to conceptualize this political influence. Some have used the contrast between instrumental and structural power to theorize how business power varies over time (Hacker and Pierson 2002). Other scholars have pushed to broaden intellectual inquiry away from power directly exercised on actors to diffuse relations of power, in which modes of discourse allow some outcomes to be chosen and not others, thus depriving social actors of autonomy (Barnett and Duvall 2005). As Thelen (1999) has observed, this is a familiar tension from HI research, between those who focus primarily on material roots of political change (Swenson 1991) and those who look more at its ideational roots (Katzenstein 1985).

The governance space, which I have briefly discussed in this chapter, is one analytical approach that combines the insights of HI analysis with a concern for business power and the role of the voters in setting political agendas. There are surely others that merit further elaboration and scrutiny. The way for political economy to build on the edifice to which HI research has contributed substantially over the past 30 years is to continue to think about the mechanisms that link democratic decision-making and the uneven distribution of economic power in capitalism. These vary over time and across policy areas, but there are features that hold true across different varieties of capitalism. There is still much to be learned about the extent and limits of the political power of business.

Notes

* This chapter has benefited from the comments of Tulia Falleti and of participants in the panel discussion on "Historical Intuitionalism and European Politics" at the 20th International Conference of Europeanists, Amsterdam, June 25–27, 2013.

1. These claims were already foreshadowed in Shonfield (1965).
2. Pontusson and Swenson (1996) showed in later work that the cross-class coalition was also the causal force in decentralizing wage bargaining in Sweden.
3. Indeed, the governance space helps make sense of the puzzling finding of research by Baumgartner et al. (2009), that expenditures on lobbying do not seem to be correlated with policy success.
4. The following paragraphs draw on findings from Culpepper (2014).

References

Baccaro, Lucio and Chris Howell. 2011. "A Common Neoliberal Trajectory: The Transformation of Neoliberalism in Advanced Capitalism." *Politics & Society* 39 (4): 521–563.

Bachrach, Peter and Baratz, Morton S. 1962. "Two Faces of Power." *American Political Science Review* 56 (4): 947–952.

Barnett, Michael and Raymond Duvall. 2005. "Power in International Politics." *International Organization* 59 (1): 39–75.

Bartels, Larry M. 2008. *Unequal Democracy*. Princeton, NJ: Princeton University Press.

Baumgartner, Frank R. and Bryan D. Jones. 1993. *Agendas and Instability in American Politics*. Chicago: University of Chicago Press.

Baumgartner, Frank R., Jeffrey M. Berry, Marie Hojnacki, David C. Kimball, and Beth L. Leech. 2009. *Lobbying and Policy Change*. Chicago: University of Chicago Press.

Berger, Suzanne and Ronald Dore, eds. 1996. *National Diversity and Global Capitalism*. Ithaca, NY: Cornell University Press.

Block, Fred. 1980. "Beyond Relative Autonomy: State Managers as Historical Subjects." *The Socialist Register* 17: 227–241.

Cioffi, John W. and Martin Höpner. 2006. "The Political Paradox of Finance Capitalism." *Politics & Society* 34 (4): 463–502.

Culpepper, Pepper D. 2003. *Creating Cooperation: How States Develop Human Capital in Europe.* Ithaca, NY: Cornell University Press.

Culpepper, Pepper D. 2005. "Institutional Change in Contemporary Capitalism: Coordinated Financial Systems since 1990." *World Politics* 57 (2): 173–199.

Culpepper, Pepper D. 2007. "Small States and Skill Specificity: Austria, Switzerland, and Interemployer Cleavages in Coordinated Capitalism." *Comparative Political Studies* 40 (6): 611–637.

Culpepper, Pepper D. 2011. *Quiet Politics and Business Power: Corporate Control in Europe and Japan.* New York: Cambridge University Press.

Culpepper, Pepper D. 2014. "The Politics of Executive Pay in the United Kingdom and the United States." Manuscript.

Culpepper, Pepper D. and Aidan Regan. 2014. "Why Don't Governments Need Trade Unions Anymore?" *Socio-Economic Review* 12 (4): 723–745.

Culpepper, Pepper D. and David Finegold, eds. 1999. *The German Skills Machine.* New York: Berghahn Books.

Culpepper, Pepper D. and Raphael Reinke. 2014. "Structural Power and Bank Bailouts in the United Kingdom and the United States." *Politics & Society* 42 (4): 427–454.

Dahl, Robert A. 1961. *Who Governs?* New Haven, CT: Yale University Press.

Deeg, Richard. 1999. *Finance Capitalism Unveiled.* Ann Arbor: University of Michigan Press.

Gilens, Martin. 2012. *Affluence and Influence: Economic Inequality and Political Power.* Princeton, NJ: Princeton University Press.

Goldthorpe, John H., ed. 1984. *Order and Conflict in Contemporary Capitalism.* Oxford: Clarendon Press.

Golden, Miriam, Michael Wallerstein, and Peter Lange. 1999. "Postwar Trade Union Organization and Industrial Relations in Twelve Countries." In *Continuity and Change in Contemporary Capitalism*, ed. Kitschelt, Herbert, Peter Lange, Gary Marks, and John Stephens. New York: Cambridge University Press, 194–230.

Gourevitch, Peter A. and James Shinn. 2005. *Political Power and Corporate Control.* Princeton, NJ: Princeton University Press.

Hacker, Jacob S. and Paul Pierson. 2002. "Business Power and Social Policy: Employers and the Formation of the American Welfare State." *Politics & Society* 30 (2): 277–325.

Hacker, Jacob S. and Paul Pierson. 2010. *Winner-Take-All Politics.* New York: Simon and Schuster.

Hall, Peter A. 1986. *Governing the Economy.* London: Oxford University Press.

Hall, Peter A. and David Soskice, eds. 2001. *Varieties of Capitalism.* London and New York: Oxford University Press.

Helmke, Gretchen and Steven Levitsky. 2004. "Informal Institutions and Comparative Politics: A Research Agenda." *Perspectives on Politics* 2 (4): 725–740.

Herrigel, Gary. 1996. *Industrial Constructions: The Sources of German Industrial Power.* New York: Cambridge University Press.

Jones, Bryan D. and Frank R. Baumgartner. 2005. *The Politics of Attention.* Chicago: University of Chicago Press.

Katzenstein, Peter J., ed. 1978. *Between Power and Plenty.* Madison, WI: University of Wisconsin Press.

Katzenstein, Peter J. 1985. *Small States in World Markets: Industrial Policy in Europe*. Ithaca, NY: Cornell University Press.

Kenworthy, Lane. 2001. "Wage-Setting Measures: A Survey and Assessment." *World Politics* 54: 57–98.

Kitschelt, Herbert, Peter Lange, Gary Marks and John Stephens, eds. 1999. *Continuity and Change in Contemporary Capitalism*. New York: Cambridge University Press.

Korpi, Walter. 2006. "Power Resources and Employer-Centered Approaches in Explanations of Welfare States and Varieties of Capitalism: Protagonists, Consenters, and Antagonists." *World Politics* 58 (2): 167–206.

Lindblom, Charles E. 1977. *Politics and Markets*. New York: Basic Books.

Lowi, Theodore J. 1964. "American Business, Public Policy, Case Studies, and Political Theory." *World Politics* 16 (4): 677–715.

Mares, Isabela. 2003. *The Politics of Social Risk*. New York: Cambridge University Press.

Miliband, Ralph. 1969. *The State in Capitalist Society*. New York: Basic Books.

Offe, Claus and Wiesenthal, Helmut, 1980. "Two Logics of Collective Action." *Political Power and Social Theory* 1: 67–115.

Pontusson, Jonas and Peter Swenson. 1996. "Labor Markets, Production Strategies, and Wage Bargaining Institutions: The Swedish Employer Offensive in Comparative Perspective." *Comparative Political Studies* 29 (2): 223–250.

Przeworski, Adam and Wallerstein, Michael. 1986. "Structural Dependence of the State on Capital." *American Political Science Review* 82 (1): 11–29.

Scharpf, Fritz W. 1997. *Games Real Actors Play*. Boulder, CO: Westview Press.

Schmitter, Philippe and Streeck, Wolfgang. 1999. "The Organization of Business Interests: Studying the Associative Action of Business in Advanced Industrial Societies." MPIfG Discussion Paper 99/1.

Schulze, Robert O. 1958. "The Role of Economic Dominants in Community Power Structure." *American Sociological Review* 23 (1): 3–9.

Shonfield, Andrew. 1965. *Modern Capitalism: The Changing Balance of Public and Private Power*. Oxford: Oxford University Press.

Smith, Mark A. 2000. *American Business and Political Power.* Chicago: University of Chicago Press.

Streeck, Wolfgang. 1991. "On the Institutional Conditions of Diversified Quality Production." In *Beyond Keynesianism*, ed. Egon Matzner and Wolfgang Streeck. Aldershot: Edward Elgar, 21–61.

Streeck, Wolfgang. 1997. "Beneficial Constraints: On the Economic Limits of Rational Voluntarism." In *Contemporary Capitalism: The Embeddedness of Institutions*, ed. J. Rogers Hollingsworth and Robert Boyer. New York: Cambridge University Press, 197–219.

Streeck, Wolfgang. 2009. *Re-Forming Capitalism: Institutional Change in the German Political Economy*. Oxford and New York: Oxford University Press.

Streeck, Wolfgang and Kathleen Thelen, eds. 2005. *Beyond Continuity: Institutional Change in Advanced Political Economies*. New York: Oxford University Press.

Swenson, Peter. 1991. "Bringing Capital Back In, or Social Democracy Reconsidered." *World Politics* 43 (4): 514–544.

Swenson, Peter. 2002. *Capitalists against Markets.* Oxford and New York: Oxford University Press.

Thelen, Kathleen. 1999. "Historical Institutionalism in Comparative Politics." *Annual Review of Political Science* 2(1): 369–404.

Thelen, Kathleen. 2004. *How Institutions Evolve: The Political Economy of Skills in Germany, Britain, the United States, and Japan*. New York: Cambridge University Press.
Vogel, David. 1987. "Political Science and the Study of Corporate Power: A Dissent from the New Conventional Wisdom." *British Journal of Political Science* 17 (4): 385–408.
Woll, Cornelia. 2014. *The Power of Inaction: Bank Bailouts in Comparison*. Ithaca, NY: Cornell University Press.
Zysman, John. 1983. *Governments, Markets, and Growth: Financial Systems and the Politics of Industrial Change*. Ithaca, NY: Cornell University Press.

CHAPTER 28

RELIGION AND EUROPEAN POLITICS

ANNA GRZYMALA-BUSSE

THE comparative study of religion and politics, both in Europe and beyond, has benefited from many of the critical emphases of historical institutionalist analyses: the importance of timing and historical sequences, and how these temporal orderings have unfolded over time to affect current outcomes and generate lasting legacies; the stickiness of earlier institutional decisions and coalitions; and the importance of ideas in generating preferences over outcomes and strategies. Thus, many aspects of contemporary European church–state relations have been shown to have their roots in historical legacies of earlier conflicts and interactions between church, state, and the nation, which persist beyond the circumstances that initially gave rise to them.

This chapter argues that historical institutionalist approaches *complement* existing studies of religion and politics by emphasizing temporality and the role of ideas (specifically, religious doctrine and religious nationalism) in shaping preferences. An emphasis on doctrine as an explanatory variable helps to account for the origin of secular institutions, ranging from contemporary welfare state institutions to education to the European Union itself, and for the persistence of particular political cleavages. Conversely, historical institutionalist analysis also *revises* our understanding of the different patterns of religiosity in contemporary developed democracies: a focus on historical conflict helps to explain why religion and its claims resonate so much more in some countries than in others, accounting for discrepancies and analytical gaps that less historically careful approaches have been unable to answer satisfactorily.

Yet much, if not most, of the research on religion and politics does not make explicit references to historical institutionalism, or its emphases on ideas and historical analyses. In this chapter, I show where historical institutionalism has nonetheless informed the study of religion in politics in several interconnected areas of European politics, ranging from religious influence on policy to political party competition to institutional development. I emphasize the role of religious ideas—and how they have shaped states, parties, welfare, and European integration. I then show how greater sensitivity to history and historical legacies can improve the study of religiosity itself.

This chapter is limited to the analysis of Christian Europe, neglecting the long and storied history of Islam in Southern Europe, for example. Even so, we can refine existing understandings by paying closer attention to religious doctrine, as a set of ideas that informs the preferences of both secular and religious actors over both institutional forms and strategies, and to the interaction of doctrine with the historical context of individual countries and regions.

The Importance of Doctrine

Religious doctrine matters as a coherent set of ideas and normative claims. By "doctrine," I mean the body of principles and teachings that describe both the tenets of the religion and the practices it advocates. These serve to influence both subsequent institutional creation and individual behavior by delimiting what is desirable in the eyes of God and feasible in the eyes of the doctrine's advocates. Here, doctrine acts much as ideology does in historical ideational analysis,[1] as a set of normative ideas that builds communities of believers, explicitly advocates for goals, and suggests tools with which goals are enacted and reproduced (Berman 2013). Religious doctrine here provides the mechanisms by which symbols, traditions, rituals, and myths influence social and political interactions. This specification of mechanisms is critical for cultural accounts, which have tended to underspecify these mechanisms (Johnson 2002, 227). Taking doctrine seriously thus allows us to delineate the mechanisms of cultural and religious influence: both by identifying which issues are relevant to religious organizations, and by suggesting how religious doctrine and its secular context interact. As we will see in the subsequent sections, by attending to doctrine as a set of religious ideas informing secular politics, we can better understand the neglected aspects of variation in the welfare state, the differences in secular organization, and the propensity of some religions to influence politics.

Doctrine affects the preferences over institutions and policy of both religious and secular actors. The modern European welfare state and educational systems have been profoundly shaped by ideas about religious charity and instruction—ideas that reflect the doctrinal differences between Catholics, Lutherans, and Calvinists in early modern Europe, for example (Kahl 2005; de Swaan 1988). Doctrine further influences the internal organization of denominations: Catholic hierarchies support and are supported by the need for mediation between God and the believers, while the belief in immediate and direct relationship between God and the faithful in some Protestant denominations supports a much flatter hierarchy with no clear leadership or lines of authority. As a result, the political impact of Catholics and Protestants may vary. The Catholic Church has insisted on the universality of its doctrine and its political relevance—and has both the experience and the organization to enforce these convictions (Martin 1999,

40). Evangelicals and other Protestants have long carried on traditions of separation of church and state (and a suspicion of the corrupting influence of politics), speak with multiple voices rather than an ideological monopoly, and have far less experience in holding secular power. As a result, Catholic churches are much more likely to insist on influencing secular policy, especially in areas they view as their moral domain, while Protestant churches are less likely to do so. Doctrine and organization of religion here shapes the degree and type of influence they seek to exert on politics: it is not surprising that coherent and organized hierarchies whose doctrine compels them to act are more likely to try to influence politics, and more likely to succeed, than loosely organized and decentralized religious bodies that have no such ambitions.

Yet for the most part, neither doctrine nor religiosity itself act alone. Religion varies in its social and political resonance: the ability of the churches to gain approval for their claims to represent the nation and its moral, ethical, and political interests, its ability to retain adherents in face of their disapproval of such efforts, and its ability to forge a variety of political alliances to obtain policy goods. Some societies are more receptive to religious framing of politics due to long-standing fusion of religious and national identities. Where we see such religious nationalism, a more purely secular nationalism is replaced by new loyalties and motives for conflict that are more compelling and less negotiable than secular nationalist ones alone (Juergensmeyer 1993, 2008). Where the churches had earlier protected the nation against either a repressive domestic state or a hostile colonial power, for example, they gained the moral authority that subsequently translated into policy success (Grzymala-Busse 2015). As we will see, such protection may also lead to durable and high popular religiosity.

This historical relationship between nation, state, and the dominant religious tradition also explains why the same denomination might resonate very differently across countries. There is as much internal variation in preferences and strategies within a given religious body as there is among denominations, as the various national strategies of the Roman Catholic Church show (Philpott 2007; Warner 2000). A universal, cross-national doctrine does not presuppose the same political strategies or influence across countries. Critically, the national historical context of church–state relations, and the institutional landscape within which the churches operate, interacts with doctrine. Thus, primarily Catholic countries, from Poland to Italy to France, show very different patterns of Catholic Church political behavior, policy influence, and coalitional politics (Grzymala-Busse 2011). Where the Roman Catholic Church had extensive moral authority, as it did in Poland or in Ireland, it could rely on direct institutional access to policymaking and a favorable reception to many of its policy demands—in contrast, where it had little such reputation or historical role, its demands were marginalized, as in the Czech Republic or France (Grzymala-Busse 2015). Similarly, in Latin America, where the Roman Catholic Church supported an authoritarian regime, it lost much of its moral authority, as it did in Argentina. In contrast, where it supported the anti-authoritarian opposition or indigenous movements, as in Chile and in some regions of Mexico, respectively, it gained both authority and influence (Gill 1998; Trejo 2009).

Thus, it is the *interaction* of doctrine and historical context that helps to explain both the strategies of different organized religions, and the variation across countries within the same denomination. These interactions are also critical to understanding the contemporary differences in state development and political parties, the rise of institutions such as education and welfare, and even the patterns of European integration. They further underlie the continued popular importance of religion in some countries—and secularization in others. In short, even though many analyses of religion and church-state relations do not explicitly acknowledge so, they benefit from the classic historical institutionalist emphases on the importance of ideas, historical sequences and their irreversibility, and the importance of political memory.

Historical States and Political Parties

In medieval and early modern Europe, churches legitimated monarchical rule in Europe (and often acted as a competing source of political authority and power). Religion was thus never far from the rise of the state (itself the target of numerous historical institutionalist investigations). In one particularly nuanced argument, religious denominations influenced the regime types that arose in early modern Europe: where Calvinist insurgents could rely on strong traditions of representative government, constitutionalism was preserved. Conversely, where such a movement or traditions were lacking, absolutism prevailed (Gorski 2003).

Religious authorities then readily became involved in secular politics, relying on a more stable configuration of state institutions religions that they themselves had earlier helped to bring about. In the nineteenth and early twentieth centuries, the fundamental cleavages driving the formation of parties and broader political conflict were between church and state—and the wresting of control over education, poverty relief, and legitimation from religious authorities by the secular state. This is the familiar story of the formation of long-lasting political cleavages in European politics (Lipset and Rokkan 1967; Rokkan 1981). More recently, however, this story has been elaborated to show how clerical-anticlerical divides brought together disparate secular politicians in some countries such as France, and why parties of Catholic religious defense had an ambivalent relationship to democratization, thanks partly to the church authorities' suspicion of popular democracy (Gould 1999; Ertman 2009; Van Kersbergen and Manow 2009). Yet again, the doctrine and hierarchical structure of a denomination influenced its political role.

Religious authorities also founded political movements and political parties, as the story of Christian Democracy in Europe and Turkish Islamic parties shows (Kalyvas 1996; Altinordu 2010). Thus, the Roman Catholic Church inadvertently fomented the rise of Christian Democratic parties in Western Europe. The Roman Catholic Church attempted to stave off a liberal challenge in nineteenth-century Europe by lending its support to lay Catholic movements—only to see them acquire an autonomous life of their own and transform themselves into Christian Democratic parties that were only tenuously connected to the Church (Kalyvas 1996). These parties had both an uneasy and fundamental relationship to the church, gaining organizational autonomy while retaining doctrinal affinities (Van Kersbergen 1994; Kalyvas and Van Kersbergen 2010; Grzymala-Busse 2011). Subsequently, these Christian Democratic parties were but one potential coalition partner for the Church, as the Roman Catholic Church in Europe sought to form political alliances with incumbent parties, exchanging government policy concessions for electoral mobilization by the Church on behalf of the parties (Warner 2000).

Here, the analytical perspective of historical institutionalism alerts us to the unintended and unanticipated consequences of the Catholic Church's secular mobilization strategies—and the durability of decisions made early on, when political parties were simultaneously arising and capturing newly enfranchised voters. Subsequently, as we will see later in this chapter, the role of ideas—specifically, Catholic social teaching—shaped how these Christian Democratic (and other) political parties approached both the market and international organizations, even if the parties themselves were by that point long autonomous of the Church itself.

Education and Welfare

Differences in welfare regimes, unemployment patterns, and educational expenditures have been linked to historical differences in prevalent religious doctrine (Castles 1994; Kahl 2005; Van Kersbergen and Manow 2009). Denominational differences in doctrine bring with them specific ideas and norms regarding a whole host of appropriate institutional solutions, and the reproduction of these solutions over time. They influence both the choice of political institutions, and the long-term outcomes that result. Robert Woodberry's analyses of the impact of Protestant missionaries go the farthest here: he argues that Protestant churches and missionaries (and their Catholic counterparts where they faced Protestant competition) promoted mass literacy, printing, and the rise of several institutions: civil society (both directly and in response to their missionary efforts), rule of law (by mobilizing white colonial settlers: the more independent the missionaries from sponsor states, the more they could speak out against injustices and demand reform), and market regulation (advocated breaking monopolies, forced labor, etc.) (Woodberry 2011). Education, in turn, spurred social mobility, opportunities for women, and long-term health improvements, among other favorable outcomes. In a more moderate articulation of this thesis, Protestantism facilitates democracy: the doctrine encourages individual conscience, with the Bible as key authority rather than priests or religious authorities, and "tend towards separation and independence from ancient church structures and traditions as well as political authorities" (Woodberry and Shah 2004, 48). This approach marries careful gathering of historical data of missionary patterns with an analytical emphasis on how differences in ideas—that is, doctrinal differences—guided durable institutional choices.

Other more specific institutional legacies are laid at the hands of religion. A central bone of contention in church–state relations has been education, and the struggle to control the inculcation of historical understandings and values in generations of citizens (and religious adherents). Both actors are in effect "taking an option on the future by ensuring the control of education of children and adolescents" (Rémond 1999, 147). The gradual wresting away of education from the church and into the secular state's hands has been a signal process in the development of the state (De Swaan 1988)—and here denominational differences (and the interaction between the historical role of the church and this doctrine) played a considerable role in determining how these processes unfolded. Protestant Free and Reformed churches have held a strongly anti-state position, while Lutheran and Orthodox state churches either "never questioned the prerogative of the central state in social policy and education" (Van Kersbergen and Manow 2009, 4) or actively embraced the state as a source of resources and a close partner.

Within denominations, the historical relationship of the church to the nation-state influenced these patterns: for example, the lower the past conflict between the Roman Catholic Church and a given nation, the greater the continued influence of the Church. As we will see in the next section, the more a church or denomination can claim to have protected the nation against hostile forces, the greater its moral authority in politics—and the greater its ability to translate its doctrinal preferences into policy. The extreme example here is Ireland, where primary education remained until very recently in the hands of the Catholic Church. Here, the newly independent Irish state handed over entire institutional sectors: education, health care, and welfare, to the Church. It did so because the Church had the organizational capacity and the moral authority to represent the best interests of the nation, both moral and material. In other European Catholic countries, even where the secular state controls all aspects of education, crucifixes remain in classrooms and religious lessons remain in the curriculum.

Dominant religious doctrines shaped would-be state institutions even before the state was founded. Lutheran, Calvinist, and Catholic doctrine each views the source of poverty differently and sees its moral import in distinctive ways. Accordingly, each church imposed different regimes of poverty assistance in early modern Europe: integration, punitive work, and exclusion, respectively (Kahl 2005, 2014). These distinctions do not map directly onto Esping-Andersen's famous typology of welfare regimes (Esping-Andersen 1990). As a result, several outstanding puzzles in the study of the welfare state are resolved: for example, why the United States and United Kingdom hold individuals responsible for their own poverty, while Scandinavian countries and Germany view it as a social responsibility. Conversely, in several countries where traditional class- and party-based accounts of the welfare state would lead us to predict sparse provisions for women and children we see instead a strong, progressive role for the state in family policy. The underlying reason was church–state conflict in the nineteenth century, won by the secular Liberal forces of the nation-state (Morgan 2009). Again, these patterns are inexplicable without taking the interaction of doctrine and historical context into account.

The very success of these welfare regimes, however, has had an unanticipated consequence. The paradox is that welfare states have religious origins—but religious electorates are less likely to support welfare state provisions (Gill and Lundsgaarde 2004). These voters are presumably confident in religion's capacity to protect individuals from the vicissitudes of economic downturns (Scheve and Stasavage 2006; Dehejia, DeLeire, and Luttmer 2007). Religion and the welfare state thus substitute for each other in insuring individuals against adverse life events; more religious individuals will prefer lower levels of social insurance (Scheve and Stasavage 2006; Gill and Lundsgaarde 2004). Religious charities may substitute for the welfare state, leading to poor religious voters opposing the welfare state (Huber and Stanig 2009). Finally, some religious doctrines lead their adherents to emphasize hard work and individualism, creating opposition to welfare programs that decouple work and reward (Benabou and Tirole 2006). Exemplifying this recent turn in political economy, De la O and Rodden (2008) argue that religion serves to distract voters from voting in their class interests, by acting as a cross-cutting cleavage. The more the poor attend church, the more likely they are to vote *against* Left parties.[2] In short, the very success of religious denominations in facilitating the rise of welfare state regimes has led to the undermining of support for these regimes—an unanticipated (and presumably unintended) consequence that is as paradoxical as it is familiar from other historical institutionalist analyses.

European Integration

Beyond shaping domestic coalitional politics and state institutions, religious doctrine influences trans-national relations. Elements of Roman Catholic doctrinal teaching, such as subsidiarity and the universalism of humanity in Catholic doctrine, have informed the organization and development of institutions such as the European Union. Building on interwar pan-European movements, the postwar push for European integration was informed by Catholic teaching. For one thing, several of the very founders of the EU, such as Robert Schuman, Alcide de Gasperi and Konrad Adenauer, were both Christian Democrats and committed Roman Catholics (Nelsen and Guth 2003; Nelsen 2005; Kaiser 2011). Their efforts in integrating Europe were informed by a deep skepticism regarding nationalism, the need for forgiveness and reconciliation, and the need to preserve what they saw as the core of European identity: a Christian civilization (Nelsen 2005). The Christian Democratic parties that dominated the postwar political landscape in Europe stood firmly behind these integrationist plans (Thomas 2005). As Wolfram Kaiser shows, these parties formed the cross-national networks that served as exchanges of contacts, information, and ideas. Just as (or perhaps, even more) importantly—these parties and these fora provided guarantees for integrationist leaders of political support and insurance against political risk domestically (Kaiser 2011). Conversely, religious groups themselves organized in the Commission of the Bishops' Conferences of the European Community (COMECE), the Conference of Christian Churches (CEC) and the Federation of Islamic Organizations in Europe (FIOE), all of which served as reminders to EU leaders of the continued importance of religion in the European community, and that "religious actors are there and willing to be consulted" (Silvestri 2009). Churches themselves are not simply non-state actors: they are transnational agents, who form identities and shape popular preferences (Mudrov 2011).

Religious ideas further had specific policy consequences: for example, the widely held European tenet of subsidiarity—that the lowest appropriate level of secular authority, closest to the individual and to the policy problem, ought to be the key to addressing those policy needs—is a restatement of Catholic social teaching. Similarly, the principle of proportionality—that the content of a measure and its application must be in keeping with the target of the action or policy—is an application of Catholic (and subsequently more broadly Christian) notion of "just war," and how such wars may be conducted (Childress 1978). Such guiding principles of an ostensibly secular international organization have their roots in the religious thinking and doctrinal loyalties of their Catholic founders, and are inexplicable without closer attention to religious doctrine.

Religious ideas continue to resonate in today's Europe, even as they are contested and questioned by advocates of a more cosmopolitan and/ or secular order, and the widespread lack of religious participation and belonging on the popular level (Minkenberg 2009). Even as the impact of religiosity on *popular* political behavior such as voting matters only for some parties and in particular religious contexts (van der Brug, Hobolt, and de Vreese 2009), political *elites* repeatedly clash over religious identities and launch political crusades in the name of higher national and historical values. The rise of Islam in Europe, and its challenge to European identity and integration, has been a potent weapon in both domestic politics and EU debates. Not surprisingly, religious references abound in discussions of the European Union: and these references have actually increased in frequency since the 2000s (de Vreese et al. 2009). The 2002–03 controversy over the inclusion of God in the European constitution was not simply a clash of secular and religious forces—it was also a rhetorical battle over the identity of Europe itself, and the continued relevance of a Christian culture to this identity. The signatories of a prominent 2003 statement on the inclusion of Europe's Christian roots ranged from former presidents of Germany and Portugal to Hungarian and Italian Nobelists, and argued for including "the double heritage of humanist and Christian values" in the constitution (Reuters, November 14, 2003). Elsewhere, as in Poland, domestic political battles raged over the inclusion of "God" and "Christian" references in the European constitution—and while there was a critique of such "religious interventionism" by the secular Left, the trope of a historically Christian Europe was not questioned by any of the major players.

In short, religious doctrine here has infused secular organizations, guiding how policymakers would identify policy challenges, and how they would choose "appropriate" policy solutions. Religious ideas and historical interpretations also produced a communal identity of sorts—a tenuously, but nonetheless identifiably, "Christian Europe." Both the lack of popular religiosity, and the rise of Islam as a European religion, challenge this identity—but numerous domestic elites, whether politicians or philosophers, continue to uphold it.

Contemporary Patterns of Religiosity

If historical institutionalist approaches incorporating religious doctrine and history *complement* our understanding of the rise and development of European secular institutions, they also offer a compelling *alternative* to the dominant tradition in explaining patterns of religiosity. Considerable variation in both the intensity and the scope of religious practice and belief persists. Even within supposedly secular Europe, Poland is very different from the Czech Republic, and Ireland (even after the recent Church scandals) is far more religious than France, just to take the extremes of the variation. These differences beg the question of the political determinants of religiosity itself—why are some countries, groups, and individuals so much more religious (as measured by belief, observance, and belonging) than others? Many states have attempted to harness religion, to sanction some beliefs and not others, and to regulate, control, and coerce religious denominations into supporting particular political options. Such attempts took on a great variety of form and intensity, even within ostensibly same state ideology and regime type (such as the communist one-party states) (Ramet 1998).

The impact of such state attempts to control religion has led to the flowering of a "political economy of religion" (see Clark (2010) and Gill (2001) for stimulating and concise overviews). In a quest to provide the micro-foundations of religious behavior, these approaches focus on the regulatory environment: how states favor a particular religion over others, and the impact that such regulation has on religions' ability to meet consumers' preference heterogeneity. Where the religious market can freely offer diverse alternatives to heterogeneous religious beliefs and preferences, rates of religious participation and denominational affiliation increase (Finke and Stark 1992; Chaves and Cann 1992; Stark and Iannaccone 1994; Iannaccone 1998; Gill 2001; Clark 2010). Competition among religions leads to better meeting consumer "demand," and subsequently to innovation and efficiency. Religious pluralism thus breeds religious fervor. In contrast, where the state regulates religious markets (by financially or politically supporting a state religion), the levels of religious pluralism and participation decrease. Specifically, where costs of market entry are high and the state favors particular religions, religious participation drops. These differences in regulation explain why only some countries have succumbed to secularism, most notably those that extend state privileges to established religions, as in northwest Europe.[3]

Two implications follow: first, both de Tocqueville and Marx earlier noted, "it was the caesaropapist embrace of throne and altar under absolutism that perhaps more than anything else determined the decline of church religion in Europe" (Casanova 1994, 29). Second, given the heterogeneity of religious preferences, religious monopolies cannot occur "naturally," in the absence of state mandate (Gill 2001; Stark 1992).

Yet as powerful and innovative as these accounts are, they leave several persistent inconsistencies unexplained, which a more historically and institutionally grounded approach can help to resolve. First, several religious monopolies flourish without state support, while newly liberalized markets do not result in a religious upsurge. It is not the case that monopolies cannot occur "naturally" (Gill 2001). Ireland, Croatia, Lithuania, Malta, and Poland are all naturally occurring monopolies, ones that survived *despite* state efforts to undermine them. Stark and Finke (2000) then argue that conflict can act as a substitute for competition, "religious firms can generate high levels of participation to the extent that the firms serve as primary organizational vehicles for social conflict" (Stark and Finke 2000, 202). This proposition has been used to explain the high levels of observance in Catholic Poland—yet Croatia and Lithuania, both of which faced similar levels of social conflict, show lower levels of religiosity (Froese and Pfaff 2001, 490). As one scholar warns against confusing causes with consequences, "perhaps the religious monopoly just means that people have not felt the need to set up rival religious bodies" (Jenkins 2007, 50). What needs explaining, then, is the *success* of these religious monopolies, and why some are so much more successful than others.

Second, the absence of regulation, or the liberalization of religious markets, does not result in the predicted religious upsurge. This is partly because the political economy approach does not conceptually differentiate between regulation as repression and regulation as subsidy. "State regulation" is almost inevitably measured as the state *support for* a given church, but not as the *active repression* of other denominations (for an important exception, see Grim and Finke 2007). Yet if we are interested in the constraints on religious participation, the question is not of privileging one religion over others, but of *preventing* others from arising. Anti-proselytizing laws, for example, explicitly and directly constrain religious participation in ways that subsidizing a dominant religion does not. This is especially the case since state support for a given religion actually frees up potential consumers for other denominations: it makes the favored religion less popular. After all, even in countries with established churches, disaffected believers are free to move to other denominations, as in nineteenth-century England with its flourishing of nonconformist sects.[4] As a result, this account fails to explain why state support for one religion would mean that other denominations fail to attract adherents or sacralize politics.

Conversely, why does the absence of regulation not result in greater observance? The political economy of religion has difficulties in explaining the low rates of religiosity in states with no state support for a particular religion, such as France, the Czech Republic, or Estonia. In these free markets, we should see high rates of observance, if the assumptions of high and heterogenous demand for religion hold. Why do we not see religious entrepreneurs move in and the rates of religious observance go up accordingly? If the assumption of a universal and varied need for religion is true, then "the sacred should have returned ... where secularization had gone the furthest and the absence of religion created the greatest need. Accordingly, we should have witnessed religious revivals in highly secularized societies such as Sweden, England, France, Uruguay, and Russia. Yet the public resurgence of religion took place in places such as Poland, the United States, Brazil, Nicaragua, and Iran, all places which can hardly be characterized as secularized wastelands" (Casanova 1994, 224–225).

The answer given by the political economy of religion is that previous state support for a given religion prevents current conversions to other religions in a liberalized market (Iannaccone 1994). Yet this is having it both ways: if state-supported religions are so inefficient in satisfying consumer demand, how could they bind adherents so successfully? Put differently, the relationship of the political economy of religion to history—and the determinism of the past—is contradictory. On the one hand, believers are said to freely move between religions. On the other hand, actions taken in the past (i.e., state support for a religious monopoly) preclude them from doing so.

More broadly, without a clearer appreciation of doctrine (other than as a strict practice) or how it matters, the political economy literature operates within unstated and unacknowledged boundary conditions of (American) Protestantism. The political economy approach argues that reaffiliation (change within religious tradition) is much less costly and more frequent than conversion (change of religious traditions) (Stark and Finke 2000, 114). Yet this is true for American Protestants far more than for other denominations, or other religious markets. If anything, the punishments meted out to apostates and heretics in many religious traditions suggest that the closer the chosen alternative, the higher the cost paid by the convert. Indeed, assuming fungibility leads to the conclusion that markets are a "natural state"—but where products (religious or otherwise) are highly differentiated, oligopolies are a common outcome.

Finally, these explanations do not examine why some individuals and by extension, some societies, may be more or less receptive to religious mobilization and belief. Yet empirical testing of the political economy models shows that there is significant variation in the demand for religion (Montgomery 2003). And it is not the case that simple insecurity—material, economic, psychological, and political—explains why people turn to religion and why some societies are more religious than others (Norris and Inglehart 2004). This account suggests that countries undergoing massive transitions and upheavals, such as those after the collapse of communism in East Central Europe, ought to turn to religion. Yet the insecurity and uncertainty that followed the fall of (secular!) communism has not resulted in an increase in religious observance or belief *anywhere* in the post-communist region (and in fact, where we observe change, it is in the opposite direction). As with the political economy of religion, the fundamental problem with this approach is that structural conditions are held responsible for behavior—yet even when market structures or levels of security change, behavior does not.

One solution to these anomalies is to develop a richer, more nuanced account of the historical relationship of churches to the nation-state: an analysis that takes into account both critical moments where identities and loyalties can be established, and the mechanisms by which these are then sustained and reproduced over time. As noted earlier, political economy accounts view the state as a market regulator that privileges certain religions over others. Yet state repression, and the sustaining myths that it generates over time, can make national martyrs out of religious bodies—subsequently creating both powerful attachment to monopoly religions and popular resonance to their claims. We thus need a more nuanced view of the state and its roles, including both support for and oppression of religion.

More fundamentally, we cannot take for granted the "nation-state" as a coherent entity: the state may have opposed the nation-building project (as it did in colonial and communist regimes). Where the administrative state and an existing nation historically opposed each other, churches could serve as protectors of national identity against the state, as they did in Ireland or Poland. They could do so through informal education, sheltering the opposition, providing physical and spiritual space for opponents to gather, and by imbuing religious symbols (such as icons and saints' relics) with national meaning. The close alignment of religious and national identities then catalyzes religiosity, and provides resonance to subsequent political claims by religious authorities (Grzymala-Busse 2015).[5] By dint of historically siding with the nation, churches gain moral authority and religion fuses with national identity, reinforcing rather than undermining the vigor of religious monopolies. Public religiosity became a political act, and patriotism blurred with religious loyalty (Martin 1991). In short, the alliance between nation and religion matters for church vitality—and earlier hostile state regulation (as oppression) strengthens it.

Where, in contrast, churches had historically opposed national aspirations and the nation-state project, we see a very different set of outcomes in both religious behavior and religious influence on policy. The Roman Catholic Church and the papacy, for example, explicitly and vigorously battled liberal or nationalist revolutions in the Czech Lands, Italy, and France. The nation-state and the Church in these countries had a subsequently uneasy relationship: private religious beliefs coexisted with secular political identities, but the church had only a tenuous claim to moral national authority. In some countries, such as the Czech Republic or France, religious participation itself did not survive the conflict between Church and nation, turning these countries into some of the most secular in the world.

Thus, a historical analysis of the role of religion in the rise of nation-states suggests distinct logics of state and national formation. The formation of *states* tended to be a secular process, often at odds with established churches. Both states and churches attempted to create a hierarchy of control and their claims often competed. In contrast, *nation* building can be imbued with religious meaning and the active participation of religious authorities. Religion can then become a protector of the nation, closely aligning religious and national identities—and providing resonance to subsequent political claims by religious authorities.

Two mechanisms reproduce such religious nationalism, or the fusion of national and religious identities, over time and through institutional contexts. The first is repeated conflict with the secular state, as suggested earlier. For example, across East Central Europe, communism was seen as an alien and unwelcome imposition: but only in some countries did the Church and the anti-communist opposition form an alliance. The more the communist authorities tried to repress societal protest, and the more the Church stood in defense of the opposition, the more opportunities for the fusion of nation and religion. Here, education and indoctrination within the family and religious community, often in the face of considerable political repression from the state (Darden and Grzymala-Busse 2006; Wittenberg

2006) also reproduced the equation of nation with religion as part of the resistance to communist rule.

A second mechanism stems from religion's unique ability to withstand secular onslaught. Religious organizations are much harder to repress than unions, newspapers, political groups, or student organizations (Sahliyeh 1990, 13). The clergy often have little to lose: for them, the benefits of joining the anti-regime opposition are far greater than the costs of inaction, since the latter means they stand to lose their congregations (Gill 1998). This may be why the more public the protest of local clergy under communism, the greater their authority and legitimacy (Wittenberg 2006). And, if the church(es) represent the nation, rather than a specific constituency, they make secular "divide and conquer" strategies even more difficult. If a domestic national movement is under church protection, eradicating such movements means crossing over into the sphere of the sacred: a move even Stalin was reluctant to make. Thus, fusion of nation and religion is reproduced through conflict with a hostile secular actor, whether a repressive state (as in the communist cases) or a colonial power (as in Ireland).

This historical relationship between nation and religion matters for contemporary church vitality—and previous state oppression can strengthen the church's current moral claims. Religious bodies can symbolically infuse the nation with religious significance, and physically protect important national symbols and representatives. Conversely, national myths can serve to fuel religious belief and participation. A homogenous nation can more easily sustain (and be sustained by) one dominant church.

As a result, in contrast to the more narrow focus on competition alone, a historical institutionalist perspective demonstrates how and when natural monopolies not only exist—but they can flourish, if sustained by the intertwining of nationalism and religious belief. Religious participation does not drop, and churches can retain both their monopoly status and influence on politics. These monopolies have roots not in state regulation, but in the historical relationship between nation and church, and the fusion of national and religious identities, as in Poland or in Ireland (Breuilly 1983; Ramet 1998; Martin 2005). Levels of both participation and belief are high, given the church's nurturing, and the double bind of betraying the nation by leaving the religion. Conversely, where the church is perceived to have earlier opposed the nation, even the absence of regulation will not result in greater religiosity, as in the Czech Republic or France.

Movement between religions is no longer devoid of transaction costs: instead, the costs of conversion will vary directly with the degree of fusion. Apostasy or conversion can be perceived as betraying the nation: "heresy becomes a national definition of treachery" (Martin 2005, 131). National identity and community ties also mean that individuals may disagree with church teachings, and with church political activity, yet remain loyal to the faith itself. As a result, extensive objections to church political activity coexist with high religiosity. This dynamic is clearest in Catholic churches, but it is also visible in Protestant denominations (Hertzke 1988, 147). Above all, churches can now enter the political arena, and find that their claims resonate both with society, and with secular politicians. Offending religious sensibilities blurs into national treason, and politicians are anxious about offending a powerful societal actor. Secular elites fear electoral backlash and increased costs of governing that would come with church opposition, and their risk aversion is exacerbated by the informational asymmetries between elites and voters.

Finally, churches can now enter the political arena, and find that their claims resonate, so long as they live up to the standards of national protection they set out for themselves. The deep historical roots of such religious nationalism and the moral authority of the churches do not mean that they are impervious, of course. If a church's moral authority (and religious monopoly) is developed through nation-state conflict, it must be sustained through its subsequent behavior. For example, the Catholic Church lost much of its moral authority—and participation—in Ireland in the 1990s, with the revelation of the pedophilia and other abuse scandals within the Church, which belied its claim to protect the common good. The moral authority, and national identification of a church is bound up with a specific organization, the standards it sets out for itself, and how its representatives fulfill this standard (Grzymala-Busse 2015). In contrast, doctrinal legacies such as "subsidiarity" that are not embodied by specific churches or other actors are more likely to persist, because they are not as closely tied to the behavior and performance of specific actors.

Future Research

Despite the elective affinities of historical institutionalism and the study of church and state relations, the scholarship on religion and politics has not always systematically incorporated a historically sensitive perspective, as the discussion of the political economy of religion shows. Yet attention to both religious doctrine as an ideational variable and sequences and critical moments in which the historical relationship between nation, state, and religion has unfolded can help to account for not only patterns of current religiosity, but the impact of religion on institutional development and contemporary policy.

By the same token, historical institutionalist analyses, whether of state development and trasnformation, welfare systems, political cleavages, or European integration hesitate to explicitly incorporate aspects of religion, whether as doctrine or a set of historically conditioned political actors. Yet as we have seen, religious doctrine, and the sequence of historical conflict between nation, state, and religion, has the potential to profoundly shape institutional solutions, their persistence, and the factors that shape their survival.

To improve our understanding of religion and politics in Europe and beyond, we need a more deliberate and rigorous understanding of the role of the historical development of doctrine, religious participation, the relationship of the state to religious participation and religious influence—and the mechanisms that reproduced and sustained these patterns over the decades and centuries. This chapter has begun to sketch how we can address the numerous anomalies that more ahistorical perspectives have been unable to resolve: for example, by paying attention to the ways in which religious doctrine informs institutional choices, or how the historical fusion of religious and national identities sustains religious monopolies that are inexplicable from the perspective of existing explanations. The focus of the EU on subsidiarity, or the curious influence of Polish or Irish Catholic churches on policy, are among the puzzles that become tractable once we pay careful attention to ideas (in the form of religious doctrine and religious nationalism), and how religious doctrine and religious actors interact with the historical sequences of secular institutional development.

Notes

1. See the seminal works of Hall (1993), Blyth (1997), and Berman (2001).
2. What is less clear is the adjudication between the two hypothesized mechanisms: either that religious beliefs act as a *substitute* for economic preferences (for poor religious voters, the psychic benefits of religion act as a substitute for the welfare state) or that religious beliefs act as a *distraction* from economic preferences (by creating a second issue dimension that proves more compelling). Partly, this is because the observable implications of each are empirically difficult to disentangle—and partly, it is because the two are logically compatible with each other. Here, one way to potentially resolve this equivalence is to examine the historical sequence of the provision of welfare benefits, the creation of political cleavages, and voter behavior.
3. The regulation of religious markets is said to depress participation for several reasons: consumers have no control over the quantity or quality of the religious goods provided, state interests are unlikely to converge with consumer preferences, one publicly sponsored religion can never provide variety of religious choices demanded by diverse individuals, and finally, even if religious alternatives arise, individuals are already bound to the inefficient state religion (Iannaccone 1991; Chaves and Cann 1992).
4. From 1840 to 1960, sects outnumbered the official Anglican population in several regions of England (Jenkins 2007, 51).
5. In different historical circumstances, the state could arise when no coherent national identity yet exists, and religion fulfills that role: this was the case in the United States, where a broad consensus on the role of religion in American identity both unified the new nation-state and legitimated subsequent religious influence on politics.

References

Altinordu, Ates. 2010. "The Politicization of Religion: Political Catholicism and Political Islam in Comparative Perspective." *Politics and Society* 38 (4): 517–551.

Benabou, Roland and Jean Tirole. 2006 "Belief in a Just World and Redistributive Politics." *Quarterly Journal of Economics* 121 (2): 699–746.

Berman, Sheri. 2001. "Ideas, Norms, and Culture in Political Analysis." *Comparative Politics* 33 (2): 231–250.

Berman, Sheri. 2013. "Ideational Theorizing in Political Science." *Governance* 23 (6): 217–237.

Blyth, Mark. 1997. "Any More Bright Ideas? The Ideational Turn of Comparative Political Economy." *Comparative Politics* 29 (2): 229–250.

Breuilly, John. 1983. *Nationalism and the State*. Manchester: Manchester University Press.

Casanova, Jose. 1994. *Public Religions in the Modern World*. Chicago: University of Chicago Press.

Castles, Francis 1994. "On Religion and Public Policy: Does Catholicism Make a Difference?" *European Journal of Political Research* 25 (1): 19–40.

Chaves, Mark and David Cann. 1992. "Regulation, Pluralism, and Religious Market Structure." *Rationality and Society* 4 (3): 272–290.

Childress, James F. 1978. "Just-War Theories: The Bases, Interrelations, Priorities, and Functions of Their Criteria." *Theological Studies* 39: 427–445.

Clark, William Roberts. 2010. "Toward a Political Economy of Religion?" *The Political Economist* 12 (1): 2–10.

Darden, Keith and Anna Grzymala-Busse. 2006. "The Great Divide: Precommunist Schooling and Postcommunist Trajectories." *World Politics* 59 (1): 83–115.

Dehejia, Rajeev, Thomas DeLeire, and Erzo Luttmer. 2007. "Insuring Consumption and Happiness through Religious Organizations." *Journal of Public Economics* 91: 259–279.

De La O, Ana and Jonathan Rodden. 2008. "Does Religion Distract the Poor?" *Comparative Political Studies* 41 (4–5): 437–476.

de Swaan, Abram. 1988. *In Care of the State: Health Care, Education and Welfare in Europe and the USA in the Modern Era*. New York: Oxford University Press.

De Vreese, Claes, Hajo Boomgaarden, Michael Minkenberg, and Ries Vliegenthart. 2009. "Religion and the European Union." *West European Politics* 32 (6): 1182–1189.

Ertman, Thomas. 2009. "Western European Party Systems and the Religious Cleavage." In *Religion, Class Coalitions, and Welfare States*, ed. Kees Van Kersbergen and Philip Manow. Cambridge: Cambridge University Press, 39–55.

Esping-Andersen, Gøsta. 1990. *The Three Worlds of Welfare Capitalism*. Princeton, NJ: Princeton University Press.

Finke, Roger and Rodney Stark. 1992. *The Churching of America: Winners and Losers in Our Religious Economy*. New Brunswick: Rutgers University Press.

Froese, Paul and Steven Pfaff. 2001. "Replete and Desolate Markets: Poland, East Germany, and the New Religious Paradigm." *Social Forces* 80 (2): 481–507.

Gill, Anthony. 1998. *Rendering unto Caesar: The Catholic Church and the State in Latin America*. Chicago: University of Chicago Press.

Gill, Anthony. 2001. "Religion and Comparative Politics." *Annual Review of Political Science* 4: 117–138.

Gill, Anthony and Lundsgaarde, Erik. 2004. "State Welfare Spending and Religiosity: a Cross-National Analysis." *Rationality and Society* 16 (4): 399–436.

Gorski, Philip S. 2003. *The Disciplinary Revolution: Calvinism and the Rise of the State in Early Modern Europe*. Chicago: University of Chicago Press.

Gould, Andrew. 1999. *The Origins of Liberal Dominance*. Ann Arbor: University of Michigan Press.

Grim, Brian and Roger Finke. 2007. "Religious Persecution in Cross-National Context: Clashing Civilizations or Regulated Economies?" *American Sociological Review* 72: 633–658.

Grzymala-Busse, Anna. 2011. "Why There Is (Amost) No Christian Democracy in Post-Communist Europe." *Party Politics* (June 10). Available at <http://ppq.sagepub.com/content/early/2011/06/09/1354068811407596> (accessed September 1, 2015).

Grzymala-Busse, Anna. 2015. *Nations Under God: How Churches Use Moral Authority to Influence Policy*. Princeton, NJ: Princeton University Press.

Hall, Peter. 1993. "Policy Paradigms, Social Learning, and the State."*Comparative Politics* 25 (April): 275–296.

Hertzke, Allen. 1988. *Representing God in Washington: the Role of Religious Lobbies in the American Polity*. Knoxville: University of Tennessee Press.

Huber, John and Piero Stanig. 2009. "Church State Separation and Redistribution." Annual Meeting of the Association for the Scientific Study of Religion, Economics, and Culture, Arlington, VA.

Iannaccone, Laurence R. 1991. "The Consequences of Religious Market Structure: Adam Smith and the Economics of Religion." *Rationality and Society* 3 (2): 156–177.

Iannaccone, Laurence R. 1994. "Why Strict Churches Are Strong." *American Journal of Sociology* 99 (5): 1180–1121.

Iannaccone, Laurence R. 1998. "An Introduction to the Economics of Religion." *Journal of Economic Literature* 36: 1465–1496.

Jenkins, Philip. 2007. *The Next Christendom: The Rise of Global Christianity*. New York: Oxford University Press.

Johnson, James. 2002. "How Conceptual Problems Migrate: Rational Choice, Interpretation, and the Hazards of Pluralism." *Annual Review of Political Science* 5: 223–248.

Juergensmeyer, Mark. 1993. *The New Cold War? Religious Nationalism Confronts the Secular State*. Berkeley: University of California Press.

Juergensmeyer, Mark. 2008. *Global Rebellion: Religious Challenges to the Secular State*. Berkeley: University of California Press.

Kahl, Sigrun. 2005. "The Religious Roots of Modern Poverty Policy: Catholic, Lutheran, and Reformed Protestant Traditions Compared." *European Journal of Sociology* 46 (1): 91–126.

Kahl, Sigrun. 2014. "Poverty and Eternity: How Religion Shapes Assistance to the Poor, from Early Church to Modern Welfare State." Book Manuscript, Yale University.

Kaiser, Wolfram. 2011. *Christian Democracy and the Origins of the European Union*. Cambridge: Cambridge University Press.

Kalyvas, Stathis. 1996. *The Rise of Christian Democracy in Europe*. Ithaca, NY: Cornell University Press.

Kalyvas, Stathis and Kees van Kersbergen. 2010. "Christian Democracy." *Annual Review of Political Science* 13: 183–209.

Lipset, Seymour and Stein Rokkan, eds. 1967. *Party Systems and Voter Alignments: Cross National Perspectives*. New York: Free Press.

Martin, David. 1991. "The Secularization Issue: Prospect and Retrospect." *British Journal of Sociology* 42 (3): 465–474.

Martin, David. 1999. "The Evangelical Protestant Upsurge and its Political Implications." In *The Desecularization of the World*, ed. Peter Berger. Washington, D.C.: Ethics and Public Policy Center, 37–50.

Martin, David. 2005. *On Secularization: Towards a Revised General Theory*. Aldershot: Ashgate.

Minkenberg, Michael. 2009. "Religion and Euroscepticism: Cleavages, Religious Parties and Churches in EU Member States." *West European Politics* 32 (6): 1190–1211.

Montgomery, James. 2003. "A Formalization and Test of the Religious Economies Model." *American Sociological Review* 68 (5): 782–809.

Morgan, Kimberly. 2009. "The Religious Foundations of Work-Family Policies in Western Europe." In *Religion, Class Coalitions, and Welfare States*, ed. Kees van Kerbergen and Philip Manow. New York: Cambridge University Press, 56–90.

Mudrov, Sergei. 2011. "The Christian Churches as Special Participants in European Integration." *Journal of Contemporary European Research* 7 (3): 363–379.

Nelsen, Brent. 2005. "Is the European Union a Christian Club?" *An Uncertain Road: Muslims and the Future of Europe*. Report for the Pew Forum on Religion and Public Life, December 2004. Available at <http://pewforum.org/publications/reports/MuslimsinEurope2004.pdf> (accessed May 12, 2012).

Nelsen, Brent and James Guth. 2003. "Religion and Youth Support for the European Union." *Journal of Common Market Studies* 41 (1): 89–112.

Norris, Pippa and Ronald Inglehart. 2004. *Sacred and Secular: Religion and Politics Worldwide*. Cambridge: Cambridge University Press.

Philpott, Daniel. 2007. "Explaining the Political Ambivalence of Religion." *American Political Science Review* 101 (3): 505–525.

Ramet, Sabrina. 1998. *Nihil Obstat: Religion, Politics, and Social Change in East-Central Europe and Russia*. Durham, NC: Duke University Press.

Rémond, René. 1999. *Religion and Society in Modern Europe*. Oxford: Blackwell.

Rokkan, Stein. 1981. "Territories, Nations, Parties: Toward a Geoeconomic-Geopolitical Model for the Explanation of Variations within Western Europe. In *From National Development to Global Community*, ed. Richard Merritt and Bruce Russett. London: Allen and Unwin, 70–95.

Sahliyeh, Emile, ed. 1990. *Religious Resurgence and Politics in the Contemporary World*. Albany, NY: SUNY Press.

Scheve, Kenneth and John Stasavage. 2006. "Religion and Preferences for Social Insurance." *Quarterly Journal of Political Science* 1: 255–286.

Silvestri, Sara. 2009. "Islam and Religion in the EU Political System." *West European Politics* 32 (6): 1212–1239.

Stark, Rodney. 1992. "Do Catholic Societies Really Exist?" *Rationality and Society* 4 (3): 261–271.

Stark, Rodney and Roger Finke. 2000. *Acts of Faith: Explaining the Human Side of Religion*. Berkeley: University of California Press.

Stark, Rodney and Laurence R. Iannaccone. 1994. "A Supply-Side Reinterpretation of the 'Secularization' of Europe." *Journal for the Scientific Study of Religion* 33 (3): 230–252.

Thomas, Scott M. 2005. *The Global Resurgence of Religion and the Transformation of International Relations*. New York: Palgrave Macmillan.

Trejo, Guillermo. 2009. "Religious Competition and Ethnic Mobilization in Latin America: Why the Catholic Church Promotes Indigenous Movements in Mexico." *American Political Sicence Review* 103 (3): 323–342.

van der Brug, Wouter, Sara B. Hobolt, and Claes H. de Vreese. 2009. "Religion and Party Choice in Europe." *West European Politics* 32 (6): 1266–1283.

Van Kersbergen, Kees. 1994. "The Distinctiveness of Christian Democracy." In *Christian Democracy in Europe*, ed. David Hanley. London: Pinter Press, 31–47.

Van Kersbergen, Kees and Philip Manow, eds. 2009. *Religion, Class Coalitions, and Welfare States*. Cambridge: Cambridge University Press.

Warner, Carolyn. 2000. *Confessions of an Interest Group*. Princeton, NJ: Princeton University Press.

Wittenberg, Jason. 2006. *Crucibles of Political Loyalty.* Cambridge: Cambridge University Press.

Woodberry, Robert. 2011. "Religion and the Spread of Human Capital and Political Institutions." In *The Oxford Handbook of the Economics of Religion*, ed. Rachel McCleary. New York: Oxford University Press, 111–131.

Woodberry, Robert and Timothy Shah. 2004. "The Pioneering Protestants." *Journal of Democracy* 15 (2): 47–61.

CHAPTER 29

SUPRANATIONALISM

TIM BÜTHE*

POLITICAL authority is supranational if consequential decisions are made by legislative, executive, or adjudicative bodies of several countries jointly, or by a single body above the level of the nation-state. Supranationalism, then, is the *process* of creating or strengthening such authority, either de novo or by shifting authority from the national (or possibly sub-national) to the supranational level.

Supranational governance should be rare and unlikely, especially in Europe, where the modern state has literally and figuratively created a common language, and fostered or elevated founding myths that create a sense of belonging among those on whom the state bestows citizenship, as well as a sense of difference vis-à-vis non-citizens (Krasner 1988). Supranationalism therefore has long been expected to face strong emotional resistance in Europe's long-established nation-states (Hoffmann 1966). The transformation of the night watchman states of the nineteenth century into modern democratic welfare states, moreover, turned the nation-state in Europe into the focal point for public goods provision, as well as distributional and regulatory politics. Consequently, we should also expect rational-materialist resistance to supranationalism. Even when supranational governance is necessary to achieve joint gains, the difficulty of committing to a distribution of those gains, which is fair in the long run, may lead the losers from supranational governance in a particular case to fiercely resist supranationalism, recognizing a conflict over the site of governance as "a conflict over policy, once removed" (Kahler and Lake 2009, 253). And yet, supranationalism in Europe has—from long-held but unfulfilled aspirations (Kant 1984 [1795]; Rich 1996) and innovative but humble beginnings in the early postwar years (Gillingham 1991; Rittberger 2001)—become a reality. The process has been often slow and highly uneven, but has gone much further than even its champions expected at the outset (Milward, Brennan, and Romero 2000).

What can historical institutionalism contribute to explaining supranationalism in Europe? A supranationalist research program should seek to explain the variation in the degree of supranationalism across issue areas and across executive, legislative, and judicial functions, including the variable degree to which European Union (EU) decision-making is supranational and the increasing range of issues governed supranationally.

To be compelling, an account of what Leuffen, Rittberger, and Schimmelfennig (2013) call "differentiated integration" also should allow us to explain this institutional development over time, including the uneven pace of European integration, with its overall monotonic institutional development toward more supranational governance—in fits and starts but without real setbacks.

A discussion of all of these aspects of supranationalism in Europe, to discern and assess what historical institutionalism has contributed to explaining the various facets of supranationalism, is impossible within the constraints of a short handbook entry. Instead, the chapter begins with a sketch of an agent-centric historical institutionalism, developed to achieve most of the explanatory tasks specified above in a way that is highly contextualized but not post hoc. Since previous work has shown the analytical power of this approach for explaining the creation of supranational executive authority (Büthe 2007, 2016a, 2016b), the remainder of this brief chapter illustrates the usefulness of agent-centric historical institutionalism for explaining legislative and judicial authority.

Historical Institutionalism

Thelen and Steinmo originally identified historical institutionalism (HI) as an approach by isolating the distinctive characteristics of then-recent institutionalist research in Political Science by scholars who were rejecting key assumptions of both rational choice institutionalism and sociological institutionalism, such as Ruth and David Collier, Peter Hall, Peter Katzenstein, Stephen Krasner, and Stephen Skowronek. Numerous recent works, discussed more fully in the Introduction to this volume, have sought to clarify, elaborate, and refine the core elements of HI, including the analytical leverage it provides for the study of European integration (Bulmer 2009; Meunier and McNamara 2007). Even after these refinements, historical institutionalism is a broad analytical approach, encompassing a variety of theories with diverse explanatory foci. What historical institutionalists have in common, in my reading, is a motivating interest in how institutions shape politics and policy—in specific cases as well as at a high level of abstraction—based on a broad notion of institutions and three core heuristic assumptions.

First, historical institutionalists assume that preferences, especially second-order preferences over policy or institutional arrangements, are malleable (and indeed likely to change over time) rather than being fixed. This implies that we need theoretical models that explicitly specify temporal context and sequences, and studies that examine institutional development as a process over a substantial span of time instead of treating history as a pool of independent, timeless observations (Büthe 2002; Farrell and Newman 2010; Thelen 1999).

Second, while institutions generally reflect the distribution of power at the time of their creation, they do not remain tightly linked to the distribution of power. Institutional equilibria are neither quickly nor efficiently established or adjusted, because institutions often have unintended and indeed unanticipated "feedback" effects. Due to such feedback effects, institutions have an independent causal effect—empowering and/or constraining political actors and thus shaping policy and outcomes. Prior institutional choices not only change how political actors pursue their goals, but also change interests or possibly even constitute new actors. These feedbacks allow historical institutionalist scholars to provide endogenous explanations of institutional development over time.

Third, historical institutionalists see any particular rule or organization as part of a broader institutional "configuration" (Pierson and Skocpol 2002).[1] Recognizing this embeddedness of each institution in a larger institutional context reinforces the expectation that institutions change according to a different logic than the distribution of power and suggests that analyzing a particular institution in isolation will lead to bias. The composition of the European Parliament (EP), for instance, which today affects not only EU policies across a broad range of issues but also the choice of Commission President, reflects the distribution of preferences in the electorates of the member states, but only at the time of the election and as deflected by voting rules. It does not incrementally change with shifts in popular or even electoral majorities in the member states until the next election. And anyone who wants to change the rules that give the EP influence over EU policy and personnel needs to do more than "just" bring about a change in political majorities in the EP.

Agent-Centric Historical Institutionalism as an Explanation of Supranationalism

Traditionally, historical institutionalist scholars have emphasized self-reinforcing feedback mechanisms and change-resistant elements of the broader institutional context, resulting in path-dependent institutional development, including in explicitly historical institutionalist accounts of European integration (see, e.g., Pierson 1996, 123, 140–144). Learning, for instance, how to lobby decision-makers effectively—or how to avoid detection of rule violations in a particular institutional environment—increases over time the benefit one experiences from those institutions. Such "positive" feedback from institutions to the interests and strategies of policymakers and socioeconomic actors increases the "returns" to these stakeholders and consequently should strengthen their commitment to those institutions and increase institutional stability. Emphasizing self-reinforcing feedback and change-resistant elements of the broader institutional context, such as requirements for large super-majorities to change the fundamental rules of the political game, has allowed historical institutionalists to provide powerful endogenous explanations of institutional stability or persistence, even when the conditions that led to the initial creation of those institutions no longer hold (e.g., Büthe and Mattli 2011; Ertman 1997; Hall and Soskice 2001; Spruyt 1994).

Different kinds of institutional development, however, are hard to explain by reference to self-reinforcing feedback. Recent scholarship has sought to address this weakness by exploring endogenous processes such as self-undermining feedback, which over time weakens the commitment to the institutional status quo and hence facilitates institutional change. Some have also noted that the broader context of any particular institution may in principle facilitate change as easily as impede it; it depends upon the particular institutional context. Especially noteworthy in this newer literature is the typology of gradual institutional change developed by Kathleen Thelen with Wolfgang Streeck and James Mahoney. The change processes identified by their typology should resonate well with scholars of the history of the EU, which contains many examples of, for instance, "conversion"—defined as reinterpreting nominally unchanged rules, altering their meaning and effect by "redirect[ing them] to new goals, functions, or purposes" (Streeck and Thelen 2005, 26). At the same time, supranationalism, as defined above, does not readily fit into their typology of institutional change, and the typology only identifies permissive conditions, rather than provide a fully developed explanation of institutional change.

What these newer attempts to explain institutional change show clearly, however, is that institutional change requires agency, which is barely visible for instance in Pierson's pioneering historical institutionalist analysis of European integration (1996). To address this issue, Büthe (2016a), building upon Mayntz and Scharpf (1995), proposes "agent-centric historical institutionalism" as an historical institutionalism theory of institutional change.

An agent-centric historical institutionalist analysis requires the analyst to identify the key stakeholders and determine the interests that such potential actors are likely to pursue, then theorize how those actors, their interests, and the way in which they pursue those interests will be affected by the opportunities and constraints of the broader institutional configuration and by institutional feedback. To avoid explaining supranationalist institutional development by simply assuming preferences for supranationalism, actors' initial core interests are assumed to be the interests conventionally attributed to all composite actors (Mayntz and Scharpf 1995, 54): self-preservation (survival or physical well-being), power (or freedom), and plenty (possession of at least basic resources and a general preference for more over less). Actors are also assumed (at any given moment) to pursue their interests strategically. This conventional assumption about first-order preferences is qualified by historical institutionalism's core insight that institutions—over time—can reshape interests or even constitute new actors. What having these interests means for second-order preferences over institutions should therefore depend greatly on how actors are constituted and on the institutional context in which they operate.

Change Agents

1. Research on public and private bureaucracies from Michels (1989 [1915]) to Carpenter (2001) suggests that the institutional position of *the supranational bodies of the EU*—the Court of Justice (ECJ), the European Commission, and in more recent decades the European Parliament—transforms their core interests of self-preservation, power, and plenty into a preference for doing more interesting and more substantively important work and hence influence (e.g., Pollack 1994). This should make them strong supporters of supranationalism.[2]

The broader institutional configuration of the EU, in which the supranational bodies are embedded, provides them with both formal and informal opportunities to pursue those second-order preferences for supranationalist institutional development. At the same time, the broader institutional configuration also constrains the supranational bodies. The Commission, for example, has agenda-setting power vis-à-vis the Council, i.e., the representatives of the member state governments acting jointly, but its proposals for institutional change need approval from the member states to proceed. Proposals that overtly, formally shift power to the supranational level should run up against the member states' fundamental interest in safeguarding their autonomy (see below) and therefore be unlikely to succeed.

The supranational bodies also have informal or "covert" (Héritier 2001) means of seeking institutional change, which range from fostering ideas and social conventions that, over time, encourage decision-making at the EU level (e.g., Jabko 2006) to the outright "creation" of pro-integration actors, for instance by providing start-up assistance to EU-level industry or professional associations. As Posner (2005, 22) warns, however, these informal methods may be well suited to "trigger[ing] change" but not to controlling the outcome "once an issue migrates to the public arena and draws additional powerful actors into the fray." We therefore need to carefully analyze other actors even in cases when supranational actors are the initial drivers of change.

2. The *member states* are the original Parties to the founding treaties of the EU, and the broader institutional configuration of the EU gives them wide latitude to be agents of institutional change—if they agree. It also gives them numerous ways to veto or constrain institutional change.

For member state governments, the most important institutional context that shapes how their core interests of self-preservation, power, and plenty translate into second-order preferences regarding supranationalism, is likely to remain national-level democratic politics. Each government's focus on winning the next election should give it a strong *ex ante* preference for preserving its policy autonomy and lead to support for supranationalism only if such a change is in the interest of its domestic constituents and electorally salient.[3] Even then, actual institutional change is constrained by the distribution of preferences and power among the member states, *given the broader institutional context*, that is, EU decision rules, which for major changes require unanimous support. An agent-centric historical institutionalist approach thus leads to the expectation that member state-driven supranationalism will only happen under very restrictive conditions.

3. Recent research has put *public officials who hold specialized positions within their respective countries*—and hence may have divergent interests from their countries' governments—back on the agenda of international relations research. For such public officials, career incentives, professional norms, and ideological commitments often reinforce each other to make achieving the stated objectives of their agencies, such as consumer or environmental protection, a core interest (Carpenter 2001; Coen and Thatcher 2005). As a consequence, they should support supranationalism if (and only if) the expected gains for achieving those objectives, given interdependence, outweigh the loss in autonomy (Farrell 2003; Simmons 2001).

The institutional context of the EU can reshape these actors and their interests over time in two ways. First, European integration was intended from the start to increase economic interdependence, which should increase over time the expected gains from supranationalism, as separate regulatory policies become less efficient and possibly even ineffective. Moreover, public officials with specialized expertise can at times of high uncertainty even strategically "create" negative externalities for otherwise resistant member states and thus create political support for supranational governance (Newman 2008, 119f, 124f). Second, if policymakers take up a new policy issue at the European-level first, national-level agencies are often created to implement the new policies or design complementary policies at the national level after supranational policymaking has begun. For such agencies, regional trans-governmental collaboration is part of their bureaucratic culture from the start, which should reduce the perceived costs of supranationalism. The creation of the Franco-German brigade and later the Euro-Corps, for instance, was explicitly intended to habitualize trans-governmental collaboration among mid-level military officers.

4. *Sub- and transnational private actors* are ignored in much of the literature but are potent change agents in an institutional context that empowers them. Situating such actors in EU-induced processes of increasing interdependence, moreover, yields theoretical expectations about the conditions under which private actors are most likely to become agents of institutional change: The institutionalization of *economic* interdependence through the EU common market project, for instance, turned firms in any one member state into stakeholders of regulatory policies in the other EU member states (see also Stone Sweet and Sandholtz 1998,

esp. 11f). EU policies that increase or intensify interdependence thus feed back to change the cast of characters and reshape their interests.

For many private actors, change in their own countries' policies will not (or only poorly) address their concerns; others will not be able to achieve such change at all, given the distribution of preferences and power in domestic politics. For all of these actors, the EU, with its various administrative and legal procedures, offers a plethora of "political opportunity structures" (Kitschelt 1986), even if those procedures may not have been intended for any such use. The importance of this broader institutional configuration goes far beyond the economic realm. The preamble and scattered articles of the Treaty of Rome, for instance, articulate numerous lofty principles, such as a commitment to reducing regional difference in economic development or gender equality. While most of these commitments appear to have been little more than declamatory politics in 1957, they were embedded in the broader institutional context of the incipient EU. This broader institutional structure, most prominently the quasi-constitutional court, has on numerous occasions enabled private citizens to make those commitments actionable vis-à-vis their own governments and even vis-à-vis other private parties by shifting governance to the supranational level *without prior negotiations or agreement among the member states* (e.g., Caporaso and Jupille 2001).

In other words, the EU allows sub-national private actors to pursue their interests through inter- or supranational rather than (only) domestic political institutions. It provides an opportunity to achieve with a different political coalition at the European level what they may be politically too weak to achieve at the domestic level. Even though most private actors might otherwise be indifferent about the locus of policymaking, their preferences concerning specific policies provide them in this context with second-order institutional preferences for, or against, supranationalism. *When* specific private actors will act on those preferences—with regard to specific rights or obligations and with enough force to bring about institutional change—might be hard to predict. Yet, insofar as the institutional context favors a shift of authority to the supranational level (see the section entitled Support and Opposition over Time, below), the argument yields a clear prediction about the direction of change.

Support and Opposition over Time

The actor-centric historical institutionalist logic of institutional development explored here implies that the creation of supranational authority is never automatic but arises out of political conflict—although those who seek supranational governance may attempt to minimize opposition by framing it as apolitical: presenting supranationalism as the most efficient solution to an economic or technical, administrative problem rather than a change in political institutions and the distribution of power. Such conflict implies that there will be both proponents and opponents of any institutional change. Opponents, however, are unlikely to form lasting coalitions: Opposition to governance beyond the nation-state provides a poor normative foundation for establishing lasting transnational political coalitions, so opposing coalitions are likely to dissolve once the particular common interest-generating issue has passed. Opponents also lack the political opportunity structures, in the broader institutional context of the EU, to translate demands for less supranational governance into actual institutional change even if the specific coalition underpinning such a demand at a particular moment in time does not last. By contrast, proponents of supranational governance may well form lasting coalitions, although the formation and persistence of political coalitions is never automatic.

Importantly, member state governments' ability to reverse supranationalist institutional changes that they do not like is constrained by the broader institutional configuration in which they operate. First, if a shift of authority to the supranational level has at least some domestic political support, democratic governments may find it harder to re-nationalize such authority than not to grant it. Second and most importantly, once a supranationalist institutional change has occurred, institutional retrenchment to the *status quo ante* via intergovernmental bargaining would require a supermajority or even unanimity. A blocking minority of member governments can therefore ensure the persistence of the new status quo even if they could not have brought it about through an intergovernmental bargain (see also Scharpf 1985). As a consequence, change toward more supranationalism should be more likely than the opposite, and an increase in supranational authority should be the trend, even though there might be periods of stalemate and conceivably even reversals.

Explaining Supranationalism for EU Law and Court(s)

The creation and strengthening of unambiguously supranational authority at the EU level occurred earliest for EU law and the European Court of Justice (ECJ). The 1957 Treaty of Rome did not explicitly create any rights and obligations for natural or legal persons, and subsequent conflicting domestic laws would in most member states have superseded any provisions in the Treaty of Rome (Weiler 1991, 2412). Within seven years, however, the ECJ put forth (a) the doctrine of direct effect in its 1963 *van Gend en Loos* decision, according to which at least some parts of the Treaty created rights and obligations for individuals and legal persons such as firms, without a need for implementing legislation at the domestic level, and (b) the doctrine of supremacy-of-EU-law in its 1964 *Costa v. ENEL* decision, according to which even subsequent domestic law cannot abrogate any rights and obligations that arise from the Treaty. In a series of decisions over the following years, the ECJ extended direct effect to an ever broader range of issues, and its views of the relationship between European and domestic law (and the

ECJ's role as a quasi-constitutional court) became mostly accepted by governments and domestic courts alike.

What needs to be explained here is, above all, what Weiler (1991) called the "constitutionalization" of the EU, the process by which the 1957 Treaty—a document recording an elaborate but otherwise seemingly unexceptional agreement between six European states—was given supranational constitutional status, with the ECJ as the supranational arbiter over its correct interpretation. What also needs to be explained is how the supremacy of EU law over the domestic law of the member states was extended to an ever broader range of issues (Burley and Mattli 1993, 43).

Agent-centric historical institutionalist theory would explain how and why these changes occurred by specifying the preferences of proponents and opponents of supranationalism and identifying how the broader institutional context empowers some actors vis-à-vis others—and how that context enables and constrains institutional development. The empirical literature strongly supports this agent-centric historical institutionalist approach:[4] Existing accounts of European legal integration are compelling precisely because, or to the extent that, they identify the key actors and specify how feedback effects and the broader institutional context endogenously (re)shaped preferences and opportunities to make these actors agents of supranationalism.

The ECJ's main task, as envisioned in the Treaty, was to serve as a dispute settlement mechanism to foster member states' compliance with their obligations vis-à-vis each other (Burley and Mattli 1993, 58). The other key objective in setting up the ECJ was to provide a safeguard against overreach by the Commission and possibly the Council. As Alter (1998, 124, 126) notes, neither of these tasks created a functional need for supremacy or direct effect of EU law, but it required granting the ECJ some power to interpret the meaning of the Treaty so as to allow it to solve the incomplete contracting problem that is an inherent feature of even the most formal, legal agreements (Shapiro 1981; Farrell and Héritier 2007). Specifically, Article 177 assigns the ECJ the task of interpreting the Treaty when a court or tribunal of a member state requests such an interpretation in the form of a "preliminary ruling."[5]

In its preliminary rulings, the ECJ has been deliberate and at times cautious but quite consistent in its support of an expansive, supranationalist reading of the Treaty (e.g., Alter 1998, 130f), consistent with the theoretical framework above.[6] At the same time, European legal integration illustrates the importance of the larger institutional configuration: Even though the ECJ's independence and status give it considerable leeway to advance institutional change, it cannot bring about change on its own, since it does not have agenda-setting power. It can only pass judgment on the cases others bring before it: Article 177-based opportunities for the ECJ to advance its interests through supranationalism arise only if private parties are unable to resolve a conflict of interest through compromise—and if at least one of them invokes European law in an appeal to a third party (the domestic court) whose decision will make one party a winner and the other a loser (see also Alter 2001, 52f). That third party is the domestic court, which then may refer questions concerning European law to the ECJ.[7]

This raises the question under which conditions we should expect domestic courts to provide the ECJ with such opportunities to (re)interpret the status of European law—and under which conditions we would expect opponents to succeed in blocking or undoing such developments. The question has been examined at some length for the lower-level domestic courts, which have been the source of the vast majority of Article 177 references (Golub 1996; Stone Sweet and Brunell 1998). Weiler (1991, 2426), Burley and Mattli (1993), and Alter (1996) all emphasize "judicial empowerment" as the key reason: By invoking EU law as the basis for their decisions, lower court judges can minimize their vulnerability to being overturned on appeal, increasing their autonomy within the national judicial hierarchy, though at the cost of giving up some autonomy vis-à-vis the ECJ.

If this reasoning is correct, then we should expect Article 177 references only if there is uncertainty about how EU law applies in the case at hand and the lower court judge is confident that the ECJ's preliminary ruling will allow him/her to reach the desired conclusion. A judge's expectations of how the ECJ will rule are naturally difficult to discern ex post, but the empirical record is at least consistent with this logic insofar as the cases sent to the ECJ for a preliminary ruling clearly constitute only a fraction of domestic court cases in which EU law is invoked. Also consistent with this reasoning is the record of unease, hesitation, and outright opposition from the positional losers—member states' higher courts and governments—to lower courts' use of Article 177 (e.g., Alter 2001, 21–25, 37f, 58–63). Attempts to sanction the lower-level national courts or the ECJ for judicial activism, however, all failed whenever the lower courts pushed back, because it proved ultimately impossible for governments, national legislatures, and higher courts to challenge the ability of lower courts to interpret the law (and the Treaty) with the assistance of the ECJ, without calling into question the very principles of rule of law and judicial independence that ostensibly motivated the opposition.

The decision whether or not to make a claim based on European law is of course usually made by the litigants. While the ECJ ("the Court") clearly sought to foster the practice (Mancini 1989, 605f), litigants appear to have done so (or refrained from or opposed it) only when doing so promised to help them achieve their particularistic, often commercial interests (Alter 2001, 3, 52f; Büthe 2016b; Mattli and Slaughter 1998, 186–190), not out of an ideological commitment or opposition to supranationalism. The pattern of cases that advanced legal integration therefore seems idiosyncratic, but it is entirely consistent with an agent-centric historical institutionalist approach. And it was the irregular stream of such cases that allowed the ECJ to advance supranationalism without any change in the Treaty and while most member state governments—especially of the largest, most powerful ones—clearly opposed specific changes such as direct effect, as well as the broader trend toward the supranationalism of EU law and Court.

Why then did the member states not put a stop to it, if necessary by revising the Treaty to restrict the Court's ability to advance supranationalism? While amending the treaties is in principle always possible, it is "the nuclear option" (Pollack 1997, 118f), since it would risk unraveling the carefully negotiated compromise of which the provisions concerning law and Court are only one part. And given preference heterogeneity among the member states, the status quo ante would likely be unattainable through intergovernmental agreement.

Explaining Legislative Supranationalism

The above account of EU legal integration provides, inter alia, an explanation for how European law came to acquire authority over national law. But it does not follow that law-*making* needed to become more supranational in the process or as a consequence. And although the Treaty of Rome already envisioned majoritarian adoption of secondary legislation in the Council, legislative supranationalism has generally, though variably, lagged behind legal integration. The key institutional developments here are the European Parliament's "remarkable journey from talking-shop to [real legislative] powerhouse" (Rittberger 2005, 3) and the shift toward actual majoritarian decision-making on EU secondary legislation in the Council.[8] Given space constraints, I will focus on the former.

"The Assembly," as the European Parliament was originally known, has existed since the beginning of the European Coal and Steel Community (ECSC). Rittberger (2005, esp. 94–107) attributes its creation to the desire to make the new High Authority (the predecessor of the Commission) accountable in a way that would ensure democratic legitimacy, without undermining the innovation of a supranational executive. Consistent with this interpretation, the Assembly was given oversight powers over the High Authority, including the right to launch inquiries that the High Authority was required to answer promptly, and even the right to censure, but it was given neither legislative nor budgetary authority.

The European Economic Comunity largely followed the blueprint of the ECSC, with the Assembly still envisioned primarily as a check on the executive power of the Commission. The Treaty of Rome, however, also assigned an advisory legislative function to the Assembly—which renamed itself the "European Parliament" (EP) in 1962. Specifically, the treaty reserved for the member states, acting jointly in the Council, the right to adopt secondary legislation after "consulting" the EP. What such consultations would entail—and whether the EP would use its Art.141-based majoritarian procedures to provide its advice—was not specified in the treaty. Such vagueness or ambiguity provided opportunities for an expansive interpretation later, but for the first two decades, the EP was generally understood as having no power over EU legislation (nor the process of European integration) beyond whatever the rhetorical brilliance of its more articulate members might achieve. Beginning in the late 1970s, however, the EP began to acquire substantially greater legislative authority in a series of (often individually small) supranationalist institutional changes. As a consequence, today's EP with its 751 directly elected members, sitting (and generally voting) by political party group rather than by nationality, is a largely equal and clearly supranational second chamber in what is now the bicameral EU legislative branch.

From Consultation to Cooperation to the New Normal of Co-Decision

The EP's supranational legislative powers have arisen out of inter-institutional conflict, with an important role for endogenous change of preferences. Key developments here are the introduction of the so-called cooperation procedure for adopting EU Regulations and Directives in the Single European Act (SEA) of 1985 and of the co-decision procedure (now known as the "ordinary legislative procedure") in the Maastricht and Amsterdam Treaties of 1992 and 1999.

Prior to the SEA, the legislative function of the EP under the consultation procedure was no more than advisory, earning the EP the "talking shop" label. The cooperation procedure constituted a major advance in legislative supranationalism because it allowed the EP to amend proposed legislation related to the single market by majority voting. This right to amend was powerful because, amendments that gained the backing of the Commission required no more than qualified majority support in the Council to take effect, whereas their rejection required unanimity in the Council. It gave the EP what Tsebelis (1994) calls "conditional agenda-setting" power. And the empirical literature, initially characterized by skepticisms, by now had clearly shown "that the EP was able to exercise [under this new procedure] considerable influence on the substance of important pieces of Community legislation" (Rittberger 2005, 143f). The introduction of co-decision in the Maastricht Treaty was a further advance in legislative supranationalism since co-decision entails a conciliation process, if the Council does not accept the Parliament's amendments. It also includes an opportunity for the EP to veto any final text by the Council. It thus brings EU law-making (when co-decision applies) more fully in line with standard procedures in bicameral legislatures—even if the gain in EP influence may be limited to cases where EP and Commission disagree (Tsebelis et al. 2001).

Several member states long opposed an increased legislative role for the EP. Occasional calls by the EP for greater equality between EP and Council in European law-making therefore went nowhere, just as most Commission proposals for institutional reforms that would have strengthened the supranational executive. How, then, did legislative supranationalism nonetheless come about when it did? Rittberger (2005, esp. 143ff.) provides a compelling historical institutionalist account: Member state governments, urgently seeking efficiency and welfare gains (an electorally highly salient benefit), decided in the SEA and the Maastricht Treaty to pool sovereignty through majority voting in the Council for an increased range of issues and to delegate sovereignty by increasing the regulatory authority of the Commission. However, these changes, Rittberger notes, created the widespread perception of a new and growing "legitimacy deficit."[9] Giving the EP greater legislative powers allowed them to address this largely domestic but shared, new political problem. Yet, why did the member states consider it necessary to actually address this legitimacy deficit when the low electoral salience of the closely related "democratic deficit" of the EU had at other times been insufficient to motivate institutional changes (Hix 2002, 267)—and how did they come to see increasing the power of the Parliament as the most desirable way to address it?

The literature on European legislative supranationalism suggests that the actors emphasized by agent-centric historical institutionalism here, too, have been the key agents of change. Treaty-based institutional reform should not be a hospitable terrain for sub- and transnational private actors since the institutional context of the EU provides no opportunities for them to exercise any direct influence. However, private actors, especially from within the business community, exercised substantial indirect influence. Their self-interested calls for achieving the long-promised common market were crucial in prompting European political leaders to seek greater economic growth and competitiveness through further economic integration (Sandholtz and Zysman 1989). It was ultimately private actors who turned even virulent anti-EU-federalists such as Britain's Lady Thatcher into cheerleaders for greater supranationalism: Since achieving the extensive requisite changes in EU secondary legislation was clearly impossible by unanimity rule, the private sector's clamoring for the Common Market endogenously changed the domestic political costs and benefits of supranationalism and consequently member states' institutional preferences. Yet, since such simultaneous domestic political demands (and promise of electoral rewards) existed only for the Common Market, the shift to qualified majority voting was limited to issues directly related to the Common Market program. Accordingly, the demands to give a more prominent legislative role to the EP in order not to exacerbate the legitimacy deficit—which might also have been made by some private actors but were articulated above all by national parliaments (e.g., Corbett 1998, esp. 185–194)—also arose only for an important but narrow slice of EU law, lowering the perceived cost of the change.

The change nonetheless gave the EP leverage, which it used not just to influence the content of legislation but also to advance its own cause vis-à-vis the Council. This dynamic of inter-institutional conflict is well documented, for instance in Hix's study of the shift from the Co-Decision I Procedure to the Co-Decision II Procedure (2002, esp. 273–279): The EP engaged in a unilateral supranationalist reinterpretation of Co-Decision I, as well as strategic changes to its own Rules of Procedure to ensure the rejection of Council legislative proposals that would have brought improvements over the legislative status quo but would have continued the hierarchy of the Council over the EP in legislative matters. Through these actions, the EP brought about de facto changes in legislative procedures that put it fully on par with the Council. The Co-Decision II procedure in the Amsterdam Treaty, which created full procedural equality between Council and EP, then merely codified institutional changes that had in practice already occurred. Subsequent changes extended the applicability of co-decision to various issue areas previously excluded from its operation, now under the label "ordinary legislative procedure," which suggests further acceptance of the changes by the member state governments.

Conclusion

Historical institutionalism, Simon Bulmer wrote in his 2009 review of the contributions of historical institutionalism to understanding the "longer-term dynamics" of the EU, "has untapped potential to shed new light on the integration process" (2009, 311). The biggest challenge in reaching that untapped potential is how to overcome the weaknesses of historical institutionalism without sacrificing its strengths, most importantly its ability to provide carefully contextualized explanations of institutional development and of endogenous changes in preferences. It has often been claimed that historical institutionalism lacks the ability to make ex ante predictions. This perceived weakness has prompted many scholars to question whether it warrants the status of a theoretical approach or tradition at all. A more explicitly agent-centric historical institutionalism promises to allow historical institutionalist scholars to derive stronger ex ante predictions while honing the strength of the historical institutionalist tradition. Büthe (2016a, 2016b) has demonstrated the promise of an agent-centric historical institutionalism by using it to explain the development of the Commission's supranational authority in competition policy. Drawing on existing analyses but re-telling their accounts in more explicitly agent-centric historical institutionalist terms, this chapter suggests that this approach similarly renders a more complete and analytically powerful account of supranationalism in the EU's law, court(s), and legislative process.

Notes

* For fruitful discussions and feedback on earlier drafts of this chapter, I thank Karen Alter, Orfeo Fioretos, William Phelan, Berthold Rittberger, and participants of the mini-symposium on historical institutionalism at the Council for European Studies 2013 Conference in Amsterdam, none of whom of course bears any responsibility for flaws and omissions.

1. This assumption is often not made explicit but in my reading is a core assumption of historical institutionalism.
2. European integration may thus endogenously shape second-order preferences. Note that identity and loyalty may act as constraints on EU civil servants' desire for a supranational EU, see Hooghe (2005).
3. The appearance of supranationalism might also be attractive as it allows them to shift blame for unpopular or failed policies without giving up autonomy.
4. This section draws on the work of Alter, who was the first to explicitly invoke the historical institutionalist tradition (2001)—primarily, as she explains in later work, out of dissatisfaction with neofunctionalism (2009, 12–14)—but I also draw on the neofunctionalist analysis of Burley and Mattli (1993) and Mattli and Slaughter (1995) and the Haas-inspired analyses of European legal integration by Stone Sweet (2004), Stone Sweet and Brunell (1998) and Stone Sweet and Caporaso (1998), and Stone Sweet and Sandholtz (1998), which I see as essentially historical-institutionalist analyses.

5. Other provisions may also be read as giving the ECJ authority to interpret the Treaty, but only implicitly.
6. Phelan (2014) argues that the Court's primary goal in those early years was actually not supranationalism per se but safeguarding against GATT/WTO-style decentralized and hence often chaotic and ineffective enforcement. Even in that account, however, the Court chose supranationalism as the way to achieve this objective.
7. The final sentence of Art.177 makes asking for a preliminary ruling mandatory for each member state's highest court if the question reaches a court at that level; for lower courts, it is a discretionary decision of the judge/tribunal.
8. "Secondary" EU law is law beyond the founding treaties and their revisions. It primarily refers to unilateral acts, such as regulations, directives, and decisions.
9. The "deficit" arises from the lack of intrinsic "procedural" legitimacy for executive-branch supranational decision-making rules and procedures without corresponding changes on the parliamentary/legislative side to ensure the democratic accountability of supranational governance.

References

Alter, Karen J. 1996. "The European Court's Political Power." *West European Politics* 19 (3): 458–487.

Alter, Karen J. 1998. "Who Are the Masters of the Treaty?" *International Organization* 52 (1): 125–152.

Alter, Karen J. 2001. *Establishing the Supremacy of European Law*. New York: Oxford University Press.

Alter, Karen J., ed. 2009. *The European Court's Political Power: Selected Essays*. New York: Oxford University Press.

Bulmer, Simon J. 2009. "Politics in Time Meets the Politics of Time: Historical Institutionalism and the EU Timescape." *Journal of European Public Policy* 16 (2): 307–324.

Burley, Anne-Marie and Walter Mattli. 1993. "Europe Before the Court: A Political Theory of Legal Integration." *International Organization* 47 (1): 41–76.

Büthe, Tim. 2002. "Taking Temporality Seriously: Modeling History and the Use of Narratives as Evidence." *American Political Science Review* 96 (3): 481–494.

Büthe, Tim. 2007. "The Politics of Competition and Institutional Change in the European Union: The First Fifty Years." In *Making History: European Integration and Institutional Change at Fifty*, ed. Sophie Meunier and Kathleen McNamara. Oxford: Oxford University Press, 175–193.

Büthe, Tim. 2016a. "Agent-Centric Historical Institutionalism as a Theory of Institutional Change: The Politics of Regulating Competition and Mergers in the European Union, 1955–2010." *International Organization* (forthcoming).

Büthe, Tim. 2016b. "Historical Institutionalism and Institutional Development in the EU: The Development of Supranational Authority over Government Subsidies (State Aid)." In *Historical Institutionalism and International Relations: Explaining Institutional Development in World Politics*, ed. Thomas Rixen, Lora A. Viola, and Michael Zürn. Oxford: Oxford University Press, forthcoming.

Büthe, Tim and Walter Mattli. 2011. *The New Global Rulers: The Privatization of Regulation in the World Economy*. Princeton, NJ: Princeton University Press.

Caporaso, James A. and Joseph Jupille. 2001. "The Europeanization of Gender Equality and Domestic Structural Change." In *Transforming Europe*, ed. Maria Green Cowles, James A. Caporaso, and Thomas Risse. Ithaca, NY: Cornell University Press, 21–43.
Carpenter, Daniel P. 2001. *The Forging of Bureaucratic Autonomy*. Princeton, NJ: Princeton University Press.
Coen, David and Mark Thatcher. 2005. "The New Governance of Markets and Non-Majoritarian Regulators." *Governance* 18 (3): 329–346.
Corbett, Richard. 1998. *The European Parliament's Role in Closer EU Integration*. New York: St. Martin's Press.
Ertman, Thomas. 1997. *Birth of the Leviathan*. New York: Cambridge University Press.
Farrell, Henry. 2003. "Constructing the International Foundations of E-Commerce." *International Organization* 57 (2): 277–306.
Farrell, Henry and Adrienne Héritier. 2007. "Introduction: Contested Competences in the European Union." *West European Politics* 30 (2): 227–243.
Farrell, Henry and Abraham L. Newman. 2010. "Making Global Markets: Historical Institutionalism in International Political Economy." *Review of International Political Economy* 17 (4): 609–638.
Gillingham, John R. 1991. *Coal, Steel, and the Rebirth of Europe, 1945–1955*. New York: Cambridge University Press.
Golub, Jonathan. 1996. "The Politics of Judicial Discretion." *West European Politics* 19 (2): 360–385.
Hall, Peter A. and David Soskice, eds. 2001. *Varieties of Capitalism*. New York: Oxford University Press.
Héritier, Adrienne. 2001. "Overt and Covert Institutionalization in Europe." In *The Institutionalization of Europe*, ed. Alec Stone Sweet, Wayne Sandholtz, and Neil Fligstein. New York: Oxford University Press, 56–70.
Hix, Simon. 2002. "Constitutional Agenda-Setting Through Discretion in Rule Interpretation." *British Journal of Political Science* 32 (2): 259–280.
Hoffmann, Stanley. 1966. "Obstinate or Obsolete?" *Daedalus* 95 (3): 862–915.
Hooghe, Liesbet. 2005. "Several Roads Lead to International Norms, But Few Via International Socialization: A Case Study of the European Commission." *International Organization* 59 (4): 861–898.
Jabko, Nicolas. 2006. *Playing the Market*. Ithaca, NY: Cornell University Press.
Kahler, Miles and David A. Lake. 2009. "Economic Integration and Global Governance: Why So Little Supranationalism?" In *The Politics of Global Regulation*, ed. Walter Mattli and Ngaire Woods. Princeton, NJ: Princeton University Press, 242–275.
Kant, Immanuel. 1984 [1795]. *Zum ewigen Frieden*. Stuttgart: Philipp Reclam Jun.
Kitschelt, Herbert P. 1986. "Political Opportunity Structures and Political Protest." *British Journal of Political Science* 16 (1): 57–85.
Krasner, Stephen D. 1988. "Sovereignty: An Institutional Perspective." *Comparative Political Studies* 21 (1): 66–94.
Leuffen, Dirk, Berthold Rittberger, and Frank Schimmelfennig. 2013. *Differentiated Integration*. London: Palgrave Macmillan.
Mancini, G. Federico. 1989. "The Making of a Constitution for Europe." *Common Market Law Review* 26 (3): 595–614.
Mattli, Walter and Anne-Marie Slaughter. 1995. "Law and Politics in the European Union: A Reply to Garrett." *International Organization* 49 (1): 183–190.

Mattli, Walter and Anne-Marie Slaughter. 1998. "Revisiting the European Court of Justice." *International Organization* 52 (1): 177–209.

Mayntz, Renate and Fritz W. Scharpf. 1995. "Der Ansatz des akteurzentrierten Institutionalismus." In *Gesellschaftliche Selbstregelung und politische Steuerung*, ed. Renate Mayntz and Fritz W. Scharpf. Frankfurt: Campus Verlag, 39–72.

Meunier, Sophie and Kathleen R. McNamara. 2007. "Making History." In *Making History: European Integration and Institutional Change at Fifty*, ed. Sophie Meunier and Kathleen McNamara. Oxford: Oxford University Press, 1–20.

Michels, Robert. 1989 [1915]. *Zur Soziologie des Parteiwesens in der modernen Demokratie*. 4th Edition. Stuttgart: Alfred Kröner Verlag.

Milward, Allen S., with George Brennan and Federico Romero, eds. 2000. "The Lives and Teachings of the European Saints." In *The European Rescue of the Nation-State*. London: Routledge, 318–344.

Newman, Abraham L. 2008. "Building Transnational Civil Liberties: Transgovernmental Entrepreneurs and the European Data Privacy Directive." *International Organization* 62 (1): 103–130.

Phelan, William. 2014. *In Place of Inter-State Relations: The European Union's Rejection of WTO-Style Trade Sandctions and Trade Remedies*. Oxford: Oxford University Press.

Pierson, Paul. 1996. "The Path to European Integration: A Historical Institutionalist Analysis." *Comparative Political Studies* 29 (2): 123–163.

Pierson, Paul and Theda Skocpol. 2002. "Historical Institutionalism in Contemporary Political Science." In *Political Science: The State of the Discipline*, ed. Ira Katznelson and Helen V. Milner. New York: W. W. Norton: 693–721.

Pollack, Mark A. 1994. "Creeping Competence: The Expanding Agenda of the European Community." *Journal of Public Policy* 14 (2): 95–145.

Pollack, Mark A. 1997. "Delegation, Agency, and Agenda Setting in the EC." *International Organization* 51 (1): 99–134.

Posner, Elliot. 2005. "Sources of Institutional Change: The Supranational Origins of Europe's New Stock Markets." *World Politics* 58 (1): 1–40.

Rich, Paul. 1996. "Visionary Ideas of European Unity after World War I." In *Visions of European Unity*, ed. Philomena Murray and Paul Rich. Boulder, CO: Westview Press, 21–34.

Rittberger, Berthold. 2001. "Which Institutions for Post-War Europe? Explaining the Institutional Design of Europe's First Community." *Journal of European Public Policy* 8 (5): 673–708.

Rittberger, Berthold. 2005. *Building Europe's Parliament*. Oxford: Oxford University Press.

Sandholtz, Wayne and John Zysman. 1989. "1992: Recasting the European Bargain." *World Politics* 42 (1): 95–128.

Scharpf, Fritz W. 1985. "Die Politikverflechtungs-Falle." *Politische Vierteljahresschrift* 26 (4): 323–356.

Shapiro, Martin. 1981. *Courts*. Chicago: University of Chicago Press.

Simmons, Beth A. 2001. "The International Politics of Harmonization." *International Organization* 55 (3): 589–620.

Spruyt, Hendrik. 1994. *The Sovereign State and Its Competitors*. Princeton, NJ: Princeton University Press.

Stone Sweet, Alec. 2004. *The Judicial Construction of Europe*. New York: Oxford University Press.

Stone Sweet, Alec and Thomas L. Brunell. 1998. "Constructing a Supranational Constitution." *American Political Science Review* 92 (1): 63–81.

Stone Sweet, Alec and James A. Caporaso. 1998. "From Free Trade to Supranational Polity." In *European Integration and Supranational Governance*, ed. Wayne Sandholtz and Alec Stone Sweet. New York: Oxford University Press, 92–133.

Stone Sweet, Alec and Wayne Sandholtz. 1998. "Integration, Supranational Governance, and the Institutionalization of the European Polity." In *European Integration and Supranational Governance*, ed. Wayne Sandholtz and Alec Stone Sweet. New York: Oxford University Press, 1–26.

Streeck, Wolfgang and Kathleen Thelen. 2005. "Introduction." In *Beyond Continuity: Institutional Change in Advanced Political Economies*, ed. Wolfgang Streeck and Kathleen Thelen. New York: Oxford University Press, 1–39.

Thelen, Kathleen. 1999. "Historical Institutionalism in Comparative Politics." *Annual Review of Political Science* 2 (1999): 369–404.

Tsebelis, George. 1994. "The Power of the European Parliament as a Conditional Agenda Setter." *American Political Science Review* 88 (1): 128–142.

Tsebelis, George, Christian B. Jensen, Anastassios Kalandrakis, and Amie Kreppel. 2001. "Legislative Procedures in the European Union." *British Journal of Political Science* 31 (4): 573–599.

Weiler, Joseph H. H. 1991. "The Transformation of Europe." *Yale Law Journal* 100 (8): 2403–2483.

CHAPTER 30

EVOLUTIONARY DYNAMICS IN INTERNAL MARKET REGULATION IN THE EUROPEAN UNION

MARK THATCHER AND CORNELIA WOLL*

An unusual political system, the European Union (EU) is frequently criticized by policymakers and often has a negative image in public opinion. It is seen as overly complex, unable to adapt to changing political conditions, imposing centralized rules that are oftentimes inadequate for local conditions and subject to a high degree of squabbling and disagreement among EU member states. Meanwhile, scholars see the EU as slow moving and weak. Its institutional structures are traditionally analyzed as the outcomes of decisions of powerful actors, be these through periodic intergovernmental "grand bargains" (Moravcsik 1998) or through pressures from transnational firms, the European Court of Justice (ECJ) and the European Commission (Sandholtz and Stone Sweet 1998).

We focus on internal market regulation to highlight two puzzles about European integration that these two traditional theories have difficulties resolving. First, the scope of European regulatory authority has expanded considerably in the last three decades in ways that nobody would have predicted in the 1970s. To be sure, much of this expansion built on initial agreements among member states, as intergovernmentalism highlights, and benefited from spill-overs and the activities of institutional European and private actors, as supranational institutionalism stresses. Yet it has also been led by public bodies, whose institutional features have evolved over time. Second, many of the dramatic changes over time emerged out of formal institutions that would be expected to have frustrated policy innovation. In a highly complex political system such as the EU, most formal agreements can only happen on the lowest common denominator, which rarely allows moving substantially away from the status quo. But seemingly insignificant advances opened the way for substantial incremental change in a variety of areas that shifted the preferences of powerful actors.

Historical institutionalism provides tools to account for the evolutionary dynamics of internal market regulation and to explain how and why EU institutions have been greatly extended in scope, detail, and depth over time. Change has been marked by endogenous processes, as liberalization has stimulated re-regulatory rules and new organizations have sought to extend EU regulation. Although the processes have been slow and marked by bargaining, negotiation, and compromise, they have led to profound transformations. We demonstrate how a historical institutionalist approach both helps to reveal and to explain these features, and hence can offer deep insights into the nature of the development of EU institutions.

The chapter begins by setting out key elements of a historical institutionalist approach applied to the EU. It then sets out key characteristics of EU institutional development in the field of regulation of economic markets, since these are at the core of the EU. Several of these characteristics differ from both popular views of the EU and several academic analyses. Finally, it looks at how an historical institutional analysis helps to explain the features found.

Analyzing European Integration and Regulation

Historical institutionalism is a well-developed framework of analysis that focuses our attention on the influence of past institutional developments on present ones, on crucial junctures and ensuing path-dependence, and on the value of examining long time periods to capture slow-moving processes (Steinmo, Thelen, and Longstreth 1992; Hall and Taylor 1996; Thelen 1999; Pierson 2000; Capoccia and Kelemen 2007). It has demonstrated that preference formation is an endogenous process produced by the wider institutional context in which political actors are situated (see Fioretos, Falleti, and Sheingate, Chapter 1, this volume).

The key insights of the historical institutional approach were developed to explain patterns within nation-states. Yet the scope for path dependence is likely to be great also in the development of EU institutions (cf. Pierson 1996). All four factors posited by Pierson (2000) for the importance of path dependence in politics apply in spades to the EU. To begin with, the nature of the EU is highly collective: many of the policies produced by the EU involve coordination of multiple participants, especially as interdependencies are high. The EU is marked by very dense politics, due to the high number of veto points and players. Equally, the reallocation of powers is likely to reinforce certain actors. Finally, the costs of setting up new institutions can be high, given the large number of actors involved. When taken into account, these factors underscore the value of using historical institutionalism for understanding the evolution of EU regulation.

First, a high number of veto players are a crucial feature of EU decision-making. Legislation can only be proposed by the Commission, but then must be passed by a qualified majority (with elements of a supermajority) by the Council of Ministers, and today also by the European Parliament in most cases. The ECJ can strike down legislation. The Commission itself is divided into Directorate Generals (DGs), headed by Commissioners nominated by national governments, which the Commission President cannot remove. National governments face their own domestic veto players and points. Coordination among these actors is therefore key to the success of a policy proposal, but equally difficult to achieve.

This is linked to a second feature: the complexity and opacity of EU legislation, and especially European Community (EC) regulation.[1] The subject matter of regulation is often highly technical. Its legal form can vary, from Directives that member states have to transpose into domestic legislation to Regulations and some Treaty Articles that have direct effects in member states. Most EU regulation is implemented by member states by national regulatory authorities, which may be government departments or independent regulatory agencies. Nevertheless, some areas, such as competition policy, are predominately managed by the Commission. To add complexity, different forms of coordination of national bodies are possible, from informal networks of regulators to formal European regulatory agencies (Coen and Thatcher 2008).

Over time, the need for coordination, technical cooperation, and integration among multiple organizations has grown. These have resulted in a third feature: interdependencies and inter-linkages between formally separate national institutions and actors. Domestic agencies now connect in order to share information and coordinate their action. Regulatory ideas are frequently shared among strong professional and epistemic communities. By encouraging comparisons and creating competitive contexts, the EU provides a political setting where developments in one member state increasingly affect the evolution of its neighbors.

Fourth, there are multiple and often competing institutional legacies. This explains both the fault lines of individual conflicts, but also highlights that the costs of adaptation to a new EU regime can be unequally shared depending on the respective institutional fit. Each member state has its own specific institutional past. Thus for instance, France's statist institutions and traditions stand in contrast with Britain's economically liberal past and strong position in favor of finance capital, which in turn differ from neo-corporatist features seen in Germany and other northern European countries (e.g., Schmidt 2002; Fioretos 2011). In addition, there are competing legacies at the EU level: for example, between DGs in the Commission, where some sectoral DGs are more "interventionist," while others, such as DG Competition, are more economically liberal.

Fifth, supranational law adds an additional layer of complexity that affects both the strategy of actors advocating or opposing policy change and the costs that can be incurred. More specifically, the highly legalized nature of the EU means that courts, especially the ECJ, provide a source of change (Weiler 1991; Kelemen 2011). This possibility is often used strategically by member states or European institutions such as the Commission to push for regulatory reform (Schmidt 1998). As Kelemen (2011) highlights in a comparison between the adversarial legalism distinctive of the US and "eurolegalism" that characterizes the EU, European courts now play a crucial role in determining political conflict in ways comparable to the American system. Regulatory dynamics are no longer just cooperative and informal, marked by bureaucratic solution-finding. With the increasing possibility for private actors and other stakeholders to take cases to the European courts, litigation strategies profoundly shape regulatory development. This stands in contrast to some Western countries where political institutions have dominated regulation.

These five features—a high number of veto-players, a complex EU regulatory process, interlinkages between national actors, competing institutional legacies, and supranational law—have lasting effects on policy change that unfold over time and underscore the relevance of historical institutionalism. Studying the empirical development of EU regulatory institutions reveals that the EU has evolved through a combination of periods of gradual change and specific events that created critical junctures where actors were able to push through more rapid changes. We argue that this is attributable to the fact that several defining features of the EU push toward the maintenance of the status quo (veto-players and complexity), while others encourage slow change (interlinkages) and can facilitate profound changes (diverse legacies and supranational law) in specific contexts.

As a general rule, EU policymaking and its regulatory process make "evolutionary" or "gradual" change the dominant feature of regulatory reform, and rapid change of direction and revolutionary reform rare. Streeck and Thelen's (2005) modes of institutional change can all be observed in the EU. Layering is a common form of institutional development, as EU governance is multi-level and contains many veto actors who contribute to new institutions being added to existing ones. Displacement is also an attractive strategy as new organizations can slowly grow and use their own resources to expand their competencies and territory. The EU's limited staffing and budget encourage "drift" (i.e., deliberate neglect) and conversion of existing organizations. In contrast, terminating existing organizations can be very difficult, not only due to incumbent organizational interests but also because new legislation must pass through a legislative process with multiple veto points and players.

Yet, as historical institutionalism points out, beyond such bounded change, new and unexpected directions of change can happen due to contingent events, which may produce "critical junctures" in which the room for reform is enlarged. The EU's political system offers several sources for such contingent events. Its powerful courts provide a non-political source of change. Equally, the youth of many of its institutions and the expansion of its regulation may allow more scope for contingent factors and new and unexpected developments than in more settled institutional systems. Finally, the contrasting and varied national institutional legacies may mean that there is more space for choice and contingency than within typical modern Western nation-states. Indeed, interactions over time among EU bodies may lead to actors altering their preferred policy positions. Many policymakers are playing at least a two-level game (Putnam 1988), if not a multi-level one (Woll 2012). Thus governments, national regulators, and firms with powerful domestic bases are operating in both national domestic and EU policy arenas (as well sometimes as international and/or regional ones), which can lead to shifting alliances across levels.

The Development of EU Regulation of Economic Markets

Until the 1970s, EC regulation of markets remained relatively limited. The focus was initially on the elimination of tariff barriers to trade. In the 1980s and especially the 1990s, competition policy became a major activity, notably regulation of state aid and dumping, which were directly handled by the Commission. However, many economic markets were left to national governments, especially public services, notably network industries such as telecommunications, energy, stock markets, and transport (Thatcher 2007). These were mostly state monopolies supplied by government-owned entities.

For decades, debates took place within the EC over the appropriate balance of state monopolies and market liberalization. These happened within a context of several important constraints. The EC was a weak regulatory body, with few legal powers. The Commission was divided, with some elements in favor of greater competition, largely inspired by German ordo-liberalism, but other elements supporting industrial policy, notably in the form of promoting national and European champion firms, who would be large enough to meet feared competition from the US or Japan. Legislative development was limited, especially due to the requirement for unanimity after the Luxembourg Compromise of 1966, which followed De Gaulle's "empty chair" approach, in which a de facto veto was given to all member states of "matters of very important national interest." The EC's main activity was the provision of agricultural subsidies.

By the early 1970s, the EC seemed to be destined to be a loose linkage of nations, at best a weak intergovernmental body. However, the 1970s and early 1980s saw a number of events concerning regulation of economic markets. Many arose from judgments of the ECJ (Weiler 1991; Caporaso and Stone Sweet 1998; Fligstein, Sandholtz, and Stone Sweet 2001). The most important was the 1979 Cassis de Dijon case, in which the court ruled that goods legally produced in one member state could be sold in other member states. In the absence of common rules, individual member states could set their own rules, and meeting these goals empowered firms to export goods and services across the EC. However, other member states could not impose national restrictions that hindered trade (Article 28 [30]) except under limited circumstances (e.g., public morality, public policy, and health and safety). Hence national rules provided a "passport" across the EC (Nicolaïdis and Schmidt 2007). In competition policy too, ECJ judgments were important, especially the 1972 Continental Can decision in which the Court offered a "backdoor" entrance for the Commission to control mergers by applying Article 86 on abuse of a dominant position (Bulmer 1994; McGowan and Cini 1999). Other similar and unexpected ECJ decisions took place in telecommunications, such as the 1982 BT case that gave the Commission ability to use its authority to regulate markets despite the absence of legislation.

The 1980s saw major changes in the European Commission. Jacques Delors, its President from 1985 to 1995 promoted the European Single Market and proposed the "1992 programme" in which EC liberalization would revitalize European economies. He formed an alliance with "economic liberals" in which greater competition led by the EC would be married with re-regulation. At first, liberalization measures appeared limited. EC legislation opened up parts of the telecommunications and energy markets, but left the bulk under national control (which often meant monopoly supply). Moreover, liberalization was counterbalanced by other "re-regulatory measures" that appeared to protect traditional "public service." A Merger Regulation was passed in 1989 giving the Commission jurisdiction over the largest mergers, but its thresholds appeared very high at the time.

The production of EC regulation was slow. The 1989 Merger Regulation took almost 20 years, while telecommunications legislation began with a Green Paper in 1987 but then took almost a decade before the whole sector was liberalized (Bulmer 1994; Thatcher 2001). Negotiations were tortuous, often pitting "liberal" states seeking extensions of EC law on competition (usually Britain and Germany) against "Southern" states (often France and Italy) who supported more scope for industrial policies of favoring selected companies and protecting traditional "public service" obligations, while the Commission sought greater powers for itself and for deepening economic integration. As a result of judicial strategies of pro-reform actors and shifting alliances, agreement was eventually reached, including on the substantive content of regulation.

Yet once seriously underway, EC regulation spread. Liberalization was extended in the late 1990s and 2000s across many economic markets. Thus by the end of the 2000s, the entire telecommunications, energy, airline, and postal markets were opened to competition under EC law (Thatcher 2007). Moreover, "re-regulatory" measures became not only increasingly detailed but also designed to ensure that competition was "fair and effective," concerning a host of matters from cost-based tariffs to interconnection. Equally, EC merger control was extended through lower thresholds. Moreover, EC legislation began to encroach on national institutional structures, notably encouraging the establishment of independent regulatory agencies (and indeed requiring them in the case of electricity). Today, EC legislation over the internal markets has been greatly extended and runs counter to traditional monopolies and highly politicized interventions by national governments. The extension of EC regulation has involved much bargaining, negotiation, and compromise, but even previously hostile countries such as France have accepted the principle of liberalization of markets.

The EC also developed its coordination capacities for the implementation of new regulations. The 1980s and 1990s saw the establishment of independent regulatory agencies in member states (Thatcher 2002). These often had detailed powers over enforcement and held many responsibilities for implementing EC regulation in practice. They had incentives to promote further EC regulation since it increased their powers and also aided them in achieving greater independence from governments. Initially, informal networks of independent regulatory agencies/authorities were created, either by the agencies themselves or helped by the Commission.[2] Over time, this process led to more formalized networks under EC law (Thatcher and Coen 2008).[3]

As the Commission (and some national governments) became concerned about consistent implementation and sought to avoid that member states "cheated" by selectively implementing EC regulations, the power of regulatory agencies increased. This created a complex relationship with the Commission, as both it and the networks sought greater EC regulation, but the network members also wished to ensure sufficient distance from the Commission. After lengthy debates, involving both actors, as well as national governments, integrated European Regulatory Agencies (ERAs) were created in 2009–2010, such as the European Banking Authority and the Agency for the Cooperation of Energy Regulators (Thatcher 2011). They were given limited formal powers, and faced many constraints, notably dual boards—one for national government representatives and another for agency representatives of independent regulatory agencies. Nevertheless, the ERAs rapidly began to extend their operations. The European Banking Authority, for example, has been an important participant in efforts to re-regulate banking in the aftermath of the financial crisis throughout Europe.

By 2012 EC regulation has been transformed in ways that were unexpected in the 1970s. It had been extended in scope and depth, covering many sectors, and including liberalization, re-regulation of competition, and implementation and coordination of national regulatory agencies/bodies. Each stage of regulatory expansion had been followed by another that built on the previous one. Development had been slow and incremental, through negotiation and compromise, strategic maneuvering and sometimes unexpected feedback loops shifted the basis of negotiation of all participants.

Insights from Historical Institutionalism

The historical institutionalist emphasis on studying longer time periods offers a very different perspective from those focusing on recent changes or isolated "grand bargains" during Treaty changes. Taking longer periods of time into account underscores that EC regulation has developed greatly over time, in terms of coverage of different markets, extension of liberalization, and provisions for implementation. This perspective offers an immensely valuable lens for understanding a polity that has grown incrementally, with a series of small steps, through limited agreements, but resulted in outcomes that were not foreseen at the start of the process.

Second, a longer-term view brings attention to the role of critical junctures in shaping the evolution of EU regulation. The path of the 1960s and 1970s stands is in sharp contrast to that of the 1980s onward. As the previous overview highlighted, a critical juncture for reform emerged following ECJ judgments and the activism of senior figures in the Commission during the early 1980s. The ECJ acted when normal legislative progress seemed impossible, offering legal alternatives through application of existing Treaty provisions. The Court rulings changed the default position that negotiators could previously fall back on. With new legal interpretation, "business as usual" was often precluded and actors who preferred the status quo had to determine new policy stances, which oftentimes brought realignments.

For its part, the Commission was able to offer new reform programs that appeared to serve the interests of national governments and to be of rather limited scope. The Commission exploited the room for reform that was created in the early 1980s to propose new legislation in response to court cases. Proposals that would previously not have passed because a majority of member states might have preferred the status quo were now able to garner more significant support. This explains many of the most significant changes in network industries such as electricity, telecommunications, and air transport (Schmidt 1998; Eising and Jabko 2001; Woll 2006).

The evolution of preferences, endogenous to the process of European integration, are thus a major motor of further institutionalization. Historical institutionalism has long drawn attention to the need to endogenize the political construction of interests into models of change. As Immergut (1998, 20) underlines, "institutions act as filters that selectively favour particular interpretations either of... goals or... means." When court judgments or Commission proposals changed default options or provided new institutional fora for negotiation, political actors adjusted their strategies, and sometimes even their overarching goals.

Third, not only the traditional decision-makers, but also new actors—such as new market entrants, policy entrepreneurs in related domains, or public officials in newly created institutions and networks—triggered positive feedback processes. Once liberalization began, it generated strong forces for the extension of EC regulation, notably for re-regulation and later concerning implementation through spill-over effects. Rules in one domain or part of a domain create pressures for further rules in adjoining domains or to re-regulate the newly liberalized market (Vogel 1996; Fligstein, Sandholtz, and Stone Sweet 2001). Moreover, new organizations, such as loose networks of national regulatory agencies, began to press for further powers. Thus, initial intervention created actors both at the EU level and at the national level, who developed their own interests, joined coalitions and pressed for changes that increased their powers and extended EC regulation. Similarly, once European networks of regulators were created, they gave rise to further processes of centralization and formalization, which contributed to the creation of European regulatory agencies. These feedback effects are vital for understanding the EU, as initial, apparently limited changes developed over time and gradually turned into far-reaching reforms.

Historical institutionalism complements neofunctionalist theories of European integration that have focused on the rise of transnational actors by pointing to the space for political actors such as the Commission, independent regulatory authorities and networks of such authorities to undertake changes which, thanks to feedback processes created dynamics that were not foreseen at the outset and that do not correspond fully to the market integration demands of the transnational actors alone. In addition, sometimes even limited agreements that correspond only to the lowest common denominator led to consequential changes in institutional design and market integration that developed their own organizational logics and paths. This does not imply that powerful actors were blind-sided or did not act strategically—on the contrary! Most decision-makers involved were large and well resourced. Rather than following scripts blindly, they continuously evaluated their interests in the face of changing political contexts and consider different institutional alternatives. They bargained hard to pursue their preferred solutions. Policy preferences had to integrate changing fall-back options and shifting alliances, the arrival of new actors, and competitive dynamics unleashed by previous decisions. This led to surprising changes in the position of countries such as France, for example, who initially opposed liberalization, or the United Kingdom, which initially resisted further integration, including financial services. The interests of some regulatory agencies also evolved, toward accepting greater formalization under EC law. Correspondingly, former monopoly providers and other private companies changed their policy stances in response to changing competition dynamics and shifts in the position of their national governments (Woll 2008).

Fourth, historical institutionalism points to the evolutionary nature of EC regulatory development. Existing organizations usually survive. They are often converted (with additional powers and formalization) or sometimes new organizational forms may be layered on top of existing ones. The process of development is fraught with conflict, as different actors jostle and find that their interests partially overlap but also partially conflict, leading to relationships of limited cooperation and also conflict. In many ways, the growing institutional complexity that arises from incrementalism and compromise can be compared to developments in American politics, where scholars have labeled the tension between overlapping sources of authority "intercurrence" (see Fioretos, Falleti, and Sheingate, Chapter 1, this volume). The American government, just like the institutions governing market regulation in Europe, grows because a multitude of actors seek to preserve their respective authorities over a policy domain and to broker institutions that allow for compromise and co-existence. The rationalization of practices is the exception.

However, there is one crucial difference between American and European regulatory developments that is linked to the policy cycle and the passage rate of legislative proposals. While the great majority of legislative proposals are abandoned in the US, Commission proposals have a very high chance of being adopted eventually, even if they undergo considerable changes during long negotiation periods.[4] This means that one should not overestimate the importance of bargaining, delay, and compromise in the EU. Paying too much attention to these features risks missing two crucial aspects that matter for outcomes in the long run: (1) most often, even protracted EU negotiations lead to some sort of agreement; and (2) however limited the agreement may seem initially, it is likely to involve greater EC regulation, in particular as it plays out over time.

Conclusion

Historical institutionalism, with the help of theoretically grounded explanatory factors, draws attention to several features of EC regulation that are unexpected or downplayed in other frameworks. The emphasis on longer time periods sheds light on two parallel and surprising evolutionary dynamics: on the one hand, the forces resisting change that lead to gradual change and layered institutions, and on the other hand, mechanisms that facilitate profound shifts. In particular, the strategic interactions of domestic actors, supranational institutions and new transnational actors and their use of European institutions create feedback loops that inform later institutional developments. Much of this evolution operates through marginal shifts in actors' preferences, and through the complex interplay of multi-level policy bargaining, these feedback loops can create quite fundamental change over time.

As the process of European integration continues and researchers aim to resolve new empirical puzzles, there is room for development within historical institutionalism. One area that future scholarship in this tradition may address concerns the definition of actor interests. As anyone doing empirical work on changing preferences will quickly find out, it is almost impossible to distinguish basic interests from altered strategies in pursuit of the same interests. Only in rare cases do actors acknowledge having completely changed their mind about fundamental goals. This may be important if deeper questions of actor objectives are at stake. Equally, it matters for discussions of whether actors' identity is altered by interactions such as bargaining and negotiations, which is at the heart of debates concerning identity in constructivism. Future historical institutionalist studies will benefit from more actively identifying the mechanisms that alter preferences over time among EU's main actors and what role legacies of past institutions and new identities play in such processes.

Finally, historical institutionalism has paid too little attention to informal arrangements that balance or off-set formal rules and organizations. On the one hand, formal institutions may only create policy effects because they are complemented by informal procedures. As Kleine (2013) shows, many formal rules alone would be unacceptable to many stakeholders in the EU and would bring integration to a stand-still. Informal governance complements formal structures and make compromises possible and viable. Such governance also reinforces learning and feedback effects in subtle ways that may have far-reaching consequences for the nature of integration. Sabel and Zeitlin (2010) argue that even non-constraining agreements, such as the open method of coordination, can create recursive processes, where comparison and learning pushes for a convergence of standards that eventually make formal arrangements possible. A more complete historical institutionalist account of European market integration needs to consider such non-constraining informal procedures on equal footing with formal institutional development.

Notes

* We would like to thank the editors, and in particular Orfeo Fioretos, for their careful readings and insightful comments on this chapter.

1. European Community (EC) is used here since most regulation is under the European Community before 1993 and then under the European Community pillar of the EU between 1993 and 2009, when the pillar system was ended.
2. Examples of informal fora largely established by the Commission include the European Electricity Regulation Forum in 1998, and the European Gas Regulation Forum in 1999 (see Eberlein 2005); examples of informal networks of independent regulatory agencies include the Independent Regulators Group (IRG) for telecommunications in 1997, and the Council of European Energy Regulators in 2000.
3. For example, the Committee of European Securities Regulators, CESR (2001), the Committee of European Banking Supervisors, CEBS (2003), and the European Regulators Group for Electricity and Gas, ERGEG (see Thatcher and Coen 2008).
4. Mahoney (2008, 64) estimated that only 10 percent of legislative proposals were passed as bills by the US Congress in 2008, compared with roughly 80 percent of European proposals which eventually turned into directives or regulations.

References

Bulmer, S. 1994. "Institutions and Policy Change in the European Communities: The Case of Merger Control." *Public Administration* 72 (3): 423–444.

Capoccia, G. and R. Daniel Kelemen. 2007. "The Study of Critical Junctures: Theory, Narrative, and Counterfactuals in Historical Institutionalism." *World Politics* 59 (03): 341–369.

Caporaso, J. A. and A. Stone Sweet. 1998. "From Free Trade to Supranational Polity: The European Court and Integration." In *European Integration and Supranational Governance*, ed. Alec Stone Sweet and Wayne Sandholtz. Oxford: Oxford University Press, 92–133.

Coen, D. and M. Thatcher. 2008. "Network Governance and Multi-level Delegation: European Networks of Regulatory Agencies." *Journal of Public Policy* 28 (01): 49–71.

Eberlein, Burkhart. 2005. "Regulation by Co-operation: The Third Way in Making Rules for the Internal Energy Market." In *Legal Aspects of EU Energy Regulation*, ed. Peter D. Cameron. Oxford: Oxford University Press, 59–88.

Eising, R. and N. Jabko. 2001. "Moving Targets: National Interests and Electricity Liberalization in the European Union." *Comparative Political Studies* 34 (7): 742–767.

Fioretos, O. 2011. *Creative Reconstructions: Multilateralism and European Varieties of Capitalism after 1950*. Ithaca, NY: Cornell University Press.

Fligstein, N., W. Sandholtz, and A. Stone Sweet. 2001. *The Institutionalization of Europe*. Oxford: Oxford University Press.

Hall, P. A. and R. C. R. Taylor. 1996. "Political Science and the Three New Institutionalisms." *Political Studies* 44 (5): 936–957.

Immergut, E. M. 1998. "The Theoretical Core of the New Institutionalism." *Politics and Society* 26 (1): 5–34.

Kelemen, R. D. 2011. *Eurolegalism: The Transformation of Law and Regulation in the European Union*. Cambridge, MA: Harvard University Press.

Kleine, M. 2013. *Informal Governance in the European Union: How Governments Make International Organizations Work*. Ithaca, NY: Cornell University Press.

McGowan, L. and M. Cini. 1999. "Discretion and Politicization in EU Competition Policy: The Case of Merger Control." *Governance* 12 (2): 175–200.

Mahoney, C. 2008. *Brussels vs. the Beltway: Advocacy in the United States and the European Union*. Washington, D.C.: Georgetown University Press.

Moravcsik, A. 1998. *The Choice for Europe: Social Purpose and State Power from Messina to Maastricht*. Ithaca, NY: Cornell University Press.

Nicolaïdis, K. and S. K. Schmidt. 2007. "Mutual Recognition 'On Trial': The Long Road to Services Liberalization." *Journal of European Public Policy* 14 (5): 717–734.

Pierson, P. 1996. "The Path toward European Integration: A Historical Institutionalist Analysis." *Comparative Political Studies* 29 (2): 123–163.

Pierson, P. 2000. "Increasing Returns, Path Dependence, and the Study of Politics." *American Political Science Review* 94 (2): 251–267.

Putnam, R. 1988. "Diplomacy and Domestic Politics: The Logic of Two-Level Games." *International Organization* 42: 427–460.

Sabel, C. F. and J. Zeitlin. 2010. *Experimentalist Governance in the European Union: Towards a New Architecture*. Oxford: Oxford University Press.

Sandholtz, W. and A. Stone Sweet. 1998. *European Integration and Supranational Governance*. Oxford: Oxford University Press.

Schmidt, S. K. 1998. "Commission Activism: Subsuming Telecommunication and Electricity Under European Competition Law." *Journal of European Public Policy* 5 (1): 169–184.

Schmidt, V. A. 2002. *The Futures of European Capitalism*. Oxford and New York: Oxford University Press.

Steinmo, S., K. Thelen, and F. Longstreth, eds. 1992. *Structuring Politics: Historical Institutionalism in Comparative Analysis*. Cambridge: Cambridge University Press.

Streeck, W. and K. Thelen, eds. 2005. *Beyond Continuity: Institutional Change in Advanced Industrial Economies*. Oxford: Oxford University Press.

Thatcher, M. 2001. "The Commission and National Governments as Partners: EC Regulatory Expansion in Telecommunications 1979–2000." *Journal of European Public Policy* 8 (4): 558–584.

Thatcher, M. 2002. "Regulation after Delegation: Independent Regulatory Agencies in Europe." *Journal of European Public Policy* 9 (6): 954–972.

Thatcher, M. 2007. *Internationalization and Economic Institutions: Comparing the European Experience*. Oxford: Oxford University Press.

Thatcher, M. 2011. "The Creation of European Regulatory Agencies and Its Limits: A Comparative Analysis of European Delegation." *Journal of European Public Policy* 18 (6): 790–809.

Thatcher, M. and D. Coen. 2008. "Reshaping European Regulatory Space: An Evolutionary Analysis." *West European Politics* 31 (4): 806–836.

Thelen, K. 1999. "Historical Institutionalism in Comparative Politics." *Annual Review of Political Science* 2: 369–404.

Vogel, S. K. 1996. *Freer Markets, More Rules: Regulatory Reform in Advanced Industrial Countries*. Ithaca, NY: Cornell University Press.

Weiler, J. H. 1991. "The Transformation of Europe." *Yale Law Journal* 100: 2403–2483.

Woll, C. 2006. "The Road to External Representation: The European Commission's Activism in International Air Transport." *Journal of European Public Policy* 13 (1): 52–69.

Woll, C. 2008. *Firm Interests: How Governments Shape Business Lobbying on Global Trade.* Ithaca, NY: Cornell University Press.

Woll, C. 2012. "Open Skies, Closed Markets: Future Games in the Negotiation of International Air Transport." *Review of International Political Economy* 19 (5): 918–941.

PART VI

INTERNATIONAL RELATIONS

Introduction

ORFEO FIORETOS

WHEN political scientists renewed their interests in the study of the state and institutions 25 years ago, international relations (IR) scholars were part of the debates that led to the crystallization of historical institutionalism. In the wake of these debates, however, the IR subfield largely looked to other traditions of institutional analysis to examine the origins and effects of international institutions. By contrast with the comparative and American politics subfields, where historical institutionalism quickly established itself as major tradition of analysis and saw steady growth, the tradition's inroads in IR are more recent. This part features chapters by contributors to early debates on institutions and the state, by scholars who maintained the sensibilities of the tradition over the years without directly invoking the historical institutionalism label, and by authors who have drawn on historical institutionalism to revisit common understandings of international relations and to chart new areas of empirical analysis. Together, the chapters demonstrate the significant potential that historical institutionalism holds for analytically sharp and empirically nuanced studies of state sovereignty, international orders, security, organization, law, trade, finance, and regulation.

In the opening chapter, Stephen D. Krasner explores the sources for the enduring nature of diverse forms of state sovereignty. Krasner notes that at no point have international systems been characterized by universal adherence to the same principles, rules, or norms of political organization, and he argues that historical institutionalism is particularly well placed to help researchers account for the persistence on diverse forms of sovereignty. Pointing to historically contingent episodes in producing instances where states have bargained away parts of their sovereignty, Krasner concludes that the modern system of state sovereignty will remain stable and only be supplanted if political entities with limited material capabilities come to possess technologies that threaten mass-scale deaths.

G. John Ikenberry participated in early debates about the state and alternative understandings of institutions, and uses his chapter to discuss historical institutionalism's contributions to study of the origins, resilience, and evolution of international orders. Ikenberry notes that international orders often prevail over long periods of time despite big shifts in distributions of state power, because institutions alter states' calculations to make them favor extant designs over radical overhauls. For this reason, Ikenberry is skeptical that shifts in global distributions of power in the early twenty-first century will upend the liberal international order that has prevailed since 1945, despite the waxing and waning of US power.

It is has been said that nowhere does state power matter more and nowhere are institutions less important than in the domain of international security. Etel Solingen and Wilfred Wan powerfully rebut such statements, documenting the central role of institutions in shaping both the trajectory of states' security strategies and in maintaining states' commitments to limit the proliferation of nuclear technology. Their account contrasts sharply with those that see international institutions as temporary arrangements with little effect on state behavior, and illustrates that states' preferences and strategies are informed and frequently transformed by international institutions. If Solingen and Wan are correct about the causal impact of institutions in shaping international security practices over time, then there are strong reasons to give historical institutionalism a more central position in IR debates about the origin and evolution of international institutions.

Noting that IR has only recently come to more seriously grapple with the contributions of historical institutionalism, Henry Farrell and Martha Finnemore encourage researchers to pay greater attention in the future to the role played by the global institutional context in shaping international affairs. Because formal international rules may be relatively weak in comparison with national ones, they argue that careful attention to how international norms and ideas shape international politics may hold the keys to why state behavior and policy choices take their particular forms. Farrell and Finnemore therefore encourage historical institutionalists to establish strong bridges to sociological institutionalism, which they see as a means to more fully incorporating the role that global social contexts, ideas, and norms play in shaping patterns of state behavior.

Changes in international normative contexts may be a product of the actions of international courts, which have grown in number over time and often impact the behavior of states, governments, and individuals. Detailing three critical junctures in the evolution of international courts, Karen J. Alter explores how incremental changes to court practices have gradually transformed states' relationships to courts in ways that have made them less likely to reject the legitimacy of courts and more likely to obey their jurisprudence. Alter makes the case that historical institutionalism holds particular promise for the grounded empirical research enterprise approach it brings to the study of international courts, as well as for its value in identifying the mechanisms that lead international institutions to shape and at times gradually transform state behavior over time.

An analytical toolbox centered on temporal concepts and research in the primary archive are hallmarks of historical institutionalism that have helped scholars provide authoritative accounts of major institutional innovations and revisit common interpretations of history. Both the chapter by Judith Goldstein and Robert Gulotty on the origins of greater trade liberalization and that by Eric Helleiner on the Bretton Woods conference illustrate the big rewards that IR stands to gain from embracing a historical institutionalist approach. Goldstein and Gulotty's analysis of how constitutional constraints and presidential strategy interacted with positive feedback effects and historical legacies to shape US and international trade liberalization help them explain why liberalization has ebbed and flowed over time without any substantial reversal since the Great Depression. Meanwhile, Helleiner's primary research revisits conventional understandings of the modern international economic system's origins by documenting how institutional arrangements proposed by New Deal supporters after the Great Depression to structure bilateral lending practices between the US and Latin America became blueprints for structuring global monetary and financial systems after the Bretton Woods conference.

The analytical toolbox of historical institutionalism has never been confined to the study of events in the distant past, but has long demonstrated its value for explaining contemporary developments. In a chapter that explores core concepts in historical institutionalism, such as temporal sequencing, practices of institutional layering, and positive feedback effects, Abraham L. Newman details the great promise historical institutionalism holds for empirical research on global market regulation in the twenty-first century. Central to Newman's account are informal international institutions, including networks of regulators that shape the structure of global markets in areas as diverse as finance and pharmaceuticals by influencing the sequence of reform within major economies, the prospects for radical and incremental reform, and the likelihood that groups with stakes in old rules will support rule changes.

CHAPTER 31

THE PERSISTENCE OF STATE SOVEREIGNTY

STEPHEN D. KRASNER*

FUNDAMENTAL changes in foundational international institutions, changes in principles, norms, rules, not the extent to which the norms and rules are honored, from one kind of structure to another have primarily been precipitated by threats to the core security interests of powerful actors. Institutions changed because old structures were destroyed by force or transformed from within to avoid conquest. The empires of the Aztecs, Incas, Fulani, Zulus, Ottomans, Manchus disappeared because their European or North American (or later Japanese) enemies defeated them in battle and dismantled their political structures. In Japan, one part of the elite destroyed the Shogunate so that Japan could be internally transformed to meet the challenge of the West. The leaders of the Meiji restoration rejected the Sino-centric hierarchical system of tributary states and embraced conventional sovereignty (Kayaoglu 2010). In Europe, sovereignty displaced empires and city-states over a period of several centuries because sovereign states were better able to tax, coerce, and defend themselves against external invaders (Tilly 1990; Spruyt 1996). The only transformation of foundational structures that has taken place through bargaining and agreement, rather than coercion, has been the European Union (EU).

In the contemporary international system there is no opportunity outside Europe for a bargaining process that could lead to a transformation of the basic norms and rules of sovereignty. There are, however, threats of force that could precipitate transformational change. In contrast to the past, these threats come not from the most powerful states in the system but rather from weaker actors, both state and non-state. The most obvious threat would be nuclear, an attack on a strong state by a weaker state or transnational terrorist group that had procured or developed nuclear weapons. There are other security threats presented by new technologies some of which are only dimly visible such as nanobots that could carry biological agents and be manipulated from thousands of miles away (Blum 2011).

An existential security threat from nuclear weapons or new technological developments could end the monopoly of sovereign statehood as the only fully legitimated institutional structure for organizing political life. Absent such a threat the sovereign state system will persist. This is not because more and more states will come to approximate the ideal of sovereign statehood; in fact, just the opposite. Departures from conventional sovereignty, which have always been present, will persist and possibly become more frequent. Sovereignty, like every other international system, has always been characterized by organized hypocrisy. There has been a decoupling of logics of appropriateness and logics of consequences (March and Olsen 1989; Brunsson 1989; Krasner 1999).

There is, however, no alternative normative structure, no alternative set of principles, norms, and rules that might displace sovereignty. The material and ideational interests of too many political leaders depend on the persistence of sovereignty. The idea of a Moslem caliphate, for instance, might appeal to a small number of leaders and to a much larger set of followers who find themselves marginalized in poorly functioning states or even wealthy Western democracies. The large number of powerful actors and forces, however, that are institutionally isomorphic with the idea of sovereign statehood will preclude the widespread acceptance of any alternative set of principles and norms absent an existential security threat to powerful states.

Consistent with historical institutionalism, changes in the sovereign state system are layered one on top of the other, but foundational norms and principles are not challenged (Fioretos 2011). Even the EU is identified by a proper noun but not a common noun. Sovereignty sticks because powerful national and even transnational actors are incorporated, legalized, legitimated, and sometimes funded by national states. These non-state entities are organized to influence state policies. They have legal departments to make sure that they do not violate the laws of the state within which they are operating; they have public relations departments to influence publics whose preferences might affect state policy; they employ lobbyists and make political donations to promote or impede legislation. In some countries they simply pay bribes. With few exceptions (such as the International Labour Organization) the constitutive members of international organizations are juridically sovereign states. While the authority and power of office holders in the Organisation for Economic Co-operation and Development (OECD) world are guaranteed by deeply embedded constitutional orders, those of political leaders in countries with limited resources and fragile institutions often depend on prerogatives associated with the rules of sovereignty. Muammar Gaddafi was killed in a ditch in Sirte, Libya in October of 2011, but two years before he was standing on the green marble dais in front of the General Assembly of the United Nations, one of the loftiest settings in the world, delivering a rambling speech that lasted more than an hour and half.

Elements of Sovereignty

Sovereign statehood has three separate and distinct elements: international legal sovereignty, Westphalian/Vattelian sovereignty, and domestic sovereignty:

- International legal sovereignty: States have international legal sovereignty when they are recognized. Recognition confers the right to enter into contracts or treaties with other states, and membership in international organizations.
- Westphalian/Vattelian sovereignty: States have Westphalian/Vattelian sovereignty when they are autonomous, when their institutional structures are autochthonously generated. The state is not subject to any external authority, even authority structures that the state has itself voluntarily created through the exercise of its international legal sovereignty. Non-intervention is a core norm.
- Domestic sovereignty: States have effective domestic sovereignty when they are able to regulate and control activities within their territory.

The three components of sovereignty are not organically linked. Logically it is possible for a geographically defined entity to have only one attribute of sovereignty, any combination of two attributes of sovereignty, or all three attributes. Empirically every variation in sovereignty attributes is present in the contemporary world system. Taiwan has effective domestic sovereignty and Westphalian/Vattelian sovereignty, but only limited international legal sovereignty as it is only recognized by about 20 states. Somalia has international legal sovereignty and Westphalian/Vattelian sovereignty, but not effective domestic sovereignty. The Solomon Islands have international recognition but lack Westphalian/Vattelian sovereignty and effective domestic sovereignty.

The two biggest classes of states that depart from conventional sovereignty are failed states and states with areas of limited statehood (Risse 2011), and the members of the EU. Failed states do not have effective domestic sovereignty, but they do have international legal sovereignty. They may or may not have Westphalian/Vattelian sovereignty. The 2014 Fragile States Index published by the Fund for Peace placed 16 states in the alert or very high alert categories and another 32 in the very high warning category (The Fund for Peace 2014).

The member states of the EU all enjoy international legal sovereignty. They all have more or less effective domestic sovereignty although there is a lot of distance between Romania, which ranks 130 on the fragile state index, and Sweden, which ranks 177 (The Fund for Peace 2014). They do not, however, have Westphalian/Vattelian sovereignty. The member states of the EU have contracted away some of their autonomy by voluntarily creating supranational institutions and agreeing to qualified majority decision voting.

The significant distance between actual practice and sovereign statehood as an ideal type might suggest that the ordering structure of the contemporary international system could crumble. Such a conclusion would be wrong. Historical institutionalism suggests that a situation in which there are many variants of some common institutional arrangement is not an aberration. Rather, because of the complexity of any international environment—the multiplicity of actors and interests and changing power configurations—patterns of layered and varied authority structures are expected to be the norm.

Sovereignty through the Centuries

The contemporary international environment is not unique. Norm violation has permeated state practice throughout the several hundred-year history of the sovereign states system. The Peace of Westphalia is often taken as the starting point of the modern state system. Leo Gross, one of the leading international lawyers of the last half of the twentieth century, described the Peace as the "majestic portal which leads from the old into the new world" (Gross 1948, 28). In fact the two treaties that comprise the Peace (Osnabruck and Münster) were far more ambivalent than Gross and many others have suggested. The Peace brought to an end the Thirty Years' War. Millions had died in the war, and the carnage had been exacerbated by religious conflict. The political leaders who met at Osnabruck (Protestants) and Münster (Catholics) were concerned about the constitutional structure of the Holy Roman Empire (the Peace redefined the rules governing the Electors who chose the Emperor), the division of land and treasure (France got Alsace Lorraine from the Empire), and containing the political consequences of religious differences.

The Peace emphatically did not recognize the Westphalian/Vattelian sovereignty, the autonomy, of all of its signatories. The treaties did reaffirm the right of the princes of the Holy Roman Empire to enter into treaties. This right had been given to them initially in the Golden Bull of 1356, and was thus nothing new. Moreover, the right to make treaties was conditioned by a clause that stated that any such "alliances be not against the Emperor, and the Empire, nor against the Publick Peace, and this Treaty, and without prejudice to the Oath by which every one is bound to the Emperor and the Empire" (Treaty of Münster 1648, Article LXV).

With regard to religious practices the Peace reconciled two conflicting objectives: affirming the prerogatives of princes and shielding politics from religion. The Peace endorsed the principle first enunciated in the Peace of Augsburg of 1555 that the prince could set the official religion of his territory (*cuius regio, eius religio*), but then, in several specific provisions of the treaties, constrained this right to minimize the danger that decisions by rulers could precipitate international conflicts over religion. The treaties stipulated that in several cities in the Holy Roman Empire, that had mixed Catholic and Protestant populations, authority had to be shared between adherents of both faiths. Religious practices were to be restored to those that existed on January 1, 1624 and could not be changed without mutual consent. Minorities, Catholics living in Protestant states and Protestants in Catholic ones, had the right to private religious observances and equal access to professions. Most important, the Peace provided that religious questions had to be decided by a majority of Protestants and Catholics voting separately in the Courts and Diet of the Holy Roman Empire. Rather than affirming the arbitrary power of the prince within his own territory, which *cuius regio, eius religio* seemed to suggest, it did just the opposite by constraining the power of rulers within Germany to act as they pleased with regard to religious practices within their own realms.

The principle of non-intervention in the internal affairs of other states, a principle clearly violated in the Peace of Westphalia, was first clearly articulated by the Swiss international jurist Emmerich de Vattel in the middle of the eighteenth century, which is why Westphalian/Vattelian sovereignty is a more appropriate designator than Westphalian sovereignty. (Vattelian sovereignty would be more appropriate still but would confuse most readers even more.) In the *Law of Nations* Vattel (1852, 154) wrote, "It is an evident consequence of the liberty and independence of nations, that all have a right to be governed as they think proper, and that no state has the smallest right to interfere in the government of another."

Throughout the eighteenth and nineteenth centuries many treaties, including major treaties like those that ended the Napoleonic and first and second Balkan wars, contained provisions for religious toleration and then in the nineteenth century for the rights of ethnic minorities. The major European power conditioned recognition of every successor state of the Ottoman Empire, beginning with Greece in 1832 and ending with Turkey in 1923 on the acceptance of such rights. These conditions were not based on commitments to liberal principles (although such commitments were important especially for Britain) but rather on the fear that ethnic conflict could destabilize all of Europe. As 1914 proved, they were very right to be worried.

As a condition of membership in the League of Nations more than 20 states had to sign international treaties or pledge to protect minority rights. Minorities were given the formal right to appeal to the League. Thus on the one hand Article 1 of the Covenant of the League of Nations stated that any "fully self-governing State, Dominion, or Colony" could become a member of the League on a vote of two-thirds of the members of the Assembly. On the other hand, the great powers were dictating the conditions under which some members would have to govern the minorities within their borders.

The Charter of the United Nations also includes provisions that are internally inconsistent. The second clause of the Preamble to the Charter states that the peoples of the United Nations are determined "to reaffirm faith in fundamental human rights, in the dignity and worth of the human person, in the equal rights of men and women and of nations large and small ..." The appeal here is not to sovereign states as the building block of the international system, but to individual human beings. Article 2.7 reaffirms the Westphalian/Vattelian principle of non-intervention stating that: "Nothing contained in the present Charter shall authorize the United Nations to intervene in matters which are essentially within the domestic jurisdiction of any state or shall require the Members to submit such matters to settlement under the present Charter."

This tension between individual rights and Westphalian/Vattelian sovereignty played itself out in recent debates over the concept of the responsibility to protect. The high-level plenary meeting of the UN General Assembly which took place in September 2005 concluded that states had the obligation to protect their own populations from genocide but, if they failed to do so, Article 139 of the Outcome Document stipulated that: "The international community, through the United Nations, also has the responsibility to use appropriate diplomatic, humanitarian and other peaceful means, in accordance with Chapters VI and VIII of the Charter, to help protect populations from genocide, war crimes, ethnic cleansing and crimes against humanity." The same document added that "we are prepared to take collective action, in a timely and decisive manner, through the Security Council, in accordance with the Charter, including Chapter VII, on a case-by-case basis and in cooperation with relevant regional organizations as appropriate, should peaceful means be inadequate and national authorities manifestly fail to protect their populations from genocide, war crimes, ethnic cleansing and crimes against humanity" (United Nations, General Assembly, 2005, A/RES/60/1).[1]

Contemporary Challenges

The three major challenges to sovereign statehood in the contemporary international system are the EU, failed states and states with areas of limited statehood, and the disconnect between underlying material capabilities and the destructiveness of weapons. The European Union offers an alternative to sovereign statehood. The question is: Will similar regional structures supplant conventional sovereignty in many parts of the globe? Governance failures in failed states and those with areas of limited statehood have prompted external actors to assume some responsibilities for domestic governance and service provision: Will these practices be legitimated as an alternative to conventional sovereignty? Actors with limited capabilities, both state and non-state, can project lethal force across long distances against states that command many more material capabilities: Will this lead to the abandonment of the principle of non-intervention and the creation of new legitimated alternatives to sovereignty such as some form of trusteeship?

The answer to the first question is no: The EU will not become a universal model even if it successfully addresses its present challenges. The answer to the second question is also no: The provision of services, including the exercise of executive authority by external actors will not become a legitimated alternative to conventional sovereignty. The answer to the third question is maybe: Security threats from weak entities, both state and non-state, could upend the way in which the international system is organized.

The European Union

In the contemporary world the European Union is a major exception to the conventional rules of sovereignty. The absence of a common noun is emblematic of the fact that the Union is still a work in progress. Its membership, authority structures, and basic principles are still in flux. The terms federal state, confederation, international organization, common market are thus not accurate descriptors.

The members of the EU have used their international legal sovereignty, their right to sign treaties, to create supranational institutions and pooled sovereignty arrangements that have violated their Westphalian/Vattelian sovereignty. In Robert Cooper 's (2003, 27) well-chosen words, "the European Union is a highly developed system for mutual interference in each other's domestic affairs, right down to beer and sausages." Europe's institutions and authority have evolved over time in ways that were not foreseen by its founding member states or even the European visionary statesmen of the early 1950s.

Most consequential, the successful assertion by the European Court of Justice of supremacy and direct effect in national courts enhanced the importance of collective decisions. The Court's assertion of authority reinvigorated what appeared to be a stalled process of integration in the 1960s. In the subsequent decades the scope of issues covered by agreements among European states has expanded dramatically. What began as a free trade area has become much more. There is free movement among the signatories of the Schengen Accord, which covers almost all members and some non-member states (Switzerland, Iceland, and Norway) as well. For the Eurozone, the European Central Bank sets monetary policy. New member states have had to accept European legislation, laws and court decisions covering tens of thousands of pages in more than 30 different issue areas.

The scope of the EU remains, however, unsettled with regard to issues and membership. Europe has been struggling to create a Common Defense and Security Policy, an effort that has been hamstrung by disagreements over basic strategies and different levels of commitment to defense, with France and the UK spending about 2.5 percent of their gross domestic product (GDP) on defense and most other member states spending between 1 and 1.5 percent. France and the UK took the European lead in pushing for an armed air intervention in Libya; Germany refused to participate. One third of the Union's members have not joined the Eurozone. The UK and Ireland have declined to join the Schengen accord and Bulgaria and Romania have not yet been admitted. Moreover, decisions taken in Brussels are not always implemented by member states. Romania's record is particularly poor. The quality of domestic authority structures varies widely, something vividly demonstrated by the financial crisis in Greece, which revealed high levels of corruption, cronyism, and tax avoidance.

The geographic scope of the EU is also still undecided. There are now 28 members. Whether the poorest countries in Europe, notably Albania and Bosnia, will be admitted is unclear. Because of sentiment in Europe and Turkey that country's membership seems unlikely. Although present arrangement could unravel, historical institutionalism suggests that this is unlikely. Too many interests depend on the Union; too many national institutions complement those in Brussels. National laws must conform to Community law. European businesses are organized to take advantage of the common market. University students expect to have at least the opportunity to study elsewhere in the Union.

The EU is an extraordinary accomplishment. Despite not having a common security and defense policy, its member states, who had fought each other for centuries, have created a security community within which war appears to be unthinkable. National rivalries have not disappeared, but their intensity has dramatically diminished. For most countries there is a single currency. For most residents movement across borders is unimpeded. Barriers to trade and investment are minimal. A new European identity has been created. At Verdun where more than 300,000 French and German troops were killed in 1916 there is a war memorial over which fly the flags of the Federal Republic of Germany, France, and the EU. It is impossible not to be moved by both the deaths and the reconciliation. This is a very different world from that of the mid-nineteenth century where the first question that any Prussian aristocrat would have asked about a colleague would have been, "Wo hat er gedient?", meaning in which regiment had he served (Steinberg 2011, 17). Such a query would seem like nonsense today, perhaps most of all in Germany.

The EU, however, will not become a model for other regions that might supplant sovereign statehood. The European project was facilitated by unique circumstances. After World War II, the United States encouraged economic integration and provided a security umbrella for Europe. Had the United States actively opposed European integration it would surely have failed. The US insisted on the creation of the Organization for European Economic Cooperation (OEEC) to coordinate the use of Marshall Plan funds, pushed for the abolition of quantitative trade restrictions, encouraged the European Coal and Steel Community (ECSC) and partially funded the European Payments Union, precursors of the Treaty of Rome. The US provided a security umbrella for Europe, creating the North Atlantic Treaty Organization (NATO) and stationing hundreds of thousands of troops thousands of miles from American soil for decades.

Finally, Germany's unique historical experience also provided support for integration. Germany, the largest state in Europe, was anxious to constrain its own freedom of action. In a world of conventional sovereigns Germany was always too big but not big enough. Not big enough because it could not, as the first and second world wars had shown, dominate Europe; too big because it always threatened to do so. But German attitudes toward integration were not just the result of some kind of sophisticated realpolitik calculus. Nazism delegitimated German nationalism even for Germans. Going it alone, or through some kind of conventional alliance structure was not the preferred strategy for most Germans. Many Germans wanted to redefine their national identity within a larger European community.

This unique set of circumstances—an offshore hegemonic power willing to guarantee security and support economic integration and the most powerful state within Europe welcoming less rather than more autonomy—will not be replicated elsewhere. Mercosur and the African Union, both of which have emphasized the importance of good governance not just economic considerations in regional integration, have embraced, in some cases copied verbatim, some of the language of the Union treaties. In the 1990s Mercosur, led by Brazil, prevented a military coup in Paraguay. The African Union created the New Partnership for Africa's Development (NEPAD) in 1991, which includes provisions for good governance and democracy. These regional organizations are consequential but they are still international organizations. The level of delegation to supranational institutions and the use of qualified majority voting does not compare with the situation in Europe. There is no external security guarantor. In Latin America, Africa, and Asia asymmetries of power matter. Brazil's GDP is far larger than that of its neighbors, as are those of South Africa and Nigeria. ASEAN was created to provide the smaller states of Southeast Asia a mechanism for coordinating their behavior with respect to China, Japan, and the United States. Within ASEAN, Indonesia has the potential to be a dominant enough actor to make other members nervous. Outside Europe, many political leaders are striving to create coherent national identities that can provide an alternative to and ultimately supersede traditional structures organized around family, clan, and tribe. Inside of Europe many citizens and voters are striving to create a new European identity.

The EU is an extraordinary historical accomplishment. The possibilities for a founding moment emerged from the bloodletting of the first and second world wars. It is an alternative to Westphalian/Vattelian sovereignty. It has been created and sustained because European leaders confronted a set of incentives, ideational and material, that made alienating Westphalian/Vattelian sovereignty more attractive than preserving domestic autonomy. In other regions, political leaders will continue to find autonomy more attractive than supra-national authority.

Failed and Badly Governed States

In the contemporary environment the EU is one major departure from conventional sovereignty; it is, in Cooper's term, the postmodern world. The second major departure is failed and badly governed states; in Cooper's terminology the pre-modern world. These states enjoy international legal sovereignty. They may or may not have Westphalian/Vattelian sovereignty. They do not, however, have effective domestic sovereignty. In a few states, central authority and control have collapsed. In many others there are what Thomas Risse has termed areas of limited statehood; some geographic regions and functional activities are not effectively controlled or regulated by recognized public authorities (Risse 2011).

Over the last two centuries states have assumed responsibility not just for international security, some legal proceedings, and coinage, but also for policing, macroeconomic policy, social safety nets, energy supplies, education, health, social security, censuses, transportation infrastructure, and many other activities. In the modern and postmodern worlds of Europe, North America, and parts of Asia, this expansion in the scope of state functions was a response to external and internal pressures. With the technological changes that began with the Enlightenment, effective security required a more efficient state apparatus that could borrow and tax. Urbanization, literacy, and social mobilization brought on by the industrial revolution expanded the size of the selectorate and generated new demands for a wider range of state services.

As John Meyer and his students have demonstrated, these same functions have been embraced by pre-modern states. There is a high degree of institutional isomorphism around the world with regard to the legal obligations of the state (Meyer et al. 1997). Developing and developed, new and old, small and large, Asian, African, European, American, all states assume formal legal responsibility for more or less the same set of tasks. Although the language differs, the ministry buildings in Khartoum have pretty much the same signs in front as those in Paris or Tokyo. This similarity was not a result of internal pressures or external threats. Rather, the world of pre-modern states, which came into being after World War II, was provided with a template of appropriate state functions. Richer, more developed countries provided this template. It was propagated by international organizations, aid agencies, international financial institutions, development experts, NGOs, and others. A modern state had to have a national research agency, even countries with no researchers (Finnemore 1993). States with no resources have legal mandates for old age pensions. Universal primary education has been guaranteed even by states that do have the resources to pay teachers, build schools, or buy equipment. In the pre-modern world there is a decoupling between logics of appropriateness, what states formally commit themselves to do, and logics of consequences, what they actually do.

The absence of effective domestic governance in the states of the pre-modern world is a major departure from conventional notions of sovereignty. One of the three core components of sovereignty, domestic sovereignty, is weak or missing. Many states do not conform to Max Weber's famous definition in "Politics as a Vocation" that "a state is a human community that (successfully) claims the monopoly of the legitimate use of physical force within a given territory" (Weber 1919, 77).

Failed states and states with areas of limited statehood will not necessarily become more like conventional sovereigns. The presence of such states will not, however, prompt a search for some alternative to sovereign statehood as the accepted and legitimated organizing principle of the international system despite numerous efforts to alter domestic authority structures in these states through coercion or bargaining. As historical institutionalism suggests, the interests of too many consequential actors, political leaders in both failed and powerful states, and the functioning of too many organizations—national, transnational, and international—would be compromised if the principles and rules of sovereignty were supplanted by some alternative like international trusteeship.

Regimes in weak states have always been potential targets for coercion. After World War II, the superpowers supported friendly regimes and opposed antagonistic ones. The wars and interventions in Korea, Vietnam, Hungary, Czechoslovakia, and Afghanistan were designed to influence regime types, not boundaries. These overt interventions, and covert ones as well such as Iran, Guatemala, and Chile violated the Westphalian/Vattelian sovereignty of target states in an effort to change their domestic sovereignty, but never challenged their international legal sovereignty.

Overall, however, the number of foreign imposed regime change (FIRCs) has been small over the last several centuries. One study identified 200 FIRCs from 1500 to the present (Owen 2010); another has identified 87 for the period 1816 to 2008 (Downes and Monten 2013); another found 33–37 for the period 1914 to 2001 (Lo, Hashimoto, and Reiter 2008). Less than one intervention every two to three years specifically aiming at changing a target regime is not a very big number. FIRCs are a clear violation of the principles and norms associated with Westphalian/Vattelian sovereignty but they have not generated an alternative set of principles, rules, and norms for the international system.

Efforts to change authority structures in failed states and those with areas of limited statehood have occurred much more often through bargaining and contracting than through coercion although we have no complete data-set. Contracting involves a voluntary agreement to change domestic authority structures. These contracts are completely consistent with international legal sovereignty. They are inconsistent with Westphalian/

Vattelian sovereignty, however, which assumes that each state is an autonomous entity with exclusive control over its own domestic institutions. Success has been uneven. Foreign assistance for governance reform is one example of contracting. With regard to promoting democracy and encouraging overall economic growth there is no compelling evidence that aid has done any good at all (Easterly 2006). Foreign aid programs to change domestic authority structures have, however, been layered on top of existing conventional principles of sovereignty rather than supplanting them.

Shared sovereignty or delegation agreements in which officials in target states have explicitly agreed to allow external actors to control some domestic authority structures are a second example of contracting (Krasner 2004; Matanock 2014). State functions have been contracted out to external entities. One example is customs. The collection of customs duties can be a sink of corruption. Public officials in some countries have responded to this problem, in many cases because of prodding from international financial institutions, by hiring private firms to run key elements of their customs service. Indonesia, for instance, used a Swiss firm to collect its customs for more than 11 years. In the late 1990s Mozambique contracted with Crown Agents, a British firm, to run the customs service and train indigenous personnel, a process that was completed in 2006 (James 2002).

There are examples of courts with shared sovereignty. In East Timor, Kosovo, and Sierra Leone mixed tribunals have been established that included both national and international judges. In East Timor and Kosovo these tribunals were initially created by a United Nations transitional authority, which exercised executive power. In Sierra Leone the Special Court was established through a formal treaty between the government of Sierra Leone and the United Nations (Burke-White 2002). In Guatemala the government contracted with the United Nations to establish a special investigator's office. The agreement, signed in 2006, created CICIG, the Comision International Contra la Impunitad en Guatemala. The Secretary General of the UN appointed the commissioner of CICIG, which was authorized to conduct independent investigations and act as a private prosecutor in Guatemalan courts. It could not, however, initiate prosecutions on its own, a power that some NGOs in Guatemala had initially hoped for. CICIG was created because some actors within Guatemala, both in and out of the government, recognized that there was no purely national solution to the deep level of corruption within the judicial system (Rearick-Hoefflicker 2010; see also Grann 2011). In 2015 a CICIG investigation contributed to the resignation and arrest of the president of Guatemala.

The Regional Assistance Mission to the Solomon Islands (RAMSI) is another example of shared sovereignty or authority delegation. In 2003 the Solomon Islands, never very effectively governed, was on the verge of collapse. Gangs had seized weapons from armories in the capital, Honoraria. The political leaders in the Solomons understood that they were about to lose power, and appealed to Australia and other Pacific countries. Acting under a Chapter VI UN resolution, legislation passed by the Solomon Islands, and the endorsement of the Pacific Island Forum, a consortium of Pacific islands states led by Australia took control of key financial activities, including the auditor general's office, as well as parts of the police and judicial systems. The cost for Australia is substantial, about $200 million a year. The success of RAMSI is not guaranteed. It is, however, one case where external actors have probably prevented state failure by assuming direct responsibility for core government activities (RAMSI n.d.; Fullilove 2006).

FIRCs, foreign aid, and authority delegation will persist. The powerful will sometimes conclude that it is in their interest to change the domestic authority structures of weaker target states. Leaders in failed states or states with areas of limited statehood will, at times, find it to be in their interest to voluntarily compromise their state's Westphalian/Vattelian sovereignty. FIRCs and sovereignty delegation will not, however, lead to the development of some new set of principles, norms, and rules that would complement or supplant those of sovereignty. Rather, public officials will continue to embrace the conventional norms of sovereignty even if they violate them in practice. As historical institutionalism suggests, the costs of moving to some new set of structures that would recognize and legitimate a permanent loss of autonomy, such as some kind of permanent trusteeship would be opposed by political leaders in more and less powerful states; in the former because they would reject any obligation to bear the cost of exercising authority; in the latter because it would deny them access to the resources and prestige that come with being the ruler of a nominally (that is, recognized) sovereign state.

Security Threats

If sovereign statehood's monopoly as the only legitimated structure for organizing political life were to end, it will be not be because of the European Union or poor governance in failed and badly governed states. The impetus for transformational change, for a new founding moment will come, if it does come, from threats to or attacks on the physical security of powerful states from actors with limited material capabilities. Until the development of nuclear and biological weapons and delivery systems that could strike across thousands of miles, there was a close connection between the material resources commanded by a state or other political entity and its ability to injure others. The most powerful states in the system were vulnerable to attacks, but only from other powerful states. This is no longer the case.

Threats and attacks from non-state actors could lead to new behaviors and these behaviors could be legitimated, institutionalized, and codified into new principles, norms, and rules. Such a change would only take place if political leaders believed that some new institutional structures would protect the security of their polities more effectively than organized hypocrisy practiced within the context of sovereign statehood.

Technology and globalizations have led to a disconnect between the underlying resources of actors, both state and non-state, and their ability to do harm. Actors with limited material capabilities can procure weapons and delivery systems that can wreak havoc on opponents commanding a much larger resource base. Some of these possibilities are clearly visible, such as nuclear and biological weapons; some are only emerging such as cyber-attacks and nanobots; others will come.

The Combined Indicator of National Capacity (CINC) used by the Correlates of War project is based on six components: total population, urban population, iron and steel production, energy consumption, military personnel, and military expenditure. According to this indicator North Korea commanded about 1 percent of the combined capabilities of all states in the international system in 2000. Despite this very modest level of resources North Korea could launch nuclear weapons that could kill millions of people in China, Russia, and Japan. Pakistan, whose CINC figure is .014 for 2000 (that is about 1.5 percent of the world total), has supported terrorist attacks against critical facilities in India, both government and public, whose CINC score is .068 and, because of Pakistan's nuclear weapons and strategic posture India has found no effective way to respond (Correlates of War 2014).

Biological weapons could also kill tens or even hundreds of thousands or even millions of people. The Office of Technological Assessment of the US Congress estimated in 1993 that a single aerial anthrax attack against Washington DC could kill 1 to 3 million people (United States Congress, Office of Technology Assessment 1993). Biologicals are easier to obtain than nuclear weapons. Many of the technologies are dual use; facilities producing non-military agents could also be used to produce weapons. The equipment and materials needed to produce biological weapons are hard to restrict because they can also be used to produce drugs and vaccines. New agents can be created through genetic manipulation. DNA synthesis could make it possible to produce the most dangerous controlled pathogens such as smallpox. The agents themselves are compact and easy to transport. Detection is difficult: The Soviet Union and Iraq both had extensive biological weapons programs that ran through the 1980s despite the fact that both countries were signatories to the 1975 Biological Weapons Convention.

Finally, there is a range of possible unconventional threats that are now only dimly perceptible. The opening page of a thought provoking paper written by Harvard Law professor Gabriella Blum is worth quoting at length:

> You walk into your shower and find a spider. You are not an entomologist. You do, however, know that any one of the four following options is possible:
>
> a. The spider is real and harmless.
> b. The spider is real and venomous.
> c. Your next door neighbor, who dislikes your noisy dog, has turned her personal surveillance spider (purchased from "Drones 'R Us" for $49.95) loose, and is monitoring it on her iPhone from her seat at a sports bar downtown. The pictures of you, undressed, are now being relayed on several screens during the break of an NFL game, to the mirth of the entire neighborhood.
> d. Your business competitor has sent his drone assassin spider, which he purchased from a bankrupt military contractor, to take you out. Upon spotting you with its sensors, and before you have had any time to weigh your options, the spider shot an infinitesimal needle into a vein in your left leg and taken a blood sample. As you beat a retreat out of the shower, your blood sample is being run on your competitor's smartphone for a DNA match. The match is checked against a DNA sample of you that is

> already on file at EVER.com (Everything about Everybody), an international DNA database (with access available for $179.99). Once the match is confirmed (a matter of seconds), the assassin spider outruns you with incredible speed into your bedroom, pausing only long enough to dart another needle, this time containing a lethal dose of a synthetically produced, undetectable poison, into your blood system. Your assassin, who is on a summer vacation in Provence, then withdraws his spider under the crack of your bedroom door and out of the house and presses its self-destruct button. No trace of the spider or the poison it carried will ever be found by law enforcement authorities.

This is the future. According to some estimates, insect-size drones will become operational by 2030 (Blum 2011).

Neither national boundaries nor a lock on the front door would offer protection from mini-drones carrying deadly toxins piloted from central Asia, or from cyber thieves sitting in West Africa from emptying a bank account in Des Moines. Blum goes on to argue that unconventional threats against private individuals, not just states, emanating from polities that either cannot or will not act against criminals within their borders would lead to a breakdown of conventional rules and norms associated with state sovereignty. There will be a greater incentive for international cooperation in policing, Blum argues, but also more unilateral action against perpetrators in weak states. The conventional norms associated with Westphalian/Vattelian sovereignty would break down. There would no longer be general acceptance that national authorities ought to be the sole source of legitimate authority within their own territory.

Conclusion

Any international environment, any environment extending beyond a single polity, will be complex, populated by different kinds of actors, with varying capacities and interests, and diverse beliefs about legitimacy and justice. Some of these environments become systems that are organized around well-defined principles, norms, and rules. The modern sovereign state system is one example; the traditional Sino-centric system is another. Because of their complexity all international systems have been characterized by organized hypocrisy: no set of principles, norms, and rules will be universally adhered to. As historical institutionalism suggests different organizational forms are layered one on top of the other. Actors are, however, reluctant to move to a fundamentally new system, to a different set of principles, norms, and rules. Too many interests and too many organizations are tied into the extant structure.

If the sovereign state system is transformed, if there is a new founding moment, it will be because of security threats emanating from polities with weak domestic sovereignty. Some of the problems presented by poorly governed states, such as disease transmission and criminal activity, can be most effectively addressed by layering new institutional forms on top of conventional sovereignty. More powerful states will focus on ways to address the health issues of their own citizens first, and to limit cyber theft by taking action within their own borders. They will provide foreign assistance to weakly governed states. If governance totally breaks down they may even assume executive authority for some limited period of time. Disease and criminality will not, however, prompt them to generate a new set of principles, rules, and norms that would displace or complement sovereign statehood.

If, however, states with limited capacity threaten the core security interests of the powerful, the international system could be transformed. A WMD attack that killed substantial numbers of people, say more than 10,000, by a transnational terrorist group operating from an impoverished state would end the monopoly over legitimated political order that conventional sovereignty now enjoys. There would not just be military retaliation; new institutional structures would also be created in which the powerful would exercise executive authority over some or all of the territory of the weak. The international legal sovereignty and Westphalian/Vattelian sovereignty of the target state would be extinguished. Attacks on private individuals, murders orchestrated from afar, would not precipitate the creation of trusteeships or some kind of shared sovereignty but could lead to the legitimation of cross-border military operations, the creation of a transnational militarized police force authorized to operate in poorly governed states, or the formal legal recognition of the right of private security firms to operate in weakly governed states under authority granted by their home countries.

The probability that sovereign statehood will be displaced is not high. Nuclear weapons are very hard to obtain and to use. Biological weapons are easier but still difficult to secure and to weaponize. The most effective measures against spider robots, drones, and other remotely controlled delivery vehicles could be some kind of electronic door lock rather than striking at the source. Nevertheless, if sovereign statehood is supplanted or complemented by some alternative structure, that structure will be put in place because of the security threat posed by actors, state or non-state, with limited material capabilities but control over weapons that could kill thousands or tens of thousands even in states commanding formidable resources.

Notes

* The author wishes to thank the editors of this project, especially Orfeo Fioretos, and the participants in the conference on New Perspectives in Historical Institutionalism held at Temple University and the University of Pennsylvania, October 25–26, 2013.

1. Glanville (2013), adopting an explicitly constructivist frame, argues that over the last several centuries the principle of non-intervention has always been limited by contrasting principles that conditioned autonomy on certain standards of domestic behavior.

References

Blum, G. 2011. "Invisible Threat." Unpublished Paper, Harvard University, December 28, 2011.

Brunsson, N. 1989.*The Organization of Hypocrisy: Talk, Decisions and Actions in Organization.* Chichester: John Wiley and Sons.

Burke-White W. W. (2002) "A Community of Courts: Toward a System of International Criminal Law Enforcement?" *Michigan Journal of International Law* 24: 1–102.

Cooper, R. 2003.*The Breaking of Nations: Order and Chaos in the Twenty-first Century* New York: Atlantic Monthly Press.

Correlates of War. 2014. *National Material Capabilities (v3.02).* Available at <http://www.correlatesofwar.org/COW2%20Data/Capabilities/nmc3-02.htm> (accessed August 21, 2013).

Downes, A. and J. Monten. 2013. "Freedom by Force: Foreign-Imposed Regime Change and Democratization." *International Security* 37 (4): 90–131.

Easterly, W. 2006. *The White Man's Burden: Why the West's Efforts to Aid the Rest Have done So Much Ill and So Little Good.* New York: Penguin Press.

Finnemore, M. 1993. "International Organizations as Teachers of Norms: The United Nations Educational, Scientific, and Cultural Organization and Science Policy." *International Organization* 47 (4): 565–597.

Fioretos, O. 2011. "Historical Institutionalism in International Relations." *International Organization* 65 (2): 367–399.

Fullilove, M. 2006. "The Testament of Solomons: RAMSI and International State-Building, Sydney: Lowy Institute." Available at <http://www.lowyinstitute.org/Publication.asp?pid=351> (accessed August 23, 2013).

Glanville, Luke. 2013. "The Myth of 'Traditional' Sovereignty." *International Studies Quarterly* 57 (1): 79–90.

Grann D. 2011. "A Murder Foretold: Unravelling the Ultimate Political Conspiracy." *New Yorker* April 4. Available at <http://www.newyorker.com/reporting/2011/04/04/110404fa_fact_grann> (accessed July 28, 2013).

Gross, L. 1948. "The Peace of Westphalia, 1648–1948." *American Journal of International Law* 42 (1): 20–41.

James, W. E. 2002. *A Note on Pre-Shipment Inspection of Imports.* Washington, D.C.: USAID. Available at <http://www.dec.org/pdf_docs/PNACQ680.pdf> (accessed August 5, 2013).

Kayaoglu, T. 2010. *Legal Imperialism: Sovereignty and Extraterritoriality in Japan, the Ottoman, Empire, and China.* New York: Cambridge University Press.

Krasner, S. 1999. *Sovereignty: Organized Hypocrisy.* Princeton, NJ: Princeton University Press.

Krasner, S. 2004. "Sharing Sovereignty: New Institutions for Collapsed and Failing States." *International Security* 29 (2): 85–120.

Lo, N., B. Hashimoto, and D. Reiter. 2008. "Ensuring Peace: Foreign-Imposed Regime Change and Postwar Peace Duration, 1914–2001." *International Organization* 62 (4): 717–736.

March, J. G. and J. Olsen. 1989. *Rediscovering Institutions: The Organizational Basis of Politics.* New York: Free Press.

Matanock, A. M. 2014. "Governance Delegation Agreements: Shared Sovereignty as a Substitute for Limited Statehood." *Governance: An International Journal of Policy, Administration, and Institutions* 27 (4): 589–612.

Meyer, J. W., J. Boli, G. M. Thomas, and F. O. Ramirez. 1997. "World Society and the Nation-State." *American Journal of Sociology* 103: 144–181.

Owen, J. M. 2010. *The Clash of Ideas in World Politics: Transnational Networks, States and Regime Change 1510–2010*. Princeton, NJ: Princeton University Press.

RAMSI (The Regional Assistance Mission to Solomon Islands). n.d. *Our Work*. The Regional Assistance Mission to Solomon Islands, Helpem Fren. Available at <http://www.ramsi.org/node/5> (accessed August 7, 2013).

Rearick-Hoefflicker, J. 2010. "CICIG's Anti-Corruption Approach in Guatemala." *Gonzaga Journal of International Law* 14 (7). Available at <https://www.law.gonzaga.edu/gjil/2011/06/cicigs-anti-corruption-approach-in-guatemala/> (accessed August 9, 2015).

Risse, T. 2011. "Governance in Areas of Limited Statehood: Introduction and Overview." In *Governance Without A State: Policies and Politics in Areas of Limited Statehood*, ed. Thomas Risse. New York: Columbia University Press, 1–35.

Spruyt, H. 1996. *The Sovereign State and Its Competitors*. Princeton, NJ: Princeton University Press.

Steinberg, J. 2011. *Bismark: A Life*. New York: Oxford.

The Fund for Peace. 2014. *Fragile States Index 2014*. Available at <http://ffp.statesindex.org/rankings-2014> (accessed August 8, 2014).

Tilly, C. 1990. *Coercion, Capital, and European States, AD 990–1990*. Cambridge, MA: Basil Blackwell.

Treaty of Munster. 1648. In *Major Peace Treaties of Modern History, 1648–1967*, vol. 1, ed. F. L. Israel. New York: McGraw-Hill.

United Nations, General Assembly. 2005. *A/RES/60/1 2005 World Summit Outcome*, October 24. Available at <http://unpan1.un.org/intradoc/groups/public/documents/un/unpan021752.pdf> (accessed August 20, 2013).

United States Congress, Office of Technology Assessment. 1993. *Proliferation of Weapons of Mass Destruction: Assessing the Risks*, OTA-ISC-559, S/N 052-003-01335-5, August 5, 1993.

Vattel, Emmerich de. 1852. *The Law of Nations; or, Principles of the Law of Nature, Applied to the Conduct and Affairs of Nations and Sovereigns*, ed. J. Chitty and E. D. Ingraham. Philadelphia, PA: T. & J. W. Jonson.

Weber, M. 1919. "Politics as a Vocation". In *Max Weber: Essays in Sociology*, trans. and ed. H. Gerth and C. Mills. New York: Oxford University Press, 77–128.

CHAPTER 32

THE RISE, CHARACTER, AND EVOLUTION OF INTERNATIONAL ORDER

G. JOHN IKENBERRY

THE world is watching a great drama of power shifts and struggles over global institutions. For over half a century, the United States has presided over a far-flung international order, organized around an array of global and regional economic and security institutions. In the last decade, however, a grouping of rising non-Western states, led by China, has emerged, seeking to translate their growing power into authority and voice while advancing various reform agendas. But this global power transition is not a simple story of rules and institutions shifting to accord with rapidly changing distributions of capacities and interests. The "old order" is not easily swept away. To understand the grand struggles between rising and declining states, it is necessary to look closely at the way in which global and regional institutions order get created and entrenched. It is not that institutional change is impossible; rather, it is that the nature of change can best be illuminated by reference to historical institutional dynamics and legacies of the past.

International order refers to the organizing rules and institutions of world politics. It is the governing arrangements that define and guide the relations among states. To speak of international order is to invoke notions of a functioning political system—however rudimentary—among states. International order is not just the crystallization of the distribution of power. It exists in the organizing principles, authority relations, functional roles, shared expectations, and settled practices through which states do business. It establishes the terms by which states command, follow, benefit, and suffer.

Scholarly theories and debate about international order—its logic and changing character—is found in various international relations (IR) literatures, including classical realist writings, diplomatic history, the English school, and theories of "system and structure." Theories and debates about international order focus on the core underlying "problems" of international relations. How is order created and maintained in a world of sovereign states? Who commands and who benefits? What are the rules and institutions that make up the governance structure of the order? State power, anarchy, insecurity—these realist features of world politics are never very far from center stage. But the focus is on how states create rules and arrangements for ongoing relations of competition and cooperation.[1] World politics is not simply states operating in anarchy—it is an active political order with rules, institutions, roles, and accumulated understandings and expectations.

From this starting point, several observations follow. First, across historical eras, international order has come and gone, risen and fallen. States have built ordering arrangements in various ways, only to see order eventually breakdown or transform itself. Indeed, scholars often mark the great eras of world politics in terms of the building and breakdown of order. Second, these great moments of order building have tended to come after major wars—1648, 1713, 1815, 1919, 1945, and 1989. Peace conferences and settlement agreements have followed these great wars, putting in place institutions and arrangements for postwar order. Victorious states have been given opportunities to organize and lead the system. Third, the actual character of international order has varied across these eras and order building moments. International order has varied in many ways, including in its geographical scope, organizational logic, rules and institutions, and the manner and degree to which coercion and consent undergird the resulting order (Ikenberry 2001, 79–118). International order has also varied in terms of its "solidarist" character, that is, the degree to which order is infused with shared notions of law and justice (Hurrell 2007).

Because international orders differ in character from one era and geographic area to another, it is possible to compare them. Some international orders have been more coherent, long-lasting, and consent-based than others. Some international orders have been organized and run "from the center" and others less so. Some international orders have been imperial and others more liberal in character. The durability of orders has also varied. Some international orders—such as the post-1815 order—lasted for nearly a century, while the post-1919 order never fully took shape. The American-led order built after World War II has had a wide range of features—economic, political, and security. More than past international orders, it has been globally expansive, organized around layers of institutions and alliance partnerships—and it has endured into the current era.

These observations suggest that a simple "rise and decline" theory of international order is inadequate. The idea that leading states periodically have found themselves in a position to build or at least shape international order is not in dispute. But the explanation for the variations in the character of orders does seem to depend on more than simply the presence of a powerful leading state. Moments of opportunity for order building open up and close. The character of the state that finds itself with the opportunity to build order also seems to matter. The rise of democracy and capitalism—and the wider and deeper transformations yielded by modernization—are also important as background conditions helping to determine what types of states actually emerge as leading states, their interests and agendas, and the international orders they build.

The task of scholarship is to explain the sources and changing character of international order. How have states turned power into order? Why have international orders taken on the character that they have—and why and in what ways have they varied across time and space? In answering these questions, a historical institutionalist approach is useful. Historical institutionalism offers ways of thinking about the origins, evolution, and consequences of international political institutions, including the origins and changing character of international order (Fioretos 2011). It directs attention to the temporal dynamics that shape institutions and institutional change. The timing and sequence of past events set the terms—creating constraints, incentives, opportunities, legacies—for subsequent political struggles. The focus is also on the various functions and roles of institutions as they are manifest across their historical life cycles, a multifaceted view of institutions that sees them reflecting and, at other moments, shaping political actors and social forces.

This chapter looks at the major episodes of modern international order-building, which occurred after great power wars of the last four centuries. World politics can be seen as a sequence of historical cycles or eras punctuated by great power wars. At periodic moments, war between the great powers has destroyed the old order and opened up opportunities for new leading states to step forward to build something new. Winners and losers emerge. The distribution of power shifts. States that win wars are given opportunities to reshape the new international order. As Robert Gilpin argues, these periodic wars "resolve the question of which state will govern the system, as well as what ideas and values will predominate" (Gilpin 1981, 203). To explain the outcomes and consequences of these order-building moments, we need to look closely at the temporal dynamics of crisis and change in global power relations.

There are several historical institutionalist concepts that are relevant to explaining the logic and change in international order: critical junctures, path dependence, increasing returns, and evolutionary change. I argue that these concepts are useful for making sense of the sequences and changing character of international order. At some moments in world politics, turning points or critical junctures emerge—typically after a major war—that loosen the constraints on at least the most powerful states, offering opportunities for these states to lay down new rules and institutions of order. But at other moments, the rules and institutions become formidable constraints and operate to reinforce and limit choices and ideas. To understand the rise, fall, and changing character of international order, the historical context matters—timing, sequencing, unintended consequences, and policy feedback.

Critical Junctures

Max Weber famously argued that politics and society run on "tracks" that are laid down at critical moments in a country's history. Occasionally, new ideas or "world images" emerge that transform the terms of struggle among societal interests. But aside from these rare moments, groups and individuals in society pursue their interests along established tracks—by which he meant a country's political institutions (Weber 1946, 280).

Weber's idea is that polities pass through founding moments or critical junctures that fix in place basic political orientations and institutions. Polities do change, of course, but the claim is that the basic organizational logic gets established at certain critical moments—and subsequent changes tend to be variations or extensions on that logic. The past determines the present, but not necessarily in a continuous way (Capoccia and Kelemen 2007; Pierson 2000).

International order-building exhibits critical junctures logic. Moments open up, giving powerful states the opportunity to lay down the "tracks" along which inter-state relations run. The moments after great power war stand out as major turning points—1648, 1713, 1815, 1919, and 1945. At these junctures, newly powerful states have been given extraordinary opportunities to shape world politics. In the chaotic aftermath of war, leaders of these states have found themselves in unusually advantageous positions to put forward new rules and principles of international relations and by so doing remake international order (Ikenberry 2001).

The great postwar junctures share a set of characteristics that make them unusually important in providing opportunities for leading states to shape international order. The war itself has destroyed the old international order. The option of "operating in the current international order" has suddenly disappeared. Moreover, the war and the struggles surrounding it have delegitimated the rules and institutions of the old order. Indeed, the war itself is evidence of the failure of the old order. The war also has ushered in a new distribution of power, creating new asymmetries between powerful and weak states. In effect, great power war—like a powerful storm—has destroyed and cleared away the old rules and institutional structures. The slate has been more or less wiped clean. A newly powerful state or group of states can now step forward to rethink and rebuild international order. The constraints of the old order are thrown off, at least temporarily and at least for the most powerful states.

During critical junctures, the leading state has choices to make. As I argue in *After Victory* (Ikenberry 2001), a state that wins a war has acquired what can be seen as a "windfall" of power assets. The winning postwar state is newly powerful—indeed, in some cases it is newly hegemonic, acquiring a preponderance of material capabilities. It has several broad choices. It can simply use its power to engage in the endless struggle over the distribution of gains. It can pull back and simply remain an isolationist state. Or it can try to build order—that is, it can try to transform its favorable postwar power position into a durable system of rules than commands the allegiance of other states. To engage in order building it needs to find ways to establish—or entrench—rules and institutions that advance its interests while also gaining the acquiescence of weaker and secondary states.

These critical junctures entail opportunities and specific sets of demands on the leading state. At each historical moment, the basic task of order building is on the table. How can the rules and institutions of order be established so as to advance and protect the interests of the leading state? In the first instance, this has involved questions of power and the restraint on power in the postwar period. If states are unable to signal restraint, the postwar order will tend to fall back on the balance of power or imperial forms of order. But if power can be restrained and states can make commitments to each other, more sophisticated and bargained forms of order are possible. Generally speaking, the ability of states to engage in what can be called "strategic restraint" has evolved over the centuries, and this has indeed changed the way in which leading states have been able to create and maintain international order. The earliest postwar order building efforts mostly entailed the separation and dispersion of power and later the counterbalancing of power. More recently, postwar states have dealt with the uncertainties and disparities in state power with institutional strategies that—to varying degrees—bind states together and circumscribe how and when state power can be exercised (Ikenberry 2001, 50–79).

Beginning with the 1815 settlement, and increasingly after 1919 and 1945, the leading states resorted to institutional strategies as mechanisms to establish restraints on state power and "lock in" a favorable and durable postwar order. The postwar order-building agendas pursued by Britain after the Napoleonic wars and the United States after the two world wars entailed increasingly expansive proposals to establish intergovernmental institutions that would bind the great powers together and institutionalize their relations after each war. In the twentieth century, the United States brought an ambitious agenda for order building that went beyond anything that had been seen before. In the post-1945 era, the United States offered a vision of order in which states would be drawn into a wide array of political, economic, and security institutions and partnerships. The critical juncture mattered in at least two respects. It mattered in the way it positioned a leading state after the war so as to take advantage of the moment. It amplified its influence—Britain in the nineteenth century and the United States in the twentieth century—and the ideas it wielded. The extent of the critical juncture itself also mattered. The break after World War II was much more dramatic and complete than the earlier junctures. The war more thoroughly destroyed the "old order" and the power disparities between the United States and the other great powers were greater. This gave the United States truly unprecedented opportunities to purvey its order building agenda.

As the sequence of order building moments suggest, change in the rules and institutions of international order has been episodic—emerging after wars or other moments of crisis or upheaval. At these junctures, the old institutional structures are most likely to be discredited or broken down. The discontinuities between underlying distribution of power and interests, on the one hand, and institutional structures, on the other, are most likely to be thrown into relief. The "tracks" along with international relations run are destroyed, and an opportunity opens up for a newly powerful state or states to lay down new tracks.

Path Dependence

International order also exhibits features of path dependence. At least when it comes to overarching international rules and institutions, change tends to be episodic rather than continuous and incremental. Institutional structures, once established, can be difficult to change even when underlying social forces continue to evolve. Within the global system, the distribution of power and social forces are continuously changing. Yet the rules and institutions of international orders, once put in place, do tend to persist, at least until a subsequent disruption shatters the old rules and institutions and opens up a new moment of order building.

Historical institutionalism relies on a variety of arguments to account for the persistence of institutional structures. One is simply that institutions tend to create privileged positions for groups and individuals who work to perpetuate those institutions, even after the interests that created the institutions have gone or changed. Within formal organizations, individuals seek to preserve their missions and responsibilities, often in the face of a radically changed environment. Others have explained institutional persistence—even when a coalition of powerful actors might benefit from a different set of institutions—in terms of costs and uncertainty. As Stephen Krasner argues, "even if there is widespread societal dissatisfaction with a particular set of institutions, it may be irrational to change them. The variable costs of maintaining the existing institutions may be less than the total costs of creating and maintaining new ones" (Krasner 1984, 235). The sticky character of institutions is also stressed in the literature on political sociology and political development—in works associated, for example, with Weber, Hintze, and Bendix. As Joseph Schumpeter put it, "[s]ocial structures, types, and attitudes are coins that do not readily melt" (Schumpeter 1960, 12). In this view, it is the "embedding" of institutions in wider realms of social and economic structures which reinforce and reproduce the institutional order.

Few scholars would argue that international rules and institutions are as "sticky" as those within stable domestic political systems. But a path dependence logic is still evident. Indeed, this presence of path-dependent effects helps explain why leading states—particularly in the last two centuries—have attempted to build order around various sorts of institutions. They have sought to entrench their interests in institutions, doing so with the anticipation that those institutions will persist. All the postwar moments—including 1648, 1713, and 1815—involved the promulgation of rules and governing arrangements. Diplomacy and rule making were on display. The great power wars that preceded these moments were themselves a ratification of the failure of the old arrangements. As a result, the rules and institutions that are established at these postwar moments take on a sort of "constitutional" significance, at least until the next geopolitical upheaval comes along. The behavior of state leaders at these moments seems to confirm this path dependent opportunity. Not all leaders were acting as Woodrow Wilson said he was at Versailles, "playing for one hundred years hence" (Knock 2009, 30). But state leaders across these postwar moments were acting as if what they did would last for more than a few generations. And indeed—with perhaps the ironic exception of Wilson's failed efforts—the settlements that followed these wars did tend to establish ordering arrangements that lasted.

Along the way, the settlements grew increasingly global in scope. The Westphalian settlement in 1648 was primarily a continental European settlement, whereas the

Utrecht settlement of 1713 saw the beginning of Britain's involvement in shaping the European state system. The Vienna settlement in 1815 brought the wider colonial and non-European world into negotiations. In the twentieth century, the settlements were truly global. The peace agreements also expanded in scope and reach. They dealt with a widening range of security, territorial, economic, and functional issues and they became increasingly intrusive, entailing greater involvement in the internal structures and administration of the defeated states; they culminated in 1945 with the occupation and reconstruction of Germany and Japan.

Postwar ordering moments also changed over time in the degree to which the leading states had available and used institutional tools. With the rise of liberal democracies over the last two centuries, the leading states have had options that did not exist previously. Particularly in the twentieth century, the United States was able to contemplate building order around quite complex forms of institutional cooperation. As states found ways to use institutions to restrain and bind themselves to each other, the possibilities for international order expanded enormously.

Leading states—poised to create order at postwar moments—have many incentives to use institutions. The pre-eminent motive has to do with power disparities. The leading state is much more powerful than other states—certainly more so than defeated states—after the war. These disparities in power create opportunities for the order building state to use institutions to lock in its advantages. At the same time, institutional agreements can also be used to bind states together and thereby reduce the risks of domination or abandonment that weaker states might face (Ikenberry 2001). In effect, institutions provide tools to help address two leading state goals—to create rules and institutions that advance and protect its long-term interests and to establish some restraints on power in ways that draw other states into the international order. In Weber's terms, the goal is legitimate domination (Weber 1968, 212–301).

It is the path dependency of postwar order building that creates incentives for leading states to calculate for the long-term and try to entrench institutions that protect their interests and legitimate their power. Historical junctures and discontinuities create variation across time in the type of "politics" that states pursue. At rare moments, they pursue the international equivalent of "constitutional politics," making choices about the basic organizing terms of order. If all "international time" was equal and change was always incremental, we would not see—or be able to explain—these moments of constitutional politics. Doing something today that will benefit you tomorrow and well into the future—these are the golden moments of international relations. With the rise of liberal democracies over the last two centuries, Britain and the United States increasingly looked to institutional agreements to do things that would create ongoing benefits. In this sense, the terms or logic of postwar path dependence has changed over time with the rise and spread of liberal democracy and advanced industrial society. State power is a sort of "asset" that can be used to project your interests in the out years. If institutions are sticky, and if they can be entrenched at postwar moments, this creates new ways to protect your interests—and new ways to build international order.

Increasing Returns

An important reason why political order can have path-dependent characteristics is the phenomenon of "increasing returns" to institutions. There are several aspects to increasing returns (Arthur 1989). First, large initial startup costs tend to exist in the creation of new institutions. Even when alternative institutions might be more efficient or accord more closely with the interests of powerful states, the gains for the new institutions must be overwhelmingly greater before they overcome the sunk costs of the existing institutions. Second, there tend to be learning effects that are achieved in the operation of the existing institutions that give it advantages over a new institution. Finally, institutions tend to create relations and commitments with other actors and institutions that serve to embed the institution and raise the costs of change. Taken together, as Douglass North concludes, "the interdependent web of an institutional matrix produces massive increasing returns" (North 1990, 95).

The notion of increasing returns to institutions means that once a moment of institutional selection comes and goes, the costs of large-scale institutional change rises dramatically, even if potential institutions, when compared to existing ones, are more efficient and desirable (Krasner, Chapter 31, this volume; Fioretos 2011). In terms of postwar settlements, this means that, short of another war or a global economic collapse, it is very difficult to create the type of historical breakpoint to replace the existing order. After the postwar institutions are in place, the cost logic shifts. At these later moments, rival institutional orders must compete with a pre-existing order, with all the sunk costs and vested interests that it manifests.

The American-led postwar international order has exhibited the phenomenon of increasing returns to institutions. At the very early moments after 1945, when imperial, bilateral, and regional alternatives to America's postwar agenda were most imminent, the United States was able to use its unusual and momentary advantages to tilt the system in the direction it desired. The pathway to the present international order began at a very narrow passage where really only Britain and the United States—and a few top officials—could shape decisively the basic orientation of the world political economy. But once the institutions, such as those erected at Bretton Woods and the General Agreement on Tariffs and Trade, were established, it became increasingly hard for competing visions of postwar order to have any viability. America's burst of institution building after World War II fits a general pattern of institutional continuity and change: crisis or war opens up a moment of flux and opportunity, choices are made, and interstate relations get fixed or settled for a while.

While institutions can serve to perpetuate institutions of many sorts, the United States purveyed institutions that particularly lent themselves to increasing returns. First, the set of principles that infused these institutions—particularly principles of multilateralism, openness, and reciprocity—are ones that command agreement because of their seeming fairness and legitimacy. Organized around principles that are easy for states to accept, regardless of their specific international power position, the institutional pattern is more robust and easy to expand. As John Ruggie argues, "[a]ll other things being equal, an arrangement based on generalized organizing principles should be more elastic than one based on particularistic interests and situational exigencies" (Ruggie 1993, 32–33). In this sense, it is both the adaptability of these institutions and their seeming legitimacy that has given them their robustness. Second, the open and penetrated character of the postwar order—its liberal character—also served to facilitate increasing returns. These characteristics encouraged the proliferation of connecting groups and institutions, and a dense set of transnational and transgovernmental channels were woven into the international order. A sort of layer cake of intergovernmental institutions was extended outward from the United States across the Atlantic and Pacific. The steady rise of trade and investment across the regions of the world made countries within the order more interdependent, which in turn expanded the constituencies within these countries for the perpetuation of the rules and institutions that support an open, multilateral system.

The institutional logic of increasing returns is useful in explaining the remarkable stability of the post-1945 order among the industrial democracies—an order that has persisted despite the end of the Cold War and the huge asymmetries of power. More than in 1815 or 1919, the circumstances in 1945 provided opportunities for the leading state to move toward an institutionalized settlement. Once in place, the open and democratic character of the states facilitated the further growth of intergovernmental institutions and commitments, creating deeper linkages between these states, making it increasingly difficult for alternative orders to replace the existing one.

Indeed, the institutional logic of post-1945 order explains both the way the Cold War ended and the persistence of this order after the Cold War. It tells us why the Soviet Union gave up with so little resistance and acquiesced in a united and more powerful Germany tied to NATO. Soviet leaders appreciated that the institutional aspects of political order in the West made it less likely that these states would take advantage of the Soviets as they pursued reform and integration. The institutional structure of the Western countries mitigated the security consequences of an adverse shift in power disparities and the rise of a united Germany, and this gave the Soviets incentives to go forward with their fateful decisions sooner and on terms more favorable to the West than they would have otherwise been. The expansive and sunk cost character of the postwar American-led international order helps account for why it continued to persist—indeed to expand outward and deepen—despite the collapse of bipolarity even if (in the case of NATO) there was no immediately apparent function for it to perform. After the Cold War, this order remained the dominant reality of world politics.

In fact, arguably, the existing international order has become more stable over time because the rules and institutions have become more firmly embedded in the wider structures of politics and society. The logic of increasing returns to institutions is at work. Over the decades, the core institutions of this increasingly global international order have sunk their roots ever more deeply into the political and economic structures of the states that participate within the order. The result is that it has become more difficult for "alternative institutions" and "alternative leadership" to seriously emerge. The American-led order has become institutionalized and path dependent—that is, more and more people will have to disrupt their lives if the order is to radically change. This has made wholesale change—absent a major historical upheaval—less likely over time (Ikenberry 1998).

The durability of this order is built on two logics. First, the institutional features of the order allow states to establish restraints on power and commitments to complex forms of cooperation. As a result, states worry less about domination or abandonment, and this lowers the risks of participation by strong and weak states alike. This in turn makes a resort to balancing and relative gains competition less necessary. Second, the institutions also exhibit an increasing returns character, which makes it steadily more difficult for would-be orders and would-be hegemonic leaders to compete against and replace the existing order and leader.

Evolutionary Dynamics

Across history, leading states that win great power wars have been presented with a common opportunity—to organize the terms of postwar order. But they have done so differently. The types of states that are doing the order building and their agendas for international order have evolved over the centuries. The scale and scope of the orders have grown, and the uses of institutions in organizing relations among states have become more extensive and sophisticated. The question arises, therefore: In the long succession of international orders, is there an evolutionary logic to their changing substantive character? Is there sequencing and development of international order in the sense that each ordering moment builds on—and in some sense incorporates and reflects—those that have come before it?

A simple rise and decline theory of international order resists the idea of an evolutionary logic. In his classic account, Robert Gilpin (1981) argues that states that win major wars bring their own ideas, values, and interests to order building. There is no evolutionary logic at work. The leading state constructs a political order around it, but these postwar efforts are all distinct, discrete, and unrelated to what came before or what will come later. Alternatively, some scholars see a trans-historical master evolutionary logic that shapes postwar orders and the overall direction of world politics (Modelski 1990).

Between these extremes, the sequence of postwar orders suggests that some sort of contingent evolutionary dynamic is at work. One possible source of evolution relates to the character of the states that win great power wars. It might be that the regime types of states that win hegemonic wars are not randomly distributed. Some kinds of states—for example, in the modern era, it might be liberal democracies—are more likely to emerge predominant after these watershed wars than others (Lake 1992; Gat 2010). Or it might be that the character of the population of states is changing over time (for reasons independent of wars), and this has an indirect effect on the types of states that are likely to be involved in order building.

There are also other possibilities. It could be that the nature of great power wars share characteristics that lead winning states to take similar sorts of order building steps after the war—and to respond to and learn from prior postwar steps. After all, as Gilpin and other scholars note, these "hegemonic wars" have been triggered by the same cause, namely aggressive states that seek to break out of and impose mastery over the wider state system. Charles V, Louis XIV, Napoleon I, and post-Bismarck Germany were the protagonists who all sought in one way or another to establish imperial dominance over other states. What unites the experiences of postwar order building states is that they were all responding to a similar sort of geopolitical aggression (Gilpin 1981; Kennedy 1987; Organski 1958).The functional tasks of order building are shared, and so states build on and learn from the sequence of prior efforts. Moreover, postwar order building states—particularly Britain after 1815 and the United States in the twentieth century—have also been focused on promoting and managing an open capitalist world economy. The functional tasks associated with doing this—as the world economy itself is evolving over the centuries—also allows us to see an unfolding logic at work in order building (Ikenberry 2014).

Two long-term "projects" of modern order building lurk in the background of these postwar moments. One is the Westphalian project, where major states over the centuries have been building on and developing rules and institutions for stabilizing the system of states. Over the centuries, the Westphalian system has evolved as a set of principles and practices expanded outward from its European origins to encompass the entire globe. Despite this unfolding, however, states have retained their claims of political and legal authority. The founding principles of the Westphalian system—sovereignty, territorial integrity, and non-intervention—reflected an emerging consensus that states were the rightful political units for the establishment of legitimate rule. Norms and principles that subsequently evolved within the Westphalian system—such as self-determination and non-discrimination—served to further reinforce the primacy of states and state authority. These norms and principles have served as the organizing logic for Westphalian order and provided the ideational source of political authority within it. Under the banner of sovereignty and self-determination, political movements for decolonization and independence were set in motion in the non-Western developing world. Westphalian norms have been violated and ignored but they have, nonetheless, been the most salient and agreed upon rules and principles of international order in the modern era (Hinsley 1963; Krasner 1999).

Over the last two hundred years, another order building project has unfolded—the liberal internationalist project. Open markets, international institutions, cooperative security, democratic community, progressive change, collective problem solving, shared sovereignty, the rule of law—all are aspects of the liberal vision that have made appearances in various combinations and changing ways over the decades and centuries. In the nineteenth century, liberal internationalism was manifest in Britain's championing of free trade and freedom of the seas. But the liberal project in international relations was limited and coexisted with imperialism and colonialism. In the twentieth century, liberal order building was pushed forward by the United States and it went through several phases. After World War I, Woodrow Wilson and other liberals pushed for an international order organized around a global collective security body in which sovereign states would act together to uphold a system of territorial peace. Post-1945 liberal internationalism went further and sought to empower states to purse progressive goals of social and economic rights and protections. FDR's Four Freedom's speech and the Atlantic Charter offered visions of a modern state system in which governments actively promoted and protected their citizens. In more recent decades, the human rights agenda has become more inconsistent with Westphalian sovereignty, as it articulates rationales for intervention into the otherwise sovereign affairs of states (Beitz 2009).

Seen in this light, we can make several general observations about hegemonic states and the rise and fall of international order. First, international orders, at least in the modern era, do exhibit a contingent evolutionary logic. Specific historical moments are created by hegemonic wars, but the "problem of order" that is thrown up at these instances is defined and shaped by the longer-term problems generated by the Westphalian state system and the liberal ascendancy. Order building states have found themselves building upon, extending, and modifying these deeply entrenched state-system and liberal internationalist frameworks of world politics. In building order, leading states are seeking to capitalize on their power advantages and build an order congenial with their interests, but they have tended to do so by trying to re-establish and strengthen the Westphalian state system and re-establishing and strengthening open, rule-based order.

Conclusion

Historical institutionalism provides a useful way of explaining broad shifts in the political organization of interstate relations. The point of departure for this sort of analysis is the problem of order in world politics. How have states created order and how do we explain variations in the types of orders that have emerged across historical eras and regions of the world? At least in the modern era, states have endeavored in various ways to build rules and institutions of order. Powerful states across the centuries have repeatedly found themselves in a position—typically after major war—to establish the terms of order. International order is not simply the crystallization of the balance of power or a byproduct of states doing other things. It is a sort of political formation. International orders have differed greatly, but each has had at least implicit in it a logic of a rudimentary political system—manifesting authority relations, principles of sovereignty and intervention, and rules and institutions of diplomacy and commerce.

What is remarkable about these ordering moments is their episodic and varied nature. It is not simply a story of powerful states that use their growing strength to organize the arrangements of global governance. Rather it is a story of openings, turning points, breakdowns, and temporally-bound opportunities. The rules and institutions of governance do not "flex" in a simple and fluid way with the ebb and flow of power and interests. Like Weber's tracks, the ordering arrangements of the system get laid down at critical moments. Openings emerge to put in place basic rules and institutions, and those moments disappear, at least for a while. The notions of critical junctures and path dependence are therefore useful analytical tools to make sense of the punctuated nature and continuous trajectories of the world's governing institutions.

Yet questions remain. Scholars need to know more about the mechanisms that make institutions resistant to change. At a "founding moment," the rules and institutions of order are indeed reflections of the power and interests of the leading state or states. Their goal is to entrench institutional arrangements that perpetuate their advantages into the future. Institutions are attractive because of the way in which they can—variously and to some extent—lock in those advantages. Indeed, this may be the most elemental attraction of political institutions, as such. They are social mechanisms that allow actors with assets to establish the circumstances that will allow them to hold on to those assets. This is true within political systems—and it seems to be equally true for states in the international system. So when states find themselves in a position to organize relations within regional and global systems, they seek to organize relations for the long term, including in the out years when their power wanes. So institutions tend to persist because of the state power that stands behind them. But institutions also tend to persist for other reasons as well—they are, or at least can potentially be, semi-independent of the powerful states that create them. As we have seen, this semi-dependence may arise from mechanisms such as sunk costs and increasing returns. It may arise because of the accumulation of vested interests and constituencies that array themselves around these founding institutions. And it may arise because of increasing returns to institutional investments, as more states see greater benefits from supporting established institutions for economic, security, and moral reasons. Sorting out these mechanisms and logics remains an important task.

These observations about the logic and character of international order are visible on the world stage today. A cohort of non-Western states, led by China, is rising up within the global system. A global power transition is underway. The "old order" put in place by the United States and its Western allies over the last 65 years is under pressure. The distribution of power that was in place at the "moment of creation" of this American-led order has eroded, and states with different interests and values are seeking to exert influence and shape international political order. This contemporary drama will put to the test the various arguments put forward in this chapter about the logic and character of international order. The old order will not exit the global stage easily. Rising states will be confronted with a complex array of constraints, opportunities, incentives, and legacies from the past that weigh on their capacities and interests. There is also the issue of great power war—or its absence. In the past, the old order tended to be weakened, delegitimated, and ultimately swept away by major war. But war as an instrument of global change has, in the age of nuclear weapons, been thankfully thrown into doubt. As a result, it is not clear that China and other rising states will be given the sort of critical juncture that past rising states have had and used to great effect. China and other rising states face an existing order with a more elaborate and world-spanning array of peoples and societies with a stake in keeping it going. As historical institutionalists suggest, change is episodic, contingent, complex, and full of unanticipated outcomes. The shifts underway in the global system today will no doubt confirm this view.

Note

1. Studies that take "the problem of order" as the defining issue of international relations include: Bull (1977), Gilpin (1981), Ikenberry (2001), Hurrell (2007), and Lake (2011).

References

Arthur, Brian. 1989. "Competing Technologies, Increasing Returns, and Lock-in by Historical Events." *Economic Journal* 99 (March): 116–131.

Beitz, Charles R. 2009. *The Idea of Human Rights*. New York: Oxford University Press.

Bull, Hedley. 1977. *The Anarchical Society: A Study of Order in World Politics*. London: Macmillan.

Capoccia, Giovanni and Daniel R. Kelemen. 2007. "The Study of Critical Junctures: Theory, Narrative, and Counterfactuals in Historical Institutionalism." *World Politics* 59 (3): 342–369.

Fioretos, Orfeo. 2011. "Historical Institutionalism in International Relations." *International Organization* 65 (2): 367–399.

Gat, Azar. 2010. *Victorious and Vulnerable: Why Democracy Won in the 20th Century and How It Is Still Imperiled*. New York: Rowman & Littlefield.

Gilpin, Robert. 1981. *War and Change in World Politics*. Cambridge: Cambridge University Press.

Hinsley, F. H. 1963. *Power and the Pursuit of Peace*. Cambridge: Cambridge University Press.

Hurrell, Andrew. 2007. *On Global Order: Power, Values, and the Constitution of International Society*. Oxford: Oxford University Press.

Ikenberry, G. John. 1998. "Institutions, Strategic Restraint, and the Persistence of American Postwar Order." *International Security* 23 (3): 43–78.

Ikenberry, G. John. 2001. *After Victory: Institutions, Strategic Restraint, and the Rebuilding of Order after Major War*. Princeton, NJ: Princeton University Press.

Ikenberry, G. John. 2011. *Liberal Leviathan: The Origins, Crisis, and Transformation of the American World Order*. Princeton, NJ: Princeton University Press.

Ikenberry, G. John, ed. 2014. *Power, Order, and Change in World Politics*. New York: Cambridge University Press.

Kennedy, Paul. 1987. *The Rise and Fall of the Great Powers*. New York: Random House.

Knock, Thomas. 2009. "'Playing for a Hundred Years Hence,' Woodrow Wilson and his Would-Be Heirs." In *The Crisis of American Foreign Policy: Wilsonianism in the Twenty-First Century*, ed. G. John Ikenberry, Thomas J. Knock, Anne-Marie Slaughter, and Tony Smith. Princeton, NJ: Princeton University Press, 25–52.

Krasner, Stephen D. 1984. "Approaches to the State: Alternative Conceptions and Historical Dynamics." *Comparative Politics* 16: 223–246.

Krasner, Stephen D. 1999. *Sovereignty: Organized Hypocrisy*. Princeton, NJ: Princeton University Press.

Lake, David A. 1992. "Powerful Pacifists: Democratic States and War." *American Political Science Review* 6 (1): 24–37.

Lake, David A. 2011. *Hierarchy in International Relations*. Ithaca, NY: Cornell University Press.

Modelski, George. 1990. "Is World Politics Evolutionary Learning?" *International Organization* 44 (Winter): 1–24.

North, Douglass. 1990. *Institutions, Institutional Change and Economic Performance*. New York: Cambridge University Press.

Pierson, Paul. 2000. "Not Just What, but *When*: Timing and Sequence in Political Processes." *Studies of American Political Development* 14 (Spring): 72–92.

Organski, A. F. K. 1958. *World Politics*. New York: Knopf.

Ruggie, John Gerard. 1993. "Multilateralism: The Anatomy of an Institution." In *Multilateralism Matters: The Theory and Praxis of an Institutional Form*, ed. John Gerard Ruggie. New York: Columbia University Press, 3–50.

Schumpeter, Joseph A. 1960. *Capitalism, Socialism and Democracy*. 3rd Edition. New York: Harper and Row.

Weber, Max. 1946. "The Social Psychology of World Religions." In *From Max Weber: Essays in Sociology*, ed. H. H. Gerth and C. Wright Mills. New York: Oxford University Press, 267–301.

Weber, Max. 1968. *Economy and Society: An Outline of Interpretive Sociology*, ed. Guenther Roth and Claus Wittich. Los Angeles: University of California Press.

CHAPTER 33

CRITICAL JUNCTURES, DEVELOPMENTAL PATHWAYS, AND INCREMENTAL CHANGE IN SECURITY INSTITUTIONS

ETEL SOLINGEN AND WILFRED WAN*

It would be an exaggeration to say that historical institutionalism (HI) pervades the study of international relations (IR), let alone international security (IS). Prima facie historical institutionalism appears to have less distinct or explicit a place in the international security area than in other subfields of Political Science, the "institutional turn" in IR notwithstanding (Fioretos 2011). And yet concepts central to HI have nonetheless permeated studies in IS. Its core themes emerge in studies of sovereignty (Krasner 1991, 2001); of 1989 as a critical (world historical) juncture that brought unipolarity and a big discontinuity in the international system (Haftendorn, Keohane, and Wallander 1999); 9/11 as another critical juncture resulting in the overhaul of global security practices (Hurd 2002); and path dependence in United Nations Security Council composition, among others (Argomaniz 2009).

Inattention to security institutions in IR may have stemmed from long-standing assumptions that security issues present the most fundamental challenge to international cooperation generally, and to institutions as handmaidens of cooperation in particular (Keohane 1993; Lake 2001). Accordingly, states create institutions as little more than vessels upon which states imprint their pre-constituted interests. This instrumental view of institutions is especially strong in neorealist narratives connecting the absence of a central authority above sovereign states to the uncertainty and fear that characterize international politics. Security cooperation here takes the shape of voluntary, ad hoc agreements between sovereign states relying on institutions to bargain on behalf of their self-interest (Jervis 1999; Mearsheimer 2001). Security institutions are thus little more than marriages of convenience, lacking the potential for longevity and autonomy, marked by fluidity and transience, and summarily discarded when national considerations require it. Path dependence is hardly a factor; great powers can overcome the obstacles to reversal, altering pathways as they see fit, sometimes turning security institutions into the "velvet glove" of hegemonic iron fists (Ruggie 1994). The centrality of states as units of analysis defies policy inertia. States do not delegate to institutions; they regulate them. Security institutions enhance information and transparency much less than their economic counterparts and lack the latter's strength, complexity, or depth (Jervis 1982; Lipson 1984).

Neoliberal institutionalism questioned neorealism's rigid view of institutions, suggesting that failure to employ institutions as mechanisms to move states toward the Pareto frontier overlooks meaningful cooperation (Krasner 1991; Jervis 1999). This functionalist turn accommodates security institutions with explicit rules, consistency in expectations, and monitoring and enforcement powers that can transcend anarchy (Koremenos, Lipson, and Snidal 2001). It is also more sensitive to temporality insofar as shared expectations alter states' cost-benefit calculations in the long run. Iterated interactions can change incentive structures, rendering defection less feasible or likely. This notion of the "shadow of the future" (Axelrod and Keohane 1985) contains surface similarities with the HI concept of "increasing returns," which describes the enhanced benefits stemming from familiarity gained with established arrangements (Thelen 1999). However, the neoliberal institutionalist approach ultimately pales in comparison to historical institutionalism's commitment to temporality. States still act ultimately at the behest of their expected utility calculations, sidelining the broader impact of institutions (Fioretos 2011). Intrinsic institutional change—independent from state fiat—does not effectively enter the calculus. The stasis ontology and instrumentality of neorealism thus remains.

Sociological perspectives focused attention on the power of institutions to form identities, shape interests, and constitute agents (Wendt 1992; Ruggie 1998). Constructivists challenged the dominant neorealist and neoliberal paradigms that viewed institutions as passive, efficient solutions to market imperfections (Barnett and Finnemore 1999). They focused, instead, on how institutions and norms reflect and imprint the collective identities of member states, changing beliefs and identities and altering the very definition of interests (March and Olsen 1998; Johnston 2001). Security institutions are no exception, highlighting and perpetuating similarities among participants, at times overriding material conditions. The more complex interplay between structure and agency here echoes themes in historical institutionalism but the overlap is hardly perfect. Furthermore, various constructivist strands do not constitute a coherent IR theory but rather a method and epistemology (Klotz and Lynch 2007).

These different approaches employ various definitions of security institutions. Neorealism and neoliberal institutionalism largely focused on formal institutions (e.g., North Atlantic Treaty Organization, World Trade Organization, alliances) whereas constructivist work addressed a wider spectrum often found in historical institutionalism including patterned interactions, embedded or informal procedures, conventions, and codes of conduct (cf. Hall and Taylor 1996).[1] The more inclusive definition is well suited for the study of international security, which features few centralized, formal mechanisms but rather various regularized behavioral patterns and shared expectations (Keohane 1989; Wallander and Keohane 1999). Furthermore, it is particularly suitable for avoiding the pitfalls of case selection in studying only formal institutions (Lake 2001).

Our chapter proceeds by applying concepts in historical institutionalism to two empirical realms in an effort to illustrate their utility beyond existing topical, geographical, and ontological foci in security studies. The primacy accorded to "temporality" is the distinguishing hallmark of historical institutionalism, a commitment to thorough examination of the timing, sequence, and context within which institutions emerge and develop (Fioretos, Falleti, and Sheingate, Chapter 1, this volume). The first application explains variation in regional orders along the conflictive/cooperative spectrum. The second explains continuity and change in arguably the most crucial global security institution, the non-proliferation regime. They both address big questions spanning the subnational, regional and global levels of analysis. Whereas a strong state-centric focus has naturally been most entrenched in the study of security, our cases broaden the scope of existing work to a wider range of domestic and international institutions that include, but also transcend, states.

Domestic Coalitions, Institutions, and Regional Orders

A promising conceptual tool for the study of security comes via a tradition with roots in Polanyi (2005 [1944]), Gerschenkron (1992), Moore (1966), and Skocpol (1979), among others, that explores the impact of class, sectoral or other coalitional dynamics on long-term institutional outcomes. This tradition has been alive and well in international and comparative political economy (e.g., Katzenstein 1978; Gourevitch 1986; Mahoney and Thelen 2010) but entered IS much later, with pioneering work by Snyder (1991) among others, largely devoted to understanding imperial overexpansion by great powers. Using the distributional consequences of the second major wave of globalization as a point of departure, Solingen (1998) identified two competing models of domestic political survival. Advanced by rival coalitions of both state and private actors, these ideal-typical models promote political-economy strategies with important implications for security outcomes. Inward-looking coalitions logroll statist and protectionist forces, including expansive military-industrial complexes that displace private sector activities. Internationalizing coalitions privilege economic growth driven by competitive export-oriented sectors and firms. A strategy hinging on integration in the global political economy makes these coalitions averse to regional conflict that might disrupt its objectives, including macroeconomic and regional stability.

Diverging trajectories in East Asia and the Middle East provide a useful window into the crucial consequences of timing, sequence, and coalitions' institutional choices for regional orders.[2] Whereas East Asia has become the engine of the twenty-first global economy, avoiding wars for several decades now, the Middle East exhibits failed states, civil wars that spill over across borders, and stunted development. Between 1973 and 1994 ballistic missiles were used in battle ten times, with Middle East states accounting for eight instances; East Asia for none (Karp 1995). Since the 1960s Egypt, Iraq, Syria, and Libya have used chemical weapons; no states have done so in East Asia. This contrast is puzzling because both regions shared common initial conditions in the mid-twentieth century: colonialism as formative experiences, comparable state-building challenges, economic crises, low per-capita gross national product (GNP)s, heavy-handed authoritarianism, low intra and extra-regional economic interdependence, and weak or non-existing regional institutions.

The underlying sources for diverging state trajectories are in critical junctures that led to the embrace of different models of political survival by ruling coalitions in each case. The typical model in East Asia hinged on economic performance and growth, which entailed an emphasis on competitive export-led manufacturing and promotion of private entrepreneurship. By contrast, the reigning model in the Middle East hinged on inward-looking self-sufficiency, nationalism, and state and military entrepreneurship, buttressed by oil rents where available. Once adopted, both models became self-reinforcing, perpetuated by embedded and complementary institutions emanating from initial choices.[3] The critical junctures, often triggered by wars or political-economy crises, began in East Asia with the inception of postwar Japan's economic miracle, followed by crucial shifts in Taiwan and South Korea, and progressively others. The critical junctures in the Middle East were Egypt's Free Officers 1952 revolution and analogous shifts throughout that region. Choices made during those defining years were embedded in the respective permissive and catalytic conditions that drove the regions in different directions. In brief, early and effective land reform, a relatively brief period of import-substitution, and natural resource scarcity weakened domestic political opposition to export-led growth in East Asia. By contrast, late, inefficient or nonexistent land reform; longer exposure to import-substitution through extensive state and military entrepreneurship; and abundant oil resources or second-order rentierism (among neighboring non-oil economies) empowered opponents of export-led growth throughout much of the Middle East.

Put differently, politically stronger beneficiaries of relative closure, import-substitution, state entrepreneurship, and natural resource monopolies—mostly within the state itself—constituted powerful veto points against alternative models in the Middle East for decades. Alternative models would have entailed appealing to different sources of legitimacy—based on new relations with international markets and institutions—than those typical of 1950s–1960s-style pan-Arab politics. Some trace this profound suspicion of external influences to colonial domination and exploitation. Yet the latter was very much present in East Asia, and did not preclude that region's profound transformation. China's yoke under colonial arrangements, Japan's imperial colonial violence and subsequent occupation by the US, and Vietnam's victimization by various external powers, among others, warn against excessive concentration on colonialism as the main barrier to change. The exhaustion of import-substitution in industrializing states created a critical juncture, a crisis that restricted choices going forward (Hirschman 1968). Differences in oil resources and land reform led to distinctive options, each relying on different coalitions of state and private interests. Abundant natural resources hindered the prospects for competitive manufacturing; enhanced patronage funds for beneficiaries of import-substitution; and eroded private sector wherewithal in the Middle East. Natural resource scarcity and effective land reform favored proponents (and weakened opponents) of labor-intensive manufacturing and private entrepreneurship in East Asia. Once in place, each model reinforced the coalitional networks between state and private actors that benefited from each path.

Political forces unleashed by Nasserism, Ba'athism, and rentier economies constituted formidable barriers to change due to overwhelming incentives to retain rents and disincentives to alter dominant models. Logics of path dependence, including reproduction of political forces invested in extant institutional arrangements and self-perpetuating mechanisms of exclusion, go far in explaining the durability of regimes. Middle Eastern leaders' rejection of export-led growth in the 1960s may not have been unusual for that "world-time." Yet subsequent opportunities introduced by the 1970s oil windfalls, the 1980s crises, the widespread global economic transformations of the 1990s, and the ensuing dramatic expansion of capital flows were also willfully missed (Henry and Springborg 2001). Potential critical junctures pregnant with possibilities for change were deflected. Declining oil windfalls in the 1980s denied Middle East leaders resources erstwhile available to avoid adjustment, yet path-dependent legacies continued to burden change. Even more recent efforts to liberalize trade and investment encountered fierce opposition to reversing deep-seated biases.

Despite broad divergence, competing models in East Asia and the Middle East shared three important features regarding state, military, and autocratic institutions. First, both relied on states, yet differences in the character of that reliance would have differing effects on the respective evolution of states over time. The two models differed in the extent to which states replaced or enhanced private capital. East Asian states were active lenders and regulators but significantly less active entrepreneurs than Middle East states. East Asian leaders watchfully steered states to macroeconomic stability and proper conditions for sustained export-led growth. States thus evolved into relatively adaptable institutions linking across the domestic, regional, and global economies. Buffeted by a very severe crisis in 1997–98, East Asian states rebounded. By contrast, rigid, exhausted, and depleted Middle East states presided over current account and budget deficits; high inflation and unemployment; and scarce foreign exchange. They became too weak to exert control over society except through force, as remains the case today.

Notwithstanding significant differences among them (and outliers like North Korea), East Asian states approximated ideal-typical developmental states ushering in industrial transformation through Weberian-style meritocratic bureaucracies able to extract resources from society and convert them into public goods (Evans 1995). Despite wide variation across the Middle East, predatory states undercutting development even in the narrow sense of capital accumulation remained largely dominant, relying on patronage-based bureaucracies primarily supplying private goods to rapacious ruling coalitions (United Nations Development Program 2009). Rents, cronyism, and corruption afflicted both types of states to different degrees. Both types were vulnerable, albeit to different challenges. East Asian states became more susceptible to global economic trends (e.g., declines in global demand) and evolving risks of capital liberalization. Middle East states, though not completely immune to the same vulnerabilities (including lower demand for oil), were also buffeted by the exhaustion of import-substitution and subsequent balance of payments, high inflation, unemployment, inefficient industries, and weak private enterprise.

Second, military institutions played important roles initially in both models, particularly as repressive mechanisms of political control. Yet the military itself evolved along different lines in tandem with prevailing political-economy models. The requirements of each model imposed different constraints on: (1) the relative size and missions of military-industrial complexes; and (2) the extent to which these complexes replaced private enterprise beyond arms production. In the Middle East, dismal economies notwithstanding, arms races typical of inward-looking models consistently attracted the highest levels of military expenditures relative to GNP worldwide. Though the average for the two regions was not dramatically different in the 1960s, with the onset of internationalization East Asian averages declined to nearly half those of the Middle East by the 1970s and 1980s. Military expenditures as a percentage of central government expenditures were historically high in both regions, arenas of Cold War sensitivity. Yet they remained 20 percent on average for Middle East states by the 1990s, nearly double the developing world average, and about 50 percent higher than East Asia's by the 2000s.

The typical Middle East state had militarized economies of the kind that were not permissible with the onset of internationalization in most East Asian cases. The former entailed gargantuan military-industrial complexes producing items either remotely or wholly unrelated to military demand; owned vast portions of land, natural resources, and sprawling networks of state enterprises; and employed the largest proportions of population relative to other regions, a pattern that lingers today from Egypt to Syria. Most importantly, this model replaced and often decimated the private sector. Unsurprisingly, military elites appropriating such rents were major opponents of privatization and key veto points blocking broader economic transformation (Halliday 2005). These were veritable instances of a *Wehrwirtschaft* (war economy) even after internal repression—*mukhabarat* regimes—had largely replaced external wars as their core "mission." By contrast, East Asian growth models sought to develop private sectors; required stable macroeconomic policies and predictable environments; and minimized the potential for inflationary military allocations that might endanger those core objectives (Chan 1992). The result was increasingly more professional militaries with declining political control over the economy and polity.

Third, both models relied on authoritarian institutions. Yet each would foreshadow differential paths regarding democratization, stemming from variations in the nature and role of military institutions and private entrepreneurship described earlier. Export-led models introduced by authoritarian leaders and ruling coalitions in East

Asia were not precisely designed to advance democracy but to curb it. Yet they unintentionally encouraged democratic institutions via several causal mechanisms: fostering economic growth, stronger private sectors and civil societies, and more professionalized militaries attuned to outward-oriented growth. By contrast, the nature of Middle East models engendered higher barriers to the development of democratic institutions. Weaker private sectors and weakened civil societies were less able to demand political reform. Furthermore, more entrenched military industrial complexes spread throughout vast segments of the economy were better able to resist those demands for political reform. Over time, the initial common dominance of authoritarian institutions in both regions gave way to increased differentiation. Various authoritarian regimes in East Asia, including South Korea, Taiwan, Indonesia, Thailand, Malaysia, and Philippines, evolved into full-fledged democracies.

Those three institutional features of domestic models had implications for the nature of relations within regions. The inability to deliver resources and services to constituencies previously mobilized through revolutionary or nationalist fervor; and efforts to divert attention from failed, economically depleted, entropic, crisis-prone, militarized and de-legitimized models led Middle East regimes to: (a) Emphasize nationalism and military prowess; (b) Externalize conflict; (c) Exacerbate arms races; and (d) Engage in competitive outbidding at the regional level. Each of these vectors individually enhanced the prospects for intended or unintended war and militarized intrusions in the domestic affairs of neighboring states. Collectively they made those even more likely, creating a structural tendency toward militarized conflict even where it may not have been the most favored preference. Mobilizations, overt subversions, and cross-border invasions were certainly intended, but not always controllable. Lacking institutional power and legitimacy domestically and regionally, Middle East leaders deployed violence at home and abroad, evoking Tilly's arguments on the use of force (Dodge 2002). Domestic fragility hidden behind pan-Arab or pan Islamic rhetoric fueled mutual assaults on sovereignty among Arab states (Halliday 2005). By contrast, East Asia's developmental states model required: (a) Contained military-industrial complexes and limited military competition; (b) Regional stability; (c) Domestic stability, predictability, and attractiveness to foreign investors; and (d) Taming arms races that might affect (a) through (c). Each of these requirements individually dampened the prospects for war and militarized conflict. Collectively they made them even less likely despite lingering hostility and nationalist resentment.

The regional context reinforced each region's respective models via different structural mechanisms: (1) Hegemonic coercion (Nasserism, Ba'athism, and equivalents in the Middle East; coups and external interventions in East Asia); (2) Diffusion (second-order "Dutch disease" effects in the Middle East flowing from oil producers to regional clients; "flying geese" and bandwagon effects in East Asia); and (3) Emulation (Japan in East Asia; competitive outbidding among pan-Arab and pan-Islamic visions in the Middle East). In time, regional agglomeration of specific models imposed neighborhood effects or network externalities that reinforced prevailing models. Regional institutions in each case could not but reflect those background conditions: East Asian institutions conformed to cooperative "open regionalism" (i.e., openness to the global economy) unlike their Middle East counterparts.

Finally, the models also explain contrasting nuclear trajectories in both regions since the inception of the Nuclear Non-Proliferation Treaty (NPT) in 1970. Middle East models entailed stronger incentives to pursue nuclear weapons than East Asian ones, for which nuclearization has been much less attractive (except for North Korea, the autarky-seeking regional anomaly). Heavy regional concentration of internationalizing models in East Asia reinforced each state's incentives to avoid nuclearization. Conversely, heavy regional concentration of inward-looking models throughout the Middle East exacerbated mutual incentives to develop nuclear weapons. Iraq, Iran, Libya, and Syria violated their NPT commitments to advance their nuclear weapons capabilities. Here as well, propositions linking models to nuclear decisions are bound by historical timing and temporal sequences in the acquisition of nuclear weapons. Disincentives stemming from an internationalizing model may be stronger at deliberative or incipient stages of nuclear weapons consideration, as was the case historically in Japan, South Korea, and Taiwan. Once nuclear thresholds have been crossed (often in the form of nuclear tests), as under inward-looking Maoist China in 1964, path dependence and "endowment effects" trump other incentives.[4] As expected from prospect theory, it is far more costly politically to eliminate existing nuclear weapons entirely than to reverse steps prior to their acquisition (Jervis 1994; McDermott 1998). Put differently, when nuclearization precedes the inception of internationalizing models, subsequent denuclearization may be much harder. Temporal sequences and context matter, which points to useful exchanges between prospect theoretic and historical institutionalist perspectives.

Our account thus far illuminates the importance of temporality and downstream effects of early choices. However, new critical junctures and learning can provide mechanisms for change even in processes heavily burdened with path dependency. Sadat used crisis to introduce *infitah* (economic reform) facing incalculable political risks, struggling to reverse Nasserism and stressing growth, foreign investment, exports, military conversion, and new relations with international markets and institutions. The political landscape Sadat inherited and his own eventual assassination continued to trump Egypt's transition, as have recent developments since the Arab uprisings that also unleashed new socio-political configurations. Non-oil producers (Morocco, Tunisia, Turkey) began promoting private sectors in the 1980s and signing trade and investment agreements to promote and protect foreign investments. Praetorian states such as Egypt, Syria, and Iraq, which had mobilized revolutionary nationalist-populist zeal, swept competitive private capital more forcefully than monarchies, creating higher barriers to reform in the former, beyond those imposed by rentierism (Henry and Springborg 2001). Gulf sheikhdoms incepted new models on the foundations of old colonial and semi-feudal states, particularly in the last decade. Dubai pioneered early diversification away from oil as far back as the 1970s, promoting outward-oriented free-trade zones, tourism, financial, shipping, stock exchanges and greater appeal to foreign companies. Other emirates in the United Arab Emirates (UAE) as well as Qatar, Bahrain, and Kuwait embraced their own variants designed to diversify, privatize, and relax foreign ownership rules. After decades of public sector expansion, import-substitution, high inflation, mounting external debt, and political violence in the 1970s, Turkey's military brutally altered the relative strength of political forces in the early 1980s, enabling Premier Turgut Özal to consolidate support for a new model based on competitive export-led growth (Waterbury 1983). The European market was a prime incentive (as was the absence of oil). Turkey could also count on a more robust and institutionalized business class fostered under Kemal Atatürk.

These and other experiences weaken deterministic views that path dependence poses insuperable barriers to alternative models. Differences in oil endowments, institutions, and private-firm incentives toward openness shape different contexts and opportunities. But Sadat forged new opportunities and advanced them in a fairly constraining context that outlived him. Özal leaned on allies in key state agencies, Korean-style private conglomerates, and popular wariness of violence and economic disarray to launch a new model. Sheikh al-Maktoum used oil endowments to replicate Singapore in Dubai. And yet the continued relevance of timing and historical context is brought to relief by the fact that East Asia's competitiveness stemming from earlier decisions compounds the difficulties that Middle East leaders confront today (Noland and Pack 2005). The favorable global and regional, political and economic circumstances that lubricated the inception of East Asia's model cannot be taken for granted. Amsden's (2001, 286) reformulation of Gerschenkron's theory has potentially ominous implications for nationalist models: "the later a country industrializes in chronological history, the greater the probability that its major manufacturing firms will be foreign-owned." Though such prospects have not deterred Eastern European states or East Asia's newcomers as Vietnam, they are far more politically menacing for Middle East leaders struggling to transcend inward-looking models. As Binder (1988, 83) notes regarding the Middle East, "no other cultural region is so deeply anxious about the threat of cultural penetration and westernization." Difficulties may not be insurmountable, however. Assessing the transformation of state power in Egypt and Turkey, Waterbury (1983, 261) suggested that "economic and class structures ... acted as retardants to processes of change but did not determine or cause them ... Rather, narrowly based political leadership, assisted by insulated change teams, drove forward *both* [our emphasis] the import- substitution strategy and the subsequent introduction of market-conforming policies."

The presence of within-region variation, outliers and anomalies has important substantive and methodological implications for the analysis of coalitions, institutions and regional orders. First, it provides further support for the relationship between models of political survival and external conflict. Outliers strove to adopt alternatives to regional models and exhibited dissimilar conflict behavior. Second, it questions micro-phenomenological theories emphasizing local cultural origins and regional uniqueness, and counters deterministic views about inevitable outcomes in any region, drawing attention to contingency. Third, anomalies place limits on "universalizing comparisons" assuming that the same internal causal sequence recurs in all regions. History and path dependency supply enough warnings against temptations to overemphasize invariant common properties across all regions. Fourth, contrasts between Southeast

Asian and Middle East states also highlight wide variation among Muslim countries and the centrality of context and sequence. The former, once labeled the "Balkans of the East" (under Sukarno's inward-looking model), were subsequently able to transform rentier political economies, follow a more flexible and "modern" Islam, and spearhead cooperative regional institutions. A key quandary in East Asia is whether the archetypical model is robust enough—particularly in China—to reproduce the low levels of militarized conflict observed in recent decades. Some paths are more dependent than others. Finally, the models described in this section provide more complete accounts than any of the approaches to security institutions reviewed in our introductory section for why different regional institutions emerged, in whose interest they operated, when they were allowed to play a significant role, and why they may not have been vital to regional cooperation.

Institutional Change in the Nuclear Non-Proliferation Regime

Our second empirical case enables us to address more pointedly the concern with institutional order and change in historical institutionalism through a focus on a nearly universal international institution, the nuclear non-proliferation regime (NPR). The NPR offers ideal grounds for understanding durability and change in highly subscribed security institutions. The regime's current makeup reflects a long-term layering process that saw the introduction of new rules atop existing ones since the Non-Proliferation Treaty opened for signatures in 1968 (see Wan 2014). This includes additions to the official treaty review process with the extension of preparatory committees and the creation of a third main committee and subsidiary bodies. Such changes have allowed for a more prescriptive regime; action plans developed at recent review conferences have served as barometers for non-proliferation activity among parties. Another example of layering are updated guidelines from the Nuclear Suppliers Group and the Zangger Committee that flesh out the safeguards agreements undergirding the NPT, specifying the items that require International Atomic Energy Agency (IAEA) attention prior to interstate transfer. These independent structures thus both implement and extend treaty principles. Further, the lone alteration to the NPR's legal framework—the 1997 Additional Protocol—provided the IAEA with "complementary access" to inspections, beyond its long-standing comprehensive safeguards agreements. These are but a few of the ways in which procedures, rules, and organizations have been built atop the regime's backbone treaty (Dunn 2007).

Historical institutionalism's analytical toolbox can also improve our understanding of the particular timing and character of change in the NPR. In their exploration of critical junctures, Capoccia and Kelemen (2007, 355) underline the impact of short-term causes of change; junctures can serve to relax the "'normal' structural and institutional constraints on action." The evolution of the NPR indeed reveals the presence of such trigger events. These include a number of nuclear tests and findings regarding non-compliance with IAEA safeguards. Yet these events by themselves are insufficient for understanding why incremental change versus transformative change emerged in their aftermath, or why the NPR was reinforced rather than completely overhauled during these periods of heightened political contestation.

An early critical juncture for the NPR emerged shortly after the 1970 entry into force of the Non-Proliferation Treaty. Even as a negotiating committee drafted the full-scope and comprehensive safeguards agreement (concluded in 1972), a select group of states sought to supplement the treaty by other means. Nuclear weapon states had long called for a strong IAEA-centered system with enforcement capabilities, but the need to secure the support of the non-nuclear weapon states had prevented tighter obligations within the NPT itself. Beginning in 1971, a group of 15 nuclear exporting states met informally—as the Zangger Committee—to find common ground on the technical components that would fall under the umbrella of safeguards agreements. Such a move would effectively govern state-to-state transfers of nuclear materials at the pass. These concerns were inextricably linked to the expansion of nuclear trade in that particular "world-time."[5] The South American market was about to open via a 1975 West Germany–Brazil cooperation agreement, while a series of impending transfers involved sensitive cases including Pakistan, South Korea, and Taiwan.

If the emergence of the Zangger Committee in 1971 marked the beginning of this critical juncture, then India's "peaceful" nuclear explosion in May 1974 provided the tipping point. While a non-party to the NPT, India had long expressed interest in a weapons program. It was part of the very group of advanced industrial and industrializing states with research and production capabilities that the NPT was designed to target. Thus, membership or not, India's surprising progress in its nuclear development signified a major failure on the part of the regime. The confluence of external circumstances further explains the significance of its test. In the midst of nuclear trade expansion, with regional instability surrounding the would-be recipients, the appearance of a worst-case scenario confirmed obvious concerns on the part of supplier states. After all, the Indian device used plutonium produced with the help of peaceful materials from Canada and the US, in the form of a research reactor and a heavy water moderator (Fuhrmann 2012).

In the aftermath of India's test, states acted decisively. The Zangger Committee concluded and released its trigger list, thus adopting self-imposed export restrictions on nuclear-specific exports. Within the IAEA, the Director-General pushed for stronger institutionalization of the safeguards agreements. This included the establishment of a committee that would interpret technical terms and impose timelines and efficiency goals, as well as the release of annual implementation reports. This incremental change to the NPR structure was supplemented by more fundamental overhauls. The Nuclear Suppliers Group emerged in 1975, reaching agreement on even more stringent controls, with safeguards encompassing not just materials but facilities. President Jimmy Carter led a global initiative in 1977 to evaluate proliferation risks across the entire fuel cycle. It was a system-level response that far outstripped those to subsequent rogue nuclear tests—including India and Pakistan in 1998 and North Korea's transgressions in the 2000s. But as demonstrated, India's 1974 test did not occur in a vacuum. Instead, it marked the culmination of a critical juncture that effectively began in 1971 with the Zangger Committee, and reflected long-term processes and developments in global nuclear trade that haven't been replicated since. These are the types of phenomena often highlighted by historical institutionalism.

Long-term institutional developments were similarly linked to a second critical juncture in the life of the NPR. The IAEA experienced a period of sustained success in the 1980s. Safeguards agreements grew to encompass an overwhelming majority of nuclear facilities within non-nuclear weapon states. The Agency flourished under the direction of Hans Blix, with the Reagan presidency calling for its further strengthening and China showing support via membership and submission to a voluntary safeguards agreement, before acceding to the NPT in 1992 (Negm 2009). The high standing of the IAEA was evident at the 1990 NPT Review Conference, with states encouraging the Agency to utilize its special inspections power under the NPT and develop new safeguards approaches (Sloss 1995). This unprecedented activism thus marked the beginning of another critical juncture—with events in 1990 and 1991 providing the roots for jurisdictional expansion. In 1991, the UN Security Council tasked the IAEA with special missions in Iraq and South Africa, assigning safeguards-related activities that nonetheless far exceeded the scope of existing agreements. This included drawing up action plans for future monitoring, imposing short-notice inspections, and using qualitative analysis to ensure the "completeness" of information provided.

The tipping point in this critical juncture was similarly apparent. In the aftermath of the first Persian Gulf War, the IAEA-UN Special Commission joint mission in Iraq discovered numerous violations: with discrepancies in declared activities, previously undeclared nuclear material, and unknown hidden enrichment facilities. The noncompliance case in 1991 marked a first for the NPR. The IAEA Board of Governors immediately elaborated procedural remedies that would tighten the reporting requirements of states, while parties reaffirmed the Agency's special inspections power. Then, an intensive formal review by the IAEA yielded Programme 93+2, which would endow the Agency with much more authoritative powers vis-à-vis NPT parties. Under the terms of the voluntary Additional Protocol, states would provide broad-based information regarding their nuclear programs, well beyond the existing scope of inspections. Combined with the complementary access discussed, and building upon the newly established Information Review Committee, NPT parties delegated a greater analytical role to the IAEA within the NPR. The expanded focus on nuclear programs was underscored with the new dual-use trigger lists offered by the Nuclear Suppliers Group and the Zangger Committee.

That Iraq's violations sparked the reevaluation of the NPR in the mid-1990s is undeniable. Yet this short-term trigger explains only the timing of change, not its character. The hallmarks of Programme 93+2 and the Additional Protocol were already delegated to the IAEA in 1991 for its special missions. The trajectory of enhanced influence was thus underway prior to the discoveries of Iraqi violations, a product of the Agency's success within the NPR in the late 1980s. As with India's test, Iraq's non-compliance exposed the already-loosened constraints for institutional change. Members then decided that the IAEA's expanded powers would no longer be limited to special circumstance, and altered the legal framework of the NPT accordingly. It is notable that a series of non-compliance cases in the 2000s—Iran and Libya in 2003, Egypt and South Korea in 2004—did not elicit more than operational tweaks within the IAEA. Again, only by considering long-term developments can we explain why the same trigger (non-compliance) in separate critical junctures (post-1991, post-2001) resulted in different outcomes, and just the one instance of widespread change.

Most empirical studies on gradual institutional change in international relations are in the field of international political economy. Yet this brief overview demonstrates that historical institutionalism has much to contribute to our understanding of the evolutionary pathway of the NPR. Grasping the dynamics between short-term trigger events within critical junctures and longer-term institutional developments helps explain variance in outcomes related to institutional change in security regimes. Other examples from the NPR case underscore that historical institutionalism can illuminate important phenomena related to institutional durability and change in international security. The notion of lock-in effects as a primary mechanism of path dependence is especially pertinent in a treaty that designates two classes of states, separating the nuclear-haves from the have-nots. Given the perfect overlap between the nuclear weapon states and the permanent members of the UN Security Council, there certainly exists the perception that the group of five continue to set forth rules that protect extant policies, turning them into veto players against change—especially on the issue of disarmament. The possibility of expanding the permanent membership of the UN Security Council could thus have reverberations within the NPR. Ultimately, the jury is still out on whether layering will remain the modal pattern of change in the NPR or, alternatively, "drifting" and "exhaustion" will overwhelm this core security institution (Mahoney and Thelen 2010).

Conclusions

Empirical incursions into divergent regional paths in East Asia and the Middle East and incremental transformations of the nuclear non-proliferation regime illustrate the value of historical institutionalism for the study of security in a number of ways. First, these cases draw attention to big questions with an explicit temporal scope that relates to the creation, reproduction, development, and makeup of evolving domestic and international institutions relevant to security outcomes (Pierson and Skocpol 2002; Fioretos 2011). Second, they affirm historical institutionalism's relative epistemological neutrality or eclecticism, enabling an emphasis on agents and material conditions as well as on ideas and other mechanisms of institutional change (Hall 2010; Sil and Katzenstein 2010). The cases thus open a window onto second-order questions such as the relationship between interests and institutions at the subnational, state, and international levels. They address individual preferences not as constants or given but endogenous to earlier historical processes and institutional arrangements that endowed some groups with power and resources in one spatial or temporal context but not another (Thelen and Steinmo 1992; Fioretos, Falleti, and Sheingate, Chapter 1, this volume). Third, they defy hyper-structural accounts that remove much of the agency from individual actors. Instead, they offer more nuanced portrayals of the relationship between institutions and individuals, a hallmark of historical institutionalism. Further, they control for world-systemic effects—those enabling conditions residing in global historical circumstances or "world-time"—that affect domestic coalitions, regional trajectories, and international institutions. These macro-level causal mechanisms help explain why and how timing and sequence contribute to wide variation in regional outcomes; why reversals become more difficult; why, when, and how wars, economic crises, revolutions, waves of nuclear market expansion, and nuclear tests have lasting effects; why alternatives forgone may have been more efficient; and why some paths are more dependent than others.

Three additional points stand out that may help advance further applications of historical institutionalism to the understanding of international security. First, our focus spanning sub-national, regional, and international levels emphasizes the utility of the tradition's insights beyond the standard, sometimes single-minded focus on state-centric approaches to international security. The preferences of ruling coalitions within a single state can vary over time. Hence they can shape a wide range of policies irreducible to abstract and putatively invariant notions of maximization of *state* power and "national security." Systemic shocks can lead a wide range of agents—including states but also IAEA Director Generals and extra-institutional actors—to advance institutional change in major security institutions. Second, while reviewing the centrality of critical junctures to evolving security arrangements, our cases illustrate how historical institutionalism enables us to both recognize what counts as a critical juncture as well as explore those junctures' varying effects. Some junctures lead to significant changes in models of regime survival, security-related outcomes, and NPR mandates while others enable no more than operational tweaks within existing models and procedures. This point suggests a promising research path for deepening our understanding of those critical junctures that matter for security trajectories. Responses to crises (nuclear tests, exhaustion of import-substitution) are embedded in longer-term permissive conditions born earlier within the critical juncture or even at previous critical junctures. Third, the cases also point to the utility of historical institutionalism for understanding regions beyond Europe and North America—more frequent loci of empirical work in this tradition. For instance, regional institutions constitute a significant thematic component of historical institutionalist studies in international security. Yet most of these studies, as well as those of international institutions more broadly, retain an emphasis on a European anomaly that obscures proper understanding of institutions elsewhere in the world (Solingen 2014). As our cases suggest, historical institutionalism can inform more relevant comparisons of emerging states with each other. This is an especially fertile research horizon as international security arguably moves unto new spatial and temporal terrains with the diffusion of power from West to East and North to South.

The analytical toolbox and empirical focus of historical institutionalism can thus help move the study of international security beyond standard work on state-based security and "great powers." In so doing, the tradition sheds light on novel causal mechanisms, allowing scholars to revisit conventional wisdoms, and clarify new or intractable puzzles. For instance, the extensive literature on the sources of World War I is steeped in references to the role of timing, sequence, critical junctures, and path dependence as underlying the outbreak of the Great War. The explicit integration of historical institutionalism categories can improve our understanding of that particular critical juncture in 1914, pregnant with implications for 2014 and beyond (see Lebow 2014). The enduring legacy and institutionalization of Germany's "iron and rye" coalition backed by its military-industrial complex precluded its replacement by a different political-economy model with different security corollaries, a model that became feasible only in the aftermath of two cataclysmic wars (Solingen 2014). From this standpoint, temporality and sequences explain much of the history of war and peace in the twentieth century. Whether or not China will follow comparable sequences in the twenty-first century is a subject of high contemporary concern in the study and praxis of international security (Tang 2014).

Historical institutionalism can also open up new research frontiers of relevance to twenty-first-century international security. Our analysis of diverging regional trajectories highlights the deep connections and synergies that accrue to applications of historical institutionalism resting at the intersection of comparative politics, comparative political economy and international security. As agents straddling all three domains, domestic political coalitions acquire particular relevance for explaining security outcomes. For instance, the possibility that path-dependent legacies from the Great Recession might alter the nature of ruling coalitions—possibly in an inward-looking direction—with corresponding security externalities, provides another important research frontier for understanding first- and second-order effects of critical junctures. Finally, as the cluster of institutions regulating ownership of nuclear weapons—the imputed *inner sanctum* of national security—one can hardly think of a least-likely case for institutional change than the NPR. Yet new sources of potential transformation pushing toward reductions in existing nuclear arsenals and visions of a nuclear-free world suggest that the non-proliferation regime could have a Sinatra effect ["if I can make it there, I can make it anywhere"] on the study of historical institutionalism in international security: if revolutionary institutional change were to happen there (the non-proliferation regime), change could arguably happen anywhere.

Notes

* The authors would like to thank the editors, especially Orfeo Fioretos, as well as participants at a workshop at the University of Pennsylvania and Temple University (October 2013) for very helpful suggestions.

1. Leeds and Mattes (2010) define alliances as formal agreements among independent states to cooperate militarily in the face of potential or realized military conflict.
2. For the full argument, empirical evidence and references, see Solingen (1998, 2001, 2007a, 2007b, 2008), on which this section builds.
3. This stylized account depicts Weberian ideal-types; neither model characterizes the universe of cases in its region nor fits any particular case wholesale but some approximate ideal-types better than others. Significant differences within each region introduce useful methodological advantages explored elsewhere (Solingen 2007a, 2007b).
4. "Path dependence" operates through causal mechanisms that explain why and how hypothesized causes yield particular outcomes (Falleti and Lynch 2009). Those mechanisms include positive feedbacks, increasing returns, self-reinforcement, lock-in effects, learning, reactive effects and competition (Pierson 2000, 2004; Mahoney 2000).
5. For more on the concept of "world-time," see Skocpol (1979).

References

Amsden, Alice H. 2001. *The Rise of "The Rest": Challenges to the West from Late Industrializing Economies*. Oxford: Oxford University Press.

Argomaniz, Javier. 2009. "Post-9/11 Institutionalisation of European Union Counter-Terrorism: Emergence, Acceleration and Inertia." *European Security* 18 (2): 151–172.

Axelrod, Robert and Robert O. Keohane. 1985. "Achieving Cooperation under Anarchy: Strategies and Institutions." *World Politics* 38 (1): 226–254.

Barnett, Michael and Martha Finnemore. 1999. "The Politics, Power, and Pathologies of International Organizations." *International Organization* 53 (4): 699–732.

Binder, Leonard. 1988. *Islamic Liberalism: A Critique of Development Ideologies*. Chicago: University of Chicago Press.

Capoccia, Giovanni and R. Daniel Kelemen. 2007. "The Study of Critical Junctures: Theory, Narrative, and Counterfactuals in Historical Institutionalism." *World Politics* 59 (3): 341–369.

Chan, Steve. 1992. "Military Burden, Economic Growth, and Income Inequality: The Taiwan Exception." In *Defense, Welfare, and Growth*, ed. Steve Chan and Alex Mintz. New York: Routledge, 163–178.

Dodge, Toby. 2002. "Bringing the Bourgeoisie Back In: Globalisation and the Birth of Liberal Authoritarianism in the Middle East." In *Globalization and the Middle East: Economy, Society and Politics*, ed. Richard Higgot and Toby Dodge. London: Brookings Press, 169–187.

Dunn, Lewis A. 2007. "Leveraging Proliferation Shocks." In *Over the Horizon Proliferation Threats*, ed. James J. Wirtz and Peter R. Lavoy. Stanford, CA: Stanford University Press, 205–220.

Evans, Peter B. 1995. *Embedded Autonomy: States and Industrial Transformation*. Princeton, NJ: Princeton University Press.

Falleti, Tulia G. and Julia F. Lynch. 2009. "Context and Causal Mechanisms in Political Analysis." *Comparative Political Studies* 42 (9): 1143–1166.

Fioretos, Orfeo. 2011. "Historical Institutionalism in International Relations." *International Organization* 65 (2): 367–399.

Fuhrmann, Matthew. 2012. *Atomic Assistance: How "Atoms for Peace" Programs Cause Nuclear Insecurity*. Ithaca, NY: Cornell University Press.

Gerschenkron, Alexander. 1992. "Economic Backwardness in Historical Perspective." In *The Sociology of Economic Life*, ed. Mark Granovetter and Richard Swedberg. Boulder, CO: Westview Press, 111–130.

Gourevitch, Peter. 1986. *Politics in Hard Times: Comparative Responses to International Economic Crises*. Ithaca, NY: Cornell University Press.

Haftendorn, Helga, Robert O. Keohane, and Celeste A. Wallander, eds. 1999. *Imperfect Unions: Security Institutions over Time and Space*. New York: Oxford University Press.

Hall, Peter A. 2010. "Historical Institutionalism in Rationalist and Sociological Perspective." In *Explaining Institutional Change: Ambiguity, Agency, and Power*, ed. James Mahoney and Kathleen Thelen. New York: Cambridge University Press, 204–224.

Hall, Peter A. and Rosemary C. R. Taylor. 1996. "Political Science and the Three New Institutionalisms." *Political Studies* 44 (5): 936–957.

Halliday, Fred. 2005. *The Middle East in International Relations: Power, Politics and Ideology*. New York: Cambridge University Press.

Henry, Clement M. and Robert Springborg. 2001. *Globalization and the Politics of Development in the Middle East*. New York: Cambridge University Press.

Hirschman Albert O. 1968. "The Political Economy of Import-Substituting Industrialization in Latin America." *The Quarterly Journal of Economics* 82 (1): 1–32.

Hurd, Ian. 2002. "Legitimacy, Power, and the Symbolic Life of the UN Security Council." *Global Governance* 8 (1): 35–51.

Jervis, Robert. 1982. "Security Regimes." *International Organization* 36 (2): 357–378.

Jervis, Robert. 1994. "Political Implications of Loss Aversion." In *Avoiding Losses/Taking Risks: Prospect Theory in International Politics*, ed. Barbara Farnham. Ann Arbor: University of Michigan Press, 23–40.

Jervis, Robert. 1999. "Realism, Neoliberalism, and Cooperation: Understanding the Debate." *International Security* 24 (1): 42–63.

Johnston, Alastair Iain. 2001. "Treating International Institutions as Social Environments." *International Studies Quarterly* 45 (4): 487–515.

Karp, Aaron. 1995. "Ballistic Missiles in the Middle East: Realities, Omens and Arms Control Options." *Contemporary Security Policy* 16 (1): 111–129.

Katzenstein, Peter J. 1978. *Between Power and Plenty: Foreign Economic Policies of Advanced Industrial States*. Madison: University of Wisconsin Press.

Keohane, Robert O. 1989. *International Institutions and State Power: Essays in International Relations Theory*. San Francisco, CA: Westview Press.

Keohane, Robert O. 1993. "Institutional Theory and the Realist Challenge after the Cold War." In *Neorealism and Neoliberalism*, ed. David A. Baldwin. New York: Columbia University Press, 269–300.

Klotz, Audi Jeanne and Cecelia M. Lynch. 2007. *Strategies for Research: In Constructivist International Relations*. New York: M. E. Sharpe.

Koremenos, Barbara, Charles Lipson, and Duncan Snidal. 2001. "The Rational Design of International Institutions." *International Organization* 55 (4): 761–799.

Krasner, Stephen D. 1991. "Global Communications and National Power: Life on the Pareto Frontier." *World Politics* 43 (3): 336–366.

Krasner, Stephen D., ed. 2001. *Problematic Sovereignty: Contested Rules and Political Possibilities*. New York: Columbia University Press.

Lake, David A. 2001. "Beyond Anarchy: The Importance of Security Institutions." *International Security* 26 (1): 129–160.

Lebow, Richard N., ed. 2010. *Forbidden Fruit: Counterfactuals and International Relations*. Princeton, NJ: Princeton University Press.

Lebow, Richard Ned. 2014. *Archduke Franz Ferdinand Lives!: A World without World War I*. New York: St. Martin's Press.

Leeds, Brett Ashley and Michaela Mattes. 2010. "Political Survival, Policy Distribution, and Alliance Formation." *Journal of Peace Research* 47 (4): 407–419.

Lipson, Charles. 1984. "International Cooperation in Economic and Security Affairs." *World Politics* 37 (1): 1–23.

McDermott, Rose. 1998. *Risk Taking in International Politics: Prospect Theory in American Foreign Policy*. Ann Arbor, MI: University of Michigan Press.

Mahoney, James. 2000. "Path Dependence in Historical Sociology." *Theory and Society* 29 (4): 507–548.

Mahoney, James and Kathleen Thelen, eds. 2010. *Explaining Institutional Change: Ambiguity, Agency, and Power*. New York: Cambridge University Press.

March, James G. and Johan P. Olsen. 1998. "The Institutional Dynamics of International Political Orders." *International Organization* 52 (04): 943–969.

Mearsheimer, John. 2001. *The Tragedy of Great Power Politics*. New York: W.W. Norton.

Moore, Barrington. 1966. *The Social Origins of Dictatorship and Democracy*. Boston, MA: Beacon Press.

Negm, Namira. 2009. *Transfer of Nuclear Technology under International Law: Case Study of Iraq, Iran and Israel*. Leiden: Koninklijke Brill NV.

Noland, Marcus and Howard Pack. 2005. "The East Asian Industrial Policy Experience: Implications for the Middle East." Working Paper Series WP05-14. Peterson Institute for International Economics.

Pierson, Paul. 2000. "Increasing Returns, Path Dependence, and the Study of Politics." *The American Political Science Review* 94 (2): 251–267.

Pierson, Paul. 2004. *Politics in Time: History, Institutions, and Social Analysis*. Princeton, NJ: Princeton University Press.

Pierson, Paul and Theda Skocpol. 2002. "Historical Institutionalism in Contemporary Political Science." In *Political Science: State of the Discipline*, ed. Ira Katznelson and Helen V. Milner. New York: W. W. Norton, 693–721.

Polanyi, Karl. 2005. *The Great Transformation: The Political and Economic Origins of Our Time*. 4th Edition. Princeton, NJ: Beacon Press.

Ruggie, John Gerard. 1994. "Third Try at World Order? America and Multilateralism After the Cold War." *Political Science Quarterly* 109 (4): 553–570.

Ruggie, John Gerard. 1998. "What Makes the World Hang Together? Neo-Utilitarianism and the Social Constructivist Challenge." *International Organization* 52 (4): 855–885.

Sil, Rudra and Peter J. Katzenstein. 2010. *Beyond Paradigms: Analytic Eclecticism in the Study of World Politics*. New York: Palgrave Macmillan.

Skocpol, Theda. 1979. *States and Social Revolutions: A Comparative Analysis of France, Russia and China*. Cambridge: Cambridge University Press.

Sloss, David. 1995. "It's Not Broken, So Don't Fix It: The International Atomic Energy Agency and the Nuclear Nonproliferation Treaty." *Virginia Journal of International Law* 35: 841–893.

Snyder, Jack L. 1991. *Myths of Empire: Domestic Politics and International Ambition*. Ithaca, NY: Cornell University Press.

Solingen, Etel. 1998. *Regional Orders at Century's Dawn: Global and Domestic Influences on Grand Strategy*. Princeton, NJ: Princeton University Press.

Solingen, Etel. 2001. "Mapping Internationalization: Domestic and Regional Impacts." *International Studies Quarterly* 45 (4): 517–555.

Solingen, Etel. 2007a. *Nuclear Logics: Contrasting Paths in East Asia and the Middle East*. Princeton, NJ: Princeton University Press.

Solingen, Etel. 2007b. "Pax Asiatica versus Bella Levantina: The Foundations of War and Peace in East Asia and the Middle East." *American Political Science Review* 101 (4): 757–780.

Solingen, Etel. 2008. "The Genesis, Design and Effects of Regional Institutions: Lessons from East Asia and the Middle East." *International Studies Quarterly* 52 (2): 261–294.

Solingen, Etel. 2014. "Domestic Coalitions, Internationalization, and War: Then and Now." *International Security* 39 (1): 44–70.

Tang, Beijie. 2014. "Internationalization's Discontents: Domestic Coalitions and the Future of China's Peaceful Rise." Ph.D. Dissertation, University of California Irvine, Department of Political Science.

Thelen, Kathleen. 1999. "Historical Institutionalism in Comparative Politics." *Annual Review of Political Science* 2 (1): 369–404.

Thelen, Kathleen and Sven Steinmo. 1992. "Historical Institutionalism in Comparative Politics." In *Structuring Politics: Historical Institutionalism in Comparative Analysis*, ed. Sven Steinmo, Kathleen Thelen, and Frank Longstreth. New York: Cambridge University Press, 1–32.

United Nations Development Program. 2009. *Challenges to Human Security in the Arab Countries*. Arab Human Development Report. New York: United Nations Publications.

Wallander, Celeste A. and Robert O. Keohane. 1999. "Risk, Threat, and Security Institutions." In *Imperfect Unions: Security Institutions over Time and Space*, ed. Helga Haftendorn, Robert O. Keohane, and Celeste A. Wallander. New York: Oxford University Press, 21–47.

Wan, Wilfred. 2014. "Firewalling Nuclear Diffusion." *International Studies Review* 16 (2): 217–228.

Waterbury, John. 1983. *The Egypt of Nasser and Sadat: The Political Economy of Two Regimes*. Princeton, NJ: Princeton University Press.

Wendt, Alexander. 1992. "Anarchy Is What States Make of It: The Social Construction of Power Politics." *International Organization* 46 (2): 391–342.

CHAPTER 34

GLOBAL INSTITUTIONS WITHOUT A GLOBAL STATE

HENRY FARRELL AND MARTHA FINNEMORE*

INTERNATIONAL relations (IR) scholars have increasingly embraced historical institutionalism (HI) to good effect in recent years (Fioretos 2011a). However, historical institutionalism has not yet grappled with the deeper intellectual challenges of "going global." Most of historical institutionalism's forays into IR to date investigate national bureaucracies tasked with international jobs (Fioretos 2011b; Farrell and Newman 2010, 2014; Raustiala 2009). In contrast, understanding international, particularly global, institutions requires additional tools. It requires attention to and theorizing of a global social context, one that does not rely on a national government in the background, ready to enforce laws and rules under which people strategize and act both inside and outside the institution. It also requires theories about the global organizations themselves. As social forms, these global organizations have distinctive properties and differ from national public bureaucracies in important ways.

In this chapter we make two claims about how historical institutionalism scholars could enrich their own theoretical repertoires with insights from scholars working on international organizations.[1] First, historical institutionalism could expand its analytical range by theorizing more fully institutional contexts beyond the state. Global organizations obviously operate in such an environment but so, too, do a wide range of informal institutions that have loose, if any, reliance on state-based order and enforcement, including epistemic communities and professional networks. Expanding historical institutionalism's toolbox so that it can better address change in institutions not governed by or dependent directly on an overarching national state could greatly enhance the tradition's reach in a globalizing world.

Historical institutionalism's current focus on national level contexts and state institutions is hardly surprising given its own history. Like the institutions it studies, historical institutionalism is a product of path dependence. Its roots lie in the state-centered analysis of Barrington Moore (1966) and Evans, Rueschemeyer, and Skocpol's influential volume, *Bringing the State Back In* (1985), which emphasized "the explanatory centrality of states as potent and autonomous organizational actors" vis-à-vis their societies (Skocpol 1985, 6). Over time, historical institutionalists have largely moved away from the macrohistorical approach, but instead of broadening their view in a globalizing world, they focused instead on the role of micro-relations between specific agents within the nation-state. Current historical institutionalism scholarship largely takes politics *within* well-established states as its starting point (Levitsky and Murillo 2010) and explores mechanisms that lead national level institutions to persist, change, or wither away. Hacker's (2004) examination of mechanisms of change in welfare politics and Mahoney's (2010) work on "change agents" are representative in that both assume a political context dominated by a hierarchical state, which different actors seek to capture or influence. Formal state institutions such as constitutional rules, laws, regulations or policy frames have received much more attention than informal societal ones (Helmke and Levitsky 2004). Indeed, some work (e.g., Streeck and Thelen 2005) seems actively to doubt that informal institutions have any great relevance in modern society.

Second, to facilitate this broader contextual theorizing, historical institutionalism needs to engage more systematically with the role of norms and ideas and the most obvious source that HI can draw on for this purpose is the broad literature on sociological institutionalism (SI), both within sociology itself and in other disciplines, including international relations. While historical institutionalism has always acknowledged sociological institutionalism's existence, its intellectual energy has been focused on engagements with rational choice (Blyth, Helgadóttir, and Kring, Chapter 8, this volume). This is in many respects unsurprising; the first self-consciously historical institutionalist work explicitly defined itself in contradistinction to rationalism (Thelen et al. 1992). Early work in the tradition made room for ideas and sociological accounts (Hall and Taylor 1996), but over time, the historical institutionalist approach increasingly bifurcated into two accounts (see Thelen 1999, footnote 12). One of these accounts, which emphasized power and interest and engaged with rational choice, came to dominate, while the other, emphasizing ideas, largely withered away (Blyth, Helgadóttir, and Kring, Chapter 8, this volume).

Re-engaging with organizational sociology and IR constructivism, in particular, could be useful in applying historical institutionalism to global institutions. Formal rules and institutions may be thin or hobbled in a global context with no hierarchical state. Norms and ideas can become important ordering mechanisms in such situations, making SI and constructivists natural partners for historical institutionalism. Conversations with these scholars could highlight neglected mechanisms of power and change in these institutions that are of interest to all three groups. Expertise and its role in organizations is one promising area of collaboration; informal institutions (including norms created by informal or semi-formal networks) are another, and we discuss both in the context of two international institutions, the International Monetary Fund (IMF) and the European Central Bank (ECB).

Conceptual Challenges for a Global Historical Institutionalism

The most glaring conceptual challenge for historical institutionalism, as it investigates global institutions, is the lack of any international equivalent of the hierarchical state. Much historical institutionalism theorizing rests on an assumption that some reasonably competent state stands in the background and can be relied upon to enforce property rights, quell violence, and provide order for actors shaping institutional development. In fact, most of historical institutionalism's core theoretical mechanisms require a pretty deep foundation of social structures to operate (Levitsky and Murillo 2010). "Increasing returns" are problematic and precarious without guaranteed property rights or reliably enforced legal outcomes. There is no "lock-in" if institutional structures can be overturned by violence at the whim of one or more players. John Ikenberry (2000) has argued that dominant hegemons can build an international equivalent to an enduring constitutional order but sustaining such orders requires the hegemon to carry out a very tricky balancing act: it must enforce the order's rules while reassuring weaker states that it considers itself to be bound by these rules as well. Ikenberry is optimistic that enlightened hegemons will both perceive the benefits of such self-restraint, and successfully resist temptation to break rules. The patchy record of the post-World War II United States on everything from human rights and democracy to cybersecurity suggests that this may be more difficult than he believes (Farrell and Finnemore 2013). Incentives for hypocrisy loom large and such hypocritical behavior undermines the social legitimacy of the hegemon's order (Finnemore 2009).

Thus, in the international realm, many of the basic incentive structures that underpin historical institutionalism's core mechanisms are weak or absent because there is no state to provide them. This is true in two senses. There is no global state to provide global public goods for international organizations (IOs). Indeed, this absence has long been described as *the* core analytic issue for theory in IR. Lack of a "global state" (sometimes called "anarchy") is what distinguishes the international realm analytically and makes IR distinct from other branches of Political Science in the minds of many IR scholars. The fact that international institutions exist at all has been treated as an anomaly to be explained in IR and much research energy was devoted to "the cooperation problem" underpinning international institutions in the 1970s–1990s. Scholarship on international institutions and "regimes" coming out of this effort bears the mark of this historical sequence in ways historical institutionalism scholars will appreciate. It focused heavily on moments of IO creation, since that was the theoretical anomaly. Little attention was paid to what IOs did after they were created, how they evolved, or whether they performed as their founders intended—concerns central to historical institutionalism research and with which its analytical toolbox can help.

The absent state is more than an analytic challenge for HI. It is also a challenge for IOs, themselves, as they carry out their missions. Many member states in which these global institutions do their work lack basic institutions and expertise and, for many practical purposes, simply cannot or do not govern. As the United Nations (UN) tries to deliver services, harmonize policies, or ensure rights around the world it often confronts a diverse array of national institutional contexts, varying greatly in their structure and, more important, in their basic capacity. Violence may dominate bargaining in these situations, so that formal rules and institutions are tangential to outcomes and evolving patterns of behavior. The number of states that have "failed," in whole or in significant part, is now quite large, making historical institutionalism's basic assumptions about how or even whether its institutional mechanisms work in these contexts suspect.

A second conceptual challenge for historical institutionalists is that the fundamental structure of international organizations is often unlike anything in the domestic arena. Most of the flagship intergovernmental organizations (IGOs) are membership organizations. Members write the mission statements for these organizations and contribute the resources for their work. This is quite different from the situation of government departments or national agencies with delegated powers specified in a piece of national legislation or executive order. There are no external legislators who can rewrite enabling statutes, no executive branch sitting on high outside the organization, no voters to please. Instead, these IOs are governed by structures and in ways that have no clear domestic analog. Executive Boards populated by Executive Directors are chosen in diverse ways with a bewildering array of powers (or lack thereof) to steer the organization. Funding and resource flows for these organizations are similarly diverse and rarely have parallels with domestic institutions. The UN peacekeepers and their equipment are provided on a pass-the-hat basis. Indeed, over time the UN dues system has been eclipsed in importance by voluntary funding mechanisms for a great many UN programs. The World Bank raises money directly from financial markets. The IMF works more like a credit union, with members paying "quotas" in order to join and the Fund making loans on the strength of its holdings. None of these has the political dynamics of a national taxation system.

International institutional structures have evolved over time in response to crises, changing membership, and changing missions in ways that beg for good analysis by historical institutionalists. In some instances, applying historical institutionalism tools might be relatively straightforward. "Sunk costs" in existing structures probably shape global institutions similarly to domestic ones. In other situations, the application will require more thought. Expanding membership is a frequent challenge for many IOs that has no clear analog in a national administrative agencies, yet it has huge implications for the evolution of these institutions in patterned ways historical institutionalism might study. Decentralized resource flows from unreliable payment of membership dues is another common challenge for IOs and informal institutions that requires more theorizing by the tradition. In short, applying historical institutionalism to international organizations could plausibly help us understand the dynamics of international organizations, but could also help historical institutionalists themselves develop better theory. Applying historical institutionalism to non-standard institutional environments would help establish the scope conditions of historical institutionalism's existing toolbox, and very possibly lead to the development of new and valuable tools.

One consequence of the structures of IOs and of absent states is that international organizations often use *means and methods* that are understudied by historical institutionalists. Some of the work of international organizations—the steady, dull accumulation of detailed formal standards and the like—is quite easy for historical institutionalists to understand, because it has close domestic equivalents. Even if these standards are often not formally binding, they can shape domestic law, or even be transposed into it, becoming binding at the level of the nation state. But IOs do more than just make rules. They also spread values and norms of behavior. The "teaching of norms" (Finnemore 1993; Barnett and Finnemore 2004) and promotion of certain social values—democracy, human rights, fiscal discipline, nuclear restraint—is part of the mission of these organizations, and they take it seriously. They promulgate these to national and sub-national actors, sometimes coercively using sticks and carrots to change those actors' understanding of what is appropriate and what is inappropriate. National bureaucracies may do this too, but not in the type of splendid national isolation suggested in typical historical institutionalism accounts of institutional change. As the tradition has moved further away from sociological institutionalism, it has focused on how institutions distribute the benefits of policy, rather than how they inculcate norms and values. Given the accretive nature of building habits, changing beliefs, and developing norms, historical institutionalism might have much to contribute to investigations of these norm-teaching processes if it can help us understand how the IOs, themselves, change—how layering, drift, and other historical institutionalism mechanisms shape the content of the norms and values IOs promote.

Through their work IOs are explicitly trying to reshape the preference functions, strategies, and worldviews of other actors and other institutions. Indeed, IOs often understand their task as reconfiguring the institutional structures and goals of the states with whom they work. The IMF sends missions to member states to set up central banks and bond markets to facilitate entry into the global economy. Various parts of the UN assist states in setting up environmental protection bureaucracies to further new environmental goals. The World Bank helps states reconfigure their institutions to root out corruption as norms against such behavior strengthen.

Both international and domestic organizations establish bureaucratic rules and set standards. Both spread values, or try to. But the international organizations face a more difficult task of persuasion than do national bureaucracies. Very rarely can they coerce and force compliance as national agencies often do. They sometimes have resources to dangle as bait. The IMF and the World Bank, not surprisingly, are often able to get impoverished borrowers to buy into their prescriptions. But few UN agencies have big monetary inducements and none of these organizations have hierarchical or law enforcement authority analogous to their domestic counterparts. They have to establish authority through other sources such as expertise or legitimacy. They then use this to shape the ideas and expectations of other actors in ways sociological institutionalism might predict but which historical institutionalism often overlooks. To understand this properly, historical institutionalism needs to build intellectual bridges with sociological institutionalism, adopting a thicker account of what institutions are and how they work.

The World Bank, for example, has established itself as a repository of expertise about international development (the "Knowledge Bank"), and showcases its expertise and knowledge functions as a currency for influencing others to adopt favored practices.[2] This is not mere "information asymmetry" as understood by various versions of rational choice, and historical institutionalists might be particularly interested in changes in the Bank's use of this tool over time. When the Bank first got into the business of deploying staff to projects in the field, expertise was understood by the organization explicitly as a one-way street. The Bank knew how to do things and borrowers learned from the Bank. Over time and following long strings of project failures, the Bank has changed its understanding of expertise and how best to use it. The old understanding has been deemed by both outsiders and insiders to be ineffective and illegitimate, tainted by paternalism and neocolonialism. In its new approach to deploying expertise, the Bank works hard to emphasize more collaboration and sharing, with itself at the center as a clearinghouse.

The Organization for Security and Cooperation in Europe (OSCE) has assiduously developed a set of norms around free and fair elections, which facilitate its efforts to cultivate democracy, and to send observers. States can, of course, refuse to accept these observers, but only through breaching these norms and paying the associated costs. ODIHR, the OSCE's Office for Democratic Institutions and Human Rights, compiles regular reports on elections with recommendations for how to improve procedures. It also provides training and technical assistance to help participating states with the technical business of running elections well. In fact, most "technical assistance," a major activity for virtually all IOs, is implicitly but more often explicitly about teaching norms and transmitting knowledge designed to further the values or goals of the organization.

Another common result of working in a global context is that IOs often aim to promote informal rather than formal institutional change, and to understand this better historical institutionalist scholars could learn a great deal from sociological institutionalism. The norms and practices that are taught by international organizations are not necessarily written ones. Even when there is a written set of principles, associated informal understandings may be quite as important, or even more important. For example, the OSCE's High Commissioner on National Minorities has few formal powers to intervene forcefully, but has played a key role in advising countries not only on how to deal with minority rights through formal reforms, but also in informally brokering compromises in which minority and majority communities learn practical norms for how to live with each other in a mutually acceptable *modus vivendi*. Similarly, the IMF has an array of "IMF Institutes" around the world. Countries send their national bureaucrats there for training in IMF "best practices" in everything from how to compile national accounts to how to run a central bank or combat money laundering. By using their legitimacy and authority to shape these actors' intellectual and social worldviews in this way, international organizations can have an important, and sometimes profound, effect on the social institutions and practices that these actors create, even in the absence of coercion.

These more informal modes of work allow IOs to navigate another central feature of the international context—huge power asymmetries that have no real domestic analog. Sometimes recognition of these asymmetries is explicit, formal, and baked into the design of these organizations. Security Council vetoes, for example, guarantee that the permanent five member states on the Council will be treated differently than others by the UN and have no good domestic equivalent. Other perks of power are largely unwritten but have been very sticky for all that. The "gentlemen's agreement" that the US appoints the head of the World Bank and that the head of the IMF is a European has persisted for more than six decades and is only now showing signs of fraying.

Power asymmetries may also create crucial variations in effects of these IOs when the same rules are applied by an international organization across dissimilar members. For example, many countries in the developing world have states with relatively weak regulatory capacity. The Conference of Parties for the Convention on International Trade in Endangered Species (CITES) may agree on what species to designate as endangered at what level of threat (Appendix I vs II), but the relevant management authorities in member states differ wildly in their funding and capacity to license and force CITES rules. Some species in some countries receive far better protection than others. Large portions of countries like Congo and Somalia have no functional state presence at all. In other countries where territory is being contested, there may be partial control of parts of the country by a state and this only part of the time (Avant 2004).

It is difficult to use standard historical institutionalism to describe the consequences of international organizations for states with limited regulatory capacity, which may have little expertise and capacity directly to resist the suasion of international organizations (Sell 2010). However, they may be able to resist unwanted mandates passively, failing to conform to international standards, precisely because they do not have the bureaucratic resources to implement them properly (Mosley 2010). Contested and non-existent states present a vacuum of government, which international organizations (e.g., aid agencies, human rights agencies, and so on) may seek to fill, more or less inadequately. In other words, historical institutionalism faces the challenge both of explaining how international organizations work in a world without a global equivalent of a state, and explaining how they may have consequences in a world where the extent and nature of "stateness" can vary dramatically.

To address the global arena, historical institutionalism needs to retool to analyze and explain international organizations, themselves—how they work and how they change over time. This should be do-able. The organizations' headquarters and centers of power exist in worlds not unfamiliar to historical institutionalists. Prominent players tend to be powerful states of the capitalist West and the organizations' headquarters (and often much of their staff) tend to be located in comfortable developed country capitals served by functional state machinery. Rethinking lines of power and causal chains for organizational development at the center will be challenging but the patterns of crisis, "lock-in" and change one might want to explain in the organizations, themselves, at least look familiar, even if the underlying causal mechanisms may be somewhat different. By contrast, applying historical institutionalism outside of reasonably settled governing structures looks much harder.

To illustrate the gains from attending to ideas and norms in international institutions, we offer two sketches. One highlights the dynamics of expertise and problem solving knowledge inside the IMF and connects these to changes in the organization's behavior and structure in countries with limited state capacity. The second sketch traces the way experts and ideational entrepreneurs built support for creation for the European Central Bank and how the ECB uses its expertise as an important tool of influence in countries with extensive state capacity.

Ideas and Expertise at the International Monetary Fund

The IMF we have today is not the organization its founders intended. Not only has its original raison d'être disappeared with the end of fixed exchange rates, but today's Fund is intimately involved in member states' domestic economies in ways specifically rejected by its founders. [3] This is the kind of evolution that that should interest historical institutionalists but it cannot be understood without close attention to the intellectual technologies and expertise at work inside the organization. The very creation of an IMF depended upon the development of new, largely Keynesian, ideas about the workings of the global economy—ideas that had not been dominant or even much present at earlier periods. Once established, the Fund's expansion and mission creep were driven, not by demands from member states, but by new intellectual connections made by Fund staff as they wrestled with recalcitrant member economies, trying to stabilize their currencies. New ideas about connections between domestic economic policies and balance of payments position created new policy opportunities, even imperatives, which staff pursued as they tried to fulfill their mandate and mission.

The Fund was created in 1944 to make short-term loans to members experiencing temporary balance of payments problems and to oversee the system of fixed exchange rates agreed upon by members at Bretton Woods. Balance of payments adjustment was a new public policy problem at the time,[4] but there was little detailed knowledge about what policies would correct a payments deficit. Operating the system created at Bretton Woods required knowledge economists simply did not have. How did one distinguish between a fundamental exchange rate disequilibrium and a temporary one? What was the relationship between the size of a par value change and the size of the balance of payments effect it would cause? Detailed and practical knowledge about these questions did not exist, yet was essential for the Fund to act and do its job.

Creating that knowledge was left largely to IMF staff (Bernstein 1991; Polak 1997a; DeVries 1987; James 1996).[5] Two conceptual tools developed at the Fund were particularly important and illustrate the transformative effects of new intellectual technologies for the organization's development: the absorption approach and the monetary approach to balance of payments.

Economists today working on exchange rate and balance of payments issues all use some descendent of the absorption approach as part of their basic toolbox, but at the time the Fund was created, it did not exist. In the 1940s, analysis of the effects of an exchange rate change on a country's payments position would have focused on its effect on the trade deficit and on the elasticity of supply and demand in both the devaluing country and in the rest of the world. Estimating these many elasticities was technically challenging by itself; doing so in the absence of good data—a common difficulty in countries facing payments difficulties—was even harder. With the advent of the Fund, these were no longer abstract academic problems. They were also pressing practical problems for the staff tasked with devising programs and policy for the new organization and defending those recommendations to member states. The logic of the old approach made some sense in the abstract but was completely unworkable as a guide to crafting practical programs with extant data.

Seeds of an alternative approach were developed by Jacques Polak of the Fund's research department as early as 1948 during negotiations over Mexico's proposed devaluation and were elaborated by him and others in following years. In a 1952 paper Polak described the core insight:

> I submit that the analysis of exchange rate changes would become much more useful if it did not start out from two, four, or eight elasticities, but from a simple social accounting identity, viz., that the existence of a balance of payments deficit implies that the country absorbs more resources in consumption and investment than it produces. Therefore, if devaluation is to cure this deficit, it must either increase production with consumption and investment constant, or decrease consumption and investment with output constant, or achieve some combination of the two. (Polak 1952; quoted in Frenkel, Goldstein, and Khan 1991, 8–9)

As a policy tool, the absorption approach was attractive because it depended on domestic expenditures and income data which were just then appearing as part of the new national accounts data that states were beginning to collect systematically after World War II, instead of import and export data which were thin to non-existent. However, the approach also changed the focus of analytic thinking about exchange rate policy. It focused attention on the structure of domestic economies—domestic consumption, investment, and output—and linked those analytically to a state's payments position. It thus provided Fund staff with a strong basis for concern about what had been previously understood as purely domestic economic policy decisions.

The monetary approach to balance of payments built on the absorption approach and was attractive for similar reasons. Relocating attention to domestic economics created new challenges since staff still lacked good ways to model these economies and tease out the linkages among variables and links to policy tools one could hope to manipulate. Polak, again, was a leader in developing new ways of thinking. In a 1957 paper, written again in response to events in Mexico, he constructed a balance sheet of assets and liabilities in the banking system and linked it to simple behavioral relationships involving income in such a way as to yield a unique relationship between domestic credit creation and foreign reserves (Polak 1957; DeVries 1987, 27–30.)

The result was a simple model that was flexible and versatile. It could be (and has been) extended in many ways. It was also dynamic in that it linked *changes* in reserves to *changes* in income and credit creation. For practitioners, it had the advantage of relying primarily on banking and trade data, which were more available than most other types. Above all, it pointed to workable policy prescriptions. It linked domestic credit to international reserves analytically, and domestic credit creation was a variable that national governments could control. The model thus gave governments and the Fund a focus for policy interventions (Polak 1997a, 1997b; Frenkel, Goldstein, and Khan 1991; James 1996, chapter 5, esp. 140–142; DeVries 1987, chapter 1; Stiles 1981, 4–16; David 1985, chapter 3; Eckaus 1986, 239–242).

These intellectual connections shaped much of the Fund's activity and organizational development going forward. For example, conditionality and technical assistance are two major Fund activities that are nowhere in the Fund's Articles of Agreement but are a logical, even necessary, outgrowth of these new intellectual understandings. Conditions on lending that intrude on domestic policy choices, such as demands for budget restraint or ends to subsidies, are justified by these connections. Borrower states often complain, sometimes bitterly, about these conditions but for Fund staff, these are not punitive or arbitrary exercises of power. Quite the contrary. From the Fund's perspective, these domestic measures are simply sound economics, necessary to put the country back on a path to financial stability. In fact, to recommend otherwise would be arbitrary and irresponsible, since economic wisdom clearly shows that these domestic measures are necessary. Ideas and expertise, in this situation, not only create power but discipline and direct it. They also constrain it since experts can only legitimately recommend actions supported by the content of their expertise.

Technical assistance activities might be of particular interest to institutionalists since they often involve creating new institutions. Throughout decolonization and again after the end of the Cold War, the Fund has been asked to provide "technical assistance" to new, or newly marketized, states seeking to join the global economy. The IMF Institute and other subunits of the Fund specialize in this. They help members with such diverse tasks as setting up a central bank and structuring bond markets and have preferred blueprints for these institutions. They also have strong opinions about "best practices" when it comes to reorganizing a state's banking sector or taxation apparatus. These opinions are rooted in the staff's understanding of "sound economics" and the intellectual connections they perceive institutional structures and economic outcomes.

One notable feature of these ideationally driven behaviors is their expansionary dynamic, often fueled by policy failure, not success. As the Fund busily tries to create stable economies among its members, it repeatedly finds its tools to be inadequate. Budget restraint does not create stability; technical assistance does not create smooth functioning domestic financial machinery. What's a Fund to do? Like most conscientious bureaucratic organizations, the Fund's answer is often "try harder" and try more things. When budget restraint is not sufficient, the Fund recommends additional conditions—ends to subsidies for food and energy or the imposition of wage restraints on public unions, matters which intrude deeply into domestic policy. When seminars at Fund headquarters are not imparting the necessary technical skills, staff may be stationed in the member state's finance ministry to supervise domestic decisions more closely. This dynamic of expertise is hardly unique to economists or the Fund and seems very much the type of motor for institutional change that interests HI. It speaks to institutional reproduction and change (Fioretos 2011a, table 1) but is driven primarily by ideational and normative forces, especially the changing structure of expert knowledge, and in this way expands the historical institutionalism toolbox.

Ideas and the European Central Bank

A second example of how ideas and norms can play a key role in explaining institutional development over time can be found in the history of the ECB. The ECB is unusual among international organizations in that it has unambiguous regulatory authority. The European Union is something between a state and an international organization, combining elements of intergovernmental negotiation with areas in which bodies such as the European Commission, European Court of Justice, and ECB have direct rule-making authority.

Historical institutionalists have paid remarkably little attention to the ECB. The most influential historical institutionalism work on European integration (see especially Pierson 1996b), has emphasized how "gaps" in member state control open up, allowing some EU institutions to become partly autonomous. However, historical institutionalists have argued that the ECB is far more strictly trammeled by rigid constitutional rules than, for example, the European Court of Justice or European Commission, and hence less likely to change over time (Heisenberg and Richmond 2002).

Arguments from sociological institutionalism show how such arguments can seriously underestimate the ability of international institutions to shape international and domestic politics (Barnett and Finnemore 2004). Norms and ideas can allow international organizations to reshape the understandings of the states that are supposed to be their masters. Indeed, norms and ideas played a key role both in shaping the ECB and in allowing it to shape politics and economic decision-making in turn. If certain key ideas had not been widely circulated, the ECB would likely have never come into being. Key experts (central bankers) and ideational entrepreneurs (like European Commission President Jacques Delors) gradually built a new consensus for economic and monetary union that framed economic decision-making in ways that took the venom out of certain relationships while generating long-term political and economic problems. Finally, much of the ECB's power comes not from its decision-making authority, but from its expertise, and associated ability to shape the categories that policymakers use to make sense of the world.

There is a strong consensus in the existing literature that the ECB's form and purpose were substantially shaped by prevalent ideas about monetary policy in the 1970s and 1980s. Kathleen McNamara (1998) shows how neoliberal ideas about monetary policy were crucial to the iterated process of political decision-making that led to European economic and monetary union, and hence to the creation of the ECB. Amy Verdun (1999) shows that the Delors Committee was an "epistemic community," in which actors largely agreed about the appropriate role of central banks. Harold James's (2012) historical account of the making of economic and monetary union (which we rely on in our analysis of the ECB, below) provides additional support for McNamara's and Verdun's argument, demonstrating, for example, the importance of Hayekian ideas about the need to remove currency decision-making from the hands of politicians. James furthermore uses archival data to document the bureaucratic processes of consensus building and accumulation of authority that turned these ideas into the organizing principles of policy. The creation of the ECB thus combined the formulation of new ideas with bureaucratic processes of accumulation of expertise and effective authority.

Initially, relations among European central banks were largely informal. The central banks themselves "were for the most part politically controlled and there existed no well-developed conceptual framework as to why or how central banks could be independent" (James 2012, 43). As European economies began to become more intertwined, central bankers came under increasing pressure to coordinate monetary policy, which they feared would limit their informal and rather casual style of governance. The European Economic Community (as it was then) created a Committee of Governors (CoG) in 1964, to encourage increased consultation and information exchange among European central bankers, who continued to see their role as non-political.

Over the succeeding three decades, the CoG came to serve a crucial role in reshaping European monetary policy. First, its regular discussions reshaped central bank governors' understanding of their role. While they continued to disdain the vulgarities of overt politics, they increasingly made policy that had important political consequences. Although they continued to disagree strongly on many aspects of economic and monetary governance, they gradually converged on a new set of concepts, most enthusiastically promoted by Germany, about how central bankers should behave. These ideas emphasized both monetary stability and the crucial importance of central bank independence.

Much of the project of economic and monetary union involved a process of bureaucratic accretion, through which divisive political issues were assimilated and redefined in technical ways. The urgent question of European monetary relations was always: who adjusts? Europeans faced the external challenge of a United States that typically had no compunction in offloading the burden of monetary adjustment onto its allies, and the internal problem of dealing with Germany's economic strength. Closer monetary cooperation promised both to make the European Union stronger vis-à-vis the US, and to turn repeated political confrontations between Germany and other countries (most prominently France) into technocratic questions of decision-making over interest rates.

New ideas about the role of central banks led to changes in the policies adopted by governments to deal with recurring tensions in monetary relations, which in turn reshaped the initial ideas. At first, many central bankers had seen their role as responding to the needs of government. Hayekian ideas that stressed the importance of central bank independence as a source of economic stability gradually eroded these assumptions, and provided European central bankers with a new collective identity. Over the longer term, this created a self-reinforcing tendency among members of the CoG toward ever greater central bank independence from national authorities, and ever greater jealousy in guarding their appurtenances. The initially unthinkable idea of a truly European central bank and a true monetary union, in successive stages became thinkable, plausible, attractive, and urgently necessary. In contrast to the policy feedback mechanisms stressed by historical institutionalists such as Paul Pierson (1993), in which new policies create constituencies that press to defend and extend these policies, the crucial feedback loop was between central bankers' idea of what they should be doing and what, in actuality, they did. As bankers came to play new roles based on new ideas, these ideas were increasingly taken for granted by their executors, and given material form through a multitude of bureaucratic routines.

This surely reflected some degree of institutional self-interest within the perpetual bureaucratic games of national politics. Yet it also reflected a genuine change in central bankers' self-conception and understanding of what their appropriate role should be. Certainly, the central bankers who started to explore policy discussions in the 1960s would have found the idea of a European central bank abhorrent, because of what it would mean for both national politics and their own bureaucratic identity. Over the longer term national central banks certainly became less dependent on national politicians, but only through being subsumed in the larger organizational structure of the ECB. Discussions in the CoG paved the way for the Delors Committee in which central bankers, somewhat to their surprise, found themselves proposing a quick transition to economic and monetary union. After the Delors Committee had issued its report, the CoG was clearly no longer a bureaucratic body, but an "epistemic community," applying consensual knowledge to promote "an idea or a vision" (James 2012, 266).

Both ideas and the establishment of bureaucratic procedure were necessary precursors to the creation of the ECB. The development of the two went hand in hand—changes in ideas promoting changes in bureaucratic practice, which, as it encountered new problems and issues, led to further changes in ideas. This led, through a process of iterated steps, to an ECB with an extraordinary degree of independence from European governments. This was at the insistence of Germany, but would have been impossible without the agreement of central bankers. This agreement reflected academic arguments (which had come to emphasize the importance of independent monetary policy) and the conversion even of holdouts like France to the belief that central bank independence was appropriate. The Bank's emphasis on monetary stability (it has a more restrictive mandate than the Federal Reserve) was also in large part a product of intellectual debates about monetary policy that were strongly influenced by the battles over inflation of the 1970s.

When the ECB was established, it not only exemplified ideas about central bank independence and monetary policy but sought actively to promote and extend them. Emulating the Federal Reserve, it speedily and deliberately established itself as the center of a network of academic and policy discussions.[6] Although it has kept its internal deliberations secret, it has also at times sought to influence public debate through regular press briefings and speeches given by its president and board members.

As the European economic crisis of 2008–2012 developed, the ECB has occupied an unusual role, on the one hand seeking to preserve its nominal independence from politics while on the other being increasingly drawn into directly political interventions. Despite early claims that the ECB was bound by a treaty "embod[ying] the best tradition of the Deutsche Bundesbank," it has found itself issuing hundreds of billions in loans to banks, and offered the possibility of "outright monetary transactions" to support member states in difficulty (Farrell 2012).[7] This has placed the ECB in an increasingly awkward position. While acknowledging that it has turned toward unorthodox tools, the ECB has insisted that it continues to preserve its independence and to work toward its basic goal of monetary stability.[8] Yet it obviously cannot achieve this goal given existing political structures, leading it to intervene both in national politics (through letters indicating that it will withdraw its support if certain political decisions are not taken) and European-level debates about whether major institutional reform is needed.

As its actions become more politicized, the ECB has sought to cloak its newly political role in technocratic jargon, describing, for example, its agreement to back national governments under certain conditions with the coinage of "outright monetary transactions." It cannot achieve monetary and economic stability through conventional means, but is incapable of changing its organizing ideas. Hence, it has sought to change the world it works in to make it more compatible with these ideas, arguing against increased government debt, helping to promote austerity politics, and more generally to create a European system which seeks as far as possible to exclude or marginalize political decision-making from economic policy. The ECB's ideational project, of becoming a central bank "above" politics, and hence insulating economic decision-making from democratic pressures, has failed. It is responding to this failure by trying to extend and generalize the Hayekian logic of decision-making far more widely than was ever anticipated.

Conclusion

Historical institutionalists could deal better with the challenge of "going global" if they re-engaged in dialogue with sociological institutionalists as well as rationalist institutionalists. This is, of course, not to say that historical institutionalism should reject its recent history—rather that, as Hall and Taylor (1996) stressed, historical institutionalism is at its best when it engages both traditions. By drawing on sociological institutionalism, historical institutionalists can better understand how organizations work in a world where there is no over-arching state. Much sociological work, especially in economic sociology (although see Fligstein and McAdam 2011) is better suited to dealing with such a world, since it does not take state mandated authority for granted, instead theorizing how actors can construct both social legitimacy and relevant knowledge. Very obviously, there is a rich tradition of work in sociological institutionalism on the power of norms, routines, and bureaucracies that historical institutionalists could turn to in order better to understand international organizations. Finally, scholars such as John Meyer and his colleagues have created a wide body of work examining how norms spread or do not spread in a world where different countries have different degrees of state capacity, and of compatibility with global norms (Meyer et al. 1997; Boli and Thomas 1998; Finnemore 1996). Equally, there is much that sociologically minded institutionalists can learn from historical institutionalism. Helpful as these sociological institutionalism arguments are, they lack the attention to temporality and its role in organizational evolution that is the hallmark of historical institutionalism. Work by Meyer and colleagues for example, focuses on diffusion of largely static institutional templates. It offers less theoretical purchase on evolution of these forms over time. Processes of norm building and norm spread are processes over time, in which sequencing very obviously matters.

Building better accounts of international organizations will require scholars of both historical and sociological institutionalism to engage with each other, as well as with the rational choice scholarship that both tend to orient themselves toward and against. Because international organizations work through instilling norms, in a context where there is no hierarchical state, historical institutionalists need to learn from sociological institutionalism. And because these organizations evolve over time, in ways that can be understood as mechanism-driven processes, sociological institutionalists need to learn from historical institutionalism.

Notes

* We are grateful to Orfeo Fioretos and the participants in the Historical Institutionalism in Political Science Conference at Temple University and the University of Pennsylvania in October 2013, for helpful comments and suggestions.

1. Our focus in this chapter is on intergovernmental organizations (IGOs) but many of the arguments presented might also be applied to NGOs. Following Barnett and Finnemore (2004), we define IOs as "organizations that have representatives from three or more states supporting a permanent secretariat to perform ongoing tasks related to a common purpose."
2. See, for example, the Bank's self presentation on its website: <http://documents.worldbank.org/curated/en/2011/01/15560820/state-world-bank-knowledge-services-knowledge-development-2011> (accessed August 14, 2015).
3. This section draws on Barnett and Finnemore (2004, chapter 3).

4. Under the old gold standard, these adjustments were supposed to happen automatically. It was only after the standard was discredited and abandoned that states confronted this new task entailed by the Bretton Woods order.
5. Bernstein was the Fund's first research director. Polak was his deputy and later succeeded him.
6. Interview with senior ECB official, 2011.
7. Despite this, the ECB continues to insist that it is bound by the principles of German "ordoliberalism," including a separation between political and non-political decision-making. See, e.g., <https://www.ecb.int/press/key/date/2013/html/sp130618.en.html> (accessed August 14, 2015).
8. See <https://www.ecb.int/press/key/date/2013/html/sp130625_1.en.html> (accessed August 14, 2015).

References

Avant, Deborah. 2004. "Conserving Nature in the State of Nature: the Politics of INGO Policy Implementation." *Review of International Studies* 30 (3): 331–382.

Barnett, Michael and Martha Finnemore. 2004. *Rules for the World: International Organizations in Global Politics*. Ithaca, NY: Cornell University Press.

Bernstein, Edward. 1991. "The Early Years of the International Monetary Fund." In *International Financial Policy: Essays in Honor of Jacques J. Polak*, ed. Jacob A. Frenkel and Morris Goldstein. Washington, D.C.: International Monetary Fund, 58–63.

Boli, John and George M. Thomas, eds. 1998. *Constructing World Culture: International Nongovernmental Organizations Since 1875*. Stanford, CA: Stanford University Press.

David, Wilfred. 1985. *The IMF Policy Paradigm*. New York: Praeger.

DeVries, Margaret Garritsen. 1987. *Balance of Payments Adjustment, 1945–1986: The IMF Experience*. Washington, D.C.: International Monetary Fund.

Eckaus, R. S. 1986. "How the IMF Lives with Its Conditionality." *Policy Sciences* 19: 237–252.

Evans, Peter B., Deitrich Rueschemeyer, and Theda Skocpol. 1985. *Bringing the State Back In*. New York: Cambridge University Press.

Farrell, Henry and Martha Finnemore. 2013. "The End of Hypocrisy: American Foreign Policy in the Age of Leaks." *Foreign Affairs* 92 (November/December).

Farrell, Henry. 2012. "A More Imperfect Union: On the European Central Bank." *The Nation* 295 (26) (December 24) 27–31.

Farrell, Henry and Abraham L. Newman. 2010. "Making Global Markets: Historical Institutionalism in International Political Economy." *Review of International Political Economy* 17 (4): 609–638.

Farrell, Henry and Abraham L. Newman. 2014. "Domestic Institutions beyond the Nation State: Charting the New Interdependence Approach." *World Politics* 66 (2): 331–363.

Finnemore, Martha. 1993. "International Organizations as Teachers of Norms: UNESCO and Science Policy." *International Organization* 47 (4): 565–597.

Finnemore, Martha. 1996. "Norms, Culture, and World Politics: Insights from Sociology's Institutionalism." *International Organization* 50 (2): 325–347.

Finnemore, Martha. 2009. "Legitimacy, Hypocrisy, and the Social Structure of Unipolarity." *World Politics* 61 (1): 58–85.

Fioretos, Orfeo. 2011a. "Historical Institutionalism in International Relations." *International Organization* 65 (2): 367–399.

Fioretos, Orfeo. 2011b. *Creative Reconstructions: Multilateralism and European Varieties of Capitalism after 1950*. Ithaca, NY: Cornell University Press.

Fligstein, Neil and McAdam, Doug. 2011. "Toward a General Theory of Strategic Action Fields." *Sociological Theory* 29 (1): 1–26.

Frenkel, Jacob A., Morris Goldstein, and Mohsin S. Khan. 1991. "Major Themes in the Writings of Jacques J. Polak." In *International Financial Policy: Essays in Honor of Jacques J. Polak*, ed. J. Frenkel and M. Goldstein. Washington, D.C.: International Monetary Fund, 3–39.

Hacker, Jacob S. 2004. "Privatizing Risk without Privatizing the Welfare State: The Hidden Politics of Social Policy Retrenchment in the United States." *American Political Science Review* 98 (2): 243–260.

Hall, Peter and Rosemary Taylor. 1996. "Political Science and the Three Institutionalisms." *Political Studies* 44 (5): 936–957.

Hall, Peter A. and Kathleen Thelen. 2009. "Institutional Change in Varieties of Capitalism." *Socio-Economic Review* 7 (1): 7–34.

Heisenberg, Dorothee and Amy Richmond. 2002. "Supranational Institution-Building in the European Union: A Comparison of the European Court of Justice and the European Central Bank." *Journal of European Public Policy* 9 (2): 201–218.

Helmke, Gretchen and Steven Levitsky. 2004. "Informal Institutions and Comparative Politics: A Research Agenda." *Perspectives on Politics* 2 (4):725–740.

Ikenberry, John. 2000. *After Victory: Institutions, Strategic Restraint, and the Rebuilding of Order after Major Wars*. Princeton, NJ: Princeton University Press.

James, Harold. 1996. *International Monetary Cooperation since Bretton Woods*. New York: Oxford University Press.

James, Harold. 2012. *Making the European Monetary Union*. Cambridge, MA: Harvard University Press.

Levitsky, Steven and María Victoria Murillo. 2010. "Building Institutions on Weak Foundations: Lessons from South America." Paper Presented at a Conference in Honor of Guillermo O'Donnell, Buenos Aires, March 26–27.

Mahoney, James. 2010. *Colonialism and Postcolonial Development: Spanish America in Comparative Perspective*. Cambridge: Cambridge University Press.

McNamara, Kathleen. 1998. *The Currency of Ideas: Monetary Politics in the European Union*. Ithaca, NY: Cornell University Press.

Meyer, John W., John Boli, George M. Thomas, and Francisco O. Ramirez. 1997. "World Society and the Nation-State." *American Journal of Sociology* 103 (1): 144–181.

Moore, Barrington. 1966. *Social Origins of Dictatorship and Democracy: Lord and Peasant in the Making of the Modern World*. Boston, MA: Beacon Press.

Mosley, L. 2010. "Regulating Globally, Implementing Locally: The Financial Codes and Standards Effort." *Review of International Political Economy* 17 (4): 724–761.

Pierson, Paul. 1993. "When Effect Becomes Cause." *World Politics* 45 (4): 595–628.

Pierson, Paul. 1996a. "The New Politics of the Welfare State." *World Politics* 48: 143–179.

Pierson, Paul. 1996b. "The Path to European Integration: A Historical Institutionalist Analysis." *Comparative Political Studies* 29 (2): 123–163.

Polak, Jacques J. 1952. "International Trade Theory—Discussion. American Economic Association Annual Meetings, December 1951." *American Economic Review, Papers and Proceedings* 42 (May): 179–181.

Polak, Jacques J. 1957. "Monetary Analysis of Income Formation and Payments Problems." *IMF Staff Papers* 6 (November) 1–50.

Polak, Jacques J. 1997a. "The IMF Monetary Model at Forty." Working Paper of the International Monetary Fund, April. Available at <http://www.imf.org/external/pubs/ft/wp/wp9749.pdf> (accessed September 1, 2015).

Polak Jacques J. 1997b. "The IMF Monetary Model: A Hardy Perennial." *Finance and Development* 34 (December): 16–19.

Raustiala, Kal. 2009. *Does the Constitution Follow the Flag?* Oxford: Oxford University Press.

Sell, Susan K. 2010. "The Rise and Rule of a Trade-Based Strategy: Historical Institutionalism and the International Regulation of Intellectual Property." *Review of International Political Economy* 17 (4): 762–790.

Skocpol, Theda. 1985. "Bringing the State Back In: Strategies of Analysis in Current Research." In *Bringing the State Back In*, ed. Peter B. Evans, Deitrich Rueschemeyer, and Theda Skocpol. New York: Cambridge University Press, 3–37.

Stiles, Kenneth. 1981. *Negotiating Debt: The IMF Lending Process.* Boulder, CO: Westview Press.

Streeck, Wolfgang and Kathleen Thelen. 2005. *Beyond Continuity: Institutional Change in Advanced Political Economies.* Oxford: Oxford University Press.

Thelen, Kathleen. 1999. "Historical Institutionalism in Comparative Politics." *Annual Review of Political Science* 2 (1): 369–404.

Thelen, Kathleen. 2012. "Varieties of Capitalism: Trajectories of Liberalization and the New Politics of Social Solidarity." *Annual Review of Political Science* 15: 137–159.

Thelen, Kathleen and James Mahoney, eds. 2010. *Explaining Institutional Change: Ambiguity, Agency, and Power.* Cambridge: Cambridge University Press.

Thelen, Kathleen, Sven Steinmo, and Frank Longstreth. 1992. *Structuring Politics: Historical Institutionalism in Comparative Analysis.* New York: Cambridge University Press.

Verdun, Amy. 1999. "The Role of the Delors Committee in the Creation of EMU: an Epistemic Community?" *Journal of European Public Policy* 6 (2): 308–328.

CHAPTER 35

THE EVOLUTION OF INTERNATIONAL LAW AND COURTS

KAREN J. ALTER*

Many studies of international cooperation proceed as if the world were a blank slate with governments coming together to make rational decisions about building international institutions to achieve functional objectives. But when examining the history of empire, colonialism, and post-colonialism, and the small and very traditional world of international diplomacy, it becomes immediately obvious that functional explanations would be insufficient, and that historical institutional analysis would have much to offer.

This chapter uses the issue of the post-Cold War proliferation of international courts to show how historical institutional approaches provide insight into international systemic change.

The creation and increased usage of permanent international courts to deal with a broad range of issues is a relatively new historical phenomenon. A quick perusal of the founding dates of international courts (ICs) suggests that three critical junctures were important in the creation of the contemporary international courts: the Hague Peace conferences and with it the larger movement to regulate inter-state relations through international legal conventions (1899–1927); the post-World War II explosion of international institutions (1945–52); and the end of the Cold War (1990–2005). The best way to understand the creation, spread, and increased usage of ICs today is to think of the proliferation of "new style" ICs as a form of international institutional evolution emanating from earlier historical junctures.

Reframed as international institutional evolution, the question becomes; How can historical institutional approaches help us understand why groups of governments decided to add or change the design of international courts in the context of pre-existing international institutions? And why is there cross-regional variation in the willingness of governments to submit to international judicial oversight? The next section, "The Creation of International Courts," juxtaposes the adoption and rejection of proposals for international courts across time, discussing how historical institutionalism asks different questions about this pattern and generates fundamentally different expectations compared to rationalist approaches that have long dominated the study of international institutional creation and design. The following two sections, "The Role of Critical Junctures," and "Antecedent and Permissive Conditions in the Timing and Design of ICs" explain how critical junctures intersect with permissive and antecedent conditions to contribute to the spread of a more intrusive "new style" model of an international court. Bringing together critical junctures, permissive and antecedent conditions, "Variations in International Human Rights Courts" charts in greater depth the variegated pattern of creating international human rights courts. The Conclusion argues that the growing role of international courts is generating a paradigmatic and structural change in international relations, transforming international law from a breakable contract between governments to a system of laws that legitimate governments must obey.

The Creation of International Courts

Rationalist approaches search for functional reasons that might account for past decisions. In researching the proliferation of international courts, rationalist scholars ask, "What benefits accrue from delegation to ICs?" and "Which countries delegate authority to ICs?" The analysis that then follows tends to be static, with scant attention to the timing of the decisions.

Scholars have identified a range of functional benefits from states delegating authority to ICs. For example, scholars argue that collective binding to the authority of international institutions, under a rule of law, eases concerns that powerful actors will wield law and power unfairly (Ikenberry 2001). Agreeing to international oversight makes commitments more credible, and states can use delegation to fill in incomplete contracts and coordinate the application of international rules across jurisdictions (Cooley and Spruyt 2009; Garrett and Weingast 1993). Self-binding to international judicial oversight helps to lock in the preferences of today, creating costs should governments in the future be tempted to walk away from international agreements (Moravcsik 1995). Scholars have also tested and documented the functional benefits that accrue from the decision to empower ICs to adjudicate legal disputes involving states (Allee and Huth 2006; Simmons 2002, 2009).

These functional benefits surely exist, but they should have always existed. Historical institutional approaches, by contrast, begin with temporal and regional variation that calls for explanation. Looking at the same basic facts about international courts, historical institutional scholars ask about the timing of institutional creation and raise questions such as "Why were governments so much more open to the idea of self-binding to international judicial oversight in the post-Cold War era?" Rationalist scholars also care about explaining variation, but their accounts tend to be more of a snapshot than a moving picture (see Pierson 2004). Whereas rationalist scholars might ask "Which states make decision x and why do they make this decision?," historical institutional scholars are more likely to investigate "Why was choice in time 1 'not x' whereas the choice in time 2 was 'x'."

When analyzing basic information about the founding and design of international courts today, the issue of timing and IC design presents itself as a puzzle. *The New Terrain of International Law: Courts, Politics, Rights* (Alter 2014) documents a fundamental change in government willingness to self-bind to international judicial oversight. In the first half of the twentieth century, there were few international courts and most international courts allowed states to opt into their jurisdiction and then later opt out. The vast majority of countries did not fall under the compulsory jurisdiction of a single international court. And most ICs only allowed states to initiate international litigation.

Following the end of the Cold War, many more ICs were created. Today's ICs tend to emulate the design of Europe's international courts. They have compulsory jurisdiction for all member states, and they allow non-state actors to initiate litigation involving states. In Europe, Latin America, and Africa, most countries fall under the compulsory jurisdiction of multiple international courts. Indeed, very few countries today fall under the compulsory jurisdiction of no international courts (Alter 2014, 101).

Figure 35.1 juxtaposes parts of Alter's (2014) periodization of the creation of ICs with Romano's (2014, 113) list of "nipped in the bud" ICs where proposals were abandoned, and Katzenstein's (2014, 159) discussion of proposals for ICs that were rejected in the early part of the twentieth century. The figure is organized around critical junctures. The timespan of each critical juncture is long because it can take a long time for a proposal to be ratified by a sufficient number of member states, and for the court to be created. The key insight is the limited experimentation before World War II, the large number of abandoned proposals before and during the Cold War, and the large number of implemented proposals following the end of the Cold War.[1]

The first experiments in creating and using ICs occurred in the context of the Hague Peace Conferences, where diplomats dared to imagine that legalized inter-state dispute settlement might replace war as a tool of international politics. The Hague conferences generated a number of legal ideas that endured, and by some accounts marked the beginning of a new world order (Reus-Smit 1997). The Hague Peace Era established "old-style" ICs, where the focus was inter-state dispute settlement. These ICs lacked compulsory jurisdiction, only states could initiate litigation in front of the courts, and the larger objective of a system of ICs failed (O'Connell and VanderZee 2014). Indeed, more proposals to create ICs failed than succeeded during the Hague Peace Conference era (Katzenstein 2014).

Although the grandiose aspects of Hague Peace vision failed, the Hague Peace process sowed seeds that later germinated. Negotiating, creating, and using the Hague-era ICs helped proponents hear and address logistical questions and concerns. Many of the proposals that were rejected in the 1940s and 1950s came to fruition much later, in some cases carried forward by the very people who had been involved in Hague Peace era conversations.[2] The International Court of Justice, the World Trade Organization's

Critical Juncture	International Courts (year created)	Inoperative or abandoned ICs (year proposed)
Hague Peace Conference Juncture (1899–1935)	Permanent Court of Arbitration (1899) Central American Court of Justice (1908–1918) Permanent Court of Justice (1922–1946)	Central American Arbitration Tribunal (1902) International Prize Court (1907) Central American Tribunal (1923) Terrorism Court (1937) Inter-American Court of International Justice (1938)
Post-WWII Juncture (1945–1960)	1. International Court of Justice (1945) International Criminal Tribunal of Nurnberg (1945) *General Agreement on Tariffs and Trade 1948–1994 2. European Union's Court of Justice (1952) 3. European Court of Human Rights (1958) 4. Benelux Court (1974) 5. Inter-American Court of Human Rights (1979) 6. Andean Tribunal Of Justice (1984)	Arab Court of Justice (1945) European Nuclear Energy Tribunal of the OECD (1957) *Arbitral College of the Benelux Economic Union (1958) *Court of Arbitration of the French Community (1959) *Arbitration Tribunal of the Central American Common Market (1960) European Tribunal on State Immunity (1972) *Judicial Board of the Organization of Arab Petroleum Exporting Countries (1980) Court of Justice of the Economic Community of Central African States (1983) International Islamic Court of Justice (1987) Court of Justice of the African Maghreb Union (1989)

FIGURE 35.1 Periodization of Established vs. Proposed ICs

Critical Juncture	International Courts (year created)	Inoperative or abandoned ICs (year proposed)
Post-Cold War Juncture (1990–2010)	7. European Free Trade Area Court (1992) 8. Central American Court of Justice (1992) 9. International Criminal Tribunal for the Former Yugoslavia (1993) 10. Economic Court of the Commonwealth of Independent States (1993) 11. International Criminal Tribunal for Rwanda (1994) 12. World Trade Organization Appellate Body *(formerly GATT)* (1994) 13. West African Economic and Monetary Union Court of Justice (1995) 14. International Tribunal for the Law of the Seas (1996) 15. Organization for the Harmonization of Corporate Law in Africa Common Court of Justice and Arbitration (1997) 16. Southern Common Market (1999) 17. Eastern and Southern Africa Common Market Court of Justice (1998) 18. Central African Economic and Monetary Community Court of Justice (2000) 19. East African Community Court of Justice (2001) 20. Caribbean Court of Justice (2001) 21. Economic Community of West African States Court of Justice (2001) 22. International Criminal Court (2002) 23. Arab Investment Court (2003) 24. Southern African Development Community (2005) 25. African Court on Human and Peoples' Rights (2006)	Court of Justice of the African Economic Community (1991) Court of Conciliation and Arbitrage for the OCED (1994) ASEAN Appellate Body (2005) *Court of Union State between Russian Federation & Belarus (1999) Court of Justice of the African Union (2003)

Italics = non-permanent court. *= that were later created in a different form. # = 25 permanent ICs.

FIGURE 35.1 Continued

Appellate Body, International Criminal Court (ICC) and International Tribunal of the Law of the Sea are in many respects modern incarnations of the Hague vision.

The Role of Critical Junctures

World War II and the onset of the Cold War was a critical juncture in the creation of international courts. Critical junctures are moments of political flux in which structural constraints are relaxed, and new opportunities for institutional change present themselves (Capoccia and Kelemen 2007, 343). Following World War II, international diplomats worked to create stable national and international institutions that could avoid the repeat of a global market crash and the return of nationalist governments. The International Court of Justice, the dispute resolution system of the General Agreement on Tariffs and Trade, and Nuremberg-style international criminal prosecutions were all efforts to overcome the interwar years and World War II. Europe's Court of Justice and Human Rights system were also inspired by the goal of avoiding another European war.

The more idealistic aspirations following World War II soon gave way to the Cold War political reality. No ambitious proposal could garner support from states on opposite sides of the Cold War, and international law proposals that did make it through the diplomatic labyrinth were often filled with compromises that advocates found distasteful. The clear limits of a global approach fueled the drive for regional approaches to international adjudication. There were real benefits to a regional approach. Because regional courts rely on judges from the region, the economies and fates of countries tend to be more interlinked. Equally important, regional cooperation initiatives did not need to satisfy US and Soviet concerns. Regional courts and the "new style" IC model thus emerged during and in part because of the Cold War freeze (Alter 2011, 393–399).

The end of the Cold War, when the political order created by Cold War alliances unfroze, provided a third critical juncture. It triggered a rush of countries wanting to join the institutions of the West, which spurred Western countries to adopt long discussed institutional changes before accepting new members. The end of the Cold War also ushered in the Washington Consensus, where international institutions, the US, and Europe all advocated for the adoption of democracy, liberal economic policies, and rule of law institutions (Alter 2011, 401–408). After the Cold War, a number of existing ICs were amended to widen jurisdiction and access to the court, and the number of operational permanent international courts grew from 6 to 25.

The post-Cold War critical juncture was different from the World War II juncture in part because of evolutions in legal practice, which changed the decision-making context. Europe's Court of Justice (ECJ, now called the CJEU) was an exception to the rule for international courts because member states had to accept the ECJ's compulsory jurisdiction and both private litigants and the supranational High Authority (later redefined as the Commission) could initiate litigation against states. The ECJ, through activist rulings in cases raised by private litigants, transformed the Treaty of Rome into a constitution for Europe by declaring the direct effect and supremacy of European law (Weiler 1991).

Europe's legal revolution had a systemic effect by introducing a model of an effective "new-style" IC that has been widely emulated. This "new-style" model, which includes compulsory jurisdiction, access for non-state actors, and understandings about what contributes to effective supranational adjudication, was then emulated when the next critical juncture—the end of the Cold War– created political openings in other settings (Alter 2014, 127–132).

A second important change in legal practice concerns unilateral enforcement action on the part of American and European judges. The United States passed legislation (the so-called "Super 301" provision) that authorized American authorities to sanction countries if the United States Trade Representative determined that the country was violating the rules of the General Agreement on Tariffs and Trade. American judges also used the revived Alien Tort Statute to sanction human rights abuses by foreigners committed abroad. Belgium declared universal jurisdiction over mass atrocities committed abroad, and Britain's House of Lords revoked the sovereign immunity of Augusto Pinochet because of credible allegations of torture committed in Chile vis-à-vis Spanish nationals. These changing legal practices meant even where governments did not consent to jurisdiction, foreign judges might be adjudicating their compliance with international law (Alter 2014, 138–142).

If legal practice can lead to institutional and systemic change, then what is the role of government's rational decisions in the design of ICs? Systemic change, like that which occurs during critical junctures, surely transforms the preferences of states. But international relations scholars tend to assume that states are in the driver's seat of international institutions, controlling international institutions through appointments, budgets, political vetoes, or threats of non-compliance (Bradley and Kelley 2008; Hawkins et al. 2006). Historical institutionalism brings attention to additional actors, including actors above and below the state such as international and domestic judges, who may also be forces for institutional change.

Historical institutionalism also considers that actions by governments may have unintended downstream affects that come to shape future decision-making. In a detailed analysis of the transformation of the Economic Community of West African State's (ECOWAS) Court of Justice, Alter, Helfer, and McAllister (2013) focus on how government preferences evolved from 1975, when ECOWAS governments agreed in principle but made no moves to create an ECOWAS court, to 1993 when governments agreed to create the ECOWAS court yet rejected a proposal to allow direct private access, to 2005 when ECOWAS member states agreed to allow direct private access for human rights violations. They argue that collective decision to use ECOWAS forces to intervene in the Sierra Leone and Liberian conflicts generated a cascade of events that members of the ECOWAS court, the ECOWAS secretariat, and human rights activists later drew upon when they argued for allowing direct private access to adjudicate human rights violations.

Regardless of whether key decisions about institutional change came from judges, sub-state actors, or governments, the central point is that historical institutional approaches focus us on how world-historical forces interact with state-level and international incentives, and on how sub-state behavior of litigants and advocacy groups make international law more enforceable. This dynamic has made ICs more independent, increased the number of cases raised, facilitated law-making, and allowed ICs to connect with actors within the state to promote greater respect for international law (Alter 2006, 2014; Keohane, Moravcsik, and Slaughter 2000; Stone Sweet 1999). This is a different political dynamic from that which rationalist scholars tend to study, which is focused on the "problem structure" of international cooperation, the sovereignty concerns of governments, and the tools governments use to try to control international institutions.

Antecedent and Permissive Conditions in the Timing and Design of ICs

Critical junctures may generate openings and incentives for change, but how these incentives get channeled varies based on the permissive and antecedent conditions in a given context. To understand the variegated change following critical junctures, we need to think about how permissive and antecedent conditions interact with critical junctures. Permissive conditions are factors that can occur at any time and that facilitate a specified change (Soifer 2012).

Before the advent of permanent ICs, countries relied on ad hoc arbitration or the creation of specialized legal bodies—mass claims courts—to handle their disputes (Crook 2006; Martinez 2012). These bodies could be created as needed, staffed by specialized judges, and they would be dismantled as soon as demand for adjudication dissipated. The idea of a system of permanent international courts, set up by multilateral agreements, with broad, ongoing, and adjustable jurisdiction, to be staffed by judges from many countries who would be appointed in advance of an actual dispute, was a radical notion.

When legal advocates first proposed the creation of a permanent international court, governments had many questions and concerns. How would judges be selected? How could litigants be certain that international judges were sufficiently neutral and qualified to deal with the variety of complex legal and political issues that might arise? How would the jurisdiction of the IC be defined in practice? What would happen if a government refused to file their papers or otherwise participate?

Through legal practice by Hague-era ICs—by appointing judges and adjudicating cases—these "how," "what," and "if" questions were addressed. Having addressed these concerns, and having showed that permanent ICs were in fact feasible, the Hague Peace Conferences thus created an important permissive condition that shaped subsequent decisions regarding ICs.

The Hague Peace experience influenced subsequent ICs in a number of ways. First, the Hague Peace era bequeathed a permanent International Court of Justice that can be designated as the legal body competent to interpret disputes involving bilateral and multilateral treaties. From 1946 on, international treaty negotiations included a conversation about whether to stipulate that the International Court of Justice or some other adjudicatory mechanism as the venue for interpreting the treaty. Second, the Hague ideals were not simply hopes and aspirations; they also survived in the minds of legal advocates. Concrete and fundamental legal precepts of the Hague Peace era endured, such as the Geneva Conventions governing war and the idea of requiring peaceful change of borders. The larger vision of subordinating power to the law also endured. Diplomats involved in the Hague Peace Conferences transferred legal practices and aspirations into regional movements in Europe and Latin America.

Development of ICs did not, however, proceed in a linear or progressive way following the Hague Peace era. Many countries drew the lesson that the Hague experience was a failure. After World War II it became clear that most governments were not interested in a system of international courts, even fairly modest courts with many political checks (Allain 2000). For most of the Cold War, governments instead displayed a clear aversion to generating new ICs or to consenting to compulsory dispute adjudication (Katzenstein 2014; Levi 1976; O'Connell and VanderZee 2014).

This is where antecedent conditions become important. Antecedent conditions are "factors or conditions preceding a critical juncture that combine with causal forces during a critical juncture to produce long-term divergence in outcomes" (Slater and Simmons 2010, 889). In Europe, World War II provided the antecedent condition that made many people unwilling to return to the Hague approach of voluntary inter-state dispute adjudication. Pierre-Henri Teitgen, a drafter and proponent of the European Court of Human Rights, famously summarized the lesson Europe's anti-fascist elite had learned:

> Democracies do not become Nazi countries in one day. Evil progresses cunningly, with a minority operating, as it were, to remove the levers of control. One by one freedoms are suppressed, in one sphere after another. Public opinion and the entire national conscience are asphyxiated. And then, when everything is in order, the 'Führer' is installed and the evolution continues even to the oven of the crematorium. It is necessary to intervene before it is too late. A conscience must exist somewhere which will sound the alarm to the minds of a nation, menaced by this progressive corruption, to war[n] them of the peril and to show them that they are progressing down a long road which leads far, sometimes even to Buchenwald or Dachau. (cited in Bates 2011, 7)

Pierre-Henri Teitgen did not just make stirring speeches. He helped draft the European Convention on Human Rights, and worked within French and European politics, as a Minister of Justice, international diplomat and a professor, to make these ideas into reality (Madsen 2007, 141).

The functional benefits and costs of submitting to international judicial review remained largely constant across time. What changed were the models and ideas about ICs. Overall the Cold War generated two models with clearly divergent outcomes. Europe's supranational courts were proving helpful in promoting respect for the legal rules they oversaw. Meanwhile in the rest of the world, advocates, governments, and opposition parties had quite a long time to evaluate the limitations of relying on international treaties that lacked compulsory judicial oversight. For example, the problems of the dispute settlement system for the General Agreement on Tariffs and Trade became very apparent. The failure of the international community to deal with war crimes during the Cold War period provided additional lessons on the limits of government respect for international legal rules. Lawyers observed these failings, standing ready to offer legal solutions designed to address growing concerns about legal violations and non-compliance with international conventions.

The three critical junctures triggered variegated IC creation that "encapsulate the shift from "old style" to "new style" ICs," and "[t]he path-dependent nature of institutional change meant that the form and nature of international judicial institutions did not repeat; rather, it evolved across iterations" (Alter 2014, 112–114, 117). This evolution is evident when observing the changing design of ICs that were eventually created. Courts that emulate key features associated with the success of Europe's supranational courts are "new-style" ICs with many similarities to European models (Alter 2014, 81–85).

There is still great variation in the willingness of governments to consent to the jurisdiction of new-style ICs. African, European, and Latin American countries are most willing to submit to compulsory international judicial oversight, committing to the compulsory jurisdiction of up to seven different ICs. Island states, Middle Eastern countries, and to a lesser extent Asian countries reveal a significant aversion to compulsory international judicial oversight. Today only 13 countries fall under the compulsory jurisdiction of no ICs, and 21 countries have only consented to the compulsory jurisdiction of the WTO's dispute adjudication system, of which the United States, China, Cuba, and Israel are prime examples (Alter 2014, 91–109 and chapter 4).

Variations in International Human Rights Courts

This section raises questions that are yet to be answered about the design choices for human rights oversight mechanisms, including whether design decisions that shape a commitment to IC oversight become politically meaningful in practice. The architects of international human rights bodies have a pretty good sense of how certain design choices help or hinder the enforcement of human rights obligations. The key issue for human rights adjudication is whether or not private litigants have access to an international legal system, and on what terms. Human rights advocates prefer a maximalist approach of direct private access to international judicial institutions that can offer binding legal remedies. The more minimalist approach is to rely on UN Treaty Bodies, under-resourced and highly politicized institutions that can generate findings but not binding legal rulings. There are also in-between models, as well as a number of creative ways to limit the extent of international human rights review, which is why the design of adjudicatory mechanisms is important. Figure 35.2 discusses in simplified terms three international oversight models for international human rights conventions. The figure indicates when design choices promote the maximalist goals of human rights advocates (+) or the more minimalist goals of sovereignty jealous states (-).

Historical institutionalism provides a useful way to explore the origins of these variations, and it raises fundamental questions about why states vary in their design choices over time. The debate over how to enforce human rights obligations began immediately following World War II. The UN Treaty Body model emerged in the 1960s when states negotiated what became a series of human rights treaties that UN members could ratify. All negotiating parties agreed in principle to the Treaty Body structure, a decision that was easier because countries could then decide whether or not to opt-into these oversight mechanisms. In what follows I explain the emergence of the European Court model, versions 1.0 and 2.0.

In 1950, dismayed by the limited UN initiatives to protect human rights, distrustful of government promises to respect human rights, and wanting to demarcate West European practices from Soviet practices in the East, the Council of Europe decided to create its own human rights system (Madsen 2010, 36–39). National sovereignty concerns and European engagement in decolonization wars then interceded, leading to a greatly constrained human rights court. The first European human rights model—European Court of Human Rights (ECtHR) version 1.0—let either the European Commission on Human Rights or a member state refer a case to the court. Governments had to first consent to the jurisdiction of the ECtHR, and separately agree to allow private litigants to complain to the European Commission on Human Rights. Originally only Sweden, Ireland, Denmark, Iceland, Germany, and Belgium accepted ECtHR's compulsory jurisdiction and only Sweden, Ireland, and Denmark accepted the right of individual petition. Moreover, a number of acceptances were provisional, made for only a few years at a time.

The Commission proceeded with great caution, so as to encourage more states to sign on and avoid future opt-outs. Between 1954 and 1961, less than 0.5 percent of the 1,307 applications filed with the Commission were declared admissible—with the result being that in its first ten years of operation, the ECtHR ruled on only seven cases (Schermers 1999, 825). The caseload increased slowly; but after 24 years of operation the ECtHR had still only issued 37 binding rulings!

Over time, more governments joined the Council of Europe's human rights system and it became politically more difficult for these governments to later withdraw their conditional acceptance of ECtHR jurisdiction (Bates 2011; Madsen 2010). The Commission began to refer more cases to the Court, leading to the overburdening of

Institutional choices	Essential features	Human rights pros & cons	Sovereignty pros & cons
UN treaty bodies	States selectively opt in. Periodic oversight results in non-binding findings.	– Process is slow and politicized. – Findings of violations are not binding.	– No obligation to comply. – Governments can repudiate the process as political and not legal.
European Court of Human Rights v 1.0 (1952)	States opt in to court and private access. Commission vets complaints, issues non-binding findings, and negotiates solutions. Unresolved cases sent to the Court.	– Commission gatekeeping slows process, and blocks cases. + Cases referred to Court lead to binding legal rulings.	+/– Court adjudicates state-initiated suits. – Commission vets private suits. – Commission process provides opportunity for negotiated solutions.
European Court of Human Rights v 2.0 (post–1994)	Club model that does not allow state opt-in. Direct private access to Court. Binding legal rulings.	+ Direct access provides quickest and least politicized process. + Legal rulings are binding (eliciting compliance remains a challenge).	+ Inconvenient cases reach court. +Outcome is a binding finding of a human rights violation. +Legal process can be hard to sway.

– = Preferred by sovereignty jealous states

+ = Preferred by human rights advocates

FIGURE 35.2 The Choice Regarding International Human Rights Oversight

the part-time Court. In 1994, just before the broad expansion of the Council of Europe, existing member states accepted Protocol 11, creating the ECtHR version 2.0. The new version eliminated the gate-keeping and screening role of the Commission and required all Council of Europe members to accept the ECtHR's compulsory jurisdiction and direct access for private litigants. ECtHR 2.0 reflects the reality that the Council's human rights system had become irreversibly embedded in Western democracies, and the desire to bind post-Soviet states to this model (Helfer 2008; Moravcsik 1995).

The European Court of Human Rights began operation in 1958. The first three UN Treaty Bodies began operation in the mid-1960s.[3] Figure 35.3 maps the membership of states in human rights courts and Figure 35.4 puts on a timeline the creation of these institutions and models.

Historical institutionalist approaches use this type of variation to identify the permissive and antecedent conditions that might have led Latin American leaders to embrace the European model in the 1960s, and African leaders to embrace European models in the 1990s. Meanwhile, Asia continues to discuss yet resist the creation of an Asian human rights charter.

Latin American countries copied the ECtHR version 1.0, but later in time. The IACtHR was created by treaty in 1969, came into existence in 1979 after a sufficient number of states had ratified the relevant legal instruments, and issued its first ruling in 1987. The delay is surprising in that the American Declaration on the Rights and Duties of Man preceded the 1948 United Nations Universal Declaration of Human Rights by six months.

Historical institutionalist approaches could be used to investigate both the delay and the design choices for the IACtHR, which can be seen as the ECtHR version 1.1. The IACtHR includes a government right to opt in and out of the court's optional compulsory jurisdiction, and the Commission serves as a gatekeeper to the court. Since the pre-existing Commission allowed individual complaints, the Inter-American system did not include a separate protocol authorizing private litigant access. As occurred in Europe, Commission screening greatly limits the number of cases proceeding to court. The IACtHR issued only eight rulings in its first ten years of operation. In 2001 the Commission decided to forward all unresolved cases to the court, contributing to the court's greater activation.

Africa resisted the pressure to adopt regional human rights instruments for even longer than Latin American countries. Following World War II, African governments and peoples were focused on decolonization and expelling European influences rather than promoting respect for human rights. Politicians asserted that national rule would ameliorate the human rights violations of the past, and this promise at first sufficed.

However, as atrocities in civil wars mounted, governments violently outstayed their welcome, and as Latin American governments moved ahead with their own regional human rights regime, African leaders asked a committee of experts to create a human rights charter that was analogous to the European and Latin American charters, though specific to the African context. The committee drafted what became the "Banjul

	UN proposal for a human rights court rejected	European Convention on Human Rights ratified, with plan to create a ECtHR	ECtHR created	American Convention on Human Rights signed, with plan to create a Inter-American Court of Human Rights	Inter-American Human Rights Court created
Cold War Era	1949	1953	1958	1969	1979
Design Model			ECtHR v 1.0		ECtHR v 1.1
	ECtHR reformed to allow direct private access	Organization of African Unity agrees to create an African Human Rights Court (1998)	People's charter calls for the establishment of an Asian Human Rights Charter, with a court or a commission	Economic Community of West African States adds a human rights competence to its court	African Court of Peoples' and Human Rights created
Post-Cold War Era	1994	1998	1998	2005	2006
Design Model	ECtHR v. 2.0			ECtHR v. 2.0	ECtHR v. 1.0

FIGURE 35.3 Creation of International Human Rights Courts Over Time

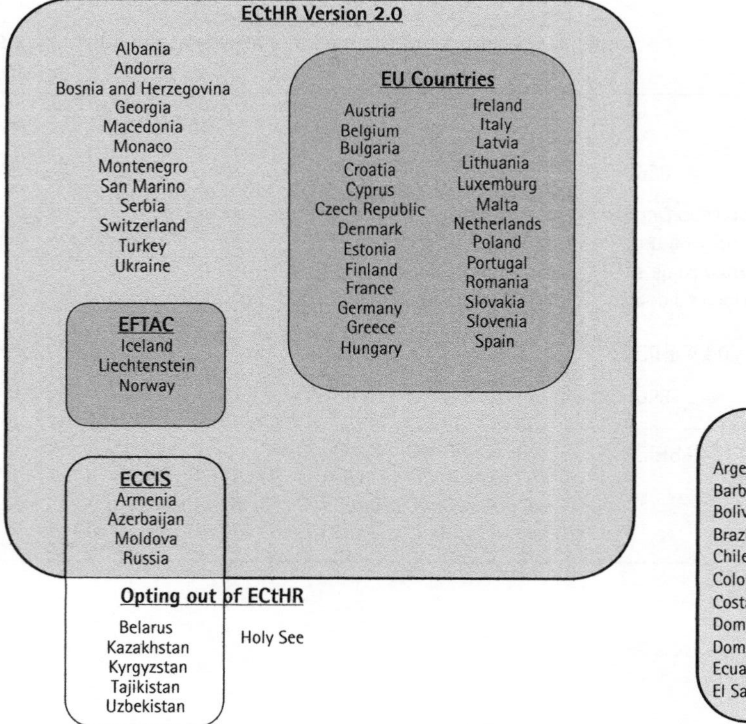

FIGURE 35.4 Membership in Human Rights Courts in Europe, Latin America, and Africa (2013)

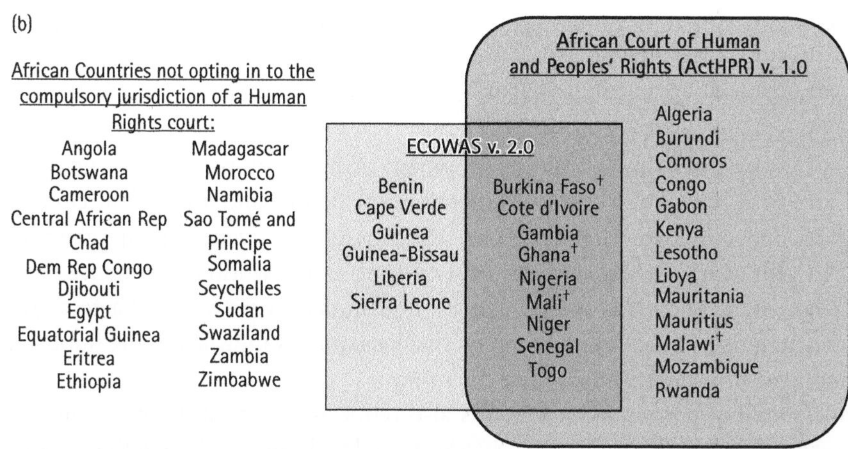

FIGURE 35.4 Continued

Charter," which emphasizes the rights of "peoples" and the duties of individuals and peoples.

The Committee's drafters considered Africa "not ready for a supranational judicial institution at that time," and recommended the creation of an African Commission on Human Rights to oversee respect of the African Charter (Viljoen and Louw 2007, 2). Only after the Cold War ended did African states agree to add a court to their human rights system. The African Court of Human and Peoples' Rights (ACtHPR) emulated the ECtHR version 1.0, allowing governments to opt in and out of the court's compulsory jurisdiction and limit private actor access to the ACtHPR.[4]

The African Union's (AU) human rights system today resembles the European system of the 1960s. Fewer than half of African countries (26 out of 54) have consented to the court's jurisdiction and only seven have authorized direct private access to the court. Commission decisions are not considered binding, and the AU's Human Rights Commission worries that African governments will not join, or that current "joiners" will opt out of the system. These concerns contribute to the Commission's gatekeeping caution. Nine years into the court's operation, the ACtHPR's had issued final rulings in only 19 cases, and most of the rulings dismiss the application for various jurisdictional, standing, and evidentiary reasons.

The limitations of the AU system, in the post-Cold War pro-human rights context, has led regional integration courts in Africa to address human rights violations. Human rights advocates have been engines of this institutional change as they seized the momentum created when ECOWAS security forces committed human rights abuses. Their mobilization led to a proposal, implemented via a vote of ECOWAS governments, to authorize private litigants to raise violations of human rights in front of the ECOWAS Court. ECOWAS essentially copied the design of the ECtHR version 2.0 (e.g., no opt out allowed, no Commission gatekeeper, direct private access). Meanwhile governments in Eastern and Southern Africa have yet to endorse a human rights jurisdiction for their regional courts, though advocates have raised cases and judges have been adjudicating human rights claims (Ebobrah 2009).

This cursory discussion of the development of international human rights courts illustrates how attention to critical junctures, permissive and antecedent conditions, and path-dependent development help explain regional variation in international human rights oversight. Developments in one part of the world do influence developments elsewhere, and ideas and models are transmitted by networks of actors. But the delays in adopting foreign models suggest that local intervening factors are important in explaining institutional diffusion and evolution.

Understanding permissive conditions also requires investigating proposals that do not succeed. Why, for example, has ASEAN created a Charter of Human Rights but not a court? Given that Asian countries have yet to embrace human rights review, while poor and authoritarian African countries have embraced international human rights review, one can reject the notion that capitalism, the growing strength of the middle class, or threshold GDP levels account for the success of human rights movements in establishing international judicial review. An historical institutional approach encourages scholars to instead focus more deeply on the tactical choices of local movements and the permissive conditions that create openings that groups seize upon as they promote change within existing institutions.

Conclusion

As governments have submitted to international judicial review by new-style ICs, systemic changes have occurred in the world of international courts. The Hague era approach and conception of international adjudication is quite different from what we find today. In the 1920s, ICs were essentially voluntary inter-state dispute resolution bodies. Governments could decide treaty by treaty, and often case by case, whether to consent to judicial resolution of a dispute. Or governments could commit for a specified number of years to allow specific courts to adjudicate any dispute that arose between states that had also assented to the specific court's compulsory jurisdiction. Even with optional provisions, however, most of the Hague era proposals failed. A larger and deeper ontology underpinned the Hague era approach to international adjudication. The inter-state dispute settlement approach conceived of international law as contract among states. Since contracts primarily bind the signatory parties, it makes sense to limit access to legal suits raised by states.

The contractual perspective allows a country to abrogate legal treaties. This decision is not costless, but repudiating treaties also does not per se mean that a country is a law-breaker. For example, in 2001 George W. Bush notified Russia, Belarus, Kazakhstan, and Ukraine that the United States intended to withdraw from the Anti-Ballistic Missile

Treaty. The world had changed very much since 1972, Bush noted, and he wanted to find new ways to protect the American people. Some may think this was a bad and perhaps unduly costly decision. But it certainly was not an illegal decision. Rather, the United States was exercising its legal right under the treaty to give a six-month notification of its decision to abrogate the Treaty.

Some scholars cling to the contractual approach to international law. Eric Posner and Alan Sykes, for example, posit the seemingly modest heuristic that international law be seen through an economic contractual perspective. They advocate for a principle of "efficient breech," suggesting that governments should violate international agreements once "the benefits to the breaching party exceed the costs to all non-breaching parties" (2013, 25). Posner and Sykes do not explain how costs are measured, and they certainly do not advocate turning over decisions about whether or not to allow a violation to independent international courts. Bundled into the contractual perspective is the idea that non-signatories gain few legal rights under international law. This contractual approach is quite different from a rule-of-law approach, where the law is binding regardless of what other states do. The new-style features of ICs, namely their compulsory jurisdiction and the ability of non-state actors to initiate litigation, signals and serves to instantiate a shift to a rule of law ontology.

Most ICs today reflect a shift toward a rule of law perspective. International courts have been delegated a broader range of judicial roles, including assessing state compliance with international rules and treaties. Governments, commissions, prosecutors, and private litigants have raised thousands of cases claiming legal violations. International judges repeatedly reject government arguments that suggest that violations by others provide them licence to retaliate.

The claim here is not that governments in the past violated international law, and today regularly respect international law. Nor is the claim that power has become irrelevant in international relations. Instead, the argument is that state decision-making over time has evolved. Systemic-level changes, such as the end of the Cold War, combined with smaller incremental changes, such the ECJ's legal revolution and changing practices regarding extraterritorial national enforcement of international law, to alter state preferences regarding international courts. In 1950, governments faced the choice of no international judicial oversight or creating untested international courts. In 1989, many countries wanted to join the institutions of the West, and governments around the world found that that American and European legal actors were, in fact, making unilateral determinations about their compliance with international law. The cumulative changes in the choices facing governments, alongside a rising sense that good governance requires the rule of law, and that legitimate governments respect the rule of law, made embracing compulsory international judicial oversight more attractive. Together these changes created a more profound evolution in the understanding of the legal obligations generated by international law.

This changing environment has also shaped IC behavior and influence. Many domains of international law–international human rights law, criminal law, investment law, intellectual property law and more–generate rights and obligations that are binding regardless of what other states do. International courts follow the law. It is inconceivable that the International Criminal Court or a human rights court would absolve an accused war criminal of his legal responsibility just because Syria's human rights violations remain unpunished. Moreover, increasingly courts adjudicating economic claims reject the notion that states can raise or impose tariffs and duties in response to another country's breech of an economic agreement.

The proliferation of ICs adjudicating legal cases involving a broad range of international legal rules reflects an expectation and a desire for a different world. This desire led to the creation of new-style ICs, and it is, to a large extent, a realization of the idealistic Hague-era vision of subordinating international politics to a rule of law.

Notes

* The author wishes to thank Orfeo Fioretos and Steve Nelson for comments on earlier versions of this chapter.

1. For abandoned ICs, the dates reported denote the year states agreed in principle to create an IC. For ICs created, there can be a time lag because it can take a long time for a sufficient number of states to ratify international proposals, to then commit and collect the resources to found a court, and to collectively select international judges. An asterisk signals an abandoned court that later appeared in a much different form.
2. Scholars have traced juris-diplomats from the interwar years, to the post-World War II prosecution of war collaborators, to the founding of European integration projects (Guieu 2012; Madsen and Vauchez 2005). It is likely that a careful tracing of legal networks would reveal a direct lineage between the Hague Peace project and the creation of subsequent ICs.
3. The Committee on Racial Discrimination began operations in 1965. In 1966, the Human Rights Committee (the oversight body for the International Covenant on Civil and Political Rights) and the Committee on Economic, Cultural and Social Rights began operation. Available at <http://www.ohchr.org/EN/HRBodies/Pages/TreatyBodies.aspx> (accessed August 3, 2015).
4. The African system is a little different in that in Europe states were opting to allow individual complaints to the Commission, whereas in Africa the 'opt in' concerns access to the Court. See Viljoen (2007).

References

Allain, Jean. 2000. *A Century of International Adjudication: The Rule of Law and Its Limits*. The Hague: T.M.C. Asser Press.

Allee, Todd and Paul Huth. 2006. "Legitimizing Dispute Settlement: International Legal Rulings as Domestic Political Cover." *American Political Science Review* 100 (2): 219–234.

Alter, Karen J. 2006. "Private Litigants and the New International Courts." *Comparative Political Studies* 39 (1): 22–49.

Alter, Karen J. 2011. "The Evolving International Judiciary." *Annual Review of Law and Social Science* 7: 387–415.

Alter, Karen J. 2014. *The New Terrain of International Law: Courts, Politics, Rights*. Princeton, NJ: Princeton University Press.

Alter, Karen J., Laurence Helfer, and Jacqueline McAllister. 2013. "A New International Human Rights Court for West Africa: The Court of Justice for the Economic Community of West African States." *American Journal of International Law* 107 (4): 737–779.

Bates, Ed. 2011. *The Evolution of the European Convention on Human Rights*. Oxford: Oxford University Press.

Bradley, Curtis A. and Judith G. Kelley. 2008. "The Concept of Delegation." *Law and Contemporary Problems* 71 (1): 1–36.

Capoccia, Giovanni and R. Daniel Kelemen. 2007. "The Study of Critical Junctures in Historical Institutionalism." *World Politics* 59: 341–369.

Cooley, Alexander and Hendrik Spruyt. 2009. "Contracting States: Sovereign Transfers in International Relations." Princeton, NJ: Princeton University Press.

Crook, John. 2006. "Mass Claims Processes: Lessons Learned Over Twenty-Five Years." In *Redressing Injustices through Mass Claims Processes*, ed. The International Bureau of the Permanent Court of Arbitration. Oxford: Oxford University Press, 41–61.

Ebobrah, Solomon. 2009. "Litigating Human Rights before Sub-Regional Courts in Africa: Prospects and Challenges." *African Journal of International and Comparative Law* 17: 79–101.

Garrett, Geoffrey and Barry Weingast. 1993. "Ideas, Interests and Institutions: Constructing the EC's Internal Market." In *Ideas and Foreign Policy*, ed. J. Goldstein and R. Keohane. Ithaca, NJ: Cornell University Press, 173–206.

Guieu, Jean-Michel. 2012. "The Debate about a European Institutional Order among International Legal Scholars in the 1920s and Its Legacy." *Contemporary European History* 21 (3): 319–338.

Hawkins, Darren, David Lake, Daniel Nielson, and Mike Tierney. 2006. "Delegation under Anarchy: States, International Organizations and Principal-Agent Theory." In *Delegation and Agency in International Organizations*, ed. Darren Hawkins, David Lake, Daniel Nielson, and Mike Tierney. Cambridge: Cambridge University Press, 3–38.

Helfer, Laurence R. 2008. "Redesigning the European Court of Human Rights: Embeddedness as a Deep Structural Principle of the European Human Rights Regime." *European Journal of International Law* 19 (1): 125–159.

Ikenberry, G. John. 2001. *After Victory Institutions, Strategic Restraint, and the Rebuilding of Order after Major Wars*. Princeton, NJ: Princeton University Press. Reprint.

Katzenstein, Suzanne. 2014. "In the Shadow of Crisis: The Creation of International Courts in the Twentieth Century." *Harvard Journal of International Law* 55: 151–209.

Keohane, Robert, Andrew Moravcsik, and Anne-Marie Slaughter. 2000. "Legalized Dispute Resolution: Interstate and Transnational." *International Organization* 54 (3): 457–488.

Levi, Werner. 1976. *Law and Politics in the International Society*. Beverly Hills, CA: Sage Publications.

Madsen, Michael Rask. 2007. "From Cold War Instrument to Supreme European Court: The European Court of Human Rights at the Crossroads of International and National Law and Politics." *Law & Social Inquiry* 32 (1): 137–159.

Madsen, Mikael Rask. 2010. *La Genese de l'Europe des droits de l'Homme: Enjeux juridiques et stratégies d'État*. Collection Sociologie politique européenne. Strasbourg: Presses Universitaires de Strasbourg.

Madsen, Mikael Rask and Antoine Vauchez. 2005. "European Constitutionalism at the Cradle: Law and Lawyers in the Construction of a European Political Order (1920–1960)." In *In Lawyers' Circles: Lawyers and European Legal Integration*, ed. A. Jettinghoff and H. Schepel. The Hague: Elzevir Reed, 15–34.
Martinez, Jenny S. 2012. *The Slave Trade and the Origins of International Human Rights Law*. Oxford: Oxford University Press.
Moravcsik, Andrew. 1995. "Explaining International Human Rights Regimes: Liberal Theory and Western Europe." *European Journal of International Relations* 1 (2): 157–189.
O'Connell, Mary Ellen and Lenore Vander Zee. 2014. "The History of International Adjudication." In *Oxford Handbook on International Adjudication*, ed. C. Romano, K. J. Alter, and Y. Shany. Oxford: Oxford University Press, 40–62.
Pierson, Paul. 2004. *Politics in Time*. Princeton, NJ: Princeton University Press.
Posner, Eric A. and A. O. Sykes. 2013. *Economic Foundations of International Law*. Cambridge, MA: Belknap Press of Harvard University Press.
Reus-Smit, Christian. 1997. "The Constitutional Structure of International Society and the Nature of Fundamental Institutions." *International Organization* 51 (4): 555–589.
Romano, Cesare. 2014. "The Shadow Zones of International Judicialization." In *Oxford Handbook on International Adjudication*, ed. C. Romano, K. J. Alter, and Y. Shany. Oxford: Oxford University Press, 90–110.
Schermers, Henry G. 1999. "Acceptance of International Supervision of Human Rights." *Leiden Journal of International Law* 12: 821–831.
Simmons, Beth. 2002. "Capacity, Commitment and Compliance: International Institutions and Territorial Disputes." *Journal of Conflict Resolution* 46 (6): 829–856.
Simmons, Beth. 2009. *Mobilizing for Human Rights: International Law in Domestic Politics*. Cambridge: Cambridge University Press.
Slater, Daniel and Erica Simmons. 2010. "Informative Regress: Critical Antecedents in Comparative Politics." *Methodology Forum* 43 (7): 886–917.
Soifer, Hillel David. 2012. "The Causal Logic of Critical Junctures." *Comparative Political Studies* 45 (12): 1572–1597.
Stone Sweet, Alec. 1999. "Judicialization and the Construction of Governance." *Comparative Political Studies* 32 (2): 147–184.
Viljoen, Frans. 2007. *International Human Rights Law in Africa*. Oxford: Oxford University Press.
Viljoen, Frans and Lirette Louw. 2007. "State Compliance with the Recommendations of the African Commission on Human and Peoples' Rights, 1994–2004." *American Journal of International Law* 101 (1): 1–34.
Weiler, Joseph H. 1991. "The Transformation of Europe." *Yale Law Journal* 100: 2403–2483.

CHAPTER 36

THE LIMITS OF INSTITUTIONAL REFORM IN THE UNITED STATES AND THE GLOBAL TRADE REGIME

JUDITH GOLDSTEIN AND ROBERT GULOTTY*

As a new nation, America relied on tariffs to fund its nascent government. Seeing the tariff as a tax, the Founders granted primary responsibility for rate-setting, and thus trade policy, to the House of Representatives. This choice was unproblematic from the perspective of the crafters of the Constitution. The frontier in 1789 was sparsely populated and although the new nation faced a British government willing and able to undermine commercial activity in the colonies, early elected officials worried little about international markets. Instead, they looked west. In the early years, the Founders looked prescient—America grew in isolated splendor.[1] Isolationism, however, proved to be a short-lived panacea. By the end of the nineteenth century, US central decision-makers had to deal with growing demands from constituents for access to foreign markets; by the mid-twentieth century, US commercial policy had moved center stage as the US orchestrated a widespread globalization in production and trade.[2]

Creating that internationally oriented trade policy, however, was problematic. The "appropriate" policy from the perspective of economic theory would have been to reduce barriers to trade in line with a rise in productivity. But, the constitutionally imposed arrangement for tariff-setting made high, and not low, tariffs the norm. Thus, with the end of the Civil War and the demise of the pro-trade Southern voting bloc, tariff-setting became the quintessential example of unfettered congressional logrolling. Tariffs moved up and not down. Famously, when the 1930 Smoot-Hawley tariff was making its way through congress, over 1,000 economists signed on to a document decrying its content. As Schattschneider (1935) later wrote in his famous analysis of the Act, congressional behavior was as predictable as it was problematic—in the face of powerful interest groups and the authority to set rates, high tariffs were inevitable.

Yet post-World War II tariff policy followed a path far afield from what would have been expected from a reading of Schattschneider's book. The US systemically changed its trade policy and opened its borders to foreign goods. Instead of being the textbook example of poor public policy, trade politics became increasingly bi-partisan and de-politicized. And although academics and pundits often cite the lack of forward movement in twenty-first century trade agreements as the first step in a "slippery slope" to the protectionism and economic decline associated with the Smoot-Hawley era, there is scant evidence of that happening. Looked at from the long view, the US continues to have one of the most liberal trade policies in the world, and far more open than at any previous moment in US history.

How did this happen? Given reform under explicit constitutional constraints, US trade policymaking does not appear to be a prime example of path dependency (see, e.g., David 1994; Pierson 2004). Yet, as we illustrate below, the transformation in US policy is a quintessential example of historically directed outcomes. While earlier work has focused on institutional redesign in the US, and in particular, delegation of authority to the Executive Office from the legislature, we suggest that congress retained authority on tariffs in line with their constitutional prerogative. The assumption that delegation explains US policy, we argue, is an example of *post hoc ergo propter hoc* reasoning. Our revisionist explanation begins with the observation that constitutional constraints were finessed, not undermined: the allocation of power to small districts was never negated through constitutional reform. In this issue domain, we argue, contemporary policy must be understood in the context of constitutionally created structures.

To demonstrate how institutional rigidity constrained policy reform and thus shaped subsequent behavior, we organize our chapter into three sections. In each section, our baseline for behavior is derived from market pressures; deviation from behavioral expectations is then argued to reflect institutional constraints. The first section, "Creation and Reform of Tariff-setting Procedures," explicates the key changes in tariff-setting that occurred in 1934 and the ways that delegation did, and did not, undermine congressional authority. The next section, "Internationalization of US Trade Policy," looks more closely at the US efforts to create international rules on trade, suggesting that the rules that have facilitated cross-border trade flows mimic US norms and rules on commerce. Being constrained to rely on "American centered rules" then helps to explain why international treaties have functioned well only for the reduction of international tariffs, the problem which they were created to fix, but faltered in addressing newer problems, such as non-tariff measures. In the "Conclusion," we reflect on the more general issue of institutional evolution and the lessons learned from this case study.

In order to avoid *post hoc ergo propter hoc* fallacious reasoning, we focus not only on the institutional changes, but also on the range of alternative policies that were viable at any one time, and the political support that made one and not another institutional reform possible. Even so, the telling of this history often sounds as if politicians reacted rationally to underlying changes in US interests in the world. As we suggest in our Conclusion, this is far from what occurred. There is an "optimal" arrangement for trade policy in order to maximize consumer surplus. This is the baseline around which we craft our argument and it is one that is far afield from America's policy positions.

Creation and Reform of Tariff-setting Procedures

Tariff-setting by the new US government was constrained by three concerns, evident from earliest congressional debate. On one side were those who saw the tariff as merely a revenue instrument, collected at the border, making it the least intrusive of possible taxes to balance the budget. On the other side were those who advocated using the tariff to build domestic industry and infrastructure and not merely, as suggested by the opposition, a tax necessary to pay off war debts. A third position, backed by one or the other at different times, advanced alternative views on the responsibility of government to workers and capital displaced by market forces, especially those from abroad.[3]

The low tariff rate, balanced budget position was advocated by those fearful of big government. Among the founding generation both Benjamin Franklin and Thomas Jefferson were such advocates, fearful of a large manufacturing sector, the alternative to an agriculturally based nation, on economic as well as moral grounds. Those who had spent time in Europe feared that American democracy could not prosper with an impoverished working class selling their labor to factory owners. Madison, in 1789, would articulate what became the dominant position: "However much we may be disposed to promote domestic manufactures we ought to pay some regard to the present policy of obtaining revenue" (The Founders' Constitution).

Arguing against this view was Alexander Hamilton and later, the Whig party, who envisioned a powerful and industrialized America, a future that would be predicated on near term tariff protection. A reading of Hamilton's *Report of Manufactures* in 1791 suggests that like Franklin and Jefferson, he was familiar with European theorists, but his reading of the US situation and British imperialism led him to defend tariffs although only as a temporary necessity that would eventually give way to free trade. In congress, this position was more often heard from representatives from the Middle States—for example, FitzSimmons of Pennsylvania took to the floor during the First Congress and argued that the tariff should be used to "encourage … production … and protect our infant manufactures" (Register of Debates in Congress 1833, 201).

Even given this ideological distance, tariffs of this era reflected institutional procedure: Congress directly set tariff levels, product by product, which favored particularism, even among the free traders. Thus while post-1846 tariffs would begin a descent as result of regional conflict, the average rate until that time was 40 percent, no matter the party control of congress. This is not to suggest that interests aligned on the tariff.[4] The fight over the tariff was acrimonious and wide ranging, in congress, in the press, and among elites. In this debate, regional interests and party position were not always in sync. Southern farmers and western agricultural producers both favored low tariffs on economic grounds. But southern farmers remained the backbone of the Democratic Party while western farmers moved into the Republican Party.[5] Budding northern manufactures remained wedded to the tariff and when the Whig party disappeared, they ended up in an urban–farm coalition in the new Republican Party. And while northern commercial interests sided with the South until the 1850s, ten years later they aligned with the Union and abandoned the Democratic Party.

The US grew rapidly after the Civil War. The completion of the railroad, Western expansion, and increased trade enriched the nation. These changes in economic circumstance had little effect on tariff rates, which after a short period of reduction prewar had moved back to the 40 percent + range. As the US moved into its "gilded age," it faced fewer tariff barriers abroad and productivity gains at home. Lower worldwide tariffs would have served the nation's interests. Instead, tariffs moved in the opposite direction. By 1875, the un-weighted average of European tariffs was 9 percent; the US average rate was 44 percent. As result, between 1870 and 1880, exports increased 148 percent measured in constant dollars. Imports rose as well, almost 91 percent in this same period, and the US ran a budget surplus in every year from 1870 to 1895.[6] From the perspective of Washington, economic policy was a success; from the perspective of economic theory, high tariffs should have disappeared.

This did not occur, even though debate reveals that individual politicians understood that tariffs were problematic. Why? The simple answer is that congress relied on the tariff as a policy tool—the constitution had granted the legislature few economic levers to use in response to constituent complaints. In good and hard times, the tariff was the pork that they could offer supporters. Republicans claimed that high tariffs protected American wages. Free trade, they argued, would swamp the US market with goods produced by cheap but impoverished foreign labor.[7] The Democratic Party took the opposite line and said that protection had little to do with wages. Rather, the tariff supported monopolies, hurt consumers, and reinforced trusts, which degraded American labor. Yet, like their Republican Party colleagues, they agreed that tariffs were necessary on at least some products. Which items could legitimately be taxed was the issue. As vulnerable to particularistic concerns as was the opposition, Democrats tended not to lower rates on goods produced in Democratic districts. Instead, they targeted goods not produced at home or products necessary for the manufacture of finished goods.

Given this institutional dynamic, it is not surprising that the tariff schedule grew in size and height. In 1890 the schedule went through an extensive expansion and for the first time, specified rates for agricultural products as well as for non-agricultural goods. Congress legislated more specific rules on product imports and exports, including the use of bounties to aid industries, in three key industries: sugar, maple sugar, and sorghum. The definition of an infant industry was expanded to include "potential industries" when congress came to the aid of the tin-plate industry. It is not that Americans ignored the changed views in Europe but rather, that the form of tariff-setting, characterized by an item-by-item product focus made it impossible to lower a rate, once set. Primary products did better than finished goods but that often reflected either a lack of domestic production or very concentrated production and limited coalition possibilities.

Institutional Reform

Congressional policy changed little as the nation entered the twentieth century. The average tariff rate came down under the Democratic president, Woodrow Wilson, but the onset of World War I abbreviated its effect and, postwar, a Republican congress returned rates to their earlier level. While politics remained mired in this partisan difference on tariff policy, the American economy was going through rapid structural change. Major innovations in business organization and manufacturing technology, along with the rise of auto use and production, an expanded electricity network, and communication innovations that connected the rural and urban population led to unprecedented growth of economic activity. Trade politics and economic forces, while somewhat out of sync in the Gilded Age, became increasingly problematic to a growing number of sectors of the economy whose interests required access to international markets.[8]

Tariff reform is often portrayed as a reaction to failed policy, that is, the economic downturn that occurred after passage of the Smoot-Hawley Act in 1930. That Act was notorious for its height and its timing. Whether or not the Depression was "caused" by US tariffs is debatable; what is uncontestable, however, is that the Depression ended the era of Republican hegemony. Again in power, it was no surprise that the Democratic Party turned its attention to tariff reform. The Party, however, had changed and was now more urban, blue collar and immigrant. Reflective of the variation in interests of this new coalition, the Trade Act that congress took up in 1934 did not stipulate any individual tariffs, but instead focused on the procedures by which rates were set.

Sidestepping Article 2 of the Constitution, the Reciprocal Trade Agreements Act of 1934 (RTAA) granted the president new authority to lower rates by up to 50 percent if he received reciprocal reductions in a partner's tariff. The authority required no *ex post* Congressional vote, enabling the president to conclude 32 agreements before 1947.[9] This authority required regular congressional renewal and both Democratic and Republican party majorities reauthorized the program.[10] In fact, nothing occurred outside the shadow of congressional reauthorization and thus when the General Agreement on Tariffs and Trade (GATT) came into force on January 1, 1948, it was based on a congressional grant of negotiating authority.[11]

While institutional change was evolutionary, not revolutionary, attitudes on trade changed more dramatically. By the early 1960s, trade lost its partisan nature and both parties had platforms that endorsed the trade liberalization program. Of the original argument about the tariff, what remained was the question of whether or not and to what extent did the government have a responsibility for market dislocation that results from a trade agreement. How did tariffs go out of vogue? A review of the procedures for setting trade, before and after 1934, illuminates how change was possible.

First, the 1934 Act and subsequent renewals stipulated that in place of congress vetting producer interests, the President needed to seek advice from the Tariff Commission, the Departments of State, Agriculture, and Commerce, and from all other appropriate sources before lowering a tariff. To accommodate this mandate the Committee for Reciprocity Information was assembled to give interested parties the opportunity to present views. They took briefs and held public hearings. Until 1937, a formal announcement of intent to negotiate was accompanied by a list of the principal producers who could potentially get a tariff cut; afterward, this was replaced by the "public" list, which signaled all items that were under consideration in any negotiation. The change in venue increased the costs of political activity on the part of producer groups, and their presence in the halls of the legislature declined rapidly in these years.

Second, the 1934 Act dictated a particular form of tariff-setting. All agreements were bilateral but their effect extended beyond the two signatories because of most favored nation provisions. After 1923, the US was bound by Executive Order to grant Most Favored Nation (MFN) privileges to nations with whom it signed a trade agreement. The effect was that once the US lowered rates for one nation as part of a bilateral process, others with whom it had a MFN agreement benefited immediately from the lower rate. The treaty process in the GATT would become multilateral in essentially the same way. Although not its intent, trade expansion via a MFN clause also undermined group resistance by increasing uncertainty about the effects of tariff agreements.

Third, the 1934 Act mandated that the Executive was to negotiate *reciprocal* agreements, meaning that import access necessitated an immediate and monetarily equal export gain. The logic of reciprocity extended as well to parties withdrawing from a treaty. Reciprocity changed the complexion of trade policymaking by bringing new groups to Washington—exporters now balanced the power of import competing groups dislodged by cheaper foreign goods.

Finally, the products on which the reciprocal agreements centered were those to which the trading partner was the "principal supplier." Governments initiated negotiations with a declaration of a set of products they sought access for in the foreign market. Each partner would look at the list of "demands" and make counter "offers." The process thus focused reductions on products that represented considerable importance in their markets and would concentrate negotiations on the members with the most at stake. The president knew which products and thus which districts would be affected by a tariff reduction; the RTAA procedures allowed him to finesse resistance by excluding politically problematic districts.

Retrospective

Tariff reform is too often classified with other examples of delegation and/or the aggrandized power of the president. While presidential preferences may have weighed in more centrally after 1934, congressional preferences were still key since congress did not abdicate control of its constitutional prerogative over tariff policy. The explanation for reform, therefore, cannot be based on a direct comparison of congressional and presidential interests, but rather, must be based on why congressional preferences changed. A simple metric illustrates this point. A delegation explanation would lead us to expect that the tariff cuts would be greatest on the highly protected products, i.e., on those that congress had favored in the past because of undue pressure or at minimum, about the same across all products post-1934. If delegation did nothing else, it should have shielded congress from protectionist pressures. Yet, while overall tariffs were reduced by almost 60 percent under the RTAA program, products that were highly protected in 1930 (defined as over 50 percent AV equivalent) came down less than 1/3 of that amount. Most reductions, in fact, came from products relatively under-protected (Goldstein and Gulotty 2014).

If the effect of delegation was not a more shielded congress, what then explains tariff reductions? The institutional innovations of 1934 were not about delegation but about changing the incentives of congress. Presidents understood that congress was constrained by constituents but that he needed to garner approval for his trade program. For a strategic president, one that wanted to open up the US market, the fear of interest group pressures on congress remained a constant concern. He did, however, have agenda control: he could choose *when* to negotiate, *who* to negotiate with and *what products* to place in a tariff bundle. These were the "tools" he used to undermine congressional mobilization.

Looking back at treaties and product negotiations, we see that presidents were wary of mobilizing anti-trade forces. Negotiators tended to stay away from the most highly protected products and those that were highly concentrated in particular districts. The principal supplier rule allowed negotiators to predict the effect of a particular treaty and they ignored nations with politically charged import patterns. And as necessary, negotiators appear to have regularly removed sensitive products from consideration by re-classification of the tariff schedule.

But, while the RTAA created a mechanism that ensured a congressional majority in favor of tariff reform, it was poorly suited to solve a set of policy problems that would ensue in later years. Looking ahead, we see that institutional reform in this domain was never complete; presidents could never independently orchestrate trade as a part of a large set of US foreign policy interests. New problems were met with a panoply of different responses, with international institutions limiting American degrees of freedom and ultimately the success of the WTO.

Internationalization of US Trade Policy

In its inception, the GATT was created to be a bargaining forum and its origins are closely associated with the timing of RTAA renewals. In 1945, the president received the grant of a 50 percent negotiating authority, which needed to be used by the time of the next renewal in 1948. In that time he needed to make progress on tariff cuts, and given limited time the US invited a number of countries to simultaneously negotiate in Geneva. The result of these bilateral negotiations was the GATT, which was merely the tariff rates that were agreed to in Geneva and a set of rules about those obligations stapled in front.

The "thinness" of the GATT, and the lack of attention to formal rules, was due in large part to participants' assumption that the agreement was temporary. The framers, most of whom were in State Department, were instead focusing on the design for a multilateral trade organization that was to be the "sister" to the other Bretton Woods institutions: the International Trade Organization (ITO). The ITO, however, was unable to find majority support in congress and the GATT became the default forum for international trade negotiation. Growth was incremental. At the second Round in Annecy, 11 new members began the process of acceding to the GATT. In the third Round in Torquay in 1950–1951, the US announced its decision to rely only on the GATT mechanism and not to re-send the ITO Charter to congress. By 1952, 34 countries were GATT members, representing 80 percent of world trade. Thereafter, the organization was the cornerstone of the liberal trade regime.

The GATT's rules and norms changed little even as the organization grew, continuing to reflect its origins in US legislature and America's bilateral treaties. Parts I and II of the GATT mimicked earlier US agreements: the MFN provision; a prohibition against monetary manipulation; specific rules for nullification; an escape clause; and the exception for economic development. The substantial differences in the GATT from earlier agreements were found in Part III, which entailed rules that had developed out of the consultative process over the creation of the ITO.

The article that would eventually garner the most attention was the escape clause, written so as to allow governments a safety valve for periods of pressure on particular industries. The rules allowed nations to impose temporary measures to protect industries that exhibited "serious injury" as a consequence of "increased quantities of imports." Over time, however, the article became increasingly incoherent; a review of its invocation reveals repeated problems in knowing what was, and was not, an acceptable response to market dislocation. A safeguard would allow a government to enact temporary legislation, compensate their trade partners, and ensure that a conflict remain temporary. However, as the GATT evolved, it became clear that the language in Article XIX was not well defined. Given problems with invoking the escape clause, it lost relevance, and GATT members resorted to extra-legal measures (Sykes 2003). By the start of the Uruguay Round in 1986, the escape clause had been invoked only 132 times (Trebilcock and Howse 1995). As a consequence, the long running debate over how to deal with job loss and firm displacement remained unsettled in the GATT as it had in domestic legislation.

While the question of just what was the "optimal" tariff policy had ended with party unity, dissonance remained on the question of responsibility for dislocation. US trade policy reform had not ignored the problem of economic injury. The executive office had legislated that all treaties include an escape clause in 1948 and protections from unfair trade were ingrained in law even before passage of the RTAA. Congress also passed legislation to address specific injury in 1962 but the idea of direct transfer payments because of market competition was never popular. Trade Adjustment Assistance (TAA) was regularly re-legislated but it had a limited budget and a relatively high bar for aid. As the Government Accounting Office would later report—the program was expensive and did little to adjust workers to import competition.[12]

Without a domestic or international mechanism to reduce protectionist pressure, labor and environmental groups ultimately defected from the pro-free trade coalition. While TAA was offered as part of the North American Free Trade Agreement (NAFTA) and other agreements as the appropriate response to international market forces, pro-trade legislation became increasingly difficult to pass. While legislative "tricks" such as fast track authority (the promise to not amend a trade bill once it hit the floor), facilitated passage of some trade legislation, fast track authorization itself became a legislative battle. Domestic politics would once again constrain even the most free trade president.

Limits to the GATT System and the Creation of the WTO

The GATT regime was remarkably successful in its early years. Tariffs were at historical lows and by 1973 the organization began to reorient itself so as to address the variations in national practices that were undermining commerce. By then the membership of the GATT had vastly expanded to 102 members, most of whom were classified as developing countries. In preparation for what would be the Tokyo Round, GATT members agreed to a far-reaching agenda, including the elimination of all barriers to trade in particular sectors and to negotiate the reduction of non-tariff measures, the evaluation of the issue of worker and firm injury by reworking the safeguard system, and an attempt to expand the GATT into new sectors such as agriculture and tropical products (Winham 1986). The Kennedy Round had introduced a new method of dealing with non-tariff measures in the "plurilateral" Antidumping Code, which the Tokyo Declaration set out to apply to non-tariff issues. As the Round progressed, however, it became apparent that the decision to negotiate each issue in isolation limited the range of trade-offs at the bargaining table. When it came time to extend the deals beyond the main negotiating countries, few countries were willing to join.

As result, the Tokyo Round agreement was a hybrid or what was later called an *à la carte* approach to trade rules. New agreements were signed but few were universal. The anti-dumping codes, for example, was adopted by 46 of the 73 members; agreements on government procurement, subsidies, safeguards, and the provisions for special and differential treatment of developing nations, similarly, had limited participation. Moving away from universal rules had facilitated the conclusion of numerous new agreements, but the strategy came with a cost. Not only did the form of negotiation preclude crosscutting deals, each code had a different dispute settlement mechanism and a different adjudicating body. Some of the codes operated on purely consultative grounds, while others authorized potential compensation for violation, limiting effective enforcement.

Further, bringing "domestic" regulations into the GATT opened up a virtual Pandora's Box of problems in the US. Tariff reductions had occurred with an *ex ante* authorization by congress to the president to negotiate agreements. Congressional representatives could delegate tariff-setting authority under a "veil of secrecy" as to which products were to be reduced. Non-tariff barriers negotiations were not amendable to this institutional "fix." All agreements needed to return to congress for approval and a change in a domestic statute. Agreements initialed in Geneva were public, facilitating the mobilization of groups adverse to the new codes. Rule changes activated a range of groups beyond firms and labor and included those interested in the environment, health and safety, as well as other border protections. In addition, given the broad range of non-tariff measures, legislation was now vetted beyond the traditional House Ways and Means and Senate Finance committees. While fast track authority finessed some of these problems by focusing congressional authority on the write-up phase of legislation, the president was increasingly pressured to invoke trade sanctions outside the GATT framework, such as Section 301 and Special 301 of the 1974 Trade Act, creating new frictions between the US and her trading partners. The US increasingly turned to "voluntary export restraint agreements" and other discriminatory practices to an extent unforeseen by negotiators.

Given these challenges to plurilateral agreements, and the limited scope of GATT disciplines, why were discriminatory side agreements, rather than changes to the original GATT, adopted in the Tokyo Round? Improvements to the agreement had to deal with 40 years of political change since the wartime negotiation of the GATT and constraints inherited in the GATT itself. Further, the GATT set significant procedural obstacles for amending the agreement. Even developing proposals for amendment was difficult, as the GATT had no regular mechanism for direct negotiations that are necessary for rule change and no regular legislative mechanisms. Ministerial meetings were organized ad hoc, sporadically, and without significant agenda control. Moreover, a number of developing member states were increasingly militating to shift negotiations to other forums, such as the United Nations Conference on Trade and Development (UNCTAD), that were thought to be more amenable to their interests.

Legislative Action at the Uruguay Round

The problem with the lack of an institutionalized legislative mechanism came to a head at the first Ministerial meeting after the Tokyo Round in November of 1982. The meeting was intended to start a new round of negotiations, but the agenda was too large and contentious, which not only led to a negotiation breakdown but also threatened to cause the whole GATT to collapse. Ironically, it may have been the failure to start negotiations that persuaded many governments of the need to address the rules of the GATT.

Going into the new Round, there was more agreement on what had gone wrong than on the right policy to pursue. All agreed that the combination of discriminatory rules and the fact that agriculture policy remained significantly unconstrained made the "semi-judicial panel procedures" of the GATT dispute resolution process inappropriate for further liberalization of non-tariff barriers (Croome 1995, 4). Governments remained divided on whether or not to extend new obligations on regulations, services, investment, or intellectual property to the entire membership, whether to allow individual governments to decide among a subset of obligations *ex ante*, and whether to allow governments to retain the right to block the application of an obligation in the course of a dispute. Governments also disagreed on whether each agreement would have implications across substantive obligations. For example, would an adverse action in restricting services allow the harmed state to retaliate on another agreement? Allowing cross-compensation was thought to help address the apparent inequality in the capacity to enforce tariff obligations, but it ruled out plurilateral arrangements with separate procedures of the kind established under the Tokyo Round (Croome 1995, 125).

Unsaid at the negotiating table but well understood was that automatic adoption and cross retaliation in disputes would constrain the US from its policy of unilateralism. With the US needing to find markets for its increasingly service-oriented and high-tech products, American negotiators had little to offer, other than support for new rules that constrained their capacity to unilaterally determine punishments for trade infractions. US negotiators also understood that support for rules that limited member autonomy sent a needed signal of continuing US commitment to a self-enforcing liberal international trading order (Goldstein and Gowa 2002).

The Uruguay Round ultimately achieved the automatic adoption of reports, and centralized dispute settlement. This occurred through what Richard Steinberg refers to as the power play—the Round ended with what amounted to a "closed rule" take-it-or-leave-it offer (Steinberg 2002). Developing countries were among the main proponents of this *single undertaking* idea, embodied in paragraph B (ii) of the Punta del Este Declaration. Their support, somewhat surprising in retrospect, was based on their assumption of no change in the special treatment for developed countries, and the expectation that they would *not* be obliged to offer concessions as part of any final agreement. The developing countries thought that a single undertaking rule would avoid the sort of pyramidal schemes seen in the Tokyo Round. In that round, negotiations started between the US and EU or other small group settings, and then the results of the negotiation were presented to the rest of the membership. Instead, the Uruguay Round would take into account developing country interests by forcing the US and the EC to agree to agricultural reform as part of a final package.

Initially, the strategy seemed to succeed. During the Brussels Ministerial meeting in 1990, a group of Latin American agriculture exporters were able to reject progress obtained in Montreal in 1988 on non-agricultural issues. The coalition of developing countries, including the Latin American members of the Cairns Group, cited the insufficient attention to agriculture, insisting that the US and the EC come back to the table as part of a *single undertaking* and ensure that the agenda would include agriculture.

During the period between the Montreal and the Brussels Ministerial meetings, the EC and Canada redeployed the concept of a *single undertaking* to new ends. The new reading of the single undertaking linked issues in trade in goods with those in trade in services. This allowed the EC and the US to maximize their negotiating leverage and ensure that a single, binding dispute settlement system would apply to all of the agreements produced at the end of the Uruguay Round. Countries prepared to accept the results of the Uruguay Round would withdraw from the GATT and join the new organization. Countries not prepared to do so would remain contracting parties to an agreement without the major trading partners, and without reassurances that the US would not use unilateral Section 301 actions, particularly Special 301 on intellectual property.

This change was a significant revision to the conceptualization of the *single undertaking* promoted by developing countries in Punta del Este, but it was not a significant deviation from the previous practice of GATT negotiations. Even before the "power play," developing country negotiators had little to no say on the institutional development of the GATT. The effort to constrain unilateral activity on the part of the most powerful states ended up serving, unintentionally, the interests of those same governments. This positive feedback mechanism was fueled by investment on the part of the incumbent Western nations in what Acemoglu and Robinson (2006) refer to as de facto political power, that is, the ability to leverage channels of power outside of the existing political institutions. As Paul Pierson points out, institutions can create powerful inducements to reinforce their own stability, in this case establishing a set of states that could use the threat of a parallel institution to avoid political reform (Pierson 2004).

Retrospective

While the Uruguay Round made significant headway on non-tariff issues by incorporating all of the plurilateral agreements into a single body, developing countries' efforts for an agreement on agriculture was not fully successful. Under the "Uruguay Round reform program" and the 1994 Agreement on Agriculture, governments did make some progress, but many programs in the US and Europe survived by governments shifting their agricultural support programs to "Green-box subsidies" that were not bound by negotiations. The adoption of a single trade instrument (instead of a number of plurilateral accords) was the consequence of an expansion of the multilateral system to non-tariff areas, rather than the outcome of developing countries pushing through reforms in the agricultural area.

The creation of the WTO occurred within the institutional conditions of the previous 60 years. Commitments to limit unilateral retaliation were joined with an expansive dispute settlement system. This system provides corrective sanctions across agreements that before relied on ad hoc enforcement. This expansion of the dispute settlement system enabled the incorporation of non-tariff issues, and by rejecting collective retaliation, avoided changing the fundamental self-help nature of the GATT.

Conclusion

The history of commercial policy offers scholars unique insights into the interdependence of institutions and societal interests. In particular, the trade liberalization case presented here exemplifies the pitfalls of static models of institutional design and demonstrates the benefits of an historical institutional approach to economic policymaking. Here and in other cases of economic policymaking, we see that markets create interests, aggregated in response to existing institutional incentives. Those incentives, however, are reflective of social organization of an earlier era, maintained because of the benefits they confer on particular groups. Scholars should not be surprised that from the perspective of traditional models of economic theory, rules and social interests are often out of sync; old procedures bias change in not necessarily optimal directions.

Our view of trade politics has been influenced by questions that arise when scholars assume a historical institutional approach. Instead of assuming that "institutions and behavior... evolve through some form of efficient historical process" (March and Olson 1989, 5), we sought examples of institutional outcomes that were, "off the equilibrium path." As we unpacked the history of trade policymaking, we found that institutions were reformed, but never transformed; problems were finessed but never overcome. Even assuming that actors were rational, we found that policies led to unanticipated outcomes, and current behavior is influenced by archaic and often dysfunctional decisions of the past. If institutions are "congealed tastes" (Riker 1980, 445), those "tastes" reflect a small nation with no thought of a globalized economy. In short, this case illustrates how behavior is constrained by the past and how moving forward is never a linear process.

In the case of the US, the 1789 Constitution placed protectionist interests in a privileged position by granting tariff-setting authority to the Congress. This created a bias toward closed borders, even as the interests of business and labor shifted. Institutions responded in an evolutionary, not revolutionary manner. Delegation in 1934 granted limited power to the president by which he was able to finesse, not change, the role of congress in trade policymaking. He was successful in reducing tariffs by having the authority to choose when to negotiate, with whom to negotiate, and what products to liberalize. As result, congressional mobilization was undermined. This institutional "fix" survived the failure of the ITO, and then thrived through the GATT era. However, unlike what one would expect if institutions could be intentionally selected to efficiently achieve the functional goals of governments, reform was constrained and incomplete: the "fix" never addressed the lack of a redistributive mechanism to compensate the losers from trade, and thus there was continued pressure from protectionist interests that challenged the extension of negotiations beyond tariffs. Domestic efforts, such as the TAA, were subject to congressional limits, and the GATT itself had no mechanisms to address those displaced by trade. Historically inherited domestic institutions established positive feedback mechanisms that enabled protectionism and constrained reform.

The evolution of the GATT into the WTO reflects the same reciprocal relationship between interests and institutions. While remaining a thin agreement without disciplines on regionalism, large exemptions for developing countries, and a little-used set of renegotiation clauses, the regime was enormously successful in reducing tariffs and developing a robust dispute settlement system centered on explicit and informal threats of unilateral retaliation. However, the organization failed to address fundamental issues that undermined cross-border trade. Non-tariff barriers, in part because of their complexity, and in part because of continued protectionist pressure from groups at home, were initially dealt with in a series of plurilateral agreements that excluded developing countries from the decision-making process as well as from the substantive obligations. Expanding membership, shifting economic power to developing and emerging countries, and limitations of the plurilateral approach set the stage for how and when the GATT would reform its rules and procedures. The new WTO not only expanded the coverage of the multilateral trade regime to services, intellectual property, and new subsidies obligations, but the creation of the WTO represented a shift from trade via a set of plurilateral arrangements to a single multilateral agreement with enforcement provisions.

The structure of the RTAA, the GATT, and the WTO all reflect the difficult nature of creating commonly accepted rules for economic exchange. Groups face uncertainty about the effects of market pressures and risk adverse individuals become wary of change. Instead of being an optimal response to market pressures, policy is often a series of compromises and side payments that put off decisions to the future. Neither the RTAA, which was thought to concentrate decision-making power in the hands of the Executive, nor the WTO, which moved enforcement to a single body, escaped particularistic pressures.

The institutional constraints on American trade policymaking today, and the continued political influence of anti-internationalist forces at home and abroad is a reminder of the oddity of trade reform in the US. Yet, despite institutional constraints, trade reform did succeed in the latter part of the twentieth century. In part, success was due to good fortune. Economic good times diffused political resistance in the US and facilitated the movement of labor into new industries; as result the expansion of neoclassical economics was consistent with America's international goals. Not surprisingly, when the US economy slowed, so too did trade liberalization. This is not to say that protectionism became the alternative. Years of trade openness created pro-trade groups who counter moves to close the US market. It is to say, however, that contemporary policy is a hybrid that reflects contradictory political instruments, legal constraints and social interests. The result is policy incongruity; trade actions by the US government are less predictable and trade reforms are at best episodic.

Notes

* We thank all the participants at the Conference on Historical Institutionalism, Philadelphia, 2013, for comments and suggestions and in particular, Orfeo Fioretos and the other editors of these volumes who went through the draft carefully, suggesting

valuable improvements. We want to also thank Miles Kahler, Karen Alter, and the other participants in the 2014 APSA meeting for providing well-appreciated feedback and suggestions for improvement.

1. George Washington, in his 1796 farewell address, noted that "The East, in a like intercourse with the West, already finds, and in the progressive improvement of interior communications by land and water will more and more find, a valuable vent for the commodities which it brings from abroad or manufactures at home."
2. Goldstein (2014) also argues for an initial constitutional constraint as explanation for contemporary regulatory commercial policy issues.
3. As Madison noted: "it is not possible for the hand of man to shift from one employment to another without being injured by the change" (The Founders' Constitution, 1962).
4. In the standard economic accounts, the political coalitions that promote or oppose the tariff depend on assumptions about the ability of economic agents to adjust. In the Stolper-Samuelson-Hecksher-Ohlin formulation, individual laborers, land owners, and capital owners can easily switch from producing one good to another, allowing the development of factor or class based interests, see Rogowski (1987). By contrast, in a specific factors model, some economic agents cannot easily change their industry of employment, leading to industry based coalitions for and against free trade, see Frieden (1991).
5. Western farmers had interests akin to those of Southern farmers—US farm products were competitive on international markets and would have benefited from low tariff rates.
6. Paul Bairoch (1976), cited in Goldstein (1993).
7. Although labor was scarce in the US making wages higher than the world average, open immigration policy and productivity differences suggest that open markets would not have depressed wages, as suggested by a classic Hecksher–Ohlin formula.
8. Real GDP growth in the 1920s averaged 4.2 percent and real GNP per capita grew at 2.7 percent, rapid rates by nineteenth- and twentieth-century standards.
9. For the classic history of this era's trade policy see Brown (1950); for a historical review of the RTAA period see Goldstein (1993) and Irwin (2002). For a review of the early GATT see Barton et. al. (2006) and Irwin et al. (2008).
10. The RTAA program was renewed in 1937, 1939, 1943, and 1945.
11. GATT participation was authorized in 1948, 1949, 1951, 1954, 1955, 1958, and 1962.
12. GAO (2000).

References

Acemoglu, Daron and James Robinson. 2006. "De facto Political Power and Institutional Persistence." *AER Papers and Proceedings* May: 325–330.

Bairoch, Paul. 1976. *Commerce extérieur et developpement économique de l'Europe au XIX siècle*. Paris: Mouton.

Barton, J. H., J. L. Goldstein, T. E. Josling, and R. H. Steinberg. 2006. *The Evolution of the Trade Regime: Politics, Law, and Economics of the GATT and the WTO*. Princeton, NJ: Princeton University Press.

Brown, William Adams, Jr. 1950. *The United States and the Restoration of World Trade: An Analysis and Appraisal of the ITO Charter and the General Agreement on Tariffs and Trade*. Washington, D.C.: Brookings Institution.

Croome, J. 1995. *Reshaping the World Trading System: A History of the Uruguay Round.* Geneva: World Trade Organization.

David, P. A. 1994. "Why Are Institutions the 'Carriers of History'? Path Dependence and the Evolution of Conventions, Organizations and Institutions." *Structural Change and Economic Dynamics* 5 (2): 205–220.

Frieden, Jeffry A. 1991. "Invested Interests: The Politics of National Economic Policies in a World of Global Finance." *International Organization* 45 (4): 425–451.

GAO. 2000. "Trade Adjustment Assistance: Impact of Federal Assistance to Firms Is Unclear." Report GAO-01-12, Washington, D.C., December.

Goldstein, J. 1993. *Ideas, Interests, and American Trade Policy.* Ithaca, NY: Cornell University Press.

Goldstein, J. 2014. "Trade Politics and Reform." In *The Politics of Major Policy Reform in Postwar America*, ed. J. Jenkins and S. Milkis. New York: Cambridge University Press.

Goldstein, J. and J. Gowa. 2002. "US National Power and the Post-War Trading Regime." *World Trade Review* 1 (02): 153–170.

Goldstein J. and R. Gulotty. 2014. "America and Trade Liberalization: The Limits of Institutional Reform." *International Organization* 68 (02): 263–295.

Irwin, Douglas A. 2002. *Free Trade Under Fire.* Princeton, NJ: Princeton University Press.

Irwin, D. A., P. C. Mavroidis, and A. O. Sykes. 2008. *The Genesis of the GATT.* New York: Cambridge University Press.

March, James and J. P. Olson. 1989. *Rediscovering Institutions: The Organizational Basis of Politics.* New York: Free Press.

Pierson, P. 2004. *Politics in Time: History, Institutions and Social Analysis.* Princeton, NJ, and Oxford: Princeton University Press.

Register of Debates in Congress. 1833. Volume 8. Washington, D. C.: Gales and Seaton. 201–202.

Riker, William. 1980. "Implications from the Disequilibrium of Majority Rule for the Study on Institutions." *American Political Science Review* 74 (2): 432–446.

Rogowski, R. 1987. "Political Cleavages and Changing Exposure to Trade." *The American Political Science Review* 81 (4): 1121–1137

Schattschneider, E. E. 1935. *Politics, Pressures and the Tariff: A Study of Free Private Enterprise in Pressure Politics, as Shown in the 1929–1930 Revision of the Tariff.* New York: Prentice-Hall, Inc.

Steinberg, R. H. 2002. "In the Shadow of Law or Power? Consensus-Based Bargaining and Outcomes in the GATT/WTO." *International Organization* 56 (02): 339–374.

Sykes, A. O. 2003. *The Economics of WTO Rules on Subsidies and Countervailing Measures.* Chicago: University of Chicago Law School.

The Founders' Constitution. 1962. *The Papers of James Madison*, ed. William T. Hutchinson et al. Chicago and London: University of Chicago Press.

Trebilcock, M. J. and R. Howse. 1995. *The Regulation of International Trade.* London: Routledge.

Winham, G. R. 1986. *International Trade and the Tokyo Round Negotiation*. Princeton, NJ: Princeton University Press.

CHAPTER 37

INCREMENTAL ORIGINS OF BRETTON WOODS

ERIC HELLEINER*

Orfeo Fioretos (2011) has argued that historical institutionalism can help scholars of international relations better understand the prevalence of incremental change in international governance. This chapter explores this point further in the context of the governance of the international monetary and financial system. At first sight, this sector would seem an unlikely one to prove Fioretos' point. After all, global financial markets are often seen as one of the most dynamic and fast-moving sectors of the world economy. But even in the face of major global financial crises, change in the governance of international money and finance has often been surprisingly slow. The insights of historical institutionalism can help us to understand why.

The chapter develops this argument through an examination of a particularly hard case: the iconic creation of the postwar Bretton Woods international monetary and financial system. The Bretton Woods negotiations are widely portrayed as a dramatic historical event in which top Anglo-American officials—led above all by John Maynard Keynes and Harry Dexter White—designed the postwar international financial and monetary system de novo. In the language of historical institutionalism, Bretton Woods is seen as a "founding moment" from which many legacies flowed. This chapter shows how even this founding moment was shaped by processes of incremental institutional change. Challenging conventional wisdom, it demonstrates that the Bretton Woods outcomes were influenced not just by power, interests, and ideas during the well-known negotiations of 1943–44, but also by a set of institutional developments that pre-dated the negotiations and that left important legacies.

The Bretton Woods Moment

The 1944 Bretton Woods conference has come to symbolize how international monetary and financial governance can be reformed in one fell swoop by successful agents with ambitious visions such as Keynes and White. Almost without fail, postwar international financial crises have encouraged reformers to call for a "new Bretton Woods" that might rekindle this ambition.[1] These calls are misplaced. The innovative aspects of the postwar international financial architecture were not a product of just one set of decisive negotiations or of a momentous historical event, but also of a longer and more incremental process of institutional change.

What were the innovative aspects of the Bretton Woods agreements? As John Ruggie (1982) has noted, they outlined a novel "embedded liberal" vision which sought to reconcile the rebuilding of an open multilateral financial system with the new more interventionist economic practices that had emerged from the experience of the Great Depression. As part of this vision, the agreements established for the first time two public multilateral financial institutions: the International Monetary Fund (IMF) and International Bank for Reconstruction and Development (IBRD). While the former was to provide short-term balance of payments finance to governments, the latter was designed to mobilize long-term reconstruction and development lending. Governments also committed to a gold exchange standard and current account convertibility, while at the same time reserving the right to adjust exchange rates and control capital movements.

Scholars usually argue that the Bretton Woods agreements were a product of some unique circumstances. One was the fact that US policymakers had enormous power to shape the postwar world because of their country's dominant economic position at the time. That same position also gave American officials and the country's leading firms a strong economic interest in rebuilding a more open international economic order. Some analysts also highlight the shared commitment to embedded liberal values of influential Anglo-American officials at the time, particularly Keynes and White who are usually credited for their exceptional agency and vision in bringing the agreements to fruition (Ruggie 1982; Ikenberry 1992).

The US Treasury's Lead Role

All this is true. But it is also important to recognize that the innovations of Bretton Woods were a product not just of a specific configuration of power, interests, and ideas during the 1943–44 negotiations but also of some institutional pre-history. Using the language of historical institutionalism, this history emerged out of a "critical juncture"—or a period of fluidity—that dated back to the Great Depression of the early 1930s and the collapse of the liberal international monetary and financial system of the pre-1930s era. "Critical junctures" are often seen to be relatively short in duration. At the international level, however, the consolidation of a new order can take considerable time and this was certainly the case with the emergence of the Bretton Woods order, which emerged from a set of incremental institutional changes dating back to the early 1930s.

The first of these was a domestic institutional change in US foreign economic policy that emerged after Roosevelt was elected US president in 1932. Under Roosevelt's New Deal, the US Treasury was quickly assigned a much more prominent role in determining US policy toward international monetary and financial issues than it had previously held. This institutional realignment in US foreign economic policy was part of a broader New Deal effort to assert greater public authority over monetary and financial issues, and constrain the influence of the New York financial community—and its perceived allies in bodies such as the State Department and Federal Reserve Bank of New York—who were held partly responsible for the Great Depression (Helleiner 1994, chapter 2; 2014a, chapters 1–3).

Roosevelt's Treasury Secretary, Henry Morgenthau, embraced the New Deal goal with enthusiasm and he defended the Treasury's privileged position in international financial and monetary affairs in a dogged fashion throughout his long tenure that lasted until 1945. The institutional legacy of the early New Deal reforms ensured that the Treasury played a lead role in shaping US policy toward the Bretton Woods negotiations in the early 1940s. It was White, Morgenthau's top official dealing with international issues, who drafted the first US plans in early 1942 and then chaired the US interdepartmental "technical committee" that refined these plans over the next two years. Throughout the international discussions leading up to Bretton Woods between 1943 and 1944, White also served as the principal US negotiator vis-à-vis other countries. At the conference itself, Morgenthau was chair of the US delegation and president of the overall meeting. Meanwhile, White chaired the conference "commission" that drafted the IMF's articles of agreement, and he and his Treasury staff dominated the practical organization of the conference.

The fact that it was the Treasury—not the State Department or the Federal Reserve Bank of New York—that took the lead in shaping US policy toward the Bretton Woods negotiations was significant. Both Morgenthau and White were much more inclined to see the Bretton Woods plans in the light of broader New Deal politics than many officials from those other agencies. When presenting White's initial plans in 1942 to Roosevelt, Morgenthau described them as an effort to create a "New Deal in international economics" (US Government 1942, 172). He later noted that one of his objectives in the Bretton Woods negotiations was "to move the financial center of the world from London and Wall Street to the United States Treasury, and to create a new concept between nations in international finance" (quoted in Gardner 1980, 76).

White saw his Bretton Woods work in a similar way. He had joined the Treasury in 1934 and, like Morgenthau, was an "ardent New Dealer" (Van Dormael 1978, 42). His initial postwar plans in early 1942 had been very ambitious, even including a provision that IBRD members would need to subscribe to an international "bill of rights" that set forth "the ideal of freedom for which most of the peoples are fighting the aggressor nations and hope they will be able to attain and believe they are defending." As White explained, "the inclusion of that provision would make clear to the peoples everywhere that these new instrumentalities [the IMF and IBRD] which are being developed go far beyond usual commercial considerations and considerations of economic self-interest. They would be evidence of the beginning of a truly new order in the realm where it has hitherto been most lacking—international finance" (Oliver 1975, 319).

Bilateral Lending to Latin America

If the Treasury's new prominence in foreign economic policy was the first key historical institutional legacy shaping the Bretton Woods outcomes, a second was the fact that Morgenthau, White, and other US officials were influenced directly by a number of prewar institutional initiatives when developing their postwar plans. One was the 1936 Tripartite Accord between the Britain, France, and the US that established the precedent of an international agreement endorsing adjustable exchange rate pegs. More important were a set of initiatives involving the US and Latin American governments in the late 1930s and early 1940s. These are sometimes mentioned in passing in the scholarly literature on the origins of Bretton Woods, but little sustained attention has been devoted to them. This neglect is unfortunate because the content of Bretton Woods was shaped deeply by institutional innovations that were designed in this US–Latin American context.

The first was a set of bilateral currency stabilization arrangements that the US negotiated with Latin American countries after 1936 (Boughton 2004, 2009; Bordo and Schwartz 2001). These arrangements involved the extension by the US government of short-term bilateral lines of credit for balance of payments purposes from its Exchange Stabilization Fund (ESF). The ESF had been established in January 1934 for a different purpose: to help stabilize the value of the dollar vis-à-vis gold. Historian James Boughton (2004, 189) notes that White became the "chief exponent" of the idea of adapting the ESF after the mid-1930s to extend short-term currency stabilization loans to other countries (the first of which was offered secretly to Mexico in 1936). Because the ESF had been placed firmly under Treasury control with no legislative constraints, it was an ideal institution to convert for this new purpose with minimal domestic opposition.

The Treasury's control of the ESF had a direct impact on White's later proposals for the IMF's lending activities in the early 1940s. White's assistant Edward Bernstein, who was deeply involved in the drafting of White's initial (and subsequent) Bretton Woods plans, later noted that White built directly on the ESF lending practices he had pioneered in Latin America when developing his first draft of the Fund in early 1942: the proposed Fund simply multilateralized the ESF's bilateral stabilization loans (Black 1991, 35). Indeed, when the IMF began its first loans after the war, it modeled the lending after earlier arrangements that the ESF had developed with Mexico (Boughton 2004, 189–190; Gold 1988). In a memo written two weeks before the Bretton Woods conference as part of the preparation for Morgenthau's welcome speech, Bernstein also highlighted privately how the experience of bilateral currency stabilization loans to Latin America—along with the 1936 Tripartite Accord—had "convinced the Treasury" of the need for multilateral financial cooperation "involving the extension and broadening of the principles" embodied in those initiatives.[2]

The IBRD's mandate to offer public international long-term loans to promote reconstruction and development also emerged directly out of a second institutional innovation in US financial relations with Latin America in the late 1930s. From 1938 onward, the US government began to extend bilateral long-term loans to Latin American governments to support their development projects. The loans represented the first such foreign lending program ever introduced for development purposes by the US government. This innovation was implemented once again through an institution created in the early New Deal for a different purpose: the Export-Import Bank. The Bank had been established in 1934 to supply credit to support US exporters, but it was redeployed to serve this development role in 1938–39 (Adams 1976; Adamson 2005). The conversion of the Bank for new purposes proved politically more difficult than the ESF's transformation because the Bank's charter came up for Congressional renewal in February 1939, just as its development lending was expanding rapidly. When Roosevelt tried to increase its lending to $500 million, opposition from isolationalist Republicans succeeded in capping its size at $100 million (Adams 1976, 250–252).

The new lending programs of both the ESF and Export-Import Bank emerged in incremental ways in response to changing US foreign policy priorities in the late 1930s (e.g., Gardner 1964; Gellman 1979; Green 1971; Grow 1981; Pike 1995; Helleiner 2014a). At that time, the Roosevelt administration was becoming increasingly concerned about growing German political and economic influence in Latin America. US officials saw a new financial partnership with the region as a way of cultivating political alliances, offsetting the appeal of Nazi ideology, and securing US export markets, foreign investments, and access to commodities in the region. This initiative also resonated with Roosevelt's commitment to reject past US "dollar diplomacy" in favor of a new "Good Neighbor" policy toward Latin America. Supporting the region's development aspirations also represented an international extension of the New Deal's efforts to generate rising standards of living at home, particularly in poor regions within the US through initiatives such as the Tennessee Valley Authority.

Latin American policymakers largely welcomed the US initiatives to support their development goals. In the wake of the Great Depression, governments across the region had increasingly prioritized state-led economic development and industrialization goals. If the US was willing to support these goals with public funds, Latin American officials appreciated the support, particularly after the outbreak of World War II which initially caused enormous economic dislocation when trade with Europe collapsed. Although there was some lingering skepticism about US goals in light of past American policy toward the region, many in Latin America held out hope that the New Deal had opened opportunities for a new era in US–Latin American relations (Helleiner 2014a, chapters 1–3).

The Inter-American Bank

Morgenthau and White were among the strongest proponents of the new US public lending to Latin America. After the outbreak of World War II in September 1939, they also became deeply involved in an even more ambitious project to create a new multilateral "Inter-American Bank" (IAB). Because the IAB ultimately was stillborn, it has received little detailed attention by historians of Bretton Woods.[3] But a number of observers have noted in passing that it influenced later US policy toward the Bretton Woods negotiation. For example, Morgenthau's biographer John Morton Blum (1965, 57) argues that the IAB initiative "gave the Americans concerned, White in particular, an experience which was to prove useful years later in the organization of the postwar financial institutions." Historians of the World Bank similarly note that "White's exposure to the technical discussions concerning the Inter-American Bank obviously influenced his April 1942 proposal for a Bank for Reconstruction and Development of the United and Associated Nations" (Mason and Asher 1973, 16). A more detailed study of the IAB confirms the importance of these observations (Helleiner 2014a, chapters 2, 4).

The IAB proposal was designed to strengthen the US political and economic goals vis-à-vis the region already noted Indeed, it was referred to officially by the US Department of State (1940, 518) as an initiative for "the economic implementation of the Good Neighbor policy." Building directly on the Export-Import Bank and ESF lending programs, the IAB was to be empowered to provide both long-term development loans as well as short-term stabilization finance for balance of payments and currency stabilization purposes. While the ESF and Export-Import Bank loans had been bilateral, the IAB placed them in a multilateral context designed to foster broader inter-American political and economic cooperation.

The IAB thus foreshadowed White's IMF and IBRD's proposals directly, combining their multilateral lending functions into one institution. As Robert Oliver (1975, 99) put it, "in a sense, the Inter-American Bank plan was the first draft of subsequent plans for a Stabilization Fund and a World Bank." Interestingly, it was White himself—with Morgenthau's blessing and Bernstein's assistance—who played the lead role in drafting a detailed charter for the Bank in consultation with Latin American officials (Helleiner 2014a, chapter 2).

The IAB proposal also anticipated some aspects of the governance of Bretton Woods institutions. It was to be governed by a board that used a weighted voting scheme with super-majority voting rules that guaranteed the US a veto over important decisions. During the IAB negotiations, US officials also discussed the possibility of using a constituency system for representation on the IAB's main decision-making body, a system that was subsequently built into the decision-making of the Bretton Woods institutions.[4]

Even more important was the fact that the institution was to be owned and controlled by member governments and with very inclusive regional membership. These features of the proposal were advanced by the US Treasury, and they were bold ideas. At the time, the only existing multilateral financial institution at the international level—the Bank for International Settlements (BIS) established in 1930—was not directly accountable to governments since most of its members were privately owned central banks. The BIS also had a relatively narrow country membership; its founding members had included central banks from just six countries (Belgium, Britain, France, Germany, Italy, Japan) and one private banking group from the United States. The IAB was to be a publicly owned and controlled intergovernmental institution and it embraced a more inclusive conception of multilateralism in the regional context of the Americas, with all republics of the Americas to be invited as members.

Federal Reserve officials (and some Latin American officials) opposed the Treasury's idea of an intergovernmental bank, urging that the IAB be a "central bankers' bank" like the BIS.[5] Morgenthau and White, however, categorically rejected the BIS model. They saw the design of the IAB in the light of the broader New Deal struggle to wrest control of financial policy away from the Wall Street elite and the Federal Reserve Bank of New York. As one US official put it in describing Morgenthau's views, "I think probably what you really get in the Treasury is a reflection of the classic fight between Mr. Morgenthau and the Federal Reserve Bank of New York."[6] The same official noted how White had also privately expressed to him "the fear lest it [the IAB proposal] fall into the hands of the Federal Reserve which he thinks would merely throw it right back into the New York banks."[7] In early 1940, White put the issue very clearly in a meeting with some colleagues:

> we have created an instrument here and given it enormous powers for good or evil and for us to turn it over at this stage to banking groups, it seems to me we are just going back to all the evils that we wish to avoid . . . This bank, if it is successful, if it lives up to expectations with respect to power, can have a very profound degree of influence on the small countries and whether that shall be democratically used in the sense of attaining objectives of Government to Government or whether it shall be merely a bankers' attempt to use that to serve—not their own individual purposes but the general philosophy that they represent, I think is a very fundamental matter and I don't see how this Administration, with its whole New Deal philosophy and with its attitude toward those fundamental problems can support an institution that becomes a super-central bank.[8]

Morgenthau and White emerged victorious from this dispute over the governance of the IAB. It was designed as an intergovernmental institution, with the small concession that each government could choose an appointment process for its director. The US government's endorsement of the intergovernmental nature of the IAB set an important precedent for the Bretton Woods negotiations. When White wrote his initial drafts of the IMF and IBRD a few years later, he designed them as bodies controlled and owned by governments. With the IAB fight behind him, White met less opposition within the government to this part of his plans. US delegates would even back a resolution at the Bretton Woods conference calling for abolition of the BIS "at the earliest possible moment" (US Government 1948, 939). White also designed the IMF and IBRD with very inclusive membership—now on a worldwide basis—involving all countries that belonged to the United Nations (as well as "Associated Members" that were neutral in the war but had broken diplomatic relations with the Axis powers).

While Morgenthau and White won this battle over the IAB's design, they lost the larger war concerning the IAB's establishment. Although the Roosevelt administration signed the Bank's convention along with eight Latin American governments in May 1940, the IAB was never created because US Congress failed to ratify it. In addition to opposition from some New York financial interests, the main cause of Congressional inaction was the intransigence of Carter Glass, the powerful conservative Democratic Senator, who feared the IAB would undermine US sovereignty (Green 1971, 60–74).

Lock-in, Conversion, and Layering

The creation of the IMF and World Bank thus involved less innovation than conventional wisdom suggests. Rather than being designed heroically from a blank slate, the US drafts for the Bretton Woods agreements—drafts on which the final agreements were largely based—grew out of incremental institutional innovations that built upon one another through processes that historical institutionalists call "lock-in," "conversion," and "layering" (see Mahoney and Thelen 2010; Fioretos 2011). In the beginning, the boosting of the Treasury's role vis-a-vis international monetary and financial policy in the early New Deal locked-in its prominence throughout Morgenthau's tenure as Treasury Secretary. The early New Deal also brought the creation of the ESF and Export-Import Bank whose purposes were then converted in innovative ways in the late 1930s. The IAB proposal was subsequently layered on top of those innovations with a novel multilateral structure. The design of the IMF and IBRD did the same, drawing directly on this institutional pre-history while also introducing new elements, including a worldwide focus and membership obligations relating to issues such as exchange rates and currency convertibility (the IAB did not include such obligations).[9]

This historical institutionalist account does not, of course, pretend to explain the origins of Bretton Woods single-handedly. It simply complements existing accounts. US officials themselves who were involved in the Bretton Woods negotiations, however, did highlight the influence of this pre-history. Bernstein's comments on this point have already been noted. When he first saw White's initial Bretton Woods draft in 1942, Adolfe Berle—an important official involved in White's technical committee in 1942–43—also applauded the way it built directly on the IAB, an initiative that he had actively supported (Schwartz 1987, 213). Similarly, one of the key officials involved in designing the IBRD, Emilio Collado, spoke of the IAB (on which he had also worked closely) as a "predecessor" to White's initial plans for Bretton Woods (McKinzie 1974, 5). Finally, US officials involved in drafting the Bretton Woods institutions sometimes even made explicit reference to text that had been used for the IAB.[10] More generally, it is striking how many US officials involved in the IAB's drafting and US–Latin American financial relations during the late 1930s and early 1940s went on to participate in discussions surrounding the development the Bretton Woods agreements (Helleiner 2014a, chapters 1–3).

It was not just US officials who drew on Bretton Woods's pre-history. Latin American officials involved in the Bretton Woods negotiations did too. For example, in a mid-1943 meeting between the IAB and White and Brazilian officials (one of whom, Eurico Penteado, had been involved in the IAB negotiations), explicit comparisons were made between White's proposals for the IMF.[11] Another meeting with Cuban officials a few months later generated discussion about how White's Fund could take on many of the tasks that the IAB had been designed to perform.[12] During the lead-up to the Bretton Woods conference, Mexican officials studying the American IBRD proposal also compared it to the earlier IAB plan that they had supported strongly (Urquidi 1996, 35).

The Latin American role at the Bretton Woods conference itself has been downplayed in most analyses of the Bretton Woods negotiations which tend to focus on the Anglo-American relationship. Yet Latin American governments made up 19 of the 44 governments represented at the conference. Since decisions at the meeting were made on one-country-one-vote basis, they had considerable potential influence; as one British official put it, "Latin America is almost sufficient to settle any issue."[13] To get their way, Latin American delegates at the conference worked as a bloc and did not hesitate to remind other delegates that they represented "practically one-half of the nations here assembled."[14] It is not surprising, then, that White told a private meeting of US delegates on the first day of the conference that "it is the South American countries who in this are going to be important to us."[15]

Latin American countries were particularly interested in the potential of the IBRD to mobilize development loans, with Mexican officials playing a lead role on this issue. Among the key Mexican officials involved in pre-conference discussions was Eduardo Villaseñor who had earlier been one of the chief advocates of the IAB's potential development role in Latin America (Villaseñor 1941). At the conference itself, one of the top leaders of the Latin American bloc, Mexico's Antonio Espinosa de los Monteros, had also worked very closely with White in 1940 in drafting the IAB's content (Eckes 1975, 154; Helleiner 2014a, chapter 2). Under Mexico's leadership, Latin American delegates succeeded in strengthening the IBRD's mandate to support development loans (Helleiner 2014a, chapter 6).

Distribution, Opportunities, and Preferences

If the institutional pre-history of Bretton Woods was significant, in what precise ways did it shape outcomes? To begin with, institutional innovations had lasting distributional effects. This phenomenon was most apparent in the way that the Treasury benefited from early New Deal reforms that strengthened its role within US international monetary and financial policymaking. Morgenthau's success in locking in the initial advantage—reinforced by his close personal relationship with Roosevelt—gave his department a very prominent role in determining US policy toward Bretton Woods.

Institutional changes also created new opportunities for political action. The fact that the ESF and Export-Import Bank had been created in the early New Deal enabled White and other US officials to act more quickly and decisively in pioneering new kinds of international public lending in the late 1930s. Those institutions could be quickly "converted" to new purposes with minimal bureaucratic hassle in ways that attracted less political resistance than would have been generated by an effort to build new institutions.

Institutional innovations also generated ready-made templates for advocates of change. The drafters of the IAB were able to draw directly on the experience of the new lending activities of the ESF and Export-Import Bank. The detailed provisions of the IAB's charter and activities of the ESF and Export-Import Bank also constituted blueprints on which the architects of the Bretton Woods institutions could draw during negotiations over the postwar international financial system. These blueprints were particularly significant in the case of White's initial Bretton Woods plans in early 1942. He produced detailed plans extremely rapidly after an initial request from Morgenthau in mid-December 1941. What scholars have described as their "unclear" (Ikenberry 1992, 300) and "somewhat mysterious" (Moggridge 1992, 682) origins are much easier to understand when this institutional pre-history is taken into account. White was able to act quickly by building directly on existing institutional templates from his Latin American experience.[16] His speedy response effectively gave him a first-mover advantage by making the Treasury's initial drafts the focal point for internal US government discussions.

Opportunities were also created by the fact that institutional innovations encouraged new political coalitions. Within the US, the new US public lending to Latin America benefited US exporters and internationally-oriented manufacturing firms in ways that contributed to a widening of domestic political support for a more internationalist US foreign economic policy. At the international level, the new institutions of US–Latin American financial cooperation in the late 1930s and early 1940s also helped to build Latin American support for the subsequent US Bretton Woods plans. As one Treasury official later put it, the US could count on Latin American support at the 1944 conference partly because White was "popular" with the Latin American delegates as a result of their close working relationship with him in the past: "having dealt with the man for years in various problems," they "had confidence that here is the man who will understand our problem and who, if he sees our problem, will fight, and he's not afraid to fight" (Oliver 1961, 18–19).

In addition to their distributional effects and creation of opportunities, institutional changes also shaped government preferences over time. Through their involvement with the ESF, Export-Import Bank and IAB, a large number of US policymakers accumulated experiences with international financial cooperation that increased their enthusiasm for it. Specific norms also emerged out of these experiences that shaped preferences. For example, White and Morgenthau's victory in the struggle over the governance model for the IAB established the idea of an intergovernmental international financial institution as a new norm.

At a more general level, the IAB can be seen to have also served as an incubator for the Bretton Woods policy paradigm of embedded liberalism. Like the later Bretton Woods agreements, the IAB combined a commitment to liberal multilateralism with support for new interventionist economic practices that had become popular during the 1930s. Indeed, US officials such as Berle were very explicit in arguing that they saw the IAB as pioneering a new kind of economic philosophy. As Berle put it in early 1940, he hoped the IAB could be "a nucleus around which things will grow'" and "a laboratory study" in how the worldwide economic relations would need to be rebuilt after the war.[17] In a June 1941 speech that anticipated the Bretton Woods' ideology of embedded liberalism, he explained the content of those relations in the following way: "Carried to its logical conclusion, all this must require a higher degree of economic planning and, at the same time, a higher degree of open trade between the American nations ... In the combination of the new conceptions with the new mechanisms we have already gone a long way towards establishing the foundation of what will be the cooperative international economics of the future" (Berle 1941, 760–761).

Conclusion

The 1944 Bretton Woods conference is legendary for establishing the constitution for the postwar international monetary and financial order. Within historical institutional scholarship, the meeting has been seen as an important "founding moment" that generated important long-term institutional legacies. But the Bretton Woods agreements should be of interest to historical institutionalists for a second reason as well: those agreements themselves were a product of a set of incremental institutional innovations that pre-dated the formal negotiations. These innovations emerged from an extended critical juncture that began in the early 1930s and involved processes well known to historical institutionalists such as "lock-in," "conversion," and "layering." Equally familiar are the effects that such modes of institutional change had on the distribution of political power, the creation of new opportunities for political action, and the preferences of governments.

This study of the origins of Bretton Woods thus reinforces key insights of historical institutionalist scholarship. It is particularly significant for Fioretos' argument about the prevalence of incremental change in international governance. The Bretton Woods agreements are usually seen as a product of a particular constellation of power, interests, and ideas at a unique historical moment. Those analyses overlook that the agreements themselves also grew out of an institutional pre-history and processes of incremental change. These kinds of processes are not always easy for scholars to detect. They require careful process tracing through archival work. In doing that work, researchers must be open to exploring the potential significance of events and phenomena that have often been overlooked by historians and even by historical actors at the time.

The importance of recognizing the incremental nature of change that generated Bretton Woods lies not just in the realm of scholarly theorizing. It also has direct policy relevance for the contemporary period. In advance of the first G20 leaders meeting at the height of the 2008 financial crisis, analysts such as Joseph Stiglitz hoped for a "Bretton Woods moment" in which the international monetary and financial system would be quickly and radically redesigned (quoted in Bases 2008). The analysis in this chapter suggests that this analogy presents too optimistic a view about the prospects for major international reforms. While the 2008 crisis may have ushered in a new critical juncture, the process of building a new international monetary and financial order is likely to be a slow and extended one. Indeed, the incrementalist content of the G20-led international reforms since 2008 provides considerable evidence of this point already (Helleiner 2014b). Historical institutionalism thus has much to contribute to understanding not just historical change but also the future trajectory of international monetary system.

Notes

* I am very grateful to Orfeo Fioretos for his helpful comments and encouragement as well as to the Social Sciences and Humanities Research Council of Canada for helping to fund research underlying this chapter.

1. See for example French President Nicolas Sarkozy and British Prime Minister Gordon Brown at the height of the 2008 financial crisis (Kirkup and Waterfield 2008).
2. E. M. Bernstein to Mr. Smith, June 12, 1944, Morgenthau Diary (MD), Book 748, p. 170, The Papers of Henry Morgenthau Jr, 1866-1960, Franklin D. Roosevelt Library, Hyde Park, New York.
3. The most detailed accounts can be found in Bordo and Schwartz (2001), Oliver (1975), Green (1971), and Helleiner (2014a, chapter 2).
4. See Gardner to Board of Governors, "The Inter-American Bank Proposal," December 20, 1939, Board of Governors Central Subject Files (CSF), 301.23–9. Record Group 82, Records of the Federal Reserve System, United States National Archives, College Park, Maryland.
5. Gardner and Goldenweiser, "Suggestions Relative to Proposed Inter-American Bank," January 18, 1940, p. 1, CSF, 301.23–9.
6. "Conversation between Dr. Goldenweiser and Mr. Berle, January 25, 1940," p. 9, CSF, 301.23–9.
7. "December 8, 1939," p. 3, Berle Papers (BP), Box 211, Franklin D. Roosevelt Library, Hyde Park, New York.
8. MD, Book 237, p. 259.
9. Since the IAB was never created, I am using the term "layering" in a broader sense than in some historical institutionalist literature to describe a situation where past blueprints (i.e., new ideas about appropriate economic rules), rather than institutions themselves, shaped later outcomes.
10. See for example "Bank for Reconstruction and Development: Points to be Discussed by American Technical Committee," April 11, 1944, p. 2; Harry Dexter White Papers, Box 8, folder 4, Public Policy Papers, Department of Rare Books and Special Collections, Princeton University Library, Princeton, NJ, USA; LC.A. and R.B., "Agreement to Form an

International Stabilization Fund of the United and Associated Nations," October 18, 1943, pp. 28, 30–31, 34, 36; Ansel Luxford Papers, "International Stabilization Fund, Memoranda, Correspondence," Box 8/7, International Monetary Fund Archives, Washington D.C., USA.

11. "Memorandum of a Meeting on the International Stabilization Fund in Mr. White's Office, May 14, 1943," Bretton Woods Conference Collection (BWCC), Box 4/7, IMF Archives, Washington D.C., USA.
12. "Memorandum of meeting on the International Stabilization Fund in Mr. White's office, Aug. 23, 1943," BWCC, Box 5/1.
13. "From Bretton Woods British Delegation (Monetary Conference) to Foreign Office," p. 12, No.50 REMAC, July 10, 1944. United Kingdom Treasury Records, 247/29, The National Archives of the United Kingdom, Kew, Richmond, Surrey, UK.
14. Luis Machado from Cuba quoted in "Informal Minutes: Commission 1, United Nations Monetary and Financial Conference at Bretton Woods, July 1944," p. 121, BWCC, Box 13/1. For their efforts to work as a bloc, see Suárez (1977, 277) and MD, Book 752, p. 5.
15. MD, Box 749, p.3.
16. The influence of his Latin American experience is also clear from the fact that his early drafts also included ideas that had arisen in the Latin American context relating to commodity price stabilization, debt restructuring, and support for infant industry protection (Helleiner 2014a, chapter 4). On the question of the speed of White's reply, some scholars have suggested that White had already begun to draft his plans in advance of Morgenthau's request (Oliver 1975, 110; Horsefield 1969, 11–12). But it is clear from reading his early drafts that he did not have a full blueprint ready before January 1942.
17. Quotes from "Conversation between Dr Goldenweiser and Mr Berle, January 25, 1940," p. 8, CSF 301.23–9.

References

Adams, Frederick. 1976. *Economic Diplomacy: The Export-Import Bank and American Foreign Policy 1934–39*. Columbia: University of Missouri Press.

Adamson, Michael. 2005. "'Must We Overlook All Impairment of Our Interest?' Debating the Foreign Aid Role of the Export-Import Bank, 1934–41." *Diplomatic History* 29 (4): 589–623.

Bases, Daniel. 2008. "World Faces New Bretton Woods Moment: Stiglitz." *Reuters UK*, November 6. Available at <http://uk.reuters.com/article/idUKTRE4A58BI20081106> (accessed September 1, 2015).

Berle, Adolfe. 1941. "The Economic Interests of the United States in Inter-American Relations." *Department of State Bulletin* 4 (105) (June 28): 756–760.

Black, Stanley. 1991. *A Levite among Priests: Edward M.Bernstein and the Origins of the Bretton Woods System*. Boulder, CO: Westview.

Blum, John Morton. 1965. *The Morgenthau Diaries: Years of Urgency 1938–1941*. Boston, MA: Houghton Mifflin Company.

Bordo, Michael and Anna Schwartz. 2001. *From the Exchange Stabilization Fund to the International Monetary Fund*. NBER Working Paper 100. Cambridge: National Bureau of Economic Research.

Boughton, James. 2004. "New Light on Harry Dexter White." *Journal of the History of Economic Thought* 26 (2): 179–195.

Boughton, James. 2009. "American in the Shadows: Harry Dexter White and the Design of the International Monetary Fund." In, *American Power and Policy*, ed. Robert Leeson. Basingstoke: Palgrave Macmillan.

Department of State. 1940. "Inter-American Bank." *Federal Reserve Bulletin* (June): 517–525.

Eckes, Alfred. 1975. *A Search for Solvency: Bretton Woods and the International Monetary System, 1941–1971*. Austin: University of Texas Press.

Fioretos, Orfeo. 2011. "Historical Institutionalism in International Relations." *International Organization* 65 (2): 367–399.

Gardner, Lloyd. 1964. *Economic Aspects of New Deal Diplomacy*. Madison: University of Wisconsin Press.

Gardner, Richard. 1980. *Sterling Dollar Diplomacy in Current Perspective*. New York: Columbia University Press.

Gellman, Irwin. 1979. *Good Neighbor Diplomacy*. Baltimore, MD: John Hopkins University Press.

Gold, Joseph. 1988. "Mexico and the Development of the Practice of the International Monetary Fund." *World Development* 16 (10): 1127–1142.

Green, David. 1971. *The Containment of Latin America*. Chicago: Quadrangle Books.

Grow, Michael. 1981. *The Good Neighbor Policy and Authoritarianism in Paraguay*. Lawrence: The Regents Press of Kansas.

Helleiner, Eric. 1994. *States and the Reemergence of Global Finance*. Ithaca, NY: Cornell University Press.

Helleiner, Eric. 2014a. *Forgotten Foundations of Bretton Woods*. Ithaca, NY: Cornell University Press.

Helleiner, Eric. 2014b. *The Status Quo Crisis: Global Financial Governance After the 2008 Meltdown*. New York: Oxford University Press.

Horsefield, J. Keith. 1969. *The International Monetary Fund 1945–1965: Twenty years of International Monetary Cooperation—Volume 1*. Washington, D.C.: IMF.

Ikenberry, John. 1992. "A World Economy Restored: Expert Consensus and Anglo-American Postwar Settlement." *International Organization* 46 (1): 289–321.

Kirkup, James and Bruno Waterfield. 2008. "Gordon Brown's Bretton Woods Summit Call Risks Spat with Nicholas Sarkozy." *The Telegraph*. October 15.

Mahoney, James and Thelen, Kathleen. 2010. "A Theory of Gradual Institutional Change." In *Explaining Institutional Change: Ambiguity, Agency, and Power*, ed. James Mahoney and Kathleen Thelen. Cambridge University Press, 1–37.

Mason, Edward and Robert Asher. 1973. *The World Bank since Bretton Woods*. Washington, D.C.: Brookings.

McKinzie, Richard. 1974. *Oral History Interview with Emilio Collado*. Harry S. Truman Library and Museum. Available at <http://www.trumanlibrary.org/oralhist/collado1.htm> (accessed October 15, 2012).

Moggridge, Donald. 1992. *Maynard Keynes: an Economist's Biography*. London: Routledge.

Oliver, Robert. 1961. *Transcript of Interview with Ansel F. Luxford*. The World Bank/IFC Archives Oral History Program, Oral History Research Office, Columbia University, July 13. Interview by Robert Oliver. Available at <http://siteresources.worldbank.org/EXTARCHIVES/Resources/Ansel_Luxford_Oral_History_Transcript_44_01.pdf> (accessed July 29, 2012).

Oliver, Robert. 1975. *International Economic Co-operation and the World Bank*. London: Macmillan.

Pike, Frederick. 1995. *FDR's Good Neighbor Policy*. Austin: University of Texas Press.
Ruggie, John. 1982. "International Regimes, Transactions and Change: Embedded Liberalism in the Postwar Economic Order." *International Organization* 36: 379–415.
Schwartz, Jordan. 1987. *Liberal: Adolfe A.Berle and the Vision of an American Era*. New York: The Free Press.
Suárez, Eduardo. 1977. *Commentarios y Recuerdos (1926–1946)*. Mexico: Sendo de la Republica. Mexico: Editoria Porrúa.
Urquidi, Victor L. 1996. "Reconstruction vs. Development: The IMF and the World Bank." In *The Bretton Woods-GATT System*, ed. Orin Kirshner. New York: M. E. Sharpe.
US Government. 1942 (published in 1963). *Foreign Relations of the United States: Diplomatic Papers*, vol. I. Washington, D.C.: US Government Printing Office.
US Government. 1948. *Proceedings and Documents of the United Nations Monetary and Financial Conference, Bretton Woods, New Hampshire, July 1–22, 1944*. Washington, D.C.: US Government Printing Office.
Van Dormael, Armand. 1978. *Bretton Woods: Birth of a Monetary System*. London: Palgrave Macmillan.
Villaseñor, Eduardo. 1941. "The Inter-American Bank." *Foreign Affairs* 20 (1): 165–174.

CHAPTER 38

SEQUENCING, LAYERING, AND FEEDBACKS IN GLOBAL REGULATION

ABRAHAM L. NEWMAN*

CAPITAL reserves held by banks, environmental impact assessments, and standards of how personal information may be shared are increasingly shaped through debates transpiring outside national capitals. Regulation—the rules that govern the behavior of public and private actors—has entered the lexicon of international affairs (Drezner 2007; Mattli and Woods 2009; Farrell and Newman 2010). The stakes of these debates are particularly high as such rules determine core features of markets, including who has access to them and on what terms. And given the legacies of existing domestic regulation, the potential for global rules to create conflict or generate switching costs is high.

Unlike traditional political economy issues such as trade or currencies, however, there are few formal treaty-based international organizations that resolve disputes or set the rules for the world. Instead, global regulation is frequently shaped by informal networks of regulators (both public and private) cooperating across borders or at times by the extraterritorial extension of domestic law by large markets (Slaughter 2004; Putnam 2009; Kaczmarek and Newman 2011; Bach and Newman 2010a; Büthe and Mattli 2011). How then can we understand the global politics of regulation? When are we likely to get agreement on key rules? Who shapes their content? And what are the distributional consequences?

Scholars as well as policy observers tend to highlight the importance of structural power when explaining who sets global rules. On the one hand, research emphasizes the policy position of large markets—when great powers agree global standards emerge and when they disagree they do not (Drezner 2007; Simmons 2001). A second literature emphasizes the role that large internationally active firms play in defining the terms of cooperation and capturing global regulation (Strange 1996; Underhill and Zhang 2008). It is clear that such structural power matters, but these accounts often have difficulty explaining complex empirical realties, such as when persistent great power stalemate gives way to cooperation, why one great power succeeds in setting the agenda over another, or the reasons for why the influence of industry shifts over time or across forums. Moreover, they often overlook the critical role that institutions play in channeling and transforming the preferences of and resources available to private sector actors.

Drawing on work from historical institutionalism, this chapter argues that the global politics of regulation is in important respects the product of domestic and international institutions (frequently informal) interacting over time and across space. By focusing on the institutional origins of preferences, temporal dynamics in global negotiations, and incremental processes of institutional change, historical institutionalism helps address lacunae in extant approaches to global regulation. It brings attention to how institutions constrain and enable actors engaged in global regulation by shaping the power resources available to them, their access to the rule-creation and rule-implementation process, and ultimately why they prefer one set of rules over another.

Because global regulation takes place within and across jurisdictional boundaries, regulatory politics cannot be isolated within one single state. Instead, regulatory politics transpire between states as well as within transnational regulatory bodies (Posner 2010; Newman 2008; Farrell and Newman 2014). The global politics of regulation, then, is less about simple rule clash between major markets and more about complex interactions and alliances forged as actors engage global markets. The core of the chapter develops a set of mechanisms—relative sequencing, cross-national layering, and transnational feedbacks—that explicate the dynamics of global regulatory politics.

Relative sequencing focuses on the timing of institutional development between major markets in relation to one another (Newman 2008; Bach and Newman 2010b; Posner 2010). It embeds traditional market power concepts within regulatory capacity—the ability to define, monitor, and enforce a set of market rules. Given the idiosyncratic nature of domestic institutional paths historically, it brings attention to relative differences in the timing of such institutional developments across economies. It then uses these differences in timing to help resolve empirical puzzles such as variations in influence between the European Union (EU) and the United States (US) in setting regulatory standards despite similarities in their overall market size. Relative sequencing can also produce an event chain that helps identify the nature of policy convergence dynamics globally. In contrast to functionalist arguments emphasizing problem/solution dynamics, the argument here is that jurisdictions often react to and copy institutional designs from powerful institutions that exert extraterritorial influence. Relative sequencing, then, helps better specify the character, timing, and nature of diffusion processes.

Cross-national layering and transnational feedback effects are mechanisms that help account for endogenous processes of change. In cases of cross-national layering, transnational alliances may use global forum to construct alternative rule-sets to domestic regulations. Over time, global rules can siphon away support from domestic regulations and open up opportunities for policy change domestically and in turn globally (Farrell and Newman 2014, 2015). Transnational feedbacks, by contrast, concern the ways in which transnational institutions may alter the power resources and preferences of actors. For example, transnational regulatory cooperation can become a site for preference homogeneity as jurisdictions use the "best practices" developed within them to modernize their domestic regulatory rules (Newman and Posner, forthcoming). In both mechanisms, globalization opens a new opportunity structure for change that had previously been blocked at the domestic level. These mechanisms then help develop causal arguments about globalization and address important puzzles such as preference change and policy reversal.

For the study of International Relations (IR), the chapter emphasizes the critical role that institutions and temporality play in an area of global politics that lack many formal treaty-based rules. It underscores the role of domestic law and regulation while at the same time highlighting the role of informal institutions such as regulatory networks. Drawing on the toolbox of historical institutionalism (Fioretos 2010; Farrell and Newman 2010), it shows that institutions may be more than simple focal points and that they also can be sources of endogenous change. For the study of comparative politics, the chapter reaches outside national jurisdictional boundaries to consider the role of cross-border interactions as well as how the relative timing of events help account for diverse developments in polities (Callaghan 2010). This chapter, then, suggests that the toolbox of historical institutionalism assists in generating better understandings of IR debates such as the origin of negotiation stalemate, policy convergence, and agenda setting, and hopes to spark debate within the historical institutionalism community on the importance of integrating cross-border and transnational interactions into studies that take temporality and context seriously. Finally, by articulating endogenous processes of institutional change that stress the nexus between domestic and global politics, the chapter hopes to stimulate further study of global regulation.

Global Regulation and the International Political Economy

Regulation was long considered the domain of domestic politics—national rules governed the behavior of domestic market participants. But since at least the 1970s with the rise of global travel, information technology, and cross-national business, firms and consumers increasingly engage in activity that spans jurisdictional boundaries (Lutz 2011; Newman and Posner 2011; Vogel 2012). At the same time, states have reacted to these developments by enacting laws that have extraterritorial provisions, reaching outside the bounds of their physical borders (Putnam 2009; Raustiala 2009; Kaczmarek and Newman 2011). Economic globalization and interdependence creates a situation in which the boundaries of market as well as the boundary of authority often extend beyond the territorial nation-state. This means that rules in one country—from food labels to financial disclosures—may have significant consequences for market actors based in other countries. Indeed, because domestic rules in previous eras developed largely within distinct national contexts, the potential for conflict in the new era of interdependence is high (Berger 2000; Farrell and Newman 2014).

Since the progressive era in the early twentieth century, governments in advanced industrial economies have moved from command and control economies to those in which the state engages in arm's length oversight (Jordana and Levi-Faur 2004; Gilardi 2005). In the course of the latter part of the twentieth century, the state increasingly got out of the business of running companies and into the business of setting the rules by which companies compete (Vogel 1996). But given the sequencing of major national regulatory initiatives such as financial reforms of the 1930s, the open government policies of the 1960s, the environmental movement of the 1970, or even the market liberalization efforts of the 1980s, most of these rules were constructed with nearly exclusive attention to parochial domestic concerns. And given distinct partisan compositions, interest group strength, and institutional configurations, different bargains were often struck across countries (Vogel 2012; Pollack and Shaffer 2009), which meant that as economic interdependence increased so did conflicts between domestic rule systems.

Research in economics on border effects demonstrates the significant amount of trade that is disrupted by regulatory mismatches (McCallum 1995; Trefler 1995). This does not include the loss in foreign direct investment or cross-national production that is due to regulatory differences. These costs become even more important to the advanced industrial economies as tariff levels have already been reduced to historically low levels on most goods. Among other illustrations, negotiations over a Transatlantic Trade and Investment Partnership between the US and Europe and the Strategic Economic Dialogue between the US and China, in which parties seek to resolve major regulatory hurdles between the jurisdictions, underscore the central role that regulation has taken in international political economy (Pollack 2005).

How regulatory conflicts get resolved has major implications for the economic competitiveness of firms as well as the quality of markets that consumers experience. Changing the calculation of bank capital reserves may benefit firms located in one jurisdiction over another and make loans less available to some types of consumers (Wood 2005; Singer 2007). Similarly, altering rules about how personal information can be exchanged and collected on the Internet will have distributional and societal consequences (Newman 2008; Farrell 2006). Far from a simple win-win coordination game, resolving global regulatory conflict can entail significant switching costs for the losers and may undermine their existing business models (Mattli and Büthe 2003; Sell 2010). There may also be significant societal consequences for consumers as new global rules change the quality of consumer protection (Young 2003). At the extreme, policy actors in foreign jurisdictions may alter the terms of fundamental democratic principles, as seen by the scandal involving the National Security Agency's monitoring of global Internet traffic.

Given the rise in regulatory conflicts and the stakes involved, it is critical to understand how regulatory disputes get resolved, on what terms, as well as the sources of persistent stalemate. Because a core feature of the postwar economic bargains embodied in the concept of embedded liberalism was to allow domestic intervention in the economy and promote global trade liberalization, the major international economic organizations focus on issues of trade and currencies, not regulation (Raustiala 1997, 2004; Alter and Meunier 2009). As a result there is no clear global regime for regulation. Instead, much of the politics of global regulation transpires through two relatively unconventional channels.

One channel through which global regulation takes shape is through major markets such as the US or Europe using domestic law to shape the behavior of firms and consumers globally (Raustiala 2009; Putnam 2009). This typically occurs through market effects as firms participating in these markets seek to minimize production costs across their products. Labeled "trading-up" by David Vogel (1995), this market mechanism plays a powerful role in shifting regulation globally. But in many cases where regulatory conflict is more intense, the state can play an active role in leveraging their market to alter firm incentives. Most notably, the US and Europe have come to rely on extraterritorial laws to transform global regulation. Equivalency clauses, which condition economic exchange on the level of legal compatibility between regulatory regimes, or the "effects doctrine," in which domestic laws apply to activities that affect national markets but do not necessarily transpire within them, add sanctions to those jurisdictions or firms that maintain divergent rules from these large markets (Posner 2009; Kaczmarek and Newman 2011).

A second channel through which global regulation takes shape is through non-treaty-based cooperation within regulatory networks (Keohane and Nye 1974; Slaughter 2004; Zaring 1998). Starting in the 1970s, a host of organizations have emerged across a range of sectors and have had important consequences for policy reform as well as firm behavior, including the International Organization of Securities Commissions, the International Conference for Environmental Compliance and Enforcement, the International Competition Network, the International Accounting Standards Board, or the International Conference of Data Protection and Privacy Commissioners. Comprised of various combinations of public and private regulators, these organizations are informal as they are not legally delegated authority through treaty-law by states. They frequently have small secretariats that serve to coordinate communication between the members, who take care of much of the substantive work. Despite their relatively informal organization, these bodies have become important sites for global regulatory governance, engaging in rule-development as well as increasingly in rule-implementation and oversight (Bach and Newman 2010a; Brummer 2011; Damro 2006).

With the rise of regulation as a major site of political contestation in the international political economy, one strand of research has increasingly turned to understand the political dynamics involved. Existing work has tended to emphasize the role of structural power in shaping global regulation. Drawing on earlier power-based work, IR scholars have emphasized the role that large markets play. Daniel Drezner (2007), for example, argues that global regulation is set primarily by the interests of the US and the EU, given their relative weight in the global economy. When the two agree, there is a set of global rules that diffuse widely and shape the behavior of market actors. When they disagree, sham standards or rival rules are likely to result. Other scholars in this tradition have applied a similar logic to a range of issues areas including financial regulation, foreign direct investment, and agriculture (Simmons 2001; Aggarwal 1985; Shambaugh 1996).

A second prominent strand of research emphasizes the role of private actors, largely internationally active firms, and their ability to capture the regulatory process (Lall 2012; Underhill and Zhang 2008; Cutler, Haufler, and Porter 1999). These arguments stress the ability of private actors to provide the expertise to regulatory agencies and set the agenda. In many cases, such private actors use the revolving door between government and business to shape market regulation.

While structural arguments definitely provide insight into the character of global rules, they tend to equate demand side factors with outcomes, which is to say that powerful actors always get what they want. These arguments face a number of challenges. Most important, they ignore supply-side factors—institutions, rules, and processes that filter or channel structural power (Mattli and Woods 2009). Relatedly, they have little ability to account for variation in influence across domains or time. More fundamentally, they focus on how powerful states or firms get what they want but have few mechanisms to understand what these actors want in the first place and what informs their preferences (Woll 2008).

Shortcomings in existing strands of research leave many empirical puzzles unanswered. For example, what explains whether the US or EU exert more influence over global rules in the face of preference divergence. Standard explanations predict rival or sham standards, but from financial services to chemicals to information technology, there are a host of examples where one jurisdiction is able to set global standards even in the face of opposition from another great power. Similarly, what accounts for changing preferences of major regulatory actors over time such as the sudden adoption of international accounting standards by the European Commission after years of resistance, or the acceptance by the US Securities and Exchange Commission of EU regulatory oversight after a long stalemate (Posner 2010).

Historical institutionalism's toolbox provides useful tools in resolving empirical puzzles in the history of global regulation. This tradition highlights the importance of acknowledging that the institutional context in which regulatory battles occur is the product of contingent socio-historical processes that shape the interests and authority resources of actors. In contrast to rationalist approaches and strong path-dependent arguments, these causal mechanisms highlighted by historical institutionalists underscore the transformative role institutions may have as sites for endogenous change.

Relative Sequencing and Regulatory Capacity

While structural factors such as market size no doubt matter in global regulatory debates, it is indeterminate with respect to many regulatory outcomes. It is true that large markets like the US, the EU, Japan, and perhaps soon China play a disproportionate role in the setting, implementation, and extra-territorial enforcement of regulatory agendas. But there are many cases where great economic powers have divergent preferences, yet one is able to outmaneuver the other in setting global standards. Similarly, jurisdictional use of extraterritoriality varies considerably across issue area. For these reasons, we need tools that allow for dynamic temporal and sectoral variation.

Institutional structures (often of the state but frequently of private actors as well) condition the ability of a jurisdiction to influence global rules. In particular, regulatory capacity—the ability to define, defend, monitor, and enforce a particular rule set—plays a critical role in the external projection of domestic regulation (Newman 2008; Bach and Newman 2007). Regulatory capacity depends on the expertise to develop and oversee a particular rule set, the delegated authority to penalize non-compliance such as control of market access, and finally ties to other regulators and constituents that can be mobilized to defend a rule set. Research across issue areas has underscored the importance of regulatory capacity for such debates. Lutz (1998), for example, argues that the self-regulatory nature of stock market oversight in Germany hampered its ability to engage in global standard setting. Similarly, Newman (2008) finds that extensive expertise and control over market access provided the European Union outsized influence in global privacy negotiations.

In contrast to much existing work on sequencing in comparative politics, which focuses on institutional timing within a single jurisdiction, relative sequencing emphasizes how distinct trajectories of state and regulatory development create powerful regulatory capacities in certain markets and deficient capacities in others. The relative timing of such capacities in one jurisdiction vis-à-vis another can produce power asymmetries that affect negotiating dynamics over long periods of time (Newman 2008; Posner 2010; Bach and Newman 2010b). With attention to relative sequencing, historical institutional scholarship can build on and extend earlier work on state capacity, which was criticized for viewing jurisdictions as unitary actors and in relative isolation from one another (Ikenberry 1988; Katzenstein 1976).

Owing to a combination of socio-historical factors including the progressive movement, government fragmentation, and the New Deal, for example, the US was among the first jurisdictions to construct independent regulatory agencies (Skowronek 1982; Carpenter 2001; Sheingate 2003). Long before globalization brought advanced industrial economies into contact with one another, US regulators built extensive regulatory capacity with arm's length regulators tasked to oversee market activity. Over time, some of these regulators developed extensive expertise in their domain and critical ties to market participants. By contrast, many European states followed either a command and control model of regulation that placed the reigns of regulation in the hands of ministries or self-regulatory organizations, such as trade associations that coordinated regulation within national contexts (Jordana and Levi-Faur 2004). These differences in domestic regulatory architectures became consequential when neoliberal market policies came to dominate global regulation. From finance to pharmaceuticals, US agencies like the Securities and Exchange Commission or the Food and Drug Administration led debates on the structure of global policy (Bach and Newman 2010a; Carpenter 2010). While the size of US markets has allowed its regulators to exert significant power, the size and expertise of these agencies cannot be underestimated. The SEC, for example, entered the era of globalization with thousands of employees, compared to the UK that lacked an independent regulator in the issue area.

The socio-historical context is far from uniform across sectors, and thus relative sequencing arguments can explain variation in influence across policy domains. For a number of reasons ranging from political fragmentation to veto points, the US failed to centralize regulation over issues such as insurance and data privacy (Singer 2007; Quaglia 2013; Newman 2008). By contrast, Europeans were among the first to construct arm's length oversight of these sectors. As would be expected by the relative sequencing argument, the development of regulatory capacity in some jurisdictions gave Europeans an advantage in promoting its domestic standards outside its borders. Variation in extraterritorial authority across markets and sectors, then, is directly tied to distinct domestic historical trajectories of institutional change.

While historical institutionalism offers novel means to consider power differentials between jurisdictions based on trajectories of regulatory development, this approach offers a somewhat static model. It risks being criticized as overly wedded to concepts such as path dependence, and for presenting countries with weak institutions as locked into being permanent rule-takers. At first blush, this might not present much of a problem as domestic regulatory trajectories (and by extension global regulation) are characterized by considerable stability. Yet there are a host of domestic models of institutional change as well as arguments about exogenous sources of change that allow the relative sequencing argument to take on a more dynamic character and for scholars working within historical institutionalism to escape an overly static notion of path dependence.

Studying global regulatory interactions allows for innovations in historical institutional arguments by focusing on relative sequencing as a source of endogenous institutional change. As jurisdictions interact, early policy trajectories in one come to interact with the policies of other jurisdictions. This does not guarantee a simple diffusion of regulatory models. Rather, the frictions that emerge from the interaction of alternatives models open up opportunity structures for change agents in jurisdictions with weak regulatory capacities (Mahoney and Thelen 2009; Sandholtz 2007; Börzel and Risse 2003; Joachim 2003). They can use the interaction to mobilize for domestic institutional change, and when successful may be in a position to challenge first-mover jurisdictions. Posner (2010) documents such a sequence in his work on accounting standards, in which US regulatory capacity challenged European influence, producing internal reforms within Europe. The end result was neither US dominance nor sham standards, but growing accommodation between the two regulatory authorities.

Relative sequencing arguments provide two important innovations for scholars of global regulation. First, they embed market power within historical institutional trajectories across the major economies. Here, both internal institutional developments and their relative timing vis-à-vis other markets matter in shaping global rules. Second, relative sequencing arguments identify causal event chains (Mahoney 2000) in which regulatory developments in one jurisdiction may influence the terms of reform in another and thereby shape global rules.

Transnational Feedbacks and Cross-National Layering

Sequencing arguments relate primarily to the ways in which historical institutional tools reorient our understanding of the role of domestic institutions in shaping global regulatory outcomes. This section adapts arguments about policy feedbacks and layering to the transnational setting, emphasizing the role of sub-state actors as advocates of change and the endogenous role of institutions in enabling changes in global rules from financial to environmental domains.

Because informal institutions typically lack the treaty-backed legitimacy of international law, scholars from the neo-functionalist camp and more power-based approaches have tended to circumscribe the effects of such informal institutions. For neo-functionalists, institutions serve primarily as focal points for coordination problems (Abbott and Snidal 2000; Shaffer and Pollack 2009). In instances where enforcement is not necessary, informal institutions offer a fast and flexible response to coordination problems. Power-based accounts tend to emphasize the epiphenomenal status of such networks highlighting their complementary role in managing regulatory issues in cases where powerful states largely agree (Drezner 2007; Shaffer and Pollack 2009). Historical institutionalism offers an important extension and at times alternative by showing how informal institutions over time may become sites of endogenous change. It offers means to explain how institutions at times have autonomous and independent affects even when they fail to solve a cooperation problem or when they lack great power support or even face opposition by such powers.

Policy feedbacks have long been a mainstay of historical institutional analysis that stress the ways in which policies adopted at an earlier time period shape the power resources, preferences, and identities of actors in future periods (Pierson 1993, 2000). Work on the welfare state, for example, focuses on how policy shapes interest groups. Campbell (2003) shows that social security in the US mobilized elder American and organized them into the American Association of Retired Persons, which became one of the most powerful lobbies in the US. Other work has focused on how similar feedback effects shape the development of the state. Levy (1999), for example, explains how dirigiste policies in postwar France gutted the necessary institutions to allow for decentralization in later periods. Relatedly, Evans (1994) argues that particular historical relationships between the bureaucracy and society facilitated innovation in Korea, while not in other countries such as Brazil.

Studies on domestic feedback effects that highlight how past policies alter the opportunities, resources, and interest of critical political actors offer a foundation for a new perspective on transnational regulatory networks as sites for policy feedbacks (Newman and Posner, forthcoming). From this perspective, a regulatory network such as the Basel Committee is not simply a focal point for capital adequacy rules for banks, but may alter the interests of those organizations with which it interacts. For example, many banks holding mortgage debt viewed such debt as a highly secure asset, which created a strong incentive for commercial banks to have mortgages on their books. Basel rules, however, transformed mortgage debt into a liability for which banks needed to hold more reserve capital. This policy change, then, increased the incentive for banks to securitize mortgages; that is, to package home loans and sell these pooled loans to investors (Jones 2000). Such regulatory arbitrage helped commercial banks reduce their required capital reserves. But at the same time, it transformed the policy preferences of commercial banks as they moved out of deposit-based assets toward more market-based products, so as to bring them closer to those of investment banks (Wood 2005). In this way, then, transnational regulatory cooperation transformed economic interests for commercial banks.

Historical institutionalist arguments concerning actor change strategies help refocus attention on transnational cooperation away from coordination mechanisms to regulatory networks as sites of endogenous change. Thelen (2004) and Shickler (2001) have shown that in the face of legislative barriers to policy repeal, actors seeking to overturn the status quo may layer new rules on top of existing ones. Over time, these new rules may slowly siphon off support for status quo rules and bring important policy change. Jurisdictions are frequently populated with actors that both support and hope to change the regulatory status quo. Transnational networks are sites that provide opportunities for change actors to forge alliances across borders (Farrell and Newman 2014, 2015). In those instances where change actors are able to do so, they may develop a set of standards or rules in opposition to similar rules in their home markets. As interdependence produces regulatory friction, market actors may look to such transnational rules as a means to resolve regulatory uncertainty. Over time, then, cross-national layers may leach away support for domestic regulations and facilitate domestic institutional change (Bartley 2011; Farrell and Newman 2015). As domestic rules change, this can alter the terms of transnational cooperation as well.

Transnational feedbacks and cross-national layering emphasize the critical role that regulatory institutions may play in reorganizing interests and power resources. By integrating dynamics over time, these mechanisms help historical institutionalists identify ways in which even informal institutions may have independent and autonomous effects on global regulatory politics.

Conclusion

Global regulatory politics is deeply shaped by domestic regulatory trajectories as well as informal transnational regulatory institutions. These two features make this domain of international politics particularly ripe for exploration through historical institutionalist tools. From accounting standards to food safety, decisions made over decades of policy development within jurisdictions sets the stage for global debates. As globalization brings these jurisdictions into contact with one another, the result is not simply rule clash or convergence. Instead, interdependence offers actors interested in altering the status quo a number of strategies to use transnational institutions to transform their domestic regulatory status quo. Historical institutionalism provides means to explain both the sources of common interests and conflict, as well as the way in which transnational institutions may transform those conflicts.

Applying historical institutional tools to global regulatory politics offers scholars of International Relations and Comparative Politics a new area of research. First, historical institutional tools—cross-national layering and transnational feedbacks—offer insights into the role of informal institutions and how these impact patterns of change. Much of the IR literature on informal institutions consider them to be a second-best solution to formal rules (Abbott and Snidal 2000; Shaffer and Pollack 2009). Lacking binding enforcement, these institutions serve primarily as information mechanisms and not as compliance tools. Historical institutional approaches shift our attention from the static functionalist role that such institutions serve toward their role in dynamic and potentially transformative processes. Both cross-national layering and transnational feedbacks underscore that informal institutions may serve to alter the preferences of actors involved. Adding a temporal component, then, expands scholars' understanding of the potential impact of informal rules.

Second, transnational regulatory issues offer a chance to overcome caricatures of historical institutional arguments as only exploring continuity. While it is vital to understand the sources of institutional continuity, critics have focused on path dependence arguments associated with early work in historical institutionalism as being unable to explain variation. In IR, much of the work that has looked to historical institutional tools has emphasized such reinforcing processes. By contrast, this chapter demonstrates that more recent work on institutional change can be applied to transnational regulatory phenomenon and thus underscores the central role of agency, alliances, and strategy within contemporary historical institutionalism.

The arguments in this chapter offer the basis to spark research focusing on inter-societal interactions along more traditional work emphasizing inter-jurisdictional interactions. Much existing work on global regulation focuses on national differences and conflict between jurisdictions. This view obscures the internal heterogeneity of preferences within jurisdictions. This chapter, by contrast, suggests that there are a host of actors below the level of the state that are dissatisfied with their regulatory status quo. Globalization offers them an opportunity to forge alliances cross-nationally and in transnational regulatory forum. As global interdependence grows, research will need to explore the scope conditions for such alliances (Farrell and Newman 2015). At the same time, the approach used in this chapter hopes to challenge those working from the historical institutional tradition in comparative politics to see the benefit of incorporating transnational and global processes into their arguments (Farrell and Newman 2014).

Finally, there exists a rich opportunity to link research from American Political Development on the regulatory state to work on transnational regulation (Fioretos 2011). Much of the most insightful work on domestic regulatory developments has employed a historical institutionalist lens and offers fertile ground for IR scholars (Skowronek 1982; Carpenter 2001; Sheingate 2003). This will allow for a more fine-grained understanding of sources of extraterritorial influence as well as a better specification of regulatory capacity. The chapter also challenges existing historical institutional work to move outside of siloed national jurisdictions. As markets and authority break free of traditional geographic borders, so too must arguments about institutional change. It is to be hoped that more interaction between those that work on domestic and transnational regulation will benefit both.

Note

* This chapter has benefited from extensive comments by the editors, in particular Orfeo Fioretos. I would also like to thank David Bach, Henry Farrell, and Elliot Posner, who have been intimate collaborators on many of the ideas expressed here.

References

Abbott, Kenneth W. and Duncan Snidal. 2000. "Hard and Soft Law in International Governance." *International Organization* 54 (03): 421–456.

Aggarwal, V. 1985. *Liberal Protectionism: The International Politics of Organized Textile Trade*. Berkeley: University of California Press.

Alter, Karen J. and Sophie Meunier. 2009. "The Politics of International Regime Complexity." *Perspectives on Politics* 7 (1): 13–24.

Bach, David and Abraham L. Newman. 2007. "The European Regulatory State and Global Public Policy: Micro-Institutions and Macro-Influence." *Journal of European Public Policy* 16 (4): 827–846.

Bach, David and Abraham L. Newman. 2010a. "Transgovernmental Networks and Domestic Policy Convergence: Evidence from Insider Trading Regulation." *International Organization* 64 (03): 505–528.

Bach, David and Abraham L. Newman. 2010b. "Governing Lipitor and Lipstick: Capacity, Sequencing, and Power in International Pharmaceutical and Cosmetics Regulation." *Review of International Political Economy* 17 (4) (October): 665–695.

Bartley, Tim. 2011. "Transnational Governance as the Layering of Rules: Intersections of Public and Private Standards." *Theoretical Inquiries in Law* 12 (2): 517–542.

Berger, Suzanne. 2000. "Globalization and Politics." *Annual Review of Political Science* 3: 43–62.

Börzel, Tanja A. and Thomas Risse. 2003. "Conceptualizing the Domestic Impact of Europe." In *The Politics of Europeanization*, ed. Kevin Featherstone and Claudio M. Radaelli. Oxford: Oxford University Press, 57–80.

Brummer, Chris. 2011. *Soft Law and the Global Financial System: Rule Making in the 21st Century*. Cambridge: Cambridge University Press.

Büthe, Tim and Walter Mattli. 2011. *The New Global Rulers: The Privatization of Regulation in the World Economy*. Princeton, NJ: Princeton University Press.

Callaghan, Helen. 2010. "Beyond Methodological Nationalism: How Multilevel Governance Affects the Clash of Capitalisms." *Journal of European Public Policy* 17 (4): 564–580.

Campbell, Andrea Louise. 2003. *How Policies Make Citizens: Senior Political Activism and the American Welfare State*. Princeton, NJ: Princeton University Press.

Carpenter, Daniel. 2001. "The Political Foundations of Bureaucratic Autonomy: A Response to Kernell." *Studies in American Political Development* 15 (01): 113–122.

Carpenter, Daniel P. 2010. *Reputation and Power*. Princeton, NJ: Princeton University Press.

Cutler, A. Claire, Virginia Haufler, and Tony Porter. 1999. *Private Authority and International Affairs*. Albany, NY: State University of New York Press.

Damro, Chad. 2006. "Transatlantic Competition Policy: Domestic and International Sources of EU–US Cooperation." *European Journal of International Relations* 12 (2): 171–196.

Drezner, Daniel W. 2007. *All Politics Is Global: Explaining International Regulatory Regimes*. Princeton, NJ: Princeton University Press.

Evans, Peter. 1994. *Embedded Autonomy: States and Industrial Transformation*. Princeton, NJ: Princeton University Press.

Farrell, Henry. 2006. "Governing Information Flows: States, Private Actors, and E-Commerce." *Annual Review of Political Science* 6: 353–374.

Farrell, Henry and Abraham L. Newman. 2010. "Making Global Markets: Historical Institutionalism in International Political Economy." *Review of International Political Economy* 17 (4): 609–638.

Farrell, Henry and Abraham L. Newman. 2014. "Domestic Institutions beyond the Nation State: Charting the New Interdependence Approach." *World Politics* 66 (2): 331–363.

Farrell, Henry and Abraham L. Newman. 2015. "The New Politics of Interdependence: Cross-National Layering in Trans-Atlantic Regulatory Disputes." *Comparative Political Studies* 48 (4): 497–526.

Fioretos, Orfeo. 2010. "Capitalist Diversity and the International Regulation of Hedge Funds." *Review of International Political Economy* 17 (4): 696–723.

Fioretos, Orfeo. 2011. "Historical Institutionalism in International Relations." *International Organization* 65 (02): 367–399.

Gilardi, Fabrizio. 2005. "The Institutional Foundations of Regulatory Capitalism: The Diffusion of Independent Regulatory Agencies in Western Europe." *The Annals of the American Academy of Political and Social Science* 598: 84–101.

Ikenberry, G. John. 1988. *Reasons of the State: Oil Politics and the Capacities of American Government*. Ithaca, NY: Cornell University Press.

Joachim, Jutta. 2003. "Framing Issues and Seizing Opportunities: The UN, NGOs, and Women's Rights." *International Studies Quarterly* 47 (2): 247–274.

Jones, David. 2000. "Emerging Problems with the Basel Capital Accord: Regulatory Capital Arbitrage and Related Issues." *Journal of Banking & Finance* 24 (1–2) (January): 35–58.

Jordana, Jacint and David Levi-Faur. 2004. *The Politics of Regulation: Institutions and Regulatory Reforms for the Age of Governance*. Cheltenham: Edward Elgar.

Kaczmarek, Sara and Abraham L. Newman. 2011. "The Long Arm of the Law: Extraterritoriality and the National Implementation of Foreign Bribery Legislation." *International Organization* 65 (4): 745–770.

Katzenstein, Peter J. 1976. "International Relations and Domestic Structures: Foreign Economic Policies of Advanced Industrial States." *International Organization* 30 (Winter): 1–45.

Keohane, Robert O. and Joseph Nye. 1974. "Transgovernmental Relations and International Organizations." *World Politics* 27 (October): 39–62.

Lall, Ranjit. 2012. "From Failure to Failure: The Politics of International Banking Regulation." *Review of International Political Economy* 19 (4): 609–638.

Levy, Jonah D. 1999. *Tocqueville's Revenge: State, Society, and Economy in Contemporary France*. Cambridge, MA: Harvard University Press.

Lutz, Susanne. 1998. "The Revival of the Nation-State? Stock Exchange Regulation in an Eve of Globalized Financial Markets." *Journal of European Public Policy* 5 (1): 153–168.

Lutz, Susanne. 2011. "Back to the Future? The Domestic Sources of Transatlantic Regulation." *Review of International Political Economy* 8 (4): iii–xxii.

McCallum, John. 1995. "National Borders Matter: Canada–US Regional Trade Patterns." *American Economic Review* 85 (3): 615–623.

Mahoney, James. 2000. "Path Dependence in Historical Sociology." *Theory and Society* 29 (4): 507–548.

Mahoney, James and Kathleen Thelen. 2009. *Explaining Institutional Change: Ambiguity, Agency, and Power*. 1st Edition. Cambridge: Cambridge University Press.

Mattli, Walter and Tim Büthe. 2003. "Setting International Standards: Technological Rationality or Primacy of Power." *World Politics* 56 (1): 1–42.

Mattli, Walter and Ngaire Woods. 2009. *The Politics of Global Regulation*. Princeton, NJ: Princeton University Press.

Newman, Abraham L. 2008. *Protectors of Privacy: Regulating Personal Data in the Global Economy*. Ithaca, NY: Cornell University Press.

Newman, Abraham, L. and Elliot Posner. 2011. "International Interdependence and Regulatory Power: Authority, Mobility, and Markets." *European Journal of International Relations*. 17 (4): 589–610.

Newman, Abraham, L. and Elliot Posner. Forthcoming. "Transnational Feedbacks, Soft Law, and Preferences in Global Financial Regulation." *Review of International Political Economy*.

Pierson, Paul. 1993. "When Effect Becomes Cause: Policy Feedback and Political Change." *World Politics* 45 (4): 595–628.

Pierson, Paul. 2000. "Increasing Returns, Path Dependence, and the Study of Politics." *American Political Science Review* 94 (2): 251–267.

Pollack, Mark A. 2005. "The New Transatlantic Agenda at Ten: Reflections on an Experiment in International Governance." *Journal of Common Market Studies* 43 (5): 899–919.

Pollack, Mark A. and Gregory C. Shaffer. 2009. *When Cooperation Fails: The International Law and Politics of Genetically Modified Foods*. New York: Oxford University Press.

Posner, Elliot. 2009. "Making Rules for Global Finance: Transatlantic Regulatory Cooperation at the Turn of the Millennium." *International Organization* 63 (4): 665–699.

Posner, Elliot. 2010. "Sequence as Explanation: The International Politics of Accounting Standards." *Review of International Political Economy* 17 (October): 639–664.

Putnam, Tonya L. 2009. "Courts without Borders: Domestic Sources of U.S. Extraterritoriality in the Regulatory Sphere." *International Organization* 63 (03): 459–490. doi:10.1017/S002081830909016X.

Quaglia, Lucia. 2013. "The European Union, the USA and International Standard Setting by Regulatory Fora in Finance." *New Political Economy* 19 (3): 427–444.

Raustiala, Kal. 1997. "Domestic Institutions and International Regulatory Cooperation: Comparative Responses to the Convention on Biological Diversity." *World Politics* 49 (4): 482–509.

Raustiala, Kal. 2004. "The Regime Complex for Plant Genetic Resources." *International Organization* 58 (2): 277–309.

Raustiala, Kal. 2009. *Does the Constitution Follow the Flag? The Evolution of Territoriality in American Law*. New York: Oxford University Press.

Sandholtz, Wayne. 2007. *Prohibiting Plunder: How Norms Change*. Oxford: Oxford Univeristy Press.

Sell, Susan. 2010. "The Rise and Rule of a Trade-based Strategy: Historical Institutionalism and the International Regulation of Intellectual Property." *Review of International Political Economy* 17 (4): 762–790.

Shaffer, Gregory C. and Mark A. Pollack. 2009. "Hard vs. Soft Law: Alternatives, Complements, and Antagonists in International Governance." *Minnesota Law Review* 94: 706.

Shambaugh, George. 1996. "Dominance, Dependence, and Political Power: Tethering Technology in the 1980s and Today." *International Studies Quarterly* 40 (4): 559–588.

Sheingate, Adam. 2003. "Political Entrepreneurs, Institutional Change, and American Political Development." *Studies in American Political Development* 17 (2): 185–203.

Shickler, Eric. 2001. *Disjointed Pluralism*. Princeton, NJ: Princeton University Press.

Simmons, Beth. 2001. "The International Politics of Harmonization: The Case of Capital Market Regulation." *International Organization* 55 (03): 589–620.

Singer, David Andrew. 2007. *Regulating Capital: Setting Standards for the International Financial System*. Ithaca, NY: Cornell University Press.

Skowronek, Stephen. 1982. *Building a New American State: The Expansion of National Administrative Capacities, 1877–1920*. Cambridge: Cambridge University Press.

Slaughter, Anne-Marie. 2004. *A New World Order*. Princeton, NJ: Princeton University Press.

Strange, Susan. 1996. *The Retreat of the State: The Diffusion of Power in the World Economy*. Cambridge: Cambridge University Press.

Thelen, Kathleen. 2004. *How Institutions Evolve: The Political Economy of Skills in Germany, Britain, the United States, and Japan*. Cambridge: Cambridge University Press.

Trefler, Daniel. 1995. "The Case of Missing Trade and Other Mysteries." *American Economic Review* 85 (5): 1029–1046.

Underhill, Geoffrey R. D. and Xiaoke Zhang. 2008. "Setting the Rules: Private Power, Political Underpinnings, and Legitimacy in Global Monetary and Financial Governance." *International Affairs* 84 (3): 535–554.

Vogel, David. 1995. *Trading Up: Consumer and Environmental Regulation in a Global Economy*. Cambridge, MA: Harvard University Press.

Vogel, David. 2012. *The Politics of Precaution: Regulating Health, Safety, and Environmental Risks in Europe and the United States*. Princeton, NJ: Princeton University Press.

Vogel, Steven Kent. 1996. *Freer Markets More Rules: Regulatory Reform in Advanced Industrial Countries*. Ithaca, NY: Cornell University Press.

Woll, Cornelia. 2008. *Firm Interests: How Governments Shape Business Lobbying on Global Trade*. Ithaca, NY: Cornell University Press.

Wood, Duncan Robert. 2005. *Governing Global Banking: The Basel Committee and the Politics of Financial Globalisation*. Aldershot: Ashgate Publishing, Ltd.

Young, Alasdair. 2003. "Political Transfer and 'Trading up'? Transatlantic Trade in Genetically Modified Food and US Politics." *World Politics* 55 (July): 457–484.

Zaring, David. 1998. "International Law by Other Means: The Twilight Existence of International Financial Regulatory Organizations." *Texas International Law Journal* 33 (281).

Index